The
Bed & Breakfast Book

New Zealand 2004

New Zealand's leading guide to accommodation with character

Self-contained Chalet, Kuaotunu, Whitianga

Hayman
Tasman Downs
Lake Tekapo

page 437

Kawatea, Okains Bay, Banks Peninsula

Published by...

The B&B Book
P.O. Box 6843, Wellington, New Zealand
Tel: +64 4 385-2615
Fax: +64 4 385-2694
Web: www.bnb.co.nz
Email: info@bnb.co.nz

© The B&B Book, 2003
Printed in China by Bookbuilders
ISBN 0-473-09714-1

Cover photo...
Edgewater Boutique Homestay
Karaka Bay, Wellington

Every effort has been made to ensure that the information in this book is as up to date as possible at the time of going to press. All listing information has been supplied by the hosts. The publishers do not accept responsibility arising from reliance on any contents in the book.

Introduction

Welcome to this edition of *The Bed & Breakfast Book*

The popularity of bed & breakfast in New Zealand has increased each year since *The New Zealand Bed & Breakfast Book* was first published in 1987. The amazing growth is not only a reflection of changing holiday trends but a response by New Zealanders to open their homes and share their experiences with travellers. Bed & breakfast in New Zealand means a warm welcome and a unique holiday experience. Most B&B accommodation is in private homes with a sprinkling of guesthouses and small hotels. Each listing in the guide has been written by the host themselves and you will discover their warmth and personality through their writing. *The Bed & Breakfast Book* is not just an accommodation guide – it is an introduction to a uniquely New Zealand holiday experience.

The best holidays are often remembered by the friends one makes. How many of us have loved a country because of one or two memorable individuals we encountered? For the traveller who wants to experience the real New Zealand and get to know its people, bed and breakfast offers an opportunity to do just that. If you have time, we recommend you don't try to travel too far in one day. Take time to enjoy the company of your hosts and other local people. You will find New Zealand hosts friendly and generous, and eager to share their local knowledge with you.

All properties inspected

All B&Bs which are newly listed are inspected to ensure that they meet our standards. We expect that all B&Bs in *The Bed and Breakfast Book* will offer excellent hospitality. Some B&Bs are members of associations which undertake inspections also.

Qualmark is New Zealand tourism's official quality agency. All guest and hosted accommodation businesses that carry the Qualmark quality mark have been independently assessed as professional and trustworthy. For more details, see www.qualmark.co.nz.

NZ Association of Farm and Home Hosts members have adopted the brand '@home NEW ZEALAND'. This new brand is your guarantee that hosts displaying this logo offer quality service and warm hospitality. You will be welcomed into their home, invited to share their facilities and your privacy will be respected as well.

Finding your way around - using *The Bed & Breakfast Book*

We travel from north to south listing the towns as we come to them. In addition, we've divided New Zealand into geographical regions, a map of which is included at the start of each chapter. In some regions, such as Southland, our listings take a detour off the north-to-south route, and follow their nose - it will soon become obvious.

Your comments

We welcome your views on *The Bed & Breakfast Book* and the hosts you meet. Please visit our website www.bnb.co.nz or write to us at PO Box 6843, Wellington, New Zealand.

Happy travelling
The B&B Book Team

Comment Forms

Please help us to maintain our high standards by sending us comments about where you stayed.

- You may submit your comment on our website www.bnb.co.nz
- Or your hosts will give you a comment form.
- Or simply cut one from the back of the book.
- Each comment returned will be in our ongoing monthly draw for a free night's B&B.
- Each person staying can submit a comment for an increased chance of success.
- Guest comments are displayed on the hosts' pages at www.bnb.co.nz

Peak View Farm, Havelock North

About B&B

Our B&Bs range from homely to luxurious, but you can always be assured of superior hospitality.

Types of accommodation

Traditional B&B; generally small owner-occupied home accommodation usually with private guest living and dining areas.

Homestay; a homestay is a B&B where you share the family's living area.

Farmstay; country accommodation, usually on a working farm.

Self-contained; separate self-contained accommodation, with kitchen and living/dining room. Breakfast provisions usually provided at least for the first night.

Separate/suite; similar to self-contained but without kitchen facilities. Living/dining facilities may be limited.

Bathrooms

Ensuite and private bathrooms are for your use exclusively.

Guests share bathroom means you will be sharing with other guests.

Family share means you will be sharing with the family.

Tariff

The prices listed are in New Zealand dollars and include GST. Prices listed are subject to change, and any change to listed prices will be stated at time of booking. Some hosts offer a discount for children - this applies to age 12 or under unless otherwise stated. Most of our B&Bs will accept credit cards.

Reservations

We recommend you contact your hosts well in advance to be sure of confirming your accommodation. Most hosts require a deposit so make sure you understand their cancellation policy. Please let your hosts know if you have to cancel, they will have spent time preparing for you. You may also book accommodation through some travel agents or via specialised B&B reservation services.

Breakfast & Dinner

Breakfast is included in the tariff, with each host offering their own menu. You'll be surprised at the range of delicious breakfasts available, many using local produce. If you would like dinner most hosts require 24 hours notice.

Smoking

Most of our B&Bs are non-smoking, but smoking is permitted outside. Listings displaying the no smoking logo do not permit smoking anywhere on the property. B&Bs which have a smoking area inside mention this in their text.

Accessibility

Certified as being wheelchair accessible.

Can accommodate guests in wheelchairs, but not certified.

The difference between a hotel and a B&B...
is that you don't hug the hotel staff when you leave.

New Zealand – Regions

Northland

Coromandel

Bay of Plenty

Auckland

Waikato, King Country

Taranaki, Wanganui,
Ruapehu, Rangitikei

Gisborne

Manawatu, Horowhenua

Hawkes Bay

Nelson, Golden Bay

Wairarapa

West Coast

Wellington

Marlborough

Canterbury

South Canterbury,
North Otago

Chatham Islands

Otago, North Catlins

Southland,
South Catlins

Stewart Island

Contents

Northland

Houhora

Mangonui
Coopers Beach
Awanui
Kaitaia
Ahipara
Kaeo
Mahinepua
Kerikeri
Okaihau
Paihia
Russell
Kohukohu
Opua
Rowene
Pakaraka
Oakura Bay
Opononi
Omapere

Kauri
Whangarei
Onerahi
Parua Bay
Whangarei Heads
Ruakaka
Dargaville
Waipu
Waipu Cove
Langs Beach
Paparoa
Matakohe
Mangawai
Kaiwaka
Te Hana
Wellsford
Warkworth
Sandspit
Snells Bea
Puhoi
Orewa
Silverdale
Kaukapakapa
Whangapa
Okura
Helensville
Albany
Auckland

Towns listed generally follow
a north to south route. Refer
to the index if required.

| 0 | Kilometres | 45 |

| 0 | Miles | 27 |

Houhora *Homestay 44km N of Kaitaia*

Houhora Lodge & Homestay
Jacqui & Bruce Malcolm
3994 Far North Rd, Houhora, RD 4, Kaitaia

Tel (09) 409 7884 Fax (09) 409 7884
Mob 021 926 992 houhora.homestay@xtra.co.nz
www.topstay.co.nz

Double $145 Single $90 (Continental & Full Breakfast)
Dinner $30 by arrangement Credit cards accepted
Children welcome
2 King/Twin 1 Single (3 bdrm) 2 Ensuite 1 Private

We have fled our largest city to live on the shores of Houhora Harbour, and look forward to sharing this special part of New Zealand with you. Come and enjoy the remote coastal walks, shell-collecting, Cape Reinga, 90 mile beach and other attractions. We can arrange 4x4 trips, sport or game fishing and provide relaxed and quality accommodation on your return. Homemade bread, homegrown fruit, home-pressed olive oil, vegetables and eggs. Fresh or smoked fish a speciality. Email, internet and fax facilities available.

Ahipara - Ninety Mile Beach *B&B Self-contained Guesthouse 16km W of Kaitaia*

Siesta Lodge
Carole & Alan Harding
PO Box 30, Ahipara, Northland

Tel (09) 409 2011 Fax (09) 409 2011
Mob 025 293 9665 ninetymile@xtra.co.nz
www.ahipara.co.nz/siesta

Double $150-$190 (Continental Breakfast) Dinner by arrangement apartment $150-$190 Credit cards accepted
3 Queen 1 Twin (4 bdrm) 3 Ensuite

The Siesta is a Mediterranean style house set in private grounds with panoramic views overlooking the sheltered Ahipara Bay, sand-dune wilderness and the magnificent Ninety Mile Beach. Each room has private balcony, queen-size bed and ensuites. Sleep to the sound of the sea with sea-views from your bed, enjoy spectacular sunsets from your balcony. The adjacent villa has a luxury self-contained, spacious apartment with spectacular views, and is an ideal base for longer stays. We have a very friendly cat and dog. Phone for directions.

Ahipara - Ninety Mile Beach *B&B Self-contained 17km W of Kaitaia*

Foreshore Lodge
Maire & Selwyn Parker
269 Foreshore Road, RD 1, Kaitaia

Tel (09) 409 4860 Fax (09) 409 4860
www.ahipara.co.nz/foreshore

Double $70-$100 Single $70 (Continental Breakfast)
Breakfast extra $7.50 pp Credit cards accepted
Children welcome
1 King/Twin 1 King 2 Double 2 Single (4 bdrm)
1 Ensuite 1 Private

Two self-contained units with fully equipped kitchens, situated on the water's edge at Ahipara Bay, the southernmost sheltered end of 90 mile beach. BBQ on your covered terrace. Relax and enjoy lovely sea views from your comfortable unit. Safe swimming, fishing, surfing and walking just across the road. All tours can be arranged. Front door pick-up Cape Reinga and Reef Point tours. Golf course - five minutes away. Restaurants, takeaways and dairies nearby. Enquire about tariff for long stays or extra guests. Children very welcome. Sorry no pets.

Kaitaia - Ahipara   *B&B Homestay 15km W of Kaitaia*

Beachside
Maire & Brian Veza
72 Foreshore Road, RD 1, Kaitaia

Tel (09) 409 4819 Fax (09) 409 4819 www.bnb.co.nz/
beachside.html

Double $70-$80 Single $50-$55 (Full Breakfast) Child
$20 Dinner $20 Credit cards accepted
1 Twin 2 Single (2 bdrm)
1 Ensuite 1 Host share

Welcome to our comfortable house. Relax and enjoy views from the deck of Ninety Mile Beach stretching to the Cape. A private walkway 50 metres leads to the beach. Activities Ahipara offers are surfing, swimming, horse riding, quad bike hire, fishing. Golf course 2km drive. For those interested in farming, visit our beef farm at Herikino. Dinner available on request. Directions: Take road to Ahipara from Kaitaia. Turn left at Ahipara School, follow road around corner, 3rd house on beach side.

Awanui - Lake Ngatu   *B&B Countrystay 14km N of Kaitaia*

Lake Ngatu Lodge
Diane & Graeme Jay
27 Sweetwater Road, RD 1, Awanui, Northland

Tel (09) 406 7300   Fax (09) 406 7300
lakengatulodge@hotmail.com
lakengatulodge.homestead.com/ngatu2.html

Double $100 Single $80 (Continental Breakfast)
Credit cards accepted
2 King/Twin (2 bdrm)   1 Private

Our lakeside home, set on 10 acres of mature garden, orchard and paddocks, is the ideal centralised Northern
retreat. Relax in your upstairs room or private lounge, swim, walk or kayak the lake, three minutes to 90 Mile Beach - the choice is yours! 100 kilometres to Cape Reinga, bus tours passes by daily, three golf-courses and Okahu Estate winery within a half hour drive, fishing/diving trips can be arranged. Special continental breakfast with home grown organic produce, undercover parking and saltwater pool top off the experience - Diane, Graeme and Jif the dog welcome you!

Kaitaia - Pamapuria   *B&B Homestay Self-contained 7min S of Kaitaia*

Plane Tree Lodge
Rosemary & Mike Wright
State Highway 1, Pamapuria Kaitaia, Northland

Tel (09) 408 0995 Fax (09) 408 0959
Mob 025 338 859
reservationsplanetreelodge@xtra.co.nz
www.plane-tree-lodge.net.nz

Double $110-$135 Single $85-$100 (Special Breakfast)
Child negotiable self-contained cottage $175 - $195
Credit cards accepted Children welcome
3 Queen 1 Twin 1 Single (5 bdrm)   3 Ensuite 1 Private

Imagine waking up to the sound of birdsong and the smell of coffee and bacon. Plan your day's activities from the many options this natural, unspoilt area has to offer. At the end of each day come home to the peaceful serenity of our 2 acre parklike garden. Wash the sand of 90 Mile Beach from your hair, and enjoy a delicious meal at one of our local restaurants. Alternatively, savour a glass of wine in the spa pool & watch the sun setting over a peaceful landcape. Our four cats will ensure you a mouse-free environment.

The difference between a B&B and a hotel
is that you don't hug the hotel staff when you leave.

Coopers Beach   *Homestay 3km N of Mangonui*

Mac'n'Mo's
Maureen & Malcolm MacMillan
PO Box 177, Mangonui

Tel (09) 406 0538   Fax (09) 406 0538
MacNMo@xtra.co.nz
www.bnb.co.nz/macnmos.html

Double $80 Single $60 (Continental Breakfast)
Dinner $25
1 Queen 1 Double 1 Twin (3 bdrm)
2 Ensuite 2 Guests share

Enjoy a "million dollar" view of Doubtless Bay while you enjoy Mac's smoked fish on your toast. The bus to Cape Reinga stops at our gate, you may go on a craft or wine trail, swim with dolphins, go fishing, diving or just relax on our unpolluted uncrowded beaches, there's one across the road. There are several fine restaurants and the "world famous" fish and chip shop nearby. Have a memorable stay with Mac'n'Mo, they will take good care of you.

Coopers Beach   *B&B 3km N of Mangonui*

Doubtless Bay Lodge
Warren & Naomi Johnston
33 Cable Bayblock Road, Coopers Beach, Mangonui 0557

Tel (09) 406 1661   Fax (09) 406 1662
Mob 025 859 700   enquiries@doubtlessbaylodge
www.doubtlessbaylodge

Double $98 Single $73 (Full Breakfast) Child $20
Credit cards accepted
3 Queen 2 Single (4 bdrm)
4 Ensuite

Our B/B is 800 mtrs north of the Coopers Beach shops. We are 1 hour north of Paihia. Each room has ensuite bathroom, Sky-Cable TV, fridge, tea and coffee making facilities. We have a guest laundry and barbecue and two pussy cats. We arrange scenic bus tours to Cape Reinga, fishing trips and dolphin watching. Enjoy the sea and rural views of this lovely place where you can visit the many isolated beaches in the area, knowing you are 150 kms from the nearest traffic lights.

Coopers Beach *B&B Homestay 2km N of Mangonui*

Rudi Heinzelmann
47 Spicer Road, Coopers Beach, Mangonui 0557
Tel (09) 406 2035 Fax (09) 406 2035
Mob 021 154 9813
www.bnb.co.nz/heinzelmann.html

Double $60-$100 Single $50 (Full Breakfast) Dinner
$20 - $35 Sleep out / tent site $20 pp
1 King 2 Queen 1 Twin 1 Single (5 bdrm)
1 Ensuite

The Bella Vista guesthouse is located on the hilltop of
Coopers Beach. We are first to see the sun! Our
commanding views take your eyes over the whole Doubtless Bay area, it's totally relaxing. Visitors are
most welcome to share all this beauty with us. A range of sports and leisure activities are waiting for
you and we can arrange this for you. Stroll the beach and watch the sunset, dine out with your best
friend. Enjoy your stay at Bella Vista. We'll take care of you.

Mahinepua - Kaeo *Homestay 22km E of Kaeo*

Waiwurrie
Vickie & Rodger Corbin
Mahinepua, RD 1, Kaeo/ Whangaroa, Northland
Tel (09) 405 0840 Fax (09) 405 0854
Mob 021 186 7900 wai.wurrie@xtra.co.nz
www.coastalhomestay.co.nz

Double $150-$175 Single $150 (Full Breakfast) Dinner
$40 pp Credit cards accepted
1 King 1 Queen (2 bdrm)
1 Ensuite 1 Private

Want something a little special? Have we the place for you! Situated on Northland's East coast surrounded
by forestry and private farmland, with magnificent Pacific Ocean views, Cavailli Islands and deep sea
fishing grounds. Golfers paradise, Kauri Cliffs, Waitangi, Ahipara, Carrington. Sightsee to Cape Reinga,
visit the Bay of Islands, Kerikeri, Whangaroa Habour or just relax. We have Benson the dog and
Moppet the cat. We love to entertain and would enjoy meeting you. Good Kiwi Hospitality! For more
information please phone us.

Kerikeri *B&B Homestay 3km E of Kerikeri*

Matariki Orchard
Alison & David Bridgman
14 Pa Road, Kerikeri, Bay of Islands
Tel (09) 407 7577 Fax (09) 407 7593
Mob 0274 080 621 matarikihomestay@xtra.co.nz
www.bnb.co.nz/matarikiorchard.html

Double $120 Single $70 (Full Breakfast)
Child $20 Dinner $40pp Credit cards accepted
1 King 1 Queen 2 Single (3 bdrm)
1 Ensuite 1 Guests share

We welcome guests to our home, large garden, swimming pool and subtropical orchard, within walking
distance to historic area. Four minutes by car to township. David has a vintage car that is used for
personalised tours. A short complimentary tour is offered of historic area to guests. We are retired
farmers and David a local tour operator for nine years loves to help with ìWhere to go and what to doî.
Can arrange tour bookings. We enjoy providing dinner with NZ wine. Will meet coach or plane, no
cost. Directions please phone.

Kerikeri - Okaihau   *B&B Farmstay 12km W of Kerikeri*

Clotworthy Farmstay
Shennett & Neville Clotworthy
Wiroa Road, RD1, Okaihau, Bay of Islands
Tel (09) 401 9371   Fax (09) 401 9371
www.bnb.co.nz/clotworthyfarmstay.html

Double $80 Single $40 (Full Breakfast) Dinner $25 by
arrangement Credit cards accepted
1 Queen 2 Single (2 bdrm)
1 Guests share

We farm cattle, sheep, and horses on our 310 acres. There
are panoramic views of the Bay of Islands area from our home 1,000 ft above sea level. Of 1840's
pioneering descent, our interests are travel, farming, genealogy and equestrian activities. We have an
extensive library on Northland history and families. Directions: SH10 take Wiroa/Airport Road at the
Kerikeri intersection. 9kms on the right OR SH1, take Kerikeri Road just south of Okaihau. We are
fourth house on the left, past the golf course (8kms).

Kerikeri   *B&B Self-contained Orchardstay 8km S of Kerikeri*

Puriri Park
Paul & Charmian Treadwell
Puriri Park Orchard, State Highway 10, Box 572,
Kerikeri
Tel (09) 407 9818 Fax (09) 407 9498 puriri@xtra.co.nz
www.bnb.co.nz/puriripark.html

Double $95 Single $75 (Full Breakfast) Child $10
Dinner $30 Credit cards accepted
3 Double 2 Twin 1 Single (4 bdrm)
1 Private 2 Guests share

Puriri Park has long been known for its hospitality in the Far North. Guests are welcome to wander
around our large garden, explore the orange and kiwifruit orchards, sit by the lilypond or feed our flock
of fantail pigeons. We have five acres of bird-filled native bush, mostly totara and puriri. We are in an
excellent situation for trips to Cape Reinga and sailing or cruising on the beautiful Bay of Islands. We
can arrange tours for you or pick you up from the airport.

Kerikeri   *B&B Farmstay Homestay 10km Kerikeri Central*

Kerikeri Inlet View
Trish & Ryan Daniells
Inlet Road, RD 3, Kerikeri
Tel (09) 407 7477   Fax (09) 407 7478
Mob 025 612 0021
www.bnb.co.nz/kerikeriinletview.html

Double $70 Single $45 (Full Breakfast) Child $15
Dinner $18 by arrangement Backpackers (not on hill)
$15 - no breakfast Children welcome
1 Queen 2 Double 2 Single (3 bdrm)
2 Ensuite 1 Guests share

We welcome you to our 7 bedroom home on top of our 1100 acre beef and sheep farm. Enjoy the superb
views of the inlet and the Bay of Islands while you relax in our spa pool. Join us for breakfast consisting
of seasonal fruit and juice, homemade bread and butter, free-range chook eggs, our own sausages,
before exploring the many attractions around Kerikeri. Backpackers has 5 lockable bedrooms, large
lounge, kitchen and laundry. Note: please phone first for bookings, detailed directions or pick-up. We
speak Japanese.

Kerikeri   *B&B Homestay 7km N of Kerikeri*

Sunrise Homestay B&B
Judy & Les Remnant
140 Skudders Road, Skudders Beach, RD 1, Kerikeri

Tel (09) 407 5447   Fax (09) 407 8448
Mob 021 774 941   sunrisehomestay@xtra.co.nz
www.bnb.co.nz/sunrisehomestaybb.html

Double $90 Single $60 (Full Breakfast) Dinner $30pp
by arrangement Credit cards accepted
1 Double 4 Single (3 bdrm)
1 Ensuite 1 Guests share

A warm welcome awaits you at our restful homestay ovelooking Kerikeri inlet, magnificent water views and often spectacular sunrises and sunsets. Occasional visits from dolphins. Plenty to see and do in Bay of Islands. We are only too happy to help arrange your trips. Tea and coffee available at all times. Laundry facilities available. Courtesy pick up from bus or airport. Phone, fax or leave phone number on answer phone, we will call you back. One of the best locations in Kerikeri. Do come and share it with us. Non smokers. We have no pets.

Kerikeri   *B&B 3km S of Kerikeri*

Graleen
Graeme & Colleen Wattam
578a Kerikeri Road, RD 3, Kerikeri, Bay of Islands

Tel (09) 407 9047   Fax (09) 407 9047
Mob 025 940 845   graleen@xtra.co.nz
www.kerikeri.co.nz/graleen

Double $70 Single $50 (Full Breakfast) Credit cards accepted
1 Queen 1 Double 2 Single (3 bdrm)
3 Ensuite

After extensive travel we have designed and built a new home with guest accommodation and comfort in mind. All bedrooms have ensuites and TV with direct access to our lovely sheltered veranda. Breakfast in our large guest lounge. Historic Kerikeri is surrounded by orchards, farms, and is centrally situated to Bay of Islands and Northland's many tourist attractions. "Graleen" is 200 metres from SH10, only 20 minutes from historic Waitangi and Paihia beaches, 3 minutes from the township, restaurants, golf course and many craft galleries.

Kerikeri   *Homestay 2.6km N of Kerikeri*

Glenfalloch
Evalyn & Rick Pitelen
Landing Road, Kerikeri

Tel (09) 407 5471   Fax (09) 407 5473
Mob 025 280 0661   glenfall@ihug.co.nz
www.bnb.co.nz/glenfalloch.html

Double $80-$90 Single $60 (Full Breakfast) Child $20
Dinner $30pp b/a Credit cards accepted   Children welcome
1 King 1 Queen 1 Double 1 Single (3 bdrm)
2 Ensuite 1 Private

Venture down Glenfalloch's tree lined driveway to a peaceful garden paradise. Evalyn and Rick welcome guests with refreshments to be enjoyed in the lounges or outdoors on the decks. You are welcome to wander about the garden, use the swimming pool and tennis court, or just relax in our private retreat. Breakfast can be enjoyed at your leisure outdoors, weather permitting. Laundry facilities available. Directions: travel 0.6km from the Stone Store to second driveway on left after Department of Conservation sign.

Kerikeri *B&B Homestay 3km E of Kerikeri*

Holmes Homestay
Jane & Tony Holmes
30b Blacks Road, Kerikeri

Tel (09) 407 7500   Fax (09) 407 7500
Mob 025 241 9448   tony_holmes@xtra.co.nz
www.bnb.co.nz/holmeshomestay.html

Double $75-$90 Single $50 (Full Breakfast) Dinner
$30 Credit cards accepted
1 Queen 1 Twin (2 bdrm)
1 Ensuite 1 Private 1 Host share

If you want tranquillity, relaxing on the deck watching boats come up the Inlet, a warm welcome awaits you, in our large, comfortable bungalow. The adventurous can paddle canoes up to the Stone Store. Our yacht is close by. Bush walks, night kiwi walks, fishing, horse trekking can be arranged. Bird life is abundant, sheep munch next door and we have two pet calves. At Kerikeri roundabout turn right into Hobson, left into Inlet - at 2.3km turn left into Blacks. We're half way down the hill. See you.

Kerikeri *Homestay Coastal 12km E of Kerikeri*

Oversley
Maire & Tone Coyte
Doves Bay Road, RD 1, Kerikeri

Tel (09) 407 8744   Fax (09) 407 4487
Mob 025 959 207   oversley@xtra.co.nz
www.bnb.co.nz/oversley.html

Double $120-$160 Single $90-$130 (Full Breakfast)
Dinner $50   B/A Credit cards accepted
1 King 1 Queen 2 Single (3 bdrm)
2 Ensuite 1 Private

'Oversley' offers magnificent panoramic water views, sweeping lawns and private native bush walks to the water. Our spacious, comfortable home, set in 18 acres, has a friendly relaxed atmosphere with quality accommodation. Laundry facilities available.   We are an easy going, well travelled, retired couple, enjoy all sports, sailing and fishing on our 13 metre yacht, golfing on Kerikeri's first class course 15 minutes away (Kauri Cliff's course only 35 minutes) and are animal lovers. Your company at dinner, to share good food and wine with us, is most welcome. (Dinner includes pre dinner drinks and wine).

Kerikeri *B&B Homestay 2km S of Kerikeri*

Gannaway House
Jill & Roger Gardner
Kerikeri Road, RD 3, Kerikeri

Tel (09) 407 1432 Fax (09) 407 1431 Mob 025 798 115
gannaway@xtra.co.nz
www.bnb.co.nz/gannawayhouse.html

Double $85-$105 Single $55-$75 (Full Breakfast) Child
$30 Dinner $30 by arrangement Credit cards accepted
2 Queen 1 Twin (3 bdrm)
1 Ensuite 1 Guests share

Jill and Roger welcome you to Gannaway House. Our comfortable home, set in 2 acres of garden and orchard is situated down a tree-lined driveway, close to town but in the quiet of the country. We offer one large ground floor room with ensuite and private entrance. Upstairs, two rooms (1 Queen and 1 Twin) with shared facilities. Enjoy our beautiful tranquil garden - also the sheep and lambs in the orchard. We are also breeders of pedigree cats. Directions: From S.H. 10 - first driveway on left past Makana Chocolate Factory.

Kerikeri   *Homestay*

Pukanui Lodge B&B
Dale Simkin & Dale Hutchinson
322 Kerikeri Road, Kerikeri

Tel (09) 407 7003   Fax (09) 407 7068
Mob 0274 444 955   pukanui@igrin.co.nz
www.bnb.co.nz/ .html

Double $120-$140 Single $60-$90
(Continental Breakfast) Child   Dinner
2 Queen 1 Twin (3 bdrm)
3 Ensuite

Tranquility 400m from Kerikeri township. Subtropical gardens and citrus orchard have influenced both decor and cuisine of Pukanui. Generous breakfast can be served on private decks off your ensuite bedroom in garden setting or overlooking pool in summer. Cosy lounge in winter. Local produce features significantly in our culinary delights with dinner by prior arrangement. Friendly hosts will help plan your visit to make it memorable. Fax and email facilities available. Complimentary airport/bus transfers.

Kerikeri   *B&B 15km NE of Kerikeri*

The Anchorage
Norm & Bev Little
Anchorage Heights, Doves Bay, Kerikeri

Tel (09) 407 6696   Fax (09) 407 6696
Mob 021 188 0750   www.bnb.co.nz/little.html

Double $130 (Continental Breakfast)
1 Queen 1 Twin (2 bdrm)
1 Private

Million Dollar views taking in the Bay of Islands and Kerikeri Inlet. Set in bush overlooking the Kerikeri

Cruising Club Marina. A magic place, where dolphins often visit our bay, and kiwi live in the bush below. Relax and enjoy the view or bushwalk or swim in safe beaches close by. Sailing, fishing, and diving trips can be arranged. Only 15 minutes to shops and cafes. Your hosts, Bev and Norm, extend a warm welcome to you.

Kerikeri Central   *B&B Self-contained 800M N of kerikeri*

Peacock Gardens Bed & Breakfast
Sally & Ken Climo
1 Peacock Gardens Drive, Kerikeri, Bay of Islands

Tel 09 407 5070 Fax 09 407 5070   Mob 027 4311 312
ksclimo@paradise.net.nz
www.bnb.co.nz/peacockgardens.html

Double $90 Single $70 (Continental Breakfast)
1 Queen (1 bdrm)
1 Ensuite

800m from Kerikeri township offering a tranquil location with rural views. Enjoy a short walk to quality cafes and restaurants, a variety of shops,historical Stone Store and Maori Pa. 20 minutes to Paihia/Waitangi, fishing, golf, beaches, tourist attractions. Amenities include offstreet parking, own entrance, TV, Microwave, Fridge, Tea/Coffee making facilities, private ensuite, iron, hairdryer. View the sunset from the decks or relax in the Spa Pool. Continental breakfast provisions supplied daily to enjoy at your leisure. Winter rates apply.

Pakaraka
B&B Farmstay 20km S of Pahia/ Kerikeri/Kaikohe

Jarvis Family Farmstay & Equestrian Centre
Frederika & Douglas Jarvis
State Highway 1, Pakaraka, RD2 Ohaeawai, Bay of Islands
Tel (09) 405 9606 Fax (09) 405 9607 Mob 021 259 1120
baystay@igrin.co.nz   www.nzbaystay.com

Double $100-$120 Single $60
(Continental Breakfast) (Full Breakfast) Child half price
Dinner $30 B/A Children welcome Pets welcome
Smoking area inside
1 King/Twin 1 Double (2 bdrm)
3 Private/Spa bath room

For a charming and relaxing break, look no further! Beautiful subtropical gardens with water features surround our spacious family home where you can choose between indoor and outdoor dining. Our four-poster suite includes its own lounge with two single beds, TV/video plus a private deck in the 'Wishing well' garden.

Fredi and Douglas emigrated from the UK in 1990, where they ran one of England's top country inns: so they are no strangers to hospitality. We have 30 acres for you to enjoy with extensive equestrian facilities and walks. Just bring a smile with you.

Here are some quotes from our visitors book: "A wonderful retreat in a tranquil environment, hospitable hosts," USA. "I enjoyed last evening and the dinner with you. Everything was perfect!" Montpellier, France. "A wonderful retreat: a privilege to share your hospitality and beautiful home," South Africa.

Pakaraka is centrally based for touring the Bay, West and North Coasts with all the popular tourist, dolphin and marine discoveries. We are a pet friendly country stay.

17

Pakaraka - Paihia *B&B Farmstay 10km N of Kawakawa*

Bay of Islands Farmstay - B&B Highland Farm
Glenis & Ken Mackintosh
Pakaraka, 6627 State Highway 1, RD 2, Kaikohe 0400

Tel (09) 404 0430 Fax (09) 404 0430
Mob 027 249 8296 Ken@infobiz.co.nz
www.bnb.co.nz/bayofislandfarmstaybb.html

Double $85-$90 Single $60 (Full Breakfast) Child $10
Dinner $20 - $30 (byo & comp.) twin room $80 - 85
Credit cards accepted Children welcome
1 Double 1 Twin 3 Single (2 bdrm)   2 Ensuite

Beautiful 51 acres, stone walls, barberry hedges. Sheep,
cattle. Ken a sheep-Dog Trialist, trains dogs and pups daily! Enjoy watching help shift animals. Meet and photograph with animals on your farm walk.Enjoy your visit. Swimming pool or cosy warm home in winter.Access to Internet. Good Central Base! Five golf courses, beaches, hot pools, shopping! Situated 15 minutes Paihia, Kerikeri, Kaikohe. Welcome to Bay of Islands. Book early or take pot luck! (10 minutes North Kawakawa or 2 south Pakaraka Junction). "Highland Farm" on entrance.

Paihia *Countrystay 8km N of Paihia*

Puketona Lodge
Heather and Maurice Pickup
769 Puketona Road, RD 1, Paihia 0252

Tel (09) 402 8152 Fax (09) 402 8152 Mob 025 260
7058   puketonalodge@xtra.co.nz
www.bnb.co.nz/puketonalodge.html

Double $120 Single $90 King $120 (Full Breakfast)
Dinner $35 Credit cards accepted
1 King/Twin 1 Double (2 bdrm)
1 Ensuite 1 Private

Our home, on 10 acres, is large and modern, built by
Maurice of native timbers. Of English/NZ origins, we have American connections too. Our bedrooms are spacious and private and open onto our large garden. We are close to Haruru Falls, Waitangi, beaches, walks, golf and historic places. Our breakfasts feature homemade breads, preserves, fresh fruit, and more. We can book tours and cruises. Complimentary refreshments on arrival. Heather teaches ceramics and enjoys showing guests over the studio. We have two dogs and one cat.

Paihia *Countrystay 7km N of Paihia*

Lily Pond Estate B&B (Est 1989)
Allwyn & Graeme Sutherland
725 Puketona Road, RD 1, Paihia,
Lily Pond Estate sign at gate

Tel (09) 402 7041
www.bnb.co.nz/lilypondorchardbb.html

Double $85 Single $45 (Full Breakfast)
1 Double 1 Twin (2 bdrm)
1 Guests share Separate toilet

Drive in through an avenue of mature Liquid Amber trees
to our comfortable timber home on our five acre Country Estate growing citrus and pip fruit. The guest wing has views of the fountain, bird aviary, small lake and black swan with the double and twin rooms having private verandah access. Fresh orange juice, fruit and homemade jams are served at breakfast. We are born NZ'ers, sailed thousands of miles living aboard our 50ft yacht in the Pacific and will gladly share our Bay of Island knowledge to make your visit most memorable.

Paihia *B&B Homestay 1.5km S of Paihia*

Te Haumi House
Enid & Ernie Walker
12 Seaview Road, Paihia

Tel (09) 402 8046   Fax (09) 402 8046
enidanderniewalker@xtra.co.nz
www.bnb.co.nz/tehaumihouse.html

Double $80 Single $55 (Continental Breakfast)
Credit cards accepted
2 Queen 1 Single (2 bdrm)
1 Guests share 1 Host share

Millennium Sunrise. Welcome to our modern waterfront home, set amongst subtropical gardens with expansive harbour views, just minutes from tourist activities and town centre. Guests enjoy privacy through a clever split-level design. Buffet breakfast with a choice of dining room, garden deck or courtyard. Laundry facilities, ample off-street parking and courtesy pickup from bus available. Descendants of early settlers, we have a good knowledge of local history. Ernie is a Masonic Lodge member.

Central Paihia *B&B Self-contained*

Cedar Suite Spas
Jo & Peter Nisbet
5 Sullivans Road, Paihia

Tel (09) 402 8516   Fax (09) 402 8555
Mob 025 969 281   enquiry@cedarspaspaihia.co.nz
www.cedarspaspaihia.co.nz

Double $89-$150   Single $81-$150   (Continental Breakfast)   Breakfast extra, $10.50 pp   Credit cards accepted
3 Queen 1 Single (3 bdrm)   3 Ensuite

The Cedar Suite Spas offers first class accommodation in our modern cedar home amidst beautiful native trees. Suites are separate, 3 with PRIVATE SPAS, and their own superior ensuites. Both of us enjoy music, Peter managing the New Zealand Symphony Orchestra for over twenty years, and Jo enjoys photography and interior design. Breakfast we call Kiwi: - continental plus - and local fruit plays a big part in that. There is private parking, comfortable beds, fine linen, a French style room, filtered water and TV.

Paihia *Separate/Suite Self-contained Central Paihia*

Craicor Accommodation
Garth Craig & Anne Corbett
PO Box 15, 49 Kings Road, Paihia, Bay of Islands

Tel (09) 402 7882   Fax (09) 402 7883
craicor@actrix.gen.nz
www.craicor-accom.co.nz

Double $120 Single $90 (Continental Breakfast optional $7.50 each) Credit cards accepted
2 King 2 Single (2 bdrm)
2 Ensuite

The perfect spot for those seeking a quiet, sunny and central location. Discover the Garden Suite and Tree House. Self contained modern units nestled in a garden setting with trees that almost hug you, native birds and sea views. Each unit has ensuite bathroom, fully equipped kitchen for self catering, super king bed, TV, insect screens and is tastefully decorated to reflect the natural colours of the surroundings. Safe off street parking, all within a five minute stroll to the waterfront, restaurants and town centre.

Paihia   *Self-contained Paihia Central*

Iona Lodge
Mary & Malcolm Sinclair
29 Bayview Road, Paihia, Bay of Islands
Tel (09) 402 8072 Fax (09) 402 8072 ionas@xtra.co.nz
www.bnb.co.nz/ionalodge.html

Double $85-$115 Single $70 (Continental Breakfast)
Credit cards accepted
2 Double 1 Single (2 bdrm)
2 Ensuite

Share with us the best views in the Bay, from the comfort of your quiet sunny units, situated in Bayview Road, overlooking Central Paihia. Conveniently situated to shops, wharf and restaurants. One unit has a double and single bed. Upstairs are the bathroom, lounge, and kitchen. The studio has a double bed, kitchen and ensuite. Both are fully equipped with TV, BBQ and decks for you to relax on and enjoy the panoramic views. We supply generous breakfast provisions each day for you to enjoy at your leisure.

Paihia   *B&B Homestay 1km N of Paihia*

Bay of Islands Bed & Breakfast
Laraine & Sid Dyer
48 Tahuna Road, Paihia, Bay of Islands
Tel (09) 402 8551   Fax (09) 402 8551
larained@ihug.co.nz
www.bnb.co.nz/bayofislandsbedbreakfast.html

Double $80 Single $40 (Continental Breakfast)
1 Queen 2 Single (3 bdrm)
1 Host share

We invite you to stay and relax in our home, only minutes from the beach, with bush walks and golf course nearby. On arrival a warm welcome awaits you, with tea or coffee and a chance to unwind. Assistance with your itinerary is offered should you need help. We look forward to the pleasure of your company and ensuring your stay is as comfortable and memorable as possible. Our courtesy car will meet you if travelling by bus. We have a dog named Katie.

Paihia   *B&B Self-contained Paihia Central*

Marlin House
Christopher & Angela Houry
15 Bayview Road, Paihia, Bay of Islands New Zealand
Tel +64 (09) 402 8550 Fax 09 402 6770
Mob 021 487 937 marlinhouse@xtra.co.nz
www.bnb.co.nz/marlinhouse.html

Double $130-$155 Single $100 (Continental Breakfast)
(Special Breakfast) Child Negotiable Dinner Big choice
in town Credit cards accepted
1 King/Twin 2 King (3 bdrm)
3 Ensuite

Marlin House is a neo-colonial building with spacious luxury accommodation for five persons in three (One Super Luxury with bath) self-contained ensuites with fridge TV and off-road parking. Situated in a quiet tree-clad spot above Paihia with beautiful sea views and only three minutes walk to the beach shops and lots of restaurants. We serve special continental breakfasts in your suite or on the deck, or order a full cooked breakfast. Ask us for discounts on most excursions. "Benny" Cat outside.

Paihia
B&B Separate/Suite Self-contained Paihia Central

Admiral's View Lodge
Robyn & Peter Rhodes
2 McMurray Road, Paihia, Bay of Islands
Tel (09) 402 6236   0800 247 234
Fax (09) 402 6237   Mob 025 779 997
admiralsview@actrix.gen.nz
www.bnb.co.nz/admiralsviewlodge.html
Double $85-$150 (Continental Breakfast)
Spa suites 2, 3, 4 bedrooms $130 - $250
Credit cards accepted
4 King 6 Queen 3 Double 9 Twin 11 Single   (13 bdrm)
9 Ensuite 2 Private   3 - 4 bedroom holiday home

Opened October 2002, Pahia's newest five-star self-contained and serviced (exceptional - among the best available in NZ). Set in a peaceful location off the busy main road with views across to historic Russell and beyond. Executive one and two bedroom apartments, luxury studios some with two-person spa baths, all with Italian style ensuites with extra large showers and double vanities. Plus our popular B&B suites. Sunny sea view terraces and balconies. Also a separate 3-4 bedroom holiday home with panoramic sea views and pool - POA. Ideal for business, pleasure or that ROMANTIC time out.
Swim with the dolphins, sail the bay, visit the Hole in the Rock, golf at Waitangi. Tarrif includes a self-service buffet breakfast. Season/unit rates apply. Restaurant adjacent, cafes and town centre all within walking distance. We have two very friendly Siamese cats, Cinnamin and Shilo.
Robyn and Peter would love to welcome you to Admiral's View Lodge.

Features and attractions:
- well equipped kitchens, dining/lounge areas
- rooms air-conditioned and serviced daily
- special honeymoon suites
- Sky TV and self-dial phones
- business & Internet facilities in rooms
- disabled facilities • guest laundry
- free bikes and tennis
- guest BBQs
- tour desk and courtesy car

Paihia   *B&B   Separate/Suite   3km N of Paihia*

Villa Casablanca
Barbara & Derek Robertson
18 Goffe Drive, Haruru Falls, Paihia
Tel (09) 402 6980   Fax (09) 402 6980
Mob 021 666 567   derek@bestprice.co.nz
www.bestprice.co.nz

Double $100-$180 Single $70-$150 (Special Breakfast)
Child n/a Dinner $45 Credit cards accepted
2 King/Twin 3 Queen 4 Single (4 bdrm)
3 Ensuite 1 Private

Our romantic villa was inspired by the grand haciendas
of Spain and Mexico. Set on the Haruru Falls ridge, it has sweeping views over Russell, the Bay of
Islands, and the shipping channel to Paihia. It is an ideal honeymoon hideaway surrounded by private
gardens and sundecks. Our accommodation consists of two suites and two bedrooms all with en-suite or
private facilities, a short walk to the waterfall, restaurants, brewhouse and shops and only 3 minutes
drive to Paihia's sandy beaches.

Paihia   *B&B   Self-contained   Private entrance   0.5km NW of Paihia*

Windermere
Richard & Jill Burrows
168 Marsden Road, Paihia, Bay of Islands
Tel (09) 402 8696   Fax (09) 402 5095
windermere@igrin.co.nz
www.windermere.co.nz

Double $100-$175 Single $80-$150 (Continental
Breakfast) Child $25 Credit cards accepted
2 Queen 4 Single (2 bdrm)
2 Ensuite

'Windermere' is a large modern family home set in a bush setting and yet located right on one of the best
beaches in the Bay of Islands. Superior accommodation is provided with suites having their own ensuite
and kitchen facilities. For longer stays one suite has its own laundry, dryer and fully equipped kitchen.
The other suite has microwave and fridge only. Each suite has its own decks where you can sit and
enjoy the view enhanced by spectacular sunsets. Sky TV. Jill and Richard would welcome your company
to enjoy our own little part of paradise.

Paihia   *B&B   Homestay   Self catering Riverside Cottage   6km W of Paihia*

Appledore Lodge
Janet & Jim Pugh
Puketona Road, Paihia, Bay of Islands
Tel (09) 402 8007   Fax (09) 402 8007
Mob 021 179 5839   appledorelodge@xtra.co.nz
www.appledorelodge.co.nz

Double $80-$150 Single $70-$100 (Special Breakfast)
Child N/A Self contained Riverside Cottage
$150 - $225 Credit cards accepted
1 King/Twin 1 King 1 Queen 1 Double (4 bdrm)
4 Ensuite

Welcome and relax in our home with our outdoor spa pool. Waitangi River gently tumbles over miniature
waterfalls and rapids just 25 metres away. Spellbinding river views from all our ensuite rooms including
the romantic four-poster. Special home made breakfast served on our antique Kauri table or grand deck.
Brand new for 2003, absolute riverside, self-contained cottage: sleeps four adults. We enjoy classic
cars, golf, travel and meeting new guests. Janet, Jim and our Golden Retriever look forward to making
your stay memorable. "Yours to enjoy."

Paihia   *B&B Homestay 3km Paihia*

Fallsview
Shirley & Clive Welch
4 Fallsview Road, RD 1, Haruru, Paihia

Tel (09) 402 7871   Fax (09) 402 7861
Mob 025 627 1652
www.bnb.co.nz/fallsview.html

Double $75-$90 Single $40-$50 (Full Breakfast)
Child negotiable Credit cards accepted
1 Queen 1 Twin 1 Single (3 bdrm)
1 Guests share

Our studio apartment has all the comforts of home, a beautiful sunny lounge with fridge, microwave, stereo, TV, tea/coffee facilities, laundry, barbecue and undercover parking. All surrounded by a semi tropical garden. With breakfast upstairs you will enjoy the beautiful panoramic view of the surrounding countryside. Extra twin beds are available upstairs if in a group.   We share our home with a small gregarious poodle and 3 reclusive cats. Situated only 3km from main tourist attractions. We offer you a warm welcome.

Paihia   *B&B Homestay 6km W of Paihia*

Blue Heron Country Lodge
Beverly and George Barke
621B Puketona Road, R.D.1 Paihia, Bay of Islands

Tel (09) 402 8195   Fax (09) 402 8194
george.barke@xtra.co.nz
www.bnb.co.nz/blueheron.html

Double $100-$120 Single $60-$90
 (Continental Breakfast)
1 Queen 1 Twin (2 bdrm)
1 Ensuite 1 Guests share

Our home is set in a large garden on 15 acres of peaceful, rural land. We invite you to join with us and experience unequalled comfort, peace and tranquillity, delicious breakfasts on the patio, fascinating bird life, picturesque rural views, totally relaxed privacy and revitalising country living. Historic sights, fabulous beaches, dolphins, a fantastic golf course, interesting walks and a wide choice of restaurants are just minutes away. We offer a warm welcome with complementary refreshments on arrival.

Paihia   *B&B Self-contained Paihia-Central*

Allegra House
Heinz & Brita Marti
39 Bayview Road, Paihia, Bay of Islands

Tel (09) 402 7932   Fax (09) 402 7930
 allegrahouse@xtra.co.nz
www.allegra.co.nz

Double $125-$160 Single $125-$160
(Continental Breakfast) Child neg apartment $140 - $200
1 King/Twin 2 Queen (3 bdrm)
3 Ensuite

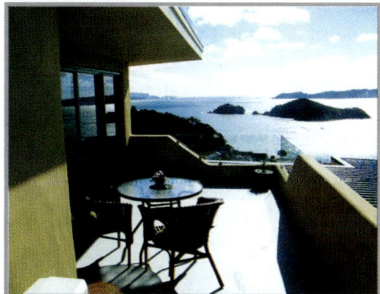

Allegra House is located in our own native bush setting, just above central Paihia, with expansive views over the Bay of Islands from each room. Our spacious home has modern furnishings enhancing the light, airy atmosphere, with plenty of balcony space to relax on and enjoy the views. We have a self-catering one-bedroom apartment as well as bed and breakfast rooms. Outdoor spa. Telescope. We are happy to help you choose the best options for your time with us and can book activities for you.

Paihia - Opua   *B&B 5km S of Paihia*

Rose Cottage
Pat & Don Jansen
37a Oromahoe Road, Opua 0290, Bay of Islands
Tel (09) 402 8099   Fax (09) 402 8096
Mob 025 605 9560
www.bnb.co.nz/rosecottageopua.html
Double $80-$100 (Continental Breakfast)
1 King/Twin 1 Double (2 bdrm)
1 Private

Welcome to our home set in a lovely bush garden and enjoying picturesque upper harbour and rural views. Our guest wing offers a private entrance and deck area, comfortable rooms, TV, fridge, microwave and tea/coffee facilities. Both rooms enjoy sea views. Don is a retired carpenter and Pat a retired nurse. Our interests include local history, gardening, walking, fishing and sailing. We have been hosting guests for many years and look forward to helping you enjoy your stay. Inspection welcome.

Paihia - Opua   *B&B Homestay Self-contained 300m E of Opua*

Margaret Sinclair
7 Franklin St, Opua
Tel (09) 402 8285 Fax (09) 402 8285
bbopua@xtra.co.nz
www.bnb.co.nz/sinclair.html
Double $70 Single $40 (Continental Breakfast)
S/C Flat 1 double 2 single $70 - $90 Double
$10 Single
1 Double 2 Single (2 bdrm)
1 Host share

Welcome to my lovely home above Opua harbour. Enjoy panoramic views of water and boat activities - always something happening. Tourist activities are nearby. Relax in the spa after your day's outing. You may like to wander in my garden - my big interest. Downstairs is a 2 roomed unit, separate shower, toilet and private deck with stunning views. Take the Whangarei - Paihia road. Turn right for Opua - Russel ferry. This is Franklin St. My house is clearly visible on the seaward side.

Paihia - Opua   *B&B Homestay Self-contained 5km S of Paihia*

Seascape
Vanessa & Frank Leadley
17 English Bay Road, Opua, Bay of Islands
Tel (09) 402 7650   Fax (09) 402 7650
Mob 027 4756 793   frankleadley@xtra.co.nz
www.bnb.co.nz/leadley.html
Double $90-$100 Single $60 (Special Breakfast)
S/C flat $90 - $100 Credit cards accepted
1 Queen 2 Single (2 bdrm)
1 Ensuite 1 Host share

"Seascape" is on a tranquil bush-clad ridge. Enjoy spectacular views, stroll through bush to the coastal walk-way, enjoy our beautifully landscaped garden, experience the many activities in the Bay, or relax on your deck. We are keen NZ and international travellers. Other interests include music, gardening, fishing, boating, and Rotary. Our fully self-contained flat has queen size bed, TV, laundry, kitchen, own entrance and deck. Join us for breakfast, or look after yourselves. Guest Room with shared facilities also available.

Paihia - Opua   *B&B Self-contained 3 b.room cottage & 2 b.room unit 5km S of Paihia*

Waterview Lodge
Antionette & Jess Cherrington
14 Franklin Street, Opua, Bay of Islands 0290
Tel (09) 402 7595   Fax (09) 402 7596
Mob 021 102 3950   waterviewlodge@hotmail.com
www.bnb.co.nz/waterview.html

Double $140-$220 Single $90-$120
(Continental Breakfast) Child $20 Dinner $30 - $40
7 Queen 1 Twin 5 Single (8 bdrm)
3 Ensuite 2 Private

Overlooking the picturesque Port of Opua, Waterview Lodge is a quality accomodation establishment. The Harbour and River suites, with private balcony's, have expansive sea views of Opua and the upper harbour. Our 3 bedroom cottage also has beautiful sea views. Our 2 bedroom Garden unit is located downstairs next to the Garden suite, with access to a private garden and native bush backdrop. Both my husband & I are originally from the Bay of Islands. We enjoy living at Waterview Lodge with our 2 sons, Ben 15 and Oliver 8, and our little dog Amy.

Paihia - Opua   *B&B Self-contained Lodge 5km N of Paihia*

Mako Lodge & Fishing Charters
Graeme & Jean McIntosh
18 Pt Veronica Drive, Opua 0290, Bay of Islands
Tel (09) 402 7957   0800 625 669   Fax (09) 402 5957
Mob 025 739 787   makolodge.charters@xtra.co.nz
www.makolodge.co.nz

Double $140 Single $140 (Full Breakfast) Child N/A
Dinner By arrangement Garden Suite From $195
Credit cards accepted Pets welcome
2 Queen 2 Single (3 bdrm)   2 Ensuite

Fabulous cliff top location in quiet cul de sac with breathtaking views over harbour, just five minutes from Paihia. Choose from our B&B unit or the garden suite (both due for completion September 2003). Services include own ensuites, TV/video with extensive video library, fridges, tea & coffee making, outdoor BBQ area and lookout. Pets and children by arrangement. Resident Golden Labrador (Tessa). Optional light tackle, saltfly, game fishing or sightseeing trips on our modern fully equipped charter vessel ìMakoî (see www.makocharters.co.nz)

Paihia - Opua   *B&B Homestay 5km S of Paihia*

Pt. Veronica Lodge
Audrey & John McKiernan
11 Pt. Veronica Drive, Opua, Bay of Islands
Tel (09) 402 5579   Fax (09) 402 5579
Mob 021 1820697   pt.veronicalodge@xtra.co.nz
www.bay-of-islands.co.nz/accomm/veronica.html

Double $100-$160 Single $70-$120
(Special Breakfast) Credit cards accepted
3 Queen (3 bdrm)
2 Ensuite 1 Private

Qualmark 4 star Guest & Hosted property at Veronica point between Paihia & Opua. Access to the coastal track and views of the bay towards Paihia & Russell; this is our special place. Peaceful, romantic and restful with wonderful bush and coastal walks from the house.   Soak in our Spa or rest on the decks. T.V. in your room and Sky channels in the lounge. Golf, sailing, fishing & historic buildings within 10 minutes drive. Audrey & John and Bonnie & Clyde, our friendly dogs welcome you.

Russell *B&B Self-contained Russell Central*

Te Manaaki
Sharyn & Dudley Smith
2 Robertson Road, Russell
Tel (09) 403 7200   Fax (09) 403 7537
Mob 025 292 4345   triple.b@xtra.co.nz
www.bay-of-islands.co.nz/accomm/tmanaaki.html
Double $150-$250 Single $150-$250 (Full Breakfast)
Child $20 Credit cards accepted
2 Superking (2 bdrm)
2 Ensuite

"Te Manaaki" overlooks the picturesque harbour and village of historic Russell with its delightful seaside restaurants, shops and wharf a gentle stroll away. Magnificent harbour, bush and village views are a feature of guests private accommodation. The Villa is an attractively appointed sunny spacious de-luxe unit set in its own grounds (with garden spa) adjacent to the main house. The Studio is a self contained suite-styled apartment on the ground floor of our new modern home. Both units have mini-kitchen facilities and off-street parking.

Russell *B&B Homestay Separate/Suite Self-contained 5km S of Russell*

Treetops
Vivienne & Andy Nathan
6 Pinetree Lane, Te Wahapu, Russell
Tel (09) 403 7475   Fax (09) 403 7459
Mob 027 272 8881   vnathan@xtra.co.nz
www.bnb.co.nz/treetopsrussell.html
Double $100 Single $85 (Full Breakfast) Dinner $35
S/C Cottage $110 Credit cards accepted
1 King 1 Double (2 bdrm)
1 Guests share

Our home is situated at the end of Te Wahapu Peninsula. We are surrounded by native bush and tuis & fantails are our constant companions. Kiwis are sometimes heard during the night. Both upstairs bedrooms have beautiful sea views from your bed. Guests are welcome to sit in the spa pool and watch the sun set over Paihia across the Bay. A track through the bush leads down to the beach and the self-contained historic cottage, where you are welcome to use the dinghy and barbecue.

Russell *B&B Separate/Suite 19km E of Russell*

Gasthaus Waipiro Bay
Beate & Thomas Lauterbach
Waipiro Bay - Manawaora Road 392,
PO Box 224, Russell
Tel (09) 403 7095   Fax (09) 403 7095
gasthaus@ihug.co.nz   www.lauterbach.co.nz
Double $165-$185 Single $135-$150
(Special Breakfast) Child $45pp Dinner $48 pp b/a
Credit cards accepted Children welcome
2 Queen 1 Single (2 bdrm)
1 Ensuite 1 Private

Dream of a place, an artist's home above a bay, the Pacific Ocean on the horizon, islands, beaches, forests - nature at your doorstep. This world of space and light inspires artist Thomas Lauterbach to paint strong images of land, sea and the Maori people. A warm, imaginative home, comfortable bedrooms with spectacular views. Enjoy your private living-room with open fire place and works of art. We love to cook gourmet meals with flavours from Italy to the South Pacific. For a taste of heaven on earth - come and let us spoil you a little.

Russell - Matauwhi Bay *B&B Self-contained Historic Guesthouse 1km E of Russell*

Ounuwhao B&B
Marilyn & Allan Nicklin
Matauwhi Bay, Russell

Tel (09) 403 7310   Fax (09) 403 8310
thenicklins@xtra.co.nz
www.bnb.co.nz/ounuwhaobb.html

Double $185-$225 Single $135-$170
(Full Breakfast) Child $45 under 12 yrs
Detached garden-suite $200-$250   S/C Cottage $175-$250
Credit cards accepted
1 King/Twin 4 Queen 2 Twin 2 Single (6 bdrm)
4 Ensuite 1 Private

Welcome to historic Russell; take a step-back into a bygone era and spend some time with us in our delightful, nostalgic, immaculately restored Victorian Villa (Circa 1894).

Enjoy your own large guest lounge; tea/coffee and biscuits always available, with open fire in the cooler months, and wrap-around verandahs for you to relax and take-in the warm sea breezes. Each of our four queen rooms have traditional wallpapers and paintwork, with handmade patchwork quilts and fresh flowers to create a lovingly detailed, traditional romantic interior.

Breakfast is served in our farmhouse kitchen around the large kauri dining table or al-fresco on the verandah if you wish. It is an all homemade affair; from the freshly baked fruit and nut bread, to the yummy daily special and the jam conserves.

Our self-contained cottage is set in park-like grounds for your privacy and enjoyment: with two double bedrooms, it is ideal for a family or two couples travelling together. It has a large lounge overlooking the reserve and out into the bay, a sun-room and fully self-contained kitchen.

Wonderful for people looking for that special place for peace and time-out. Max 4 persons. Breakfast is available if required. Complimentary afternoon tea on arrival. Laundry service available.

We look forward to meeting you soon.

Our homes are *smoke-free*

We are closed June and July.

We are a member of NZ Heritage Inns Group.

Experience out historic B&B
Enjoy a world of difference

Russell - Okiato
B&B Self-contained holiday house 9km S of Russell

home
NEW ZEALAND

Aimeo Cottage
Annie & Helmuth Hormann
Okiato Point Road, RD 1, Russell
Tel (09) 403 7494   Fax (09) 403 7494
Mob 025 272 2393   aimeo-cottage.nz@xtra.co.nz
www.bnb.co.nz/aimeocottage.html
Double $115-$145 Single $105-$135 (Full Breakfast)
Child $25 Three bedroom holiday home on request
Credit cards accepted Children welcome
4 King/Twin 1 Single (2 bdrm)
1 Ensuite 1 Private

"A quiet place to relax." We have sailed half way around the world to find this beautiful quiet place in the heart of the Bay of Islands and would be happy to share this with you for a while. Aimeo Cottage is built on the hill of Okiato Point, a secluded peninsula overlooking the Bay. In 10 minutes you are in New Zealand's first capital, Russell, the site of many historic buildings, an interesting museum and art galleries. Children are welcome. For golfers, a complimentary complete set of clubs available.

Russell
Homestay 1km E of Russell

Lesleys
Lesley Coleman
1 Pomare Road, Russell, Northland
Tel (09) 403 7099   Mob 021 108 0369
three.gs@xtra.co.nz
bay-of-islands.co.nz/accomm/lesley.html
Double $115 Single $75 (Special Breakfast)
Child $30 Dinner $20 Credit cards accepted
1 Double 1 Single (1 bdrm)
1 Private

Our home is 10 minutes walk to historic Russell and the
design inspired by having lived in Greece. In warm weather breakfast on the verandah looking out to Matauwhi Bay and Russell Boat Club otherwise relax in the glassed-in breeze way with fresh waffles and maple syrup. Or you may like a traditional English breakfast using fresh eggs from our chickens. We have only one guestroom with its own entrance, large bathroom and antique bath. Our combined interests include travelling, art, sport and our dog Billie. Welcome!

All our B&Bs are non-smoking
unless stated otherwise in the text.

28

Russell - Te Wahapu
B&B Self-contained 7km S of Russell

Brisa Cottages
Jenny & Peter Sharpe
92B Te Wahapu Road, RD 1, Russell
Tel (09) 403 7757 Fax (09) 403 7758
brisa@xtra.co.nz
www.bay-of-islands.co.nz/accomm/brisa.html
Double $160 Single $140 (Special Breakfast)
Dinner by arrangement $40pp Credit cards accepted
1 King/Twin 3 Queen 1 Single (4 bdrm)
4 Ensuite

Our home and garden are hidden among the trees at the water's edge. In the morning wake to the sound of the birds and the sunrise over Orongo Bay.

We offer warm hospitality and quiet, clean, high quality accommodation with safe off street parking. Our guests can enjoy total privacy within a self contained cottage which has a kitchenette, a spacious bedroom/lounge area and ensuite bathroom.

Each cottage has its own area of flowers shrubs and trees, a separate entrance and large deck that overlooks the bay. The emphasis is on tasteful, comfortable surroundings with all the essential extras such as fresh flowers, home baking, toiletries and bathrobes. Top quality beds and bedding, cotton sheets and soft absorbent towels ensure a feeling of luxury. In each suite a television, books and magazines are provided for your enjoyment.

Our breakfast table is set with white linen, silver and fine china and features fresh baking, home grown fruit, our own preserves and eggs from our free range hens. The menu changes daily. Picnic hampers and dinners are also available by arrangement. A dinghy is at hand for a leisurely paddle from our beach and historic Russell's museum, restaurants and galleries are just seven minutes away by car.

Come and enjoy this private and tranquil place with us.

Russell   *Homestay 0.5km N of Russell*

La Veduta
Danielle & Dino Fossi
11 Gould Street, Russell, Bay of Islands
Tel (09) 403 8299   Fax (09) 403 8299
laveduta@xtra.co.nz   www.laveduta.co.nz
Double $150-$180 Single $110-$130 (Full Breakfast)
 Child $45 Dinner by arrangement
Credit cards accepted
4 Double 1 Single (5 bdrm)
2 Ensuite 2 Private 1 Guests share

LA VEDUTA (the view). Enjoy our mix of traditional European culture in the midst of the beautiful Bay of Islands. Historic heartland of New Zealand. La Veduta is the perfect pied a terre for your Northland holiday. We offer our guests a warm welcome and personalised service. A delicious breakfast is served on the balcony. Enjoy refreshments watching the sunset over the Bay. Relax or we can arrange tours and activities. Restaurants, beach and ferries handy, transport available. French & Italian spoken. TV room, billiard room, laundry.

Russell   *B&B Self-contained Studio Russell Central*

A Place in the Sun
Pip & Oliver Campbell
57 Upper Wellington Street, Russell, Bay of Islands
Tel (09) 403 7615   Fax (09) 403 7610
Mob 025 777 942   sailing@paradise.net.nz
www.aplaceinthesun.co.nz
Double $100-$150 Single $90 (Continental Breakfast)
Group of four $250
1 Queen 1 Double 1 Single (3 bdrm)
2 Ensuite

'Romantic Russell, where the present meets the past', is this retired sailing couple's perfect anchorage. Our home (and your separate accommodation) overlooks the village, with great views across the bay. Close to uncrowded beaches, heritage trails and restaurants. Convenient departure for all cruises and activities. Two new ensuite apartments plus studio (for longer stay), open onto a covered terrace garden (no stairs). You will find a peaceful setting, bordering on a native bush reserve, comfortable beds, bathrobes, toiletries. We serve a substantial continental breakfast.

Kohukohu   *B&B Homestay Guesthouse 80km S of Kaitaia*

Harbour Views Guest House
Jacky Kelly & Bill Thomson
Rakautapu Road, Kohukohu, Northland
Tel (09) 405 5815   Fax (09) 405 5865
www.bnb.co.nz/harbourviewsguesthouse.html
Double $90 Single $45 (Full Breakfast) Dinner $20
1 Queen 2 Single (2 bdrm)
1 Private

Historic Kohukohu, now a friendly and charming village,is situated on the north side of the Hokianga Harbour. Our beautifully restored Kauri home is set in two acres of gardens and trees and commands a spectacular view of the harbour. The guest rooms, opening on to a sunny verandah, are in a private wing of the house. Meals are prepared using home-grown produce in season. We are interested in and knowledgeable about the history and geography of the area. We have two cats.

Rawene   *B&B Homestay 43km W of Kaikohe*

Searell's
Nellie & Wally Searell
Rawene 0452, Nimmo Street West, Rawene
Tel (09) 405 7835 Fax (09) 405 7835
Mob 021 268 7150 www.bnb.co.nz/searells.html
Double $80 Single $45 (Continental Breakfast)
Child $15 - $20 Dinner $20 Triple $120
Full breakfast $5
1 Queen 1 Single (2 bdrm)
1 Private

The view of harbour and hills beautiful - sunsets breathtaking. Our one acre garden includes tropical flowers and fruit trees. Fresh fruit picked almost everyday. We are retired, Wally an ex naval man. Interests meeting people, gardening, wine making, photography, exploring New Zealand. Zola, friendly 2 year old german sheppard bitch. 1km to shops, hotel, ferry, petrol, hospital. Turn off main road, motor camp sign over hill veer left. At Nimmo Street West turn left to top of hill, flat parking area, easy access. Warm welcome.

Opononi   *B&B Homestay 50km W of Kaikohe*

Koutu Lodge
Tony and Sylvia Stockman
Koutu Loop Road, Opononi, RD 3, Kaikohe
Tel (09) 405 8882 Fax (09) 405 8893
koutulodgebnb@xtra.co.nz
www.bnb.co.nz/koutulodge.html
Double $100 Single $60 (Full Breakfast)
Dinner $35 by arrangement Credit cards accepted
1 King 1 Queen (2 bdrm)
2 Ensuite

Situated on Koutu Point overlooking the beautiful Hokianga Harbour, our quiet home has views both rural and sea. Both rooms have private entrance, decks, ensuites, and are tastefully decorated. We are a friendly Kiwi couple, and our aim is to provide a memorable stay in the true B&B tradition. We have Digital TV and offer email service. Our friendly dog lives outside. Koutu Loop Rd is 4.3 kms north of Opononi then left 2.3 kms on tar seal to Lodge on right.

Opononi   *B&B Homestay 57km W of Kaikohe*

Opononi Dolphin Lodge
Rob & Pam Jensen
Cnr SH12 & Fairlie Cres, PO Box 28, Opononi
Tel (09) 405 8451 Fax (09) 405 8451
shirley@xtra.co.nz
www.bnb.co.nz/dolphinlodge.html
Double $65-$85 Single $50 (Continental Breakfast)
Credit cards accepted
1 Queen 1 Double 1 Twin 1 Single (3 bdrm)
2 Ensuite 1 Private

Situated on the corner of SH12 and Fairlie Cres, opposite a beach reserve on the edge of the pristine Hokianga Harbour, only 20 minutes from 'Tane-Mahuta' the largest Kauri tree in the world. From our decks there are picture postcard views up and down and across the harbour to the huge golden sand dunes. Machine embroidery, patchwork, quilting, fishing, boating, service clubs activities and indoor bowls are our main interests. Come to the Hokianga - the West Coast diamond.

Omapere   *B&B 60km W of Kaikohe*

Harbourside Bed & Breakfast
Joy & Garth Coulter
State Highway 12, 1 Pioneer Walk, Omapere

Tel (09) 405 8246 harboursidebnb@xtra.co.nz
www.bnb.co.nz/harboursidebedbreakfast.html

Double $85 Single $60 (Continental Breakfast)
Credit cards accepted
1 Queen 2 Single (2 bdrm)
2 Ensuite

Our beachfront home on corner State Highway 12 and
Pioneer Walk overlooking the Hokianga Harbour is within walking distance of restaurants and bars.
The beach is 50 metres away. Both rooms have ensuites, tea making facilities, refrigerators and TV
with separate entrances onto private decks to relax and enjoy superb views. We're close to the Waipoua
Forest, West Coast beaches, sand hills and historic Rawene. We have an interest in farming, forestry and
education. Stay and share our home and cat.

Omapere   *B&B 60km W of Kaikohe*

Hokianga Haven Omapere Beachfront
Heather Randerson
226 State Highway 12, Omapere, Hokianga

Tel (09) 405 8285   Fax (09) 405 8215
Mob 021 393 973   tikanga2000@xtra.co.nz
www.hokiangahaven.co.nz

Double $130-$180 (Full Breakfast)
1 Queen (1 bdrm)
1 Private

Snuggled into this peaceful private, beachfront location,
our comfortable home embraces the continuously inspiring sea scape of the dramatic harbour entrance
and magnificent dune. Simply relaxing in this harbourside haven is reviltalizing. Bush and forest
walks, horse riding, harbour cruising, fishing, river and coastal swimming are some of the natural delights
to be enjoyed in this historic area. Our dog will be a willing walking companion. Star gazing in the
warmth of the hot tub is a wonderful way to finish the day. Range of healing therapies available.

Omapere   *B&B 55km W of Kaikohe*

McKenzie's Accomodation
Leonie & Doug McKenzie
4 Pioneer Walk, Omapere, South Hokianga

Tel (09) 405 8068   Fax (09) 405 8068
dlmk@xtra.co.nz
www.bnb.co.nz/mckenzie.html

Double $85 Single $60 (Continental Breakfast)
Child $15 Children welcome
1 Double 1 Single (1 bdrm)
1 Private

Our home is right on the beach of the scenic Hokianga Harbour. This photo is taken from just outside
the house. The B&B room has separate outside entrance, double and single beds, TV, fridge and jug.
Separate bathroom and toilet exclusively for guests. We also have a separate two bedroom self-contained
unit, this can be self-catering or B&B. Stop a night before or after visiting the Waipoua Kauri Forest or
stay a few days and enjoy this unique environment. Your friendly hosts have extensive local knowledge.

Dargaville *B&B Luxury Farmstay Accommodation 1.5km S of Dargaville*

Kauri House Lodge
Doug Blaxall
PO Box 382, Bowen Street, Dargaville
Tel (09) 439 8082 Fax (09) 439 8082 Mob 025 547 769
kaurihouse@infomace.co.nz   www.bnb.co.nz/kaurihouselodge.html
Double $200-$275 Single $200 (Full Breakfast) Credit cards accepted
1 King/Twin 2 King (3 bdrm)
3 Ensuite

Kauri House Lodge sits high above Dargaville amongst mature trees. The 1880's villa retains all it's charm, style and grace with original kauri panelling and period antiques in all rooms.
Start your day woken by native birds, walk through extensive landscaped grounds or read in our library. In summer enjoy a dip in the large swimming pool. In winter our billiard room log fire is a cosy spot to relax for the evening.
Join us to explore beautiful mature native bush on our nearby farm overlooking the Wairoa River and Kaipara Harbour. The area offers many activities including deserted beaches, lakes, river tours, horse treks, walks and restaurants. We have been hosting bed and breakfast for 30 years.

The most common comment in our visitor book: *"Save the best to last."*

Dargaville *Separate/Suite Self-contained Self contained suites 2km Dargaville*

Awakino Point Boutique Motel
June & Mick
PO Box 168, Dargaville
Tel (09) 439 7870   Fax (09) 439 7580
Mob 025 519 474 awakinopoint@xtra.co.nz
www.awakinopoint.co.nz
Double $85-$95 (Continental Breakfast)
Dinner by arrangement 2/brm, 4 persons $145 - $155
Rates seasonal Credit cards accepted
3 Queen 4 Twin (5 bdrm)   3 Ensuite

This unique property set on its own acreage surrounded by attractive gardens is just 2kms from Dargaville on SH14 (The Whangarei Road). The best features of a motel scheme and a New Zealand bed and breakfast have been amalgamated to produce something a little different. You will enjoy your own self contained suite with private bathroom, friendly personal service and a good breakfast. Three well appointed one and two bedroom self contained ground floor units. One of them has a kitchen, bath and log fire.   Smoking outdoors please.

Dargaville - Bayly's Beach *12km W of Dargaville*

Ocean View
Paula & John Powell
7 Ocean View Terrace, Baylys Beach, RD7, Dargaville
Tel (09) 439 6256   Mob 021 0400 511
baylys@win.co.nz
www.bnb.co.nz/oceanview.html
Double $80 Single $45 (Continental Breakfast)
Child $10 under 12yrs Credit cards accepted
1 Double 1 Single (1 bdrm)
1 Ensuite

Just off the trail, this sometimes wild, always wonderful, expansive west coast beach is a fine place to relax. With a glimpse of the sea, your cottage is two minutes walk to the beach and clifftop walkways. We have two great cafes and 18-hole golf locally, with Kai Iwi Lakes and forests an easy day trip. Enjoy your sunny, comfortable cottage (great shower!) and breakfast at your leisure - provided in cottage for you. With our two children and Ruby the cat we look forward to welcoming you. Directions: Drive through the village, you will see our sign at the foot of the big hill.

Dargaville *B&B*

Birch's B&B
Anson & Pat Clapcott
18 Kauri Street, Dargaville,
Tel (09) 439 7565   Fax (09) 439 7520
Mob 027 252 2564 birch@kauricoast.co.nz
www.bnb.co.nz/birchs.html
Double $70 Single $45 Child Neg
Dinner By arrangement
2 Queen 2 Twin (4 bdrm)

You will need several days in the Dargaville area to fully appreciate the Kauri bungalow is the place to stay. We have two queen and two twin rooms for your comfort. There is a large family lounge with fireplace and a modern kitchen with dining area. Enjoy a complimentary afternoon beverage from the balcony overlooking beautiful gardens and native trees. We're close to the town centre with excellent dining facilities or dinner by arrangement. Friendly dog on property.

Dargaville   *B&B 2km S of Dargaville*

Turiwiri B&B
Jennifer & Bruce Crawford
Turiwiri RAPID 6775, State Highway 12, Dargaville
Tel (09) 439 6003   Fax (09) 439 6003
crawford@igrin.co.nz
www.bnb.co.nz/turiwiribb.html

Double $70 Single $35 (Continental Breakfast)
2 Queen (2 bdrm)
1 Guests share

We enjoy sharing our local knowledge with guests in our
modern, one level home two kilometres south from Dargaville on SH 12, minutes from quality restaurants.
Excellent parking for vehicles and an expansive garden in the midst of our 37-acre farmlet. Our family
of three grown children all live away from home, and interests include family, farming, Rotary
International, gardening and big game fishing. We have two friendly cats.

Paparoa   *B&B 1km S of Paparoa Township*

Pioneer B&B
Rowie & Pete Panhuis, The Pines Road, Paparoa,
Tel (09) 431 6033   Fax (09) 431 6677
officeworkshop@xtra.co.nz
www.bnb.co.nz/pioneer.html

Double $95-$120 Single $85 (Full Breakfast)
Child $25 Dinner $30 by arrangement
Children welcome Smoking area inside
1 Queen 1 Twin (2 bdrm)   1 Ensuite

Pete and Rowie welcome you to their historic homestead.
Step back in time and relax in our charmingly restored
cottage with ensuite and open fireplace.   Enhanced by
surrounding native bush and cottage gardens, this is a delightful place to enjoy some country hospitality.
Evening meals are cooked on our coal range using fresh local produce if you care to join us, or local
restaurants are nearby. We have a passion for local history and memorabilia with the famous Kauri
Museum close by.   Pets on property.

Just as we have a variety of B&Bs
you will also be offered a variety of breakfasts,
and they will always be generous.

Matakohe   *B&B Homestay 9km S of Matakohe*

Petite Provence
Linda & Guy Bucchi
703c Tinopai Road, RD1, Matakohe

Tel (09) 431 7552
Fax (09) 431 7552
petite-provence@clear.net.nz
www.bnb.co.nz/petiteprovince.html

Double $100 Single $80
(Continental Breakfast)
Dinner $25 - $35 by arrangement
2 Queen (2 bdrm)
2 Ensuite

Bienvenue to Petite Provence our new colonial style home (French provencal interior) set amongst rolling farmland with adjacent native bush and views of Kaipara Harbour. Relax on covered decks, play petanque or go for a bush walk. We are 9km South of Matakohe Kauri museum and 13km from Tinopai. Guy is French, I am a New Zealander, and our family home in the South of France was also a homestay. Mediterranean/vegetarian/local cuisine (home grown produce and local seafood when possible). Smoking outdoors. Pets: Loopy our friendly outside dog. Bookings preferred.

Directions: from Matakohe Kauri Museum travel 2km south, take Tinopai Road and after 7km you will come to a private road on your left, we are at the end (500m). Sign on Street frontage. Hukatere Scenic Reserve is adjacent to our private road.

Oakura Bay   *Homestay Self Contained Studio 45km NE of Whangarei*

Robin's Nest
Robin & Peter Cusdin
32 Ohawini Road, Oakura Bay, Whangaruru South
Tel (09) 433 6035   Fax (09) 433 6039
Mob 021 188 9000   robin@robinsnest.co.nz
www.robinsnest.co.nz

Double **$90-$130** (Continental/Full Breakfast)
Self-Contained Studio $130-$190
Breakfast available by arrangement
Dinner $30pp by arrangement Credit Cards accepted
1 King/Twin 1 Queen (2 bdrm) 2 Ensuite

Our studio is self-contained with superb sea views, TV, CD player, underfloor heating,private decks with gas barbecue. Breakfast is available if required at extra cost. The double room in our home has tea making facilities, ensuite, heated towel-rail, TV, with breakfast included, plus glorious sea views. There are scenic, coastal and native forest drives to the Bay of Islands, Chartered fishing trips, boat & kayak hire, horse trekking, beach & rock walks. Guests are greeted by two old retired retrievers, Cagney and de Lacey

Whangarei   *B&B Homestay Self-contained 10km E of Whangarei*

Waikaraka Harbourview
Marrion & John Beck
477 Whangarei Heads Road, Waikaraka, RD 4, Whangarei
Tel (09) 436 2549   Fax (09) 436 2549
becksbb@xtra.co.nz
www.bnb.co.nz/waikarakaharbourview.html

Double **$60-$80** Single $40-$60 (Full Breakfast)
Credit cards accepted Pets welcome
1 King/Twin 1 Double (2 bdrm)
1 Ensuite

Our homestay suits one to four persons. We have a king/twin studio with ensuite and a double studio with conservatory and share bathroom. Spectacular sea and landscape views - tea/coffee facilities, refrigerator, table and chairs. Enjoy garden, beach and forest walks, golf, fishing, boating and swimming. Choice of breakfast menu on arrival. Directions: from city centre, head east to Onerahi (5km), at BP station, turn left onto Whangarei Heads Road, 4.77km to B&B (sign on left). Phone answered 24 hours.

Whangarei   *Farmstay Homestay 17km E of Whangarei*

Parua House
Pat & Peter Heaslip
Parua Bay, RD 4, Whangarei
Tel (09) 436 5855
Fax (09) 436 5105
paruahomestay@clear.net.nz
www.paruahomestay.homestead.com

Double $125 Single $75
(Full Breakfast)
 Child 1/2 price Dinner $35
Credit cards accepted
2 Queen 3 Single (4 bdrm)
2 Ensuite 1 Private

Parua House is a classical colonial house, built in 1883, comfortably restored and occupying an elevated site with panoramic views of Parua Bay and the Whangarei Harbour.

As featured on TV's "Corban's Taste NZ" & "Ansett NZ Time of Your Life".

The property covers 29 hectares of farmland including two protected reserves, which are rich in native trees (including kauri) and birds. Guests arc welcome to explore the farm and bush, milk the Jersey cow, explore the olive grove and subtropical orchard, or just relax in the spa-pool or on the veranda. A safe swimming beach adjoins the farm, with a short walk to the fishing jetty; two marinas and a golf course are nearby.

Our wide interests include photography, patchwork quilting and horticulture.   The house is attractively appointed with antique furniture and a rare collection of spinning wheels.

Awake to home-baked bread and freshly squeezed orange juice. Dine in elegant surroundings with generous helpings of home produce with our own meat, milk, eggs, home grown vegetables, olive and subtropical fruit (home-made ice cream a speciality). Pre meal drinks and wine are provided to add to the bonhomie of an evening around a large French oak refectory table.

Whangarei - Onerahi *B&B Self-contained Luxury 9km Whangarei*

Channel Vista
Jenny & Murray Tancred
254 Beach Road, Onerahi, Whangarei
Tel (09) 436 5529   Fax (09) 436 5529
Mob 025 973 083   tancred@igrin.co.nz
www.bnb.co.nz/channelvista.html

Double $90-$150 (Full Breakfast)
Credit cards accepted
2 Queen (2 bdrm)
2 Ensuite

'Channel Vista' is situated on the shores of Whangarei Harbour. We have 2 luxury self contained units each with their own private decks where you can relax and watch the boats go by. We offer a smoke free environment and have laundry, fax and email facilities available. Salty (dog) and Pepe (cat) are our friendly pets. Local shopping centre is only 3 minutes away. All sports facilities (eg golf, diving, walks, game fishing, bowls etc) nearby. We are only 1 hour from the Bay of Islands, so it is a good place to base yourself for your Northland holiday.

Whangarei *B&B Homestay 16km W of Whangarei*

Taraire Grove
Jan & Brian Newman
Tatton Rd, RD 9, Whangarei
Tel (09) 434 7279   Fax (09) 434 7279
cooper@igrin.co.nz
www.bnb.co.nz/tarairegrove.html

Double $80 Single $50 (Full Breakfast)
Child 1/2 price Dinner $12 - $20 pp
Credit cards accepted Children welcome
1 Queen 2 Single (2 bdrm)   1 Guests share

We welcome you to our charming country residence at Maungatapere, within easy driving distances to East and West Coast beaches. We are a semi-retired couple, and welcome the opportunity to return hospitality experienced overseas. Our home overlooks a stream and we are gradually developing the 3 1/2 acres into lawns, gardens and ponds. The guest wing is private - TV room - tea\coffee making facilities - smoke free area. Whangarei, 15 minutes away, has excellent restaurants or you can choose to dine with us and enjoy hospitality.

Whangarei *B&B Separate/Suite 4.5km NE of Whangarei*

Graelyn Villa
Joanie Guy
166 Kiripaka Road, Whangarei
Tel (09) 437 7532   Fax (09) 437 7533
graelyn@xtra.co.nz
www.bnb.co.nz/graelynvillla.html

Double $85 Single $65 (Full Breakfast)
Child by arrangement Credit cards accepted
Children welcome Pets welcome Smoking area inside
2 Queen 2 Single (3 bdrm)
3 Ensuite

Welcome to my turn-of-the-century villa, which has been lovingly restored to offer comfort and luxury. My rooms offer superbly comfortable beds, TV, tea/coffee, heaters and electric blankets. FOR YOUR PRIVACY, ALL ROOMS ARE SEPARATE TO OWNERS ACCOMMODATION AND ALL HAVE ENSUITES. Five minutes to city centre with a wide variety of top class restaurants, 25 minute drive to Tutukaka Coast, handy to spectacular Whangarei Falls. I have two quiet dogs and a cat named Koko. Your pets welcome. Laundry facilities available.

Whangarei *Self-contained 10km NE of Whangarei CBD*

Country Garden Tearooms
Margaret & John Pool
526 Ngunguru Road, RD 3, Whangarei
Tel (09) 437 5127 Mob 025 519 476
www.bnb.co.nz/countrygarden.html
Double $70 Single $50 (Full Breakfast)
Dinner $20 by arrangement
2 Queen (2 bdrm)
2 Ensuite

Enjoy a warm friendly welcome. We have over three acres
of beautiful trees, shrubs, bulbs, perennials, succulents
and a large variety of bird life. Feel at home in a spacious self-contained unit with fridge, microwave
and tea making facilities. Enjoy cooked or continental breakfast in our dining room overlooking the
garden. We are 10km from central Whangarei on Ngunguru-Tutukaka highway. 5km from Whangarei
Falls. Beautiful beaches, restaurants, diving, fishing and golfing within 10km.

Whangarei *B&B Homestay 12km SW of Whangarei*

Owaitokamotu
M & G Whitehead
727 Otaika Valley Road, Otaika, Whangarei
Tel (09) 434 7554 Fax (09) 4347554
minniegeorge@xtra.co.nz
www.bnb.co.nz/owaitokamotu.html
Double $75 Single $55 (Full Breakfast) Dinner $20
Children welcome Pets welcome
2 King/Twin 2 Queen (3 bdrm)
2 Guests share

Come and enjoy the absolute tranquillity of "Owaitokamotu" which is a place of water, magnificent
rocks of all shapes and sizes, and pristine native bush awaiting your rambling walks, all set on 10 1/2
acres of easy contour and newly created gardens. Our home is newly built and is wheelchair friendly.
Bedrooms have private access form exterior. TV, tea, coffee and cookies. A wide verandah offers
pleasant relaxation. Smoking outside only please. Laundry facilities available.

Whangarei *B&B Homestay Self-contained In House 6km W of Whangarei*

The Stranded Mariner
Errol & Sharon Grace
State Highway 14, RD 9, Whangarei
Tel (09) 438 9967 Fax (09) 438 7967
Mob 027 414 2006 info@strandedmariner.co.nz
www.strandedmariner.co.nz
Double $90-$120 Single $90 (Full Breakfast)
Dinner by arrangement Extended stay discounts apply
Bankcard accepted
3 Queen 1 Twin 3 Single (3 bdrm)
1 Ensuite 2 Private

îStranded Marinerî, 6km from central Whangarei. In a very peaceful country, native bush surrounding.
Walkways lead from boundaries to Museum, 18th century Clarke homestead, Bird Recovery Centre, Kiwi
house. Sherwood Golf Course, 3km. Errol handcrafted our home from native timbers (floors, ceilings),
featuring leadlight windows, bricked fireplaces. Cottage garden waterwheel, organic vegetables. Breakfast,
and evening meals prepared in our kitchen emphasizing freshness-top quality. Whangarei is a great base to
explore Northland, Bay of Islands, Kauri forest, Kauri Museum, Poor Knights Islands are all easy day trips.

Whangarei- Glenbervie *B&B Homestay 12km NE of Whangarei*

Lupton House Homestay B&B
Marie & John Dennistoun - Wood
555 Ngunguru Road, Glenbervie, RD 3, Whangarei

Tel (09) 437 2989   Fax (09) 437 2989
 Mob 025 203 9805   dennistoun-wood@xtra.co.nz
www.truenz.co.nz/luptonhouse

Double $95-$140   Single $70-$90 (Full Breakfast)
Dinner By arrangement Smoking area inside
2 Queen 2 Single (3 bdrm)
3 Ensuite

Welcome to our home which is located in the dry-stone
walled farmland of Glenbervie, between Whangarei and the beautiful beaches of Tutukaka coast. Lovingly restored and furnished and with extensive gardens, swimming pool and games room, our colonial villa offers guests comfort and relaxation in a friendly old-world country atmosphere which we share with our grandson, golden retriever dogs and two donkeys. We offer a full breakfast and by arrangement, dinner. Diving, fishing, golf, watersports and country walks within a 15km radius.

Whangarei *B&B Homestay Self-contained 25km SE of Whangarei*

Vealbrook B & B
Bob and Pre Sturge
2013 McLeod Bay, Whangarei Heads,
RD 4 Whangarei Heads Road, Whangarei

Tel (09) 434 0098   Fax (09) 434 0098
pretoria@clear.net.nz
www.bnb.co.nz/vealbrook.html

Double $100   Single $65 (Special Breakfast)
Child $20 Dinner $25 Self Contained Unit $120
Children welcome
1 Queen 1 Double 1 Twin 3 Single (3 bdrm)

Stunning sea views. Interesting coastal scenic walks. We are 20 metres to the beach, quiet and peaceful with safe swimming, snorkeling, kayaking and good fishing. Ten minute walk to the jetty and and local dairy. 20 minutes to the nearest town. Courtesy car available. Enjoy original paintings of NZ artists and antique furniture. Bob's turned timber furniture, antique lace garments on view. Hair dryer, laundry. Dinner by arrangement. Meals served with wine. Warmth and friendliness.

Whangarei Heads *B&B Self-contained 31km SE of Whangarei*

Manaia Gardens
Audrey & Colin Arnold
2487 Whangarei Heads Road, Taurikura, Whangarei

Tel (09) 434 0797   arnoldac@igrin.co.nz
www.bnb.co.nz/manaiagardens.html

Double $75   Single $60 (Continental Breakfast)
Child under 5 free Self-catering $60
Extra Person $15 Credit cards accepted
Children welcome Smoking area inside
2 Queen 1 Single (3 bdrm)
2 Private

We have a small farm and a large garden, with two quaint old self-contained cabins in the garden. They have comfortable beds and basic cooking facilities. We have a rowboat you are welcome to borrow, nearby shops and galleries. Laundry available. This is a beautiful area with rocky bush clad hills, harbour and ocean beaches, lots of Conservation land for walks. Or just relax in private. We are the only buildings in the bay. Mailbox 2487 on the Whangarei Heads Road.

Whangarei Heads *Homestay 28km SE of Whangarei*

Bantry
Karel & Robin Lieffering
Little Munro Bay, RD 4, Whangarei
Tel (09) 434 0751   Fax (09) 434 0754
lieffering@igrin.co.nz
www.bnb.co.nz/bantry.html

Double $105 Single $55 (Full Breakfast)
Child 1/2 price under 12yrs Dinner $30
1 Queen 2 Single (2 bdrm)
1 Guests share

We are a semi-retired couple with a dog. We speak Dutch, French,
German, Japanese and we like to laugh. Our unusual home with some natural rock interior walls is on
the edge of a safe swimming beach, and bush reserve with walking tracks and several good fishing
spots. A photographically fascinating area with wonderful views of coastal 'mountains'. Guests have
own entrance and sitting room with all sea views. Enjoyable food and NZ wine. Phone, fax or email us
for reservations and directions. One party bookings only.

Ruakaka *B&B Farmstay Self-contained 30km S of Whangarei*

Bream Bay Farmstay
Joyce & Vince Roberts
Doctor's Hill Road, RD 2, Waipu
Tel (09) 432 7842   Fax (09) 432 7842
Mob 025 419 585   robertsb.b@xtra.co.nz
www.bnb.co.nz/breambayfarmstay.html

Double $80 Single $50 (Full Breakfast) Child $20
Dinner $25 Credit cards accepted Children welcome
Pets welcome
2 Queen 2 Single (3 bdrm)
1 Private 1 Host share

We offer awesome sea views from your own private terrace plus a free tour by arrangement, over our
160 acre dry stock farm & bush. Cooking facilities available. Our wetland area is home to the rare
brown bittern. Beautiful beaches, golf course, racetrack where Vince trains our racehorses and good
restaurants are a short drive from our home. As ex dairy farmers with a grown up family of four
children, other interests include B&B for the past 13 years, travel, golf gardening.

Waipu *Farmstay Self-contained 10km S of Waipu*

Andre & Robin La Bonte
PO Box 60, Waipu, Northland
Tel (09) 432 0645   Fax (09) 432 0645
labonte@xtra.co.nz
www.bnb.co.nz/labonte.html

Double $80 Single $50 (Continental Breakfast)
Dinner $20 B/A Credit cards accepted
1 King 2 Double 2 Single (3 bdrm)
2 Private

Sleep to the sound of the ocean in a separate efficiency
apartment or in guest bedrooms on our 36 acre seaside
farm. Explore our limestone rock formations or just sit and relax under the mature trees that grace our
shoreline. The beach at Waipu Cove is a ten minute walk along the sea. We are a licensed fish farm,
graze cattle and have flea free cats. Glow worm caves, deep-sea fishing, scuba diving and golf available
locally. No smoking please. American spoken. Bookings recommended.

Waipu   *B&B Farmstay Self-contained 6km SE of Waipu*

The Stone House
Gillian & John Devine
Cove Road, Waipu

Tel (09) 432 0432   0800 007 358   Fax (09) 432 0432
stonehousewaipu@xtra.co.nz
www.bnb.co.nz/thestonehouse.html

Double $60-$100 Single $60 (Full Breakfast)
Child $20 Dinner $25 Credit cards accepted
Children welcome Pets welcome
1 King/Twin 2 Queen 1 Double 3 Single (4 bdrm)
1 Ensuite 3 Private

Relax in a charming seaside cottage or with your hosts Gillian and John in their unique solid Stonehouse. Either way you will enjoy the green pastures of our farm, fringed with mature pohutakawa trees and the sound of surf on our magnificent ocean beach. Picturesque rock gardens, croquet lawn and sheltered patios complete the setting. Canoes and dinghys are available for exploring the adjacent lagoon and bird sanctuary. A touch of Cornwall with warm company around a log fire. German spoken.

Waipu Cove   *B&B Self-contained Downstairs Flat 8km SE of Waipu*

Flower Haven
Shirley & Brian Flower
53 St Anne Road, Waipu Cove, RD 2, Waipu 0254

Tel (09) 432 0421   bnb@flowerhaven.com
www.flowerhaven.com

Double $95-$115 (Continental Breakfast)
Credit cards accepted
2 Double (2 bdrm)
1 Private

Flower Haven is elevated with panoramic coastal views,
being developed as a garden retreat. The accommodation is a self-contained downstairs flat with separate access; kitchen includes stove, microwave, fridge/freezer. Washing machine, radio, TV, linen, duvets, blankets and bath towels provided. Reduced tariff if continental breakfast not required. Our interests are gardening, genealogy and meeting people. Near to restaurants, museums, golf, horse treks, fishing, walking tracks, oil refinery. 5 minutes to shop, sandy surf beach, rocks. Whangarei 35 minutes, Auckland 1 1/2 hours.

Langs Beach   *B&B 12km SE of Waipu*

Lochalsh Bed & Breakfast
Graham & Billie Long
Cove Road, Langs Beach, Waipu

Tel (09) 432 0053   Fax (09) 432 0053
Mob 025 203 1660   lochalsh@clear.net.nz
www.lochalsh.co.nz

Double $85-$120 Single $60 (Full Breakfast)
Child POA Dinner $25 by arrangement
Credit cards accepted Children welcome
1 King/Twin 1 King (2 bdrm)
2 Ensuite

Our great grandfather settled this area in 1853. Our home
is the original Lang home, right beside this most beautiful of white surf beaches, lined by Pohutakawa trees. There is modern facilities, sunny guest lounge/kitchen/dining area running right along the front of the house, looking over the beach, bay and Hen and Chicken Islands. Comfortable rooms with ensuites make this a delightful place for rest and relaxation. Billie & Graham provide friendly but unobtrusive hosting. From our visitors book: 'Our best stay in New Zealand!'

Auckland

Waipu
Waipu Cove
Langs Beach
Paparoa
Mangawai
Kaiwaka
Te Hana
Wellsford
Matakana
Warkworth
Sandspit
Snells Beach
1
Puhoi
Orewa
Kaukapakapa
Auckland City
enlargement next page
Helensville
Waiheke Island
Huapai
Waitakere
Beachlands
Bethells Beach
Whitford
Piha
Clevedon
Papakura
Kaiaua
Drury
Towns listed generally
follow a north to south
route. Refer to the index
if required.
Patumahoe
Pukekohe
Bombay
1
2
Waiuku

0 Kilometres 20
0 Miles 12
Mercer

AUCKLAND

Silverdale

Whangaparaoa

Okura

Auckland City

Browns Bay

Coatesville
28
Albany
1

Mairangi Bay

18

Kumeu
Herald Island
Greenhithe

16
Hobsonville
Beach Haven

Takapuna

Rangitoto Island

Waitemata Harbour

Herne Bay
Devonport

Mission Bay

Freemans Bay
Ponsonby
Auckland
Central
Parnell
Orakei
St Heliers

Swanson
Western Springs
Glendowie

Ranui
Mt Eden
Remuera
Bucklands
Beach

Epsom
1
Ellerslie

Avondale
One Tree Hill
Howick

Pakuranga

Titirangi

Mangere Bridge
Otahuhu

Manukau Harbour
Mangere

Manukau City

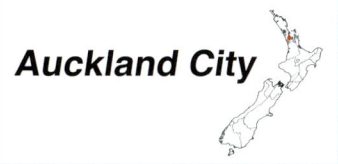

Towns listed generally follow
a north to south route. Refer
to the index if required.

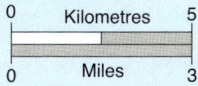

Auckland
International
Airport

1

Manurewa

0   Kilometres   5

0   Miles   3

Mangawhai   *Homestay 7km S of Mangawhai*

Fallowfield
Jean & Don Goldschmidt
Staniforth Road, RD 5, Wellsford

Tel (09) 431 5096 Fax (09) 431 5063 Mob 0274 829
736 goldschmidt@xtra.co.nz
www.beach-holidays.co.nz

Double $95-$105 (Full Breakfast) Dinner $30 Credit
cards accepted
1 Queen 1 Twin (2 bdrm)
1 Private 1 Guests share

'A little out of the way, quite out of the ordinary'. Breathtaking views over rolling pasture to a Pacific ocean dotted with islands can be seen from our eyrie tucked into the hills above the seaside haven of Mangawhai. After a game of croquet or a beach visit for swimming or fishing, we can share the evening meal. Within our home built with architectural flair the guestroom is private, has tea and coffee facilities, a bed with a firm mattress, good heating and good lighting.

Mangawhai Heads   *boutique bed and breakfast Inn 1km SE of Mangawhai Heads*

Mangawhai Lodge - Boutique B&B Inn
Jeannette Forde
4 Heather Street, Mangawhai Heads

Tel (09) 431 5311 Fax (09) 431 5312
mlodge@xtra.co.nz
www.seaviewlodge.co.nz

Double $120-$150 Single $95-$130
(Full Special Breakfast) Credit cards accepted
3 King/Twin 2 Queen 8 Single (5 bdrm)
3 Ensuite 2 Private

Indulge yourself - escape to the tranquility and magic that's Mangawhai Lodge. Five stylish guest rooms open onto wrap-around verandahs of this colonial Inn. Spectacular sea and island views of the Hauraki Gulf, and white sandy beaches ensure Mangawhai Lodge is the ultimate "room with a view". Spend your days on the championship golf course, exploring the beaches and walkways or curled up reading or watching the boats sail by. Ideal for social golfing groups. Adjacent to award winning cafe, bowls/golf. Water access 3 minutes.

Mangawhai Heads   *B&B 30km NE of Wellsford*

Fairways Bed & Breakfast
Val & Rob Cleaver
240 Molesworth Drive, Mangawhai Heads,

Tel (09) 431 4042 Fax (09) 431 4042
Mob 021 619 311 cleaver@fairways.co.nz
www.fairways.co.nz

Double $100-$110 Single $75-$85 (Full Breakfast)
1 King/Twin 1 Queen 1 Double 1 Single (4 bdrm)

Fairways is a brand new modern Bed & Breakfast offering a relaxing retreat in friendly comfortable accommodation, located adjacent to the Golf Course, walking distance to beach, shops, cafe & restaurants. You can enjoy full breakfast on the deck with views right across the Hen & Chickens Islands. Alternatively there is spectacular views of the award winning Golf Course with its beautiful rural views. Guests have the comfort of their own lounge with TV & tea & coffee facilties.   We look forward to welcoming you at Fairways.

Wellsford - Te Hana   *Farmstay 6km N of Wellsford*

The Retreat
Colleen & Tony Moore
Te Hana, RD 5, Wellsford
Tel (09) 423 8547
booking@sheepfarmstay.com
www.sheepfarmstay.com
Double $95 (Full Breakfast) Dinner $25pp
Self-contained cottage $85
Credit cards accepted
2 Queen 1 Double 1 Single (3 bdrm)
1 Ensuite 1 Private

Tony and Colleen welcome you to The Retreat, a spacious 1860's farmhouse built for a family with 12 children. Set well back from the road, the house is surrounded by an extensive landscaped garden, including a productive vegetable garden and orchard. Fresh produce from the garden is a feature in our home cooking.

Colleen is a spinner and weaver and our flock of sheep provides the raw material for the woollen goods that are hand made and for sale from the studio. If you haven't got close up to a sheep this is your chance, as we always have friendly sheep to hand feed.

We have hosted guests at The Retreat since 1988 and appreciate what you require. We know New Zealand well, our families have lived in NZ for several generations and we have visited most places in our beautiful country, so if you have any questions on what to see or do, we are well equipped to provide the answers.

We host only one group at a time, so you won't have to share a bathroom with someone you don't know.

The Retreat is very easy to find. Travelling North on SH 1, we are 6km North of Wellsford, look for the Weaving Studio sign on your left. You will pass through Te Hana before arriving at The Retreat. Kaiwaka is 13km north of The Retreat.

Wellsford   *B&B Farmstay 7km N of Wellsford*

Rosandra Homestay
Ross & Sandra Williams
557 SH1, RD5, Wellsford,
Tel (09) 423 9343   Fax (09) 423 9343
Mob 021 179 9311   rosandra@xtra.co.nz
www.bnb.co.nz/rosandrahomestay.html
Double $100 Single $80 (Full Breakfast)
3 Queen 1 Twin (4 bdrm)
1 Ensuite

Welcome to our 90 acre lifestyle farm.   Beautifully
covered with mature trees, where our sheep and beef cattle graze. Privately set in landscaped gardens
our modern home offers you warm spacious guest rooms with ensuite, private lounge, opening on to a
sunny outdoor deck area. Swim all year round in the indoor 15m heated pool or watch the big screen
TV while relaxing in the spa pool. Situated close to golf courses and East Coast beaches, find us easily
on SH1, 7km north of Wellsford and opposite Mangawhai turn off. Two cats.

Warkworth   *B&B 0.5km N of Warkworth*

Homewood Cottage
Ina & Trevor Shaw
17 View Rd, Warkworth
Tel (09) 425 8667   Fax (09) 425 9610
Mob 025 235 7469
www.bnb.co.nz/homewoodcottage.html
Double $90 (Special Breakfast) Credit cards accepted
1 Queen 1 Twin (2 bdrm)
2 Ensuite

Our home is in a peaceful, quiet garden with views of Warkworth and the hills. The bed-sitter style
rooms are a good size. Each has own entrance, tea making, TV and patio with car parking. No cooking.
The rooms are private but feel free to come in and chat. Breakfast is substantial continental with choice.
We enjoy walking and golf. Ina is an artist. Close to town and a selection of restaurants. Our home is
smoke free. Please phone. View Road is off Hill Street.

Warkworth - Sandspit   *Homestay 7km E of Warkworth*

Belvedere Homestay
M & R Everett
38 Kanuka Road, RD 2, Warkworth
Tel (09) 425 7201   Fax (09) 425 7201
Mob 027 284 4771   belvederehomestay@xtra.co.nz
www.belvederehomestay.co.nz
Double $110-$130 Single $80 (Special Breakfast)
Dinner $35
2 Queen 1 Twin (3 bdrm)
1 Ensuite 2 Private

'Sandspit' the perfect stop to and from The Bay of Islands. 'Belvedere' has 360-degree views, sea to
countryside; it's 'awesome'. Relaxing decks, barbecue, garden, orchards, native birds and bush, peace
and tranquillity with good parking. Air-conditioned, spa, games room, comfortable beds are all here for
your comfort. Many attractions are within seven kilometres and Margaret's flair with cooking is a great
way to relax after an adventurous day with pre-drinks, two course meal and wine. Come and stay with
Margaret, Ron and our friendly dog 'Nicky'.

Warkworth *Homestay Self-contained 13km E of Warkworth*

Barbara & John Maltby
Omaha Orchards, 282 Point Wells Road, RD 6,
Warkworth

Tel (09) 422 7415   Fax (09) 422 7419
jandbmaltby@value.net.nz
www.bnb.co.nz/maltby.html

Double $60-$80 Single $50-$70 (Continental
Breakfast) Dinner $15 - $20 by arrangement In-house
accommodation available Extra persons $12
1 Queen 1 Double (1 bdrm)
1 Ensuite

Our home and self-contained unit (built 1999) is set on 11 acres nestled beside the Whangateau Harbour. Relax in the extensive gardens and swim in the beautifully appointed pool. Nearby is Omaha Beach, golf course, tennis courts, restaurants, art and craft studios, pottery works, museum, Sheep World, Honey Centre and Kawau Island. This is some of the prettiest coastline in New Zealand. John and Barbara look forward to sharing their little slice of paradise with you.

Warkworth *B&B Homestay Self-contained 4.5km W of Warkworth*

Willow Lodge
Paddy & John Evans
541 Woodcocks Road, Warkworth

Tel (09) 425 7676   Fax (09) 425 7676
Mob 025 940 885   paddywarkworth@xtra.co.nz
www.bnb.co.nz/willowlodgewarkworth.html

Double $100-$120 Single $60-$80 (Full Breakfast)
Child $20 Dinner $30
1 Queen 2 Double 4 Single (4 bdrm)
2 Ensuite 1 Private

Your hosts, John & Paddy have more than 30 years experience in the hospitality field and have lived in Warkworth for the past 27 years. Our wealth of local knowledge will ensure your stay is both memorable and enjoyable. Willow Lodge boasts tranquil rural views over rolling farmland and is set in two acres of landscaped gardens. We offer superior self-contained accommodation complete with own ensuite, kitchen facilities, TV, BBQ all of which opens onto your own private courtyard. We are well know for our fabulous breakfasts.

Warkworth *Farmstay 6km S of Warkworth*

Ryme Intrinseca
Elizabeth & Cam Mitchell
121 Perry Road, RD 3, Warkworth

Tel (09) 425 9448   Fax (09) 425 9458
Mob 021 033 2750   rymeintrinseca@xtra.co.nz
www.bnb.co.nz/rymeintrinseca.html

Double $100 Single $60 (Full Breakfast)
Child 1/2 price Dinner $30 by arrangement
Credit cards accepted Children welcome
2 Queen 2 Single (3 bdrm)
1 Private

Our sheep and cattle farm is 50 minutes from Auckland just 1km off SH1, and our spacious home is set in a quiet, secluded valley overlooking native bush and surrounded by gardens. Join in farm activities or just relax. The upstairs guest bedrooms, with extensive farm views, open into a large guest sitting room with TV and tea/coffee making facilities. Local sightseeing attractions include historic Kawau Island, vineyards, Sheep World, horse riding, and many lovely beaches. We are widely travelled and warmly welcome visitors to our home. We take only one party at a time.

Warkworth *Self-contained studio loft apartment 9km E of Warkworth*

Island Bay Retreat
Joyce & Bill Malofy
105 Ridge Rd, Scotts landing, RD 2, Warkworth
Tel (09) 425 4269   Fax (09) 425 4265
Mob 025 262 8358
www.bnb.co.nz/islandbayretreat.html
Double $115
1 Queen (1 bdrm)
1 Ensuite

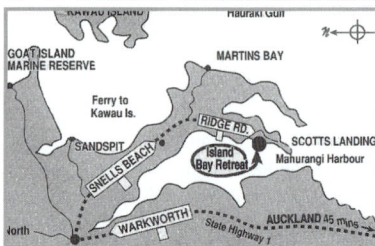

Secluded intimate retreat on the beautiful Mahurangi Peninsula. Set amongst 2 acres of lovely gardens right on Mahurangi Harbour's foreshore. Idyllic magical place to relax in total privacy, captivating panoramic sea & rural views from our cosy open plan accommodation. Facilities for weekend or longer stays (self-catering). Sundecks, reclining chairs, bbq, kitchen, TV, ensuite (own entrance). Stroll along the bays to historic Scott's Landing, bush trails, swimming, boating, fishing (rods provided). Friendly village atmosphere, licensed restaurants, shopping and attractions. (Auckland 1 hour)

Warkworth - Sandspit *B&B Self-contained 10km E of Warkworth*

Sea Breeze
Di & Robin Grant
14 Puriri Place, RD 2, Sandspit Heights, Warkworth
Tel (09) 425 7220   Fax (09) 425 7220
Mob 021 657 220   robindi.grant@xtra.co.nz
www.bnb.co.nz/seabreeze.html
Double $120 Single $100 (Continental Breakfast)
Credit cards accepted
1 Queen (1 bdrm)
1 Ensuite

Sea Breeze is a self-contained luxury apartment with magnificent sea views and surrounding bush. Breakfast is provided in the kitchenette to be enjoyed at your leisure and a bedsettee in the lounge doubles for extra guests. There are lovely bush walks to the beaches immediately below the property. Take a cruise to Kawau Island or visit the many vineyards, galleries and cafes. Your hosts have travelled extensively and now enjoy gardening and boating in their spare time. Phone/fax for directions.

Warkworth - Snells Beach *B&B 9km E of Warkworth*

Wings and Waves B&B
Sue Bunce
25 Fidelis Ave., Snells Beach, Warkworth
Tel (09) 425 6399   Mob 025 403 299
pinkperil@xtra.co.nz
www.bnb.co.nz/bunce.html
Double $90-$110 Single $60 (Continental Breakfast)
1 Queen 1 Double (2 bdrm)
1 Guests share

Awake to beautiful sea views from your room and sounds of birdsong. Walk uphill in the adjoining nature reserve for panoramic views of Kawau Island and beyond. Attractions include: Kawau Island, Wineries, Snorkelling at Goat Island, beautiful beaches and scenic walks. Rooms have TV and coffee facilities. I'm a Commercial Pilot and keen sailor, walker and kayaker. I live the outdoor Kiwi life to the full. I've travelled extensively in NZ and worldwide. Bill & Ben are my tame chooks. Sorry, no children or smoking.

Warkworth   *B&B Private entrance/patio 2.5km S of Warkworth*

Warkworth Country House
Alan & Pauline Waddington
18, Wilson Road, RD1, Warkworth

Tel (09) 422 2485   Fax (09) 422 2485
Mob 025 680 6016   paulalan@xtra.co.nz
www.bnb.co.nz/warkworthcountry.html

Double $110-$130 Single $80-$100 (Full Breakfast)
Child neg.
1 Queen 1 Twin (2 bdrm)
2 Ensuite

Set in 2 peaceful acres,45 mins north of Auckland. Each tasteful room has en-suite, private entrance and patio with tea/coffee making facilities, hairdryer, electric blankets, radio alarm, T.V. and toiletries. Enjoy delicious cooked or continental breakfasts in the dining room or alfresco,weather permitting. Visit historic Warkworth Museum, Kawau Island, antique and craft shops, vineyards and pottery. Enjoy horse riding, golf, fishing, or just strolling on the nearby sandy beaches. We look forward to welcoming you to our country home.

Warkworth - Matakana   *B&B Luxury Country Lodge 3km NE of Warkworth*

Stargate Lodge
Jane & Neil Peterken
139 Clayden Road, PO Box 275, Warkworth 1241

Tel (09) 425 9995   Fax (09) 425 9778
Mob 025 991 115   info@stargate-lodge.co.nz
www.stargate-lodge.co.nz

Double $180-$275 Single $150-$225 (Full Breakfast)
1 King/Twin 1 King 2 Twin (2 bdrm)
2 Ensuite

Relax and indulge! Wake up to birdsong, ease into your day...have a delicious breakfast on your own balcony or our guest dining room whilst enjoying the beautiful countryside vistas...perhaps a stroll through our native bush. Your suite is privately appointed, designed with your comfort in mind, offering restful decor, fresh flowers, white linen,TV,tea/coffee, fridge and ensuite. At night a comfortable guest lounge with log fire - a real pleasure! Great location..only minutes to golf courses, cafes, wineries, shops. (Chalet suites opening late spring '03)

Warkworth - Sandspit   *B&B Studio room 7km E of Warkworth*

Shoalwater
Don & Jocelyn Adolph
1 Kanuka Road (entrance between 7 & 9 Kanuka Rd),
Sandspit, RD2, Warkworth

Tel (09) 425 0566   0800 110 925   Fax (09) 425 0566
Mob 021 126 0081   shoalwater@xtra.co.nz
www.shoalwater.co.nz

Double $100-$150 Single $90-$120 (Continental
Breakfast)
2 Queen (2 bdrm)
2 Ensuite

Situated on the waterfront with breathtaking views of the tidal movements and moored boats at Sandspit. Our brand new architecturally designed home has two luxurious B&B studios, completely private with their own entrance, in a truly peaceful setting. Tastefully decorated with spacious tiled ensuites, queen size beds, lounge chairs, dining table, tea/coffee, fridge, microwave, stereos, TV, video, etc. Boutique vineyards, restaurants, cafes, potteries, art galleries, and beaches nearby. A short walk to Kawau ferry. Home to Beesha our small dog. Entrance down right of way to 7 & 9A Kanuka Road and is sign-posted.

Warkworth - Sandspit *B&B Self-contained 6km E of Warkworth*

Jacaranda House B&B
Gillian Irons & Richard Bray
1186 Sandspit Road, RD2, Warkworth

Tel (09) 422 2394 Fax (09) 422 2395
Mob (027) 283 7772 or (0274) 976 314
jacarandahouse@xtra.co.nz
www.bnb.co.nz/jacaranda.html

Double $100-$120 Single $80-$90 (Continental Breakfast) (Full Breakfast)
1 Queen (1 bdrm)
1 Ensuite

We are on the Matakana Estuary and a short walk to the Sandspit Wharf, gateway to Kawau Island. A few minutes drive to restaurants, cafes, vineyards and pottery in the Matakana region. Enjoy your breakfast choice on our north facing deck with 180 degree view of the estuary, or enjoy the privacy of the self-contained unit. You will have your own ground level entrance and parking.

Warkworth *B&B 8km W of Warkworth*

home

Yankiwi Lodge B&B
Vicki and Jon Mathers
26 Dennis Road, RD 1, Warkworth 1241,
North Auckland

Tel (09) 422 2083 Fax (09) 422 2084
yankiwi-lodge@paradise.net.nz
www.yankiwi-lodge.co.nz

Double $115 (Full Breakfast) Child N/A Dinner $35pp
4 King (4 bdrm)
3 Ensuite 1 Private

Jon (Yank) and Vicki (Kiwi) warmly welcome you to enjoy our relaxed hospitality at Yankiwi Lodge. Situated on seven acres of tranquil countryside. Four guest rooms are well set up - three with ensuites, one with private bathroom; all with private entrances and patio area, refrigerators, heaters, ceiling fans, tea & coffee. Our large living area is surrounded with decks to enjoy the sunsets after a day visiting local shops and wineries, beaches or fishing. Mini conference facilities: up to eight people. One dog, two cats.

Puhoi *Homestay Separate/Suite 9km N of Orewa*

Westwell Ho
Fae & David England
34 Saleyards Road , Puhoi ,

Tel (09) 422 0064 Fax (09) 422 0064
Mob 025 280 5795 dhengland@xtra.co.nz
www.bnb.co.nz/ .html

Double $95 Single $75 (Full Breakfast) Child $35
Dinner Credit cards accepted Children welcome
1 Queen 1 Double 1 Single (2 bdrm)
1 Ensuite 1 Private

We welcome you to our sunny colonial style home in the lovely Puhoi Valley. We are only 2 minutes by car west of Main North Highway up a small road behind the old pub in this historic Puhoi Village. The homestead has wide verandahs around 3 sides where you can relax as you view the gardens, winding paths and beautiful trees. Nearby are the fantastic Waiwera Thermal Pools, or you could hire a canoe and paddle down the Puhoi River to Wenderholm Beach and Park. Sky TV available.

Puhoi   *Farmstay 20km N of Orewa*

Nichola(s) & Peter Rodgers
Krippner Rd, Puhoi, Auckland
Tel (09) 422 0626   Fax (09) 422 0626
Mob 021 215 5165
ofp@friends.co.nz
www.farmstaynz.com

Double $105-$190 Single $90-$150
(Full Breakfast)   Child under 16 free
Dinner included   Guest Wing
Credit cards accepted   Children welcome
1 Queen 2 Twin (2 bdrm)
1 Private

Farmstay, the gentle, organic way. Tariff includes taste-filled organic meals; fruit & vegetables; fresh baking ... very comfortable beds. Children welcomed (babysitting?).
Come relax (no children if not yours), sleep off 'jet-lag'. Share panoramic views, fresh air, clean water; share expreiences, ideas and knowledge over dinner. Walk in the hills through trees streams, bird life & native flora & fauna, secluded private places.
Use our library and business facilities ... We farm with kindness sheep, Belted Galloway

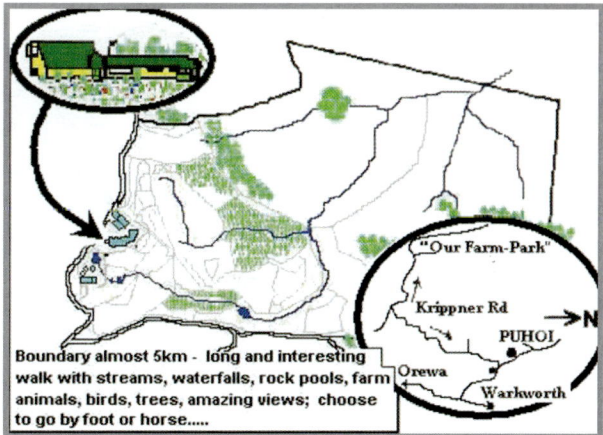

Boundary almost 5km - long and interesting walk with streams, waterfalls, rock pools, farm animals, birds, trees, amazing views; choose to go by foot or horse.....

"Our Farm-Park"
Krippner Rd
PUHOI
Orewa
Warkworth
N

Orewa   *B&B Homestay 20min N of Auckland Central*

Villa Orewa
Sandra & Ian Burrow
264 Hibiscus Coast Highway, Orewa, Auckland
Tel (09) 426 3073   Fax (09) 426 3053
Mob 021 626 760   rooms@villaorewa.co.nz
www.villaorewa.co.nz

Double $150 Single $150 (Continental Breakfast)
Dinner by arrangement Credit cards accepted
1 King/Twin 2 Queen (3 bdrm)   3 Ensuite

Welcome to our beautifully appointed unique new Mediterranean style home, with white-washed walls and blue vaulted roofs, purpose built as aboutique Bed and Breakfast for the discerning traveller - a taste of the Greek Isles here in New Zealand on beautiful Orewa Beach, just 20 minutes drive north of downtown Auckland. Stay in one of our self-contained rooms, each with private balcony, and enjoy the panoramic beach and sea views, or socialise with us in ourspacious living areas as you wish.Orewa offers a great range of activities and amenities, and the cafes, reataurants, and shopping are all within a few metres walk (see the Orewawebsite at www.orewa-beach.co.nz)

Orewa Beach   *B&B Orewa*

Orewa Bach
Lesley & Grahame Gilbertson
309A Hibiscus Coast Highway, Orewa Beach,
Auckland 1461
Tel (09) 426 3510   Fax (09) 426 3509
Mob 025 237 9567   grahame.g@xtra.co.nz
orewabach.co.nz

Double $150-$200 Single $130-$180
(Special Breakfast)
2 Queen (2 bdrm)   2 Ensuite

Welcome to Orewa Bach, situated on the picturesque Hibiscus Coast, with absolute beach frontage to popular Orewa Beach. The central shopping area with a variety of cafes, restaurants and bars is immediately adjacent. Our luxurious bedrooms feature ensuites, heated towel rail, hairdryer, toiletries and quality bed linen. The guest lounge has modern furniture, Sky TV, complimentary refreshments are provided. Enjoy delicious breakfasts served in the dining alcove or outdoors on the patio. Local attractions include golf courses, hot pools, factory and craft shops and wineries.

Orewa   *Homestay 3.5km SE of Orewa*

Red Beach Homestay
Loretta Austin
13a William Bayes Place, Red Beach, Orewa
Tel (09) 426 7204   Fax (09) 426 7204
Mob 025 619 5659   l.austin@xtra.co.nz
www.bnb.co.nz/redbeachhomestay.html

Double $85 Single $50 (Continental Breakfast)
1 Double 1 Single (2 bdrm)
1 Ensuite

Escape the city. Relax by the park! Walk to our safe surf beach (body boards available). Red Beach is 30 mins north of the harbour bridge, one hour from Auckland Airport and has easy access to highways north. It is a casual, relaxed seaside suburb, with 3 golf courses, yacht marina, hot pools, and beach and bush walks. My house is light and sunny, the beds have electric blankets and the double ensuite room has tea and coffee facilities and TV. Off-season discount. Some German spoken.

Silverdale *B&B Separate/Suite 1km S of Silverdale*

The Ambers
Gerard & Diane Zwier
146 Pine Valley Road, Silverdale, Auckland
Tel (09) 426 0015 Fax (09) 426 0015
diane@the_ambers.co.nz
www.the-ambers.co.nz
Double $130-$150 Single $90-$110 (Continental Full Special Breakfast) Child $25 under 12 Credit cards accepted
2 King/Twin 2 Double (4 bdrm) 3 Ensuite

Looking for a romantic weekend away or just wanting to relax in elegant surroundings during your travels around New Zealand, then come and stay at The Ambers. Share our tranquil country atmosphere and warm hospitality - unwind with complimentary pre-dinner drinks. We have travelled extensively and enjoy meeting people. Three friendly German Shepherd dogs are part of our family. We are 30 minutes north of Auckland and are minutes from beaches, restaurants and shops. Please phone for reservations and directions. Warm regards, Di and Gerard.

Whangaparaoa *Self-contained 40km N of Auckland*

Jan & Ernest's Place
Jan Collins & Ernest Davenport
18A Brixton Road, Manly, Whangaparaoa
Tel (09) 424 7281 Mob 025 264 2962
codav@xtra.co.nz
www.bnb.co.nz/janandernests.html
Double $65-$95 Single $55-$75 (Continental Breakfast) $5 pp optional continental breakfast
2 Single (1 bdrm)
1 Private

We offer a comfortable twin studio unit with private bathroom and mini-kitchen with fridge, microwave and top-cook stove. Separate guest entrance and private patio surrounded by trees and garden. TV, linen and towels are provided. Beds have electric blankets and duvets. We are within walking distance to beaches, shops, bowling club and restaurants. Within 5km is Shakespeare Park, Gulf Harbour Marina and golf course. Our home is smoke-free and we have two Balinese cats 'Chino' and 'Phoebe'. Directions - please phone.

Whangaparaoa *Self-contained 40km N of Auckland*

Seashell View
Margriet & Adriaan van der Lee
1312 Whangaparaoa Road, Army Bay, Whangaparaoa
Tel (09) 424 8555 Fax (09) 444 3634
Mob 021 441 309 seashellview@slingshot.co.nz
www.seashellview.com
Double $120-$150 (Breakfast not provided)
1 Queen 1 Double (1 bdrm)
1 Private

This self-contained unit is set among a peaceful tropical garden with a spa pool. The Whangaparaoa Peninsula offers many interesting activities including safe swimming beaches, golf courses, fishing, and walking tracks. Seashell View is close to restaurants, cafes, shops and cinema. There is a ferry service at nearby Gulf Harbour Village that takes sightseeing tours to neighbouring islands Tiritiri Matangi a bird sanctuary and Kawau Island. The ferry service also goes directly to Auckland City. Directions: from Auckland motorway, exit at Silverdale, take Whangaparaoa Road and continue to Army Bay (15km). Not suitable for children under 12.

Whangaparaoa   *B&B 4km Ea of Orewa*

Duncansby
Kathy & Ken Grieve
72 Duncansby Road, Whale Cove, Stanmore Bay,
Whangaparaoa
Tel 09 424 0025   Fax 09 424 0025
Mob 025 200 96 88 or 027 4422278
duncansby@xtra.co.nz
www.bnb.co.nz/duncansby.html

Double $90 Single $60 (Full Breakfast)
2 Queen (2 bdrm)
2 Private

Duncansby, our brand new home opening February 2004, offers the chance to relax and enjoy beautiful sea views of the Hibiscus Coast. Located at Whale Cove between Red Beach and Stanmore Bay, we offer well appointed private rooms with own entrance, TV, decks, white linen and off street parking. Closeby are 3 golf courses, boating marina, rock fishing, superb beaches and plenty of excellent local restaurants and cafes. We are 35 minutes north of Auckland. A warm welcome awaits you.

Kaukapakapa   *Homestay 14km N of Kaukapakapa*

Kereru Lodge
Mrs B Headford
Arone Farm, RD 3, Kaukapakapa
Tel (09) 420 5223   Fax (09) 420 5223
Mob 021 420 522   Bheadford@xtra.co.nz
www.bnb.co.nz/kererulodgekaukapakapa.html

Double $70 Single $45 (Full Breakfast) Dinner $20
Credit cards accepted
1 Queen 1 Double 2 Single (3 bdrm)
1 Ensuite 1 Guests share

Relax in comfort and enjoy the warm hospitality of our large Kiwi country home. Set in a large much loved garden, in a quiet rural valley our home has lots of indoor/outdoor living. You may wish to play petanque or darts or pool, or just relax with a drink in the Summerhouse. Locally there are bushwalks, golf and tennis. We have many interests from shell collecting to geology and fossils. We enjoy sharing the delights of country living and meeting people from around the world.

Silverdale - Wainui   *B&B Self-contained 8km SW of Silverdale*

Whitehills Country Stay
Maureen & Dennis Evans
224 Whitehills Road, RD 1, Kaukapakapa
Tel (09) 420 5666   Fax (09) 420 5666
Mob 021 042 7958   d-mevans@xtra.co.nz
www.bnb.co.nz/whitehillscountrystay.html

Double $90 Single $50 (Continental Breakfast)
Child neg. Dinner $25 by arrangement Self-contained
studio $110 Children welcome
1 Twin 4 Single (3 bdrm)
2 Private

Relax and unwind at Whitehills situated 25 minutes from Auckland and 7 minutes from the Silverdale motorway exit. Enjoy quality B&B accommodation in the main house with a choice of twin or queen room. The comfortable self-contained studio has its own entrance and deck. Breakfast provisions will be provided. You are most welcome to wander around our garden, walk in the 6 acres of native bush or simply relax on the covered verandah. We, and our friendly border collie, look forward to meeting you.

Helensville   *B&B Self-contained 4km SW of Helensville*

Rose Cottage
Dianne & Richard Kidd
2191 State Highway 16, RD 2, Helensville

Tel (09) 420 8007   0800 755 433   Fax (09) 420 7966
Mob 025 599 135   kidds@xtra.co.nz
www.bnb.co.nz/rosecottagehelensville.html

Double $110 Single $80 (Full Breakfast) Credit cards
accepted
1 Queen (1 bdrm)
1 Ensuite

"Rose Cottage" offers comfort and privacy set within peaceful gardens. Whenuanui is a 350 ha Helensville sheep and beef farm providing magnificent farm walks. The family homestead and gardens have panoramic views over Helensville and the Kaipara Valley. Tasteful accommodation includes ensuite, TV and kitchenette. All-weather tennis court available for guests to use. Just 35 minutes from downtown Auckland on State Highway 16. A base to explore the Kaipara region or a great start or end to your Northland tour. Smoking outdoors appreciated.

Huapai - Kumeu   *B&B Farmstay Homestay 15km W of Auckland*

Foremost Fruits
Andrea & Jim Hawkless
45 Trigg Road, Huapai, Auckland

Tel (09) 412 8862   Fax (09) 412 8869
jrhawkless@xtra.co.nz
www.bnb.co.nz/foremostfruits.html

Double $80 Single $60 (Full Breakfast) Child $25
Dinner $20 Credit cards accepted Children welcome
2 Queen 3 Single (3 bdrm)   1 Guests share

Foremost Fruits is surrounded by several top NZ wineries
and is on a small orchard with a greenhouse growing export table grapes. We provide comfort and relaxation plus use of a swimming pool. Guests have upstairs to themselves - all bedrooms have TV. Breakfast is of choice and we offer selection of homemade breads and jams. There are several top restaurants in the area plus casual dining and take-away. Local attractions: top wineries, beaches, gannet colony, horse riding, golf. Directions from Auckland: take North Western motorway to end. Turn left to Kumeu (8km) past garden centre, over railway line to Trigg Road (left before 100km sign), No. 45 on left (30 minutes).

Just as we have a variety of B&Bs
you will also be offered a variety of breakfasts,
and they will always be generous.

Kumeu *B&B Homestay Countrystay 26km NW of Auckland*

Calico Lodge
Kay & Kerry Hamilton
250 Matua Road, RD 1, Kumeu
Tel (09) 412 8167   0800 50 18 50   Fax (09) 412 8167

Mob 025 286 6064   bed@calicolodge.co.nz
www.calicolodge.co.nz
Double $110-$130 Single $85 (Full Breakfast)
Dinner $30 by arrangement Credit cards accepted
1 Queen 1 Double 2 Single (3 bdrm)
1 Ensuite 1 Guests share

Kerry and Kay, Zippy our little dog, three cats and tame sheep welcome you to Calico Lodge. Amidst the wineries and cafes, near west coast beaches, 25 minutes NW of Auckland our new home on four acres has established trees and gardens. Hand made teddy bears and patchwork quilting adorn the bedrooms and guest lounge. Two minutes from SH16, peace and beautiful bush views complete the picture. We love it here and wish to share our little piece of paradise. Airport pickup and meals available.

Hobsonville *B&B Homestay 15mins NW of Auckland*

Eastview
Joane & Don Clarke
2 Parkside Road, Hobsonville, Auckland
Tel (09) 416 9254   Fax (09) 416 9254
eastview@xtra.co.nz
www.bnb.co.nz/eastview.html
Double $95-$120 Single $80-$90 (Full Breakfast)
(Special Breakfast) Child $30 Dinner By arrangement
Exta adult discount Credit cards accepted Children welcome
2 Queen 2 Single (3 bdrm)   2 Private 1 Guests share

Our EASY-TO-Find location is well situated for exploring Auckland. Stunning, panoramic water/city views. Two accommodation areas. Ground level has own lounge opening into garden, studio kitchen, two bedrooms, one queen, one twin, and private bathroom. Upstairs one bedroom (queen) and private bathroom. Spacious bedrooms and lounges soak up all-day sun. Enjoy tea/coffee, home-baked cookies anytime, watch Sky/TV. Stroll to nearby marina, discover superb beaches, wineries, great restaurants, thermal pools, native bush clad hills, gannet colony, golf courses.

Bethells Valley - West Auckland *Farmstay Self-contained 15km W of Henderson*

Greenmead Farm
Averil & Jon Bateman
115 Bethells Road, RD 1, Henderson
Tel (09) 810 9363   Fax (09) 810 8363
jabat@greenmead.co.nz
www.greenmead.co.nz
Double $110 Breakfast additional charge Extra guests
$20 each Children welcome
4 Single (2 bdrm)
1 Private

Guests have sole use of comfortable holiday home - two bedrooms, bathroom, lounge (TV) and large kitchen/dining room with excellent cooking facilities. Additional guests $20 each. Breakfast extra. The main house and guest cottage are surrounded by a large country garden - swings for children. Cattle, two Border collie working dogs. Peaceful location in rural valley in the Waitakere Ranges. Good walking tracks in the area - forest, beach and lake. 30 minutes drive west of central Auckland. Beach six minutes.

Bethells Beach
Self-contained Cottages   15km W of Swanson

Bethell's Beach Cottages & 100 Seater Summer Pavilion
Trude & John Bethell-Paice
PO Box 95057, Swanson, Auckland
Tel (09) 810 9581   Fax (09) 810 8677
info@bethellsbeach.com   www.bethellsbeach.com
Double $195-$295 Child under 12yrs 1/2 price
Dinner 2 course $35pp + gst   3 course $45pp + gst
Breakfast extra $25pp
Credit cards accepted   Children welcome
2 Queen 2 Double 3 Single (3 bdrm)
2 Private

"To Give is to Love & To Love is to Live"
Trude Bethell-Paice

Drive 30 minutes from Auckland city to one of the most unique parts of the West coast. The Bethell's settled this area 6 generations ago and Trude and John continue the long family tradition of hospitality. They have created two magic cottages and venue in this spectacular place where the best sunsets and seaviews are to be experienced - as seen in magazines: *Grace, & Elle Aus, Feb 2000, Elle Singapore, March 2000.* Both cottages have a sunny north facing aspect and are surrounded by 200-year-old pohutukawa's (NZ Christmas tree). Each one is totally separate, private and has a large brick barbecue. The vast front lawn is ideal for games and the gardens are thoughtfully designed for relaxation.

The cottages are made up with your holiday in mind - not only are beds made and towels/linen put out, but Trude and John have attended to too many details to mention and laundry facilities are available. Even the cats will welcome you. As seen in *Vogue Australia 1998. Life/The Observer (Great Britain 1998)* - 'one of twenty great world wide destinations'. *British TV Travel Show 1998. She magazine (February 1999)* - 'one of the 10 most romantic places to stay in NZ'. *North and South magazine (January 1999)* - 'one of the 14 best Bed and Breakfasts in NZ' Oct 2002 - USA Fodors travel guide.

'Turehu' Cottage has a studio atmosphere with double bi-folding doors from the conservatory. For outdoor dining sit under a pohutukawa tree at your own bench and table on the hillside with views over the beach and Bethell's valley. Cork floor in the kitchen, TV and bedroom area, gentle cream walls and white trim. Warm slate floors in the conservatory with lounge, dining table and bathroom (shower and toilet). Kitchen has microwave, large fridge/freezer, stove and coffee plunger, with all kitchen and dining amenities. Suitable for a couple and one child or two friends.

'Te Koinga' Cottage, this superb home away from home is 80sqm and has two bi-folding doors onto a 35sqm wooden deck for outdoor dining and relaxation in this sun trap. Set under the shade of a magnificent spralling pohutukawa tree and surrounded by garden. A fireplace for winter warmth and sixteen seater dining table. The two bedrooms have carpet and terracotta

tiles expand to the dining, kitchen, bathroom and toilet. Wood panelled and cream/tan rag rolled walls for a relaxing atmosphere. The bathroom offers a bath and shower. Open planned kitchen has microwave, large fridge/freezer, stove, dishwasher and coffee maker. Suitable for a family, 2 couples or a small function. Trude is a marriage celebrant and Trude and John specialise in weddings, private functions and company workshops. A local professional chef is available for these occasions.

Local adventures - Bethell's beach is a short drive or walk. Pack a picnic lunch and discover Lake Wainamu for fresh water swimming and expansive sand dunes or go on a bush walk with excellent examples of New Zealand native flora. If you head in the direction of the beach you may enjoy exploring the caves (at night the magic of glow worms and phosphorescence in the shallows), or go surfing and fishing. You are close to many world class Vineyards and restaurants/cafes. You may fancy a game of golf - two courses within 10-20 minutes drive from your cottage. Many more activities in a short driving distance. No pets please. Children under 12 half price.

Waitakere Ranges - Swanson
B&B Guesthouse 4km W of Swanson

Panorama Heights
Allison & Paul Ingram
42 Kitewaho Road, Swanson, Waitakere City, Auckland
Tel (09) 832 4777   0800 NZBNB4U
Fax (09) 833 7773   Mob 025 272 8811
nzbnb4u@clear.net.nz
www.panoramaheights.co.nz
Double $115-$125 Single $80-$90 (Full Breakfast)
Dinner by request Credit cards accepted
2 Queen 1 Twin 1 Single (4 bdrm) 3 Ensuite 1 Private

Private and peaceful with breathtaking panoramic views located high in the Waitakere Ranges on the "Twin Coast Discovery Route". Watch the sun rise across native kauri trees, bush and Auckland City beyond.Within easy access to over 200 km of walking tracks through 17,000 hectares of native rainforest. 10-15 minutes from West Coast beaches (Piha, Bethells, Karekare, Muriwai),West Auckland Wineries and two scenic golf courses, art trails, shopping centers. Indoors non-smoking. A warm welcome awaits you. Please phone for bookings and directions. Airport pick up available.

Ranui
B&B Homestay Detached B&B 15mins W of Auckland

The Garrett
Alma & Rod Mackay
295 Swanson Road , Waitakere City , Auckland 8
Tel (09) 833 6018   Fax (09) 833 6018   Mob
www.bnb.co.nz/ .html
Double $75 Single $45 (Continental Breakfast)
Child $22   Dinner $20
2 King/Twin 1 King 2 Single (2 bdrm)   1 Ensuite

Just 15 minutes form Auckland City and five minutes from historical Henderson, The Garrett offers villa style accommodation with ensuite and private terrace. Twin beds or king size if you prefer. We can accommodate extra guests with folding beds on request. High ceilings and period furniture and decor create an atmosphere of old in this delightful Homestay, just minutes away from Waitakere City. Leading attractions include wine trails, Art Out West Trail - including Lopdell House Gallery. Waitake Ranges, bush walks, Aratiki Heritage and Environment Centre, golf courses. West City Shopping Centre, Lynn Mall and St Lukes. No pets; no campervans.

Piha
Self-contained 20km W of Henderson

Piha Cottage
Tracey & Steve Skidmore
PO Box 48, Piha, Waitakere City, Auckland
Tel (09) 812 8514   Fax (09) 812 8514
piha_cottage@yahoo.co.nz
www.pihacottage.co.nz
Double $95-$120 Single $95-$120
(Continental Breakfast) Child $20 Children welcome
1 Double 1 Single (1 bdrm)
1 Private

Beautiful Piha Cottage is secluded in a quiet bush setting within easy walking distance of beach and tracks. This open plan home has a well-equipped kitchen and spacious dining, living and sleeping areas. We have two young children and a friendly cat. Piha Cottage is on the rugged West Coast, nestled into native bush. So leave the city behind. Go surfing, swimming or choose from a network of outstanding walking tracks, through lush rainforest or spectacular coastline. We welcome you warmly and then leave you in peace to enjoy the tranquility.

Piha   *Self-contained 40mins W of Auckland*

Piha Lodge
Shirley Bond
117 Piha Road, Piha
Tel (09) 812 8595   Fax (09) 812 8583
Mob 021 639 529   pihalodge@xtra.co.nz
www.pihalodge.co.nz
Double $140-$200 (Continental Breakfast) Child $20
Additional adults $30   Credit cards accepted   Children
welcome   4 Queen 1 Double 1 Single (5 bdrm)
1 Ensuite 2 Private

Awarded Best Accommodation. Our two quality self-contained units plus one large apartment with fireplace, full kitchen (couple only), have stunning panoramic sea and bush views and give you all the comforts of home plus privacy and security. Situated in the subtropical rainforest of the Waitakere Ranges and on the wild West Coast, Piha has one of New Zealand's top surfing beaches and magnificent sunsets that are legendary. Enjoy the bush walks, climb Lion Rock, visit the fairytale Kitekite Falls or relax in the swimming pool, hot spa or games room. Complimentary breakfast, homemade bread.

Piha   *Self-contained 25km W of Henderson*

Westwood Cottage
Dianne & Don Sparrow
95 Glenesk Road, Piha, Auckland
Tel (09) 812 8205   Fax (09) 812 8203
Mob 021 278 8110
westwoodcottage.piha@clear.net.nz
www.bnb.co.nz/westwoodcottage.html
Double $120 (Continental Breakfast) Child $20
Children welcome
1 Queen 1 Single (2 bdrm)
1 Private

Westwood Cottage offers a unique experience. Nestled in a secluded corner of our property, amongst beautiful bush overlooking Piha Valley. The Cottage is self-contained, open plan design, flowing on to a private deck. Full kitchen facilities with continental breakfast supplied. A cozy log fire for your enjoyment on cooler evenings. Off road parking provided. Children 5 and over welcome. A short walk leads to Piha Surf Beach and bush walks include Kitekite Waterfall and Black Rock Dam.

Okura   *B&B Self-contained 20km N of Auckland Central*

Okura B&B
Judie & Ian Greig
20 Valerie Crescent, Okura, North Shore City,
Auckland
Tel (09) 473 0792   Fax (09) 473 1072
ibgreig@clear.net.nz
www.bnb.co.nz/okurabb.html
Double $95 Single $70 (Continental Breakfast)
(Full Breakfast) Credit cards accepted
1 Queen 1 Single (2 bdrm)
1 Private

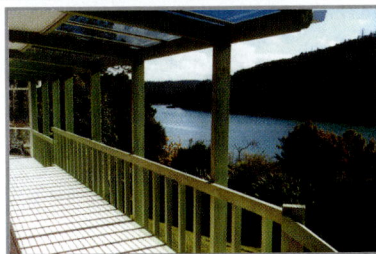

Situated on Auckland's North Shore, Okura is a small settlement bounded by farmland and the Okura River, an estuary edged with native rain-forest. If you like peace, quiet, with only bird song nearby, estuary and forest views, then this is for you. Accommodation includes your own, not shared, TV lounge, tea-making facilities, fridge, shower and toilet. Nearby are a wide variety of cafes, shops, beaches, walks, North Shore Stadium, Massey University and golf courses. Okura - one of Auckland's best kept secrets.

Coatesville - Albany
B&B Homestay Country Homestay 10km N of Albany

Ki Swara Country Homestay
Susan Beer
77 Wake RD, RD3 Coatesville, Albany

Tel (09) 415 9358 Fax (09) 415 9358
Mob 025 312 156 kiswara@xtra.co.nz
www.kiswara.co.nz

Double $130 Single $80 (Continental Breakfast)
(Full Breakfast) Child $40 Dinner $30 Children
welcome Pets welcome
1 Queen 3 Single (2 bdrm)
1 Ensuite 1 Host share

Ki Swara provides the best of both worlds: the quiet of the country and the culture of the city,(25 mins).
Our lively Border Collie watches over our 10 acres grazed by sheep and horses. Guests have a large
room with bath in their wing of the house which also has TV, separate entrance, and private deck. Star
gazing from bed is an extra delight. Come join us for a ride up the road or a game of tennis. Enjoy our
homebaking and fresh produce for your meals. No smoking please.

Coatesville - Albany
Farmstay 7km N of Albany

Camperdown
Chris & David Hempleman
455 Coatesville/Riverhead Highway, RD 3, Albany,
Auckland

Tel (09) 415 9009 0800 921 479 Fax (09) 415 9023
chris@camperdown.co.nz www.camperdown.co.nz

Double $130 Single $90 (Full Breakfast) Child $45
Dinner $40 Children welcome
1 King/Twin 1 King 2 Queen 2 Single (4 bdrm)
2 Private 1 Guests share

We are only 20 minutes from Auckland City. Relax in secluded tranquillity, our home opens into
beautiful gardens, native bush and stream offering the best of hospitality in a friendly relaxed atmosphere.
On the farm we have sheep, cattle and pet lambs Our spacious guest areas consist of the entire upstairs.
Guests may use our games room, play tennis on our new court, row a boat on the lake, or just stroll by
the stream. Camperdown is easy travelling to the main tourist route north. Directions. travel North to
Albany, onto Highway 17, turn left at 'BP' into Coatesville/Riverhead Highway (28).

Albany - Coatesville
B&B Country Homestay 3km N of Albany

Te Harinui Country Homestay
Mike & Sue Blanchard
102 Coatesville/Riverhead Highway, RD 3, Albany,
Auckland

Tel (09) 415 9295 sue@teharinui.co.nz
www.teharinui.co.nz

Double $90 Single $75 (Full Breakfast) Child by
arrangement Dinner $35 by arrangement
1 Queen 2 Single (2 bdrm)
1 Guests share

A home from home in the country only 20 minutes from the city. Stroll in the bush and paddocks; feed
our pet coloured sheep, two dog and cats all very friendly. Learn to spin and browse our craft shop. We
can arrange outings to local attractions including gardens, orchards and beaches. Close to stadium and
Massey University. Generous breakfasts; coffee and teas are always available. Sue speaks French and
is learning Mandarin.

Coastal Beach Haven
B&B Homestay 15 min N of Auckland Central

Port O' Call
Jill & Bernie Cleal
12 Amelia Place, Coastal Beach Haven, Auckland
Tel (09) 483 4439 Fax (09) 483 4439 Mob 025 227
2639 portocall.b&b@xtra.co.nz
www.bnb.co.nz/portocall.html

Double $150-$160 Single $100-$120 (Full Breakfast)
Credit cards accepted
1 King 1 Queen (2 bdrm)
2 Ensuite

Welcome to "Port O'Call", a secret hideaway
overlooking the tranquil waters of the Waitemata Harbour. Come and enjoy our relaxed hospitality in our spacious, tastefully decorated bedrooms with a nautical theme with TV/CD, ensuites featuring hair drier, toiletries, bathrobes, all leading to a salt water pool and spa pool. Tea/coffee making facilities. Discover the "Secret Garden" amongst the tropical palms and native plants, or cuddle up in front of the log fire during winter. The ultimate place to unwind. P.S. There are three resident cats.

Greenhithe
B&B Homestay Rural Homestay 15km N of Auckland

@ home

Waiata Tui Lodge (The Song of the Tui)
Therese & Ned Jujnovich
177 Upper Harbour Drive, Greenhithe, Auckland
Tel (09) 413 9270 Fax (09) 413 9217
theresewa@xtra.co.nz
www.bnb.co.nz/waiatatuilodge.html

Double $85-$100 Single $70 (Special Breakfast) Child
Negotiable Dinner $25 Credit cards accepted
2 Queen 1 Twin 2 Single (3 bdrm)
2 Private 1 Guests share

You will be warmly welcomed to Waiata Tui Lodge. Our haven of nine acres is only fifteen minutes to Auckland City and six minutes to Albany University and stadium. A handy starting off place for traveling North. Relaxing and refreshing. Waken to bird song. Look out over Kauris to the tranquil water below and the more distant Waitakere Ranges. Walk in our lush rain forest with massive trees, a few centuries old. Swim in our pool. Therese is a keen winemaker. We have both traveled extensively in New Zealand and overseas. Homestay since 1986. Five kilometres to Albany and Glenfield

Herald Island
B&B Homestay 6km NW of Henderson

Harbour View Homestay
Les Pratt
84 The Terrace, Herald Island
Tel +64 (9) 416 7553 Fax +64 (9) 416 7553
harbourviewhomestay@nznet.gen.nz
www.bnb.co.nz/harbourview.html

Double $80-$110 Single $45-$65 (Full Breakfast)
Child under 12 half price Dinner $25 Credit cards
accepted Children welcome Pets welcome Smoking
area inside 1 Queen 4 Single (3 bdrm) 1 Ensuite 1 Private

Your host has a two storey home with superb accommodation, right on waters edge. Upstairs has 2 bedrooms, 1 Queen, 1 Twin, each with its own sundeck, with views of harbour. Own lounge, bathroom, and tea & coffee making facilities. Downstairs has 1 Twin (large) with own ensuite. Very homely. Easy access. Within 20 mins radius, wine tasting, horse riding, golf course, bush walks, vintage car museum & model world. Rooms serviced daily, laundry available. We have 1 dog Emma, 1 cat Tiger, both very friendly. Herald Island is joined to the mainland.

Browns Bay *B&B 1.5km W of Browns Bay*

Amoritz House
Carol & Gary Moffatt
730 East Coast Road, Browns Bay, Auckland
Tel (09) 479 6338   0800 936 338   Fax (09) 479 6338
Mob 025 806958   amoritz@ihug.co.nz
www.aucklandaccommodation.co.nz

Double $90-$200 Single $70-$90 (Full Breakfast)
Dinner $10 - $30 pp
2 King/Twin 1 Double 1 Single (3 bdrm)
2 Ensuite 1 Private

Spend some peaceful nights in our quiet guest bedrooms with Sky TV, garden and rural outlooks. Separate guest entrance leads into kitchenette with fridge, microwave, washing machine, dryer etc. Adjoining dining room. Internet, e-mail, fax etc available. Minutes from North Harbour Stadium, Millennium Stadium, Massey University, a variety of cafes, restaurants, beaches, shopping and Auckland City Centre with all its attractions. Bus stop at door. Large garden, barbeque. Off street parking, 2 minutes to Motorway. Non smoking. Dinners $10, $20, $30 pp with prior notice.

Mairangi Bay *B&B Separate/Suite 13km N of Auckland*

Bays Cottage B&B
Jean & Brian Henstock
7 Matipo Road, Mairangi Bay, Auckland
Tel (09) 479 3822   Fax (09) 479 3822
Mob 021 268 9308   bayscottage@xtra.co.nz
www.bayscottage.co.nz

Double $100-$120 Single $80-$90 (Continental Full
Special Breakfast) Child Negotiation Dinner $15 - 30
by arrangement Credit cards accepted Children welcome
1 King/Twin 1 King 1 Queen (3 bdrm)   3 Ensuite

Our refurbished cottage is a short stroll from shops, restaurants, cafes, sandy beaches and cliff top walkways. Golf, bowling and other attractions are adjacent. We offer warm friendly hospitality in our comfortable home with idiot cat on site. Amenities include ensuite bedrooms, guest entrance and TV lounge, tea/coffee, laundry, E-mail access, phone/fax, barbecue area and off-road parking. Relax in our secluded tranquil garden with solar heated pool and native bird life. Breakfast is a scrumptious indulgence and evening meals can be requested.

Takapuna *B&B 300met SW of Takapuna*

Ambience
Marie   Hitchfield
1/16 Napier Ave, Takapuna 1309, Auckland
Tel (09) 489 5542   Fax (09) 489 5581
Mob 027 405 3032   mhitchfield@pcconnect.co.nz
www.bnb.co.nz/.html

Double $95 Single $65 (Continental Breakfast)
Child $10 extra.   Dinner
1 King/Twin (1 bdrm)   1 Private

Enjoy our large attractive double bedroom (twin or superking), TV, fridge, tea and coffee-making facilities. Private bathroom, use of laundry. Drive-in with private access through carport. Superbly situated near harbour bridge and motorway, we are a stone's throw from Takapuna Beach and the vibrant shops and restaurants of Takapuna City. A few minutes drive south is the Victorian seaside charm of Devonport and, over the harbour bridge, the Auckland CBD. Despite its proximity to all this, the B&B is exceptionally quiet.

Bayswater - Auckland *B&B Separate/Suite 5km S of Takapuna*

Matuku Lodge
Rhondda & Les Sweetman
39A Beresford St., Bayswater, North Shore
Tel (09) 445 6649   0800 80 0 537   Fax (09) 445 6659
Mob 025 912 281   rhondda@xtra.co.nz
www.bnb.co.nz/matukulodge.html

Double $150-$190   Single $90-$110   (Full Breakfast)
(Special Breakfast) Child $60 Dinner $45 pp
Credit cards accepted Children welcome
1 King 2 Queen 1 Twin (3 bdrm)
2 Ensuite 1 Private 1 Guests share

Tranquil Matuku Lodge on the water's edge of Shoal Bay, Bayswater Peninsula. Only 9 minutes by ferry to Downtown Auckland. Sail, row, canoe, birdwatch, relax. Beautiful architect designed home complemented by original Art [www.kiwiartz.co.nz]. Special concessions on our sailing catamaran [www.kowhaicat.co.nz] King br/ensuite, and Queen br/private bath, open onto deck to the sea. 3rd Br/ensuite has Queen and twin singles. Expect a warm welcome from our border collie, Jess.

Devonport   *Homestay 8km N of Auckland*

Cheltenham-By-The-Sea
Gayle and Mark Mossman
2 Grove Road, Devonport, Auckland
Tel (09) 445 9437   Fax (09) 445 9432
Mob 021 251 6920   mgmossman@clear.net.nz
www.cheltenhambythesea.co.nz

Double $100-$130 Single $75-$100
(Continental Breakfast) Child $50
1 Queen 1 Double 1 Twin 1 Single (4 bdrm)
1 Ensuite 1 Private 1 Guests share

Mark & Gayle welcome you to Cheltenham By The Sea, one minute walk to the beach. A large contemporary home set amongst native trees and garden. Close to public transport and a short stroll to the village with cafes, restaurants, art galleries, antique shops and much more. Location: we are located 45 minutes from the International Airport. Airport shuttle available to our doorstep.   12 minutes via ferry to downtown Auckland City. Courtesy pick-up from Devonport wharf. We welcome longer stays and can arrange favourable rates accordingly. We offer experienced advice for your NZ pursuits.

Devonport   *B&B Separate/Suite*

Rainbow Villa
Judy McGrath
17 Rattray Street, Devonport, Auckland
Tel (09) 445 3597   Fax (09) 445 4597
rainbowvilla@xtra.co.nz
www.bnb.co.nz/.html

Double $130-$160   Single $100-$130   (Full Breakfast)
Credit cards accepted
1 King 1 Queen 2 Twin 2 Single (3 bdrm)
3 Ensuite

Welcome to our pretty Victorian Villa (1885) nestled in a quiet cul-de-sac on the lower slopes of Mt Victoria. there are three elegant spacious rooms with ensuites and Sky TV. A hot Spa Pool is available in the garden. We serve a delicious full breakfast and coffee and tea are available at all times. Situated just 100 metres from the Historic Devonport Village, 5 minute walk to the ferry which is a 10 minute ride to downtown Auckland. Directions: Rattray street is the first on the left past the Picture theatre. Shuttles are available at the airport. Not suitable for children or pets.

Devonport   *B&B Separate/Suite Self-contained & Cottage 4km N of Auckland Central*

Karin's Garden Villa
Karin Loesch & Family
14 Sinclair Street, Devonport, Auckland 1309
Tel (09) 445 8689 Fax (09) 445 8689
stay@karinsvilla.com   www.karinsvilla.com

Double $145-$175 Single $90-$135
(Continental Breakfast) Child $25 Dinner B/A
S/C cottage $185 Credit cards accepted
Children welcome   Cot available
1 King/Twin 2 Double 3 Single (4 bdrm)
1 Ensuite 1 Private 1 Guests share

Tucked away at the end of a quiet cul-de-sac, Karin's Garden Villa - *a Devonport Dream* - offers real home comfort with its light cosy rooms, easy relaxed atmosphere and the warmest of welcome from Karin and her family.

A beautifully restored spacious Victorian villa surrounded by large lawns and old fruit trees. Karin's Garden Villa has also been featured on NZ and Australian television advertising for its relaxed, peaceful setting. Just 5 minutes stroll from tree-lined Cheltenham Beach, sailing, golf, tennis, shops and restaurants and only a short drive or pleasant 10 minute walk past extinct volcanoes to the picturesque Devonport centre with its many attractions.

Your comfortable room offers separate private access through French doors, opening onto a wide verandah and cottage garden. And for those visitors wanting ultimate comfort and privacy, there is even a self-contained studio cottage with balcony and full kitchen facilities to rent (min. 3 days).

Sit down to a nutritious breakfast in the sunny dining room with its large bay windows overlooking everflowering purple lavender and native gardens. Guests are welcome to join the family barbecue and relax on our large lawn. We welcome longer stays and can arrange favourable discounts accordingly. Help yourself to tea and German-style coffee and biscuits anytime, check your e-mail and feel free to use the kitchen and laundry.

Karin comes from Germany and she and her family have lived in Indonesia for a number of years. We have seen a lot of the world and enjoy meeting other travellers. Always happy to help you arrange island cruises, rental cars, bikes and tours.

From the airport take a Shuttle Bus to our doorstep or to Downtown Ferry Terminal. Courtesy pick-up from Devonport Wharf. By Car: After crossing Harbour Bridge, take Takapuna-Devonport turnoff. Right at T-junction, follow Lake Road to end, left into Albert, Vauxhall Road and then first left into Sinclair Street. ***Come as guests - leave as friends***

Devonport
B&B Separate/Suite 2km N of Auckland Central

Villa Cambria
Kate & Clive Sinclair
71 Vauxhall Road, Devonport, Auckland
Tel (09) 445 7899 Fax (09) 446 0508
Mob 025 843 826
info@villacambria.co.nz   www.villacambria.co.nz

Double $150-$250 Single $150-$250 (Full Breakfast)
Credit cards accepted
3 Queen 1 Double 1 Twin (5 bdrm)
5 Ensuite

Villa Cambria is among one of the finest Bed & Breakfast Inns in Devonport. The elegant, historic Villa is a typical Devonport Victorian home. Built in 1904 of native kauri timber, it has been lovingly restored to its former glory and tastefully furnished with an eclectic mix of antique, asian, interesting and homely items. The Villa is situated in an unbeatable location, just a few minutes walk to beautiful Cheltenham Beach and the picturesque Waitemata Golf Course (18 holes).

Each of the guest rooms is decorated individually. Choose from the romantic Garden Loft with its own balcony, or one of our four beautifully appointed guest bedrooms. From the hand-selected sprigs of lavender in the bathrooms to the complimentary tea, coffee, port and toiletries, you'll be pampered during your stay. All our rooms have phone connections, irons and hairdryers.

Breakfast is wholesome, enjoy hand selected fresh fruit, yoghurt, a choice of cooked breakfasts and a selection of continental favourites. Breakfast is made with fresh produce from the market and is accompanied by home made bread, followed by freshly brewed coffee and a choice of teas. The finishing touch though, is without a doubt the warm, friendly spontaneity of owners Clive and Kate, who live in a completely separate part of the house. After breakfast you can enjoy the many nearby attractions, take a 12 minute ferry ride into the centre of the city (ferries cross every 30 minutes), or explore the many islands in the Hauraki Gulf. Devonport boasts more than 30 restaurants and offers excellent shopping, a cinema, many lovely walks and one of 49 extinct volcanic cones dotted around Auckland. Indeed Devonport has the enviable reputation of being the 'Jewel in Auckland's Crown' and one of the safest places to live within the city. Visit our web site at www.villacambria.co.nz for full details and room descriptions.

Directions: From the airport take a shuttle bus door to door service. By car: Travelling north, cross Auckland Harbour bridge. Travel 1.5kms and take the Esmonde Road exit Highway 26 to Takapuna-Devonport. Follow signs to Devonport along Lake Road. At the roundabout turn left into Albert Road, then at the T junction turn left into Vauxhall Road, Inn on left.

Devonport *B&B Homestay 1.5km N of Devonport*

Ducks Crossing Cottage
Gwenda & Peter Mark-Woods
58 Seabreeze Road, Devonport, Auckland
Tel (09) 445 8102 Fax (09) 445 8102
duckxing@splurge.net.nz
www.bnb.co.nz/duckscrossingcottage.html
Double $90-$120 Single $65-$85 (Full Breakfast)
Child $30
1 Queen 1 Double 2 Single (3 bdrm)
1 Ensuite 2 Private

Welcome to our charming modern home, built in 1994, surrounded by trees and gardens. Peaceful, spacious and sunny bedrooms with attractive country decor. All rooms have TV and clock radios. Tea and coffee facilities available with delicious home cooking. we are adjacent Waitemata Golf course and 5 minutes from Narrow Neck Beach. Swim, sail and explore. Devonport village is 2 minutes by car and has a variety of restaurants, cafes and antique shops. Hosts are well travelled,and enjoy hospitality. Directions: From Airport shuttle direct (door to door). If driving take Route 26, into Seabreeze Road, 1st house on left.

Devonport *Homestay Separate/Suite*

Amberley B & B
Mary & Michael Burnett
3 Ewen Alison Avenue, Devonport, Auckland 1309
Tel (09) 446 0506 Fax (09) 446 0506
Mob 025 288 0161 amberley@xtra.co.nz
www.bnb.co.nz/amberleybb.html
Double $110-$140 Single $80-$110 (Full Breakfast)
Child neg Credit cards accepted
3 Queen 2 Single (4 bdrm)
2 Guests share

Our home is a charming colonial villa within easy walking distance of Devonport's numerous cafes, shops, safe swimming beaches, golf course and ferry terminal. Spectacular panoramic views from nearby summit of Mt Victoria. Spacious bedrooms with exceedingly comfortable beds! Double spa bath in one bathroom. Bathrobes provided. Large guest lounge with sky TV, tea/coffee making facilities, fridge and homebaking. Laundry facilities. Outside smoking only. We have travelled extensively both here and overseas and look forward to making your stay in our beautiful country an enjoyable experience.

Devonport *B&B Separate/Suite Self-contained Quality Accommodation*

Badgers of Devonport
Heather & Badger Miller
30 Summer Street, Devonport, Auckland
Tel (09) 445 2099 Fax (09) 445 0231
badgers@clear.net.nz
www.badger.co.nz
Double $130-$175 Single $100-$135 (Full Breakfast)
Dinner $35pp Credit cards accepted
2 Queen 3 Double 4 Twin 2 Single (5 bdrm)
4 Ensuite 1 Private

Welcome to our home. Let us pamper you in our quiet, sunny Victorian Villa furnished with antiques, oriental carpets and memorabilia from our extensive travels. Laze on your Victorian brass bed, soak in your Victorian claw footed bath. Complimentary drinks, chocolates. All bedrooms have ensuite, private bathrooms, bathrobes, toiletries, flowers, TVs, cuddly teddy bears. Self-contained guest wing complete with kitchen facilities. Laundry, airport transfers available. Off-street parking. Sumptuous breakfast for vegetarians and meat lovers. Stroll to beaches, restaurants, cafes, art galleries, shops, museums.

Devonport   *B&B Separate/Suite 8km N of Auckland*

Devonport Villa B&B Inn
Keith & Lesley Wilkinson
46 Tainui Road, Devonport, Auckland

Tel (09) 445 8397   Fax (09) 445 9766
dvilla@ihug.co.nz   www.bnb.co.nz/devonportvillabbinn.html

Double $175-$245 (Full Breakfast)   Credit cards accepted   Children welcome
2 King 4 Queen 2 Twin 1 Single (7 bdrm)
7 Ensuite

Devonport Villa Inn, winner of the NZ Tourism Awards for hosted accommodation, is in the heart of Devonport, 2 minutes walk from Auckland's best kept secret, sandy and safe Cheltenham Beach. There is something special about every aspect of this exquisite historic home built in 1903 by a wealthy retired English doctor. Edwardian elegance, spacious individual rooms with king and queen beds, extensive guest library, rich woollen carpets, restored colonial furniture, outstanding stained glass windows and the guest lounge with its amazing vaulted ceiling and polished native timber floor.

Choose from the unique upstairs Turret Room, the romantic and sunny Rangitoto Suite with its private balcony, the colonial style Beaconsfield Suite with antique clawfoot bath and four-poster king bed or the Oxford and Gold rooms. Each cosy room is individually decorated with firm beds, soft woollen blankets, flowers from the garden, plump pillows and crisp white linen.

And in the morning you will be cooked a delicious full breakfast, including freshly squeezed juice, natural yoghurt, nutritious muesli, muffins baked daily, pancakes, double smoked bacon with eggs and preserves.....join other guests in the dining room overlooking the garden, or if you like we can serve breakfast in some rooms at a time to suit. Please ask when booking.

Sit in the sunny shell courtyard overlooking the Edwardian style garden with lavender hedges, old roses and spacious lawns. Enjoy a moonlit stroll along the beach to North Head and dinner at a nearby restaurant. Devonport Villa is within easy walking distance of the major wedding reception venues and the historic sights of Devonport. Let us help you to make your stay in Devonport relaxing, pleasant and unique. Fax and E-mail available. Smoking is not permitted in the house

Devonport Villa Inn, winner of the NZ Tourism Awards for hosted accommodation

Devonport   *B&B Self-contained Cottage 4km N of Auckland Central*

The Jasmine Room
Joan & John Lewis
20 Buchanan Street, Devonport, Auckland

Tel (09) 445 8825   Fax (09) 445 8605
Mob 021 120 9532   joanjohnlewis@xtra.co.nz
www.bnb.co.nz/thejasmineroom.html

Double $100   (Full Breakfast)
1 Queen (1 bdrm)
1 Ensuite

Welcome to our cosy smoke-free quiet and private guest cottage. We are right in the heart of historic Devonport Village with all its attractions, cafes, beaches, golf course, scenic walks. The ferry to Auckland City and the Hauraki Gulf is 3 minutes walk away. A breakfast basket is delivered to your door and provides fruit juice, cereals, home made muesli and yoghurt, a platter of seasonal fruits, breads, English muffins, jams, spreads, cheeses, free range eggs, breakfast teas and freshly brewed coffee. TV, fax.

Devonport   *1km NE of Devonport*

The Devon
Gayle & Tom Kalaugher
41 Tainui Rd, Devonport, Auckland

Tel (09) 445 7304   Fax (09) 445 7394
Mob 025 656 0784
devonportcouple@hotmail.com
www.bnb.co.nz/thedevon.html

Double $110 Single $100 (Continental Breakfast)
1 Queen (1 bdrm)
1 Private

Our comfortable friendly home is situated within minutes of all Devonport's desirable amenities, Cheltenham Beach, North Head, and for golfers, Waitemata golf Course. A short pleasant stroll along the waterfront takes you to Devonport village with it's many cafés restaurants and shops. For those who wish to travel further afield the ferry leaves from the centre of Devonport. Continental breakfast includes home baked muffins. Television in your room, Off street parking, Bathrobes provided.

A homestay is a B&B
where you share the family's living area.

Waiheke Island *Self-contained .01km Oneroa Village*

Hillside Holiday Apartment
Cheryl & Maurie Keeling
57 Church Bay Road, Oneroa, Waiheke Island

Tel (09) 372 8897 Fax (09) 372 8897
Mob 027 255 8897 mckeeling@xtra.co.nz
www.bnb.co.nz/treeways.html

Double $185 Single $165 (Full Breakfast)
1 King/Twin (1 bdrm)
1 Ensuite

Luxury one bedroom apartment with sea and vineyard views and only a ten minute easy walk into Oneroa village restaurants and wineries. Full breakfast includes home grown fruits and vegetables, home grown breads, jams, yoghurts and treats; served on your terrace over looking the village and Oneroa Bay. Spa pool, email and off street parking. We have travelled extensively, enjoy the outdoors, garden, beach and arts. Builder and ESL teacher and Digby (the Jack Russell dog) welcome you to our part of this beautiful island. Free transfers from ferry.

Waiheke Island *B&B*

Blue Horizon
David & Marion Aim
41 Coromandel Road, Sandy Bay, Waiheke Island

Tel (09) 372 5632
www.bnb.co.nz/bluehorizon.html

Double $80-$95 Single $55-$70
(Continental Breakfast)
2 Queen (2 bdrm)
1 Ensuite 1 Host share

We live above Sandy Bay which is 2-3 mins walk away with spectacular sea views. All the rooms of our modest home face due north catching the sun all day. Waiheke caters for adventuring, dining out, sandy beaches, rock pools, which we enjoy after farming and owning a garden centre which our 4 children helped with. We really enjoy our B & B and look forward to sharing our beautiful island with you. Directions: Ferry from Auckland. Car ferry Howick. Complimentary ferry transfers.

Herne Bay - Auckland Central *B&B 2.5km W of Auckland central*

Moana Vista
Tim Kennedy & Matthew Moran
60 Hamilton Road, Herne Bay, Auckland

Tel (09) 376 5028 0800 213 761 Mob 021 376 150
info@moanavista.co.nz
www.moanavista.co.nz

Double $140-$220 Single $120 (Full Breakfast)
Credit cards accepted Children welcome
2 Queen 1 Twin (3 bdrm)
2 Ensuite 1 Private 1 Guests share

Just minutes stroll from the Waitmata Harbour, nestled in the exclusive enclave of Herne Bay in Auckland, sits Moana Vista. This charming, renovated two-storey villa is owned and operated by your friendly and well-travelled hosts, Tim and Matthew. Moana Vista has three double bedrooms, two ensuites and one private bathroom. Two of the upper rooms have lovely harbour views. The bathrooms feature high-pressure showers and monogrammed Moana Vista toiletries. We also offer complimentary use of multi-channel TV, high-speed Internet/email services, mineral water, tea, coffee and even a glass of wine.

Herne Bay - Auckland   *B&B   Auckland Central*

Sunderland House Bed & Breakfast
Donald & Kathy Sunderland
1a Cox Street, Herne Bay, Auckland

Tel (09) 376 6336   Mob 025 249 9025
sunderlandhouse@ihug.co.nz
www.bnb.co.nz/sunderlandhousebb.html

Double $185-$215   Single $140   (Special Breakfast)
Traditional NZ roast by request
2 King (2 bdrm)
2 Ensuite

Television personality & interior designer Donald Grant Sunderland, wife Kathy and springer spaniel Ben, invite you to share their elegant and sumptuous replica Victorian villa. Your privacy and comfort is paramount in beautiful, spacious ensuite rooms. For romantics, the principle suite features a claw-foot bath set luxuriously in the bedroom. The second suite has an ensuite spa-bath for two. Stroll to local cafes, trendy shopping and great restaurants, then relax on the verandah or in the library with complimentary port. Just 3kms to the central city.

Ponsonby - Auckland Central   *Self-contained Auckland Central*

Ponsonby Potager
Marsha & Ray Lawford
43 Douglas Street, Ponsonby, Auckland 2

Tel (09) 378 7237   Fax (09) 378 7267
raywarby@xtra.co.nz
ponsonbypotager.co.nz

Double $120   Single $90 (Special Breakfast)
2 Double (2 bdrm)
1 Private

Prepare to be pampered at the "Ponsonby Potager". Enjoy a self-help breakfast "breakfast provisions provided" in the garden room or on one of the two private decks. You have your own entrances, bathroom, lounge (with video and book library), fully equipped kitchen, fresh fruit and flowers, off-street parking and Sky TV. It is peaceful here but only a 3 minutes stroll to the shops, cafes and restaurants of Ponsonby. Marsha, Ray and Danny (4 legged son) respect your privacy but are here if you need advice.

Ponsonby - Auckland Central   *B&B Homestay Auckland Central*

Colonial Cottage
Grae Glieu
35 Clarence Street, Ponsonby, Auckland 1034

Tel (09) 360 2820   Fax (09) 360 3436
www.bnb.co.nz/colonialcottage.html

Double $100-$120   Single $80-$100
(Special Breakfast) Dinner $25 by arrangement
1 King 1 Queen 1 Single (3 bdrm)
1 Guests share

Delightful olde-world charm with modern amenities to assure your comfort - accent on quality. Hospitable and relaxing. Quiet with green outlook. Close to Herne Bay & Ponsonby Road cafes & quality restaurants. Airport shuttle service door-to-door. Handy to public transport, city attractions and motorways. Smoke free indoors. Alternative health therapies & massage available. Special dietary requirements catered for. Organic emphasis. Single party bookings available.

Ponsonby - Auckland Central   *B&B Small hotel Auckland Central*

The Great Ponsonby
Sally James & Gerry Hill
30 Ponsonby Terrace, Ponsonby, Auckland

Tel (09) 376 5989   0800 766 792   Fax (09) 376 5527
great.ponsonby@xtra.co.nz
www.ponsonbybnb.co.nz

Double $180   Double Suites $190 - $325
Separate/Suite   Credit cards accepted
6 King/Twin 5 Queen (11 bdrm)
11 Ensuite

Ponsonby is the liveliest area of Auckland, full of cafes, restaurants, boutiques, ceramics. The Great Ponsonby is in a cul-de-sac in the middle of all this. No traffic noises here as we are not on the main road.
Centrally located, close to all major attractions, walk or bus to the harbour and down town. Plenty of off street parking. Link bus passes our corner every ten minutes.
Large, restored 1898 villa tucked away in a quiet street. The white exterior is deceptive. Inside is a bold profusion of colour with art from the Pacific. There is a choice of accommodation from queen rooms to roomier courtyard studios courtyard or palm garden suites.
Colourful, understated modern design. They have their own bathroom with heated mirror and towel rails, hairdryer. Tea & coffee making facilities in all rooms, Sky TV, DDI phones, internet access, clock radio. Studios also have a fridge for the bubbly, king or twin beds, leather couch, cd player, video player. Suites have a bath tub.
Leisurely breakfasts served from our extensive menu in the dining room or alfresco on the verandah. Resident cat and dog. We can take pets under some conditions so please phone to make a booking. Ask about our winter rates.

Jason Cochrane, editor of Arthur Frommer's Budget travel magazine, November 2002 said in his article on Auckland *"my top choice is Great Ponsonby B&B"*. Leading English travel guide Footprint says *"one of the best B&Bs in the city"*. The Great Ponsonby topped the list of accommodation chosen by the NY Times 26/1/03.

Ponsonby - Auckland Central *B&B 2km W of Auckland Central (Queen Street)*

Lodge 33
Selwyn Houry
33 Peel Street, Westmere, Auckland 2002
Tel (09) 361 3715 Fax (09) 361 3715
Mob 021 535 635 selwyn_houry@hotmail.com
www.bnb.co.nz/summerstreet.html

Double $90-$135 Single $70-$90 (Continental
Breakfast) Child by arrangement
1 King/Twin 3 Queen (4 bdrm)
4 Ensuite 1 Guests share

Situated in a quiet residential area only ten minutes from
the centre of Auckland and five minutes from the famous Ponsonby Road with all it's exciting bistros,
cafes, restaurants and boutique shops. Public transport is a short three minute walk. Quality linen and
towels are provided. A continental buffet breakfast is served in the dining area or in our lanscaped
garden around the swimming pool. Otherwise you have a huge range of cafes on Ponsonby Road. There
is off street parking.

Ponsonby - Auckland *B&B 1km W of Inner City*

Amitee's on Ponsonby
237 Ponsonby Road, Ponsonby, Auckland
Tel (09) 378 6325 Fax (09) 378 6329
relax@amitees.com
www.amitees.com

Double $145 Single $145 (Continental Breakfast)
Queen $170 Penthouse $235
1 King/Twin 5 Queen 1 Double 1 Twin (8 bdrm)
8 Ensuite

Cool and contemporary - the only boutique Hotel
accommodation on vibrant Ponsonby Road. Eight
attractive comfortable bedrooms with ensuites designed
with flair. Two suites with awesome city views. Private
garden, wine cellar with guest selection, free internet, DD phones, guest kitchen, cosy fireplace in
winter. Small friendly family-owned in great neighbourhood. Restaurants, cafes, bars, boutiques a step
away. "Link" bus at gate every 10 mins around city and all the sights.Credit Cards Visa/MC.

Ponsonby - Auckland *B&B Self-contained 2km NE of Auckland*

PonsonBynB
Kyria Mailman
9 Picton Street, Ponsonby, Auckland
Tel (09) 376 0250 Fax (09) 376 0250
Mob 021 766 607 kyria@xtra.co.nz
www.ponsonbynb.co.nz

Double $210 Single $180 (Continental Breakfast)
Child $30 Children welcome Pets welcome
1 King 1 Double (1 bdrm)
1 Private

Welcome to your home away from home. Our quiet
elevated studio has great views over Central Auckland.
New and modern fully equipped kitchen, bathroom, fine linen and plenty of everything. Friendly hosts
and little son Jordan - nothing is too hard, just ask! Amazing section with full security pin-code gates,
BBQ and private sun bathing area available. Just minutes walk to Ponsonby to dine at all our favourite
restaurants, cafes and bars. Book in a massage or walk to the park and have a flying fox ride with the
kids, its all here.

Parnell - Auckland   *Separate/Suite Small Hotel 1.5km E of Auckland Central*

Ascot Parnell
Therese & Bart Blommaert
St Stephens Avenue, Parnell, Auckland 1
Tel (09) 309 9012   Fax (09) 309 3729
info@ascotparnell.com
www.ascotparnell.com

Double $195-$325 Single $135-$295
$60 extra person   ask about Winter rates
Credit cards accepted
1 King/Twin 2 Queen 3 Twin 2 Single (3 bdrm)
3 Ensuite

The Ascot Parnell
The Ascot Parnell is a charming **centrally located B&B** in a tranquil garden setting. A moment's stroll from Parnell Village; with its numerous cafes, restaurants, art galleries and boutiques, and 1.5 km to Auckland city centre. The Rose Gardens and Auckland Museum is an easy 5 minute walk.

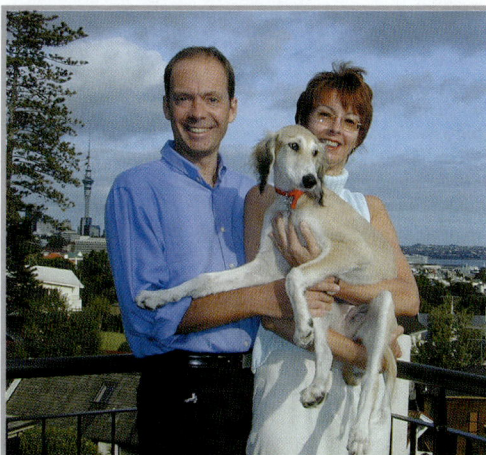

The Airport Shuttle-Bus stops at the door
Bedrooms are bright and spacious, with large windows that open, some with balconies and have either garden or harbour views. Rooms are all non-smoking, have TV, air-conditioning, phone and internet-connection. **Breakfast** is a five-course feast with freshly squeezed juice, seasonal or tropical fruits, yoghurt, cereals and homemade muesli, gourmet omelettes, bacon and eggs, Belgian crepes, pancakes, French toast etc.

The cosy guest-lounge
The cosy guest-lounge opens onto a large balcony with views on the harbour, city skyline and the Sky-Tower, which is beautifully lit at night. A Mac-PC offers free Internet. **Car parking is free and secure inside building.**   The hosts, Bart and Therese are well travelled and offer gracious yet down-to-earth friendly hospitality. They can help you book tours, rental cars and accommodations for your onward journey. **Reservations are essential.**

Auckland Central   *B&B   Auckland Central*

Redwood Vista Bed & Breakfast
Dawn Feickert
4D Kingsbridge, 72 wellesley street, Auckland
Tel (09) 373 4903   0800 349 742
Fax (09) 373 4903   Mob 0274 758 996
kotuku@wave.co.nz
www.redwood-bed-breakfast.ws

Double $135-$165 Single $100-$135
(Special Breakfast) Credit cards accepted
2 Queen 2 Twin (2 bdrm)
1 Ensuite 1 Host share

The Redwood Vista is a convenient central location in the heart of Auckland City with stunning views day and night. Walk to all the city attractions including art galleries, museums, theatres, cinemas, restaurants, shopping arcades, try your luck at Harrah's casino. Go sailing, stroll around the Viaduct yacht basin, along the waterfront, and through the renowned parks and reserves. Run down to the heated baths and gym. Ideal for the business traveller where everything is close by in the CBD plus walk to the Auckland University and Hospital.

The Auckland Airport shuttles are available door to door on request 24 hours a day. The Ferry terminal is 15 minutes walk away. The link bus and city buses are close by to take you to places like the Parnell Village the Rose Gardens, Ponsonby, Kelly Tartlton's under water world. We are also close to motorways-North and South. You have several golf courses available, close to beaches.

From our 4th floor spacious and private apartment with views of the Harbour Bridge, Sky Tower and Waitemata Harbour enjoy a gourmet breakfast with choices of fresh fruit, yoghurt, cereals, daily baked muffins, scones, breads and pastries as well as special dishes. This is served in the dining room or you can wander onto the verandah. Our rooms are non-smoking, comfortable and have queen and single beds with all the conveniences you would expect, including colour T.V. plus tea and coffee making facilities.

We are well travelled with a great interest in wine and every effort has been made to ensure your stay - be it business or pleasure is an enjoyable one. Email and office facilities available. Please phone for directions to the apartment.

Freemans Bay - Auckland *B&B*

Freemans B&B
Seema & Raj Chatly
65 Wellington Street, Freemans Bay, Auckland
Tel (09) 376 5046   0800 437 336   Fax (09) 376 4052

Mob 021 677 544   freemansbb@xtra.co.nz
www.freemansbandb.co.nz

Double $85 Single $55 (Continental Breakfast)
(Special Breakfast) Dinner $10pp Family room -
sleeps 4 $119 Children welcome
1 King/Twin 2 King 3 Queen 1 Single (7 bdrm)
1 Private

Hosts: Seema and Raj. Top location: walk to city centre, harbour, casino and markets. Near Ponsonby cafes and restaurants. Fully refurbished guest rooms with new beds and posturepaedic mattresses. Plus big TV, lounge, laundry, leafy garden, internet available. (1-4 persons).

Parnell - Auckland *Separate/Suite B&B Hotel 1.5km E of Downtown Auckland*

Chalet Chevron Bed & Breakfast
Brett & Jennie Boyce
14 Brighton Road, Parnell, Auckland
Tel (09) 309 0290 or (09) 309 0291   Fax (09) 373 5754
chaletchevron@xtra.co.nz   www.chaletchevron.co.nz

Double $110-$125 Single $80-$90 (Full Breakfast)
Child $25 Family room - sleeps 4 $140 - $180
Credit cards accepted Children welcome
2 King/Twin 1 Queen 5 Double 3 Twin 4 Single
(12 bdrm)   12 Ensuite 1 Guests share

Ideally positioned near Parnell Village with its restaurants, boutiques and art galleries, we are a small hotel offering quiet, well-appointed, charming guestrooms, all with own bathrooms and many boasting stunning harbour and bay views. Our typically 'kiwi' breakfast has an individually cooked course. We are conveniently close to public transport, making Downtown Auckland, harbour ferries and other city locations readily accessible. Starship Children's Hospital, University, Museum, the Domain, Wintergardens, Rose Gardens, cinemas and shopping areas are all situated within easy walking distance.

Parnell - Auckland *B&B B&B 1.5km Auckland City*

St. Georges Bay Lodge
Carol & Steven Quilliam
43 St. Georges Bay Road, Parnell, Auckland
Tel (09) 303 1050   Fax (09) 360 7392
Mob 021 214 1473   carol@stgeorge.co.nz
www.stgeorge.co.nz

Double $215-$255 Single $195-$215 $135 - $165
without ensuite (Continental & Full Breakfast)
2 King/Twin 1 Queen 1 Double 1 Twin (5 bdrm)
4 Ensuite 1 Private 1 Host share

St Georges Bay Lodge is an elegant Victorian Villa which has the charm of a by-gone era, with the comfort of modern amenities. There is no better location for your stay in Auckland City. We are minutes from: picturesque PARNELL VILLAGE, designer boutiques and speciality stores, great cafes, restaurants, and night club life, health centres, swimming pools, gardens, parks, and the Museum in Auckland Domain and Holy Trinity Cathedral. Also within walking distance: Newmarket and the business district, the Casino, more restaurants and City night life, the University of Auckland, Waitemata Harbour, watersports, island destinations, ferry tours, and beaches.

Mt Eden - Auckland *B&B Small Hotel 2km S of Auckland Central*

Bavaria B&B Hotel
Ulrike & Rudolf
83 Valley Road, Mt Eden, Auckland 3

Tel (09) 638 9641 Fax (09) 638 9665
bavaria@xtra.co.nz
www.bavariabandbhotel.co.nz

Double $135 Single $95 (Full Breakfast)
Child $12   over 2 yrs   Children welcome
Reduced rates May - Sep   Credit cards accepted
1 King/Twin 4 Queen 2 Double 2 Twin 2 Single
(11 bdrm)
11 Ensuite   Separate/Suite

We invite you to stay at our charming small hotel offering quality B&B with all modern facilities yet combined with a homely and welcoming atmosphere.

Our picturesque, colonial villa with its 11 guestrooms is tastefully decorated with contemporary native timber furniture. It is designed generously and maintained immaculately. All rooms have ensuites, quality commercial beds (extra length), telephones, suitcase racks, desks, electric blankets and internet access for your laptop computer.

Relax in our large sunny guest lounge which looks on to a private sun deck and small exotic garden. Our breakfast buffet is a house speciality offering a wide selection of freshly prepared healthy foods with a touch of German cuisine. Refreshments are offered during the day. There is plenty of off-street parking available in the court yard.

Within walking distance you will find excellent restaurants, cafes, banks, a modern supermarket, internet cafes and many other shops. Despite the proximity to the city, you will enjoy the quiet atmosphere of Mount Eden with its colonial villas, pretty gardens and Mt. Eden summit lending panoramic views over the city and harbour. Your hosts are always happy to give advice on rental cars, tours or on any other topic about New Zealand.

The city is only 2km away and can be easily reached by bus or car.

Epsom - Auckland
Homestay 5km S of Auckland City Centre

Millars Epsom Homestay
Janet & Jim Millar
10 Ngaroma Road, Epsom, Auckland 1003
Tel (09) 625 7336 Fax (09) 625 7336
Mob 027 251 3817
jmillar@xtra.co.nz
www.bnb.co.nz/millarsepsomhomestay.html

Double $80-$100 Single $60-$70 (Full Breakfast)
Child $10 Dinner $30 Credit cards accepted
1 King 1 Queen 2 Single (3 bdrm)
1 Ensuite 2 Private

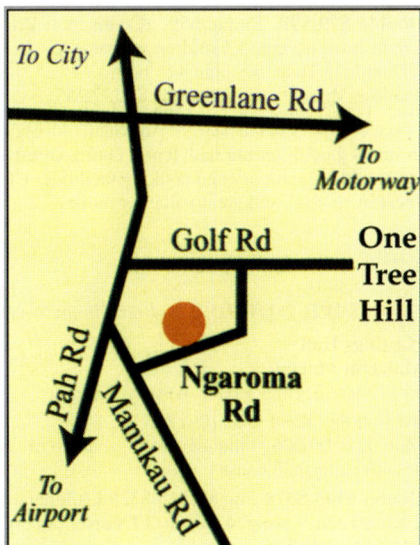

Our home, a spacious 1919 wooden bungalow, is surprisingly quiet and restful, set in a garden suburb in a tree-lined street, 200 metres from Greenwoods Corner Village with its bank, post office, reasonably priced non-tourist restaurants, and bus stop on direct route (15 minutes to the CBD).

There is a short walk to One Tree Hill, one of Auckland's loveliest parks with a playground, farm animals, groves of trees, the Observatory, and a magnificent panorama of Auckland from the summit. A 15 minute walk through the park leads to the Expo centre and Greenlane Hospital.

There are two accommodation areas - either the 'Garden Suite' with its Queen-sized double bedroom, large lounge with 3 single beds, patio, desk and TV, own bathroom, and which is the area we find really suitable for families; or the 'Upstairs' bedroom (king-size, can be converted to twin beds) with own ensuite, desk and TV.

We have travelled widely both in NZ and overseas (our son lives in Finland) and very much like conversing with guests and assisting in making their stay as pleasant as possible in our country and especially in this attractive suburb of Auckland. We are a smoke-free family. Jim and I were both born in NZ, and we belong to NZ Association Farm and Home Hosts, and also to Home and Farmstay Auckland.

Mt Eden - Auckland   *B&B Auckland Central*

811 Bed & Breakfast
Bryan Condon & David Fitchew
811 Dominion Road, Mt Eden, Auckland 1003

Tel (09) 620 4284   Fax (09) 620 4286
Mob 021 260 4184
www.bnb.co.nz/bedbreakfast.html

Double $85 Single $55 (Full Breakfast)
2 Double 1 Twin (3 bdrm)   2 Guests share

All are welcome at 811 Bed and Breakfast. Your hosts Bryan and David, Pfeni and their Irish Water Spaniels welcome you to their turn of the century home. Our home reflects years of collecting and living overseas. Centrally located on Dominion Road (which is an extension of Queen Street city centre). The bus stop at the door, only 10 minutes to city and 20 minutes to airport, shuttle bus from airport. Easy walking to Balmoral shopping area (banks, excellent restaurants). We have operated a bed and breakfast on a farm in Digby County, Nova Scotia, Canada. From north-south motorway, Greenlane off ramp, continue on Greenlane, to Dominion Road. Turn left and we are 7 blocks on your right to 811 (between Lambeth and Invermay and across from Landscape Road).

Mt Eden - Auckland   *B&B Separate/Suite B&B Hotel 3km S of Auckland Waterfront*

Pentlands B&B Hotel
Brian Hopkins
22 Pentland Avenue, Mt Eden, Auckland

Tel (09) 638 7031   Fax (09) 638 7031
hoppy.pentland@xtra.co.nz
www.pentlands.co.nz

Double $79-$99 Single $59   (Continental Breakfast)
Credit cards accepted Children welcome
7 Double 3 Twin 5 Single (15 bdrm)
4 Guests share   Extra People $20 - $25

Peace and quiet in the heart of Auckland. Ideal for travellers, families and groups. Top-rated villa style in sunny garden setting with tennis court. Guest lounge with open fire, Sky TV, internet facilities. Off street parking, laundry and cooking facilities. Close to Eden Park and to shops, restaurants etc. Rated "best by guests" and great value for money.

Western Springs   *B&B 3mins W of Town*

Hastings Hall
Malcolm Martel
99 Western Springs Road, Western Springs,

Tel (09) 845 8550   Fax (09) 845 8554
Mob 021 300 006   unique@hastingshall.co.nz
www.hastingshall.co.nz

Double $145-$375 Single $115-$325 Children welcome
2 King/Twin 1 King 4 Queen 1 Double (8 bdrm)
7 Ensuite 1 Private

Magnificently restored 1878 colonial mansion set in its own extensive grounds 5mins from the heart of Auckland City. Ideal for the tourist, businessman or a retreat away to unwind. Enjoy gourmet breakfasts in the conservatory, formal dining room, gazebo above the pool & spa pool. There are eight themed guest rooms all with marble ensuites including one designed for disabled guests. Choose from the Grand Hastings suite with private lounge to the Moulin Rouge loft suite in the Stables. Upstairs areas are ideal for families with adjoining room. Tropically landscaped grounds, formal lounge & large pool lounge with library, home theatre & computer, email & fax facilities. Furnished with antiques from the period, fine linen & warm fluffy towels. Ideal for small conferences, functions, meetings or seminars.

Western Springs - Auckland *B&B Self-contained 5km W of Auckland Central*

Phoenix House
Janine & Ray Niethe
26 Bannerman Road, Western Springs, Auckland
Tel (09) 846 7244   Fax (09) 846 7244
Mob 025 657 1756   rjniethe@xtra.co.nz
www.bnb.co.nz/phoenixhouse.html

Double $120 Single $90 (Continental Breakfast)
Child $20 Extra Person $20 Children welcome
1 Queen 1 Double (2 bdrm)
1 Private

Ray, Janine and Tigger (the cat) welcome you to Phoenix
House. A beautiful restored bungalow with tropical gardens and spa pool. Located in Western Springs, only five minutes drive from Auckland Central. Close to bus and train routes, golf course, Zoo, restaurants and cafes. Beautifully decorated we offer comfort with a queen size bed and settee in living room; can sleep up to four. Own entrance with fully equipped kitchen, stove and microwave, washing machine and iron, TV. Continental breakfast including homemade jams awaits you.

Epsom - Auckland *B&B Homestay 5km S of Auckland Central*

Auckland Homestay
Isobel & Ian Thompson
37 Torrance Street, Epsom, Auckland
Tel (09) 624 3714
aucklandhomestay@xtra.co.nz
www.aucklandhomestay.co.nz

Double $125-$145 Single $85-$110 (Full Breakfast)
Child Neg Dinner By arrangement
Credit cards accepted Children welcome
2 Queen 1 Single (3 bdrm)
1 Ensuite 1 Guests share

Experience warm, friendly hospitality in our large modern home in a quiet tree lined street. Just 5 minutes from motorway and 15 minutes from Airport and City CBD. Our central location is ideally positioned to explore the many attractions, whether by car or one of the nearby bus routes. Use of full laundry facilities. Telephone, email by request. Evening meals by prior arrangement. Off Street Parking. We look forward to sharing our non-smoking home with you.

Epsom - Auckland *B&B Homestay 5km S of Auckland*

Epsom House
Kathy & Rick
18 Crescent Road, Epsom, Auckland
Tel (09) 630 0900   0800 118 448   Fax (09) 630 0900
Mob 025 834 779   kathy@epsombb.com
www.epsombb.com

Double $200 Single $160 (Special Breakfast)
Dinner $40 Credit cards accepted
2 King 1 Twin (2 bdrm)
2 Ensuite

Nestled on the slopes of One Tree Hill in a tree-lined street, Epsom House is within 4 minutes flat walk of the local Greenlane and National Women's Hospitals, Expo and Conference Centre, Showgrounds and Collectors Markets. Luxurious suites, superior bed and bedding and quality furnishings, ensuite bathrooms with spa bath. Relax in the private sunny courtyard garden or private comfortable guest lounge. All suites have fast internet and e-mail facilities. Tariff includes complimentary continental or gourmet breakfasts, airport transfers, coffee, special teas and juices. We offer you warm hospitality and personal service. Dog Linny welcomes you.

81

Epsom - Auckland
B&B Self-contained 5km SE of Auckland CBD

Laurel Cottage
Pene & Steve Ryan
83 Ranfurly Road, Epsom, Auckland
Tel (09) 630 4384 Fax (09) 630 4384
Mob 025 986 909 enquiry@laurelcottage.co.nz
www.laurelcottage.co.nz
Double $160-$190 Single $130-$150 (Full Breakfast)
1 Queen (1 bdrm) 1 Ensuite

Welcome to our delightful, newly renovated early 1900's cottage situated in a lovely and very central suburb. Laurel Cottage has luxurious furnishings and bed linen, fully equipped kitchen, TV, stereo, phone/modem, sunny courtyard and much more for a relaxing and comfortable stay. We are 20 minutes from the airport and 5 minutes by car to Auckland City and harbour, an ideal base for all tourist attractions. Easy strolling distance to cafes, NZ Expo Centre, Greenlane/National Women's Hospitals and beautiful Cornwall Park. Shopping, entertainment, art galleries, and antiques are nearby.

One Tree Hill - Auckland
Homestay Self-contained 5km S of Newmarket

Ron & Doreen Curreen
39B Konini Road, One Tree Hill, Auckland 5
Tel (09) 579 9531 Fax (09) 579 9531
www.bnb.co.nz/curreen.html
Double $65-$75 Single $50 (Continental Breakfast)
Child $12 Dinner $25 by arrangement
1 King 1 Queen 1 Double (3 bdrm)
1 Private 1 Guests share

A warm friendly welcome awaits you at 39B. Situated 15 minutes from the airport and city centre our large contemporary home in a secluded garden setting on private right of way offers pleasant views and peaceful surroundings. We are close to Ellerslie Racecourse, One Tree Hill Domain, Alexandra Park, Epsom Showgrounds and Ericsson Stadium, Restaurants, Antique shops, Supermarket, and bus service are a short distance away. Our spacious self-contained unit has a large bedroom with king sized bed. Private bathroom lounge with TV, kitchenette, microwave, washing machine and extras.Directions: Take Ellerslie-Penrose exit on Motorway 1, North or South to Great South Road North. Rockfield 2nd on left, first right into Konini.

Ellerslie - Auckland
Homestay 8km SE of Auckland Central

Taimihinga
Marjorie Love
16 Malabar Drive, Ellerslie, Auckland 1005
Tel (09) 579 7796 Fax (09) 579 7796
mlovebnb@ihug.co.nz
www.bnb.co.nz/taimihinga.html
Double $80 Single $50 (Full Breakfast)
Dinner by arrangement Credit cards accepted
1 Double 1 Twin 1 Single (3 bdrm)
1 Guests share

Taimihinga - softly calling o'er the ocean. Answer the call - enjoy the welcome at this comfortable home in quiet garden with pleasant northerly outlook. Ellerslie offers convenient access to Auckland's Business and Entertainment Centres, Scenic and Recreational Attractions. It is close to motorway (1km), transport, racing, parks, hospitals, shops, restaurants. Interests: people, family (now in faraway places), arts, music, travel, church (Anglican), Probus, gardening. Refreshment trolley, hairdrier and bathrobes in rooms. Laundry and fax facilities (small charge). Smoking outside only, please. Directions: Please phone, fax or write.

One Tree Hill - Auckland *Homestay 6km S of Downtown Auckland*

Clare's Greenlane Homestay
Clare Boyd
21 Atarangi Road, Greenlane East, Auckland 5
Tel (09) 523 3419   0800 254 419
Mob 025 281 3222
Stay@Paradise.net.nz
www.bnb.co.nz/clares.html

Double $80 Single $50 (Full Breakfast)
2 Queen 1 Twin 5 Single (4 bdrm)
1 Ensuite 2 Guests share

For tourists and business people alike, our comfortable non-smoking home has modern facilities with a huge 400-acre treed park at the end of our short street. We are close to Great South Road, with restaurants, the NZ Expo and the Ellerslie Conference centres nearby. Off-street parking, frequent buses. Phone, TV, Internet connection and desk in rooms. Laundry, fax and computer available.

Directions: exit route 1 at Green Lane East, head west, then left at the lights, then second right.

Remuera - Auckland   *B&B Homestay   7km N of Auckland Central*

Woodlands
Judi & Roger   Harwood
18 Waiatarua Road, Remuera, Auckland 1005
Tel (09) 524 6990   Fax (09) 524 6993
Mob 025 602 5592   Woodlands@ake.quik.co.nz
www.bnb.co.nz/.html
Double $130-$145 Single $100 (Special Breakfast)
Child not suitable Dinner $45 pp Credit cards accepted
1 King 1 Double 1 Single (2 bdrm)
1 Ensuite 1 Private

Guest book comments "Absolutely purr-fect". "A superb stay". "Very comfortable with stunning food". "A lovely oasis of calm with wonderful breakfasts". "Peaceful retreat with excellent breakfasts". Our breakfasts ARE special using seasonal fruit and produce. Join us for a Cordon Bleu candlelit evening dinner - booking essential. "Woodlands" is very quiet, surrounded by native trees and palms and central to many places of interest. The two guest bedrooms have tea/coffee facilities, heated towel rails, and coloured TV's. Safe off street carparking. Arrive a guest - leave a friend.

Remuera - Auckland   *B&B Self-contained*

Lillington Villa
Carol and Peter Dossor
24 Lillington Road, Remuera, Auckland
Tel (09) 523 2035   Fax (09) 523 2036
Mob 025 927 063   caropet@xtra.co.nz
www.bnb.co.nz/lillingtonvilla.html
Double $120 Single $100 (Full Breakfast) Child $20
Dinner $40 full week $550 - $600 Credit cards accepted
Children welcome
1 Queen 3 Single (2 bdrm)   1 Ensuite

Home away from home. Two large, sunny, welcoming flats in well-restored villa ten minutes from central Auckland. Own entrances and courtyards. Lock-up garages. Security and fire alarm systems. Gas heating. Telephone and Sky TV. Full modern open-plan kitchens and well-equipped bathrooms. Dishwasher, microwave, fridge/freezer, stove, washing machine, dryer. Quality fittings and equipment. One-bedroom flat has queen and single beds and double bed-settee in living area. Two-bedroom family flat has queen and three single beds.

Remuera - Auckland   *B&B Homestay 1.5km E of Newmarket*

Green Oasis
James & Joy Foote
25a Portland Rd, Remuera, Auckland 5
Tel (09) 520 1921   Fax (09) 522 9004
Mob 021 175 8291   footes1@xtra.co.nz
www.babs.co.nz/greenoasis
Double $100-$120 Single $75 (Full Breakfast)
Child $65 Children welcome
1 Queen 1 Single (2 bdrm)
1 Private 1 Guests share 1 Host share

Green Oasis offers a secluded and tranquil location in a much-loved garden of native trees and ferns - 10 mins to city centre. We are close to the Museum, antique and specialty shops, restaurants and cafes of Remuera, Newmarket and Parnell. Ours is an informal home of natural timbers and sunny decks where you will find us relaxed and welcoming, sensitive to your needs, be it to withdraw and rest, or to engage with us. Your accommodation, entered from a private garden, is self-contained with fully equipped kitchen, tea and coffee-making facilities, washing machine and TV. A special breakfast of seasonal and homemade taste sensations!

Orakei - Okahu Bay   *B&B Homestay 5km E of Auckland Central*

Nautical Nook/Free Sailing
Trish & Keith Janes & Irish Setter
23b Watene Crescent, Orakei, Auckland

Tel (09) 521 2544   0800 360 544
nauticalnook@bigfoot.com
www.nauticalnook.com

Double $110-$120 Single $80-$85 (Full Breakfast)
Credit cards accepted Children welcome
2 Queen 1 Single (2 bdrm)   1 Ensuite 1 Private

Friendly, relaxed beachside hospitality overlooking park/
harbour, 4.8km from downtown. 100 metres from Okahu
Bay, fringed by Pohutukawa trees. Gourmet breakfast. Stroll along picturesque promenade to Kelly
Tarlton's Underwater World, Mission Bay Beach and cafes, Te PA Cultural Visitors Centre. Bus at door
to downtown, ferry terminal, museums. Unwind for 2-3 day stopover. Complimentary sailing on the
sparkling harbour on our 34' yacht. We have a wealth of local knowledge and international travel
experience and can assist with sightseeing, travel planning, rental-car. Take taxi or shuttle from airport.

Mission Bay - Auckland   *Homestay 6km E of Auckland Central*

Jean & Bryan Cockell
41 Nihill Cresent, Mission Bay, Auckland

Tel (09) 528 3809   www.bnb.co.nz/cockell.html

Double $95 Single $70 (Full Breakfast) Dinner $25
Credit cards accepted
1 Double (1 bdrm)
1 Private

We warmly welcome you to our modern split level home.
The upper level is for your exclusive use including a
private lounge. 5 minutes walk to Mission Bay beach,
cafes and restaurants and 10 minutes scenic car or bus
ride to down town Auckland and ferry terminal for harbour and islands in the Gulf. We are retired and
look forward to sharing our special part of Auckland with you. Please phone for directions or airport
shuttle bus to our door. Please no smoking.

St Heliers - Auckland   *B&B Separate/Suite 800m N of St Heliers Bay /City 12mins*

The Totara
Peter & Jeanne Maxwell
1/17 Glover Road, St Heliers Bay, Auckland

Tel (09) 575 3514   Fax (09) 575 3514
Mob 027 284 0172   maxwell.totara@clear.net.nz
www.bnb.co.nz/thetotara.html

Double $120-$140 Single $90 (Continental Breakfast)
(Full Breakfast) Child n/a Credit cards accepted
1 Queen 1 Twin (2 bdrm)
1 Private

The B&B with Comfort, Convenience and Hospitality. On holiday or business, relax in our home
overlooking Glover Park. Enjoy our great breakfasts. 5-10 minute walk from safe beach, cafes, shopping
and banks yet only 12 minute harbourside drive to the central city. Visit Kelly Tarlton's Underwater
World, Sky City Casino or cruise the Waitemata Harbour. Tea & coffee available in separate guest
lounge. Sunny bedrooms with tv. Bathrobes and hairdryer provided. Handy transport or carpark available.
Peter and Jeanne with Sophie the cat welcome you.

St Heliers - Auckland   *B&B 10km E of Auckland*

Jill & Ron McPherson
102 Maskell Street, St Heliers, Auckland
Tel (09) 575 9738   Fax (09) 575 0051
Mob 0274 752 034   ron&jill_mcpherson@xtra.co.nz
www.bnb.co.nz/mcpherson.html

Double $110 Single $75 (Continental Breakfast)
1 Queen 1 Twin (2 bdrm)
1 Private

Welcome to our modern home with off street parking in
a smoke free environment.   One group of guests is
accommodated at a time. Having travelled extensively
ourselves we are fully aware of tourists' needs. Eight minutes walk to St Heliers Bay beach, shops,
restaurants, cafes, banks and post office. Picturesque 12 minutes drive along the Auckland waterfront
past Kelly Tarlton's Antarctic and Underwater Encounter to Downtown Auckland. Interests including
all sports, gardening and Jill is a keen cross-stitch embroiderer. Not suitable for children/pets.

St Heliers - Auckland   *B&B Homestay 10km E of Auckland Central*

Pippi's Bed and Breakfast
Pippi & Philip Wells
15 Tuhimata Street, St Heliers, Auckland
Tel (09) 575 6057   Fax (09) 575 6055
Mob 021 989 643   pswells@xtra.co.nz
http://go.to/pippis

Double $120-$170 Single $100-$140 (Full Breakfast)
Credit cards accepted
1 Queen 1 Double (3 bdrm)
1 Ensuite 1 Private

Our character home with pretty cottage garden offers guests a sunny retreat only a short walk to lovely
beach, village and restaurants. Spacious bedroom with easy access, ensuite bathroom, electric blankets,
feather duvets, Sky TV, tea/coffee etc. Delicious breakfast of fruit, home-made bread/muesli, and/or
full breakfast, espresso coffee/tea. Telephone, fax, email, hairdryer, laundry, off street parking available.
With Bess (golden retriever), Bertie (toy poodle) and Rags (cat) we look forward to offering you a
warm welcome to our smoke-free home.

St Heliers   *B&B 10km E of Auckland City*

Burnt Fig
Dianne & Alister Benvie
2/1 Walmsley Road, St. Heliers, Auckland
Tel (09) 575 4150   Mob 025 281 6893
benvie@xtra.co.nz
www.burntfig.co.nz

Double $130-$165 Single $110-$130 (Full Breakfast)
1 Queen 1 Double 1 Twin 2 Single (3 bdrm)
1 Ensuite 1 Private

Welcome to Burnt Fig, a modern architect-designed house
located in beautiful St. Heliers Bay. Only minutes walk
to local beaches and great cafes. A stunning waterfront drive takes you to downtown Auckland and the
Viaduct Basin.   Among the facilities available are tea and coffee in a separate guest lounge, off-street
parking and use of laundry. Tia, the Belgian Shepherd is very popular with our guests. We both play
golf at Titirangi, one of New Zealand's finest Championship courses where tee times can be arranged.

Glendowie   *B&B Homestay 12km E of Auckland Central*

The Munro's
Margaret and Don Munro
12 Emerson Street, Glendowie, Auckland 1005
Tel (09) 528 0459 Fax (09) 528 0459
dmlmunro@xtra.co.nz
www.bnb.co.nz/munro.html

Double $120 Single $90 (Full Breakfast)
1 King/Twin (1 bdrm)
1 Ensuite

Our spacious guestroom has a king or twin comfortable
bed(s), ensuite, private entry and patio area. There are
tea/coffee facilities. Off street parking. Located only two
kilometres from St. Heliers Bay with a 10 kilometre scenic waterfront drive to central Auckland. The
airport is a 45 minute drive, or a taxi/shuttle bus will bring you to our door. Dinner is available by prior
arrangement. We are a retired Scottish couple who have lived in the tropics, enjoy travel and conversation.
No smoking please.

Titirangi - Auckland   *B&B Separate/Suite 20min W of Auckland City*

Kaurigrove
Gaby & Peter Wunderlich
120 Konini Road, Titirangi, Auckland 7
Tel (09) 817 5608 Fax (09) 817 5608
Mob 025 275 0574
www.bnb.co.nz/kaurigrove.html

Double $90-$95 Single $55 (Special Breakfast)
Credit cards accepted
1 Queen 1 Single (2 bdrm)   1 Guests share

Welcome to our home! Kaurigrove offers a tranquil
location amidst Kauri trees in a park-like setting yet close
to shops, cafes and restaurants. Situated at Titirangi we
are near Auckland's historic West Coast with its magnificent beaches and vast native bush with a wonder
world of walking tracks. Gaby and Peter, your hosts of German background, are keen trampers themselves
and are happy to introduce you to the highlights of Auckland and its surrounding areas. PS: We have
a shy cat called Coco. Non smoking inside residence.

Titirangi - Auckland   *B&B 15km W of Auckland City*

The Ferns
Kate Mora
81 Park Rd, Titirangi, Auckland
Tel (09) 817 1956 Fax (09) 817 3072
Mob 025 979 262 theferns@xtra.co.nz
www.theferns.co.nz

Double $145-$165 Single $120-$140
(Continental Breakfast)
1 Queen 1 Double (2 bdrm)
1 Private 1 Host share

Located in the lush Waitkere Ranges, 30 minutes from
central Auckland and the Airport, "The Ferns" is a stylish yet homely B&B nestled in a peaceful subtropical garden. Stroll to cafes and galleries with nature walks close by. In summer, enjoy the private
outdoor patio and in winter, a cozy log fire in the spacious guest lounge. Visit vinyards, artists studios,
or the golf club, A short drive takes you to the Manukau Harbour or dramatic West Coast beaches.
Small friendly pooch in residence.

Avondale - Auckland   *Homestay Self-contained 10km W of Auckland Central*

Kodesh Community
Kodesh Trust
31B Cradock Street, Avondale, Auckland
Tel (09) 828 5672   Fax (09) 828 5684
Kodesh_Trust@free.net.nz
www.bnb.co.nz/kodeshcommunity.html

Double $55 Single $35 (Continental Breakfast)
Child $20 Dinner $8 Flat $60 - $80
2 Queen 1 Double 4 Single (5 bdrm)
2 Private 1 Host share

Kodesh is an ecumenical, cross cultural Christian community of around 25 residents, about 8 minutes by car from downtown Auckland. Guest rooms are in a large modern home. Two self contained flats sleep four each. An evening meal is available in the community dining room Monday - Friday. Bookings essential. The atmosphere is relaxed and guests can amalgamate into the life of the community as much or little as desired. No smoking, no pets, children under 12 welcome in self contained unit.

Mangere Bridge - Auckland Airport   *Homestay 14km S of Auckland Central*

Mangere Bridge Homestay
Carol & Brian
1 Boyd Ave, Mangere Bridge, Auckland
Tel (09) 636 6346   Fax (09) 636 6345
www.bnb.co.nz/mangerebridgehomestay.html

Double $80 Single $55 (Full Breakfast) Child $20,
12 & under Dinner $25 by prior arrangement
2 King/Twin 1 Double (3 bdrm)
3 Ensuite 1 Guests share

We invite you to share our home, which is within ten minutes of Auckland Airport, an ideal location for your arrival or departure of New Zealand. We enjoy meeting people and look forward to making your stay an enjoyable one. We welcome you to join us for dinner by prior arrangement. Courtesy car to or from airport, bus and rail. Off street parking available. Handy to public transport. Short stroll to the waterfront. Please no smoking indoors. Our cat requests no pets. Inspection welcome.

Mangere   *B&B 4km Airport*

Airport Bed and Breakfast
Laurel Blakey
1 Westney Road, Cnr Kirkbride Road, Mangere
Tel (09) 275 0533   Fax (09) 275 0968
Mob 027 270 5810   airportbnb@xtra.co.nz
airportbnb.co.nz

Double $69-$89 Single $59-$79 (Continental Breakfast)

Extra person $17
1 King/Twin 2 Queen 7 Double (10 bdrm)
2 Ensuite

Just five minutes drive from Auckland Airport a friendly Kiwi welcome and great value accommodation await. Ten quality rooms, two ensuites, central heating, large TV/dining room, Internet access. Two Minutes walk to city bus stop - see Auckland by bus, train and ferry on the $12 day pass. Restaurants/ takeaways nearby. Car, cycle and luggage storage. Rental cars and NZ wise sightseeing tours booked. Courtesy airport transfers (not 24 hour), free phone at airport, dial 28. Continental breakfast included, light meals available and special diets catered for by arrangement.

Mangere - Auckland Airport   *B&B Homestay 2km Mangere*

Airport Homestay/B&B
May Pepperell
288 Kirkbride Road, Mangere, Auckland
Tel (09) 275 6777   Fax (09) 275 6728
Mob 025 289 8200
www.bnb.co.nz/airporthomestay.html
Double $65 Single $40 (Continental Breakfast)
Child $20
3 Single (2 bdrm)   1 Guests share

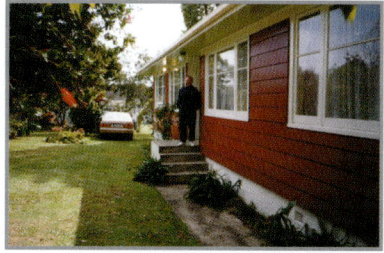

Clean comfortable home five minutes from airport but not on flight path. Easy walk to shops and restaurants. Ten minutes from shopping centres and Rainbows End amusement park. Aviation golf course near airport, winery and Lakeside Convention Centre nearby. My interests are golf, travel, Ladies' Probus and voluntary work. Beds have woollen underlays and electric blankets. There is a sunny terrace and fenced swimming pool. Courtesy car to/from airport at reasonable hour. Vehicles minded while you're away from $1 day. Bus stop very close.

Mangere Bridge - Auckland Airport   *B&B 7.5km N of Auckland Airport*

Mountain View B&B
Ian & Jenny (and cat Oscar) Davis
85A Wallace Road, Mangere Bridge, Auckland
Tel (09) 636 6535   Fax (09) 636 6126
mtviewbb@xtra.co.nz
www.bnb.co.nz/mountainviewbb.html
Double $95-$140 Single $75-$95 (Full Breakfast)
Child $20 Dinner by arrangement Credit cards accepted
Children welcome
2 King/Twin 1 King 4 Queen 3 Twin 1 Single (6 bdrm)
4 Ensuite 1 Guests share

Spacious villa with quality decor in quiet locality 8 mins. from Auckland Airport. Exit on George Bolt Drive, left into Kirkbride Road, follow through to Wallace Road. We're 1.2km on right from roundabout. Friendly, hospitable NZ hosts are aircraft builders/enthusiasts. Enjoy superb harbour views whilst eating delicious breakfasts. Convenient off-street parking, public transport at gate. Downtown Auckland/major attractions 10-25 minutes drive, typed navigational assistance to north, south or city.

Otahuhu - Auckland   *B&B 17km S of Auckland*

Jerrine & Gerard Fecteau
70 Mangere Road, Otahuhu, Auckland
Tel (09) 276 9335   Fax (09) 276 9235
oasisbb@xtra.co.nz
www.bnb.co.nz/fecteau.html
Double $70 Single $50 (Full Breakfast) Child neg
Dinner $20 Credit cards accepted Children welcome

Pets welcome
1 Queen 1 Double 1 Twin (3 bdrm)
2 Guests share

We welcome you to the Oasis in Otahuhu with the best Canuck-Kiwi hospitality. We are 15 minutes from the airport and 5 minutes from the train and motorway. We are collectors of many things: coins of the world, brass, Canadian Indian art. Cactus garden. We can help you plan your holiday and get a rental car. In addition to breakfast you can join us for dinner by arrangement or dine at one of the 35 restaurants in Otahuhu. Please phone, fax or email and our courtesy van will pick you up.

Pakuranga - Auckland   *B&B 200m E of Westfield Shopping Town*

Roydon Glen
Judy & Bill Dalziel
2A William Roberts Rd, Pakuranga 1706,
Tel (09) 576 1233   Mob 021 036 2338
roydonglen@paradise.net.nz
www.bnb.co.nz/roydonglen.html

Double **$95**   Single $50 (Full Breakfast) Dinner $20 pp
1 Queen 1 Single (2 bdrm)
1 Private 1 Host share

If you are wanting home comforts, a warm and friendly
atmosphere awaits you when you visit us. We are very
handy to restaurants, Westfield Shopping Town, and St Kentigern College, with bus stops to the city and Howick just minutes away, shuttle bus 30 minutes from airport. Off-street parking. The double room is large with ranchsliders opening to a patio and our lovely garden has its own toilet and separate bathroom. The single room has shared toilet and bathroom facilities. We look forward to meeting you.

Manukau - Auckland   *Homestay 6.5km NE of Manukau City*

Tanglewood
Roseanne & Ian Devereux
5 Inchinnam Road, Flat Bush, Auckland
Tel (09) 274 8280   Fax (09) 634 6896
tanglewood@clear.net.nz
www.bnb.co.nz/tanglewoodmanukau.html

Double **$95**   Single $60 (Full Breakfast) Child $10
Credit cards accepted Children welcome
1 Queen 1 Double 2 Single (3 bdrm)
1 Ensuite 1 Guests share

Our homely country cottage, set in two acres is close to the international airport. The garden loft is separate from the house with ensuite, TV, fridge, deck overlooking large peaceful gardens and ponds. Accommodation inside the house has its own bathroom. We are 30 minutes from downtown Auckland, close to bush walks, Regional Botanic gardens and restaurants. Delicious home cooked breakfast includes eggs from our free range hens. We have a swimming pool and a friendly dog 'Daisy'. We are non-smoking. Booking is essential.

Manurewa - Auckland   *Homestay 2km S of Manukau City*

Hillpark Homestay
Katrine & Graham Paton
16 Collie Street, Manurewa, Auckland 1702
Tel (09) 267 6847   Fax (09) 267 8718
Mob 021 215 7974   hillpark.homestay@xtra.co.nz
www.bnb.co.nz/hillparkhomestay.html

Double **$80**   Single $50 (Full Breakfast) Child $20
Dinner $15 by arrangement Credit cards accepted
Children welcome
1 Double 4 Single (3 bdrm)   1 Ensuite 1 Guests share

Welcome to our sunny, spacious home and meet our friendly Tonkinese cat. We are 15 minutes from Auckland Airport, 20 minutes from Auckland City Centre, by motorway, gateway to the route south and Pacific Coast Highway. Nearby are Manukau City Shopping Centre, Rainbow's End Adventure Park, restaurants, cinemas, souvenir shops, Community Arts Centre, Regional Botanic Gardens (Ellerslie Flowershow), and bush walks. Our interests include Red Cross, teaching, classical music, painting, gardening, photography, Christian interests, reading and travel. We're a smoke-free home. Directions: Please phone.

Bucklands Beach - Auckland   *B&B 2km N of Howick*

Bucklands Beach Bed and Breakfast
Jo and David Woolford
45B The Parade, Bucklands Beach, Auckland
Tel (09) 535 6092   Fax (09) 535 6092
Mob 027 287 5015
woolford@bucklandsbeachbedandbreakfast.co.nz
www.bucklandsbeachbedandbreakfast.co.nz
Double $150 Single $120 (Continental Full Breakfast)
1 Queen (1 bdrm)
1 Private

A warm welcome awaits you as our sole guests at our modern beachfront home. A queen size bedroom, separate private bathroom and own lounge with TV, stereo and library are provided for your comfort. Complimentary tea and coffee are available as are an iron, ironing board and hair dryer. Metres to restaurants and convenience store. Close to golf courses, bowling green and boat ramp. 30 mins from airport and 30 mins to downtown Auckland. A 15yr old Tibetan Spaniel owns us.

Bucklands Beach - Auckland   *B&B Self-contained 4KM NW of Howick*

B&B By the Beach
Barbara and Ted Meyer
6 Hostel Access Road, Eastern Beach, Auckland
Tel (09) 534 9436   Mob (021) 666 300
meyer@actrix.co.nz
www.bnb.co.nz/bbbythebeach.html
Double $90-$110 Single $70 (Continental Breakfast)
1 Double (1 bdrm)   1 Private

Welcome to our beach paradise on the beautiful Bucklands Beach Peninsula. Eastern Beach is only 50 metres away at the end of our street where you can swim, sail or sunbathe. There are many lovely coastal and cliff top walks on the peninsula. Howick Golf Course is a five minutes drive away. There are also many excellent restaurants in the area - two within five minutes walk along the beachfront. Take a 30 minute ferry ride to Auckland city or Waiheke or take the bus (bus stop is two doors away). A continental breakfast is provided and you have full cooking facilities. Off-street parking is adjacent to your own level entrance that opens into a TV room. We are a semi-retired couple with many interests including travel, art, theatre and sport. Directions: please telephone first.

Howick - Auckland   *B&B Homestay 1/2 k E of Howick*

Mellons Bay Lodge
June & Owen Williams
64 Mellons Bay Road, Howick, Auckland
Tel 09 535 0535   Fax 09 535 2713   Mob 025 504 352
ojw@takeiteasy.co.nz   www.takeiteasy.co.nz
Double $115-$125 Single $99 (Continental Breakfast)
(Full Breakfast) Child $20-$40 Credit cards accepted
Children welcome
1 Queen 1 Double 1 Single (3 bdrm)
1 Private 1 Guests share 1 Host share

We offer warm relaxed hospitality in a charming setting with excellent facilities - your own sunny lounge, private bathroom, bathrobes, hairdryer, great breakfasts with homemade foods. Offstreet parking, laundry and office facilities. Only 30 min from CBD by local ferry or motorway (offpeak) and 25 min from airport. Short stroll to beach, lookout, and Howick village with many restaurants, cafes, pubs, interesting shops. 10 min drive to 5 safe beaches, historic village, golf courses. We look forward to sharing our home with you. Qualmark accredited Three Star Plus.

Howick - Auckland   *B&B Homestay 3km S of Howick*

Cockle Bay Homestay
Jill & Richard Paxman
81 Pah Road, Cockle Bay, Howick, Auckland
Tel (09) 535 0120   0800 159 837   Fax (09) 535 0120
Mob 027 2422646   cocklebay@bnbnz.co.nz
www.bnbnz.co.nz
Double $140-$150 Single $120-$130 (Full Breakfast)
Credit cards accepted
1 King/Twin 1 Queen (2 bdrm)
1 Ensuite 1 Private

Welcome to our home above Cockle Bay Beach with
breathtaking seaviews in a quiet location. Walk beach/restaurant. Ferries run daily to Downtown a
relaxing way to view the harbour, no parking hassels. Guest rooms are comfortable, well appointed and
spacious. View our website for immediate confirmation booking. Enjoy the warm Kiwi hospitality, plus
all those little extras your hosts offer. We want to make your stay as happy and memorable as possible.
Shuttle can be arranged/Airport 25 mins. We have a small friendly dog.

Beachlands   *B&B Homestay 25km E of Howick*

Enid & Terry Cripps
51 Wakelin Road, Beachlands 1705
Tel (09) 536 5546   etcripps@xtra.co.nz
www.bnb.co.nz/cripps.html
Double $90 Single $60 (Full Breakfast)
Dinner $30 by arrangement Credit cards accepted
1 Queen (1 bdrm)
1 Private

Enid and Terry offer you a warm welcome to the Marine
Garden suburb of Beachlands which is situated on the
East Coast, 40 km South East of Auckland City. Our
converted cottage is only 3 minutes walk from the beach at Sunkist Bay, local shops and licensed
restaurant. The Formosa Auckland Golf Course and Pine Harbour marina are 5 minutes drive away.
We are both in our 60's, have travelled widely. Guest accommodation is a large upstairs bedroom with
sitting area, TV and a shaded balcony facing the sea. Shuttle bus from the Airport or phone for directions.

Whitford   *Farmstay 25km SE of Auckland*

Springhill Country Homestay
Judy & Derek Stubbs
Polo Lane, Whitford, RD, Manurewa, Auckland
Tel (09) 530 8674   Fax (09) 530 8274
Mob 021 251 2518   djstubbs@ihug.co.nz
www.bnb.co.nz/springhillfarmstay.html
Double $95 Single $70 (Full Breakfast) Child $35
Dinner $30pp by arrangement Children welcome
1 Queen 2 Single (2 bdrm)
1 Ensuite 1 Host share

Springhill is an 8 hectare farm in Whitford, an attractive rural area approximately 25km SE of Auckland.
We are close to a beautiful golf course, beaches and Auckland Airport. We farm Angora goats and free
range hens, and pets include a cat and a dog. Guest accommodation is one detached double room with
ensuite, and 1 room with twin single beds. TV, tea & coffee making facilities,and a private spa pool are
available. Directions: Left off Whitford Park Road. 1km past Golf Course.

Whitford   *Homestay 12km Howick*

Albertine
Averill & Bart Allsopp - Smith
298 Clifton Road, Whitford, RD 1, Howick, Auckland

Tel (09) 530 9441   Fax (09) 530 9441
Mob 021 974 119   albertinestay@xtra.co.nz
www.bnb.co.nz/albertine.html

Double $90 Single $65 (Full Breakfast)
Credit cards accepted
1 Double (1 bdrm)
1 Ensuite 1 Private

Enjoy a game of tennis on our peaceful rural five acre
block. Wake up in your separate self-contained loft to the sound of the birds. We are 30 minutes from Auckland City and within 15 minutes. of cinemas, shopping, restaurants, cafes and craft shops. Nearby is a Marina where sailing/boating and fishing are available by arrangement. We are close to beaches, golf courses and polo ground, or you may prefer a quiet country walk. Unsuitable for children or animals.

Whitford   *B&B Self-contained Semi-detatched Cottage 35km SE of Auckland*

Cedar Lodge
Barbara and Bela Demeter
603 Whitford Maraetai Road, Whitford, Auckland

Tel +64 9 536 5380   0800 1 LODGE or 0800 1 56343
Mob 025 888 004   cedar.lodge@clear.net.nz
www.bnb.co.nz/cedarlodge2.html

Double $150 Single $100
(Continental Full Special Breakfast)
Children welcome
1 Queen 2 Single (1 bdrm)   1 Private

Cedar Lodge is a much admired home set amongst farmland with extensive views of Auckland city, beaches, fields and Whitford Forest. Your suite comprises a bedroom and dressing room, separate lounge with tea and coffee facilities, large conservatory and your own bathroom, one level with main rooms opening onto our expansive lawn. 5 mins to good shopping, 15 mins to Botany Downs Mall, and several restaurants set in country or waterfront locations within 5 mins drive. Can accommodate up to four. Close to ferry to Auckland. Weddings welcome.

Alfriston - Auckland   *B&B 2km Manukau City*

Thistlefern
Evelyn & Patrick Scanlon
36 Cairnsvale Rise, Alfriston/Manurewa, Manukau City

Tel (09) 267 6787   Fax (09) 267 6781
Mob 027 602 6677   pateve@clear.net.nz
www.bnb.co.nz/thistlefern.html

Double $80-$100 Single $60-$80
(Continental Full Breakfast) Child Neg Dinner $20
Children welcome
1 Queen 2 Double 1 Single (3 bdrm)

Pat, Robyn the cat and I are looking forward to meeting you. we are just off Pacific Coast highway, walking distance to the Botanic Gardens/Ellerslie Flowershow. Twenty minutes from Auckland Airport, five minutes from the South/North motorway. Twenty minutes to city centre, Sky City and Viaduct. Minutes from Manukau and Botany Down Shopping Centre, Rainbow's End, Bus, trains. We are from Scotland, NZ citizens. RN & qualified Aromatherapist on site. Evening meal by arrangement. Courtesy car, airport. New residential area. Quiet and comfortable, an ideal stopover.

Kaiaua   *B&B Lodge 85km SE of Auckland*

Kaiaua Seaside Lodge
Fran Joseph & Denis Martinovich
1336 Pacific Coast Highway, Kaiaua
Tel (09) 232 2696   Fax (09) 232 2699
Mob 025 274 0534   kaiaua_lodge@xtra.co.nz
www.bnb.co.nz/kaiauaseasidelodge.html
Double $95-$110 Single $75 (Full Breakfast)
(Special Breakfast)
2 Queen 1 Double 2 Single (5 bdrm)
2 Ensuite 1 Guests share

Situated on the water's edge, 4km north of Kaiaua township, the Lodge has panoramic views of the Coromandel across the Firth of Thames. It is ideally positioned for leisurely seashore strolls or more active tramps in the Hunua Ranges. Boating and fishing facilities are available and breakfast includes flounder or snapper, in season. Ensuite rooms are spacious and the separate guest lounge has a refrigerator and television. The Seabird Coast is renowned for its birdlife, thermal hot pools, nearby Regional Parks and "fish 'n chips".

Papakura   *B&B Homestay Country stay 5km E of Papakura*

Hunua Gorge Country House
Ben, Amy & Joy Calway
482 Hunua Road, Papakura, South Auckland
Tel (09) 299 9922   Fax (09) 299 9922
Mob 021 669 922   hunua-lodge@xtra.co.nz
www.friars.co.nz/hosts/hunua.html
Double $90-$135 Single $90 (Full Breakfast)
Child depending on age Dinner $25 - $35
Credit cards accepted Children welcome
1 King 1 Queen 1 Double 2 Twin 5 Single (5 bdrm)
1 Ensuite 1 Private 1 Host share

Welcome to our wilderness on the doorstep of Auckland City. A great place to start or end your NZ holiday. Great food, magic sunsets, wild scenery, leafy greenery, starry skies, and views from all rooms. Large comfortable newly decorated home, verandahs, lawns, garden, bush and rural setting on 50 acres with cattle and birdlife. Stay a few days and discover the wonders of Auckland. Fresh food, fresh air, comfortable beds guaranteed. Please phone. Dinner from $25 or $35, 3 courses by prior arrangement.

Papakura   *Homestay 1.5km W of Papakura*

Campbell Clan House
Colin & Anna Mieke Campbell
57 Rushgreen Ave, Papakura
Tel (09) 298 8231   Fax (09) 298 7792
Mob 0274 967 754   colam@pl.net
www.campbellclan.co.nz
Double $100-$110 Single $55-$65 (Full Breakfast)
Child Neg Dinner $25/$35 by arrangement
Credit cards accepted Children welcome
2 Queen 2 Single (3 bdrm)   2 Ensuite 1 Private

Our peaceful location is close enough to Auckland to visit downtown attractions (25mins) as well as being close to the motorway system (2mins) for speedy access north, south or to the airport. Our separate upstairs guest accomodation includes 3 double bedrooms, large comfortable lounge with tea/ coffee facilities, TV, tourist information and private balcony with estuary views. We can assist you with holiday arrangements, hire vehicles & airport transfers and offer fax, internet & laundry facilities. We offer a discounted rate for 3+ nights bookings.

Hunua - Paparimu *Homestay Self-contained 20mins S of Papakura*

Erathcree Countrystay
Rob & Gillian Wakelin
10 Wilson Road, Paparimu, RD 3, Papakura, Auckland
Tel (09) 292 5062   Fax (09) 292 5062
Mob 021 128 1547   gillrob@xtra.co.nz
www.bnb.co.nz/erathcree.html

Double $110 Single $80 (Full Breakfast)
Child Under 12yrs reduced rate
Dinner $35pp by arrangement
Bed settee in lounge Additional person: $30pp
Credit cards accepted Children welcome
1 Queen 1 Double (2 bdrm)   1 Private

Self-contained cottage in 23 acres of lovely unspoiled countryside against the Hunua Ranges. A lost world amongst tall trees, spacious country gardens, streams full of eels and no city lights: yet Auckland Airport and city is only 40 minutes away. SH2 for travel South or Coromandel Peninsula is 10 minutes away. The atmosphere is relaxed, the cats and dog friendly, the cottage charming - a garden stroll from the house. Well traveled hosts guarantee a helpful warm welcome to their home.

Drury *B&B 5km S of Drury*

Tuhimata Park
Susan & Pat Baker
697B Runciman Road, Runciman, RD 2, Drury
Tel (09) 294 8748   Fax (09) 294 8749
tuhimata@iprolink.co.nz
www.bnb.co.nz/tuhimatapark.html

Double $90-$120 Single $60-$80 (Full Breakfast)
Child neg Dinner $35 - $40 Credit cards accepted
Children welcome
2 Queen 2 Single (3 bdrm)
2 Ensuite 1 Guests share

Our spacious, comfortable, and relaxing home is an ideal place to start or finish a NZ holiday. Only 20 minutes from Auckland Airport and 30 minutes from the city centre. Set in expansive lawns and giant oak trees, with wide verandahs, overlooking rolling green farmland, indoor garden and BBQ in a large conservatory, tennis court, swimming pool, spa pool, and games room. 2 or 3 course dinners, including pre dinner drinks and nibbles, wine, and liqueurs with coffee. Laundry facilities. Pets - a family cat.

Ramarama *B&B Homestay 1km N of Bombay*

Thistledown Lodge
Sue & Archie McPherson
1810 Great South Road, Ramarama, Drury RD 3
Tel (09) 236 0044   Fax (09) 237 0415
Mob 025 736 313   inquires@thistledownlodge.co.nz
www.bnb.co.nz/thistledownlodge.html

Double $100 Single $60 (Full Breakfast)
(Special Breakfast) Child Neg Dinner B/A
3 Queen 3 Single (3 bdrm)
1 Ensuite 2 Private 1 Host share

Warm country hospitality in a peaceful country setting, it's the perfect start or end to your holiday. The English colonial style home has king size second floor bedrooms with TV and tea/coffee making facilities. Guest activities include swimming and spa pools, infrared sauna, lawn croquet, petanque and horseshoes or a walk through private bush beside the Ngakoroa Stream. Find out why guests remember Archie's breakfast and keep returning for more! Easy to find from Ramarama or Bombay motorway exits. Secure off-street parking.

Drury   *3km E of Drury*

The Drury Homestead
Carolyn & Ron Booker
349 Drury Hills Road, Drury, South Auckland
Tel (09) 294 9030   Fax (09) 294 9035
Mob 021 158 5061   druryhome@paradise.net.nz
www.bnb.co.nz/user90.html

Double $90   Single $60   Child negotiable
Dinner $30
Credit cards accepted
2 Queen (2 bdrm)
2 Ensuite

The Homestead is an early colonial home (1879) with an interesting history. Lovingly restored by Ron and Carolyn this character filled family home nestles on 15 acres with mature native bush and a tumbling stream creating a wonderful peaceful haven, only 30 mins from the centre of Auckland. Close to restaurants or let us cook for you using the best of fresh local produce. Guest lounge and TV, laundry facilities. Family cat and dog. Please phone for directions. 20 mins to airport.

Drury   *Homestay 3km S of Papakura*

Southawk
Lynn Lockhart & Rod Campbell
249 Sutton Road, PO Box 203, Drury, Auckland
Tel (09) 298 0670   Fax (09) 298 0673
Mob 021 354 024   southawk@xtra.co.nz
www.bnb.co.nz/southawk.html

Double $110   Single $70   (Full Breakfast)   Child neg
Dinner $25   Credit cards accepted
2 Queen 1 Single (3 bdrm)   2 Private 1 Host share

Southawk is a secluded country home set in 10 acres with beautiful gardens, swimming pool an petanque. Only 25 mins from Auckland City; 20 mins from Auckland International Airport; 3 kilometres from the Southern Motorway. Close to all Auckland's most famous attractions. Join us for an evening meal or NZ style BBQ. Large modern guest bedrooms, own bathrooms and lounge with TV/music and tea/coffee facilities. Relax around the open fire in the winter and the pool in the summer. A warm welcome awaits you. We will be pleased to assist and advise on further travel arrangemants. Internet, fax & laundry facilities available.

Waiuku   *Homestay 5km E of Waiuku*

Totara Downs
Janet & Christopher de Tracy-Gould
Baldhill Road, RD 1, Waiuku, South Auckland
Tel (09) 235 8505   Fax (09) 235 8504
Mob 021 154 8713   totaradw@ihug.co.nz
www.totaradowns.co.nz

Double $120   Single $80   (Full Breakfast)
Credit cards accepted
1 King/Twin 1 Queen (2 bdrm)
1 Ensuite 1 Private

Just 50 minutes drive from Auckland's International
Airport and city, "Totara Downs" is found on a quiet country road. Set in large country house gardens with breath taking rural views. We offer feather and downs pillows and duvets, sitting room with open fire, swimming pool, lawn croquet. Historic Waiuku boasts wonderful peninsula beaches and country garden tours. With Flora our westie and two cats we look forward to meeting you. Not suitable for children under 12. Smoke free home.

Bombay - Auckland
B&B Self-contained Countrystay 50km S of Auckland

Pinnacle Farm Countrystay
Robin & Alton Ross
438 Pinnacle Hill Road, RD Bombay 1850, Auckland
Tel 09 236 0956 Fax 09 236 0957 Mob 021 250 5651
nzgolfing@clear.net.nz
www.bnb.co.nz/pinnaclefarm.html

Double $140 Single $90 (Continental Breakfast)
Child $30 Children welcome
2 King/Twin 1 Queen (2 bdrm)
1 Private

Self catering, two bedroom guesthouse on 10 acres, 6kms
from Southern Motorway and 4kms from SH2 to Coromandel and Bay of Plenty, 15 minutes from Pukekohe
Racetrack. Exclusive use, with private entrance, own balcony with views, sitting room, TV, kitchenette
and electric blankets on each bed. Continental breakfast tray delivered, other meals available in Bombay
(6kms), Pukekohe (12kms) or self-catering. Heated salt-water swimming pool and tennis court available.
A quiet place for your first or last nights in New Zealand as we are 40 minutes south of Auckland Airport.

Mercer
B&B Farmstay Homestay 24km SE of Pukekohe

Dorothy & Alan McIntyre
233 Koheroa Road, Mercer
Tel (09) 232 6837 Fax (09) 232 6837
www.bnb.co.nz/mcintyre.html

Double $85 Single $50
(Full Breakfast)
Child Neg
Dinner $20
1 Queen 1 Double (2 bdrm)
1 Private

We live on a cattle farm with a modern brick home. We have a large swimming pool surrounded by one
acre of interesting garden. We are 3km off the main Auckland-Hamilton highway. Our views are
panoramic. Very happy to provide dinner - alternative restaurants available. 30-40 minutes from Auckland
Airport. Directions: Travel SH1 to Mercer. At Mercer do not enter Mobil Service Centre. Travelling
from north turn left across railway line. Travelling from south turn right across railway line 3km up
Koheroa Rd - meet Kellyville Rd - House visible on left.

Please let us know
how you enjoyed your B&B experience.
Ask your host for a comment form,
or leave a comment on www.bnb.co.nz

Waikato

2

Mangatarata

1

Te Kauwhata

Glen Murray

Huntly

27

Hamilton

Raglan

23

Tamahere

Cambridge

1

Ohaupo

Te Awamutu

31

3

Otorohanga

Waitomo

Towns listed generally follow
a north to south route. Refer
to the index if required.

0   Kilometres   20

0   Miles   12

Te Kuiti

Piopio

30

3

Mangatarata   *Farmstay 13km W of Ngatea*

Clark's Country Touch
Betty & Murray Clark
209 Highway 27, Mangatarata, RD 6, Thames
Tel (07) 867 3070   Fax (07) 867 3070   Mob 021 808
992 bmclark@xtra.co.nz
www.bnb.co.nz/clarkscountrytouch.html

Double $70 Single $45 (Continental Breakfast)
Child Discount Dinner $20 Credit cards accepted
Children welcome
1 King/Twin (1 bdrm)   1 Host share

Welcome to our beef farm with views of rolling pasture, bush and Coromandel ranges. Our sunny guestroom with TV, tea, coffee, cookies is opposite the bathroom. We are handy to the Hauraki Golf Course, Bowling Club, Seabird Coast, Miranda Hot Pools, Ngatea Gemstone Factory and Thames Coromandel coast. Our friendly dog Becky lives outside and our cat Watson shares our home. We are aged 50ish and enjoy handcrafts, gardening, four wheel driving and vintage machinery. Warm country hospitality awaits you. Non-smoking indoors.

Te Kauwhata   *Farmstay Self-contained 7km E of Te Kauwhata*

Herons Ridge
David Sharland
1131 Lake Waikare Scenic Drive, RD 1, Te Kauwhata
Tel (07) 826 4646   Fax (07) 826 4646
herons.ridge@xtra.co.nz
www.huntly.net.nz/heron.htm

Double $80-$100 Single $50-$70 (Full Breakfast)
Child Discount Dinner By arrangement
S/C studio $120 Children welcome Pets welcome
1 King 2 Queen 1 Double 1 Single (4 bdrm)
2 Ensuite 1 Private

Welcome to your home in the Waikato. Our quality inhouse family suite and superb Garden Studio overlooking the pool and garden are the perfect setting for your stay. The Horse Stud, set amongst ponds and pinewoods, enhance our rural location close to Lake Waikare. Meals are served inhouse. Horse riding, country walks, golf and hot springs - the choice is yours. From SH1 go through Te Kauwhata village, 6kms East along Waerenga Road, 1km on right - Welcome.

Te Kauwhata   *B&B Farmstay Self-contained 7.5km E of Te Kauwhata*

Puriri Grove
Linda & John Morris
784 Waerenga Road, Te Kauwhata, RD 1
Tel (07) 826 7714   Fax (07) 826 7714
Mob 021 157 9138   john.mcgee@paradise.net.nz
www.bnb.co.nz/puririgrove.html

Double $110 Single $75 (Special Breakfast)
Dinner $30 Studio S/C $120
1 Queen 1 Double 1 Twin (3 bdrm)
1 Private

Built on a hilltop overlooking Lake Waikare and set on thirty acres, Puriri Grove is a five bed roomed, architect designed property with a self contained studio. It has outstanding views to the Coromandel in the east and Karioi on the west coast. The house has a spa, croquet lawn, petanque court and table tennis. We cater for vegetarians and provide evening meals. There are ten acres of native bush with trails on the property and nearby several golf courses, we can also arrange horse treks.

Glen Murray - Te Kauwhata   *Farmstay Self-contained 22km W of Te Kauwhata*

Awaroa Vineyard Cottage
Jan and Brian White
121 Insoll Rd, Glen Murray,
Tel (09) 233 3289   Fax (09) 233 3290
Mob 021 77 33 27   jan_white@xtra.co.nz
www.bnb.co.nz/awaroa.html
Double $110-$125 (Full Breakfast)
1 Queen (1 bdrm)
1 Private

Awaroa Cottage offers attractive self contained accommodation set in tranquil surroundings with panoramic rural views. Guests can relax in the lounge, around the barbecue in the private garden setting or stroll around the boutique vineyard on the property. Free range chickens supply farm fresh eggs for breakfast. We share the historic homestead with our two cats. Centrally located less than one hour from Auckland and Hamilton and within easy reach of Te Kauwhata wineries, three excellent golf courses, 'the hole adventure' and horseriding trails.

Huntly   *B&B Farmstay Self-contained 4km NW of Huntly*

Parnassus Farm & Garden
Sharon & David Payne
Te Ohaki Road, RD 1, Huntly
Tel (07) 828 8781   Fax (07) 828 8781
Mob 021 458 525   parnassus@xtra.co.nz
www.parnassus.co.nz
Double $110 Single $60 (Full Breakfast)
Child According to age Dinner by arrangement
Credit cards accepted Children welcome
2 King/Twin 2 Double 2 Single (3 bdrm)
3 Private 1 Guests share

Parnassus offers you all the calm and beauty of the New Zealand countryside yet is only minutes off SH1. We are a working farm combining dairying, forestry, sheep and beef and have an extensive (1.6ha) garden incorporating rose beds, woodland area, orchard, berryfruit courtyard and kitchen gardens. Children enjoy our range of birds and small animals. We're easy to find, from SH1 cross Waikato River just south of Huntly township, right into Harris St 2km, right into Te Ohaki Road, 1.9 kms on LHS.

Raglan   *Farmstay Self-contained 20km S of Raglan*

Matawha
Jenny & Peter Thomson
61 Matawha Road, RD 2, Raglan
Tel (07) 825 6709   Fax (07) 825 6715
Mob 025 162 6405   jennyt@wave.co.nz
www.bnb.co.nz/matawha.html
Double $60-$80 Single $30-$40 (Full Breakfast)
Dinner $20
1 King 1 Double 4 Single (3 bdrm)
1 Private 1 Host share

We are fortunate to have our own private beach and farm right on the Westcoast - panoramic views - providing surfing, fishing, hang gliding, bush and mountain walks and scenic drives. We take pride in farming this land for over 100 years. A large garden provides vegetables and flowers. Two cats are our resident pets. Separate studio and spa. Directions: 1/2 hour Raglan/1 hour Hamilton/2 1/2 hours Auckland. Take Hamilton/Raglan Road route 23. Turn left at Kauroa/Bridal Veil Falls. Turn right at Te Mata into Ruapuke Road. Turn left into Tutu Rimu Road and follow it to the junction and our entrance No. 61 on the cattlestop with our name on the letterbox.

Hamilton   *Homestay 3km N of Hamilton*

Kantara
Mrs Esther Kelly
7 Delamare Road, Bryant Park, Hamilton
Tel (07) 849 2070   Mob 025 263 9442
esther@enlighten.co.nz
www.bnb.co.nz/kelly.html

Double $90-$110 Single $55 (Full Breakfast)
Dinner $25 Credit cards accepted
1 Double 1 Twin (2 bdrm)
1 Ensuite 1 Private

I have travelled extensively throughout New Zealand and overseas and welcome tourists to my comfortable home. I live close to the Waikato River with its tranquil river walks and St Andrews Golf Course. My interests are travel, golf, tramping, Mah Jong and gardening. A member of NZ Association Farm & Home Hosts and Probus. I look forward to offering you friendly hospitality. Directions: From Auckland - leave main Highway north of Hamilton at 2nd round intersection into Bryant Road. Turn left into Sandwich Road and 2nd street on right.

Hamilton   *B&B Homestay 1.5km E of Hamilton Central*

Matthews B&B
Maureen & Graeme Matthews
24 Pearson Avenue, Claudelands, Hamilton
Tel (07) 855 4269   Fax (07) 855 4269
Mob 0274 747 758   mgm@xtra.co.nz
www.matthewsbnb.co.nz

Double $75-$85 Single $50-$55 (Full Breakfast)
Child 1/2 price Dinner $20 Credit cards accepted
1 Double 1 Twin (2 bdrm)
1 Guests share 1 Host share

Welcome to our home two seconds off the city bypass on Routes 7 and 9 at Five Crossroads. We are adjacent to the Waikato Events Centre, Ruakura Research Station and handy to the university and only three minutes from central city. Our home is a 'lived-in' comfortable home, warm in winter and cool in summer, with a pool available. We enjoy spending time with visitors from NZ and overseas . We have travelled extensively and enjoy helping to plan your holiday. Dinner by arrangement.

Hamilton   *B&B Homestay*

Ebbett Homestay
Glenys & John Ebbett
162 Beerescourt Rd, Hamilton
Tel (07) 849 2005   johnebbett@xtra.co.nz
www.bnb.co.nz/ebbett.html

Double $90 Single $60 (Full Breakfast) Dinner $25
2 Single (1 bdrm)
1 Private

Only minutes from town centre, our 12 year old home has a spectacular view of the Waikato River (New Zealand's longest) and access to Hamilton's popular river walk. We enjoy sharing travel anecdotes, but also respect our guests' wish for privacy. Your room has its own tea/coffee facility and private bathroom. Eighty-five minutes from Auckland International Airport appeals to tourists arriving or departing New Zealand. Our interests include people, music, sport, travel, gardening and community. We have had 10 years of happy hosting. We don't have children or pets.

Hamilton *Homestay Hamilton Central*

Judy & Brian Dixon
50A Queenwood Avenue, Chartwell, Hamilton
Tel (07) 855 7324 ju.dixon@xtra.co.nz
www.opotiki2.co.nz/waiotahi
Double $65 Single $45 (Continental Breakfast)
2 Single (1 bdrm)
1 Private

Haere mai - Welcome to our comfortable smoke free, homely Lockwood nestled within a quiet garden. Guests have sole access to their bathroom and bedroom. Our aim is to provide a warm environment where guests relax and enjoy themselves. Within walking distance are popular "Cafe en Q", "The Platter Place". Chartwell Square and Waikato River walks. We also have a beach home with magnificent sea views near Opotiki if requested. We share our home with a friendly cat named Zapper. Directions: please phone.

Hamilton - Ohaupo *B&B Homestay 4km SW of Hamilton*

Green Gables of Rukuhia
Earl & Judi McWhirter
35 Rukuhia Road, RD 2, Ohaupo
Tel (07) 843 8511 Fax (07) 843 8514
Mob 021 583 462 judi.earl@clear.net.nz
www.bnb.co.nz/greengablesofrukuhia.html
Double $80-$90 Single $40-$50
(Continental Breakfast) Dinner by arrangement
Credit cards accepted
2 Double 3 Single (3 bdrm) 1 Guests share

Warm, comfortable smokefree family home in a quiet rural setting, close to Hamilton, Airport and Fielddays (Mystery Creek). Free pick-up/delivery airport, bus, train terminal all part of the friendly service. 5km to Vilagrad Winery; 2 minutes walk to Gostiona Restaurant. Two storeyd house with guest rooms, lounge downstairs; dining, hosts upstairs. Fresh home baked bread and selection of coffees to suit. Judi lectures statistics, University of Waikato. Earl is a "retired" school teacher. One teenage daughter still lives at home. Non-smokers preferred.

Hamilton *Homestay Home & Garden 4km S of Hamilton*

The Poplars
Lesley & Peter Ramsay
402 Matangi Road, RD 4, Hamilton
Tel (07) 829 5551 Mob 025 668 0985
ramsay@waikato.ac.nz
www.bnb.co.nz/thepoplars.html
Double $95 Single $70 (Full Breakfast)
Dinner $30pp by arrangement Credit cards accepted
1 King 2 Single (2 bdrm)
1 Private

Just minutes from Hamilton, Mystery Creek and Cambridge, The Poplars offers a haven of peace and quiet. Set in a majestic three acre garden with internationally acclaimed daffodils, 800 roses and many water features. Each guest room has tea and coffee making facilities, electric blankets and TV. Solar heated swimming pool and spa are adjacent to guest rooms. Hosts Peter and Lesley, themselves seasoned travellers, offer you the charms of country living. A warm welcome shared with family pets awaits you. A unique and special place to stay. Directions: Please phone.

Lake Rotokauri - Hamilton *Self-cont Country Gardenstay 4km NW of Hamilton*

Cathy & David Dewes
Exelby Rd, Hamilton
Tel (07) 849 9020   Fax (07) 849 9020
Mob 027 418 0367   dcdewes@clear.net.nz
www.bnb.co.nz/dewes.html

Double $130 Single $100 (Special Breakfast)
Credit cards accepted
1 Queen (1 bdrm)
1 Ensuite

Our home is nestled in 3 acres of garden, offering privacy and relaxation. Enjoy magnificent views of Lake Rotokauri and Mt. Pirongia from our upstairs guest rooms where there is a kitchen, lounge and dining area. Our special self-serve breakfast is full of homemade treats. Soak in the hydrotherapy spa or relax having a professional therapeutic massage (available by appointment). We, with our children are keen outdoors people and can direct you to local attractions ... the Hamilton zoo with its famous 'free flight' sanctuary is just 2 minutes away. Please phone for reservations and directions.

Hamilton *B&B Homestay 28km S of Hamilton*

Country Quarters Homestay
Ngaere & Jack Waite
No 11 Corcoran Road, Te Pahu, Hamilton
Tel (07) 825 9727   graeme.waite@xtra.co.nz
www.bnb.co.nz/countryquartershomestay.html

Double $80 Single $40 (Full Breakfast) Child $10
Dinner $20 Caravan $15 Children welcome
Pets welcome
1 Queen 1 Twin 3 Single (5 bdrm)
1 Guests share

We welcome you to the peace and tranquillity of country life. Our place is central from Te Awamutu and Hamilton and are located in the little farming community of Te Pahu, right under Mount Pirongia. We are in the middle of a block of Chestnut trees and are quite secluded. We have our small dog and two fat cats. Our home is very large and roomy and we have special facilities for the elderly person. Comfort and nice meals is what we offer you.

Hamilton - Tamahere *B&B 10km S of Hamilton*

Lenvor B&B
Lenora & Trevor Shelley
540E Oaklea Lane, RD 3, Tamahere, Hamilton
Tel (07) 856 2027   Fax (07) 856 4173
lenvor@clear.net.nz
www.bnb.co.nz/lenvorbb.html

Double $100 Single $50 (Full Breakfast) Child $25
Dinner by arrangement Children welcome
2 Queen 1 Twin 1 Single (4 bdrm)
1 Ensuite 1 Guests share 1 Host share

Lenora and Trevor warmly invite you to relax and to share the comfort of our home "Lenvor", which is set in a rural area, down a country lane. Our two storeyed home has guest rooms, small lounge upstairs; dining, lounge, hosts, downstairs. 10 minutes to Hamilton or Cambridge; 5 minutes to Mystery Creek or airport. Lenora's interests are floral art and cake icing. Trevor enjoys vintage cars. Centrally situated for day trips to Coromandel, Tauranga, Rotorua, Taupo and Waitomo Caves.

Hamilton *Self-contained Country Cottage 10km E of Hamilton*

A&A Country Stay
Ann & Alan Marsh
275 Vaile Road, RD 4, Hamilton
Tel (07) 824 1908 or (07) 8241909 Fax (07) 824 1908
Mob 025 763 014   aacountrystay@xtra.co.nz
www.bnb.co.nz/aacountrystay.html
Double $90 Single $60 (Full Breakfast)
Child neg Dinner $20pp Credit cards accepted
Children welcome
1 Queen 2 Single (2 bdrm)
1 Private

Enter down our driveway treelined with London Planes to our country cottage where you will recieve a warm welcome. The Cottage is spacious, two bedrooms, self-contained including laundry and sky digital. Enjoy our peaceful surroundings set in two acres of garden short distance from our home. Sit, relax in privacy out on the deck and have our doves visit you while overlooking our 47 acres with sheep and cattle. We have two Jack Russells who will welcome you also. Long stayers are welcome.

Hamilton *Homestay*

Pukeko Landing
Penny & Gordon Irvine
1885 River Road, RD1, Hamilton
Tel (07) 854 5311 Mob 0274 190 054
pukeko.landing@xtra.co.nz
www.bnb.co.nz/pukekolanding.html
Double $90 Single $60 (Continental Breakfast)
Dinner $20 pp
1 Queen 1 Twin (2 bdrm)
1 Private

Relax and unwind in our new home set on over 1 acre,
amongst native trees and wildlife on the banks of the mighty Waikato River. Tranquil rural views across the river to the Equestrian Centre and the mountains beyond. Located just minutes north of central Hamilton, enjoy river walks and golf. Near SH1, 85 minutes from Auckland airport, also handy to main tourist attractions and beaches. We are seasoned travellers and together with our children Michael and Samantha a warm welcome awaits you.

Ohaupo *B&B 15km S of Hamilton*

Ridge House
Margaret Birtles & Mathew Harris
15 Main Road, Ohaupo,
Tel (07) 823 6555 Fax (07) 823 6550
Mob 021 156 9582   m.a.birtles@xtra.co.nz
www.bnb.co.nz/ridgehousenz.html
Double $80 Single $65 (Continental Breakfast)
Child $15 Dinner $20 B/A Children welcome
Pets welcome
1 Queen 2 Double 1 Twin 1 Single (4 bdrm)

We welcome you to come and visit our home with its wonderful lake and pastoral views. Our home is shared with our dog, Zoe - who loves to welcome visitors. We are just six minutes to Hamilton International Airport and can arrange pick up from there and car storage ($10). This is an ideal base for trips to Hamilton, Te Awamutu, Waitomo Caves, Cambridge, Rotorua and Tauranga. Mystery Creek (home of Field Days) is also close by. Accessibility for people with disabilities is being developed. Travel well.

Cambridge   *B&B Separate/Suite Cambridge Central*

Park House
Pat & Bill Hargreaves
70 Queen Street, Cambridge

Tel (07) 827 6368   Fax (07) 827 4094
Park.House@xtra.co.nz   www.parkhouse.co.nz

Double $130-$160 Single $120 (Full Breakfast)
Credit cards accepted
1 King/Twin 1 Queen (2 bdrm)   1 Ensuite 1 Private

Park House, circa 1920, is for guests of discernment who appreciate quality and comfort. For 15 years we have offered this superb setting for guests. Throughout this large home are antiques, traditional furniture, patchworks and stained glass windows creating an elegant and restful ambience. The guest lounge features an elaborately carved fireplace, fine art, library, TV and complimentary sherry. Bedrooms in separate wing upstairs ensues privacy. Unbeatable quiet location overlooking village green, two minute walk to restaurants, antique and craft shops. Member of Heritage Inns.

Cambridge   *B&B Farmstay Separate/Suite 5km SW of Cambridge*

Birches
Sheri Mitchell & Hugh Jellie
263 Maungatautari Road, PO Box 194, Cambridge

Tel (07) 827 6556   Fax (07) 827 3552
Mob 021 882 216   birches@ihug.co.nz
birches.cambridge.net.nz

Double $95 Single $60 (Special Breakfast)
Child by arrangement Dinner by arrangement
Credit cards accepted Children welcome
1 Queen 1 Double 1 Single (2 bdrm)
1 Ensuite 1 Private

Our 1930's character farmhouse offers open fires in guests' sitting room, tennis and swimming pool set in country garden amongst picturesque horse studs. Proximity to Cambridge and Lake Karapiro makes Birches an ideal base for lake users. Hugh, a veterinarian, and I are widely travelled. Olivia, 11, is happy to show her farm pets and cat. Little Cherry Tree cottage (queen/ensuite) is ideal for couples wanting privacy. The twin room in farmhouse has private bathroom with spabath. We serve delicious farmhouse breakfasts alfresco or in dining room.

Cambridge   *B&B Homestay Self-contained Cambridge Central*

White's Homestay
Diane & Paul White
7 Marlowe Drive, Cambridge,

Tel (07) 823 2142   Fax (07) 823 2143
Mob 025 963 224   paulanddi@paradise.net.nz
www.bnb.co.nz/whiteshomestay.html

Double $85 Single $55 (Full Breakfast) Child N/A
Dinner B/A Self contained cott $85
Credit cards accepted
2 Queen 1 Twin (2 bdrm)   2 Ensuite

A warm welcome awaits at our home by the Waikato River. Spacious guestrooms have TV, tea and coffee facilities and ensuite bathrooms. Five star breakfast. Easily located with tranquil gardens, a pleasant stroll to town centre. Cross bridge at the south end of Victoria Street (main street), turn right after bridge, Marlowe Drive is the first on the right. White's Cottage. Delightful, self contained, private. Two bedrooms, separate lounge, fully equipped kitchen with breakfast provisions supplied. Sleeps five. Longer term negotiable.

Cambridge *B&B Homestay 2km S of Cambridge*

Glenelg
Shirley & Ken Geary
6 Curnow Place, Cambridge,
Tel (07) 823 0084   Fax (07) 823 4279
glenelgbnb@ihug.co.nz
www.bnb.co.nz/glenelg.html

Double $100 Single $65 (Full Breakfast)
Child $20 Dinner $20 by arrangement
Credit cards accepted Children welcome Pets welcome
3 Queen 1 Twin (4 bdrm)   3 Ensuite 1 Private

Glenleg welcomes you to Cambridge to a new home with quality spacious accommodation - warm quiet and private overlooking Waikato farmland, with plenty of off street parking. Beds have electric blankets and woolrests. 200 rose bushes in the garden. Five minutes to Lake Karapiro. Mystery Creek, where NZ National Field Days and many other functions are held is only 15 minutes away. Laundry facilities available. No smoking indoors please. "Home away from Home." For a brochure and directions please phone. Evening dinner by arrangement. Pets and children are welcome.

Cambridge *B&B Countrystay 10km S of Cambridge*

Dunfarmin
Jackie & Bob Clarke
55 Gorton Road, RD 2, Cambridge
Tel (07) 827 7727   Fax (07) 823 3357
Mob 025 611 5247 dunfarmin@wave.co.nz
www.bnb.co.nz/dunfarmin.html

Double $90 Single $50 (Full Breakfast) Child $25
Dinner $25 by arrangement Credit cards accepted
1 Queen 1 Double 3 Single (3 bdrm)
1 Ensuite 1 Guests share

Welcome to our country home, situated just off State Highway One. Positioned on a commanding knoll, 20 acres sheltered by mature trees offering the weary traveller peace and tranquillity. The outlook from the spacious home provide panoramic views of the surrounding Waikato countryside. We have an inground swimming pool and floodlit tennis court. Five minutes to Lake Karapiro, twenty minutes to Mystery Creek. Within one hours drive to Tauranga, Rotorua , Waitomo Caves. Please feel at home with us, farm animals and Possum the cat.

Cambridge *B&B Self-contained 2km S of Cambridge*

Pamade B&B
Paul & Marion Derikx
229 Shakespeare Street, Leamington,
Opposite turn off to Karapiro Lake
Tel (07) 827 4916   Fax (07) 827 4988
Mob 021 261 7122 pamades@hotmail.com
www.bnb.co.nz/pamade.html

Double $75-$90 Single $50-$60 (Special Breakfast)
1 King 1 Queen 1 Twin 4 Single (3 bdrm)
2 Ensuite 1 Host share

Pamade is a character home, very comfortable with beautiful gardens. We are situated 2 minutes from central Cambridge with its wonderful selection of fascinating Art, Craft, Boutique and Antique Shops, Restaurants, Stud Farms and Golf Course. Just around the corner from Lake Karapiro (5 minutes drive), with its water-skiing, rowing and other aquatic sports. Mystery Creek (Fieldays) is only 10 minutes drive away. Self contained unit plus large double room (ensuite and coffee and tea arrangements) with private exit. Ideal for longer stays. Great breakfast guaranteed. Dinner by prior arrangement.

Cambridge   *B&B Homestay Self-contained 3km NE of Cambridge*

Gainsborough House
Julie and Michael Thorpe
1-103 Maungakawa Road, Fencourrt, Cambridge

Tel (07) 823 2473   Fax (07) 823 1678
GainsboroughHouse@xtra.co.nz
www.gainsboroughhouse.co.nz

Double $120-$150 Single $90 (Full Breakfast)
Dinner by arrangement Self-contained cottage $95
Credit cards accepted Children welcome Pets welcome
1 King 2 Double 2 Twin (5 bdrm)   3 Ensuite

Country House Living with Style: elegant, superior accommodation in a peaceful rural setting near Cambridge, in stunning gardens and furnished with quality artwork and antiques. We also offer a self-contained COTTAGE which can sleep 6. Stroll through our gardens and neighbouring farmland, or relax with a book in our library. With Thomas Gainsborough the cat we offer a haven for jet-lagged travelers: we are only 90 min from Auckland Airport, and are within easy reach of many major tourist attractions.

Cambridge   *B&B Homestay 2km S of Cambridge*

Chatfield
Kay and Kerry Miller
4 Curnow Place, Cambridge,

Tel (07) 823 1035   chatfieldbnb@ihug.co.nz
www.bnb.co.nz/chatfield.html

Double $90 Single $60 (Full Breakfast) Child $25
Dinner by arrangement Children welcome
1 Queen 2 Single (2 bdrm)
1 Private

Chatfield is situated in beautifully landscaped gardens five minutes from Cambridge. We offer a private area of our warm, comfortable home for families and people travelling together. Enjoy the privacy of your own lounge with TV and woodfire, or join us for coffee. Centrally located to Mystery Creek, Karapiro, Hamilton city restaurants and airport, and Cambridge and Tirau antiques, crafts and cafes. We have lived in Australia and Asia for 20 years, and offer friendly hospitality.

Te Awamutu   *Farmstay Guesthouse 4.5km N of Te Awamutu*

Mrs R Bleskie & C Bleskie
Storey Road, Te Awamutu

Tel (07) 871 3301   sophy@ihug.co.nz
www.bnb.co.nz/bleskie.html

Double $115 Single $60 (Full Breakfast) Child $25
Dinner $25 Children welcome Pets welcome
1 Double 8 Single (5 bdrm)
1 Ensuite 1 Guests share 1 Host share

The 85 acre farm, situated in beautiful country side with cattle, horses, pigs, poultry, sheep, goats and pets. A spacious home welcomes you with swimming pool and tennis court. Large guest rooms with doors to garden. Specials: Horseback riding and gig rides for children and adults for $10 a ride. Raspberry picking in season and access to the milking of 500 dairy cows.

Te Awamutu   *B&B Farmstay 2km S of Te Awamutu*

Leger Farm
Beverley & Peter Bryant
114 St Leger Rd, Te Awamutu

Tel (07) 871 6676   Fax (07) 871 6679
www.bnb.co.nz/legerfarm.html

Double $125-$140 Single $85-$100 (Full Breakfast)
Dinner $30
1 Queen 1 Double 1 Twin 3 Single (4 bdrm)
1 Ensuite 1 Private 1 Guests share

'Leger Farm' is a private residence with country living at
its finest. The discerning leisure traveller seeking quality
accommodation, in peaceful, relaxing surroundings, will find warm hospitality and every comfort here.
Spacious bedrooms share stunning panoramic views of surrounding countryside. Each bedroom has its
own balcony with beautiful garden vistas. We farm cattle and sheep, and are centrally based for visiting
Waitomo Caves and black water rafting, Rotorua with its thermal activity and NZ's dramatic West
Coast and ironstone sands. Golf course nearby for relaxation. Smoke free home.

Te Awamutu   *B&B Homestay 4km S of Te Awamutu*

Morton Homestay
Marg and Dick Morton
10 Brill Road, RD 5, Te Awamutu

Tel (07) 871 8814   Fax (07) 871 8865
www.bnb.co.nz/mortonhomestay.html

Double $75 Single $45 (Full Breakfast)
Dinner $20 by arrangement
Rates negotiable for more than 3 people
Credit cards accepted
1 Double 4 Single (3 bdrm)   1 Private

We welcome visitors to enjoy our hospitality and the peacefulness of our home 5 minutes from the
centre of New Zealand's "Rosetown". Waitomo, Rotorua and Lake Taupo are within easy driving
distance from us. Hamilton airport and Mystery creek are 20 minutes away. Te Awamutu is an excellent
base for bushwalking, golfing, fishing and garden visits. Gardening, philately and woodturning are
among our interests. We also have an interest in Classic cars. Direction. Please phone or fax for
reservations and directions.

Te Awamutu   *Homestay 2.5km N of Te Awamutu Post Office*

Tregamere
Bev & Chris Johnson
2025 Ohaupo Road, Te Awamutu 2400,

Tel (07) 870 1950   Fax (07) 870 1952
Mob 025 291 3162 c.b.john@xtra.co.nz
www.bnb.co.nz/tregamere.html

Double $100 Single $80 (Full Breakfast)
Child $30 Dinner $35 Campervans $30
1 Queen 3 Single (2 bdrm)
1 Ensuite 1 Guests share

A warm welcome awaits you at Tregamere, where you'll share our large, well-appointed home, and
slumber in comfort. Enjoy fabulous sunsets over Mt Pirongia, savour our lush garden, explore the
impressive Kahikatea stand, or amuse yourself in the games room. Set in tranquil surroundings on Te
Awamutu's northern boundary, our central location is great for exploring - west coast beaches, the
renowned Waitomo Caves, Hamilton and Rotorua are all within an easy drive.

Otorohanga - Waitomo District   *B&B Farmstay Self-contained*

Meadowland   *8km NW of Otorohanga*
Jill & Tony Webber
746 State Highway 31, RD 3, Otorohanga
Tel (07) 873 7729 0800 687 262 Fax (07) 873 7719
meadowland@xtra.co.nz
www.bnb.co.nz/meadowland.html

Double $75 Single $50 (Full Breakfast) Child $20
Credit cards accepted Children welcome
2 Queen 1 Double 1 Twin 2 Single (5 bdrm)
1 Private 1 Guests share

Welcome to Meadowland, on State Highway 31, on the right hand side at the top of the second hill. Our accommodation is: a self-contained unit which can sleep up to six. One twin and two double bedrooms in homestead with guest shared bathroom and separate toilet. All beds have woolrests and electric blankets. We have a tennis court, swimming pool and spa pool on site. We are five minutes from the Otorohanga Kiwi House and Aviary, twenty minutes from Waitomo Caves area. We have three outside cats. Non smokers preferred.

Waitomo Village - Waitomo District   *B&B*

Dalziel Waitomo Caves Guest Lodge
Andree & Peter Dalziel
PO Box 16, Waitomo Caves
Tel (07) 878 7641   Fax (07) 878 7466
www.bnb.co.nz/dalzielwaitomocaves.html

Double $70 Single $50 (Continental Breakfast)
Credit cards accepted
3 Queen 1 Double 2 Single (5 bdrm)
5 Ensuite

Our home is only 100 metres from the Museum of Caves information office in the centre of the village and a few hundred metres from the Glow Worm Caves. Our detached rooms with their individual ensuite facilities are of the highest standard. With a variety of cave adventure trips, excellent bush walks and a top golf course we recommend at least two days to spend with us. We will arrange your meals. You will find a place with warm and friendly hospitality.

Waitomo Caves   *B&B Self-contained 9.7km W of Waitomo Village*

Te Tiro
Rachel & Angus Stubbs
970 Caves Te Anga Road, Waitomo Village,
Tel (07) 878 6328   Fax (07) 878 6328
Mob 027 226 7681   stubbs.a_r@xtra.co.nz
www.waitomocavesnz.com

Double $80-$95 Single $60 (Continental Breakfast)
Child $15 Children welcome Pets welcome
2 Queen 5 Single (2 bdrm)
2 Private

Te Tiro (The View) 'welcomes you'. Enjoy fantastic panoramic views of the central North Island and mountains. At night enjoy glowworms nestled in lush NZ bush only metres from your cottage. Situated on an established sheep farm with 350 acres of reserve bush. Our new self-contained pioneer style cottages can accommodate up to five people in a cosy open plan room. Hosts Rachel and Angus have thirty years of tourism experience between them and would be happy to advise you on the wonders of Waitomo.

Te Kuiti - Waitomo District   *B&B Homestay 1km S of Te Kuiti*

Te Kuiti B&B
Pauline Blackmore
5 Grey St, Te Kuiti

Tel (07) 878 6686   pauline.blackmore@xtra.co.nz
www.bnb.co.nz/tekuitibb.html

Double $70-$80 Single $50 (Full Breakfast)
Credit cards accepted
2 Queen 2 Single (3 bdrm)
2 Ensuite 1 Private

We live only 50 metres off Highway 3. Expect a warm
welcome, peace and relaxation in our 1920's bungalow.
The bedrooms have tea and coffee-making facilities, quality beds and bedding and heaters. Breakfast
can be timed to suit you and includes cereals, fruit, juice and toast followed by cooked English breakfast
and brewed coffee or tea. Feel free to use the TV in one of the lounges. We can help you with advice
about local attractions including great places to walk or tramp.

Te Kuiti - Waitomo District   *Farmstay   20km NW of Te Kuiti*

Tapanui Country Home
Sue & Mark Perry
1714 Oparure Rd, Te Kuiti

Tel (07) 877 8549   Fax (07) 877 8541
Mob 025 949 873   info@tapanui.co.nz
www.tapanui.co.nz

Double $165-$180 Single $155-$170 (Full Breakfast)
Dinner By Arrangement Credit cards accepted
3 King/Twin (3 bdrm)   1 Ensuite 1 Private

Magnificent country retreat near the famous Waitomo
Caves. Enjoy elegance, peace and uninterrupted views of hill country pasture. Relax and recharge with
comfortable king/twin size beds, luxurious cotton bathrobes, hair dryers, spacious ensuite and private
bathrooms. Experience New Zealand farming hospitality and delicious cooked meals while recharging
from Waitomo adventures and activities. Meet the family of hand-reared sheep, pig and donkey on our
1900 acre sheep and cattle farm. Guests welcome after 4pm. Unsuitable for children.

Te Kuiti - Waitomo District   *B&B Farmstay Homestay 6km E of Te Kuiti*

Panorama Farm
Raema & Michael Warriner
65 Carter Road, RD 2, Te Kuiti

Tel (07) 878 5104   Fax (07) 878 8104
panoramab.b@xtra.co.nz
www.bnb.co.nz/panoramafarm.html

Double $72 Single $36 (Full Breakfast) Child $18
Dinner $20 Credit cards accepted
1 Double 3 Single (2 bdrm)
1 Guests share

Raema, Michael and the cat welcome you to our hill top home, overlooking bush clad hills, fertile
valleys and distant peaks with golden dawns and spectacular sunsets. We offer comfortable beds and
the quiet surroundings of a 30 hectare farm plus 40 years experience of the district and its attractions.
Waitomo is 25 mins away, Rotorua, Taupo 2 hours so come and enjoy the company, the scenery and a
good night's rest. Arriving or departing from Auckland - we are 2 1/2 hours to the Airport.

Te Kuiti - Waitomo District *B&B Homestay 1km S of Te Kuiti PO*

Sanaig House
Sue & Mike Wagstaff
35 Awakino Rd, Te Kuiti,
Tel (07) 878 7128   Fax (07) 878 7128
sanaig@xtra.co.nz
www.bnb.co.nz/sanaighouse.html

Double $100 Single $70 (Continental Breakfast)
2 Queen 1 Double (3 bdrm)
1 Ensuite 1 Private

Welcome to Sanaig House, one of Te Kuiti's gracious homesteads, built in 1903. Our guest bedrooms are attractive, spacious and overlook a garden of lovely mature trees. The Waitomo area, famous for its glow-worm caves, has a variety of other exciting outdoor adventures - blackwater rafting, abseiling, quad bike riding and horse riding. Relaxing bush walks, fishing, bird watching and garden visits can all be arranged. Sanaig House is only 500m from a good restaurant and there is a selection of cafes and other restaurant sin Te Kuiti.

Te Kuiti - Waitomo District *B&B Farmstay 2km N of Te Kuiti*

Margaret & Graeme Churstain
129 Gadsby Road, RD 5, Te Kuiti
Tel (07) 878 8191   Fax (07) 878 5949
Mob 025 735 853   www.bnb.co.nz/churstain.html

Double $70 Single $40 (Continental Breakfast)
Dinner $15 pp B/A Children welcome
1 Queen 1 Double 1 Twin (3 bdrm)
1 Ensuite 1 Private

Welcome to the 'peace and tranquility' of our hilltop farmlet, signposted on SH3, northern end of Te Kuiti. Having welcomed travellers for many years, come and enjoy our wonderful rural views and kiwi hospitality. Being the sheep shearing capital of the world, Te Kuiti and surrounding areas offer many leisure activities, Waitomo Caves 10 mins away. Comfortable double rooms are available with private bathrooms. Within one hour (Hamilton) and two and a half hours (Auckland) International Airports this is the place to begin or end your New Zealand journey. ...simply the best...

Piopio - Waitomo District *B&B Homestay Country Homestay 24km SW of Te Kuiti*

Bracken Ridge
Susan & Rob Hallam
Aria Road, Piopio 2555,
Tel (07) 877 8384   www.bnb.co.nz/hallam.html

Double $85 Single $50 (Full Breakfast)
Dinner $20 by arrangement
1 Queen 1 Twin 1 Single (2 bdrm)
1 Private

Enjoy a peaceful, quiet relaxing time at our large, modern home set in landscaped gardens on a small sheep and cattle farmlet. Our elevated site provides panoramic views of green pastures, trees and limestone rocks. All rooms have a garden or rural outlook. Spacious heated bedrooms have comfortable beds and electric blankets. Our interests encompass gardening, music, sailing and meeting people from all over the world. Piopio 1km and Waitomo Caves just 35 minutes away. Please phone ahead for reservations and directions.

Pio Pio - Waitomo District   *B&B Farmstay Homestay 19km S of Te Kuiti*

Carmel Farm
Barbara & Leo Anselmi
Main Road, PO Box 93, Pio Pio

Tel (07) 877 8130   Fax (07) 877 8130
Carmelfarms@xtra.co.nz
www.bnb.co.nz/carmelfarm.html

Double $100 Single $50
(Continental Breakfast) Dinner $25pp
Children welcome   Pets welcome
2 King/Twin 4 Single (4 bdrm)
1 Ensuite 1 Host share

Barbara and Leo Anselmi own and operate a 1200 acre sheep, beef and dairy farm.

You will be welcomed into a 3000 square feet modern home set in picturesque gardens, in a lovely limestone valley. You will be treated to delicious home cooked meals and the warmth of our friendship.

Whether enjoying the excitement of mustering mobs of cattle and sheep, viewing the milking of 550 cows, driving around the rolling hills on the four-wheeled farm-bike, relaxing as you bask in the sun by the pool or wandering through the gardens, you will experience unforgettable memories of breathtaking scenery, a clean green environment.   We have farm pets who love the attention of our guests. The donkeys are waiting to be fed.

We look over a beautiful 18 hole golf course which welcomes visitors. The property is a short distance from Black Water Rafting and canoeing activities, The Lost World Cavern, and the famous Waitomo Caves. Nearby are bush walks and the home of the rare Kokako bird. We can help to arrange activities for people of all ages and interests including garden visits and horse riding. Please let us know your preference. We are 140 kms from Rotorua/Taupo.

Directions: Travel 19 kms south of Te Kuiti on SH3 towards Piopio. Carmel Farm is on the right. We can arrange to pick up from Otorohanga, Te Kuiti or Waitomo, if required.

Coromandel Peninsula

Towns listed generally follow a north to south route. Refer to the index if required.

Waiheke Island

Kuaotunu

Coromandel

Whitianga

Cooks Beach

Hahei

Hot Water Beach

Coroglen

Te Mata Bay

Tairua

Te Puru

25

Thames

Beachlands

Whitford

Clevedon

Papakura

Kaiaua

rury

Bombay

Whangamata

Mercer

2

Waihi

Waihi Beach

| 0 | Kilometres | 20 |
| 0 | Miles | 12 |

Thames   *Farmstay Homestay Self-contained 8km SE of Thames*

Wharfedale Farmstay
Rosemary Burks
RD 1, Kopu, Thames
Tel (07) 868 8929   Fax (07) 868 8926
wharfedale@xtra.co.nz
www.bnb.co.nz/wharfedalefarmstay.html
Double $100-$120 Single $80 (Full Breakfast)
Credit cards accepted
1 Double 2 Single (2 bdrm)
2 Private

For 13 years our guests have enjoyed the beauty of Wharfedale which has featured in Air NZ "Airwaves" and Japan's "My Country" magazines. We invite you to share our idyllic lifestyle set in 9 acres of park like paddocks and gardens surrounded by native bush. Delight in private river swimming, abundant bird life, our dairy goats. We enjoy wholefood and organically grown produce. There are cooking facilities in the studio apartment. We have no children or indoor animals. Cool shade in summer and cozy log fires and electric blankets in winter. We look forward to meeting you.

Thames   *B&B 1.5km SE of Thames*

Brunton House
Albert & Yvonne Sturgess
210 Parawai Road, Thames
Tel (07) 868 5160   Fax (07) 868 5160
Mob 025 235 2449   asturgess@paradise.net.nz
www.bnb.co.nz/bruntonhouse.html
Double $95 Single $60 (Full Breakfast)
Credit cards accepted
2 Queen 1 Double 2 Single (3 bdrm)
1 Guests share 1 Host share

Share in Thames' early history, stay in our Lovely Victorian House which is comfortable, homely and smokefree. Our large grounds include mature trees, swimming pool (summer) and grass tennis court. The house features large comfortable bedrooms, guest lounge with TV, stereo and extensive library, billiard room, S/S tea and coffee. Our interests include travel, steam trains, embroidery, dancing, reading, gardening and our lovable cat and dog. Directions: Opposite Toyota Plant turn into Banks Street. Right into Parawai Rd and find us 200m further on left.

Thames   *Homestay 8km E of Thames*

Huia Lodge
Val & Steve Barnes
589 Kauaeranga Valley Road, Thames
Tel (07) 868 6557   Fax (07) 868 6557
huia.lodge@xtra.co.nz
www.thames-info.co.nz/HuiaLodge
Double $80 Single $50 (Full Breakfast) Child $20
Dinner $20 by arrangement Credit cards accepted
2 Queen 2 Single (3 bdrm)
2 Ensuite

Each guest has an ensuite and tea/coffee facilities. Relax and enjoy the tranquility of the Valley, hike in the nearby Forest Park or circle the Peninsula to view the famous Coromandel scenery. We're in our mid 50's, enjoy meeting travellers, love the rural lifestyle, grow fruit/vegetables and pamper Bart the cat on our 4 acre property. Turn at BP corner (south end of township) into Banks Street then follow Parawai Road into the Valley. We're 8km from BP. Just 1 1/2 hours from Auckland.

Thames   *Homestay Separate/Suite 6.4km E of Thames*

Mountain Top B&B
Elizabeth McCracken & Allan Berry
452 Kauaeranga Valley Road, RD 2, Thames
Tel (07) 868 9662   Fax (07) 868 9662
nzh_mountain.top@xtra.co.nz
www.bnb.co.nz/mountaintopbb.html

Double $90-$95 Single $50 (Full Breakfast)
Child 1/2 price Dinner $20 - $30 Credit cards accepted
Children welcome Pets welcome
1 Queen 1 Double 1 Single (2 bdrm)   1 Guests share

Allan and I grow mandarins, olives, native trees & raise
coloured sheep on a small organic farm. Our guest wing with lounge, fridge, TV and extensive library
has bedrooms with decks overlooking river and mountains. Coromandel forest park has superb walking
tracks or nearby you can amble over neighbouring farmland or swim in forest pools. We have a relaxed
garden, Jack Russell Roly and cat Priscilla. We love meeting people often cooking for guests mostly
from farm produce. Come and let us look after you.

Thames   *B&B 4km E of Thames*

Acorn Lodge
Dennis & Pat
161 Kauaeranga Valley, RD 2, Thames
Tel (07) 868 8723   Fax (07) 868 8713
AcornLodge@xtra.co.nz
www.bnb.co.nz/acornlodge.html

Double $110   Single $70 (Full Breakfast) Child Neg
Dinner $40 by arrangement Credit cards accepted
1 Queen 1 Double 1 Single (3 bdrm)
2 Private

Relax and enjoy the tranquil views from our spacious
home set in 2 acres of park-like grounds. Enjoy a pot of tea or coffee and home baking on your sunny
patio or relax in your comfortable lounge featuring an atrium and waterfall. At night marvel at the glow
worms - only 2 mins walk. Our interests include tramping in the nearby "Forest Park", fishing and
gardening. We, Dennis and Pat, along with Penny our cat and Coco our friendly German Shepherd,
assure you of a warm welcome.

Thames Coast - Te Puru   *B&B Homestay Self-contained 12km N of Thames*

Te Puru Coast Bed & Breakfast
Bill and Paula Olsen
2a Tatahi St, Te Puru, Thames Coast, Coromandel
Tel (07) 868 2866   Fax (09) 868 2866
Mob 027 656 6058
tepurucoastbnb@xtra.co.nz
www.tepurucoastbnb.co.nz

Double $85 Single $60 (Continental & Full Breakfast)
Child $10.00 Dinner $25.00 pp Children welcome
1 Queen 2 Double 1 Twin 2 Single (4 bdrm)
1 Private 1 Host share

Welcome to the beautiful Thames Coast. Our modern comfortable home is 80 metres off the main coast
road with offstreet parking. Guest lounge has TV and Tea & Coffee facilities. You may choose a
continental or cooked breakfast and evening meals are on request with a complimentary glass of New
Zealand wine or beer. Our large deck is yours to enjoy or take a short 2min walk to the beach. Fishermen
welcome. The seperate self contained unit has own laundry, kitchen/dining, bathroom, BBQ.

Te Mata Bay - Thames Coast   *Homestay 23km N of Thames*

Te Mata Bay Homestay
Helen & Charlie Burgess
29 Eames Crescent, Te Mata Bay, Thames Coast
Tel (07) 868 4754 Fax (07) 868 4757
Mob 025 233 0656
temata.hstay@xtra.co.nz
www.bnb.co.nz/tematabayhomestay.html
Double $100 Single $50
(Full Breakfast) Dinner $25
1 Queen 1 Double 2 Single (3 bdrm)
1 Guests share

We offer you the experience to stay in a real homestay situation. We are 23 kilometres from Thames, 32 kilometres from Coromandel town. Our home is one kilometre off the main coast road. Enjoy the incredible sea and mountain views from the balcony, which surrounds out large comfortable home. A three course evening meal is included in the tariff of $75 per person. Send and receive your emails. Arrive as guest and depart as friends.

Coromandel   *Homestay   11km S of Coromandel*

Coromandel Homestay
Hilary & Vic Matthews
74 Kowhai Drive, Te Kouma Bay, Coromandel
Tel (07) 866 8046 Fax (07) 866 8046
vc.hm.matthews@xtra.co.nz
www.bnb.co.nz/.html
Double $90-$105 Single $60-$70
(Continental Breakfast) Dinner $40 by arrangement
Credit cards accepted
2 Queen 1 Single (2 bdrm)   2 Ensuite

Our homestay is near an attractive safe beach. We have a bush setting and beautiful views of Coromandel Harbour. The area is very quiet and peaceful. Vic is a professional furniture/designer maker. Hilary enjoys gardening, spinning and woodturning. We have a cat. The house is unsuitable for young children. Take SH25 for 50kms travelling north from Thames. Turn sharp left into Te Kouma Road. After 3kms turn left into Kowhai Drive. We are 15 minutes drive south of Coromandel town. Dinner by prior arrangement.

Coromandel   *B&B Farmstay 3km S of Coromandel*

Jacaranda Lodge
Gayle & Gary Bowler
3195 Tiki Road, RD 1, Coromandel Town
Tel (07) 866 8002 Fax (07) 866 8002
jacarandacoromandel@xtra.co.nz
www.jacarandalodge.co.nz
Double $100-$135 Single $50-$100 (Special Breakfast)
Child Neg. Dinner $40 by arrangement
Credit cards accepted
4 Queen 1 Twin 1 Single (6 bdrm)
2 Ensuite 1 Private 1 Guests share

Welcome to Jacaranda, a warm relaxing home set on 6 acres of peaceful farmland and beautiful gardens with rural and mountain views. We offer spacious bedrooms, guest lounges and kitchen and ample verandahs. Our meals are delicious, featuring fresh home grown foods plus local seafood, served overlooking the rose garden whenever possible. Jacaranda is an excellent base close to all the peninsula's attractions. Gayle loves tramping the amazing local trails. Gary loves fishing, golf and tennis and we will happily organise these or any other activities.

Coromandel *B&B Self-contained 0.5 E of Coromandel*

Country Touch
Colleen & Geoff Innis
39 Whangapoua Road, Coromandel

Tel (07) 866 8310 Fax (07) 866 8310
Mob 025 971 196 countrytouch@xtra.co.nz
www.bnb.co.nz/countrytouch.html

Double $95 Single $65 (Continental Breakfast)
Child $10 Credit cards accepted   Children welcome
2 Queen 2 Twin (4 bdrm)
4 Ensuite

Geoff and I are a retired couple who enjoy meeting people, and invite you to a restful holiday in a country setting. With newly established trees and gardens, roses a speciality. You have the independence of 4 units situated apart from our home, all with fold out sofas, TV, fridge, tea and coffee making facilities. You have a country touch feeling with only a 10 minute stroll to Coromandel township, where you can enjoy our local arts, crafts and restaurants. Come and enjoy.

Coromandel *Homestay 10km S of Coromandel*

AJ's Homestay
Annette & Ray Hintz
24 Kowhai Drive, Te Kouma, RD, Coromandel

Tel (07) 866 7057 Fax (07) 866 7057
Mob 0274 581 624 rm.aj.hintz@actrix.gen.nz
www.bnb.co.nz/ajshomestay.html

Double $85-$120 Single $70 (Continental Breakfast)
Dinner $25 - $35 Credit cards accepted   Children
welcome   2 Queen 1 Double 1 Single (3 bdrm)
1 Ensuite 1 Host share

AJ's HOMESTAY with panoramic sea views overlooking the Coromandel Harbour, spectacular sunsets. Five-minute walk to a safe swimming beach. Most mornings breakfast is served on the terrace. Our games room has a billiard and table tennis table. Dinner can be arranged. Directions, Thames coast main road (SH25) Approx. 50 mins. At the bottom of the last hill overlooking the Coromandel Harbour. Turn sharp left, at the Te Kouma Rd sign. Travel past the boat ramp, next turn left. Kowhai Drive, we are No 24.

Coromandel *B&B 0.5km S of Coromandel*

The Green House
Gwen Whitmore
505 Tiki Road, Coromandel

Tel (07) 866 7303
whitmore@wave.co.nz
www.greenhousebandb.co.nz

Double $90-$110 Single $60-$75
(Continental Breakfast)
Credit cards accepted
1 King/Twin 1 Queen 1 Double (3 bdrm)
1 Ensuite 1 Guests share

This relaxed home has very comfortable guest facilities, views over hills and sea, great sunsets too. Upstairs are two bedrooms, bathroom and guest lounge (ideal for small groups) downstairs an ensuite queen room. Just minutes walk from excellent restaurants, shops etc this central location, from which to explore the great natural beauty and hospitality of Coromandel, offers a discount for stay of 3 nights. Help is available in planning day trips to maximise your time and enjoyment of the region. Advance bookings are advisable over summer.

Kuaotunu   *B&B   Country Stay   17km N of Whitianga*

Kaeppeli's
Jill & Robert Kaeppeli
Grays Avenue, Kuaotunu, RD 2, Whitianga,

Tel (07) 866 2445   Mob 025 656 3442
kaeppeli.kuaotunu@paradise.net.nz.
www.kaeppeli.co.nz

Double $80-$125 Single $60-$85 (Full Breakfast)
Child negotiable Dinner by arrangement $32.50
Credit cards accepted Children welcome Pets welcome
2 King 4 Single (4 bdrm)   3 Ensuite 1 Guests share

Country Living in Style and Comfort. Exquisite meals -
Robert is an excellent Swiss Chef using top quality produce and the wood fired oven. Meals served in the panoramic gazebo or guests dining room. Relax and enjoy the peace and tranquility of Kuaotunu, choice of clean safe beaches, bush walks, fishing, tennis, kayaking, swimming. Matarangi's Bob Charles designed golf course and horse trekking, nearby. Our daughter and pets make children welcome. Ideal starting point for exploring the Coromandel Peninsula. And our view?? Just the best!

Kuaotunu   *B&B   Homestay   16km N of Whitianga*

The Peachey's
Yvonne & Dale Peachey
15 Kawhero Drive, Kuaotunu RD 2, Whitianga

Tel (07) 866 5290   Fax (07) 866 5290
DYPeachey@xtra.co.nz
www.thepeacheys.co.nz

Double $100-$120 Single $80 (Special Breakfast)
Dinner $25pp Credit cards accepted
1 King 1 Queen 2 Single (2 bdrm)
2 Ensuite

Welcome. Our new home and B&B at Kuaotunu, is on SH25 between Whitianga and Coromandel. A short stroll through the reserve opposite your accommodation is Kuaotunu Beach. The place for the "travel weary" to unwind. We are a semi retired couple (and Barley the cat) who have lived in the area for many years and enjoy meeting people. Swimming, tennis, golf, fishing, cycling, bush walks and relaxation at your doorstep. Cafes and restaurants at Whitianga and Matarangi are only a 15 minute drive away.

Kuaotunu   *B&B   Homestay Self-contained 18km N of Whitianga*

Kuaotunu Bay Lodge
Lorraine and Bill Muir
State Highway 25, Kuaotunu, RD 2, Whitianga

Tel (07) 866 4396   Fax (07) 866 4396
Mob 025 601 3665   muir@kuaotunubay.co.nz
www.kuaotunubay.co.nz

Double $150-$180 Single $120
(Special Breakfast) Dinner $45pp Credit cards accepted
2 Queen 2 Single (3 bdrm)
2 Ensuite 1 Private

An elegant beach house situated 18km north of Whitianga
on a four-hectare property overlooking Kuaotunu Bay, panoramic views of the peninsula and Mercury Island. Our home has been purpose built for guest with ensuites, decks, private entrances and underfloor heating. Watch the waves from your bed or enjoy a morning swim before a hearty breakfast on the deck. Walks, kayaking, horse riding all within easy reach. Savour some of the fine restaurants in Whitianga or dine at the Lodge with prior arrangement. Spending two or three days with us gives you time to explore the whole peninsula.

Kuaotunu - Coromandel Peninsula   *B&B Self-contained 17km N of Whitianga*

Blue Penguin
Glenda Mawhinney & Barbara Meredith
11 Cuvier Crescent, Kuaotunu, RD 2, Whitianga

Tel (07) 866 2222   Fax (07) 866 0228
holidayhomes@bluepenguin.co.nz
www.bluepenguin.co.nz

Double $110-$125 Single $65 (Continental Breakfast)
Child $30 Dinner $25 B/A Credit cards accepted
Children welcome Pets welcome Smoking area inside
1 King/Twin 1 Double 4 Single (2 bdrm) 1 Guests share

We offer you our architecturally designed home with spectacular views over the beach and pohutukawa trees to the Mercury Islands and Great Barrier. The master guestroom has king bed, window seats and small private balcony. Children love the family guestroom, double, two singles, bunks, cot, TV/video, toys, games, kids' videos. We have a Retriever, Poodle and little Foxy. We are two professional women whom also manage 300 Private Beach Houses available for holiday rental - see our web site for full descriptions, colour photographs, seasonal rates and availability calendars.

Kuaotunu   *B&B Homestay 17km N of Whitianga*

Drift In B&B
Yvonne & Peppe Thompson
16 Grays Avenue, Kuaotunu, RD 2, Whitianga
Tel (07) 866 4321   Fax (07) 866 4321
Mob 025 245 3632   www.bnb.co.nz/driftinbb.html

Double $85-$95 Single $50 (Full Breakfast)
Child $30 (5-12yrs) Dinner By arrangement $25
Visa/MC accepted Children welcome
1 Queen 2 Single (2 bdrm)
1 Guests share

Welcome is assured. This tranquil comfortable modern cedar home is designed to take full advantage of the sun and breathtaking island views by day and moonlit night. An unique beach theme pervades house and garden with small dog in residence. Just a minute stroll to white sand beaches for safe swimming and fossicking. Breakfast is a memorable occasion with sight and sounds of birds and sea complementing an excellent range of home cooking. Delicious evening meals available by prior arrangement. Drift in, relax and enjoy this unique and special part of New Zealand.

Whitianga   *B&B Self contained cottage 1km S of Whitianga*

Cosy Cat Cottage
Gordon Pearce
41 South Highway, Whitianga
Tel (07) 866 4488   Fax (07) 866 4488
Mob 025 798 745   cosycat@xtra.co.nz
www.cosycat.co.nz

Double $85-$105 Single $55-$75 (Full Breakfast)
Cottage $90 - $160 Credit cards accepted
2 Queen 1 Double 1 Single (3 bdrm)
2 Ensuite 1 Private

Welcome to our picturesque two storied cottage filled with feline memorabilia! Relax with complimentary tea or coffee served on the veranda or in the guest lounge. Enjoy a good nights rest in comfortable beds & choose a variety of treats from our breakfast blackboard menu. You will probably like to meet Sylvie the cat or perhaps visit the cat hotel in the garden. A separate cottage is available with Queen beds, bathrooms and kitchen. Friendly helpful service is assured - hope to see you soon!

Whitianga *B&B Homestay*

Anne's Haven
Anne & Bob
119 Albert St, Whitianga

Tel (07) 866 5550 anneshaven@paradise.net.nz
www.bnb.co.nz/anneshaven.html

Double $65 Single $45 (Full Breakfast)
Child $20 Dinner $20
1 Double 2 Single (2 bdrm)
1 Host share

Welcome to our comfortable modern home and the tranquillity of the garden. Guests share the lounge/TV room. The shower, toilet and bathroom are each separate rooms for easy access. Breakfast includes homemade bread and jams. We are 400 metres from shops and restaurants and within walking distance to six lovely beaches. Bob enjoys building and flying radio controlled model planes. Anne makes pottery, dabbles with watercolours and gardens. Let us make your stay a memorable one. Our moggie 'Gordon Bennett' is also friendly.

Whitianga *B&B Homestay 3.5km S of Whitianga*

Camellia Lodge
Pat & John Lilley
South Highway, RD 1, Whitianga

Tel (07) 866 2253 Fax (07) 866 2253
Mob 021 217 6612 camellia@wave.co.nz
www.whitianga.co.nz/camellia-lodge

Double $90-$110 Single $65 (Full Breakfast)
Child 1/2 price Dinner $25 Credit cards accepted
1 Queen 2 Double 2 Twin (4 bdrm)
2 Ensuite 2 Guests share

Welcome to our friendly home, which is nestled in a secluded park-like garden, which includes native, and many mature trees. We also offer you a spa and swimming pool and lots of lovely gardens to relax in. You would normally be woken up to the tune of bellbirds, then you settle into a hearty breakfast which will set you up for the whole day. We have a guest lounge and tea and coffee making facilities. We can assure you of a warm friendly welcome and a comfortable stay.

Whitianga *B&B Homestay Bedsit 2km S of Whitianga*

A Hi-Way Haven
Joan & Nevin Paton
1 Golf Road, Whitianga

Tel (07) 866 2427 Fax (07) 866 2424
a-haven@paradise.net.nz
www.bnb.co.nz/ahiwayhaven.html

Double $70-$90 Single $40-$50 (Full Breakfast)
Credit cards accepted
1 King/Twin 1 Queen 1 Double 2 Single (4 bdrm)
1 Ensuite 1 Guests share

Looking for comfortable affordable accommodation 2km from Whitianga. Hearty cooked breakfast will keep you going all day. 18 hole golf course is adjacent and central to all amenities on the Coromandel Peninsula. Short drive to Whitianga township with many restaurants and your hosts will be happy to arrange all holiday wishes. Guest lounge, TV, Tea/Coffee and laundry facilities. Ensuite bedsit also available for disabled people. Friendly cat. We at A Hi-way Haven know that you will come as a visitor and depart as a friend.

Whitianga - Cooks Beach   *Homestay Rural 17km N of Tairua*

Mercury Orchard
Heather and Barry Scott
141 Purangi Road, RD1, Whitianga
Tel (07) 866 3119   Fax (07) 866 3115
mercorchard@xtra.co.nz
www.mercuryorchard.co.nz

Double $110 Single $75 (Full Breakfast) Dinner $25
S/C Cottage $130 Credit cards accepted
3 Queen 2 Single (4 bdrm)
2 Ensuite 1 Host share

Mercury Orchard is 5 acres of country garden and organic orchard close to Cooks, Hahei and Hot Water Beaches. Our large guest room opens to private garden and swimming pool, has tea & coffee facilities, ensuite bathroom and adjoining queen bedroom. Also available - Fig Tree Cottage, self contained country style comfort, opening through French doors into orchard, crisp cotton bed linen, fresh fruit and flowers, breakfast hamper and use of BBQ. We share our smoke-free home with 2 small dogs and a cat. We look forward to making your Coromandel experience a memorable one.

Whitianga   *B&B Self-contained 6km S of Whitianga*

Riverside Retreat
Maree & Richard Prestage
309 Road, RD 1, Whitianga
Tel (07) 866 5155   Fax (07) 866 5155
Mob 021 238 1921   retreat@xtra.co.nz
www.riversideretreat.co.nz

Double $120 Single $120 (Continental Breakfast)
1 Queen (1 bdrm)
1 Private

You are invited to share our Riverside Retreat beside the waters that run through the beautiful Mahakirau Valley. Your cottage, nestled amongst native trees in three acres of landscaped gardens, has a sunny kitchen and lounge, queen bedroom upstairs in loft, with views over the garden and river. You can fly-fish for trout, bush walk, or just relax by the river with a book. The perfect place to unwind, soothe the spirit and leave the world behind. Your hosts and moggy "Woz" assure you a relaxing and memorable stay.

Whitianga   *B&B Separate/Suite Hotel style 4km N of Whitianga*

At Parkland Place
Maria & Guy Clark
14 Parkland Place, Brophys Beach, Whitianga
Tel (07) 866 4987   Fax (07) 866 4946
Mob 025 291 7495   parklandplace@wave.co.nz
www.atparklandplace.co.nz

Double $135-$200 Single $100-$150 (Continental
Special Breakfast) Child Neg Dinner by arrangement
Credit cards accepted Children welcome
1 King/Twin 3 King 2 Queen 3 Single (5 bdrm)
4 Ensuite 1 Private 1 Guests share

Enjoy European hospitality in Whitianga's most luxurious Boutique Accommodation. Maria, a ships chef from Poland and New Zealand husband Guy, a master mariner, will make your stay a memorable experience. Large luxuriously appointed rooms. Magnificent breakfasts. Superb candle-lit dinners or BBQ by arrangement. Sunny picturesque outdoor area with spa pool. Large guest lounge with TV, library, music and refreshments. Situated near the beach and next to reserves and farmland ensures absolute peace and quiet. Privacy and discretion assured. You will not regret coming.

Whitianga - Coroglen *B&B Farmstay 14km S of Whitianga*

Coroglen Lodge
Wendy & Nigel Davidson
2221 State Highway 25, RD 1, Whitianga 2856

Tel (07) 866 3225 Fax (07) 866 3235
clover@wave.co.nz
www.mercurybay.co.nz/coroglen.html

Double $75-$85 Single $50-$60 (Continental Breakfast)
Child $35 Credit cards accepted Children welcome
2 Queen 2 Single (3 bdrm)
2 Guests share

Coroglen Lodge is situated on 17 acres of farmland with cattle, sheep, alpacas and friendly chickens. Surrounded by hills and nestled in a valley with views of the Coromandel Ranges, this is rural tranquillity. Halfway between Whitianga township and Hot Water Beach there is easy access to both areas and all attractions. We have a garden to roam in, barbecue area with fuel, and full cooking facilities. Two showers, two toilets and laundry facilities are available. Guest area is separate and spacious with a large sunny lounge area for your comfort.

Whitianga *B&B 500m Whitianga*

Cottage by the Sea
Max Murray
11 The Esplanade, Whitianga

Tel (07) 866 0605 Fax (07) 866 0675
Mob 025 237 6163 staying@acottagebythesea.com
www.bnb.co.nz/cottagebytheseawhitianga.html

Double $120-$160 Single $120 (Full Breakfast)
Credit cards accepted
1 King 1 Queen (2 bdrm)
1 Ensuite 1 Private 1 Guests share

The charming cottage is located opposite the wharf offering peaceful harbour views. A 1 minute stroll takes you to Buffalo Beach. The township, a 2 minute easy walk has excellent restaurants, cafes and shopping. A 4km drive takes you to the 18 hole golf course and busy airfield. Guest share the family lounge with open fire during the cooler months. Breakfast served on sunny deck or room service. Guests own entrance with safe private off street parking. Our lovely home is shared with two quiet cats.

Whitianga *B&B Farmstay Studio Apartment 22 km S of Whitianga*

Coppers Creek Farmstay
Graham & Pamela Caddy
1587 State Highway 25, Coroglen, RD 1
Whitianga 2856

Tel 07-8663960 Fax 07-8663960 Mob 025-526151
caddy.copperscreek@xtra.co.nz
www.copperscreekfarmstay.co.nz

Double $90-$70 (Full Breakfast) Children welcome
1 Queen (1 bdrm)
1 Private

Coppers Creek is a small working beef breeding farm comprising of 120 acres of pasture, bush and streams. We have the usual assortment of farm animals including the odd teenager. Enjoy the freedom of our self contained studio apartment with private entrance and BBQ area, with fresh produce available from the farm garden in season. We are only 15 min. drive from Hot Water Beach, Hahei, Cooks Beach and Whitianga. We enjoy boating, fishing, diving and bush walks.

Hahei *B&B Self-contained 38km S of Whitianga*

The Church
Richard Agnew & Karen Blair
87 Beach Road, Hahei, RD 1, Whitianga

Tel (07) 866 3533 Fax (07) 866 3055
Mob 025 596 877 hahei4ch@xtra.co.nz
www.thechurchhahei.co.nz

Double $90-$145 (Continental Breakfast) Child $10
Dinner Menu Credit cards accepted Children welcome
11 Queen 1 Double 13 Single (11 bdrm)
11 Ensuite

The Church is Hahei's most unique accommodation and
dining experience. The Church building provides a character dining room/licensed restaurant for wholesome breakfasts and delicious evening meals. Eleven cosy wooden cottages scattered through delightful bush and gardens offer a range of accommodation and tariffs, with ensuites, fridges and tea and coffee facilities. Some cottages fully self-contained with woodstoves for winter. Enjoy the wonders of Cathedral Cove, Hot Water Beach, and the Coromandel Peninsula. Seasonal rates. Smoking outside.

Hahei Beach *Homestay Separate/Suite 28km N of Tairua*

Cedar Lodge
Jenny & John Graham
36 Beach Road, Hahei, RD 1, Whitianga

Tel (07) 866 3789 Fax (07) 866 3978
cedarlodge@wave.co.nz
www.cedarlodge.gen.nz

Double $100 Single $75 (Full Breakfast)
Credit cards accepted
1 Queen 1 Single (1 bdrm)
1 Private

Come and unwind in our comfortable private upstairs studio apartment with its own entrance. Enjoy the sea views and relaxing atmosphere. Take a 200m stroll to the beautiful beach and experience the magic of Hahei. Cathedral Cove walkway and Hot Water beach are nearby. Scenic boat/dive trips are easily arranged with local operators. We have an adult family scattered around the world and two friendly cats. We thank you for not smoking indoors. We enjoy an active retired lifestyle, so please phone ahead for bookings and directions.

Hahei Beach *B&B 200m NE of Hahei shops and cafes*

Hawleys Bed and Breakfast Hahei
Peter and Rhonda Hawley
19 Hahei Beach Road, RD 1, Whitianga

Tel 07 8663272 0800 2 78783 Fax 07 8663273
Mob 025 971090 hawleysb&b@haheibeach.co.nz
www.haheibeach.co.nz

Double $120 Single $110 (Full Breakfast)
Credit cards accepted Children welcome
1 Queen 2 Single (2 bdrm)
1 Private 1 Guests share

Situated on the flat, half-way (200m) between the beach and the shops and cafes. Ideal for those who enjoy extra space and comfort. The purpose built two double bedrooms (house completed mid 2000) and spacious bathroom and take up all of the second storey at the rear of the house. The larger room has a balcony and a queen size bed and the smaller room two single beds. A cot is available. There is secure garaging. No children at home and no pets.

Hot Water Beach   *Self-contained 24km N of Tairua*

Auntie Dawns Place
Dawn & Joe Nelmes
Radar Road, Hot Water Beach, Whitianga R D 1

Tel (07) 866 3707   Fax (07) 866 3701
AuntieDawn@wave.co.nz
www.bnb.co.nz/auntiedawnsplace.html

Double $80-$100   Single $50   (Continental Breakfast)
 Credit cards accepted
2 Queen 1 Double 1 Single (2 bdrm)
2 Private

Hot Water Beach is a beautiful surf beach. At low tide hot water
bubbles up at a particular place in the sand and you dig yourself a "hot pool". Our house is surrounded
by huge Pohutukawa trees, 3 mins walk from the hot springs. We have a terrier and Joe makes home-
brew beer. Apartments are comfortably furnished and we provide tea, coffee, bread, butter, jam, milk
and cereals. Guests prepare breakfast at preferred time. Nearest restaurant 10 minutes away at Hahei.
Directions: Turn right into Radar Road 200 metres before shop.

Hot Water Beach   *B&B Homestay Separate/Suite 32km S of Whitianga*

Hot Water Beach B&B
Gail & Trevor Knight
48 Pye Place, Hot Water Beach, RD 1,
 Coromandel Peninsula

Tel (07) 866 3991   0800 146 889   Fax (07) 866 3291
Mob 025 799 620   TKnight@xtra.co.nz
www.hotwaterbedandbreakfast.co.nz

Double $160-$180   Single $140-$160 (Full Breakfast)
Dinner by arrangement Credit cards accepted
2 Queen (2 bdrm)
2 Ensuite

We have a spacious elevated home with extensive decks, on which you can have fresh coffee or juice,
while enjoying sweeping panoramic sea/beach views. Sit under the brilliant southern stars in our spa
pool or play on our full sized billiard table. You can swim, surf, dive, fish, kayak, play golf, bushwalk,
horse trek or visit spectacular Cathedral Cove or alternatively just dig a hole and soak in the natural hot
springs on our beach. We have two cats and a sociable boxer.

Tairua   *Homestay 30km E of Thames*

On the Edge - Tairua
Andrea Patten
219 Paku Drive, Tairua, Coromandel Peninsula

Tel (07) 864 8285   Fax (07) 864 8232
Mob 025 736 176   ontheedge717@hotmail.com
www.bnb.co.nz/ontheedgetairua.html

Double $140-$180   Single $100-$130 (Full Breakfast)
Child $50 Dinner $30 Credit cards accepted
Children welcome
2 Queen 2 Double (2 bdrm)   2 Ensuite

'On The Edge' of Paku Hill, panoramic views of the
Pacific Ocean and islands. Ideally situated for walks to Paku Hill with spectacular views of Pauanui
and Tairua. 20mins north - Hot Water Beach and Cathedral Cove. Close to 18 hole golf course and
good restaurants. Andrea and James have travelled extensively, spending their leisure time diving,
fishing and skiing. With their intimate knowledge of the Coromandel Peninsula they can provide a tour
of the Coromandel in their green coach. While having breakfast enjoy the sound of the sea below the
deck. Double & ensuite bedrooms with spectacular sea and island views.

Tairua   *B&B 45km E of Thames*

Harbour View Lodge
Sheryl Allan & John Goldstone
179 Main Road, Tairua

Tel (07) 864 7040   Fax (07) 864 7042
info@harbourviewlodge.co.nz
www.harbourviewlodge.co.nz

Double $120-$160 Single $110-$135
(Continental Breakfast) (Special Breakfast)
Credit cards accepted
1 King/Twin 2 Queen (3 bdrm)   3 Ensuite

Situated on the foothills of Tairua. Our B & B has been
recently refurbished with the finest of linens and interior design. All rooms have their own ensuite, hair
dryers, electric blankets, tea/coffee facilities. Guest Lounge, swimming pool, off street parking.
Continental or a full cooked breakfast is served in the dining room with its ever-changing views of
Tairua Harbour and Paku Mountain. Enjoy our beaches, bush walks,18 hole golf course. 5 min level
walk to local Restaurants. Close to Cathedral Cove & Hot Water Beach.

Tairua   *B&B Homestay 30km E of Thames*

Colleith Lodge
Maureen and Colin Gilroy
8 Rewa Rewa Valley, Tairua, Coromandel Peninsula

Tel (07) 864 7970   Fax (07) 864 7972
Mob 025 721 423
info@colleithlodge.co.nz   www.colleithlodge.co.nz

Double $220-$250 Single $220
(Continental   Full Breakfast) Dinner by arrangement
Discounts for stays 2 nights or longer
3 Queen 1 Single (3 bdrm)   3 Ensuite 3 Private

Colleith Lodge is a unique location situated on the East Coast of the Coromandel Peninsula. Set on 1.5
acres of native bush and built for your relaxation, privacy and comfort in mind. The sweeping panoramic
views encompass Tairua Estuary, Pauanui and the Pacific Ocean. Each guest room has its own private
patio. Colleith Lodge is stunning one level accommodation and offers a spa and swimming pool for
your enjoyment. Your hosts Colin and Maureen both love people and enjoy meeting others from all
parts of the world. We have two outside dogs named Jip and Sam. Golf courses, bush walks.

Tairua   *B&B 40km E of Thames*

Dell Cote   Earth Brick Homestay
Barry & Trish Oldham
37 Rewrewa Valley Road, Tairua,

Tel (07) 864 8142 Fax (07) 864 8142
homestay@dellcote.com   www.dellcote.com

Double $160-$180 Single $160
(Special Continental breakfast served)
Children by arrangement
3 Queen 1 Single (3 bdrm)
2 Ensuite 1 Private

Dell Cote has the refined rustic ambience of natural non-
toxic building materials, earth brick and macrocarpa. Set in the beautiful, secluded, bush-clad Rewarewa
Valley, on an acre of land with native bush, an abundance of birdlife and an extensive organic orchard
and vegetable garden. Bessie, our friendly little dog, is a special member of the family. We are 1.5kms
from the seaside village of Tairua, with convenience shopping, pottery/art studios, golf, fishing/diving,
plus a variety of restaurants. Inspection invited.

Whangamata (Rural) *B&B 8km N of Whangamata*

Copsefield B&B
Trish & Richard Davison
1055 State Highway 25, RD 1, Whangamata
Tel (07) 865 9555 Fax (07) 865 9555
Mob 027 289 0131 copsefield@xtra.co.nz
www.copsefield.co.nz

Double $90-$140 Single $70-$100 (Full Breakfast)
S/C rustic cottage. Sleeps 4   Credit cards accepted
2 Queen 2 Single (3 bdrm)
3 Ensuite

Character country home situated on 3 acres, at the Southern end of the stunning Coromandel Peninsula. Copsefield is purpose built for your comfort, with 3 ensuite rooms. All rooms are non-smoking. Two beaches close by . Canoes, bikes, walks, spa pool. 6 hole pitch & putt golf. Peace and tranquility beside native bush and river. Guest lounge with TV, tea and coffee . Complimentary wine. Full breakfast including locally grown eggs and fresh fruit. Your hosts Trish & Richard, & Mia our Burmese cat, offer you a warm and friendly welcome, and personal attention.

Whangamata *B&B Homestay 200m N of town centre*

Sandy Rose Bed & Breakfast
Shirley & Murray Calman
Corner Hetherington & Rutherford Roads, Whangamata
Tel (07) 865 6911 Fax (07) 865 6911
Mob 027 420 4296 sandyrose@whangamata.co.nz
sandyrose.whangamata.co.nz

Double $110 Single $85 (Special Breakfast)
Credit cards accepted
1 Queen 2 Twin (3 bdrm)
3 Ensuite

A charming B&B in the Coromandel Peninsula's popular holiday destination, we have three tastefully decorated guest bedrooms, all with ensuite bathrooms, comfortable beds and in-room TVs. Complimentary tea and coffee is available in the guest lounge. We are ideally located, close to Whangamata's shops, cafes and restaurants, and an easy stroll to the surf beach, harbour and wharf. Enjoy our extensive continental breakfast and use our home as a base to relax and enjoy the natural attractions that Whangamata and area has to offer.

Whangamata *Guest Lodge 2km W of Whangamata*

Brenton Lodge
Rosa & John Ashton
1 Brenton Place, Whangamata,
Tel (07) 865 8400 Fax (07) 865 8400
Mob 021 1200 574 brentonlodge@xtra.co.nz
www.bnb.co.nz/brentonlodge1.html

Double $295 Single $275 (Full Breakfast)
Extra person $80
3 Queen (3 bdrm)
3 Ensuite

Brenton Lodge provides superior boutique accommodation with style. A superb country retreat for the discerning visitor: intimate and personal. Escape & enjoy peace, privacy & pampering. Glorious sea views, beautiful gardens: swimming pool & spa house in the garden. Situated just 2km from the surf beach and village.   Charming guest cottages are tastefully decorated, cotton sheets, fresh flowers. Gourmet breakfasts served in the privacy of your room or alfresco on your balcony.

Waihi   *B&B Homestay 1km S of Waihi*

West Wind Gardens
Josie French & Merv Scott
58 Adams Street, Waihi

Tel (07) 863 7208   westwindgarden@xtra.co.nz
www.bnb.co.nz/westwind.html

Double $70 Single $35 (Continental Breakfast)
Child $15 Dinner $20 Credit cards accepted
Children welcome
1 Double 2 Single (2 bdrm)
1 Guests share

We offer a friendly restful smoke-free stay in our modern home and garden. Waihi is the gate way to both the Coromandel with its beautiful beaches and the Bay of Plenty. Waihi is a historic town with vintage railway running to Waikino, a working gold mine discovered 1878 closed 1952. Reopened in 1989 as a open-cast mine. Free mine tours available. Beach 10 min away, beautiful bush walks, golf courses, trout fishing. Enjoy a home cooked meal or sample our restaurants. Our interests are gardening, dancing and travel.

Waihi   *B&B Country House 5km N of Waihi*

The French Provincial Country House
Margaret van Duyvenbooden
Golden Valley - Trig Road North, RD 1, Waihi

Tel (07) 863 7339   Fax (07) 863 7330
Mob 021 130 8081   www.bnb.co.nz/thefrench.html

Double $165-$195 Single $140 (Continental Breakfast)
Credit cards accepted Smoking area inside
1 King 1 Queen 1 Double (3 bdrm)
1 Ensuite 1 Private 1 Guests share

A warm welcome awaits you at this charming elegant County Houseî with fine accommodation. Sited on farmland in a picturesque valley only five kilometers from an historic township, close to all attractions. Upstairs is a private, large luxurious suite with rural views, two private balconies, super-king bed, ensuite bathroom, TV, fresh flowers, crisp white bed linen, electric blanket, hairdryer, toiletries and big soft bath towels. This home is not suitable for children and is smoke free. In summer colourful gardens with large shade trees and front door parking for guests. Close to beautiful beaches for swimming and fishing, gold mining tours, cafes, restaurants. Please make an early reservation to save disappointment.

Waihi Beach   *Self-contained 11km E of Waihi*

Waterfront Homestay
Kay & John Morgan
17 The Esplanade (off Hinemoa Street), Waihi Beach

Tel (07) 863 4342   Fax (07) 863 4342
Mob 025 287 1104   k.morgan@xtra.co.nz
www.bnb.co.nz/waterfronthomestay.html

Double $90 Single $65 (Continental Breakfast)
Credit cards accepted Children welcome
1 King 1 Double 1 Single (2 bdrm)   1 Private

Waterfront Homestay Fully self contained two double bedrooms plus single bed. Very suitable for two couples or small family group. Unit on lower floor of family home. Situated on waterfront of beautiful uncrowded ocean beach. Walk from front door directly onto sandy beach. Safe ocean swimming, surfcasting, surfing and coastal walks. 9 hole golf course with club hire in township, 18 hole golf course 11km away. Restaurant within walking distance of accommodation or use facilities provided with accommodation. Tariff $90 per couple bed & breakfast, $10 per extra persons. Off season rates available. Hosts John & Kay Morgan.

Waihi *B&B Homestay Studio 2km W of Waihi*

Trout & Chicken at Drift House
Michael & Adrienne Muir
9137 State Highway 2, RD 2, Waihi
Tel (07) 863 6964 Fax (07) 863 6966
Mob 025 206 4080 troutandchicken@paradise.net.nz
www.troutandchicken.co.nz
Double $110-$130 Single $100 (Special Breakfast)
Dinner by arrangement Studio $50pp
Credit cards accepted
1 Queen 2 Twin (2 bdrm)
2 Ensuite

On an organic blueberry orchard, our home is 300 metres off the main highway. Quiet, peaceful and designed for your comfort. Enjoy a spacious bedroom, lounge and deck: a special breakfast in the dinning room or el fresco. Blueberry muffins and coffee on arrival then relax or walk by the Waitete Stream or in the orchard. Visit the spectacular gorge, gold mine, antique shops, art gallery and museum. Plan on at least two nights, there is a lot to see in the Waihi area. We have pets at home.

Waihi *B&B Homestay 0.5km W of Waihi*

Chez Nous
Sara Parish
41 Seddon Avenue, Waihi
Tel 07 863 7538 Sara.P@xtra.co.nz
www.bnb.co.nz/cheznous.html
Double $65 Single $45 (Continental Breakfast)
Child $20 Dinner $20pp by arrangement
Credit cards accepted Children welcome
1 Queen 1 Twin (2 bdrm)
1 Guests share

Enjoy a relaxed and friendly atmosphere in a spacious, modern home in an attractive garden setting. Shops and restaurants are within easy walking distance. Discover past and present gold mining activities (tours available), sandy surf beaches, bush walks, 9 and 18 hole golf courses, art, craft and wine trails. Waihi is an ideal stopover for the traveller who wants to explore the Coromandel Peninsula, Bay of Plenty and Waikato.

Ensuite or private bathroom is yours exclusively.
Guest share bathroom is shared with other guests.
Hosts share bathroom is shared with the family.

Bay of Plenty

Towns listed generally follow a north to south route. Refer to the index if required.

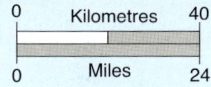

0	Kilometres	40
0	Miles	24

aotunu

Hahei
Hot Water Beach
ach
Coroglen
Tairua
es

Whangamata

Waihi

Katikati
2
Omokoroa
Tauranga
Te Puke
Mt. Maunganui
Papamoa
Maketu
Pukehina
Waihau Bay
Te Kaha
Maraenui
ta
Ngongotaha
Rotorua
Whakatane
Ohope
Opotiki
35
30 Ngakuru
5
1
2
Kinloch
Taupo
Whatatutu
Waipaoa
Ormond
Waikaremoana
Gisborne
Motuoapa
Turangi
Mahanga Beach
Wairoa

Katikati   *Self-contained 20km S of Katikati*

Jones Lifestyle
Thora & Trevor Jones
Pahoia Road, RD 2, Tauranga
Tel (07) 548 0661   Fax (07) 548 0661
joneslifestyle@clear.net.nz
www.bnb.co.nz/joneslifestyle.html
Double $90 Single $60 (Continental Breakfast)
Child $20 Credit cards accepted
1 Queen (1 bdrm)   1 Private

This modern self-contained apartment has all amenities
including lounge (with convertible divan), fully equipped
kitchen and laundry. For a larger family extra bedrooms
and a private bathroom are available in the main house. A deluxe continental breakfast is provided for
self-service. Other amenities are BBQ, dinghy, games rooms for billiards, table tennis etc. We share
our peaceful horticultural lifestyle property on Pahoia peninsula with many birds. There are spectacular
views of Tauranga harbour (water's edge 200m away) and sunset over the Kaimai Ranges.

Katikati   *B&B Farmstay 3km N of Katikati*

Aberfeldy
Mary Anne & Rod Calver
164 Lindemann Road, RD 1, Katikati
Tel (07) 549 0363   0800 309 064 Fax (07) 549 0363
Mob 025 909 710   aberfeldy@xtra.co.nz
www.aberfeldy.co.nz
Double $100 Single $60 (Full Breakfast) Child $30
Dinner By arrangement Credit cards accepted
Children welcome Pets welcome
1 Queen 1 Twin 1 Single (2 bdrm)   1 Private

Large attractive home set in extensive gardens with private sunny guest accommodation. The private
lounge opens onto a patio, and has TV and coffee making facilities. One party at a time in guest
accommodation. We farm sheep and cattle. Rod's associated with Kiwifruit and is a Rotarian. Panoramic
views of bush-clad hills, farmland and harbour. Activities include bush and farm walks, meeting tame
animals especially Sue & Lucy the Kune Kune pigs. Golf course, horse riding, and beaches nearby.
Jax, our Australian terrier will welcome you.

Katikati   *B&B 1km N of Katikati*

Waterford House (katikati.8k.com)
Alan & Helen Cook
15 Crossley Street, Katikati 3063
Tel (07) 549 0757
www.bnb.co.nz/waterfordhouse.html
Double $70 Single $45 (Full Breakfast)
Child discounted Dinner $20 by arrangement
Credit cards accepted Children welcome
1 Queen 1 Double 2 Twin 1 Single (5 bdrm)
3 Guests share

Web site: www.katikati.8k.com - Waterford House, situated in a quiet semi-rural area, provides spacious
accommodation with wheelchair access throughout. A large comfortable lounge with television, stereo-
radio, fridge-freezer, microwave and tea/coffee making facilities. Cot and highchair are available.
Local attractions include Twickenham Homestead Cafe, Morton Estate Winery, Bird Gardens, Ballantyne
Golf Course, Sapphire Springs Hot Pools, Kaimai bush walks, Uretara River Walkway and craft
workshops. 32 murals and sculptures depict the history of Katikati "Mural Town", located on Pacific
Coast Highway. Our cat is called Matilda.

Katikati *B&B Countrystay 7km N of Katikati*

Cotswold Lodge
Alison & Des Belsham
183 Ongare Point Road, RD 1, Katikati
Tel (07) 549 2110   Fax (07) 549 2109
cotswold@ihug.co.nz
www.cotswold.co.nz

Double $120-$130 Single $95 (Full Breakfast)
Dinner By arrangement Credit cards accepted
1 Queen 1 Double 2 Single (3 bdrm)
3 Ensuite

We offer warm Kiwi hospitality, a little luxury and a relaxed environment in our rural 'home away from home', Cotswold Lodge. Gourmet breakfasts. Evening meals by prior arrangement. Wander through the gardens, Kiwifruit orchard or down to the Harbour. Enjoy the views to the Kaimai Ranges or relax in the hot spa and listen to the birds. We have a friendly labrador. Rotorua and Coromandel only 1.5 hours away. Nearby: restaurants, murals, bird gardens, heritage museum, hot pools, beaches, coastal and bush walks, wineries, galleries, and several golf courses.

Katikati *B&B Private suites 9km N of Katikati*

Panorama Country Lodge
Barbara & Phil McKernon
901 Pacific Coast Highway (SH2), RD1, Katikati
Tel (07) 549 1882   Fax (07) 549 1882   Mob 021 165 5875
mckernon@xtra.co.nz www.panoramalodge.co.nz

Double $110-$130 Single $75 (Special Breakfast)
Dinner $40 by arrangement
1 Queen 1 Double 2 Single (3 bdrm)
1 Ensuite 1 Private

Perfectly situated between beautiful Waihi Beach & Katikati (Mural Town). Nestling in the foothills of the Kaimai Ranges & commanding magnificent Pacific & island views from every room! Relax in splendid & peaceful private guest suites, with ensuite & private facilities, quality furnishings, TV & CD, slippers & robes, air-con, fresh coffee & tea, delicious breakfasts, served: in-suite, terrace or dining room. Explore the grounds & orchards, swimming pool, paddocks and meet 'Our boys' the Alpacas, not forgetting our very friendly dog, Kaimai. Nearby: cafes, beaches, golf, boating, walks, etc. 'We love it here...so will you!'

*If you need any information ask your hosts,
they are your own personal travel agent and guide.*

Katikati *B&B 12km N of Katikati*

The Candys' B&B
Gloria & Neil Candy
Athenree Road, RD 1, Katikati
Tel (07) 863 1159   Fax (07) 863 1196
Mob 025 233 8116   neilcandy@ihug.co.nz
www.bnb.co.nz/athenree.html

Double $90   Single $70-$80   (Continental Breakfast)
Dinner $28pp
1 King 1 Queen 2 Twin (2 bdrm)
1 Ensuite

Take time out: relax. Our new home is on three acres, with beautiful harbour views: each room has a patio. Walk to Athenree Hotpools, drive three minutes to Waihi Surf Beach, ten minutes south to Katikati, Ballantynes Golf Course, Morton Winery, Lavender Farm. Ten minutes north to Waihi Goldmine, walks and excellent restaurants. Neil loves fishing, and is an ex chef, Gloria loves crafts. Meals on request. This is paradise and our city pets agree.

Katikati *B&B Self-contained 15km S of Waihi*

Paradiso
Theo and Gerda Blok
101 Athenree Rd., R.D.1, Katikati
Tel (07) 863 5350   Fax (07) 863 5678
paradijs@xtra.co.nz
www.paradisobb.co.nz

Double $90   Single $60 (Continental Breakfast)
Child $ 10 under 5 Children welcome
1 Queen 2 Single (1 bdrm)
1 Private

Paradiso, five acres of park-like gardens, with children's playground, nestled on the edge of Tauranga harbour. A double-seated kayak is available to explore the harbour, native bush walks nearby. Five km from Waihi beach. We offer friendly B&B in our clean, comfortable studio-style accommodation, or you can self-cater and be as private as you wish. We came from Holland 36 years ago and lived on a dairy farm for 30 years, and now we have found paradise. If you like more information, look us up on our website.

Omokoroa - Tauranga *B&B Self-contained Cottage 15km N of Tauranga*

Walnut Cottage
Ken & Betty Curreen
309 Plummers Point Road, Omokoroa, RD 2, Tauranga
Tel (07) 548 0692   Fax (07) 548 1764
walnuthomestay@actrix.co.nz
www.cybersurf.co.nz/curreen

Double $80-$95 Single $50-$70 (Continental Breakfast)
Dinner $15
1 Queen 1 Double (2 bdrm)
1 Ensuite 1 Private

Situated on scenic Plummers Point Peninsula overlooking Tauranga Harbour we invite our guests to enjoy the tranquility our "little-corner-of-the-world" has to offer. Stroll along the Peninsula with its superb views, boat jetty and reserve. In the vicinity we have mineral hot pools, golf course, fountain & quarry gardens,tramping tracks, wineries and eating houses. Walnut Cottage is selfcontained. Kowhai Suite has own entrance,conservatory with tea/coffee,T.V. Directions:Plummers Point Rd is opposite Caltex Service Station on SH2.

Tauranga - Omokoroa   *B&B Homestay 20K N of Tauranga*

Serendipity
Sarath and Linda Vidanage
77 Harbour View Road, Omokoroa, Tauranga

Tel (07) 548 2044   Mob 021 999 815
sarathv@yahoo.com
www.bnb.co.nz/vidanage.html

Double $100 Single $75 (Full Breakfast)
Child $30 Dinner $30   Children welcome
4 Double (2 bdrm)
2 Private

Welcome to our home and garden nestled above
spectacular Omokoroa Beach. The beach is a short walk down the steps. Leisurely walking treks take
you through the groves and gardens of the peninsula. A beautiful golf course and local hot pools are
minutes away. We are a well-traveled couple who have found our paradise. We love to cook and offer
a varied cuisine from traditional to exotic. In one stop you will experience the best of the Bay of Plenty.

Omokoroa   *B&B 17km N of Tauranga*

Seascape
Sue & Geoff Gripton
5 Waterview Terrace, Omokoroa

Tel (07) 548 1027   Mob 021 171 1936
grippos@xtra.co.nz
www.bnb.co.nz/seascape.html

Double $80-$90 Single $55 (Full Breakfast)
1 Double 2 Single (2 bdrm)
1 Ensuite

Come share our stunning views of Tauranga Harbour and
Kaimais. On our doorstep are beaches, walkways, golf, hot pools, boat ramps etc. Just halfway (15
minutes) between Tauranga and Katikati, we offer a double room with ensuite and TV, twin room with
shared bathroom, both with tea/coffee. Enjoy a cooked or continental breakfast with homemade bread
and jams while gazing at the ever-changing view. Only three and a half kilometres from SH2, left at
roundabout, first right, first left into Waterview Terrace. Geoff, Sue and our cat will welcome you.

All our B&Bs are non-smoking
unless stated otherwise in the text.

Tauranga *B&B 3km W of Tauranga City centre*

Be Our Guest
Aileen and Lang Pringle
257 Waihi Road, Tauranga City
Tel 07 571 8862   Fax 07 571 8862   Mob 021 0309627

beourguest@xtra.co.nz
www.beourguest.co.nz
Double $80-$100 Single $45-$55 (Full Breakfast)
Child $20 Dinner $25
2 Queen 1 Twin 1 Single (3 bdrm)
1 Ensuite

Warm Kiwi Hospitality, with itinerary help. Our rooms all have tv, electric blankets, a deck for sitting & relaxing in our garden. Laundry facilities. Just a few minutes away are shopping in the city, cafes, hot mineral pools, bush walks, water falls, beaches, volcanic mountain, fishing, golf, we have it all. We have Kayaks, therapeutic masseur, complimentary pick-up within city. Fresh coffee/tea & homemade biscuits are always available. Aileen & Lang would love to share some time with you. Contact us today.

Tauranga *B&B Homestay 2km W of Tauranga*

Christine Ross
8A Vale Street, Bureta, Tauranga
Tel (07) 576 8895   rossvale@xtra.co.nz
www.bnb.co.nz/ross.html
Double $80 Single $50 (Continental Breakfast)
(Full Breakfast)
1 Twin 1 Single (2 bdrm)
2 Private

Welcome. We are located close to town, with a golf course and licensed restaurants nearby and a park opposite. Twin room has every comfort and large private bathroom. The single guest room has own facilities and TV. You can enjoy our spacious lounge and sunny balcony, or take a short stroll to harbour edge. Your hostess Christine, is a miniaturist and doll maker and has travelled extensively and is enjoying retirement. Breakfast of your choice. Off street parking plus a garage. Will meet public transport.

Tauranga - Matua *B&B 6km N of Tauranga*

Christiansen's B&B
John Christiansen
210 Levers Road, Matua, Tauranga
Tel (07) 576 6835   Fax (07) 576 6464
Mob 021 766 835   christiansensbandb@clear.net.nz
www.bnb.co.nz/christiansensbb.html
Double $90 Single $60 (Full Breakfast)
Credit cards accepted
1 Queen 2 Single (2 bdrm)
1 Guests share

Our home in the pleasant suburb of Matua is set in a garden of NZ native trees, shrubs and ferns. The guest wing is quiet and comfortable. Please use our lounge and enjoy the garden. Our home is smoke-free. Can cater for food allergies. Close to harbour beaches and parks; seven minutes drive to Tauranga city centre and fifteen minutes to Mount Maunganui's Ocean Beach. Our interests include growing native plants, the performing arts and motorcycling.

Tauranga - Oropi   *Farmstay Homestay 9km S of Tauranga*

Grenofen
Jennie & Norm Reeve
85 Castles Road, Oropi, RD 3, Tauranga
Tel (07) 543 3953   Fax (07) 543 3951
n.reeve@wave.co.nz
www.bnb.co.nz/grenofen.html

Double $120   Single $80 (Full Breakfast)
Child by age Dinner $35
1 King 2 Single (2 bdrm)
2 Ensuite

We invite you to stay with us in our spacious home overlooking the countryside, sea, Tauranga city and Mt Maunganui. Our property is a sheltered 3 1/2 acres with trees, gardens and lawns. You may relax in quiet and privacy, enjoy the spa, or swim in our pool. both rooms have ensuite, electric blankets, TV, and comfortable chairs. Tea facility in guest area, laundry done overnight if required. We love to share our home and travel experiences with guests. Be sure of a warm welcome.

Tauranga - Bethlehem   *B&B 6km NW of Tauranga*

The Hollies
Shirley & Michael Creak
Westridge Drive, Bethlehem, Tauranga 3001
Tel (07) 577 9678   Fax (07) 579 1678
stay@hollies.co.nz
www.hollies.co.nz

Double $120-$250   Single $95-$165 (Full Breakfast)
Dinner $40 pp Credit cards accepted
2 King/Twin 1 Queen 2 Single (3 bdrm)
1 Ensuite 2 Private

Hollies, an elegant sophisticated modern country house, acre of gardens. Large luxuriously appointed rooms, panoramic views of gardens and rolling hills. The spacious suite has super king (or twin) bed, ensuite, lounge & TV, kitchenette, alternative private entrance and balcony. Hairdryers, bathrobes and toiletries. Fresh flowers, chocolates and crisp linen and every attention to detail combine to ensure your stay is truly memorable. Complimentary tea/coffee. Breakfast: home made bread, muffins, fresh fruit and tempting cooked dishes. Muffee our cat.   Children by arrangement.

Tauranga   *Homestay 6km N of Tauranga*

Matua Homestay
Anne & Peter Seaton
34 Tainui Street, Matua, Tauranga
Tel (07) 576 8083   Mob 0274 915 566
pa_seaton@clear.net.nz
www.bnb.co.nz/matuahomestay.html

Double $80   Single $50 (Continental Breakfast)
Child $25 Children welcome
1 Double 1 Twin (2 bdrm)
1 Guests share

Welcome to our quality one level well appointed home set in a peaceful garden, only 200 metres to the estuary beach. Enjoy a generous continental breakfast overlooking our picturesque garden. Tea, coffee, home baking, laundry facilities are available anytime. We have travelled extensively. Let us help you plan your sightseeing visits to local and regional places of interest . We look forward to offering you friendly Kiwi hospitality making your stay very special. Please phone for directions or the free pick up service from public transport.

Tauranga *B&B Homestay 3km N of Tauranga Central*

Harbinger House
Helen & Doug Fisher
209 Fraser Street, Tauranga
Tel (07) 578 8801 Fax (07) 579 4101
Mob 025 583 049   d-h.fisher@xtra.co.nz
www.harbinger.co.nz

Double $75-$90 Single $55-$70 (Special Breakfast)
 Child 1/2 price Dinner $25 Credit cards accepted
2 Queen 2 Single (3 bdrm)
1 Guests share

Harbinger House provides 'affordable luxury in the heart"%f Tauranga', being close to hospital, conference facilities, downtown and a new shopping mall 100m away. Our upstairs has been renovated with your comfort in mind, using quality furnishings, linen, bathrobes, fresh flowers, tea and coffee. A guest phone and laundry facilities are available. The queen rooms have separate vanities and private balconies. Breakfast is a gourmet event. We offer complimentary pick up from public transport depots and off street parking is available.

Tauranga *B&B Homestay 10km E of Tauranga*

Birch Haven
Judy & George McConnell
R403 Welcome Bay Road, RD 5, Tauranga
Tel (07) 544 2499 Mob 025 414 289
george.mcconnell@paradise.net.nz
www.bnb.co.nz/birchhaven.html

Double $80 Single $50
(Full Breakfast) Child $25 Dinner $25
1 King/Twin 1 Queen (2 bdrm)
1 Private 1 Host share

Luxurious, comfortable one-level 'home away from home' on 3 1/2 acres growing tamarillos and avocados. We enjoy meeting people, have travelled extensively and our interests include Blackie our cat, sport, reading, gardening, good food and wine. We offer a 3 course dinner option, swimming and spa pools, tour information and local courtesy pickup. Tauranga, Mt Maunganui, cafes and restaurants are a ten minute drive. Make us your base for day trips to Lake Taupo, Rotorua, Waitomo Caves or Coromandel Peninsula. Go sightseeing - have fun - return and relax!

Tauranga *B&B 0.5km SW of Tauranga*

Tauranga B&B
Jeanette & Buddy Craig
4 Ninth Avenue, Tauranga
Tel (07) 577 0927 Fax (07) 577 0954
Mob 025 297 1349 or 025 281 5649
www.bnb.co.nz/taurangabb.html

Double $85 Single $55 (Full Breakfast) Child $25
1 Queen (1 bdrm)
1 Ensuite

Welcome to our home within easy walking distance to the city's cafes, bars and restaurants. Guests may park inside, next to their room & ensuite with its own entry and court yard and are welcome to share our kitchen, lounge and laundry. A separate twin bedroom (upstairs) is available for your family but share your ensuite. Our home is pet and smoke free. We are across Devonport Road to Memorial Park which is on harbours edge. Our hobbies - motor caravaning and travel. Please, a phone call is essential.

Tauranga *B&B Homestay 12km S of Downtown Tauranga*

Floribunda
John & Sue Speirs
70 Gargan Road, RD 1, Tauranga
Tel (07) 543 0454   Fax (07) 543 0454
Mob 021 778 414   s.phillips@clear.net.nz
www.bnb.co.nz/floribunda.html
Double $95 Single $75 (Full Breakfast) Dinner $30pp
1 Queen (1 bdrm)
1 Private

A warm welcome awaits you at our elegant country home,
just 15 minutes from downtown Tauranga. Relax amongst the Bays' finest gardens, set on 5 acres with magnificent rural views. Enjoy tennis, swimming in Summer, the putting green, walking or cycling. Your room offers every facility to ensure your utmost in comfort. Restaurants, golf courses, beaches, wineries, shopping etc. all very close by.

Tauranga *B&B 3km S of Tauranga*

Fieldview 15th Avenue
Tui and Brian Henry
143c Fifteenth Ave, Tauranga,
Tel 07 579 0919
www.bnb.co.nz/bandbtauranga.html
Double $80 Single $60 (Continental Breakfast)
1 Double (1 bdrm)
1 Ensuite

Welcome to our modern, open plan townhouse, with off street parking, conveniently located close to CBD, restaurants, hospital, main highways. Our guest room, with ensuite, is on the ground floor. Join us for tea, coffee and home baking in our spacious lounge, or relax in the sunny open aspect of our courtyard. Cut lunches for travellers can be arranged. We look forward to welcoming you to our home, where your every comfort is our concern.

Tauranga *B&B Farmstay Self-contained 15km N of Tauranga*

Petersfield
Peter & Merle Bray
134 Whakamarama Road RD6, Whakamarama,
Tauranga
Tel (07) 552 5673   Fax (07)552 5673
Mob 025 273 4765   p&mbray@xtra.co.nz
www.petersfield.co.nz
Double $75 Single $45 (Continental Breakfast)
1 Queen 1 Single (1 bdrm)
1 Ensuite

A 50 acre farm, situated midway between Tauranga & Katikati with beautiful baywide views you will enjoy the peaceful countryside and warm hospitality. We farm Saler cattle, perendale sheep, mohair goats with horses a main priority! Handy to beaches, boat ramp, hot pools, wineries, good restaurants and golf course handy. A smoke free home, Rosie our border collie and Nike the tabby cat will welcome you.

Tauranga *B&B Self-contained 10km W of Tauranga*

The Lavender Patch Countrystay B & B
Mike & Pamela Mail
136 Kennedy Road, Pyes Pa RD 3, Tauranga
Tel (07) 543 2113 Fax (07) 543 2731
Mob 025 974259 mikemail@xtra.co.nz
www.bnb.co.nz/user131.html

Double $120 (Continental Breakfast)
Child $15 Dinner $30 pp Children welcome
1 Queen 1 Single (1 bdrm)
1 Ensuite 1 Private

Set amongst lavender and nestled on one acre, The Lavender Patch Countrystay Bed & Breakfast provides a charming self-catering spacious one-bedroom apartment plus lounge (with convertible divan) for guests, with fresh cotton bed linen scented with lavender. Set in a lovely cottage garden setting. 800 lavender plants are planted on the property and distilled for oil every Jan/Feb with lavender oil available for sale. Generous breakfast includes home-made muesli, yoghurt and preserves. We have one shy cat. Children welcome.

Tauranga *B&B Homestay 2km NW of Tauranga*

The Lazy Pukeko
Julie & Mark Bellette
61 Kulim Ave, Bureta, Tauranga
Tel (07) 576 3438 Fax (07) 576 3410
Mob 027 417 9607 lazypukeko@hotmail.com
www.bnb.co.nz/lazypukeko.html

Double $75 Single $50 (Continental Breakfast)
Child $25 (5-12 years)
1 Queen 1 Twin (2 bdrm)

The Lazy Pukeko is a sunny character home surrounded by gardens and 50 metres from the harbour's edge.We are very central to Tauranga's attractions, being minutes to Tauranga's marinas, Mt Maunganui surf beaches and central Tauranga shopping. We are a short stroll to Otumoetai golf course, Kulim Park ,walkways and restaurants. We offer two comfortable bedrooms with a guest bathroom, guest TV lounge, dining and off street parking.Barbecue and laundry facilities available.Pickup available.25% discount for 7 days and over.Pet; Swedish Vallhund.

Tauranga - Tauriko *B&B Self-contained 11km SW of Tauranga*

Wairoa Lodge
Wendy Broome
48 Redwood Lane, Tauriko RD 1, Tauranga
Tel (07) 543 4018 Fax (07) 543 4018
Mob 021 048 4520 broomes@clear.net.nz
www.bnb.co.nz/wairoa.html

Double $80 Single $50 (Continental Breakfast)
Child $15 Dinner $25 Children welcome
1 Double 1 Twin (2 bdrm)
1 Private

Nestled on the banks of the Wairoa River, Wairoa Lodge offers you 33 acres of peaceful seclusion just 12 minutes drive from downtown Tauranga. Enjoy local beaches, bush walks and sports facilities: swim, canoe, fish or simply relax and enjoy the view. We offer a self-contained unit with shower room and complimentary tea and coffee. Dinner by prior arrangement. Double bed is a foldout. We have two daughters and some curious beefies. Sorry no smokers.

Tauranga - Tauriko   *B&B Farmstay 10km SW of Tauranga*

Redwood Heights
Chrissy & Errol Jefferson
50 Redwood Lane, Tauriko RD1, Tauranga
Tel (07) 543 1116   Fax (07) 543 1742
Mob 027 417 2891   redwoodheights@value.net.nz
www.bnb.co.nz/redwoodheights.html
Double $95 Single $70 (Continental Breakfast)
Child $30 Dinner $25 Children welcome
1 King 2 Single (2 bdrm) 1 Guests share

Welcome to our 30-acre farm overlooking the Wairoa
River and home of our Belted Galloway Cattle, numerous animals and outside pets. Attractions include a swimming pool, spa pool, extensive gardens with ponds and waterfall, kayaking, fishing on the river and walks. Only five minutes to winery and restaurants, 12 minutes to downtown Tauranga. Guest lounge with tea/coffee etc, TV/video or join us and exchange travel experiences. Hospitality and your comfort is our priority. Come as a guest leave as a friend. No charge for children under two years. Cot available.

Tauranga   *B&B 10km SW of Tauranga*

Redwood Villa
Bridget & Rod Hill
17 Redwood Lane, Tauriko RD 1, Tauranga
Tel (07) 543 2880   Fax (07) 543 4780
redwoodvilla@xtra.co.nz
www.redwoodvilla.co.nz
Double $125 Redwood Suite, Walnut Room$85
(Continental Breakfast)
Candle lit dinner $35 Mouth-watering Full B/fast $15pp
2 Queen (2 bdrm)   1 Ensuite 1 Hosts share

Relax, enjoy, recharge amongst the ambience of the giant Redwood/Oak trees in our 100 year old villa. As the original Tauriko Trading Post (10kms from Tauranga) servicing the district at the turn of the last century, much of the yesteryear charm remains. If you are looking for a home away from home, want to be treated to something special, enjoy your own space, or are simply looking for a place to stay for a night or two, give us a call. Steffe our Schnauser will welcome you.

Mt Maunganui   *Homestay Self-contained   4km N of Mt Maunganui*

Homestay on the Beach
Bernie & Lolly Cotter
85C Oceanbeach Road, Mt Maunganui
Tel (07) 575 4879 Fax (07) 575 4828 Mob 025 766 799
bernie.cotter@xtra.co.nz
www.bnb.co.nz/.html
Double $130 Single $80 (Continental Breakfast)
Child negotiable $25pp extra guests Suite Double $160
Children welcome
2 Queen 1 Single (2 bdrm)
1 Ensuite 1 Private

Welcome to our magnificent home by the sea. Choose from our self-contained suite, sleeping 2 couples and 1 single (suitable for children) with private deck. 1 min to beach for those casual walks. Upstairs is our Queen ensuite with TV. Your continental breakfast includes eggs any style. International golf course 500 metres. The famous "Mount Walk" up or around with 360 degree views is breathtaking. 4kms are shops, hot salt water pools, and restaurants for your enjoyment. Sorry no pets. Off street parking. Look forward to having you stay.

Mt Maunganui   *Homestay Self-contained 7km S of Mt Maunganui*

Beachfront Homestay
Barbara Marsh
28A Sunbrae Grove, Mount Maunganui

Tel (07) 575 5592   Fax (07) 575 5592
Mob 021 707 243   barbmarsh1@hotmail.com
www.bnb.co.nz/beachfronthomestaymtmaunganui.html

Double $105 Single $75 (Continental Breakfast) Credit
cards accepted
1 Queen 2 Single (2 bdrm)
1 Guests share

Welcome to our absolute oceanfront Paradise, where you can relax in beautiful surroundings at one of the country's finest beaches. We are close to great restaurants, excellent shopping, bowls, golf and hot salt pools. We have one twin and one queen-sized bedroom, guest bathroom, lounge with kitchen facilities, TV etc. This unit is available to rent, also, at a separate rate. Undercover, off-street parking, laundry facilities offered, smoke-free home. Your well travelled hostess looks forward to meeting you.

Mt Maunganui   *Homestay Self-contained 3km S of Mt Maunganui*

Fairways
Philippa & John Davies
170 Ocean Beach Road, Mt. Maunganui

Tel (07) 575 5325   Fax (07) 578 2362
pipjohn@clear.net.nz
www.bnb.co.nz/fairways.html

Double $95 Single $75 (Full Breakfast)
Dinner incl. wine $35pp B/A Credit cards accepted
1 Queen 1 Double (2 bdrm)
1 Ensuite 1 Host share

A Golfer's paradise. Our comfortable, timbered, character home adjoins the 8th fairway of the Mount golf course, and is across the road from the wonderful ocean beach. Enjoy with us interesting food, wine, art, music, conversation, and a bonus golf lesson. John is a retired solicitor, teacher and former scratch golfer, and Pippa a registered nurse involved in natural health. Our leisurely dinners are fun occasions, and John's desserts legendary. We are well travelled both in New Zealand and abroad, and look forward to meeting you.

Mt Maunganui   *B&B 9km S of Mt Maunganui*

Pembroke House
Cathy & Graham Burgess
12 Santa Fe Key, Royal Palm Beach, Papamoa/
Mt Maunganui

Tel (07) 572 1000   PembrokeHouse@xtra.co.nz
www.bnb.co.nz/pembrokehouse.html

Double $90-$95 Single $70-$75 (Full Breakfast)
Child $35 Credit cards accepted
2 Queen 2 Single (3 bdrm)
2 Ensuite 1 Private

Welcome to our modern home. Cross the road to the Ocean Beach, where you can enjoy swimming, surfing and beach walks. Enjoy stunning sea-views while dining at breakfast. Near Palm Beach Shopping Plaza, restaurants and golf courses. Separate guest lounge with TV and tea-making facilities. Cathy is a primary school teacher and Graham semi-retired - your host. We are widely travelled and both enjoy meeting people. Our home is shared with a Persian cat - Crystal. (Not suitable for children under five years.)

Mt. Maunganui   *B&B Homestay 3km S of Mt. Maunganui*

Beachside
Lorraine & Jim Robertson
21B Oceanbeach Road, Mt Maunganui,

Tel (07) 574 0960   Mob 021 238 0598
jim.lorraine@ihug.co.nz
www.bnb.co.nz/beachsideocean.html

Double $90-$115 Single $75 (Full Breakfast)
1 King/Twin 2 Queen (3 bdrm)
1 Private

We are 30 seconds to NZ's most popular beach. Off-street parking & laundry facilities available. Courtesy transport from local airport, buses & information centre. Relax & enjoy great sea views from our 3rd storey lounge with tea & coffee making facilities or indulge with Jim's cappuccinos & smoothies. We are widely travelled, have a great sense of humour, and enjoy meeting people. We would love to share our modern comfortable home with you and help you to have a memorable stay in our beautiful locality.

Mt Maunganui - Papamoa   *B&B Homestay 9km SE of Mt Maunganui*

Hesford House
Sally & Derek Hesford
45 Gravatt Road, Royal Palm Beach,
Papamoa/Mt Maunganui

Tel (07) 572 2825   Mob 025 244 7021
derek.sally@clear.net.nz
www.bnb.co.nz/hesford.html

Double $85-$110 Single $45-$60
(Continental Breakfast) (Full Breakfast) Child $25
Dinner by arrangement Children welcome
2 Queen 1 Twin (3 bdrm)   1 Ensuite

We invite you to stay in our modern, architecturally designed character home. Our rooms are tastefully decorated with your comfort and pleasure being our priority. Enjoy panoramic views of the Papamoa Hills together with exquisite sunsets. A short stroll to the shopping plaza and through the lakes to the beach. Close to restaurants, cafes and popular tourist attractions. Relax in a beautiful outdoor garden setting. Courtesy pickup from public transport. Complimentary tea/coffee facilities and TVs in each room.

Te Puke   *B&B Self-contained 3km E of Te Puke*

Aotea Villa
Kay Allen
246 Te Matai Road, RD 8, Te Puke
Tel (07) 573 9433   Fax (07) 573 9463
Mob 027 270 6778 or 027 227 6240
kay2000@xtra.co.nz   www.aoteavilla.co.nz

Double $100 Single $80 (Full Breakfast) Child $30
Dinner $20 Children welcome
1 Queen 2 Double 1 Twin 1 Single (3 bdrm)
1 Ensuite

Welcome to our relaxing and comfortable character 1910 villa situated in the heart of the Bay of Plenty. Only five minutes from Te Puke, 40 minutes from Rotorua and Whakatane and 20 minutes from Tauranga and Mount Maunganui. Tranquil country setting, nestled between kiwi fruit and avocado orchards. Enjoy our spa and swimming pool, relax on our wide verandas and partake in our beautiful sunsets. Main house has double/twin bedrooms, guest lounge, ample parking. Bungalow - double/single beds with ensuite, tea/coffee facilities. Bookings preferred.

Te Puke   *Homestay 2km NW of Te Puke*

Lindenhof Homestay
Beth & Murray Allen
58 Dunlop Road, Te Puke,
Tel (07) 573 4592   Fax (07) 573 9392
Mob 025 339 405
lindenhofhomestay@wave.co.nz
www.bnb.co.nz/lindenhofhomestay.html

Double $120 Single $75 (Full Breakfast) Dinner $25
1 Queen 2 Single (2 bdrm)
1 Ensuite 1 Private

Lindenhof is an imposing building in the style of a
Georgian country home. You are able to indulge in affordable luxury. Te Puke is the heart of Kiwifruit
country. Close to town, semi rural. Tennis court, swimming pool, spa pool, billiard room, formal
lounge and dining room. No smoking in house. Not suitable for children. SH2 from Tauranga, Dunlop
Rd turns right by Gas Centre (international B/B sign) 1 km. Up Dunlop Rd on left.

Maketu Beach - Te Puke   *B&B   Sea View Unit*
8km E of Te Puke

Blue Tides Beachfront B&B/Homestay
Patricia Haine
7 Te Awhe Road, Maketu Beach, Bay of Plenty
Tel (07) 533 2023   0800 359 191   Fax (07) 533 2023
Mob 025 261 3077   info@bluetides.co.nz
www.bluetides.co.nz

Double $100-$145 Single $80 (Full Breakfast)
Dinner $25 - $35 S/C Unit $100 - $120 Pets welcome
2 King/Twin 2 Queen (4 bdrm)
4 Ensuite 1 Private

Tourism Award Winner 2002 Qualmark 3+ Enjoy an authentic NZ experience, "Stay Put" and visit
Rotorua and Tauranga 30 minutes, and exciting local tourist activities, shops and a choice of beaches.
Located on the water's edge in a multicultural village full of ancient history. Cafes and restaurants
nearby, amazing views, sunsets and night skies. Safe swimming and walks, warm and cozy year round.
Very relaxed with caring extras and genuine hospitality. Two resident cats.

Pukehina Beach   *Homestay 21km E of Te Puke*

Homestay on the Beach
Alison & Paul Carter
217 Pukehina Parade, Pukehina Beach, RD 9, Te Puke
Tel (07) 533 3988   Fax (07) 533 3988
Mob 025 276 7305   p.a.carter@pukehina-beach.co.nz
www.homestays.net.nz/pukehina.htm

Double $110 Single $70 (Continental Breakfast)
(Full Breakfast) Child 1/2 price Dinner $30 Unit $130
Credit cards accepted Children welcome
2 Double (2 bdrm)   1 Guests share

Welcome to our Absolute Beachfront Home situated on the Pacific Ocean. Your accommodation situated
downstairs, allowing complete privacy, if you so wish, includes, T.V. lounge with coffee/tea, fridge,
microwave and laundry facilities, also available at separate rate. Enjoy magnificent views from your
own sundeck, including White Island volcano and occasional visits from friendly dolphins. A Golf
course 13km. 30-40 minute drive from Tauranga, Mount Maunganui, Whakatane and Rotorua. A
licensed restaurant 2km, Surf Casting, Swimming walks or relax and enjoy our Unique Paradise.

Whakatane *Homestay 7km W of Whakatane*

Leaburn Homestay
Kathleen & Jim Law
237 Thornton Road, RD 4, Whakatane
Tel (07) 308 7487 or 308 7955 Fax (07) 308 7487
kath.law@theredbarn.co.nz
www.bnb.co.nz/leaburnhomestay.html

Double $70-$90 Single $40
(Full Breakfast) Dinner $25
Credit cards accepted
1 Queen 2 Single (2 bdrm)
1 Guests share

Whakatane is off the beaten tourist track, yet it is the centre for a wide range of activities. We can arrange sightseeing trips, including White Island and jet boat rides. We are handy to the Golf Links. Be as busy or as quiet as you like. Relax in peaceful surroundings in the homestead on our dairy farms, which are managed by our 50/50 sharemilker. No longer actively involved in dairy farming activities, we have a small citrus orchard and breed black and coloured sheep as well as managing the Red Barn Craftshop on our property. This is run in conjunction with the Tio Tio Cafe/Restaurant.
As 'young oldies', we enjoy bowls, Lions Club, genealogy and organic gardening. We no longer have domestic pets and as our family has fled we enjoy company. Our twin-bedded room is adjacent to a separate shower room and bathroom/toilet facilities. These facilities are only shared if other guests occupy the other queen-sized bedroom.

Guest's comments: "A wonderful warm bed and a yummy breakfast." Jay, Auckland. "Nice place, nice weather, great hosts." Uli, Germany. "We struck a winner; grateful thanks." Pat and Ray, Cornwall, England. "A wonderful stay and stimulation conversation." Judi, California, USA.

Whakatane   *Farmstay 18km S of Whakatane*

Omataroa Deer Farm
Jill & John Needham
Paul Road, RD 2, Whakatane
Tel (07) 322 8399   Fax (07) 322 8399
Mob 025 449 250   jill-needham@xtra.co.nz
www.bnb.co.nz/needham.html

Double $90 Single $60 (Continental Breakfast)
(Full Breakfast) Child $40 Dinner $25
1 King 1 Queen (2 bdrm)
1 Ensuite 1 Private

We invite you to stay with us in our contemporary home which sits high on a hill commanding panoramic views. We farm deer organically and grow Hydrangeas for export. You will be the only guest so you have sole use of a quiet private wing. Your evening meal will be 'special', venison - lamb or fresh seafood with home-grown vegetables. We dive, fish, tramp, ski, golf and love to travel. We have a friendly chocolate Labrador and a Burmese cat. Laundry available.

Whakatane   *Homestay Whakatane Central*

Travellers Rest
Karen & Jeff Winterson
28 Henderson Street, Whakatane 3080
Tel (07) 307 1015   Mob 025 276 6449
travrest@wave.co.nz
www.bnb.co.nz/travellersrest.html

Double $70-$80 Single $35-$40 (Continental Breakfast)
Credit cards accepted Children welcome Pets welcome
1 King/Twin 2 Single (2 bdrm)
1 Guests share

Needing Time Out? Join Jeff and Karen in their quiet home and garden beside the Whakatane River. Enjoy scenic river walks, rest in their garden, or visit the vibrant, local, art, craft, or garden trail. Take a short drive to Ohope beach, Hot Pools, River or Sea activities. Our Interests are: family, roses, gardening, photography, walking our dog, model cars, and stamp collecting. We look forward to sharing time with our guests, as does our friendly cat. Internet facility available.

Whakatane   *B&B Homestay Private Cottage 10km S of Whakatane*

Baker's
Lynne & Bruce Baker
40 Butler Road, RD 2, Whakatane
Tel (07) 307 0368   Fax (07) 307 0368
Mob 025 284 6996   bakers@world-net.co.nz
www.bakershomestay.co.nz

Double $100-$120 Single $75 (Continental Breakfast)
(Full Breakfast) Dinner $25 B/A S/C private cottage
1 King/Twin 2 Queen 2 Single (4 bdrm)
2 Ensuite 1 Private   Credit cards accepted

You will be sure of a friendly welcome to our lovely country home nestled amongst mature gardens, croquet lawn, swimming and spa pool to enjoy and relax in. Choose between our delightful fully self-contained two bedroom cottage or be pampered with bed and breakfast in our warm spacious home. Guest lounge has Sky TV, tea/coffee and treats. Lynne and Bruce are keen outdoor hosts enjoying fishing, surfing, gardening and travel. White Island tours, dolphin watching, deep-sea fishing and diving activities can be arranged for your memorable stay.

Whakatane *B&B Homestay Self-contained 1.5km S of Whakatane Post Office*

Crestwood Homestay
Janet & Peter McKechnie
2 Crestwood Rise, Whakatane, Bay of Plenty
Tel (07) 308 7554   0800 111 449   Fax (07) 308 7551
Mob 025 624 6248   pandjmckechnie@xtra.co.nz
www.bnb.co.nz/crestwood.html
Double $90-$110 Single $70-$90
(Continental Breakfast) Dinner $25 by arrangement
Credit cards accepted
1 Queen 2 Single (2 bdrm)   1 Private 1 Guests share

"Let's find someplace quiet tonight." A peaceful oasis located on a hillside just above Whakatane. Mesmerising sea, bush and island views from all rooms. Home baking and cuppa on arrival. Self contained,entire upstairs area includes comfortable beds, lounge, Internet, TV, kichenette,bathroom,separate toilet. Bathrobes,hairdryer and toiletries provided. Join us downstairs for a generous breakfast - time to share our local knowledge. Interests are trout and sea fishing, coastguard activities, travelling, Janet is learning German. Near wharf for White Island and dolphin excursions.

Whakatane *B&B Farmstay Separate/Suite 13 W of Whakatane*

Kanuka Cottage
Carol & Ian Boyd
880 Thornton Road, RD 4, Whakatane
Tel (07) 304 6001   Fax (07) 304 6001
Mob 021 883 684   kanuka1@xtra.co.nz
www.bnb.co.nz/kanukacottage.html
Double $80-$100 (Full Breakfast) Child $15
Dinner $25 B/A Credit cards accepted
1 King/Twin 1 Queen 3 Single (2 bdrm)
2 Ensuite

Enjoy expansive sea and active volcano views from our B&B and self-contained units. Set in 23 secluded acres of coastal kanuka with private access to sandy surf beach. Good surfcasting and kontiki fishing. White Island tours, deep-sea fishing, and other recreational activities arranged. Handy to golf courses. Large and interesting succulent, cacti and bromeliad gardens with plants for sale. Feed our friendly alpaca, highland cattle, goats, ducks and chickens. Sample our fresh vegetables, fruit and eggs organically produced on our property. We are on the Pacific Coast Highway.

Ohope Beach *B&B Homestay Self-contained 6km E of Whakatane*

Shiloah
Pat & Brian Tolley
27 Westend, Ohope Beach
Tel (07) 312 4401   Fax (07) 312 4401
www.bnb.co.nz/shiloah.html
Double $66-$80 Single $35-$45
(Full Breakfast)
Child 1/2 price
Dinner $18 - $25 by arrangement
S/C unit
1 Queen 1 Twin 4 Single (3 bdrm)
2 Private 1 Guests share

Homestay: Paradise on the beach - view White Island and enjoy our hospitality. Facilities available for disabled guests. Classic car enthusiasts - well travelled. Self contained unit 1 twin bedroom, 1 single bed with bed settee (2) if required. Tariff $30-$35 own bedding, $40-$45 supplied. Access to beach across road. Fishing, swimming, surfing, and bush walks.

Ohope Beach *Self-contained 8km Whakatane*

The Rafters
Pat Rafter
261A Pohutukawa Ave, Ohope Beach
Tel (07) 312 4856 Fax (07) 312 4856
The_Rafters_Ohope@xtra.co.nz
www.wave.co.nz/pages/macaulay/The_Rafters.htm

Double $80-$90 Single $75-$80
(Continental Breakfast) Dinner $30 - $45
Child $10 Children welcome Pets welcome
Smoking area inside
1 King 1 Single (2 bdrm)
1 Ensuite 1 Private

Panoramic sea views: White, Whale islands, East Coast. Safe swimming. Many interesting walks. Golf, tennis, bowls, all within minutes.
Licensed Chartered Club Restaurant opposite. Trips to volcanic White Island, fishing, jet boating, diving, swimming with dolphins arranged.
Full cooking facilities; private entrance, sunken garden, BBQ. Complimentary: tea, coffee, biscuits, fruit, newspaper, personal laundry service. By special arrangement, dinner with Host and his Weimaraner dog, Gazelle, in Library - dining room, $30 - $45, includes pre dinner drinks and wines.
Pat's interests are: philosophy, theology, history, English literature, the making of grape wines and all spirits, golf, bowls, music and tramping. I have a friendly Weimaraner dog. Courtesy car available. House trained animals welcomed.
Three restaurants and Oyster farm within 5 minutes drive. I look forward to your company and assure you unique hospitality.

Directions:
On reaching Ohope Beach turn right, proceed 2 km to 261a (beach-side) name "Rafters" on a brick letterbox with illuminated B&B sign.

Ohope Beach *B&B 5km SE of Whakatane*

Turneys Bed & Breakfast
Marilyn & Em Turney
28 Pohutukawa Ave, Ohope Beach

Tel (07) 312 5040   0800 266 269   Fax (07) 312 5040
Mob 025 960 894
turneys@xtra.co.nz
www.turneys.co.nz

Double $120-$150 Single $100 (Continental Breakfast)
Dinner by arrangement
1 King 1 Queen (2 bdrm)
2 Ensuite

Base yourselves with us and 'day trip', erupting White Island or Rotorua, fishing or golfing, to mention a few activites available. We offer luxury, multi-level accommodation, opposite a safe beach, cafe and shops. Treat yourself to the special 'Blue' room with its private deck overlooking the ocean, or the 'Garden' room. Both are spacious and tasteful with all amenities, and with little extras which make it so special. Come and share all we have to offer - you won't be disappointed.

Ohope Beach *B&B Homestay Self-contained 8km SE of Whakatane*

Oceanspray Homestay
Frances & John Galbraith
283A Pohutukawa Avenue, Ohope, Bay of Plenty

Tel (07) 312 4112   Mob 027 286 6824
frances@oceanspray.co.nz
www.bnb.co.nz/oceansprayhomestay.html

Double $100-$120 Single $60-$80 (Special Breakfast)
Child neg Children welcome
3 Queen 4 Twin (5 bdrm)
2 Private

Panoramic views and a warm welcome greet you at Oceanspray Homestay - a beachfront property with upstairs views to White Island, also East Cape. Our downstairs separate unit within our home has three attractively furnished bedrooms, lounge/kitchen. Adjacent to our house, a two bedroom, modern, self-contained cosy cottage. Home comforts - Sky TV,videos/toys for children. Special breakfasts - homemade bread, preserved fruits. John's pursuits are kayaking/longline fishing; Frances enjoys entertaining/ providing excellent cuisine. Our cat and Labrador dog also make you welcome.

Ohope Beach *Self-contained 9.5km E of Whakatane*

Beach Rest
Margaret Green
48 Ocean Road, Ohope, Whakatane

Tel (07) 312 4508   margg@xtra.co.nz
www.bnb.co.nz/beachrest.html

Double $90-$110 Single $60-$80 (Full Breakfast)
Child $40-$60
Children welcome
1 King/Twin 1 Single (1 bdrm)
1 Private

Relax in my large, bright, comfortable, fully self-contained ground floor studio unit across the road from Ohope Beach. Base yourself here while you enjoy the attractions of this exciting area. I work full time, but I will enjoy meeting you and sharing my attractive home and warm hospitality. I have been an active tramper in this area and now enjoy biking, reading, talking and relaxing. All breakfast ingredients are provided. There are restaurants and very good take-aways available nearby.

Ohope Beach *B&B Self-contained 10km Whakatane*

Tawai House
Audrey & Ray Butler
13 Tawai Street, Ohope Beach 3085,

Tel (07) 312 4332
www.bnb.co.nz/tawai.html

Double $85 Single $60
(Continental Breakfast)
1 Double 2 Single (2 bdrm)
1 Private

Our home is situated 100 metres from the ocean beach, swimming and surfing. Ray an experienced fisherman will enjoy taking you fishing. You may enjoy a game of snooker with us and enjoy our views. Only minutes from the Chartered Club, restaurants, golf, bowls and bush walks. Directions: Tawai Street left off Harbour Road.

Opotiki *B&B Farmstay Self-contained 18km E of Opotiki*

Coral's B&B
Coral Parkinson
Morice's Bay, Highway 35, RD 1, Opotiki

Tel (07) 315 8052 Fax (07) 315 8052
Mob 021 299 9757 coralsb.b@wxc.net.nz
www.bnb.co.nz/coralsbb.html

Double $90-$130 Single $52-$65
(Continental Breakfast) Child $10 Dinner $25
Children welcome Pets welcome
2 Queen 1 Double 2 Single (3 bdrm) 2 Private

We provide two self-contained accommodation options located on our hobby farm. As well as pets and farm animals we collect varied memorabilia. Enjoy the beach and bird life; swim at nearby sandy beach. Fish, ramble over the rocks, explore caves. The two storied cottage features lead-light windows, native timbers, large decks look out across the bay and native bush. The mews has separate bedroom, large lounge, all on one level. Three golf courses within an hours drive; covered packing, homemade bread and preserves.

Opotiki - Maraenui *B&B Farmstay Self-contained 40km E of Opotiki*

Oariki Farm House
Chris Stone
Maraenui Beach/Houpoto, Box 486, Opotiki

Tel (07) 325 2678 Fax (07) 325 2678
Mob 025 531 678 oariki@clear.net.nz
www.bnb.co.nz/oarikifarmhouse.html

Double $100 Single $50 (Full Breakfast) Child $25
Dinner $30 S/C Cottage $90 - $130
Credit cards accepted Children welcome Pets welcome
1 King 2 Queen 1 Double 1 Single (3 bdrm)
1 Ensuite 1 Private 1 Guests share

Nestled in bush on a secluded coastal farmlet near the mouth of the Motu River, Oariki Farmhouse offers farmhouse accommodation, bed and breakfast, or a two bedroom self contained cottage with kitchen. Our farmlet grows organic produce ,often we have fresh fish or mussels. Our dog will take you on beach walks, and our cat escorts you fishing! The perfect place to relax for a few days in peaceful surroundings. Sleep to the sound of the ocean , wake to the sound of the birds. Some maps show Maraenui as Houpoto. Directions are essential.

www.beachholidayhomenewzeala

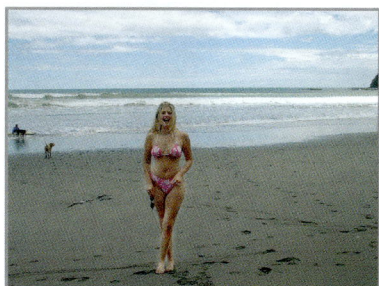

Opotiki - Tirohanga Be

Tirohanga Beach Holiday Home
jaffarian@xtra.co.nz

Natalie & Jeff Jaffarian
P.O. Box 186 (#787 State Highway 35E), Opotiki,
Tel (07) 315 8899   Fax (07) 315 8896
Mob 027 412 6411

Two Self-contained units, 7km East of Opotiki

Top Unit: One Double room and a Single room

Bottom Unit: One Queen room and a Twin room

Each Unit has a tub shower bath, full kitchen with fridge, stove, microwave, kettle, and utensils. Barbecue, washing machine, internet access and telephone may be available.

Double $90, Additional $45 each, Special Weekly and monthly rates available. Dinner by arrangement $25 per person.

Tirohanga Beach Holiday Home is an ideal get-away for all seasons. Magnificent ocean view right from your bed! Beautiful beach extends for miles in each direction. Swimming, surfing, fishing, beach walking at your doorsteps. Enjoy breathtaking sun-rises and sun-sets from the large deck overlooking White and Whale Islands.

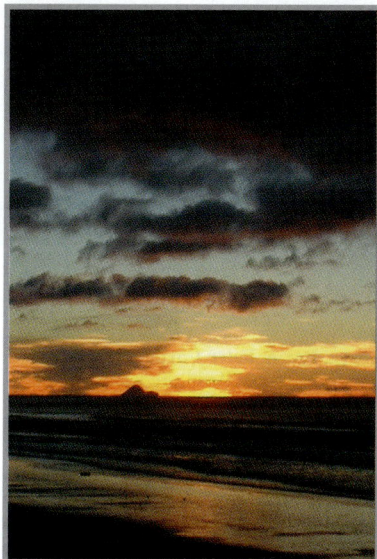

> **We offer everything you need to relax and enjoy your holiday**

Opotiki - Te Kaha   *B&B Lodge 66km E of Opotiki*

Tui Lodge
Joyce, Rex & Peter Carpenter
201 Copenhagen Road, Te Kaha, BOP 3093
Tel (07) 325 2922   Fax (07) 325 2922
jorex@xtra.co.nz   www.bnb.co.nz/tuilodge.html
Double $100-$130 Single $75-$95 Child $30
(Full Breakfast) Dinner $30pp
Credit cards accepted
4 Queen 1 Twin 4 Single (6 bdrm)
3 Ensuite 1 Private

Set in three acres of gardens Tui Lodge offers comfort and tranquillity without equal on 'the coast'. Purpose built in 1998 the lodge is in complete harmony with out native bush surrounds while affording views of volcanic While Island and the Pacific Ocean. Joyce's meals almost exclusively feature naturally grown fruit and vegetables from our own gardens. We are situated a short walk from Maungaroa Beach and can arrange fishing, horse treks, tramping, jet boating or four wheel drive excursions.

From our visitor's book: The lodge is a dream, I could stay for life. *Horst Kersten, Germany.*
Wonderful, the best hosts we have ever had. *Shirley & Stan King, Auckland.*
We'll never forget your warm hospitality; we'll be back again one day. *Balleraud family, Noumea.*
We were so lucky to find you, a wonderful stay in a glorious setting. *Pat & Jim Roy Bucks, UK.*
The best example of Kiwi hospitality ever. *Derek Henderson, Sydney.*
Beautiful gardens, even better food and great hosts. *Kitty & Paul Brennan, Ireland.*
What a paradise, how wonderful our time here has been. *Karen & Bill Lillibridge, USA.*
Can we stay forever in this little bit of paradise? *Nell & Ron Reid, Rotorua.*
Absolutely unique, great food and great people. *Marie & Jakob Lundberg, Sweden.*
We'll come back again, hospitality you can only dream about. *Corry & Peter van Meggelen, Holland.*

Opotiki   *Homestay 11km W of Opotiki*

Fantail Cottage
Meg & Mike Collins
318 Ohiwa Harbour Road, RD 2, Opotiki
Tel (07) 315 4981   0800 153 553   Fax (07) 315 4981
wendylyn@wave.co.nz
www.bnb.co.nz/fantailcottage.html

Double $85 Single $50 (Full Breakfast)
Dinner $25 pp
1 Twin (1 bdrm)
1 Ensuite

Set on a sunny bush-clad spur, your room and hot spa have breathtaking views overlooking Tern Island (see photo), Ohiwa Spit and the open sea out to Whale Island. Meg and Mike have travelled widely overseas and enjoy cooking with homegrown organic produce. 34km from Whakatane and 11km from Opotiki, this is a great place to relax, bird-watch, fish, walk and swim. From Whakatane turn left on SH2 at Waiotahi Bridge. Follow signs to Ohiwa Holiday Camp and Fantail Cottage.

Opotiki - Te Kaha   *B&B Self-contained 1hr N of Opotiki*

Waikawa B&B
Bev & Kev Hamlin
7541 State Highway 35, RD 3, Opotiki
Tel (07) 325 2070   Fax (07) 325 2070
waikawa.bnb@xtra.co.nz
www.bnb.co.nz/waikawabb.html

Double $85-$90 Single $60 (Continental Breakfast)
Child 1/2 price under 12 Dinner $25 Self-contained $90
Credit cards accepted Pets welcome
1 King/Twin 2 Queen (3 bdrm)
3 Ensuite

Welcome to Waikawa Bed & Breakfast. 200 metres down driveway off State Highway 35. Our dwelling is on the water's edge facing north in tranquil surroundings. The west views, spectacular seascapes and stunning sunsets with White Island guarding on the horizon. Our detached guest rooms have ensuites, TV, fridge, tea and coffee facilities. Stroll the 2 acre property and enjoy the farm yard animals. We also have a cat and small dog. We have fresh organic fruit and vegetables in season.

Opotiki - Waihau Bay   *B&B Homestay Self-contained 112km N of Opotiki*

Waihau Bay Homestay
Noelene & Merv Topia
RD 3, Opotiki
Tel (07) 325 3674   0800 240 170   Fax (07) 325 3679
Mob 025 674 2157   n.topia@clear.net.nz
www.nzhomestay.co.nz/topia.html

Double $85-$100 Single $55-$75 (Continental Full Breakfast) Child 1/2 price Dinner $25
Credit cards accepted Pets welcome
1 King/Twin 1 King 1 Queen 2 Twin (4 bdrm)
2 Ensuite 2 Private 1 Guests share

Surrounded by unspoiled beauty we invite you to come and enjoy magnificent views, stunning sunsets, swim, go diving, kayaking (we have kayaks) or just walk along the sandy beach. You are most welcome to join Merv when he checks his craypots each morning and his catches are our cuisine specialty. Fishing trips, horse treks and guided cultural walks are also available. We have two self-contained units with disabled facilities, and a double room with ensuite. Our cat Whiskey, and dog Meg enjoy making new friends.

Rotorua - Ngongotaha   *Farmstay Self-contained 17km N of Rotorua*

Deer Pine Lodge
John Insch
255 Jackson Road, Ngongotaha, Rotorua
Tel (07) 332 3458 Fax (07) 332 3458
Mob 025 261 9965 deerpine@clear.net.nz
www.bnb.co.nz/deerpinelodge.html

Double $85-$100 Single $70-$85 Child $20 - $25
(Continental Breakfast) Dinner $30 B/A
Credit cards accepted
3 King 1 Queen 4 Single (5 bdrm)
5 Ensuite

Welcome to Deer Pine Lodge. We farm deer, our property surrounded with trees planted by the New Zealand Forest Research as experimental shelter belts on our accredited deer farm.
The nearby city of Rotorua is fast becoming New Zealand's most popular tourist destination offering all sorts of entertainment. We have a cat and a Boxer (Jake), very gentle. Our four children have grown up and left the nest.
Our bed/breakfast units are private, own bathroom, TV, radio, fridge, microwave, electric blankets all beds, coffee/tea making facilities, heaters. Heaters and hair dryers also in all bathrooms.
Our two bedroom fully self contained units, designed by prominent Rotorua architect Gerald Stock, each having private balcony, carport, sundeck, ensuite, spacious lounge, kitchen, also laundry facilities, TV, radio, heater etc. Cot and highchair available. Security arms fitted on all windows, smoke detectors installed in all bedrooms and lounges, fire extinguisher installed in all kitchens.
Holding NZ certificate in food hygiene ensuring high standards of food preparation and serving. Guests are free to do the conducted tour and observe the different species of deer and get first hand knowledge of all aspects of deer farming after breakfast. If interested please inform host on arrival. Three course meal of beef, lamb, or venison by prior arrangement, pre dinner drinks.
Hosts John and Betty, originally from Scotland have travelled extensively overseas and have many years experience in hosting look forward to your stay with us. Prefer guests to smoke outside.

Three course meal of beef, lamb, or venison.

Rotorua   *Homestay 2km Rotorua centre*

Rotorua Lakeside Homestay
Ursula & Lindsay Prince
3 Raukura Place, Rotorua

Tel (07) 347 0140
Freephone 0800 223 624
Fax (07) 347 0107
the-princes@xtra.co.nz
www.bnb.co.nz/
rotorualakesidehomestay.html

Double $85-$100 Single $65-$75
Minimum stay 2 nights.
Discount for 3 or more nights
PLEASE TELEPHONE TO
CONFIRM VACANCY

(Special Breakfast)
1 King/Twin 1 Queen (2 bdrm)
1 Ensuite 1 Private

You can be sure of a warm welcome when you decide to stay with us at our spacious modern home right at the lakefront in Rotorua. Quiet and secluded, yet only five minutes by car from the city centre, our house is ideally situated for easy access to visitor's activities. You will find both guestrooms spacious and well appointed; with electric blankets at the cooler time of year.

While staying with us, take time to relax on the deck, as you view the tranquil lake and mountain scene; watch the waterbirds. Have fun as you make free use of our Canadian canoe. We have enjoyed sharing our home with guests from all over the world since 1988, we hope the informal atmosphere will give you too the feeling of being with friends. Your breakfast, consisting of a platter of fresh fruit, orange juice, home-made jams and preserves and a variety of cereals, is followed by toast and home-made muffins with tea or coffee. Conversations over breakfast often prove to be a highlight for both guests and hosts.

We will help you make the most of your stay in Rotorua, feel free to use our extensive range of maps and guide books.

We will be happy to arrange you local bookings. The highlight of your stay could be an evening spent learning about Maori culture and customs, as well as being treated to a delicious meal - the HANGI. If at all possible, allow yourself two full days to explore New Zealand's Volcanic Wonderland

We are an active, retired couple, enjoying life with all its challenges. We take an interest in local and international affairs, have travelled and lived overseas and are very concerned about environmental issues. We love the outdoors and are still active in canoeing, swimming, fishing, cycling, walking and camping. Being non-smokers, we thank you for not smoking in the house.

HOW TO FIND US
From Lake Road turn into Bennetts Road, then first left into Koutu Road, then first right into Karenga Street. Turn RIGHT into Haumona Street, a left turn at the end brings you down Raukura Place to our door.

Rotorua *Farmstay 4km SW of Rotorua*

Hunts Farm
Maureen and John Hunt
363 Pukehangi Road, Rotorua
Tel (07) 348 1352
www.bnb.co.nz/hunt.html

Double $100 Single $70
(Full Breakfast) Child $25
1 King/Twin 1 Queen 2 Single (2 bdrm)
2 Ensuite

Come rest awhile with us in our new home as we help
you plan your itinerary and book your local tours. Explore
our farm of 150 acres, running beef and deer, by foot or farm vehicle. Now our children have flown,
Tigger, our trusty farm dog who lives in the garden is our chief helper. The views are magical. 360
degrees of lake, island, forest, city and farm land. Guest area has private entrance; lounge with tea,
coffee making facilities, TV, fridge and laundry available. Two triple rooms, each with ensuite lead out
to sunny private terraces.

Rotorua *B&B Homestay 4km S of Rotorua*

Serendipity Homestay
Kate & Brian Gore
3 Kerswell Terrace, Tihi-o-Tonga, Rotorua
Tel (07) 347 9385   Mob 025 609 3268
b.gore@clear.net.nz
www.bnb.co.nz/serendipityrotorua.html

Double $100-$110 Single $65 (Full Breakfast)
Child $30 Dinner $30 by arrangement
Credit cards accepted Children welcome
1 Double 2 Twin (2 bdrm)
1 Private

Marvel - at unsurpassed views of geysers, city, lakes and beyond. Relax - in all day sun, on the deck, in
the conservatory or in the privacy of our garden. Indulge - in comfort, home cooked cuisine and the
friendly folk who have been enjoying hosting for many years. Our interests are, golf, tramping, travel,
antiques and sharing our extensive local and national knowledge with you. Let us advise you on the
'must see' list while in Rotorua and other highlights of our beautiful country. Welcome!

Rotorua *B&B Homestay Separate/Suite 1.5km S of Rotorua*

Heather's Homestay
Heather Radford
5A Marguerita Street, Rotorua
Tel (07) 349 4303   Mob 027 289 3059
heathermr@xtra.co.nz
www.bnb.co.nz/heathershomestay.html

Double $80 Single $50
(Full Breakfast)
Credit cards accepted Children welcome
2 Queen 1 Twin (2 bdrm)
2 Private

Haeremai - Welcome to my comfortable home in the heart of the thermal area, minutes from the city
centre yet quiet and private. Rotorua born and bred I am proud of my city and enjoy sharing what
knowledge I have with guests. A keen tramper/walker, I also enjoy showing off the lovely walks in the
area. For ten years I have been a B&B host and look forward to many more visitors to my home and
unique city. Directions - off Fenton Street.

Rotorua - Ngongotaha *Homestay Lakestay 10km N of Rotorua*

Waiteti Lakeside Lodge
Val & Brian Blewett
2 Arnold Street, Ngongotaha, Rotorua
Tel (07) 357 2311 Fax (07) 357 2311 Mob 025 615 6923
waitetilodge@xtra.co.nz
www.waitetilodge.co.nz

Double $145-$210 Single $135-$200 (Full Breakfast)
Child $35 10 & over multiple-night rates available Credit cards accepted
4 Queen 2 Single (5 bdrm)
3 Ensuite 1 Private 2 Guests share

Waiteti Lakeside Lodge is situated on the shores of Lake Rotorua at the mouth of the picturesque Waiteti Trout Stream, away from the sulphur fumes and traffic noise of Rotorua City but close to all of Rotorua's attractions, fine restaurants, and Maori culture. The timber and natural stone lodge offers luxury private accommodation in traditional style and an extremely quiet and tranquil setting.

There are five supremely comfortable bedrooms, three with ensuites, one private or two sharing a bathroom. The ensuite rooms have TVs and open on to balconies overlooking the lake, and in addition there is a private guests' lounge with satellite TV, video, library, pool table, and tea and coffee facilities. All rooms enjoy spectacular views of the lake and stream mouth, and the lodge's gardens extend to the water's edge, home to numerous native birds and waterfowl.

Enjoy trout fishing (with or without professional guide) from the lodge's grounds, on the lake in the lodge's own charter boat, or on one of the many productive local trout streams - your catch can be fresh smoked for a superb breakfast or lunch treat.

Alternatively you may prefer to take a guided boat trip to historic Mokoia Island, a sacred Maori site and wildlife sanctuary, where native flora and birdlife, including several rare and endangered species, abound.

Your experienced hosts Brian and Val Blewett are available to advise and/or guide you at all times to ensure that your stay is highly enjoyable. Brian is a professional fishing guide with more than 30 years experience, so success is virtually guaranteed.

Brian and Val will arrange bookings for all local attractions and activities including:
- Rotorua's best cafes and restaurants
- six golf courses
- white water rafting
- forest walks
- float plane trips from the lodge
- maori culture and entertainment
- back country/wilderness trout fishing
- canoeing
- mountain biking

Directions: Take Highway 5 from Rotorua to Ngongotaha, through town centre, over the railway line, turn 2nd right into Waiteti Road. At the end turn right into Arnold Street and the lodge is at the end of the street next to the footbridge.

Rotorua *B&B Homestay Self-contained 5km SE of Rotorua*

Walker Homestay & B&B
Colleen & Isaac Walker
13 Glenfield Road, Owhata, Rotorua
Tel (07) 345 3882 Fax (07) 345 3856
Mob 025 289 5003 colleen.walker@clear.net.nz
www.bnb.co.nz/walkerhomestay.html
Double $70-$75 Single $40-$45 (Continental Breakfast)
Child 1/2 price Dinner by arrangement Extra adult $15
Credit cards accepted Children welcome
2 Double 1 Twin 1 Single (3 bdrm) 1 Ensuite 1 Private

The cottage, situated in its own garden area has one double and one twin bedroom, lounge, kitchen, bathroom and laundry. Room in the house has one double; one single bed; ensuite; tea/coffee facilities; microwave; separate entrance as well as access to hosts living area. Have complete privacy or be one of the family. Colleen is a Technical Institute tutor and Ike is a NZ Maori, a keen fisherman, golfer and tour guide with a background of farming and the paper industry. Two friendly little dogs will welcome you. Off road parking. 24 hours notice if evening meal required.

Rotorua *B&B 14km E. of Rotorua*

Joy & Lin Cathcart
99 Brunswick Drive, RD 4, Rotorua 3221
Tel (07) 350 1472 Fax (07) 350 1472
joylin@clear.net.nz
www.bnb.co.nz/cathcart.html
Double $90 Single $50 (Full Breakfast)
Dinner B/A
1 King (1 bdrm)
1 Private

Having retired from dairy farming, we once again welcome guests to our new home on a 2 acre section in a quiet life-style sub- division overlooking Lake Rotorua. We are 15 minutes from Rotorua city centre and five minutes from Rotorua Airport. Our interests include gardening, golf, bridge and family. The guest room has TV and tea making facilities. We are non-smoking and have no pets. Sorry no children under 12 years. We look forward to your stay.

Rotorua *B&B Homestay 3km W of Rotorua*

West Brook
Judy & Brian Bain
378 Malfroy Road, Rotorua
Tel (07) 347 8073 Fax (07) 347 8073
www.bnb.co.nz/westbrook.html
Double $70 Single $45 (Continental Breakfast)
Child under 12 half price Dinner $25
Children welcome
4 Single (2 bdrm)
1 Host share

Retired farmers with years of hospitality involvement, live 3km from city on Western outskirts. Interests include meeting people, farming, international current affairs. Brian a Rotorua Host Lions member, Judy's interest extend to all aspects of homemaking and gardening. Both well appointed comfy guest rooms are equipped with electric blankets. The friendly front door welcome and chatter over the meal table add up to our motto "Home away from Home". Assistance with sightseeing planning and transport to and from tourist centre available.

Rotorua - Ngongotaha *B&B Homestay 10km N of Rotorua*

Alrae's Lake View Retreat
Raema & Alf Owen
124 Leonard Road, PO Box 14, Ngongotaha
Tel (07) 357 4913   0800 RAEMAS   Fax (07) 357 4513
Mob 025 275 0113   relax@alraes.co.nz
www.alraes.co.nz
Double $105-$160 Single $130-$80 (Special Breakfast)
Dinner $40 Credit cards accepted
1 King/Twin 1 Queen 1 Double (3 bdrm)
1 Ensuite 1 Private 1 Guests share

Raema & Alf welcome you to their friendly relaxing Bed & Breakfast where your comfort is our priority. There are a variety of animals on the two areas. 10 minutes to Rotorua city, restaurants, golf - five minutes to major tourist attractions. Walking distance to Lake Rotorua and trout stream. Enjoy a special breakfast in the conservatory overlooking the stunning million dollar views. Quality accommodation, comfortable beds, guest lounge, laundry, tea/coffee, fridge and many extras will make an ideal base to explore the Bay of Plenty. The home is available for extended periods of the year by negotiation.

Rotorua City *B&B Homestay 100m N of Tourism Centre*

Inner City Homestay
Susan & Irvine Munro
1126 Whakaue Street, Rotorua
Tel (07) 348 8594   Fax (07) 348 8594
Mob 025 359 923   innercityhomestay@yahoo.com
www.bnb.co.nz/innercityhomestay.html
Double $85 Single $50 (Full Breakfast) Child $30
Children welcome
1 Double 2 Single (2 bdrm)
1 Guests share

"Innercity Homestay", 1126 Whakaue Street, the most central bed and breakfast/homestay in Rotorua. In the central city close to major tourist attractions and Lake Rotorua. Comfortable home with two guest bedrooms, thermally heated (pool also available). Cooked or continental breakfasts with special diets catered for. Most restaurants, cafes and tourism centre are within a short walking distance. Buses met at tourism centre. We are happy to make reservations for tours, Maori hangi, and concerts. Laundry service available. We welcome your enquiries.

Rotorua *B&B Homestay 3km S of Rotorua*

Thermal Stay
Wendy & Rod Davenhill
367 Old Taupo Road, Rotorua
Tel (07) 349 1605   Fax (07) 349 1641
Mob 025 377 122
davenhill@clear.net.nz   www.thermalstay.co.nz
Double $95-$120 Single $65 (Full Breakfast) Child 1/2
price under 12yrs Dinner $30pp by arrangement
1 King 2 Queen 2 Single (3 bdrm) Credit cards accepted
1 Private 2 Guests share 1 Host share

"An Oasis In The City" (Scene Lifestyle magazine) Quiet, central, private. Thermally heated home and swimming pool, spa in winter. Tranquil gardens featuring waterfall, fish and native birdlife. Walking distance to city centre, thermal activities, forests and golf courses. Well travelled hosts who enjoy good food, wine and conversation. Our company, or time in the guest lounge with private patio. Dine with us or sample one of our many restaurants or Maori hangi/concerts. Off road parking, table tennis. Laundry, e-mail and fax available. Pet - Candy, a very friendly tabby cat. Discounts for multiple nights.

Rotorua *B&B Farmstay Homestay 15km N of Rotorua*

Panorama Country Homestay
Dave Perry & Chris King
144 Fryer Road, Hamurana, Rotorua
Tel (07) 332 2618   0800 303 703   Fax (07) 332 2618
Mob 021 610 949   panorama@wave.co.nz
www.bnb.co.nz/panoramacountryhomestay.html
Double $145-$170   Single $100-$110   (Continental
Full Breakfast) Child $50 Dinner $50 Credit cards accepted
Children welcome
1 King/Twin 1 King 1 Queen 1 Double 1 Twin 1 Single (3 bdrm)   2 Ensuite 1 Private

This is an ideal base to stay whilst visiting Rotorua. The architecturally designed cedar and brick home takes full advantage of the panoramic views of Lake Rotorua and surrounding countryside, away from the sulphur smells of Rotorua. All bedrooms have ensuites or private bathroom with heaters, toiletries, hair dryers and heated towel rails. Play tennis or relax in the heated jaccuzi, or go for walks to Hamurana Springs, or Redwood Forest. Five golf courses and fishing close by. There are friendly sheep and working dogs. Dinner is available. Discount for over two nights.

Rotorua *B&B Homestay 4km W of Rotorua City Centre*

The Towers Homestay
Doreen & Des Towers
373 Malfroy Road, Rotorua
Tel (07) 347 6254 0800 261 040 ddtowers@clear.net.nz
www.mist.co.uk/homestaynz/
Double $80 Single $45 (Continental Breakfast)
Child $25, 12 & under Dinner $25 by arrangement
Credit cards accepted Children welcome
1 Double 1 Twin (2 bdrm)
1 Private

Welcome to our elevated smoke free home with views over Rotorua. We really enjoy home hosting, and our lifestyle enables us to spend time (as required) with our guests. Guest bedrooms/bathroom downstairs. Breakfast is served upstairs in our spacious lounge. We offer free Public Transport pickup. Off street parking and laundry available. Des has many years experience with a national organisation providing both local and NZ touring information. Doreen, originally from South Wales, likes gardening and reading, and enjoys meeting people. We host only one party at a time.

Rotorua *B&B Farmstay Homestay Country Homestay 12km NE of Rotorua*

Eucalyptus Tree Country Homestay
Manfred & Is Fischer
66 State Highway 33, RD 4, Rotorua
Tel (07) 345 5325   Fax (07) 345 5325
Mob 025 261 6142
euc.countryhome@actrix.co.nz
users.actrix.co.nz/euc.countryhome
Double $90 Single $60 (Full Breakfast) Dinner $25
1 King/Twin 2 Queen 1 Double (3 bdrm)
1 Guests share 1 Host share

Welcome to our quiet, smokefree, high quality country home. On our small farm near Lake Rotorua, close to Lake Rotoiti and Okataina, we have a donkey, calves, sheep, chickens, rabbits, bees, organic vegetables and fruit trees. Native bush drive to clear trophy trout fishing lakes and bush walks, thermal area, Maori culture, Hotpools, horseriding, skydiving, whitewater rafting. Our hobbies are troutfishing from boat, and fly fishing in lakes and rivers, hunting and shooting. We lived in the USA, Canada, Indonesia, Mexico and Germany and speak their languages.

Rotorua - Ngongotaha *B&B Farmstay 17km N of Rotorua*

Clover Downs Estate - Separate/Suite

Lyn & Lloyd Ferris

175 Jackson Road, RD 2, Ngongotaha

Tel (07) 332 2366   0800 3687 5323

Fax (07) 332 2367   Mob 021 712 866

Reservations@cloverdowns.co.nz

www.cloverdowns.co.nz

Double $185-$250 Single $170-$235

(Special Breakfast) Credit cards accepted

Children welcome   Child neg

3 King/Twin 1 King (4 bdrm)

4 Ensuite

For the discerning, a place to unwind and rediscover the simple pleasures in life. Magnificent Deer & Ostrich farm retreat set amidst 35 acres of green pasture, only 15 minutes drive north from Rotorua city centre.

We can offer you the Governor's Suite, or one of our three beautifully appointed spacious guestrooms, complete with ensuite bathrooms. Each room is equipped with tea & coffee facilities, refrigerator, TV, video. Rooms are serviced daily and there are laundry facilities available.

After a sumptuous breakfast, join Lloyd and our friendly dogs on our farm tour, try a game of pentanque, or just relax on your individual outdoor deck and enjoy the peace and tranquility of Clover Downs Estate. There are many things to do and see in Rotorua. Visit our many cultural and scenic tourist attractions, go horse riding, play a round of golf , or try trout fishing with an experienced guide at one of the many lakes and rivers in the area. Rotorua has some wonderful restaurants and cafes or maybe enjoy a Maori hangi & concert. We have extensive overseas and New Zealand travel experience so let us help make your stay in our country relaxing, pleasant and memorable. We are proud members of Superior Inns of NZ, Boutique Lodgings of NZ, Heritage & Character Inns of NZ & Kiwi Host.

"A unique place to stay"

Rotorua *B&B Homestay 20km E of Rotorua*

Lakeside B & B
Laurice & Bill Unwin
155G Okere Road, RD 4, Rotorua
Tel (07) 362 4288 Fax (07) 362 4288
Mob 0274 521 483 laurice.bill@xtra.co.nz
www.bnb.co.nz/unwin.html
Double $120 Single $80 (Full Breakfast)
Dinner $35pp Credit cards accepted
1 King/Twin 2 Queen (3 bdrm)
2 Ensuite 1 Private

We have a new home in a beautiful setting beside Lake Rotoiti (Okere Arm). Bird life abounds and within short walking distance there are bush walks, glow worms, waterfalls, river and lake fishing. Maori concerts and hangis, plus thermal activity are nearby. Each B&B is centrally heated with ensuite, comfortable beds, TV, refrigerator, tea/coffee making facilities. We share convivial meals with many guests. Smoke free inside. Small friendly outdoor dog. We are easy to find just one minute from Highway 33. Please ring for details. Laundry facilities available.

Rotorua *B&B Homestay Separate/Suite 4km E of Rotorua*

Honfleur
Bryan & Erica Jew
31 Walford Drive, Lynmore, Rotorua
Tel (07) 345 6170 Fax (07) 345 6170
Mob 025 233 9741 honfleurmaison@xtra.co.nz
www.bnb.co.nz/honfleur.html
Double $100 Single $50-$75 (Full Breakfast)
Dinner $35 Credit cards accepted
1 Double 2 Twin (2 bdrm)   1 Ensuite 1 Host share

"Honfleur" is a French country-style home in quiet, semi-rural surroundings close to lakes and forest. We offer generous hospitality amid antique furnishings and a beautiful garden featuring roses and perennials. Downstairs double bedroom with ensuite bathroom has a private entrance. Upstairs a twin bedroom has lake views and shares family bathroom (separate toilet). We are long-term Rotorua residents with sound local knowledge - retired medical professionals with friendly Labrador dog. Interests include travel, gardening, books, bridge, music, sport and Erica's embroidery. We offer a three course dinner (with wine) by arrangement. Not suitable for young children.

Rotorua *B&B Homestay 4km E of Rotorua*

Aroden B&B Homestay
Leonie & Paul Kibblewhite
2 Hilton Road, Lynmore, Rotorua
Tel (07) 345 6303 Fax (07) 345 6353
aroden@xtra.co.nz
www.bnb.co.nz/lynmorebbhomestay.html
Double $100-$120 Single $70-$90 (Special Breakfast)
Credit cards accepted
2 Queen (2 bdrm)
1 Ensuite 1 Private

Discover real character and warmth just 4kms from the city, nestled beside beautiful Whakarewarewa Forest. Leonie, ex-teacher, and Paul, scientist, delight in being New Zealanders - share our love of this remarkable area over refreshments or a wine on the patio... And meet Taupo, Paul's engaging Guide Dog. Enjoy well-appointed rooms (quality linen and great showers); winter central heating; a lovely garden featuring native trees. Relax in the comfortable lounge or sunroom. Delicious breakfast - this couple enjoys food!   Leonie parle francais (und ein bisschen Deutsch).

Rotorua - Lake Tarawera   *B&B Homestay Self-contained 15 SE of Rotorua*

Boatshed Bay Lodge
Lorraine van Praagh
95 Spencer Road, Lake Tarawera, RD 5, Rotorua
Tel (07) 362 8441   Fax (07) 362 8441
Mob 025 279 9269   boatshedbay@xtra.co.nz
www.bnb.co.nz/boatshedbaylodge.html
Double $120   Single $90   (Full Breakfast)   Child $25
Dinner $40 pp S/C $95 Credit cards accepted
2 Queen 1 Double 2 Single (2 bdrm)
2 Ensuite

Boatshed Bay is located on the shore of scenic Lake Tarawera with its sparking waters fringed by native bush at the foot of majestic Mount Tarawera. We offer boat charter, world renowned trout fishing, tramping (mountain trek), bushwalks or just relax in peace and tranquillity only 15km from Rotorua. All facilities are available, including laundry, kitchen and nearby licensed restaurant "The Landing Cafe". We provide home style breakfast and meals on request. Your hosts Lorraine and Steve are well travelled and enjoy meeting people. Our place is your place.

Rotorua - Lake Tarawera   *B&B Homestay   20km SE of Rotorua*

Lake Tarawera Rheinland Lodge
Gunter & Maria
484 Spencer Road, RD 5, Rotorua
Tel (07) 362 8838   Fax (07) 362 8838
Mob 025 234 3024
tarawera@ihug.co.nz   www.bnb.co.nz/ .html
Double $100-$130 Single $75-$95 (Special Breakfast)
Child 1/2 price   Dinner $30
1 King/Twin 1 Queen (2 bdrm)
1 Private 1 Host share

Located at the magic Lake Tarawera renowned for its scenery and history we offer warm hospitality with a personal touch. Expect total privacy, magnificent lake views, luxurious and relaxing outdoor whirlpool, spacious bathroom with shower and bath, fitness area, stereo, TV, internet connection, lake beach 5 minutes on foot, sea 45 minutes by car, bush walks, fishing and hunting trips by arrangement, home-made bread, German cuisine on request, organic garden, German/English spoken, free pick-up from airport or city.

Rotorua   *B&B Self-contained 10km W of Rotorua*

Rhodohill
Ailsa & Dave Stewart
569 Paradise Valley Road, Rotorua,
Tel (07) 348 9010   Fax (07) 348 9041
Mob 025 672 4009   www.bnb.co.nz/rhodohill.html
Double $80 Single $60 (Continental Breakfast)
Child $20 Credit cards accepted Children welcome
1 Queen (1 bdrm)
1 Ensuite

"Rhodohill" is set in a mature 4 acre garden in picturesque Paradise Valley, 10km west of Rotorua. Its hillside setting, large trees and hundreds of rhododendrons, camellias etc and many native birds offer a relaxing retreat within easy distance of major tourist attractions, golf courses and cafes and restaurants. The renowned Ngongotaha trout stream flows through the valley. Modern, self-contained accommodation with own entrance, ensuite bathroom, fully equipped kitchen, dining room-lounge. Smoke free indoors. We operate a specialist plant nursery. Our retired sheep dog "Max" enjoys escorting guests around the garden.

Rotorua - Lake Tarawera   *B&B Self-contained 23km SE of Rotorua*

Bush Haven
Marie & Rob Dollimore
588 Spencer Road, Lake Tarawera, Rotorua
Tel (07) 362 8447   Fax (07) 362 8447
www.bnb.co.nz/bushhaven.html

Double $145 Single $115 (Continental Breakfast)
1 Queen 1 Double 2 Single (3 bdrm)   Tourist flat
2 Private 1 Guests share

Following the violent and unexpected volcanic eruption of Mount Tarawera in 1886, the land has healed and nature has restored Lake Tarawera to its former majestic beauty and serenity. Lake Tarawera is the perfect place to enjoy a wide variety of activities including New Zealand's finest trout fishing, scenic lake cruises, the buried village of Te Wairoa, guided mountain tours, nature walks and all water sports. Bush Haven is nestled in five acres of attractive gardens and bush reserve with views across Otumutu Island and bay to the south western section of the lake. Our comfortably appointed and spacious self-contained tourist flat is the ground floor. It has two bedrooms, separate bathroom, fully equipped kitchen and lounge. Extra beds can be arranged.

Hosts Marie and Rob and friendly pet spaniels live in the upper level. There is a delightful 300 metre bush walk from the garden down to a secluded bay. Native flora and fauna are in abundance. Bush Haven is quiet and peaceful, away from the main settlement. It has ample, easy access, car and boat parking. Boat launching two minutes down the road. A dinghy with outboard is available for hire. The ideal base for your Rotorua holiday. Our friendly hospitality awaits you.

Rotorua - Central *B&B Rotorua Central*

Tresco
Gwyn & John Hanson 3 Toko Street, Rotorua
Tel (07) 348 9611   0800 TRESCO (873 726)
Fax (07) 347 6551   trescorotorua@xtra.co.nz
www.bnb.co.nz/tresco.html
Double $90 Single $50 (Full Breakfast)
Single ensuie $70, Triple $115 Extra person plus $20
Credit cards accepted Children welcome
2 King/Twin 2 Queen 2 Single (6 bdrm)
3 Ensuite 1 Private 2 Guests share

Central location - A warm welcome awaits you at our
comfortable friendly home, situated on a tree-lined street only 150 metres from Central Rotorua with its
many attractions and excellent restaurants. Established for over 30 years and recently renovated, Tresco
offers all the comforts of home. We serve a substantial breakfast and 24-hour complimentary refreshments.
Genuine hot mineral pool. Free pick-up from airport or bus terminal. Off-street parking. Laundry
facility with drying room. Guest survey gives us top marks for friendliness, cleanliness and location.

Rotorua - Ngongotaha *B&B Homestay 8km N of Rotorua*

Bayadere Lodge
Cynthia and Neil Clark
38 Hall Road, Ngongotaha, Rotorua
Tel 07 3575965   Fax 07 3575965   Mob 027 2928 520
c.clark@clear.net.nz
www.bnb.co.nz/bayaderelodge.html
Double $110-$140 Single $90-$100 (Continental Full
Breakfast) Child neg Dinner $35 pp Children welcome
2 King 1 Twin (3 bdrm)
1 Ensuite 1 Private

Bayadere Lodge is 8kms from Rotorua and 200 metres from Ngongotaha Village and stream. We are
close to the world famous attractions. Rainbow Springs, Skyline Rides, Horse Trekking and the Agrodome
sheep show. The Lake front and Waiteti stream are within walking distance and Neil has local fishing
knowledge to share. Our home has king and twin rooms with a guest lounge that has lake and rural
views. Full breakfast is served. Tea/coffee complimentary, laundry service available and ample parking.
We will welcome you as special guests in our home

Rotorua *B&B Homestay 2km N of Rotorua*

Moana Rose Lakeside Bed and Breakfast
Pauline and Bruce Kingston
23 Haumoana Street, Koutu, Rotorua
Tel (07) 349 2980 Fax (07) 349 2997
Mob 027 273 2008 moanarose@bktours.co.nz
www.bnb.co.nz/moanarose.html
Double $120 Single $80 (Continental Full Special
Breakfast) Child $35 Children welcome
1 Queen 1 Twin (2 bdrm)
1 Private

Situated on the lake edge, 2km from the city centre, we offer a quiet relaxed atmosphere, including
separate entrance, comfortable spacious bedrooms, electric blankets, own bathroom and a delightful
garden spa. Enjoy our company or the privacy of your own sitting room, including Sky TV, fridge, tea/
coffee facilities. From our sun deck walk down to the lake and watch the bird life grazing on the reserve
with Lizzie our cat in hot pursuit. Bruce is a licensed tour operator and will gladly assist with your tour
options. Welcome, Kia Ora.

Rotorua *B&B Boutique Hotel / Lodge 5km NW of Rotorua City Centre*

Swiss Lodge Rotorua

Heiko & Christina Kaiser

207 - 209 Kawaha Point Road, PO Box 1600, Rotorua

Tel (07) 348 5868   Fax (07) 348 5869

Mob 021 119 1000

stay@swisslodge.co.nz   www.swisslodge.co.nz

Double $195-$295 Single $155-$195 Child $35
(Including Special Breakfast) Dinner $45 - $65
Penthouse apartment $329 self-contained
Lakeside chalet $399-$479 self-contained
Credit cards accepted   Children welcome
6 King   3 Queen   3 Twin   (12 bdrm)
9 Ensuites   1 Private

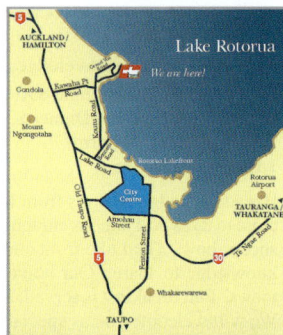

Swiss Lodge is situated near the tip of Kawaha Point, a
leafy peninsula on the Western shore of Lake Rotorua. It
is just five minutes' drive from the city centre but away
from traffic noise and sulphur fumes.

Our unique lake front retreat nestles in a peaceful garden
setting with panoramic views over the lake. It offers a
variety of luxury accommodation from ensuite bedrooms
with terrace through to a self-contained penthouse
apartment and entire lakeside chalet.

Guests can swim from the private beach, then relax in
the lakeside open-air spa and the Finnish sauna, or enjoy
a massage on site. The Lodge's jetty is an ideal starting
point for floatplane or boating excursions and a round of
golf is popular with complimentary green fees at the
nearby 18-hole golf course.

The breakfast buffet offers European breads and other
specialities prepared by one of our qualified chefs.
Finnish soapstone fireplaces throughout ensure that the
Swiss Lodge is warm and inviting summer or winter.

Lake Rotoiti - Rotorua *B&B 20km NE of Rotorua*

Kamahi
Sheryl & Kevin Jensen
137 Okere Road, RD4, Lake Rotoiti, Rotorua

Tel 07 362 4244 Fax 07 362 4244   Mob 027 4570 496
or   027 4440 321   S&KJensen@xtra.co.nz
www.bnb.co.nz/jensen.html

Double $95-$100 Single $70 (Continental Breakfast)
Child $15 Children welcome
1 Queen 1 Twin (2 bdrm)
1 Private

Kamahi (ka-ma-he) Bed & Breakfast is a cottage, among
a colourful garden, with beautiful views of Lake Rotoiti
- a few steps to the water edge. Kayaks and bicylces are available. Handy to Okere Falls, whitewater
rafting, bush walks, fishing, golf course. One room with Queen bed, TV, radio, microwave, fridge,
table/chairs, tea/coffee facilities etc. Separate bathroom, another room with twin beds. Fish smoker and
BBQ available. We are friendly NZers, Kevin's involved with animal nutrition, Sheryl's an educator.
Two friendly small dogs.

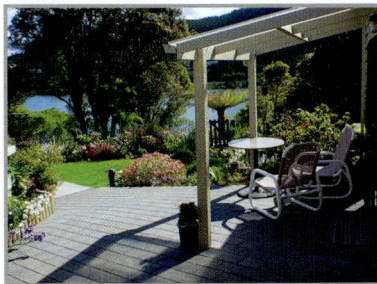

Rotorua *10km E of Rotorua*

Peppertree Farm
Robyn Panther & Barry Morris
25 Cookson Road, RD4, Rotorua

Tel (07) 345 3718   Fax (07) 345 3718
www.bnb.co.nz/peppertree.html

Double $95-$105 Single $60 Child half price
1 Double 2 Twin (3 bdrm)
1 Ensuite

Handy to the airport our quiet rural retreat overlooking
Lake Rotorua provides a picturesque and homely
welcome. Farm animals are horses, cows, sheep, a baby
donkey and chickens. Lucy, our Cavalier King Charles
Spaniel, is a house pet, and Ben, our very friendly
Labrador lives outside. We are knowledgable locals who enjoy horse-racing, rugby, most sports and
meeting interesting people! If you wish to attend a Maori concert and hangi, we can arrange pickup and
delivery back to the farm.

Rotorua *B&B Farmstay 30km S of Rotorua*

Caradoc Farm
Robyn & Bunny Stunell
466 Galatos Road, Ngakura RD1, Rotorua

Tel (07) 333 2779   Fax (07) 333 2779
Mob 025 244 4230   stunell@wave.co.nz
www.caradocfarm.co.nz

Double $95-$120 Single $70-$90 (Full Breakfast)
Child $25 - $35 Dinner B/A Children welcome
2 Queen 1 Single (2 bdrm)

While on vacation take a break at Caradoc Farm –
farm stay accommodation only a short drive to renowned trout fishing lakes, Rotorua's cultural,
thermal and adventure activities. Bunny and Robyn, our small dog Mac and Cairo the cat, offer a warm
welcome to our farm (running deer and beef cattle). Our quiet comfortable home features a guest wing
with two queen bedrooms, separate guest bathrooms and toilet facilities. Spectacular views overlook
the farming community of Ngakuru. Cooked or continental breakfast: evening meals by arrangement.

Rotorua - Glenholme   *B&B Homestay 1km S of Rotorua Central*

Innes Cottage
Chris and Gill Innes
18A Wylie Street, Glenholme, Rotorua
Tel 07 349 1839   0800 24 30 30   Fax 07 349 1890
Mob 027 498 2100   chris@clican.com
www.innescottage.co.nz

Double $100 Single $85 (Continental Breakfast)
Child $30 Dinner by arrangement Children welcome
Pets welcome
1 Queen 2 Single (2 bdrm)
1 Private

Centrally situated in easy walking distance to the city, set in a treelined quiet neighborhood only 100metres from the main road. Close to Whakarewarewa Thermal area, Rotorua Golf Club, major tourist attractions are easily accessible. After 130 years heritage in the beverage industry we have travelled extensively, have collected a wealth of knowledge and many valuable contacts. Let us assist and advise you on the most popular and "must see" attractions and other highlights of our beautiful country."Bob" is our cat.

Rotorua   *Self-contained 1.5km SW of Rotorua*

Golf View Chalet
Fred and Caroline Windner
83 Springfield Road, Rotorua,
Tel (07) 347 8168   Fax (07) 347 8134
www.bnb.co.nz/golfviewrotorua.html

Double $135 Single $80
(Continental Breakfast)
Child not suitable
1 King/Twin 2 Single (1 bdrm)
1 Ensuite

Separate private chalet, 1km west of Whakarewarewa, our famous Pohutu Geyser. Approximately 2km to the city centre. We have off-street parking and your first continental breakfast provisions are free. Not suitable for children or pets. Besides all the recreational facilities Rotorua offers, you can perfect your chipping and putting on the Springfield Golf Course. Access through our property. We are Austrian Kiwis.

Rotorua   *B&B 10km N of Rotorua*

Ngongotaha Lakeside Lodge
Lyndsay & Graham Butcher
41 Operiana Street, Ngongotaha, Rotorua
Tel (07) 357 4020   0800 144 020   Fax (07) 357 4020
Mob 021 266 1341   lake.edge@xtra.co.nz
www.bnb.co.nz/ngongotahalodge.html

Double $125-$165 Single $110-$135 (Full Breakfast)
Child Over 12 neg Dinner B/A
1 King 1 Queen 2 Twin 2 Single (3 bdrm)
3 Ensuite

Absolute lake edge, amazing views, fishing, bird watching, great food and warm hospitality are what you will find at our spacious comfortable home. The upper level is exclusively for guests with fully equipped lounge/conservatory overlooking the lake. All bedrooms have ensuite facilities with everything provided. The famous Waiteti Stream is only metres away, with Rainbow and Brown Trout waiting to be caught. Free use of fishing gear and canoes and we'll smoke your catch for you. Smoke free inside. Ample, safe parking and sulphur free.

Rotorua *B&B 17km S of Rotorua*

Pareheru Waimangu
Edith Turner
312 Waimangu Road, RD 3, Rotorua

Tel (07) 366 6796   Fax (07) 366 6796
Mob 021 474 173   edith_turner1@hotmail.com
www.bnb.co.nz/pareheruwaimangu.html

Double $100 Single $70 (Full Breakfast) Child $60
Dinner $40 includes wine Children welcome
1 King/Twin 1 Queen (2 bdrm)
1 Ensuite 1 Private

Pareheru is 17km south of Rotorua off main Rotorua/Taupo SH5. Our deer farm is 3km along Waimangu Road. We enjoy the peace and tranquility of the countryside with glorious views of Mt Tarewera. The famous Waimangu Volcanic Valley is only 3 km from Pareheru. Our family have enjoyed living here over 20 years and we look forward to welcoming you to our home. Comfortable spacious bedrooms, laundry facilities as well as fax and internet available. Price includes full English breakfast. Dinner by arrangement. I am a painter and have a gallery of NZ artists, paintings, pottery and glass.

Kinloch *B&B Country Village Accommodation 15mins W of Taupo*

Twynham at Kinloch
Elizabeth & Paul Whitelock
84 Marina Terrace, Kinloch, Taupo

Tel (07) 378 2862   Fax (07) 378 2868
Mob 025 285 6001   twynham.bnb@xtra.co.nz
www.twynham.co.nz

Double $125-$135 Single $105 (Continental Full
Breakfast) Dinner $45 Credit cards accepted
Children welcome Pets welcome
1 Queen 2 Single (2 bdrm)   1 Ensuite 1 Private

Nestled within private gardens in the picturesque lakeside village of Kinloch - Twynham is unequalled as a base for exploring the Taupo region. Golf, fishing, watersports, (all five minute stroll), snow skiing, bush and mountain walks. The north facing guest wing with private entrance, includes lounge and sunny deck. Hearty breakfasts, wholesome dinners and warm welcomes assure guests of an enjoyable stay. Paul is a NZ Kennel Club judge, golf, music, travel and sports are family interests. We have two friendly dogs Sieger and Sparky. Laundry service and delicious home baking always available.

Taupo *B&B Homestay 2km E of Taupo*

Yeoman's Lakeview Homestay
Colleen & Bob Yeoman
23 Rokino Road, Taupo 2730
Tel (07) 377 0283 Fax (07) 377 4683
www.bnb.co.nz/yeomans.html

Double $100 Single $50 (Full Breakfast) Child $25
Dinner $30 by arrangement
Children welcome
1 Queen 3 Single (3 bdrm)
1 Ensuite 1 Guests share

Bob and I have enjoyed hosting for over fifteen years, our Lakeview Homestay with beautiful mountains backdrop makes our guests' stay in Taupo very special. Our home is spacious, comfortable and relaxing. All Taupo's attractions are nearby, golf courses, thermal pools, Huka Falls and fishing. We are retired sheep and cattle farmers, Bob excels at golf and is in charge of cooked breakfasts. Home made jams and marmalade are my specialty. Turn into Huia Street from lakefront, take fourth turn on the rigth into Rokino Road. Off street parking.

Taupo *Homestay 2km S of Taupo*

Nolan's Homestay
Betty & Ned Nolan
30 Rokino Road, Taupo
Tel (07) 377 0828 Fax (07) 377 0828
Mob 027 244 9035 nolans@beds-n-leisure.com
www.bnb.co.nz/nolanshomestay.html

Double $90 Single $60 (Full Breakfast) Child 1/2 price
Dinner $30 Children welcome
2 Twin 4 Single (2 bdrm)
1 Ensuite 1 Private 1 Host share

Our one level home is located up a tree lined drive with ample parking, nestled among trees. Superb views of town, lake mountains and ranges. Retired sheep and cattle farmers we have travelled widely with many tangible reminders furnishing our home. Relax or enjoy trout fishing, tramping, sightseeing or golf. Betty loves to cook but Taupo abounds in good restaurants. This is not just a Bed and Breakfast but a HOMESTAY! Directions: Lakefront Take Taharepa Road to Hilltop shops turn left into Rokino road. No 30 is on right after Waihora Street. (One loved cat)

Taupo *Homestay Self-contained 3km S of Taupo*

Hawai Homestay
Jeanette & Bryce Jones
18 Hawai Street, 2 Mile Bay, Taupo
Tel (07) 377 3242 Mob 025 234 0558
jeanettej@xtra.co.nz
www.beds-n-leisure.com/hawai.htm

Double $80 Single $50 (Full Breakfast) Child $20
Dinner $20 Marmite Cottage $55 double
Credit cards accepted Children welcome
1 Queen 1 Twin (2 bdrm)
1 Guests share

Taupo is great for holidays any season, swimming, fishing, tramping, skiing. Our modern warm house has wonderful lake views from lounge and deck. Quiet and comfortable guest bedrooms are downstairs with shared bathroom. Home made muesli, preserves, fresh cooked bread and muffins our breakfast specialty. Two minutes walk to lake and excellent restaurants. Self-contained cottage, 3 bedrooms, sleeps seven, open plan lounge, potbelly stove, linen and firewood supplied. Great for families. Interests include church, Probus, roses, WW2 memorabilia and adorable shitzu dog.

Taupo - Acacia Bay   *Homestay 5km W of Taupo*

Pariroa Homestay
Joan & Eric Leersnijder
77A Wakeman Road, Acacia Bay, Taupo

Tel (07) 378 3861   Mob 025 530 370
pariroa@xtra.co.nz
www.bnb.co.nz/pariroahomestay.html

Double $80 Single $60 (Full Breakfast)
Credit cards accepted
1 Queen 2 Single (2 bdrm)
1 Guests share

Views views! Our home is Scandinavian style with
wooden interior. Situated in a very quiet area and minutes form the beach, we have magnificent, uninterrupted views of Lake Taupo and The Ranges from bedrooms and living room. We have travelled extensively and Eric was previously a tea planter in Indonesia, having lived in The Netherlands, Spain and Italy. Directions: Turn down between 95 and 99 Wakeman Road. We are the last house on this short road (200 metres).

Taupo - Acacia Bay   *Homestay 6km W of Taupo*

Leece's Homestay
Marlene and Bob Leece
98 Wakeman Road, Acacia Bay, Taupo 2736

Tel (07) 378 6099   Fax (07) 378 6092
www.bnb.co.nz/leeceshomestay.html

Double $90 Single $60
(Continental Breakfast)
Child neg
1 King 1 Double 2 Single (2 bdrm)
1 Guests share

Your hosts Bob and Marlene extend a warm welcome to our large wood interior home with woodfire for winter and north facing sunny deck from guest bedroom. Also magnificent view of Lake Taupo from lounge and front deck. There are bush walks and steps down to lake to swim in summer. We are awaiting your arrival with anticipation of making friends. Please phone for directions.

Taupo   *Homestay 1km S of Taupo*

Pataka House
Raewyn & Neil Alexander
8 Pataka Road, Taupo

Tel (07) 378 5481 Fax (07) 378 5461
Mob 025 473 881
www.beds-n-leisure.com/pataka/htm

Double $100 Single $70 (Full Breakfast)
Child $30 Separate suite $120
Children welcome
2 Queen 4 Twin (4 bdrm)
1 Ensuite 1 Private 1 Guests share

'Pataka House' is highly recommended for its hospitality. We assure guests that their stay lives up to New Zealand's reputation as being a home away from home. We are easily located just one turn off the lake front and up a tree-lined driveway. Our garden room is privately situated, has an appealing decor and extremely popular to young and old alike. Stay for one night or stay for more as Lake Taupo will truly be the highlight of your holiday. Toddy the cat enjoys visitors.

Taupo - Acacia Bay   *B&B Homestay 5km W of Taupo*

Paeroa Lakeside Homestay
Barbara & John Bibby
21 Te Kopua Street, Acacia Bay, Taupo
Tel (07) 378 8449   Fax (07) 378 8446
Mob 0274 818 829
bibby@reap.org.nz   www.taupohomestay.com
Double $175-$225   Single $175-$225 (Full Breakfast)
(Special Breakfast) Child $75 Dinner $40
Triple (2 Rooms) $225 - $250 Credit cards accepted
2 King 1 Queen 2 Single (3 bdrm)
3 Ensuite

Unique genuine lakefront location Paeroa's hosts Barbara and John welcome you to their spacious modern quality Homestay at sheltered **Acacia Bay,** developed on three levels to capture the **magnificent uniterrupted panoramic views** of world famous **Lake Taupo** and beyond.

The flower filled garden gently descends to the private beach, jetty where you can swim, relax. Use the rowboat or catch a **fishing charter** with John in his 30-ft cruiser. John has fished Lake Taupo and its rivers successfully for 35 years. We can cook your large **Rainbow Trout** for breakfast or smoke it for your lunch.

The house is large, comfortable and well appointed for your comfort and privacy with spacious lounge areas, sundecks, patios and outdoor seats in the garden to enjoy the abundant birdlife, flowers and Lake Views. The rooms have comfortable beds, TV, electric blankets and heaters, great views, ensuite bathrooms with heated towelrails and hairdriers - serviced daily. Laundry service is available. A large guest lounge for your use with tea and coffee facilities, TV, piano, books and comfort. Private decks off the rooms. Breakfasts are a specialty.

We are retired sheep and beef farmers enjoying living in our quiet peaceful and private home beside the beach, just minutes from the town centre, 3 golf courses, bush walks, restaurants, shops, boating, thermal hot springs, and all the many major attractions the area provides.   Plan to **stay several days** and base your **central North Island** visits to Napier, Rotorua, Tongariro National Park and ski-fields from here. Amongst your hosts' interests are travel, golf, gardening, fishing, entertaining and family. We have a detailed knowledge of the region and members of @ Home NZ.

There is so much to do in Taupo

Taupo   *Lakestay 6km W of Taupo*

Kooringa
Robin & John Mosley
32 Ewing Grove, Acacia Bay, Taupo
Tel (07) 378 8025   Fax (07) 378 6085
Mob 025 272 6343   kooringa@xtra.co.nz
www.kooringa.co.nz
Double $120 Single $100 (Full Breakfast)
Credit cards accepted
1 Queen 1 Double 2 Single (2 bdrm)
1 Ensuite

"Kooringa" is situated in sheltered Acacia Bay (2 mins walk to Lake), surrounded by native bush and gardens with magnificent views of Lake Taupo and Mt Tauhara. We are a retired professional couple, lived overseas and travelled extensively with our two sons. We are within easy distance of all major attractions. Your private guest suite includes lounge and deck. A generous breakfast with plenty of variety is served in the conservatory overlooking the Lake. Please phone, fax or email for bookings. Directions: www. kooringa.co.nz

Taupo   *Homestay Self-contained 15km W of Taupo*

Ben Lomond
Mary & Jack Weston
1434 Poihipi Road, RD 1, Taupo
Tel (07) 377 6033   Fax (07) 377 6033
Mob 025 774 080   benlomond@xtra.co.nz
www.bnb.co.nz/benlomond.html
Double $90 Single $45 (Full Breakfast) Child $22
Dinner $25 by arrangement S/C price on inquiry
Credit cards accepted Children welcome Pets welcome
1 Queen 1 Twin (2 bdrm)
1 Guests share

Welcome to Ben Lomond. Jack and I have farmed here for 40 years and our comfortable family home is set in a mature garden. There is a self contained cottage in the garden or 2 bedrooms available in the house. We have interests in fishing, golf and the Equestrian world and are familiar with the attractions on the Central Plateau. Our pets include dogs and cats who wander in and out. Taupo restaurants are 15 minutes away or dine with us by arrangement.

Taupo   *Homestay Self-contained Taupo Central*

Lakeland Homestay
Lesley, Chris & Pussycats
11 Williams Street, Taupo
Tel (07) 378 1952   Fax (07) 378 1912
Mob 025 877 971   lakeland.bb@xtra.co.nz
www.bnb.co.nz/lakelandhomestay.html
Double $100 Single $60 (Continental Breakfast)
$120 dble + $20 pp Self-contained flat
Credit cards accepted
1 Queen 2 Double 2 Twin (4 bdrm)
1 Ensuite 1 Private 1 Host share

Nestled in a restful tree-lined street, a mere five minutes stroll form the Lake's edge and shopping centre
"Lakeland Homestay" is a cheerful and cosy home that enjoys views of the lake and mountains. Keen gardeners, anglers and golfers Chris and Lesley work and play in an adventure oasis. For extra warmth on winter nights all beds have electric blankets, and laundry facilities are available. A courtesy car is available for coach travellers and there is off-street parking. Please phone for directions.

Taupo *Homestay 3km SE of Taupo*

Ann & Dan Hennebry
28 Greenwich Street, Taupo
Tel (07) 378 9483 Mob 025 297 4283
brie@xtra.co.nz
www.bnb.co.nz/hennebry.html
Double $90 Single $60
(Full Breakfast) Dinner $30
1 King 1 Single (2 bdrm)
1 Guests share

We enjoy having guests in our spacious home overlooking
farmland and bordering Taupo's Botanical gardens. We hope you will join us for dinner (maybe a
barbecue in the summer) and complimentary wine in our pleasant dining room. There are many good
restaurants in Taupo should you prefer that. Our launch "Bonita" is available for fishing or sight seeing
on the beautiful lake - Dan is an excellent skipper. We look forward to welcoming you to our warm,
comfortable, home.

Taupo - Countryside *B&B Homestay Self-contained 35km NW of Taupo*

South Claragh & Bird Cottage
Lesley & Paul Hill
South Claragh, Poihipi Road, RD 1, Mangakino
Tel (07) 372 8848 Fax (07) 372 8047
welcome@countryaccommodation.co.nz
www.countryaccommodation.co.nz
Double $120 Single $80-$90 (Full Breakfast)
Child $10-$45 Dinner $45pp Bird Cottage $90-$100
dbl, $25/$10 extras Credit cards accepted
1 Queen 1 Double 1 Single (3 bdrm) 2 Private

Turn into our leafy driveway and relax in tranquil, rambling gardens with gentle donkeys, coloured
sheep, outdoor dog. Accommodation options: 1. Enjoy bed & breakfast in our comfortable, centrally
heated farmhouse. Delicious farm breakfasts. Homegrown produce and excellent cooking make dining
recommended.   2. Settle into Bird Cottage which is self-contained and cosy, with delightful views.
Perfect for two, will sleep 3/4. Firewood and linen provided, cot available. No meals included, but
breakfast/dinner happily prepared by arrangement. Details and pictures on our web site. Children welcome.

Taupo *Homestay 3km S of Taupo*

Catley's Homestay
Beverley & Tom Catley
55 Grace Crescent, Taupo
Tel (07) 378 1403 Fax (07) 378 1402
taupo@actrix.gen.nz
www.bnb.co.nz/catleyshomestay.html
Double $100-$120 Single $70 (Full Breakfast)
Child $30 Credit cards accepted Children welcome
1 Queen 1 Double 2 Single (3 bdrm)
1 Private 1 Host share

If you want a quiet Homestay with panoramic views of
lake and mountains, generous breakfasts and warm hospitality, this is the place for you. Upstairs guest
rooms open onto a sheltered sundeck with extensive views of the lake and snow capped volcanoes. We
also have a comfortable self-contained unit with its own garden entrance. All Taupo's famous attractions
are nearby including Huka Falls and thermal pools. Laundry facilities are available. You will enjoy
your stay in this lovely area. To avoid disappointment booking is recommended.

Taupo *B&B Homestay 2km S of Taupo*

Bramham
Julia & John Bates
7 Waipahihi Avenue, Taupo,
Tel (07) 378 0064 Fax (07) 378 0065
Mob 025 240 9643 & 021 240 9643
info@bramham.co.nz
www.bramham.co.nz
Double $100-$110 Single $60-$80 (Full Breakfast)
1 Double 2 Twin 1 Single (3 bdrm)
3 Ensuite

Bramham is situated just two minutes walk form the Hot Beach of Lake Taupo and offers tremendous views of the lake and mountains to the south.   John and Julia, having spent 24 years in the RNZAF, including service with the USAF in Tucson Arizona, welcome you to our quiet, homely and peaceful atmosphere. Hearty breakfasts are our specialty. Local knowledge is our business. Bus terminal and airport service complimentary. Being non smokers our dogs, Koko and Daisy, ask you not to smoke in our home.

Taupo *Homestay Rural Homestay 14km NW of Taupo*

Minarapa
Barbara & Dermot Grainger
620 Oruanui Road, RD 1, Taupo
Tel (07) 378 1931 Mob 025 272 2367
info@minarapa.co.nz   www.minarapa.co.nz
Double $95-$125 Single $70-$100 (Full Breakfast)
Child Price on application Dinner By arrangement
Credit cards accepted
1 King/Twin 2 Queen 2 Single (4 bdrm)
2 Ensuite 1 Private

Wend your way along a tree-lined drive to enter the
tranquillity of our 11 acre rural retreat, just 12 minutes from Taupo, 45 minutes from Rotorua and central to tourist attractions. Our large home has billiard room with fridge for guest use, lounge with feature fireplace and covered verandah. The spacious, well appointed guest rooms, two with ensuite and balcony, overlook park-like grounds with colourful gardens, mature trees, grass tennis court and beyond pond and stream, friendly farm animals. Barbara speaks fluent German.

Taupo *Homestay 2km S of Taupo*

Mountain Views Homestay
Bridget & Jack Grice
17B Puriri Street, Taupo
Tel (07) 378 6136 Fax (07) 378 6134
Mob 025 200 5437 mtviews@reap.org.nz
www.bnb.co.nz/mountainviewshomestay.html
Double $80 Single $50 (Continental Breakfast)
Child negotiable Dinner by arrangement
Credit cards accepted
1 Queen 1 Twin (2 bdrm)
1 Guests share

Enjoy a warm welcome and a nice cuppa on arrival. Stay longer, stay cheaper with a 10% off after the first night when you book direct. Continental breakfast is server in the warm living room and includes Bridget's home made jams and bread. Our home is cool in the summer and warm in the winter. After 10 years in the tourist industry J & B are very knowledgeable about this area. In our free time we enjoy walking in the local forests. Off street parking. Phone for directions.

Taupo *B&B Homestay Self-contained 3km S of Taupo*

Above the Lake
Judi Thomson
59a Shepherd Road, Taupo
Tel (07) 378 4558   Fax (07) 378 4071
Mob 025 817 443
judi.thomson@xtra.co.nz
www.abovethelake.co.nz

Double $110 Single $85
(Continental Full Special Breakfast) Child POA
Credit cards accepted
1 Queen (1 bdrm)
1 Private

Welcome to our completely private guest area which includes queen size bed, television, ensuite and views over the lake to the mountains. Georgia, our social Labrador, looks forward to your company. We are happy to suggest 'what's hot and what's not' for local activities and eateries.

Taupo *B&B Separate/Suite*

Gillies Lodge
Margi Martin & Alan Malpas
77 Gillies Ave, Taupo
Tel (07) 377 2377   Fax (07) 377 2377
info@gilliesoftaupo.co.nz
www.gilliesoftaupo.co.nz

Double $95-$115 Single $75
(Continental Full Breakfast) Credit cards accepted
4 Double 12 Single (9 bdrm)
9 Ensuite

Taupo's original licensed guest house, minutes from Lake Taupo and town. A perfect base to explore and enjoy Taupo's many attractions. Warm, peaceful, sunny and quiet with ample off street parking. With a pot of good coffee or tea, relax and enjoy the views or sunsets from the lounge with log fire and library or sit outside on the lounge deck. Breakfast with you hosts Alan and Margi and share their intimate local knowledge and sense of history. A true bed and breakfast experience. Extra facilities and features provided.

Taupo *Homestay Country Homestay 6km E of Taupo*

Richlyn Homestay
Lyn & Richard James
1 Mark Wynd, Bonshaw Park, Taupo
Tel (07) 378 8023   Fax (07) 378 8023
Mob 025 908 647   richlyn.james.taupo@xtra.co.nz
www.richlyn.co.nz

Double $140-$190 Single $100-$140 (Full Breakfast)
Child Neg Credit cards accepted
1 King 2 Queen 2 Single (4 bdrm)
1 Ensuite 1 Private

We provide what we like to find when travelling, a warm welcome, spacious rooms, beds like the one at home, good breakfasts and a safe secure place to stay. Come and walk or relax in eight acres of gardens and trees, with views of mountain, forest and countryside. Enjoy our outdoor spa pool, play with our two little poodles and cat. We welcome you to our haven of peace and tranquility. Directions: From Taupo, SH5 to Napier 6km, right at Caroline Drive, 2km to Mark Wynd left, first driveway left.

Taupo   *Farmstay   12km NW of Taupo*

Whitiora Farm
Judith & Jim McGrath
1281 Mapara Road, RD 1, Taupo
Tel (07) 378 6491 Fax (07) 378 6491
mcg.whitiora@xtra.co.nz
www.bnb.co.nz/ .html
Double $100   Single $60 (Full Breakfast) Child $25
Dinner $30, lunch $15, by arrangement
1 Queen 3 Single (3 bdrm)
2 Host share   Children welcome

Three course dinner by arrangement. Breakfast: your
choice of cereal, homegrown fruit, eggs, bacon, sausages, home-made bread, conserves, coffee, English/ herb tea. Our 461 acre farm grazes sheep, cattle, deer, goats thoroughbred horses, which we breed and Jim trains and races. Judith, NZAFHH member enjoys gardening, especially organic vegetables. We enjoy sharing our large comfortable home, garden, farm, welcome children (5-12 half price, under 5 negotiable). We appreciate you not smoking in our home. Booking advisable to avoid disappointment.

Taupo   *B&B Farmstay Self-contained 13km N of Taupo*

Bellbird Ridge Alpaca Farm
Mike & Lorraine Harrison
68 Tangye Road, RD 1, Taupo
Tel +64 7 377 1996 Fax +64 7 377 1992
Mob 025 668 7754   lharrison@xtra.co.nz
www.bnb.co.nz/bellbirdridge.html
Double $100-$130 Single $90 (Full Breakfast)
Child $30 Dinner $40 pp by arrangement
Children welcome Pets welcome
2 Queen 1 Twin 1 Single (4 bdrm)
1 Ensuite 1 Private

Our one bedroom self-contained cottage is the perfect retreat to relax, unwind and enjoy the serenity of country life. The cottage has quality fittings and nestles into our extensive garden with deck overlooking the pond. We also have available in the main house a twin bedroom, a single bedroom and a large double bedroom, where you would be our only guests. Our 10 acres have sweeping rural views and only 15 minutes easy drive from Taupo and 1.5 hours from the snowfields.

Taupo   *B&B Homestay 5km S of Taupo centre*

Beside the Lake
Irene & Roger Foote
8 Chad Street, Taupo,
Tel (07) 378 5847   Fax (07) 378 5847
Mob 025 804 683   foote.tpo@xtra.co.nz
www.bnb.co.nz/besidethelake.html
Double $180 (Continental Full Breakfast)
Credit cards accepted
2 King/Twin 1 Queen (3 bdrm)
1 Ensuite 1 Private

We invite you to enjoy the tranquillity of our beautiful
property beside Lake Taupo. Our luxury accommodation offers breakfast of your choice, air conditioning, central heating, and secure garage with internal access to house and elevator. All rooms have lake views, and balcony or terrace. Relax beside the lake, in the lake (swimming), on the lake (boating, fishing) or around the lake fishing world famous trout rivers, walking trails, ski slopes, golf courses, thermal pools and unique volcanic countryside. Enjoy your break beside the lake.

Taupo   *Homestay Boutique Accommodation 2.5km S of Taupo*

Fairviews
Brenda Watson & Mike Hughes
8 Fairview Terrace, Taupo,
Tel (07) 377 0773 fairviews@reap.org.nz
www.reap.org.nz/~fairviews
Double $110-$135 Single $95-$110 (Full Breakfast)
Credit cards accepted
1 Queen 1 Twin (2 bdrm)
1 Ensuite 1 Private

You are invited to stay at our modern smoke-free homestay situated in a tranquil neighbourhood within walking distance of Hot Pools and Lake. Relax and enjoy Fairviews gardens. Be as private as you wish or socialise with hosts. Rooms are tastefully decorated and comfortable. Double room is large with private entrance, TV, fridge, tea/coffee facilities, robe and hairdryer. Generous breakfasts provided. Email facilities and laundry are available at small charge. Our regional knowledge is extensive. Interests include theatre, travel, cycling, tramping, antiques/collectables.

Taupo   *B&B Homestay 2km SE of Taupo*

Finial House
Jan & Neil Fleming
51 Ngauruhoe St, Taupo,
Tel (07) 377 4347   Fax (07) 377 4348
Mob 025 685 8255 n.j.fleming@xtra.co.nz
www.finial-homestay.co.nz
Double $100-$135 Single $70-$95 (Full Breakfast)
Dinner $20-25 Credit cards accepted
2 King/Twin 2 Queen (3 bdrm)
2 Ensuite 1 Host share

Finial House is a spacious home in a peaceful setting. Enjoy the magnificent views of the lake and volcanic mountains from our extensive lounge, or deck with a relaxing spa pool. Close to town and lake with they're many attractions. We are ex dairy farmers who enjoy talk with you about your travels and interests. Our interests are: sports, travel, music, walking, running and gardening. Out three children have families of their own and we are left with out two timid cats.

Taupo   *B&B Homestay Self-contained 16km N of Taupo*

Brackenhurst
Barbara & Ray Graham
801 Oruanui Road, RD1, Taupo
Tel (07) 377 6451   Fax (07) 377 6451
Mob 0274 456 217 rgbg@xtra.co.nz
www.bnb.co.nz/brackenhurst.html
Double $100 Single $60 (Continental Breakfast)
(Full Breakfast) Child $30 Dinner $35
Children welcome Pets welcome
1 Queen 1 Double 4 Single (3 bdrm)   2 Ensuite 2 Private

Brackenhurst is a warm modern Lockwood design home on 14 acres of peaceful countryside with fantails, tuis, bellbirds flitting from tree to tree.We have friendly highland cattle. We offer a warm welcome with peace and tranquility. You can also practise your chipping and putting. We are half a kilometre from SH1 and close to Huka Falls, geothermal activities, golf courses and in a days outing to Rotorua, Waitomo Caves or Napier. Private guests wing in the house or a separate annex offer away from home comforts. Breakfast to suit, continental style or full English. Dinner is available by arrangement.

Taupo - Acacia Bay   *B&B Homestay 7km W of Taupo*

Hazeldene Lodge
Judy & Tony Pratt
119 Acacia Heights Drive, Acacia Bay, Taupo

Tel (07) 377 0560   Fax (07) 377 0560   Mob 025 609 2647
hazeldene@xtra.co.nz   www.hazeldenelodge.co.nz

Double $175-$215 Single $150-$215   (Continental Breakfast) (Full Breakfast)
Child POA Children welcome
3 Queen 1 Double 1 Twin (5 bdrm)
5 Ensuite

Hazeldene Lodge is a stunning newly created up-market home planned specifically for the comfort of guests. Set on two acres of land on the brow of a hill in a picturesque rural setting, yet only seven kilometres drive from town.

After operating a very successful bed & breakfast in England for three years, your hosts Judy & Tony decided to immigrate to New Zealand and offer the same high standard of 'Home from Home' accommodation. All our bedrooms have been very tastefully furnished and fitted out with all the luxuries in life, such as TV's, electric blankets, hair dryers, iron and ironing board, coffee and tea-making facilities. Also from your rooms you have spectacular views during the day, and by night twinkling lights of Taupo township are gorgeous. We are within easy distance of the famous Huka Falls, and also international golf courses, geothermal activity, and also some excellent restaurants.

We assure you a warm welcome and a comfortable stay. Please phone, fax or email for bookings, or visit our website.

Taupo - Acacia Bay *B&B 5km W of Taupo*

The Loft
Grace Andrews & Peter Rosieur
3 Wakeman Road, Acacia Bay, Taupo
Tel (07) 377 1040   Fax (07) 377 1049
Mob 0274 851 347
book@theloftnz.com   www.theloftnz.com

Double $120-$175 Single $90-$120 Child $50 - $75
(Continental Full Special Breakfast) Dinner $30 - $45
3 Queen 2 Single (3 bdrm)
3 Ensuite

Situated five minutes from Taupo township, "The Loft" is nestled on a hillside that overlooks Lake Taupo. Your hosts, Grace and Peter, are relaxed friendly people who delight in the best things in life. Both have travelled extensively throughout New Zealand and the rest of the world. Their passions vary from food and fine wine to tramping and gardening.

Enjoy their scrumptious breakfast of fresh fruit salad, freshly squeezed orange juice, freshly baked muffins and croissants; wonderful scrambled eggs with mushrooms, bacon and home grown tomatoes; an experience not to be missed. Arrange an evening meal at "The Loft" and you will be treated to a pleasurable three-course dinner that will leave you with a lasting memory of New Zealand hospitality. After your dinner, join your hosts for a complimentary port before retiring for a good nights sleep.

"The Loft" boasts three very private bedrooms each with queen size beds and ensuite bathrooms. Their style is rustic, romantic and warm where attention to detail shows that your comfort takes top priority. The guest lounge, with an open fire welcomes you to relax and enjoy afternoon tea while you chat about the Taupo region and your sight seeing plans. Trout fishing trips and adventure treks can be arranged by your hosts along with a myriad of other more relaxing activities.

Grace and Peter look forward to sharing their home and their company with you, assuring you of a warm welcome and a luxurious stay. Turtle the red-eared turtle and Sweetie, the cat complete the family. **Directions:** www.theloftnz.com

Taupo - Acacia Bay   *Homestay 5km W of Taupo*

Bay View Homestay
Marion & Guy Whitehouse
50/1 Wakeman Road, Acacia Bay, Taupo
Tel (07) 378 7873   Fax (07) 378 7893
Mob 021 211 2904
www.bnb.co.nz/bayviewhomestay.html
Double $100 Single $60 (Continental Breakfast)
Dinner by arrangement
1 Queen 1 Twin (2 bdrm)

Enjoy the warm hospitality with your hosts Marion and
Guy, retired deer farmers and friendly cat 'Kita'. Our quiet, relaxing, modern, contemporary home of native timbers offers open-plan living, air conditioning, double glazing, off-road parking. Spectacular panoramic views of Lake Taupo and mountains. Taupo's shimmering lights by night. Minutes from lake, fishing, tennis, native walks, restaurant. 5km to Taupo township and local attractions, thermal pools, Huka Falls, Huka jet, chartered fishing, bungy, golf. Bookings can be arranged. Please phone for directions.

Taupo   *B&B Homestay Boutique Accommodation 3km S of Taupo*

Moorhill
Liz & Peter Sharland
27 Korimako Road, Taupo,
Tel (07) 377 1069   Fax (07) 377 1069
Mob 021 300 455   petenlizr@xtra.co.nz
www.moorhill.co.nz
Double $125-$145 Single $110 (Continental Breakfast)
(Full Breakfast) Dinner By arrangement
1 Queen 1 Twin (2 bdrm)
2 Ensuite

Moorhill is ideally situated for relaxing weekends, a base
for sightseeing or experiencing Taupo's more adventurous activities. Enjoy our peaceful, mature garden; wake to the sounds of Bellbirds and Tuis. The queen room has luxury ensuite; sitting area with garden access. Upstairs, the spacious twin room, with ensuite, has views of Lake Taupo. Rooms have electric blankets, hairdryers, tea making and ironing facilities. Breakfast style and time to suit. We enjoy sharing travel experiences, gardening, sport, music, good food and wine. Off-street parking for cars/boats.

Taupo   *B&B Self-contained 3.5km S of Taupo*

Norfolk Lodge
Elizabeth Lomas
1 Norfolk Road, Taupo,
Tel (07) 377 4318   Mob 025 605 0724
liz@norfolk-lodge.co.nz
www.norfolk-lodge.co.nz
Double $110 Single $75 (Continental Breakfast)
Self-contained $175 Children welcome
3 Double 2 Single (2 bdrm)

Discover Norfolk Lodge situated in a tranquil tree setting
with stunning lake views. Enjoy space and style in your private self-contained apartment with fully equipped kitchen and laundry. Up to 8 guests comfortably catered for (B&B also available). What could be better than watching the sunset over the lake from your secluded garden patio? Short stroll to scenic lakeside walks. Only 4 mins drive from Taupo's many top class restaurants and shops. Located in a quiet cul de sac with ample off street parking.

Taupo   *B&B Homestay 15km N of Taupo*

Maimoa House
Margaret & Godfrey Ellis
41 Oak Dr; off Palmer Mill Rd, Taupo
Tel 07 376 9000 mewestview@xtra.co.nz
www.bnb.co.nz/to follow.html
Double $80-$95 Single $60 (Continental Breakfast)
Child $30 Dinner by arrangement $30
Children welcome Pets welcome
1 Queen 1 Twin 1 Single (3 bdrm)   1 Private

Hello and welcome to our brand new rural hilltop home,
with spectacular views over the countryside, mountains and lake. You will be made very welcome in
this scenic 12 acres just 15 minutes from town, but only minutes from thermal villages and Huka Falls.
We are a semi-retired couple with a friendly flat coated retriever. Our interests include church activities
and walking.

Turangi   *B&B Homestay Self-contained + Self contained cottage 1.5km E of Turangi Central*

The Andersons'
Betty & Jack Anderson
3 Poto Street, Turangi
Tel (07) 386 8272 Fax (07) 386 8272
Mob 025 628 0810 jbanderson@xtra.co.nz
www.bnb.co.nz/anderson.html
Double $90 Single $70 (Full Breakfast)
Child in cottage only   Self-contained cottage $75-$140
Credit cards accepted
2 Queen 1 Twin (3 bdrm)   3 Ensuite

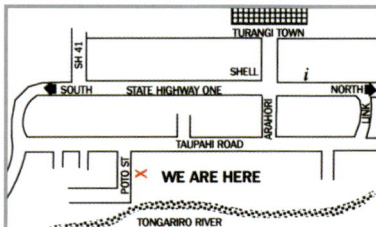

Welcome to our smoke-free home, with ensuite bathrooms for your comfort. Situated in a quiet street,
beside Tongariro River walkway, handy to restaurants and town and fishing. Arranged transport to
Tongariro National Park at your door. Lake Taupo and thermal baths five minutes drive. Upstairs
queen rooms with balconies, separated for privacy by tea/coffee making area. Downstairs has twin
suite, laundry and lounge where we'll share interests in flying, skiing, fishing, tramping, and maps, of
our volcanic area. Guest-shy cat. Cottage is suitable for families.

Turangi   *B&B Self-contained 53km S of Taupo*

Akepiro Cottage
Jenny & John Wilcox
PO Box 256, Turangi
Tel (07) 386 7384 Fax (07) 386 6838
jennywilcox@xtra.co.nz
www.bnb.co.nz/akepirocottage.html
Double $100 Single $50 (Continental Breakfast)
continental breakfast on req. $10, twin $100
Credit cards accepted
2 Queen 2 Single (2 bdrm)
1 Private

Half-acre woodland garden, featuring rhododendrons and native plants, attracting many species of birds.
Access through garden gate to Tongariro River,major fishing pools. Perfect retreat for restful break.
Close to excellent 18 hole golf course, 1/2 hour to the mountains, the Tongariro Crossing. many walking
tracks and World Heritage park. Our home and garden are adjacent, but utmost privacy maintained.
Full kitchen, laundry, all linen supplied, TV, BBQ. Breakfast must be requested if required. Come,
share this corner of nature's paradise.

Turangi
B&B Homestay Separate/Suite Self-contained 1km E of Turangi

Ika Fishing Lodge
Suzanne & Kerry Simpson
155 Taupahi Road, PO Box 259, Turangi
Tel (07) 386 5538 Fax (07) 386 5538
ikalodge@xtra.co.nz
www.ika.co.nz

Double $140-$160 Single $120-$140 (Full Breakfast)
Dinner $50pp self-contained apartment $160 - $200
Credit cards accepted
2 King/Twin 3 Queen (4 bdrm)
3 Ensuite

You open the back gate and there is the Island Pool. We can now offer 1 self contained unit with 2 bedrooms, kitchen, lounge and sun deck. 2 double rooms inside the lodge with ensuites. A spacious lounge with open fire is available along with Sky TV. Kerry, your guide has fished the area for 50 years and has been a guide for some 30 years. Suzanne, the other Simpson partner is your resident chef and is renowned for her trout sashimi. Please come and "enjoy".

Turangi - Motuoapa
B&B Self-contained 10km N of Turangi

Meredith House
Frances & Ian Meredith
45 Kahotea Place, Motuoapa, RD 2, Turangi
Tel (07) 386 5266 Fax (07) 386 5270
meredith.house@xtra.co.nz
www.bnb.co.nz/meredithhouse.html

Double $90 Single $60 (Continental Full Breakfast)
Self-contained (breakfast extra) $100 - $120
Credit cards accepted Children welcome
1 Queen 3 Single (2 bdrm) 1 Private

Stop and enjoy this outdoor Paradise. Just off SH1 (B & B Sign). Overlooking Lake Taupo, our two-storey home offers ground-floor self-contained accommodation with own entrance. Fully equipped Kitchen, Dining room, Lounge. Two cosy bedrooms (each with TV). Vehicle/Boat off-street parking. Minutes to Marina and World-renowned Lake/river fishing. Beautiful bush walks. 45 minutes to ski fields and Tongariro National Park. Our association with Tongariro/Taupo area spans over 30 years, through work and outdoor pursuits. Welcome to our Retreat.

Turangi
B&B 54km S of Taupo

Founders at Turangi
Peter & Chris Stewart
253 Taupahi Road, Turangi
Tel (07) 386 8539 0800 FOUNDERS
Fax (07) 386 8534 Mob 025 854 000
founders@ihug.co.nz www.founders.co.nz

Double $150 Single $80 (Full Breakfast) Whole lodge,
12-13 persons negotiable Credit cards accepted
1 King/Twin 3 Queen (4 bdrm)
4 Ensuite

Welcome to Turangi and to our New Zealand colonial-style home. Relax and enjoy the unique beauty of the "trout fishing capital of the world". Many outdoor activities are available at this "place for all seasons" - with Tongariro river, mountains and magnificent Lake Taupo on our doorstep. Four ensuite bedrooms open on to the veranda. Enjoy breakfast outside in the summer or pre-dinner drinks by the fire apres ski in the winter! Our friendly dog has her own kennel. Whole Lodge available - sleeps 13 self-catered.

BAY OF PLENTY

Turangi *B&B 52km S of Taupo*

The Birches
Tineke & Peter Baldwin
13 Koura Street, Turangi,
Tel (07) 386 5140   Fax (07) 386 5149
Mob 021 149 6594   tineke.peter@xtra.co.nz
www.bnb.co.nz/thebirches.html
Double $120 Single $100 (Special Breakfast)
Dinner by arrangement Credit cards accepted
1 Queen (1 bdrm)
1 Ensuite

Close to the world renowned Tongariro River we offer a charming and gracious residence in a quiet street. This unique setting has exceptional access to tramping, fly fishing, skiing, rafting or purely a retreat from life's hustle and bustle. Enjoy superior and spacious ensuite accommodation with TV and coffee/tea making facilities in a separate part of the house. Your Dutch/Canadian hosts have considerable international experience and can speak Dutch and French. Dinner by arrangement.

Turangi *B&B 16km NW of Turangi*

Wills' Place
Jill & Brian Wills
145 Omori Road, Omori,
Tel (07) 386 7339   Fax (07) 386 7339
Mob 027 228 8960   willsplace@wave.co.nz
www.laketaupo.co.nz/turangi/motels/willsplace/index.htm
Double $110 Single $80 (Full Breakfast)
(Special Breakfast) Child neg Dinner by arrangement
Children welcome
2 Queen 3 Single (2 bdrm)   1 Private

Our home is lakeside in the beautiful southwest corner of Lake Taupo with wonderful views, excellent fishing, boating, swimming, bush walks. We are off the beaten track, yet only 10-15 minutes to shops, restaurants, thermal pools, Tongariro River, rafting, kayaking, etc. 40 minutes to Tongariro National Park and ski-fields. We offer a comfortable two bedroom suite with separate entry and complete privacy. Private bathroom with bath and shower. Tea-making facilities, fridge, microwave, television, laundry. A special place we'd love to share with you.

Turangi *B&B Self-contained 15 km N of Turangi*

Plum Tree Lodge
Pauline Kerr
4 Tuki Street, Oruatua RD 2, Turangi
Tel 0064 7 3868220   Mob 0274 809622
paulker@paradise.net.nz
www.bnb.co.nz/plumtree.html
Double $85 Single $75 (Continental Breakfast)
Fisherman's Cottage $55 Children welcome
1 King/Twin 1 Queen 1 Double 2 Twin 3 Single
(2 bdrm)
2 Ensuite

Comfortable haven nestled beside Tauranga-Taupo fly fishing river famed for its runs of rainbow and brown trout. Metres from lake Taupo and boatramps. Excellent tramping rafting and skiing. The lodge has two self contained units - Fisherman's Cottage and Plum Tree Unit. Separate entrances and barbecue area. Both have ensuites and kitchen facilities. Plum Tree contains queen bed and fold down futon. Fishermans Cottage has twin/king & single. Both have TV, heating and stocked fridge/freezer with optional light meals and beverages.

Turangi   *B&B   Homestay   16km NW of Turangi*

Inukshuk Homestay
Peter and Sharon Simpson
56 TeWaaka Terrace, Kuratau, R. D. 1, Turangi

Tel (07) 386 5686   Fax (07) 386 5683
Mob 021 272 9464 or 025 811 182
inukshukhomestay@attglobal.net
www.inukshukhomestay.co.nz

Double $125-$150 Single $100-$125
(Special Breakfast)
Child Negotiable Dinner By arrangement
1 King 1 Queen (2 bdrm)   1 Ensuite 1 Private

At Inukshuk Homestay we warmly welcome guests to our new home with panoramic views of Lake Taupo. Our beautifully appointed guest rooms are furnished with your comfort in mind and include many extras. We are centrally located 10 minutes from restaurants and 40 minutes from the ski fields and National Park. Your day begins with a sumptuous special breakfast before enjoying local adventure activities, thermal pools, bush walks, and trout fishing. Friendly pet schnauzer in residence.

Turangi   *B&B Self-contained 2km N of Turangi*

Dyden Cottage
Sarah & Graeme Henshaw
Old Mill Lane, 134 Grace Road RD 2, Turangi

Tel (07) 386 6050   Fax (07) 386 6052
Mob 021 402 278   dydencottage@xtra.co.nz
www.bnb.co.nz/dydencottage.html

Double $90 Single $60 (Continental Breakfast)
Child $10 Dinner $35 B/A Children welcome
1 Queen 1 Single (1 bdrm)
1 Ensuite

Dyden Cottage offers self-contained accommodation set in five acres of mature gardens and farmland. It has a separate entrance and private outdoor area. The cottage sleeps three and includes an ensuite bathroom and living area with television. The kitchen is stocked with everything you need for a hearty breakfast ? including fresh eggs from the property. Enjoy the peace and tranquility of your surroundings or take advantage of the world class fly fishing, bush walks, golf, boating, river rafting and skiing all within easy reach of Turangi.

BAY OF PLENTY

A homestay is a B&B
where you share the family's living area.

Gisborne

Waihau Bay

Te Kaha

Maraenui

35

Anaura Bay

Whatatutu

Tologa Bay

2

Waipaoa

Ormond

Whangara

Gisborne

Tiniroto

2

Towns listed generally follow
a north to south route. Refer
to the index if required.

0	Kilometres	20

| 0 | Miles | 12 |

Anaura Bay
B&B Farmstay Homestay Self-contained Beachstay 23km N of Tol

Anaura Beachstay or Willowflat Farmstay B&B
June & Allan Hall
Tolaga Bay, Gisborne

Tel (06) 862 6341 Fax (06) 862 6371
Mob 021 267 4909 willowflat@xtra.co.nz
www.geocities.com/anaura7/

Double $90 Single $60 (Full Breakfast)
Child Half price Dinner $25 S/C Beachfront Cottage,
2 Double + $120-$180 p.n. min 2 nights
1 Queen 1 Double (2 bdrm) 2 Host share

Paradise - the best of both worlds - Breakfast at our beachfront cottage in picturesque Anaura Bay, glorious sunrises, white sand and backdrop of beautiful native bush, fishing, walkways, or at Willowflat, our sheep, cattle and cropping farm, spacious home and grounds, an hour north of Gisborne. Village, Cashmere Company, fishing charters, hunting, golf, reserves within 12 km of Willowflat or 23 km of Beachstay. Self-contained option available both venues $120-$180 per night, Beachstay 2 doubles plus, Farmstay 3 doubles plus, min. 2 nights.

Tolaga Bay
Homestay Self-contained 3km N of Tolaga Bay, Gisborne 55km

Papatahi
Nicki & Bruce Jefferd
427 Main Road North, Tolaga Bay,

Tel (06) 862 6623 Fax (06) 862 6623
Mob 025 283 7178 b.n.jefferd@xtra.co.nz
www.bnb.co.nz/papatahi.html

Double $95 Single $60 (Full Breakfast)
Child 1/2 price Dinner $25 Children welcome
1 Queen 1 Double (2 bdrm)
1 Ensuite 1 Guests share

Papatahi Homestay is very easy to find being just 3km north of the Tolaga Bay township, on the Pacific Coast Highway. We have a comfortable, modern, sunny home set in a wonderful garden. Papatahi offers separate accommodation with ensuite. A golf course, fishing charters, the Tolaga Bay Cashmere Co and several magnificent beaches are all just minutes away. Daily farm activities are often of interest to our guests. Friendly farm pets and three children add to the experience! Great country meals and good wine are a speciality. Inspection will impress!

Whangara
Farmstay Self-contained 50km E of Gisborne

The Roost
Nick Reed
Mataurangi Station, 1389 Panikau Road, Gisborne

Tel (06) 862 2858 0800 398 411 Fax (06) 862 2857
Mob 025 242 2449 mataurangi@xtra.co.nz
www.bnb.co.nz/theroost.html

Double $80 Single $50 (Continental Breakfast)
Child $25
1 Double 1 Single (1 bdrm)
1 Private

Mataurangi is a 607 Ha Hill Country sheep and cattle station situated 14km up Panikau Rd, off SH35 between Tolaga Bay and Gisborne. You will stay in "The Roost"; a secluded, fully refurbished, self contained shepherds cottage. (Full kitchen facilities, BBQ, sundeck and small garden). While we may be slightly off the beaten track, we know you will enjoy the experience, and look forward to meeting you and sharing our corner of New Zealand. Please phone for detailed directions.

Whatatutu   *Farmstay 50km NE of Gisborne*

Te Hau Station
Chris and Jenny Meban
332 Te Hau Road, Whatatutu, Eastland 3871
Tel (06) 862 1822   0800 686218   Fax (06) 862 1997
Mob 025 844 574   tehaustn@xtra.co.nz
darla.mit.edu/~mountain/te_hau/tehau.htm
Double $95 Single $70 (Full Breakfast)
Child 1/2 price Dinner $30 Credit cards accepted
Children welcome Pets welcome
1 Queen 2 Double 2 Single (3 bdrm)
1 Ensuite 1 Guests share 1 Host share

Our Colonial Farmhouse, on a 6000 acre hill country station, is an easy 40 minute drive from Gisborne, off SH2 North. Enjoy hands-on farm experiences, learning about life on a sheep and cattle station; watch the shepherds riding horses, expertly handling stock with their sheepdogs. Walking, clay-bird shooting and hunting are all options, or enjoy the many facilities we have to offer including our pool and hot spa. Our two young sons take pleasure in showing guests their many pets. Horse-riding $20/hr. All meals available.

Waipaoa   *Farmstay 20km N of Gisborne*

The Willows
Rosemary & Graham Johnson
& Montgomerie the Labrador
Waipaoa, RD 1, Gisborne
Tel (06) 862 5605 Fax (06) 862 5601
Mob 025 837 365
www.bnb.co.nz/thewillows.html
Double $80 Single $50 (Full Breakfast)
Child 10% discount Dinner $30, by arrangement
2 Queen 2 Single (3 bdrm)
1 Private 1 Guests share

Our home is situated on a hill amid a park like garden with some wonderful trees planted by our forefathers. We enjoy the amenities available in the city and also the country life on our 440 acre property involving deer, cattle, sheep, grapes and cropping. We now offer a double bedroom with a private bathroom. The bedroom has its own access so you can enjoy privacy if you so desire. We are situated 20km north of Gisborne on SH2 through the scenic Waioeka Gorge.

Ormond   *B&B Self-contained Orchard Stay, Large Self-contained Villa 18km N of Gisborne*

Kiwifruit Orchard Stay
Jenny & Greig Foster
37 Bond Road, RD1, Ormond, Gisborne
Tel (06) 862 5688 Fax (06) 862 5688
Mob 027 441 2876   jdfoster@ihug.co.nz
www.bnb.co.nz/kiwifruitorchardstay.html
Double $95-$130 Single $85-$95 (Special Breakfast)
Child $25 Dinner $35 Children welcome
3 Queen 3 Single (3 bdrm)
2 Private

Set amongst the chardonnay capital of NZ. Country Living with style and comfort. Stay in our Villa Moderna, self-contained or our home with private lounge and bathroom. Spend lazy afternoons in the sun sampling wine from our local wineries. During the chillier winter nights take a long soak in our indoor spa and watch the stars set amongst the chardonnay capital of NZ. Come relax with us and our cats and dogs on our kiwifruit orchard and sample the fruit. Five minutes to restaurant bar/grill. Fax, internet, email, spa, swimming pool available.

Ormond *Self-contained 18km N of Gisborne*

Hide-a-way Cottage
Paul and Pauline Manning
1354 Matawai Rd (SH2), Ormond RD 1, Gisborne
Tel (06) 862 5456   0800 100 430   Fax (06) 862 5802
paulandpauline@xtra.co.nz
www.bnb.co.nz/user98.html

Double $90 Single $75 (Continental Breakfast)
Child $10 Dinner $20 Credit cards accepted
Children welcome
1 Queen 1 Double 2 Single (2 bdrm)   1 Private

Your hosts, Paul and Pauline welcome you to Hide-a-
way Cottage. The cottage is situated on our mandarin orchard with a rural outlook overlooking our trees
and surrounding vineyards to the hills. The cottage captures the sun from early morning to late evening.
It is very pivate and peaceful, fully self-contained with ramps and bathroom set up for the disabled. We
breed Burmese cats and have two house cats also. By arrangement and for a small cost guests can share
dinner with us.

Gisborne *B&B Homestay Gisborne Central*

Thomson Homestay
Barbara & Alec Thomson
16 Rawiri Street, Gisborne
Tel (06) 868 9675   0800 370 505   Fax (06) 868 9675
Mob 027 420 0264
www.bnb.co.nz/thomsonhomestay.html

Double $80 Single $60 (Continental/Full Breakfast)
1 Queen 2 Twin (2 bdrm)
1 Guests share

From our spacious home it is only a five minute stroll to
the city centre, wharf complex, museum, rose gardens
etc. Secure internal garaging available. We are happy to meet bus or plane. Guests have own TV
lounge with tea and coffee making facilities etc. Alec and I enjoy a game of bridge, and are also keen
bowlers.

Gisborne *B&B Homestay Gisborne Central*

Sea View
Raewyn & Gary Robinson
68 Salisbury Road, Gisborne
Tel (06) 867 3879   0800 268 068   Fax (06) 867 5879
Mob 021 214 4316   raewyn@regaleggs.co.nz
www.bnb.co.nz/seaviewgisborne.html

Double $95 Single $70 (Continental Breakfast)
Children welcome
2 Double 1 Twin 1 Single (3 bdrm)
2 Private

Absolute luxury and comfort. Beachfront bed and breakfast. Seaview is situated on the foreshore of
Waikanae beach with unsurpassed panoramic views of Young Nicks head and beautiful Poverty Bay.
Just 50 metres from front door to golden sand, and warm blue waters of Poverty Bay. Only two minutes
drive to the city (easy walking distance) and visitor information centre. Relax and enjoy safe swimming
and great surfing. Five minutes to international golf course and Olympic pool complex. We offer 2
double bedrooms and twin room. 2 private bathrooms. Internet facilities available.

Rouse
Wainui Beach, Gisborne
Fax (06) 868 8162
Mob 025 794 929   pete.dot@xtra.co.nz
www.bnb.co.nz/beachstaygisborne.html

Double $85 Single $50 (Full Breakfast) Child $10
Dinner $25 Credit cards accepted Smoking area inside
1 Queen 2 Double 2 Single (2 bdrm)
1 Ensuite 1 Private

We welcome you to our home which is situated right on the beach front at Wainui. The steps from the lawn lead down to the beach, which is renowned for its lovely clean sand, surf, pleasant walking and good swimming. Gisborne can also offer a host of entertainment, including golf on one of the finest golf courses, charter fishing trips, wine trails, Eastwood Hill Arboretum, horse trekking etc, or you may wish to relax on the beach for the day with a light luncheon provided.

Gisborne   *Homestay 24km W of Gisborne*

Manurere
Joanne & John Sherratt
RD 2, Ngatapa, Gisborne
Tel (06) 863 9852   Fax (06) 863 9842
john.sherratt@xtra.co.nz
www.bnb.co.nz/manurere.html

Double $100 Single $60 (Full Breakfast)
Dinner $20 Credit cards accepted
1 Queen 1 Single (1 bdrm)
1 Ensuite

Manurere

We have a lovely old villa in a peaceful setting in an old established country garden, only 20 minutes from the city centre and beaches. We have a tennis court and swimming pool available in season. We enjoy meeting people and regard homestaying as a wonderful way of achieving this by sharing our home and hospitality with others. Come and enjoy the Ngatapa Valley with our famous 'Eastwoodhill Arboretum' 5 minutes away and also local crafts and furniture makers. Reservations by appointment only.

Gisborne   *Homestay   8km N of Gisborne*

Makorori Heights
Roger & Morag Shanks
36 Sirrah St, Wainui Beach, Gisborne
Tel (06) 867 0806   Fax (06) 868 7706
Mob 021 250 4918
www.bnb.co.nz/ .html

Double $80 Single $45 (Full Breakfast)   Dinner $25
Credit cards accepted
1 Double 2 Single (2 bdrm)
1 Guests share 1 Host share

Our home is 1/2 km off Highway 35 at the northern end of Wainui Beach. With beautiful sea and sunrise views, surrounded by farmland and our own young olive grove. Handy to bush and coastal walkways. We have travelled overseas and enjoy the company of others. Roger is a water colour artist with examples of his overseas and local works available for viewing or purchase. Horse trekking, fishing trips, country excursions by arrangements. We have one friendly small dog not allowed indoors.

Gisborne *B&B Homestay 1km E of Gisborne*

Fox Street Retreat
Jan & Alan Saunders
103 Fox Street, Gisborne

Tel (06) 868 8702   0800 868 8702   Fax (06) 868 8702
Mob 025 907 777   jan.saunders@clear.net.nz
www.geocities.com/fox_street_retreat

Double $70 Single $50 (Continental Breakfast)
Child $25 Dinner by arrangement
Credit cards accepted
1 Queen 1 Twin (2 bdrm)
1 Host share

Welcome to our tasteful retreat situated in our delightful gardens in a quiet location within easy walking distance of city. Relax around our pool and enjoy use of our BBQ. Sky TV in bedrooms. We play bowls and bridge and will gladly arrange games for guests. We are Tuberous Begonia enthusiasts with lovely display in gardens, pots and baskets in season. We will gladly arrange tours. Cut lunches on request. Off street parking available.

Gisborne *B&B Gisborne*

Riverbank Homestay
Judy, David and Marney Newell
100 Oak Street, Gisborne

Tel 021 633 372   Fax (06) 868 9340
Mob 021 633 372   riverbank@xtra.co.nz
www.anaura-stay.co.nz

Double $75-$85 Single $50 (Full Breakfast)
Child $20 Dinner $25 Credit cards accepted
Children welcome
1 Queen 1 Double 1 Twin (3 bdrm)
1 Ensuite 1 Private 1 Guests share

We are a retired couple used to travel during working lives-our guests now keep us (and daughter Marney) in touch with the outside world and are a welcome source of new friendships. Our home is on a quiet riverbank section 5 minutes by car from city centre. We offer a large, airy, private studio with ensuite, TV, and deck or rooms, with private bathroom, in the family living area. We also have a beachfront homestay "Rangimarie" at beautiful Anaura Bay on SH 35.

GISBORNE

Gisborne *B&B Homestay 2km NE of Gisborne*

Herons Mead Lodge
Avril & Brian Jackson
5 Island Road, Gisborne

Tel (06) 868 1224   Fax (06) 868 1224
Mob 021 189 2486   heronsmead@xtra.co.nz
www.roan.co.nz/heronsmead

Double $80 Single $55 (Full Breakfast)
Child $20 sharing family room
Dinner $25 pp By prior arrangement
2 Double 1 Single (2 bdrm)   2 Ensuite 1 Private

Herons Mead Lodge is situated on the outer boundary of Gisborne City, in a semi-rural setting. Avril and Brian offer comfortable, home from home, accommodation, where guests are welcomed as part of the family. Gisborne is New Zealand's best kept secret, with miles of clean golden beaches, and beautiful scenery. Enjoy our restaurants and cafes, where good food and a wide choice is the norm. Soak up the sunshine, the atmosphere, the history of the region, and visit local wineries and other places of interest in the area.

rne *B&B 5mins Gisborne Central*

Jula Villa
Jy Sa
1 Mill Road, Gisborne,
Tel (06) 867 5439
www.bnb.co.nz/sa.html

Double $90 Single $60 (Continental Breakfast)
1 Queen 1 Single (2 bdrm)
1 Host share

Calendula Villa is a 90 year old home offering traditional comforts with a Mediterranean twist. Guests can relax in the spacious bedroom and enjoy the quiet garden setting from the old-fashioned wisteria covered verandah. The separate guest lounge has TV, fridge, tea/coffee facilities and refreshments, while the bathroom offers a claw-foot bath as well as shower. An easy five minute drive to the centre of town ensures you will enjoy all that Gisborne has to offer.

Gisborne - Wainui *B&B 5km NE of Gisborne*

Best Beach View
Annabel Reynolds
8 Tuahine Cresent, Wainui, Gisborne
Tel (06) 868 9757 Fax (06) 867 9003
mahara_hara@family.net.nz
www.bnb.co.nz/reynolds.html

Double $95 Single $60 (Continental/Full Breakfast)
Children welcome
1 Queen (1 bdrm)
1 Ensuite 1 Private

Best Beach View sits on Tuahine Point at the southern end of Wainui Beach. Because of its elevated position it has spectacular and panoramic views overlooking all of Wainui, and seeing the early morning sunrise is fantastic. The double room and ensuite has outside access opening onto a private garden with a barbeque for your use. Tuahine Crescent is very peaceful and quiet with plenty of off street parking. Walking on the beach is a great way to unwind after travelling and you can get a wonderful meal at the Sandbar Restaurant (five minute walk away).

Gisborne - Wairoa *Farmstay Self-contained 60km SW of Gisborne*

Rongoio Farm Stay
Matt & Jude Stock
Ruakaka Rd, Tiniroto, Gisborne
Tel (06) 867 4065 Fax (06) 863 7018
rongoio@paradise.net.nz
www.bnb.co.nz/rongoiostation.html

Double $100 Single $80 (Special Breakfast)
Child $20 Dinner $30 Surcharge for 1 night only $10
1 King 1 Queen 3 Single (3 bdrm)
1 Private

Join us on our 440 hectare hill country sheep and cattle farm and enjoy all that rural NZ life offers. Very close to the homestead but secluded by established trees is a three bedroom totally self contained cottage. From this cosy home feel the remote peace and tranquillity along with the magnificent views of the trout filled Hangaroa River and waterfall. We encourage guests to participate in rural activities including fishing, wild game shooting, horse and motor bike riding, possum shooting and eeling. Warm friendly back country hospitality is our specialty. Children most welcome but no pets.

Taranaki, Wanganui, Ruapehu, Rangitikei

Te Awamutu

Otorohanga

Waitomo

Te Kuiti

Piopio

Taumarunui

Waitara

New Plymouth

Raurimu

National Park

Stratford

Raetihi   Ohakune

Hawera

Taihape

Waitotara

Mangaweka

Wanganui   Hunterville

Marton

Fielding   Colyton

Woodville

Oroua Downs

Palmerston North

Tokomaru

Foxton   Pahia

Eketahuna

Levin

Otaki
Te Horo

Towns listed generally follow
a north to south route. Refer
to the index if required.

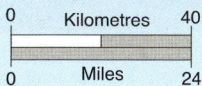

0	Kilometres	40

0	Miles	24

Waitara   *B&B Homestay Self-contained 15kms N of New Plymouth*

Trenowth Gardens
Sherril and Ken George
2 Armstrong Avenue, Waitara, Taranaki
Tel (06) 754 7674   Fax (06) 754 8884
Mob 025 736 055   sherril@trenowth.co.nz
www.trenowth.com
Double $80 Single $65 (Full Breakfast)
Child $15 Dinner $25pp Credit cards accepted
2 Double 1 Single (2 bdrm)
1 Ensuite 1 Private

Garden Homestay plus self-contained B&B cottage situated right on the main north-south Auckland/
New Plymouth/Wellington highway at historic Waitara. Large family house with guest homestay(ensuite)
plus additional B&B cottage with separate bedroom,lounge/dining/kitchen area with separate bathroom/
laundry/toilet. Fully equipped with TV/music/library; all set in 18 acres of landscaped gardens, private
lake and orchards. Close to 4 golf courses, local fishing, bush and mountain walks. Ten minutes from
New Plymouth restaurants, twenty minutes from the mountain.

New Plymouth   *Homestay 6km SE of New Plymouth*

Blacksmiths Rest
Evelyn & Laurie Cockerill
481 Mangorei Road, New Plymouth
Tel (06) 758 6090   Fax (06) 758 6078
Mob 025 678 8641
www.bnb.co.nz/blacksmithsrest.html
Double $80-$90 Single $50 (Full Breakfast)
Dinner $25 by arrangement
2 Queen 1 Twin 2 Single (3 bdrm)
1 Ensuite 1 Private 1 Host share

Relax and enjoy our rural views although we are only five minutes drive from city centre while the well
known "Tupare Gardens" are just next door.   Each guest room has a queen and a single bed with an
ensuite in the upstairs bedroom. We have a large garden, some sheep and a friendly dog called Bill who
lives outside. Interests, equestrian, sport, gardening. There is plenty of off street parking. Mangorei
Road can be easily found when approaching New Plymouth from either north or south.

New Plymouth - Omata   *B&B 5km S of New Plymouth*

Rangitui
Therese & Tony Waghorn
Waireka Road, RD 4, New Plymouth
Tel (06) 751 2979   Fax (06) 751 2985
twaghorn@clear.net.nz
www.accommodationtaranaki.co.nz
Double $70-$90 Single $60-$80 (Full Breakfast)
Portacot available Dinner $40 Credit cards accepted
1 Queen 2 Single (2 bdrm)
1 Ensuite 1 Private

10 minutes from New Plymouth. Separate chalet with ensuite, queen bed, TV, and balcony overlooking
bush and sea. Twin room with guest facilities in house. Your choice of breakfast (except kippers!)
Dinner with wine, $40 per head, by arrangement. Enjoy bush or orchard walks, relax by our pool, or
visit some of the nearby attractions: beautiful Mt Taranaki, some of the best surf in the world, famous
gardens, art gallery, museum, historic sites and golf courses. Bookings: Please phone for reservations/
directions.

New Plymouth *Homestay* *of New Plymouth Central*

Kirkstall House
Ian Hay & Lindy MacDiarmid
8 Baring Terrace, New Plymouth
Tel (06) 758 3222   Fax (06) 758 3224
Mob 025 973 908   kirkstall@xtra.co.nz
www.bnb.co.nz/ .html

Double $85 Single $65 (Continental Breakfast)
Ensuite room $95/$75
1 Queen 1 Double 1 Twin (3 bdrm)
1 Ensuite 2 Private

îKirkstall Houseî invites you to experience its old world beauty and comfort, in an atmosphere of easy hospitality and relaxed surroundings. ìKirkstall Houseî is one of surprise. Enjoy our superb mountain views, cosy open fire, and delightful garden leading down to the river. The sea, beaches, and walkways, restaurants and shops are all within easy walking distance. Lindy, a practising physiotherapist, and Ian, involved with tourism, are here to help you enjoy Taranakai to the utmost. We are smoke free, have 2 cats and a dog named Eva.

New Plymouth *B&B Homestay Farmlet 5km W of New Plymouth Central*

Birdhaven
Ann & John Butler
26 Pararewa Drive, New Plymouth
Tel (06) 751 0432   Fax (06) 751 3475
Mob 0274 167 166   info@birdhaven.co.nz
www.birdhaven.co.nz

Double $86-$110 Single $59-$90 (Special Breakfast)
Child b/a Dinner b/a Credit cards accepted
1 King/Twin 1 Queen 2 Single (2 bdrm)
1 Private 1 Guests share

Ensuring your comfort and pleasure is important to us. We have lived in three continents and enjoy travelling. We love welcoming guests to Birdhaven and endeavouring to exceed your expectations. Share our tranquil, spacious, tastefully furnished home, secluded gardens and spectacular mountain view. Relax on the patios overlooking our beautiful native bush, woodlands and birdlife. Indulge in the complimentary refreshments and the special breakfast of seasonal and homemade temptations. A peaceful retreat only five minutes from city. Cedric, our cat, is gregarious and well behaved.

New Plymouth *Farmstay Self-contained 3km S of New Plymouth*

Oak Valley Manor
Pat & Paul Ekdahl
248 Junction Road, RD 1, New Plymouth
Tel (06) 758 1501 Fax (06) 758 1052
Mob 025 420 325   kauri.holdings@xtra.co.nz
www.bnb.co.nz/oakvalleymanor.html

Double $105 Single $75 (Full Breakfast)
Child $1 per year up to 12yrs Dinner $30
Pets welcome   Credit cards accepted
2 Queen 1 Single (2 bdrm)
2 Ensuite

Your hosts, Pat and Paul, two friendly people with a wealth of experience in the hospitality industry, invite you to a unique bed and breakfast in their beautifully appointed home with views from each room to Mount Egmont. These beautiful views make an impression which we will everlasting. Guests can choose their own privacy or socialise with us. We have a variety of animals, donkey, peacocks, pigs, and dogs. Ducks and geese enjoy the lake. Golf course 10 minute drive. Laundry available.

193

New Plymouth   *Self-contained 25km N of New Plymouth*

Cottage by the Sea
Nancy & Hugh Mills
66 Lower Turangi Road, RD 43, Waitara

Tel (06) 754 7915 Fax (06) 754 7915
nancy.mills@clear.net.nz
www.bnb.co.nz/cottagebytheseanewplymouth.html

Double $120 Single $100 (Continental Breakfast)
Child neg extra person $20
1 Queen 1 Double (1 bdrm)
1 Ensuite

Go to sleep with the sound of the waves...wake with the birds. You will have this modern, peaceful cottage all to yourself. It is nestled amongst landscaped gardens and lawns, and offers complete privacy. You may take a short bushwalk down 100 steps to the beach, relax on the veranda watching ever-changing sea views, or bring your surf-casting gear. The sofabed in the lounge makes into a comfortable double bed. The kitchen is fully equipped, so subtract $10.00 per person if you wish to provide your own breakfast. Our family dog may greet you.

New Plymouth   *Homestay Separate/Suite*

The Grange
Cathy Thurston & John Smith
The Grange, 44B Victoria Road,
New Plymouth Central

Tel (06) 758 1540   Fax (06) 758 1539
Mob 027 4333 497 cathyt@clear.net.nz
www.bnb.co.nz/thegrange.html

Double $110 Single $85 (Full Breakfast)
Credit cards accepted
1 King/Twin 1 Queen 2 Single (2 bdrm)
2 Ensuite

Come and stay in our modern architecturally designed award-winning home built with the privacy and comfort of our guests in mind. With unique bush views and a house designed to take full advantage of the sun our guests can enjoy relaxing in the lounge or the extensive tiled courtyards. The Grange is centrally heated, security controlled and located adjacent to the renowned Pukekura Park and Bowl of Brooklands. The city is within a short 5 minute walk.

New Plymouth   *B&B Separate suite New Plymouth Central*

93 By the Sea
Patricia & Bruce Robinson
93 Buller Street, New Plymouth

Tel (06) 758 6555   Mob 025 230 3887
pat@93bythesea.co.nz
www.pat@93bythesea.co.nz

Double $120-$100 Single $100-$80 (Special Breakfast)
Dinner by arrangement Children welcome
1 King/Twin 1 Double (2 bdrm)
1 Private

A supremely comfortable character home, situated on the New Plymouth coastal walkway.   Just two minutes from sandy, surf beaches and swimming. Tranquil river pathway, 15 minutes stroll along the sea front to the city centre. Two large bedrooms, private entrance, off-street parking, lounge, unique bathroom (spa-bath, walk in shower) and laundry facilities are for guests' personal use, with the option of an exclusive one party booking, or shared facilities. Enjoy a special breakfast, with a view over gardens, to the ever-changing Tasman Sea.

New Plymouth *B&B Seashore Luxury Caravan 1km S of Civic Centre*

The Treehouse
Lorraine & Herbert Abel
75 Morley Street, New Plymouth
Tel (06) 757 4288 herbabel@xtra.co.nz
www.bnb.co.nz/thetreehouse.html

Double $85 Single $60 (Full Breakfast)
Dinner $25 B/A Seashore Luxury Caravan $75
Credit cards accepted
1 King 1 Queen 2 Twin (3 bdrm)
1 Guests share

Lorraine and Herb invite you to our stunning Treehouse. Our guest accommodation is situated downstairs with all rooms opening on to our attractive garden, but please feel free to join us upstairs or lounge on our sunny deck anytime. We are just minutes from all amenities and beautiful Pukekura Park. Our home is smoke free but not suitable for children or pets. Ample off street parking available. Lorraine, Herb and our friendly house cat look forward to meeting you. Beautiful beach site accommodation also available.

New Plymouth *B&B Self-contained*

Vineyard Holiday Flat
Shirley & Trevor Knuckey
12 Scott St, Moturoa, New Plymouth
Tel (06) 751 2992 Fax (06) 751 2995
Mob 025 622 3553 shirley12vineyard@xtra.co.nz
www.bnb.co.nz/vineyardholidayflat.html

Double $75 Triple $100 Single $50 (Full Breakfast)
Child $15 Dinner by arrangement
Credit cards accepted
1 Double 1 Twin (1 bdrm) 1 Ensuite

Situated in New Plymouth's port-view Moturoa suburb. Pass the hobby vines to the spacious upstairs open-plan studio, maximising 320 views of harbour, mountains, city; coast north and south. Handy to surfing and shoreline pleasures. Guests may be as self-contained as wished - with lock-up garage, separate entrance and mini-kitchen. Lounge has private balcony, dining-table, Sky TV. Extra bed(s) by arrangement. Shirley and Trevor bring their own wide traveling to their enthusiasm to ensure guests' enjoyment. There is a pet cat.

New Plymouth *Separate/Suite Guest House New Plymouth central*

Issey Manor
Carol & Lewis
32 Carrington Street, New Plymouth,
Tel (06) 758 2375 Fax (06) 758 2375
Mob 025 248 6686 issey.manor@actrix.co.nz
www.isseymanor.co.nz

Double $100-$150 (Full Breakfast)
Child by arrangement corporate rates available
Credit cards accepted
1 King/Twin 3 Queen (4 bdrm)
4 Ensuite

Issey Manor offers 4 luxury contemporary suites, all with designer bathrooms, 2 having spa baths. All rooms have beautiful bedding, refreshments, phones, work desks, data points comfortable seating, email, fax available. Separate guest dining/lounge, Sky TV. An inner city location just minutes stroll to many cafes, seaside promenade, art galleries, Information Centre, Pukekura Park and Brooklands Bowl. Enjoy our many books, artwork, collectables and relax on the enormous decking overlooking a tranquil bush and stream vista. For business or pleasure your comfort and privacy assured.

New Plymouth *B&B 5km W of City Centre*

Bradford Way B&B
Joy & Robbie Peel
186 South Road, New Plymouth,
Tel (06) 751 0551   Fax (06) 751 0551
Mob 021 038 1849
bradfordway@ihug.co.nz
www.bnb.co.nz/bradfordwaybb.html

Double $85-$95 Single $50-$75
(Special Breakfast) Dinner $25 B/A
Child half price
2 Queen 1 Twin (3 bdrm)
2 Ensuite 1 Private

We are the closest city B&B to surf highway and fabulous beaches. Also nearby to bush walks on Mt Taranaki or Pukekura and Brooklands Parks or you can take a walk along our coastal walkway.
Visit the art galleries or enjoy a game of golf at one of our excellent golf courses. We are well situated on a main road making us easy to find and we have good off-street parking. Complimentary laundry facilities available.
Our spacious well appointed guest wing has its own TV lounge/sporting library and fridge. A separate entrance is off a large courtyard with tables and chairs for your use and outdoor relaxation. Rooms have a tea and coffee tray with special teas and chocolates for the sweet tooth. Enjoy a sumptuous breakfast, continental or full cooked special breakfast served in our sunny dining room or alfresco.

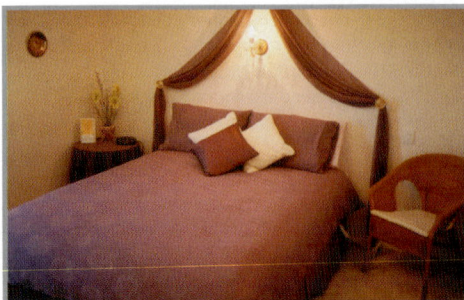

Beds are really comfortable with good linen, electric blankets, wool rest and feather duvets for winter warmth ad cosiness. Heating in all rooms.
We have travelled extensively overseas giving us a great appreciation of true hospitality.

The difference between a B&B and a hotel
is that you don't hug the hotel staff when you leave.

New Plymouth *B&B Homestay 6km N of New Plymouth*

Rockvale Lodge
Jeannette and Neil Cowley
97 Manutahi Road, R.D. 2, New Plymouth

Tel (06) 755 0750   Fax (06) 755 0750
Mob 025 682 1236   jeannette.neil@xtra.co.nz
www.bnb.co.nz/user200.html

Double $80 Single $60 (Full Breakfast) Child $30
Dinner $25 By Arrangement Children welcome
1 Queen 2 Single (2 bdrm)

We welcome you to our large, country-style home, recently renovated, surrounded by deer farm, with beautiful Mt. Egmont/Taranaki as a backdrop. Guests' double room and adjoining lounge open onto a balcony, with rural views. Relax in your private spabath, and join us for dinner, on the deck in summer, or by the fire in winter. We are close to airport, city, beaches, parks and the mountain. Six 18-hole golf courses are within 15 minutes drive. You will receive a warm welcome from Mallory, our Labrador, who lives outdoors. We look forward to sharing our home with you. Families welcome.

New Plymouth *B&B Separate/Suite Self-cont.*

Airlie House   *500m W of New Plymouth Central*
Lisa McCready & Trevor Masters
161 Powderham Street, New Plymouth

Tel (06) 757 8866   Fax (06) 757 8866
email@airliehouse.co.nz
www.airliehouse.co.nz

Double $125 Single $95 (Special Breakfast)
Child neg Credit cards accepted
1 King/Twin 2 Queen 2 Single (3 bdrm)
1 Ensuite 2 Private 1 Guests share

Airlie House is a 110 year-old character home nestled among mature trees and garden. This home has been beautifully renovated to provide two large guest bedrooms with ensuites, plus a studio apartment with its own kitchen and private bathroom. Located in central New Plymouth, Airlie House is an easy 5-minute walk from shops, restaurants, the sea front, parks and many other local attractions. All rooms have many features and amenities available for your comfort, including Sky TV and broadband Internet access.

New Plymouth   *B&B New Plymouth Central*

Kawaroa-by-the-Sea
Jan & Bruce Meachen
3a Kawaroa Close, New Plymouth 4601,
Tel (06) 759 1943   Fax (06) 759 1947
Mob 021 292 7791   b.meachen@xtra.co.nz
www.bnb.co.nz/kawaroa.html
Double $110 Single $85 (Special Breakfast)
Child by arrangement Children welcome
1 King/Twin 1 Queen 1 Twin (2 bdrm)
1 Private

Sleep to the sound of the Sea. New,spacious, peaceful and luxurious, ground level accommodation -
sleeps four (one party only) either queen or king/twin, heating, electric blankets, quality cotton bedlinen,
fresh, modern decor. Guests own lounge/office (TV, fax, email) opens on to pretty walled garden.-
Coastal walkway, the Port, CBD, restaurants, Art Gallery,New Museum & theatres just a pleasant stroll
away. Guests own tea/coffee making facility. Ask about special winter weekend rates.

Stratford   *B&B Farmstay Homestay Separate/Suite On Edge of Town*

Stallard B&B   **Billieanne & Corb Stallard**
3514 State Highway 3, Stratford Northern Boundary
Tel (06) 765 8324   Fax (06) 765 8324
stallardbb@infogen.net.nz
www.bnb.co.nz/stallardbb.html
Double $75-$80 Single $45-$50 (Special Breakfast)
Child $20 Family room sleeps 4 $95
Credit cards accepted Smoking area inside
2 Double 2 Twin 2 Single (4 bdrm)
4 Ensuite 1 Guests share

1900 "Upstairs Downstairs" comfort. Cooked or continental breakfast included. Free self catering
kitchen, tea, coffee, biscuits. Homely or private. Own key. Optional separate lounge. Restaurants,
taverns, shops nearby. Rooms are antique, romantic with TV, heaters, electric blankets, serviced daily.
Gardens, BBQ, row boat, bush bath, river walks. 15 mins Mt Egmont skifields, climbing, tramping.
Centrally located on edge of Stratford, easy distance to New Plymouth, museums, famous gardens,
tourist attractions. We are semi retired farmers. Interests include gemstones travel, art. Welcome.

Egmont National Park   *Farmstay Homestay Separate/Suite 9km W of Stratford*

Anderson's Alpine Lodge
Berta Anderson
PO Box 303, Stratford, Taranaki
Tel (06) 765 6620   0800 668 682   Fax (06) 765 6100
Mob 025 412 372   mountainhouse@xtra.co.nz
www.mountainhouse.co.nz
Double $145-$185 Single $145 (Full Breakfast)
Dinner $35 - $40 Mountain House Motor Lodge $115
Credit cards accepted Pets welcome
1 King/Twin 1 Queen 1 Double 2 Single (3 bdrm)
3 Ensuite

Swiss style chalet surrounded with native gardens and bush. Offering luxury accommodation with special
Alpine Ambiance. Spectacular views of Mount Egmont/Taranaki and Egmont National Park opposite our
front gate. Five kilometres to Mountain House and its famed restaurant, further 3km to Stratford Plateau and
skifields. Tramps, summit climbs, trout stream, gardens & museums nearby. Private helicopter summit
flights. Pet sheep, pig, ducks etc. Swiss Berta Anderson has owned Mountain Lodges since 1976, winning
many awards. Beautiful paintings from Keith, her husband (Died 1.Feb.03) are on display.

Stratford   *Separate/Suite Country Retreat 15km NE of Stratford*

Sarsen House
Bruce & Lorri Ellis
Te Popo Gardens, 636 Stanley Road, RD 24, Stratford

Tel (06) 762 8775   Fax (06) 762 8776
tepopo@clear.net.nz
www.tepopo.co.nz

Double $130-$150 Single $110-$130
(Special Breakfast) Dinner $30 - $40
Credit cards accepted
1 King 2 Queen 1 Single (3 bdrm)
3 Ensuite

If you are looking for a natural environment or a quiet and secluded spot, this is it. Sarsen House is set in Te Popo Gardens (34 acres), a charming woodland garden and park encircled by a deep river chasm and bush gully. Each of the three spacious guestrooms opens to the garden and have ensuite bathrooms, woodfires and superior beds for your comfort. Culinary delights include special breakfast, served in the sunny conservatory, and dinner (by arrangement). Self-catering available. Two wonderful dogs share our home.

Hawera   *B&B Separate/Suite Self-contained 1.5km S of Hawera Central*

Tairoa Lodge
Linda & Steve Morrison
3 Puawai Street, PO Box 117, Hawera

Tel (06) 278 8603   Fax (06) 278 8603
Mob 027 2435782   tairoa.lodge@xtra.co.nz
www.tairoa-lodge.co.nz

Double $140-$185 Single $120 (Full Breakfast)
Dinner b/a S/c Cottage - Sleeps 6 $195-$355
Credit cards accepted Children welcome
2 Queen 1 Single (2 bdrm)   2 Ensuite

TAIROA LODGE
● BED & BREAKFAST ●

Originally built in 1875 our Kauri villa has been renovated to its former Victorian glory and is nestled amongst established grounds. Polished Kauri floors add a golden glow to the tastefully decorated guest rooms. Enjoy; private garden setting, swimming pool, sumptuous breakfasts, afternoon tea or aperitif on arrival, robes, hairdryers, toiletries and fresh flowers. For peace, privacy and retreats our self-contained Tairoa Cottage is perfect for honeymooners, families or special occasions. Sleeps 6. Linda, Steve, Hannah, Caitlyn & Emma (dog) assure you a memorable stay.

Hawera   *B&B*

Linden Park
Douglas & Merilyn Tippett
69 Waihi Road, Hawera,

Tel (06) 278 5421   Fax (06) 278 5421
Mob 025 281 6216   lindenpark@inspire.net.nz
www.bnb.co.nz/lindenpark.html

Double $80 Single $60 (Full Breakfast)
Dinner $15, By arrangement Credit cards accepted
Children welcome
2 Queen 1 Double 1 Twin (4 bdrm)
1 Guests share

Welcome to our home, named after the old English Linden trees growing at the entranceway. We are situated on SH3, directly opposite King Edward Park and Hawera's aquatic centre, and are in close proximity to Hawera's amenities, restaurants and local attractions. The mountain, intensive dairy farming, trout streams, parks, gardens, beaches, golf courses, museums and local industry offer a variety of activities. We trust ours will be a home away from home as you enjoy the loveliness of South Taranaki.

Waitotara - Wanganui   *Farmstay Separate/Suite Self-contained 29km W of Wanganui*

Ashley Park
Wendy & Barry Pearce
State Highway 3, Box 36, Waitotara, Wanganui

Tel (06) 346 5917   Fax (06) 346 5861
ashley_park@xtra.co.nz
www.bnb.co.nz/ashleypark.html

Double $80-$100 Single $50 (Full Breakfast)
Dinner $25 Credit cards accepted
1 Queen 4 Single (3 bdrm)
1 Ensuite 1 Guests share

We have a 500 acre sheep and cattle farm and live in a comfortable home, set in an attractive garden with a swimming pool and tennis court. Also in the garden is an antique shop selling Devonshire teas. 100 metres from the house is a 4 acre park and lake, aviaries and a collection hand fed pet farm animals. We welcome guests to have dinner with us. Self-contained accommodation is available in the park.

Wanganui   *Farmstay 45km N of Wanganui*

Operiki Farmstay
Trissa & Peter McIntyre
3302 River Rd, Operiki, RD 6, Wanganui

Tel (06) 342 8159
www.bnb.co.nz/operikifarmstay.html

Single $35 (Full Breakfast) Child $15 Dinner $20
Credit cards accepted
1 Queen 2 Single (2 bdrm)
1 Host share

Farmstay overlooking the Whanganui River - en route to the Bridge to Nowhere - sheep, cattle and deer farming. Pottery and macadamia nuts and cat. Enjoy a country picnic and/or walk. Other activities along the river can be arranged: canoeing, jet boat rides, mountain bike riding, Marae visit and farm activities according to season.

Wanganui   *B&B Homestay 5min w Wanganui Centre*

Bradgate
Frances
7 Somme Parade, Wanganui

Tel (06) 345 3634   Fax (06) 345 3634
www.bnb.co.nz/bradgate.html

Double $75-$80 Single $40-$50 (Full Breakfast)
Dinner $25
1 Queen 1 Twin 1 Single (3 bdrm)
1 Guests share

Welcome to Bradgate, a gracious 2 storey home. With its beautiful entrance hall and carved rimu staircase which reflects the original character and gracefulness of the house. 28 years ago my husband and I came to New Zealand. We owned Shangri-La Restaurant by Virginia Lake. 20 years later the family have flown the nest. We decided to welcome guests into our home. My Mum and I share an energetic young labrador named Crunchy. I enjoy playing golf, gardening and meeting people. Non-smoking house, Dinner by arrangement.

Wanganui *B&B Homestay 2km NW of Wanganui*

Kembali
Marylyn & Wes Palmer
26 Taranaki Street, St Johns Hill, Wanganui

Tel (06) 347 1727 Mob 025 244 4347
wespalmer@xtra.co.nz
www.bnb.co.nz/kembali.html

Double $80 Single $50 (Full Breakfast)
Credit cards accepted
1 Queen 1 Twin (2 bdrm)
1 Private

In a quiet cul-de-sac, 'Kembali' is a modern, centrally heated, sunny home. Upstairs are the guest bedrooms and lounge with TV, fridge, tea/coffee facilities. The house overlooks trees and 'wetlands' where native birds roam. Semi-retired, no pets, children married, we offer a restful stay for one party/group at a time. We enjoy meeting people, gardens, travel, books and have Christian interests. Off-street parking and laundry available. Five minutes drive to restaurants and walks. We look forward to welcoming you.

Wanganui *Farmstay 20km NE of Wanganui*

Misty Valley Farmstay
Linda & Garry Wadsworth
RD 5, 97 Parihauhau Road, Wanganui

Tel (06) 342 5767 linda.garry.wadsworth@xtra.co.nz
www.bnb.co.nz/mistyvalley.html

Double $70 Single $45 (Full Breakfast) Child $20
Dinner $30 by arrangement Credit cards accepted
Children welcome
2 Double 2 Twin (2 bdrm)
1 Guests share

Misty Valley is a small organic farm at 3.7 hectares. We prefer to use our own produce whenever possible. There are farm animals for you to meet including our Brittany George and cats Alice and Calico, who all live outside. Our two grandchildren visit us regularly and children will be made very welcome. We are non-smoking, but have pleasant deck areas for those who do. Our famous river and historical city offer plenty of activities for the whole family to enjoy.

Wanganui *B&B 2 min from Wanganui centre*

Braemar House
Gail and Mike Helleur
2 Plymouth Street,
Wanganui

Tel (06) 347 2529 Fax (06) 347 2529
www.bnb.co.nz/user186.html

Double $75 Single $50 (Continental Breakfast)
Children welcome
4 Double 8 Single (8 bdrm)

Welcome to 'Old World Charm'. This restored character home was built in 1895 and has a homely atmosphere that makes your stay restful and enjoyable. The graceful entrance leads to character bedrooms, lounge and dining room, which are all centrally heated. Laundry facilities and fully equipped kitchen are available. Off-street parking is surrounded by lovely gardens. The location is close to town and many tourist attractions. We look forward to you staying here. Gail, Mike, family, and Pippin, the resident cat, will welcome you.

Taumarunui   *Farmstay 10km E of Taumarunui*

Orangi Farmstay
Gayle & Dave Richardson
Orangi Road, RD 4, Taumarunui
Tel (07) 896 6035   Fax (07) 896 6035
daveandgayle@xtra.co.nz
www.bnb.co.nz/orangifarmstay.html

Double $70 Single $50 (Full Breakfast)
Child 1/2 price Dinner $20 Campervans $20
Children welcome Smoking area inside
1 Queen 3 Single (2 bdrm)
1 Host share

Welcome to Orangi, it's your home away from home, spacious, quiet and private. Comfortable rooms with electric blankets and duvets. Toby 15 and Jana 14 and our friendly cats enjoy the company of other children. Our friendly little dog will greet you on arrival. Go trout fishing, or walk along the river bank. We look forward to enjoying your company in our friendly and casual home. Join us for a good country meal, and the kettle is always on. Laundry available.

Taumarunui   *Farmstay 5km NE of Taumarunui*

Shirley & Allan Jones
213 Taringamotu Road, Taumarunui,
Tel (07) 896 7722   costleyj@xtra.co.nz
www.bnb.co.nz/user194.html

Double $100 Single $70 (Full Breakfast)
Child half price Dinner by arrangement
1 King 1 Twin (2 bdrm)
1 Private

Our spacious home is situated 5km from the centre of Taumarunui surrounded by a peaceful one-acre garden with a native bush backdrop filled with NZ native birds. The bedrooms open on to a large verandah. Laundry available. A stream runs along one boundary of the 80 acre property suitable for walks and summertime swimming. A golf course is located within 2km, along with guided mountain walks, canoeing, hot pools, scenic flights, skiing, trout fishing and white-water rafting are all within an hours drive.

Owhango - Taumarunui   *B&B Self-contained Cottage 8km N of Owhango*

Fernleaf
Carolyn & Melvin Forlong
58 Tunanui Road, RD 1, Owhango
Tel (07) 895 4847   Fax (07) 895 4837
Mob 027 285 1441 or 027 415 3179
fernleaf.farm@xtra.co.nz
www.bnb.co.nz/fernleaf.html

Double $100 Single $60 (Full Breakfast) Child $40
Dinner $20 Outside Cottage $75 Children welcome
2 Queen 1 Double 1 Single (3 bdrm)

Relax in the tranquil Tunanui Valley just five hundred metres from SH4. Close for convenience, far enough away for peace and quiet. We are the third generation to farm 'Fernleaf' and our Romney flock has been recorded every year since the First World War. The views from various vantage point on the farm are awesome, taking in the mountains: Ruapehu, Ngaruahoe, Tongariro and Taranaki. Enjoy our generous country hospitality, wonderful breakfast, two beautiful Dalmatian and friendly cats. Other meals by arrangement.

Raurimu
B&B Homestay Self-contained cabin 7km N of National Park

Spiral Gardens
Phil & Margaret Hawthorne
Raurimu Road, Raurimu

Tel (07) 892 2997 Fax (07) 892 2997
Mob 025 753 482 spiralgardens@xtra.co.nz
www.bnb.co.nz/spiralgardens.html

Double $130 Single $110 (Full Breakfast) Child $40
Dinner by arrangement S/c cabin $130 double
Credit cards accepted Children welcome
2 Queen 3 Double 3 Single (3 bdrm)
3 Ensuite 1 Private

Our new home overlooks the Piopiotea Stream and a magnificent stand of native bush. We are 5 mins from National Park Village, gateway to Tongario and Wanganui National Parks. The Whakapapa ski area is a 25 min drive. We can organise any of the many adventure activities offered in the Ruapehu and Taupo Districts. Our luxury suits feature a queen bed, a bed settee, casual chairs, dresser and writing bureau. The bunk room sleeps 5, ideal for larger families. Our cosy cabin is self-catering.

Tongariro National Park
Self-cont B&B Lodge 2km S of National Park

Mountain Heights Lodge
Wendy and Chris Howard
PO Box 43, National Park

Tel (07) 892 2833 Fax (07) 892 2850
mountainheights@xtra.co.nz
www.mountainheights.co.nz

Double $100-$150 Single $80 (Full Breakfast)
Child $30 S/C $70 - $130 Credit cards accepted
1 King/Twin 1 Queen 2 Double 2 Twin (5 bdrm)
4 Ensuite 1 Guests share

Welcome to Mountain Heights, situated at the edge of Tongariro National Park. We offer bed and breakfast in comfortable ensuite rooms in private guest wing of lodge. Views across farmland to bush and volcanoes. Hot spa, central heating. Large lounge with log fire. Ideal for tramping, fishing, canoeing, skiing, mountain biking or just relaxing.Transport to the Tongariro Crossing organised. Our self-catering units are adjacent to the lodge and have their own bathroom and TV.Some with kitchens. Sleep 2-6.

Raetihi
B&B Homestay Separate/Suite Self-contained 0.5km N of Raetihi

Log Lodge
Jan & Bob Lamb
5 Ranfurly Terrace, Raetihi

Tel (06) 385 4135 Fax (06) 385 4835
Lamb.Log-Lodge@Xtra.co.nz
www.bnb.co.nz/loglodge.html

Double $105 Single $55 (Full Breakfast)
Child $40 Credit cards accepted
2 Double 4 Single (2 bdrm)
2 Private

A unique opportunity to stay in a modern authentic log home sited high on seven acres on the edge of town. Completely private accommodation, with own bathroom. All sleeping on mezzanine, your own lounge with wood fire, snooker table, TV/video, stereo and dining area, opening onto large verandah, with swimming pool and spa available. Panoramic views of Mts. Ruapehu, Ngauruhoe and Tongariro. Tongariro National Park and Turoa Skifield is half hour scenic drive.

Ohakune   *Farmstay Homestay   6km W of Ohakune*

Mitredale
Audrey & Diane   Pritt
Smiths Road , RD , Ohakune
Tel (06) 385 8016   Fax (06) 385 8016
Mob 025 531 916
www.bnb.co.nz/ .html

Double $90 Single $50 (Continental Breakfast)
Dinner $25pp B/A Credit cards accepted Pets welcome
1 Double 2 Single (2 bdrm)
1 Host share

We farm sheep, Bull Beef and run a Boarding Kennel in a beautiful peaceful valley with magnificent views of Mt Ruapehu. Tongariro National Park for skiing, walking, photography. Excellent 18 hole golf course, great fishing locally. We are members of Ducks Unlimited a conservation group and our local wine club. Have 2 Labradors. We offer dinner traditional farm house (Diane, a cook book author), or breakfast with excellent home made jams. Take Raetihi Road, at Hotel/BP Service Station Corner. 4kms to Smiths Road. Last house 2kms.

Ohakune   *Homestay 1km SW of Ohakune*

Kohinoor
Nita & Bruce Wilde
1011 Raetihi Road, Ohakune
Tel (06) 385 8026   Fax (06) 385 8026
Mob 021 253 3415   kohinoor@xtra.co.nz
www.bnb.co.nz/kohinoor.html

Double $110-$120 Single $60 (Full Breakfast)
Child $35 Dinner $35
1 King/Twin 2 Double (3 bdrm)
1 Ensuite 1 Private 1 Host share

Enjoy spectacular views of volcanic Mt Ruapehu while relaxing in our tranquil 3 acre garden. Kohinoor (a gem of rare beauty) is an ideal base from where you can ski Turoa or Whakapapa skifields. Tramp in the world famous Tongariro World Heritage Park and enjoy golf, trout fishing and kiwi encounters. We are just 1 km from Ohakune with its cafes, restaurants and apres ski activities. Our interests include gardening, photography, trout fishing, skiing and giving genuine kiwi hospitality. In the Ski Season, room rates apply, and midweek ski deals are available.

Taihape   *B&B Homestay 1km on hill above Taihape*

Korirata Homestay
Pat & Noel Gilbert
25 Pukeko Street, Taihape
Tel (06) 388 0315   Fax (06) 388 0315
korirata@xtra.co.nz
www.bnb.co.nz/koriratahomestay.html

Double $70 Single $50 (Special Breakfast)
Child 1/2 price under 10yrs Dinner by arrangement
Credit cards accepted
4 Single (2 bdrm)
1 Guests share

A warm welcome awaits you at the top of the hill in Taihape, where panoramic views of the mountains, ranges and surrounding countryside, add to the tranquil surroundings. Three quarters of an acre has been landscaped with shrubs. Hydroponics and orchid houses are found along with chrysanthemums in season. Meals, if desired, are with hosts, using produce from the garden where possible. Comfortable beds with electric blankets. Rafting, bungy jumping and farm visits can be arranged. One hour to Ruapehu, Lake Taupo and $2^1/_2$ - 3 hours to Wellington and Rotorua.

Taihape/Rangitikei   *B&B Farmstay Homestay Fishingstay/Retreat 26km Taihape*

Tarata Fishaway
Stephen & Trudi Mattock
Mokai Road, RD 3, Taihape
Tel (06) 388 0354   Fax (06) 388 0954
Mob 025 227 4986
fishaway@xtra.co.nz www.tarata.co.nz

Double $100-$160 Single $50-$85
(Continental Breakfast)   Dinner $30 pp
Child half price under 12 years
Children welcome
Credit cards accepted   Pets welcome
1 King/Twin 4 Queen 1 Double 4 Single
(6 bdrm)
1 Ensuite 1 Private 2 Guests share

We are very lucky to have a piece of New Zealand's natural beauty. Tarata is nestled in bush in the remote Mokai Valley where the picturesque Rangitikei River meets the rugged Ruahine Ranges. With the Ruahines towering above us, stunning views, farm pets and unique trout fishing right at our doorstep, it is the perfect environment to bring up our three children.

Stephen offers guided fishing and rafting trips for all ages. Raft through the gentle crystal clear waters of the magnificent Rangitikei River, vertical papa gorges and stunning scenery you will never forget.

Our spacious home and garden allow guests private space to unwind. Whether it is by the pool on a hot summers day with a book or spending a cosy winters night in front of our open fire with a good wine.

There is something special for the whole family and our spotlight safari, farm tour and spa pool are free for all our guests. Our new 'River Retreat' has a fully self-contained kitchen, lounge, bathroom and two bedrooms (wheelchair friendly). Soak in the spa-bath with 'million dollar views' of the river or relax on the large decking amidst native birds and trees. Peace, privacy and tranquillity at its best! We will even deliver a candle light dinner to your door if you prefer.

We think Tarata is truly a magic place and we would love sharing it with you. Approved pets welcome.

Features and Attractions
Homestead Accommodation

River Retreat	"Mini" Golf
Honeymoon Suite	Trout Fishing
Spotlight Safaris	Rafting
Claybird Shooting	Camp Outs
Bush Walks	Swimming Pool
Farm Tours	"Magic" Carpet
Farm Animals	Spa Pool

Directions: Tarata Fishaway is 26 scenic kilometres from Taihape. Turn off state highway one, six kilometres south of Taihape at the Gravity Cannon signs. Follow the Gravity Cannon and Tarata Fishaway signs (14km) to the Bungy bridge. We are six kilometres past here on Mokai Road.

TARANAKI, WANGANUI, RUAPEHU, RANGITIKEI

Mangaweka *B&B Farmstay 12km E of Mangaweka*

Mairenui Rural Retreat
Sue, David & Matt Sweet
Ruahine Road, Mangaweka 5456

Tel (06) 382 5564 Fax (06) 382 5885   Mob 025 517 545
info@mairenui.co.nz   www.mairenui.co.nz   www.nzstay.co.nz

Mairenui Rural Retreat offers three accommodation options and meals are available at the Homestead for guests in the self contained houses. On the farm there is a concrete tennis court, a full size petanque court, a croquet lawn and river swimming. There is also a trout stream for catch and release fishing only. Locally there are the renowned Rangitikei gardens, river adventure, historic home tours and four scenic golf courses. Sue, David and Matt, Bess the terrierX dog, and cats Norman & Nicky welcome guests of all nationalities. French and German are spoken.

The Homestead

Double $120-$190 Single $85-$100
(Special Breakfast) Dinner $35 Credit cards accepted
1 Queen 1 Twin (2 bdrm)
2 Ensuite

The Homestead offers quality in house accommodation for up to four people. One heritage-style double room with a small sitting area and a slate floored ensuite bathroom with sunken bath, toiletries, hairdryer and its own verandah. The twin room is larger with shower / toilet and also its own verandah.

The Retreat

Double $150 Single $50   Min.$150 max $300
Dinner $35 Breakfast $10 -$15
Credit cards accepted Children welcome Pets welcome
1 Queen 1 Double 1 Twin (3 bdrm)
1 Guests share

A 1977 Comeskey designed open plan, three and a half storey building set in a stand of 700 year old native trees. A semi circular living room leads up to a brick paved kitchen which is fully equipped with electric oven, microwave and a wood burning stove. Double-hung doors lead through to a tiled breakfast conservatory.Also on this level are the glass-roofed toilet & bathroom. The bricked central circular stair tower leads to two first storey double bedrooms, with a newly-built toilet off the landing, and the twin room which is up a vertical ladder. A "seventies" experience! Meals available at Homestead

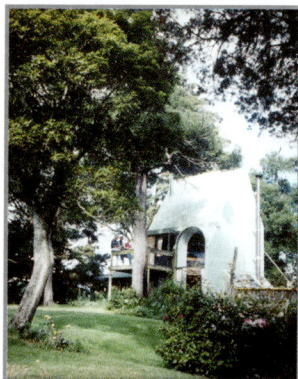

The Colonial Villa

Double $70 Single $35   Min $70 max $250
Dinner $35 Breakfast $10-$15
Credit cards accepted
Children welcome Pets welcome
3 Double 2 Twin (5 bdrm)
2 Guests share

A restored hundred year old dwelling with polished wooden floors, a wind up gramophone, a small pool table, two open fires and a wood stove. There's a refrigerator, stove,microwave, some electric blankets and heaters. The beds have duvets and blankets, there is a separate shower and the bath is an original claw foot beauty! Verandahs on two sides of the house provide plenty of room for relaxing on the comfortable seats in the sun. Meals available at Homestead.

Ensuite or private bathroom is yours exclusively.
Guest share bathroom is shared with other guests.
Hosts share bathroom is shared with the family.

Mangaweka *B&B Homestay 21km S of Taihape*

The Old Church
Mike and Sue Naylor
Raumaewa Road, Mangaweka,

Tel 06 382 5500 theoldchurch@hotmail.com
www.theoldchurch.net.nz

Double $60 Single $40 (Continental Breakfast)
Dinner $20 Children welcome
2 Twin (2 bdrm)

Mike and Sue invite you to enjoy this beautifully
restored Wesleyan church, giving the opportunity to stay
in a piece of history, (first church built in Mangaweka
in 1897). The upstairs bedrooms feature original church windows, woodwork, with rustic timbers featured
in the main dining/lounge areas. A short walk brings you to Broadway, the main street in Mangaweka
once housing thriving businesses from late eighteenth century through to the mid 1900s. All this situated
only 100 metres off State Highway 1.

Hunterville *Farmstay 10km NE of Hunterville*

Vennell's Farmstay
Oriel & Phil Vennell
Mangapipi Road, Rewa, RD 10

Tel (06) 328 6780 0800 220 172 Pin
Fax (06) 328 6780 Mob 025 407 164
www.bnb.co.nz/vennellsfarmstay.html

Double $100 Single $50 (Full Breakfast)
Child neg Dinner $30
1 King/Twin 1 Queen 1 Twin 4 Single (3 bdrm)
2 Private

We are fifth generation farmers on Richmond Station, a 1200 acre sheep/cattle hill country farm. Our
spacious home is in a tranquil setting of 100 year old trees and garden with swimming pool. You will
enjoy our large family room, cosy lounge with open fire, great farm walks and beautiful views. Central
to private gardens and river activities. We are midway Rotorua/Wellington, just off SH1 near Hunterville
on scenic SH54. We are featured in "50 Great New Zealand Farmstays". Group lunches a specialty.
Two outdoor cats.

Hunterville   *Heritage   10km S of Hunterville*

Maungaraupi
Elizabeth Robertson
Maungaraupi Country Estate, Leedstown Road,
RD 1, Marton

Tel (06) 327 7820   Fax (06) 327 8619
mcestate@xtra.co.nz
www.bnb.co.nz/.html

Double $150-$190 Single $100 (Full Breakfast)
Child $50 Dinner $40 Children welcome
5 Double 2 Twin 4 Single (9 bdrm)
3 Ensuite

Situated just off SH1 this historic home is set in bush and gardens with expansive views from the Ruahine Ranges to Kapiti. The nine bedrooms are furnished with antiques, three rooms have open fireplaces and there are two large old baths. You can play billiards, tennis or read in the library. Whether you spend a night to break your journey or a couple of days to relax in the heartland of the Rangitikei, Maungaraupi will be a unique experience.

Marton   *B&B Homestay 45km N of Palmerston North*

Rea's Inn
Keith and Lorraine Rea
12 Dunallen Avenue, Marton,

Tel (06) 327 4442   Fax (06) 327 4442
Mob 025 799589   keithandlorraine@xtra.co.nz
www.bnb.co.nz/reasinn.html

Double $80 Single $45 (Continental Breakfast)
Child Half price Dinner $20 Children welcome
1 Queen 1 Twin (2 bdrm)
1 Private

We have a warm comfortable home offering hospitality, peace and tranquility. Situated in quiet cul-de-sac with a private garden setting. Guests stay in separate wing of home. Close to Nga Tawa and Huntley Schools. Ideal for weekend retreat or stopover.(Only 2hrs from Wellington Ferry.) Organic Farm tour available by arrangement. Your comfort and pleasure are important to us. Our 2 cats like people too, and we all welcome you to come, relax and enjoy the friendly atmosphere at Rea's Inn.

Please let us know how you enjoyed your B&B.
There are comment forms at the end of the book.

Hawkes Bay

Waikaremoana

Tiniroto

Wairoa

Mahanga Beach

Mahia Beach

2

5

Whirinaki Beach

Bay View

Napier

Taradale

Hastings

HavelockNorth

50

2

Waimarama

Waipawa

Waipukurau

52

Towns listed generally follow
a north to south route. Refer
to the index if required.

0	Kilometres	40

| 0 | Miles | 24 |

Mahia Peninsula - Mahanga Beach   *Farmstay S/C cottage 50km N of Wairoa*

Reomoana
Louise Schick
RD 8, Nuhaka, Hawkes Bay

Tel (06) 837 5898   Fax (06) 837 5990
reomoana@paradise.net.nz
www.bnb.co.nz/reomoana.html

Double $100 Single $60 (Continental Breakfast)
Child $20 Dinner $30 Cottage $100
Credit cards accepted Children welcome Pets welcome
2 Queen 1 Single (3 bdrm)   1 Ensuite 1 Private

"Reomoana" - The voice of the sea. Pacific Ocean front farm at beautiful Mahia Peninsula. The spacious, rustic home with cathedral ceilings, hand-crafted furniture overlooks the Pacific with breathtaking views. Enjoy the miles of white sandy beaches, go swimming, surfing or fishing. A painter's paradise. Attractions in the area include: Morere Hot Springs, Mahia Reserve, golf course and fishing charters by arrangement. 6km to 'Sunset Point Restaurant'. Outside pets: Golden Labrador and cat. Also self-contained cottage in avocado orchard, ideal for families, 3 minutes walk to beach.

Waikaremoana   *B&B Homestay 50km W of Wairoa*

Waikaremoana Homestay
Bev Macharper
Tuai Village, RD5, Wairoa

Tel (06) 837 3701   Fax (06) 837 3709
ykarestay@xtra.co.nz
www.waikaremoanahomestay.co.nz

Double $85 Single $50 (Continental Breakfast)
Dinner $30 B/A Children welcome Pets welcome
1 Double 2 Single (2 bdrm)
1 Host share

Lake Waikaremoana is a unique native forest wilderness bordering eastern Te Urewera National Park. The homestay, set in the picturesque village of Tuai, is an ideal base for hiking, flyfishing or boating. Tuai Village is nestled around Lake Waikaremoana, 1km from Highway 38. The house, 70 years old, is cosy and comfortable and from the verandah you may view the lake and relax. Home cooking uses garden and local produce. A fishing dinghy is available. Relax in outdoor spa. House pets - three cats and a little dog.

Whirinaki Beach   *B&B 20km N of Napier*

Ocean View Retreat
Daphne & John Nichol
137 Northshore Road, RD 2, Napier

Tel (06) 836 6880   Fax (06) 836 6880
Mob 025 659 1047 the.nichols@actrix.co.nz
www.bnb.co.nz/ocean.html

Double $100 Single $80 (Continental Breakfast)
Dinner $25 B/A
1 Queen (1 bdrm)
1 Private

Ocean View Retreat has an aromatherapy environment with wonderful energies of the sea. Guests have private downstairs facilities, bathroom, spa pool and gardens. Room has electric blanket, heating, TV, fax, email, tea, coffee and laundry facilities. Guest are welcome upstairs to enjoy the balconies. Our hobbies are travel, food and wine with a philosophy of quality service. We have a cat. Two minutes from Esk Valley Wineries and close to bush walks. We have information on all Hawkes Bay has to offer. 15 Minutes from Napier - Art Deco city.

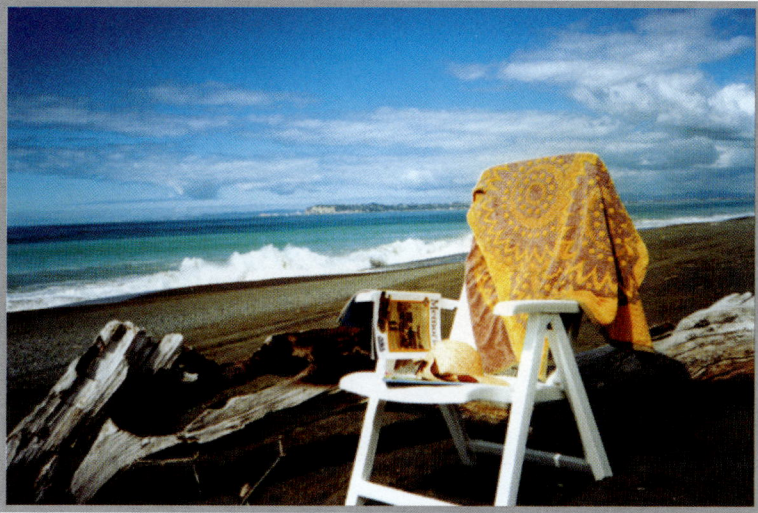

Bay View - Napier *Homestay Beach 12km N of Napier*

Kilbirnie
Jill & John Grant
84 Le Quesne Road, Bay View, Napier
Tel (06) 836 6929   Mob 025 234 7363
jill.johng@xtra.co.nz
www.bnb.co.nz/kilbirnie.html

Double $70-$90
(Full Breakfast) (Special Breakfast)
Child not suitable
Dinner $20 - $30pp by arrangement
1 Queen 1 Double (2 bdrm)
1 Ensuite 1 Private

We moved with our dog in 1996 to the quiet end of an unspoiled fishing beach by the Esk river, attracted by the beauty and position away from the traffic noise, while only 15 minutes from the main attractions. Nearby are vineyards, gardens, walks and a full range of harbourside restaurants north of Napier.

Kilbirnie is near the Taupo Road intersection with the Pacific Highway to Gisborne, with off road parking. Upstairs, guest rooms have restful views of the Pacific Ocean one side, vineyards on the other, private bathrooms, excellent showers, abundant hot water, comfortable firm beds and guest lounge.

Special breakfast overlooking the ocean is an experience which makes lunch superfluous. We are retired farmers with time to share good company, fresh imaginative food and juice, real coffee, an eclectic range of books, who invite you to enjoy our hospitality in modern surroundings. We have 13 years home hosting experience and are non-smokers.

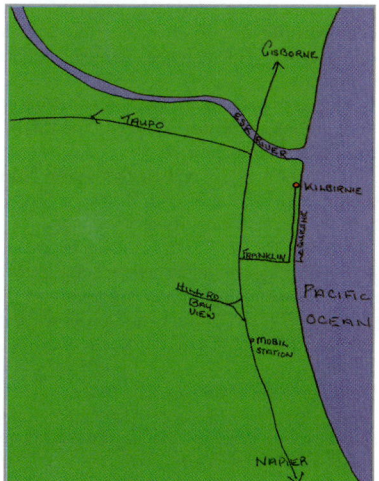

Directions: From Taupo first left after intersection Highway 2 & 5 Franklin Road to Le Quesne, proceed to far end beachfront. From Napier first right after "Mobil" Station.

The View

Bay View - Napier

B&B Farmstay & self-contained lodge 12km N of Napier

home
NEW ZEALAND

The Grange - Farmstay & Winery

Roslyn & Don Bird

263 Hill Road, Eskdale, Hawkes Bay

Tel (06) 836 6666   Fax (06) 836 6456

Mob 025 281 5738

thefarmstay@xtra.co.nz   www.thegrangelodge.com

Double $85 Single $70

(Full   Special Breakfast) Dinner $35

S/C Lodge $85 double $70 sgl, $25 extra pp

Credit cards accepted   Children welcome

2 King/Twin 1 Double 2 Single (2.5 bdrm)

2 Private

The Farm

In the heart of a thriving **wine region** overlooking the picturesque Esk Valley nestles "The Grange" our delightfully modern "Farmstay" and superior **self-contained** "Lodge". Private, spacious accommodation in relaxing peaceful surrounds with spectacular rural, coastal and city views. Feel the comforts of home as we tempt you with our farm produce, baking, and preserves.

We're an outgoing family who really enjoy the company of guests. Hospitality is guaranteed! Experience our **farm** life with Roslyn, Zac (our Weimaraner farm Pup), and Sparkie (our resident cat). Feed the sheep, cows, pigs, chickens and dairy goats. Try milking Nancy the Goat or bottle-feeding a lamb - seasonal.

Don a passionate 3rd generation **winemaker** combines 27 years knowledge with tasting over dinner or at our **Wishart Estate Winery.** You might like to try hand plunging the reds at Vintage or a Barrel sample of future releases.

Explore the world's **Art Deco Capital Napier 12 minutes** drive away and Hawke's Bay's many regional attractions within 30 minutes.

Unwind on the Deck to the soothing chorus of native birds in the surrounding gardens and trees and at day's end spend time romancing over our wonderful night sky. Taupo (Kinloch) holiday home and email access available. Share our home or retreat in the Lodge.

"Our Place Is Your Place."

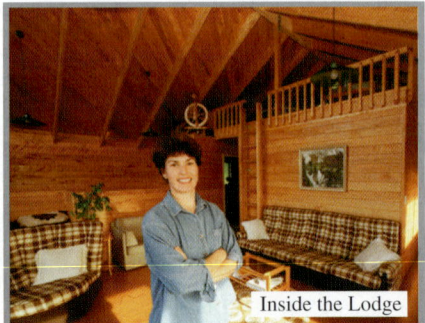

Inside the Lodge

Direction: 1km off SH5 at Eskdale or 3km off SH2 at Bay View.

Bay View   *B&B Homestay Separate/Suite Self-contained 12km N of Napier*

Beachfront Homestay
Christine & Jim Howard
20a Le Quesne Rd, Bay View, Napier
Tel (06) 836 6530   Fax (06) 836 6531
Mob 021 159 0162   j-howard@clear.net.nz
www.beachfronthb.co.nz
Double $90 Single $55 (Special Breakfast)
Child $15 Dinner $25 Credit cards accepted
1 Queen 1 Twin (2 bdrm)
1 Private

Jim, Christine and Sarcha (Jack Russell) will welcome you to their new beachfront home with breathtaking views of Hawkes Bay and walking distance to local wineries. Guests are offered self contained accommodation and own entrance on ground floor. Jim a local stock agent and Christine works at a local winery both enjoy meeting people and their interests are fishing and the outdoor life. Surfcasting and Kontiki fishing available. Beachfront homestay is just 5 mins from the Napier Taupo turn off and 12 minutes from Napiers Marine Parade & Cafes. Wine & sightseeing tours available.

Bayview - Martha's Vineyard   *B&B 10km N of Napier*

Bay View Estate
Jeff Franklin & Juanita Baldwin
Kaimata Heights, Bay View, Napier
Tel (06) 836 7516   Fax (06) 836 7517
www.bnb.co.nz/bayviewestate.html
Double $175-$195 Single $125 (Special Breakfast)
1 King/Twin 1 King 1 Queen 1 Twin
1 Ensuite 1 Private

Picture the glistening sun flickering across the expansive Pacific Ocean as you enjoy alfresco breakfast. Our architect's brief was to exploit the natural beauty and tranquility of the area. He succeeded in creating a stunning ultramodern, stylish hilltop country retreat, with first class facilities. Take your time to meander through the magical 'Esk Valley' and enjoy the world class wineries and restaurants. For your 'urban cravings' Art Deco Napier is only minutes away.

Bay View - Napier   *B&B 10km N of Napier*

Bev's on the Bay
Beverley White
32 Ferguson Street North, Bay View, Napier
Tel (06) 836 7637   bevann@paradise.net.nz
www.bnb.co.nz/bevs.html
Double $100-$120 Single $80 (Full Breakfast)
Child $30 Children welcome Pets welcome
1 King 1 Queen (2 bdrm)
1 Ensuite 1 Private

This stylish beach-front property offers large, modern rooms, each with bathroom, TV, sitting area, tea and coffee facilities and private entrances. The king room has its own balcony and sea views. The queen room has near-level access and doors to the courtyard. Step off the front lawn for swimming or surf casting. Wineries in walking distance. Five minutes drive from the airport and ten minutes from Napier town. Undercover parking is provided. Your host, Beverley White, is an amateur artist and former business woman. Elderly poodle on property.

HAWKES BAY

Napier *B&B Homestay 1km N of Napier*

Spence Homestay
Kay & Stewart Spence
17 Cobden Road, Napier

Tel (06) 835 9454   0800 117 890   Fax (06) 835 9454
Mob 025 235 9828   ksspence@actrix.gen.nz
www.bnb.co.nz/spence.html

Double $125 Single $90 (Full Breakfast)
Credit cards accepted
1 Queen 1 Single (1 bdrm)
1 Ensuite

Welcome to our comfortable near new home.   Quiet
area 10-15 minutes walk from art deco city centre. Guest suite opens outside to patio,petanque court,and colourful garden.   Lounge includes double bed settee, TV,kitchenette with tea making facilities, fridge and microwave. Bedroom has queen and single beds,ensuite bathroom. We have hosted for over 10 years, and enjoy overseas travel.   Able to meet public transport. Directions: Port end Marine Parade, Coote Road, right into Thompson Road, left into Cobden Road opposite water tower.

Napier   *Homestay 1.5km NW of Post Office*

A Room with a View
Robert McGregor
9 Milton Terrace, Napier

Tel (06) 835 7434   Fax (06) 835 1912
roomwithview@xtra.co.nz.
www.bnb.co.nz/mcgregor.html

Double $100 Single $65 (Continental Breakfast)
Credit cards accepted
1 Queen (1 bdrm)
1 Private (bath & shower)

Having hosting for 10 years with my late wife, I look forward to continued companionship, conversation and laughter with guests. Sea view, large garden and sunny hill location. Only a 15 minute walk to restaurants at historic Port Ahuriri or our world-famous Art Deco City Centre. Laundry facilities at a nominal charge. Free pick-up service. No smoking inside please. I'm interested in travel, gardening, the arts, and especially local history, as I'm Executive Director of the Art Deco Trust. Please email, write or phone first.

Napier   *B&B Homestay 1.2km N of Napier Central*

Hillcrest
Nancy & Noel Lyons
4 George St, Hospital Hill, Napier

Tel (06) 835 1812   lyons@inhb.co.nz
www.hillcrestnapier.co.nz

Double $85-$90 Single $65 (Continental Breakfast)
Credit cards accepted
1 Double 2 Single (2 bdrm)
1 Guests share

If you require quiet accommodation just minutes from
the city centre, our comfortable home provides peace in
restful surroundings. Relax on wide decks overlooking our garden, or enjoy the spectacular sea views. Explore nearby historic places and the Botanical Gardens. Your own lounge with tea/coffee making; laundry and off street parking available. We have travelled extensively and welcome the opportunity of meeting visitors. Our interests are travel, music, bowls and embroidery. We will happily meet you at the travel depots. Holiday home at Mahia Beach available.

Napier   *Homestay Self-contained 5km S of Napier*

Snug Harbour
Ruth & Don McLeod
147 Harold Holt Avenue, Napier

Tel (06) 843 2521   Fax (06) 843 2520
donmcld@clear.net.nz
www.bnb.co.nz/snugharbour.html

Double $80-$90 Single $55 (Full Breakfast)
Dinner $25 by arrangement Credit cards accepted
1 Queen 1 Twin 1 Single (3 bdrm)
1 Ensuite 1 Host share

Ruth & Don welcome you to our modern smoke free
home with its rural outlook and sunny attractive patio.
The garden studio with ensuite and tea making facilities has its own entrance. We are situated on the
outskirts of Napier City, the Art Deco City of the World, and in close proximity to wineries and many
other tourist attractions. We both have a background in teaching, with interests in travel, gardening and
photography.

Taradale - Napier   *B&B 8km W of Napier*

Kerry Lodge
Jenny & Bill Hoffman
7 Forward Street, Greenmeadows, Napier

Tel (06) 844 9630   Fax (06) 844 1450
Mob 0274 932 874   kerrylodge@xtra.co.nz
www.kerrylodge.co.nz

Double $100 Single $70 (Full Breakfast)
Child $45 Credit cards accepted Children welcome
1 King 1 Queen 2 Twin (3 bdrm)
1 Ensuite 1 Private 1 Guests share

Set in tranquil gardens, we invite guests to share the
warmth and comfort of our home. Our large rooms offer heating, refreshment facilities and colour
television. A mobility ensuite and wheelchair access is available for guests convenience. Also a laundry.
Your day with us begins with a scrumptious breakfast and a chat to help plan your day's activities.
Relax in our sparkling pool or indoor spa. Situated near Church Road and Mission wineries. Our dogs
Tess and Hogan and cat Tabitha wait to welcome you.

Napier   *B&B 1km N of Napier*

Ourhome
N & N Hamlin
4 Hospital Terrace, Hospital Hill, Napier

Tel (06) 835 7358   Fax (06) 835 7355
Mob 025 852 304   nancina@xtra.co.nz
www.bnb.co.nz/ourhome.html

Double $90 Single $60 (Continental Breakfast)
1 King/Twin 1 Double (1 bdrm)
1 Private

Kick off your shoes, put up your feet and drink in the
magical views with your cuppa or G & T while relaxing on your own patio or your private lounge. Our
superking/twin beds have been described as 'pamper' beds. Double bed-settee in lounge,
one group only. To make your stay as comfortable as possible we offer tea/coffee/cookies, TV, fridge,
iron, laundry facilities, parking and total privacy. All attractions within easy driving distance. Pick up
from public transport. Small gentle poodle has joined our household.

Napier *B&B Separate/Suite Guesthouse*

Blue Water Lodge Ltd
471 Marine Parade, Napier

Tel (06) 835 8929   Fax (06) 835 8929
bobbrown2@xtra.co.nz
www.bnb.co.nz/bluewaterlodgeltd.html

Double $70-$80 Single $40 (Continental Breakfast)
Child $10 under 14 yrs Credit cards accepted
6 Double 9 Single (9 bdrm)
1 Ensuite 2 Guests share

Blue Water Lodge is on the beach front opposite the
Aquarium on Napier's popular Marine Parade. Close to all local tourist attractions and within walking distance to the city centre, information centre, family restaurants, RSA and Cosmopolitan Club. Owner operated.

Napier *B&B Homestay 0.5km E of Napier Central*

home
NEW ZEALAND

No 11
Phyllida & Bryan Isles
11 Sealy Road, Napier Hill, Napier

Tel (06) 834 4372   Mob 021 455 572
phyllbry@xtra.co.nz
www.bnb.co.nz/nonapier .html

Double $100 Single $75 (Special Breakfast)
1 King/Twin 2 Queen (3 bdrm)
1 Guests share

The name says it all! You will score our home more than
10 for Comfort, Convenience, Conviviality. Comfort: Spacious, sunny, warm, bedrooms with TV, tea making facilities, electric blankets, sun lounge. Convenience: Quality new home with wonderful views. Easy stroll to city, cafes, and tourist attractions. Off-street parking. Conviviality: Our aim is to assist you to make your stay enjoyable. A selection of specialty breakfast choices is offered. We have a dog. Please no smoking indoors. We look forward to meeting you.

Napier *Self-contained 1km N of Napier*

The Coach House
Jan Chalmers
9 Gladstone Road, Napier

Tel (06) 835 6126   Mob 025 657 3263
www.bnb.co.nz/thecoachhouse.html

Double $100 Single $80 (Full Breakfast)
Child $25 - babies free 4 people $160 Pets welcome
1 Queen 2 Single (2 bdrm)
1 Private

On the hill over-looking a gorgeous Mediterranean garden
and sea views, the historic Coach-house is tastefully renovated and totally self-contained. It contains 2 bedrooms , open plan kitchen, dining, living rooms, bathroom and separate loo. The fridge will be full of a variety of breakfast supplies. TV and radio included and fresh flowers in all rooms. The sunny deck has a table and chairs and gas barbecue. Off-street parking and easy access plus peace and privacy complete the picture.

Taradale - Napier *B&B 8km SW of Napier*

Greenwood Bed and Breakfast
Ann & Peter Green
62 Avondale Road, Taradale, Napier
Tel (06) 845 1246 Fax (06) 845 1247
Mob 025 795 403 greenwood@clear.net.nz
www.greenwoodbnb.co.nz
Double $90-$105 Single $60-$70 (Full Breakfast)
Dinner $30 Credit cards accepted
2 Queen 2 Single (3 bdrm)
3 Ensuite

Relax in our guest lounge or on the deck as trees filter the afternoon sun. Savour Ann's homemade preserves and eggs benedict. Put the world to rights as we discuss the follies of presidents and kings. Laugh as Peter tries to converse in German and French. Our loves are family and entertaining. Our interests are history, language, art, computers and golf. A short walk takes you to Taradale shops, restaurants and wineries. Tourist attractions and golf courses within easy driving distance. Dinner by arrangement.

Taradale - Napier *B&B Self-contained 10km W of Napier*

Otatara Heights
Sandra & Roy Holderness
57 Churchill Drive, Taradale, Napier
Tel (06) 844 8855 Fax (06) 844 8855
sandroy@xtra.co.nz
www.bnb.co.nz/otataraheights.html
Double $90 (Continental Breakfast)
$30 per extra person Credit cards accepted
1 Queen 1 Double (1 bdrm)
1 Private

Comfortable, quiet apartment in the heart of our foremost wine producing area. Superb day and night views over Napier and local rural scenes. 10 minutes drive to the Art Deco capital of the world. 2km to Taradale village. Safe off-street parking. Top quality restaurants and wineries nearby. We are a friendly couple who have enjoyed B&B overseas and like meeting people. Our interests are travel, theatre, good food and wine. Bella, our cat, keeps to herself. Handy to E.I.T. and golf course.

Taradale - Napier *B&B Homestay 7.5km SW of Napier*

'279' Church Road
Sandy Edginton
279 Church Road, Taradale, Napier
Tel (06) 844 7814 Fax (06) 844 7814
Mob 025 265 6760 sandy.279@homestaynapier.co.nz
www.homestaynapier.co.nz
Double $100-$120 Single $70-$80 (Full Breakfast)
Dinner by arrangement Credit cards accepted
Smoking area inside
1 Queen 1 Double 1 Single (2 bdrm)
1 Guests share

"279", an elegant and spacious home set amongst mature trees and gardens, offers excellent hospitality in a relaxed, friendly atmosphere to Domestic and International visitors. Located adjacent to Mission Estate and Church Road wineries,restaurants and craft galleries, "279" is within a short drive of 'Art Deco' Napier, Hastings, golf courses, and tourist activities. I welcome you to "279" and will help make your visit the highlight of your travels.

Napier · *Homestay 500m from Napier Post Office*

Cameron Close
Joy & Graeme Thomas
33 Cameron Road, Napier
Tel (06) 835 5180 Fax (06) 835 4115
Mob 021 683 551 besco@xtra.co.nz
www.bnb.co.nz/cameronclose.html
Double $90 Single $60 (Special Breakfast)
1 Queen 1 Double 1 Single (3 bdrm)
1 Guests share

Come and share our 1920's home, garden and pool situated above the lovely Art Deco city of Napier. A five minute stroll will have you amongst the Art Deco buildings and town, or relax poolside and enjoy our garden. We offer home cooked goodies using fresh produce from Hawkes Bay. Our interests include food, wine, classic cars, art deco and good company. Let us share our knowldge of NZ with you. We offer laundry facilities and have bikes available. Phone for easy directions.

Napier *B&B Homestay Separate/Suite 1 N of Napier*

home

Cobden Garden Homestay
Rayma and Phillip Jenkins
1 Cobden Crescent, Bluff Hill, Napier
Tel 06 834 2090 0800 426 233 Fax 06 834 2090
Mob 025 540062 info@cobden.co.nz
www.cobden.co.nz
Double $110-$160 Single $90-$140
(Special Breakfast) Credit cards accepted
1 King/Twin 1 King (2 bdrm)
2 Ensuite

We invite you to stay in our quiet, warm and sunny colonial villa on Bluff Hill. We have two double rooms, each with its own ensuite. There is a beautiful garden for your enjoyment. We invite you to join us each evening for complimentary tastings of local wine and produce. Each morning choose your gourmet breakfast from the menu of local foods and homemade delights. We make sure your stay will be extra special and memorable. There are two unobtrusive cats in residence.

Napier Hill *B&B 1km N of Napier*

Maison Bearnaise
Christine Grouden & Graham Storer
25 France Road, Bluff Hill, Napier 4001
Tel (06) 835 4693 Fax (06) 835 4694
chrisgraham@xtra.co.nz
www.hawkesbaynz.com/pages/maisonbearnaise
Double $120-$140 Single $85-$95
(Continental Breakfast) (Full Breakfast)
2 Queen (2 bdrm)
2 Ensuite

Christine, Graham and Brewster (the cat),welcome you to our attractive, peaceful oasis. Walk to city centre, restaurants,Bluff Hill lookout. Off street parking, Internet, laundry services available. Each bedroom has tv, electric blankets, heating, and en suite for complete privacy. Relax with tea or coffee in your room or guest lounge, to read or perhaps play cards, backgammon. Delicious breakfasts served in dining room or colourful courtyard.An invitation to a warm and friendly atmosphere with helpful local, national sightseeing tips - a bonus.

Napier - Marine Parade   *B&B Separate/Suite Boutique hotel Napier*

Mon Logis
Gerard Averous
415 Marine parade, PO Box 871, Napier
Tel (06) 835 2125   Fax (06) 835 8811   Mob 025 725
332 monlogis@xtra.co.nz
www.babs.co.nz/monlogis

Double $140-$160 Single $120
(Continental Full Breakfast)   Credit cards accepted
2 King/Twin (4 bdrm)
3 Ensuite 1 Private

A little piece of France nestled in the heart of the beautiful
wine-growing region of Hawke's Bay.   Built as private
Hotel in 1915 this grand colonial building overlooking
the Pacific's breakers is only a few minutes walk from
the city centre. Now lovingly renovated Mon Logis will
cater to a maximum of eight guests and is modelled on
the small privately owned French hotel.

Of the upstairs individually furnished rooms, two have
queen beds and two have twin beds, all have their own
private facilities. Owner Frenchman Gerard Averous has
decorated each guest room differently but in a style in
keeping with the original charm of the building. Iron

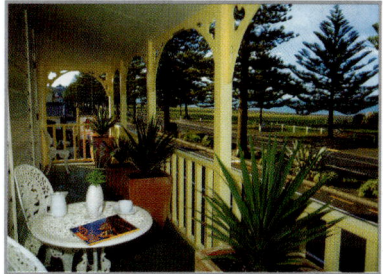

bedsteads, feather duvets, lace covers and fine cotton linen all create a special elegance and one room is
totally furnished with pieces bought from France.

Downstairs, an informal guest lounge invites relaxation, television viewing, a quiet time reading or
perhaps a game of chess or bridge. Guests can help themselves to coffee or tea and home made biscuits
any time of the day. Breakfast, served in the privacy of your own room or in the downstairs Dining
Room, could be a basket of freshly baked breads, croissants, or brioche, with a compote of locally
grown fruits or a wonderful herb omelette, with crispy bacon and grilled tomatoes. Should you want to
dine out, Gerard is happy to give recommendations and can help with insight into Napier's unique
architecture.

All perfectly designed for comfort and relaxation, Mon Logis is a non-smoking establishment and does
not cater for children. French and Spanish spoken. Exclusive customised vineyard tours with host by
arrangement. Casual elegance at a price you can afford.

Charm, personal service and French cuisine are the specialities

219

Napier *B&B 500m N of Napier Central*

The Green House On The Hill
Ruth Buss & Jeremy Hutt
18b Milton Oaks, Milton Rd, Napier
Tel (06) 835 4475 Fax (06) 835 4437
Mob 021 187 3827 ruthzmail@clear.net.nz
home.clear.net.nz/pages/ruthzmail
Double $88-$120 Single $60 (Special Breakfast)
Dinner $25
2 Queen 1 Twin (3 bdrm)
1 Ensuite

The Green House On The Hill is a Vegetarian Bed and Breakfast, 5 minutes walk from the heart of 'Art Deco Napier', yet surrounded by woodland, with plenty of native birds ... and sea views! We aim to provide a peaceful, smokefree environment for our guests.Homemade breads and preserves for breakfast! Our hillside home is built on several levels and unsuitable for wheelchairs or small children, although babies or older chidren would be very welcome. We have ample parking, or can pick up from Airport, buses etc. Internet access available.

Napier - Hastings *Farmstay Homestay 15km E of Napier/Hastings*

Heather and Bill Shaw
Charlton Road, RD 2, Hastings
Tel (06) 875 0177 Fax (06) 875 0525
www.bnb.co.nz/shaw.html
Double $150 Single $100 (Full Breakfast)
Dinner by arrangement
4 Single (2 bdrm)
1 Ensuite 1 Host share

Our home is situated in Charlton Road Te Awanga which is approximately twenty minutes form both Napier and Hastings and right next door to the gannets at Cape Kidnappers and one of Hawkes Bay leading winery restaurants. With us you can enjoy space, tranquillity, and fine hospitality while receiving every assistance to make your stay in our area as interesting and enjoyable as possible. We have two Jack Russel dogs. Directions: Charlton Road is the first road on your right after passing through Te Awanga village.

Napier - Hastings *B&B Self-contained btw Napier/ Hastings*

Copperfields
Pam & Richard Marshall
Copperfields, Pakowhai Road, Napier
Tel (06) 876 9710 Fax (06) 876 9710
Mob 021 256 7590 rich.pam@clear.net.nz
www.bnb.co.nz/copperfields.html
Double $95-$110 Single $80 (Full Breakfast)
Child $15 - babies free Dinner $30pp B/A
Credit cards accepted Children welcome
1 Double 3 Single (2 bdrm)
1 Private

Copperfields: Lifestyle orchard within ten minutes of Napier, Hastings, Havelock North and Taradale - central for all tourist attractions. Guests stay in "Glen Cottage" large self contained cottage attached to our house with your own front door. Fully equipped kitchen/dining, bathroom/laundry and large lounge with log fire. Also on property an old church converted into an antique, collectables and craft gallery. Our interests are weaving, furniture restoration and antiques. We have a pet pig and sheep. Family rates negotiable. Dogs welcome (conditions apply).

Napier - Hastings   *Homestay Separate/Suite 18km W of Napier*

Silverford
Chris & William Orme-Wright
Puketapu, Hawkes Bay

Tel (06) 844 5600   Fax (06) 844 4423
homestay@paradise.net.nz
www.silverford.co.nz

Double $145-$165 Single $115
(Full Breakfast)
Credit cards accepted
1 King 1 Queen 1 Double (3 bdrm)
1 Ensuite 1 Guests share

Situated on the Wine Trail, 'Silverford' - one of Hawkes Bay's most gracious Homesteads - is spaciously set in 17 acres of farmland, established trees and gardens. Drive through our half a kilometre long gorgeous Oak lined avenue to the sweeping lawns, bright flower gardens and ponds surrounding our elegant home designed by Natusch at the turn of the century.

We are relaxed and friendly and offer a warm ambience in private, comfortable and tranquil surroundings - a romantic haven with tastefully furnished bedrooms, charming guest sitting room and a courtyard to dream in.

Silverford is an idyllic welcoming haven for a private, peaceful and cosy stay whilst at the same time being close to all the amenities and attractions that Hawkes Bay has to offer. Friendly deer, cow, pigeons, ducks and dogs. Central Heating. Swimming Pool. Good restaurants close by.

We are smokefree and regret the property is unsuitable for children. Some French and German spoken.

Silverford is an idyllic welcoming haven

Napier - Hastings *Farmstay Homestay 50km W of Hastings - Napier*

Waiwhenua Farmstay
Kirsty Hill & Family
808 River Road, RD 9, Hastings
Tel (06) 874 2435 Fax (06) 874 2465
Mob 027 479 4094 kirsty.hill@xtra.co.nz
www.bnb.co.nz/waiwhenuafarmstay.html
Double $100 Single $50 (Continental Breakfast)
Child $50 Dinner $20 Campervan/Backpacker Lodge
2 Queen 3 Single (2 bdrm)
1 Private

Experience a genuine farmstay, delicious home produce and food, trout fishing and friendly rural hospitality at our historic homestead and farm. Our family and numerous pets enjoy meeting people and catering for individuals or families interested in the outdoor life (two nights recommended) on our large sheep, beef and deer farm, and organic apple and pear orchard. Enrich your stay by experiencing outdoor activities at our backdoor including, guided farm tours, relaxing swimming pool, trout fishing, farm walks, jet boating and extensive bush and mountain hikes.

Napier - Hastings *B&B Self-contained cottage 2.5km SE of Clive*

Kerry & Jan McKinnie
PO Box 38, Clive, Napier
Tel (06) 870 0759 Fax (06) 870 0528
Mob 027 211 0464 ker.jan@xtra.co.nz
www.bnb.co.nz/mckinnie.html
Double $80 Single $50 (Full Breakfast)
Child by arrangement Dinner by arrangement
Credit cards accepted Children welcome Pets welcome
1 Queen 1 Double 4 Single (3 bdrm)
3 Ensuite

Riverbank house is set amongst the trees on 1.5 acres of land. Our two well appointed cottages include tea/coffee facilities, fridge, microwave etc and suit all types of travellers. We are a well-travelled family who enjoy looking after our guests. We have two cats and one dog. At 2.5km south of Clive we are central to everything. See you soon!

Napier - Hastings *Homestay Self-contained 12km E of Napier/Hastimgs*

Merriwee Boutique Homestay
Jeanne Richards
29 Gordon Road, Te Awanga, Hawkes Bay
Tel (06) 875 0111 Fax (06) 875 0111
Mob 021 214 5023 merriwee@xtra.co.nz
www.merriwee.co.nz
Double $100-$180 Single $100-$130 (Full Breakfast)
Dinner B/A
1 King/Twin 1 King 1 Queen 1 Double (4 bdrm)
2 Ensuite 1 Private

Merriwee was built in 1908 and is set in an apricot orchard just a stroll from Te Awanga beach. It is close to Napier/Hastings and Havelock North, with Cape Kidnappers and wineries nearby. The home is spacious, with quality furnishings, open fires and sea views across to Napier. French doors access bedrooms to verandahs and garden. The main guest area is self contained with sitting room, open fire and kitchen. There is a swimming pool and pentanque court. Terrier 'Mags' and cat Poppy will greet you. Gorden Road is the first on the right as you enter Te Awanga Village.

Hastings - Havelock North   *Homestay Self-contained 2.5km SE of Havelock North*

Jill & Jock Taylor
134 Kopanga Road, Havelock North
Tel (06) 877 8797   Fax (06) 877 2335
jilljock@paradise.net.nz
www.bnb.co.nz/taylor.html

Double $90 Single $50 (Continental Breakfast)
1 Queen 2 Single (2 bdrm)
2 Private

Welcome to our home and garden. In rural surroundings only five minutes to Havelock North.   Hastings and Napier approximately fifteen minutes. We are gardeners and golfers and what better place to be than Hawkes Bay with four excellent golf courses, superb gardens and many wineries. Our four children have gone but we have two friendly black cats. There is a queen bed with guests' own bathroom in the house. An outside unit has two single beds, shower, toilet and tea making facilities. No smoking inside please.

Hastings - Havelock North   *Farmstay 16km S of Havelock North*

Ros Phillips
Wharehau, RD 11, Hastings
Tel (06) 877 4111   Fax (06) 877 4111
www.bnb.co.nz/phillips.html

Single $40 (Full Breakfast) Child 1/2 price
Dinner $25 Beach Bach   Children welcome
1 Queen 2 Twin 1 Single (4 bdrm)
1 Guests share 1 Host share

20 minutes from Hastings, Havelock North or Waipawa, enjoy the beautiful Hawkes Bay. We are handy to the many attractions Hawkes Bay has to offer. Gannets - wineries - art deco - golf courses - Splash Planet - a local trout river (guide available) or just relax in peace and space. Dinner (featuring local produce) available on request. If interesetd and weather permits a farm tour in 4WD.

Hastings City   *Homestay Hastings Central*

McConchie Homestay
Barbara & Keta McConchie
115A Frederick Street, Hastings
Tel (06) 878 4576   Mob 025 610 2902
barbaramcconchie@xtra.co.nz
www.bnb.co.nz/mcconchie.html

Double $80 Single $45 (Full Breakfast) Child $15
Dinner $20 B/A Credit cards accepted
1 Queen 2 Single (2 bdrm)
1 Guests share

Enjoy our peaceful garden back section, away from all traffic noises, yet central to Hastings City. My Siamese cat says 'Hi'. Nearby are parks, golf courses, wineries, orchards and the best icecream ever. Short trips take you to spectacular views, Cape Kidnapper's Gannet colony, or Napier's Art Deco. Activities include ballooning, Clydesdale wagon ride, hot pools, wine trails, or relaxing having coffee on our deck. Directions: From Wellington, take the Napier/Stortford Lodge route, left off main highway at Paki Paki. From Taupo ring. No smoking please.

Hastings   *B&B   Self-contained   9km W of Hastings*

A Cottage
Anne & Peter Wilkinson
Box 2116,
79 Carrick Road, Twyford (residential), Hastings
Tel (06) 879 9357   Fax (06) 879 9357
Mob 021 1835144   ph-aawilkinson@clear.net.nz
www.bnb.co.nz/wilkinson.html
Double $95 Single $80 (Full Breakfast)
Credit cards accepted
1 King/Twin (1 bdrm)
1 Private

We look forward to giving you a warm welcome to the Hawkes Bay which offers a wide variety of attractions, in particular wineries and the Art Deco buildings of Napier. We are close to the Ngaruroro River for good trout fishing during the season and within easy reach of a variety of other rivers and lakes. Guided fishing is offered by Peter. Our accommodation has a small kitchen and living room. Non smoking and not suitable for children. Owners have two dogs. Ring for directions.

Hastings   *Homestay   2.5km   of Hastings*

Woodbine Cottage
Ngaire & Jim Shand
1279 Louie Street, Hastings
Tel (06) 876 9388   Fax (06) 876 9666
Mob 025 529 522   nshand@xtra.co.nz
www.bnb.co.nz/ .html
Double $100 Single $70 (Continental Breakfast)
Dinner $25pp by arrangement   Credit cards accepted
1 Queen 1 Twin (2 bdrm)
1 Guests share

Our home is set in half acre of cottage garden on the Hastings boundary close to Havelock North. Swimming pool and tennis court for the energetic and a spa bath to relax in at night Hastings city centre is five minutes by car and Havelock North 2 minutes. 'Splash Planet', with its many water features and hot pools is only two minutes away We look forward to your company and can assure you of a comfortable and relaxing stay. Non smoking and not suitable for small children or pets.

Hastings   *B&B 3km S of Hastings*

Raureka
Rosemary & Tim Ormond
26 Wellwood Road, RD 5, Hastings
Tel (06) 878 9715   Fax (06) 878 9728
Mob 025 627 5887   r.t.ormond@xtra.co.nz
www.bnb.co.nz/raureka.html
Double $90 Single $70 (Full Breakfast)
1 Queen (1 bdrm)
1 Ensuite

îOne of Hawkes Bay's best kept secrets.î This is one of the many wonderful comments written in our visitor's book.'Raureka' is an apple orchard. You will enjoy all the special surprises to be found here.   Fresh flowers, superior linen, home baking are among the many treats to be enjoyed here. Your accommodation is a quiet attractive double room with ensuite, separate from the house. Relax by the pool with views of our unique property where a dozen 100-year-old trees grow.

Hastings
B&B Homestay 12km W of Hastings, 12km S of Taradale

Stitch-Hill Farm
Charles Trask
170 Taihape Road, RD 9, Hastings
Tel **(06) 879 9456**   Fax (06) 879 9806
cjtrask@xtra.co.nz
www.bnb.co.nz/stitchhill.html

Double $85 Single $50 (Continental Breakfast)
Dinner $30 by arrangement
1 Queen 1 Twin (2 bdrm)
2 Ensuite

Welcome to Hawkes Bay, the premier food and wine
region of New Zealand. Stitch-Hill invites you to relax in the quiet countryside surrounded with panoramic views. Our prime location is just minutes from the city centres, wineries, attractions, fishing and tramping. In our comfortable smoke-free home we offer the very best hospitality. Your requirements our challenge. Your choice of room, twin with ensuite, queen bed with ensuite. Stroll in our gardens or around our acres. Unsuitable for children and pets.

Hastings
B&B Self-contained 3km S of Hastings

Primefruit Orchard
Elly & Dick Spiekerman
74 Longlands Road East, Hastings,
Tel **(06) 876 4163**   Fax (06) 876 4163
Mob 027 444 8798   info@holidaynewzealand.co.nz
www.holidaynewzealand.co.nz

Double $90 Single $70 (Continental Breakfast)
Cottage $110 Children welcome Pets welcome
2 Queen 1 Double 2 Single (4 bdrm)
3 Private

We like to be your host on our orchard where we have an
abundance of fruit and guided tour in season. We offer a double bedroom with continental breakfast. Explore our indoor games room or gazebo. If you like privacy we have a self-contained cottage with two bedrooms, barbecue on deck, enjoy swimming pool, spa, table tennis, petanque and lawn croquet. All welcome.

All our B&Bs are non-smoking
unless stated otherwise in the text.

Havelock North - Hastings
Farmstay Homestay 1km S of Havelock North

PeakView Farm
Dianne & Keith Taylor
92 Middle Road, Havelock North
Tel (06) 877 7408   Fax (06) 877 7410
homestays@xtra.co.nz
www.bnb.co.nz/peakviewfarm.html

Double $75 Single $50 (Full Breakfast)
Dinner $25   Credit cards accepted
Children welcome   Child neg.
1 Double 2 Single (2 bdrm)
1 Host share

We invite you to relax in our century old home admidst large trees, gardens and lawns on 25 acres of horticulture land. Enjoy our friendly, personal and caring hospitality, or a separate lounge is available with TV and books if you want a quiet time.

Comfortable beds with firm mattresses and electric blankets make for a good night's sleep. Sit and chat, when time allows, over a generous breakfast - cooked or continental with homemade preserves and goodies. Wholesome dinners on request.

Interests include tramping, bushwalks, gardening and genealogy. We have travelled extensively and enjoy meeting local and overseas visitors. Can also advise on travel throughout New Zealand.

After nearly 16 years of "Happy Hosting", we have an ever-increasing circle of friends - with many returning. Dianne is one of few in New Zealand who has a Certificate in Homestay Management.

Panoramic views from Te Mata Peak - 10 minutes to the top. Visit the many wineries, safari trip to the gannets, trout fishing and orchard tours are just a few of the wonderful activities to enjoy. A short walk to lovely boutique shops, cafes and restaurants. Hastings and Splash Planet are only 4kms away, and Napier, the Art Deco City of the World is 20 kms.

We look forward to meeting you and our aim is to make your stay a memorable one. Be welcomed with juice, real coffee or tea.   Laundry facilities available. No smoking inside please.

Perfectly position between Hastings and Napier

Havelock North *B&B Homestay Boutique 1km N of Havelock North*

Weldon Boutique Bed & Breakfast
Pracilla Hay
98 Te Mata Road, Havelock North, Hawkes Bay
Tel (06) 877 7551   0800 206 499   Fax (06) 877 7051
pracilla@weldon.co.nz   www.weldon.co.nz
Double $120-$140 Single $80-$110
(Special Breakfast) Dinner $35 queen, $130 - $150
twin, $120 Credit cards accepted
1 Queen 2 Double 1 Twin 1 Single (5 bdrm)
2 Private 1 Guests share

In a quiet picturesque garden at the end of a lavender
lined lane, WELDON offers comfort and quality with romantic olde worlde charm. Accommodation is
offered in spacious elegantly appointed bedrooms, furnished with period and antique furniture. TV &
tea/coffee are provided in each room. Fresh flowers, fine linen and fluffy towels reflect the luxury of
fine accommodation. Breakfast of fresh local fruits & gourmet cooked options is served outdoors
among the roses in summer or in the dining room during winter. Two toy poodles (James and Thomas).

Havelock North *B&B Homestay 6km E of Hastings*

Redwood
Shirley & Mervyn Pethybridge
8 Redwood Close, Brookvale Estate, Havelock North
Tel (06) 877 4551   Fax (06) 877 4550
pethybridge@actrix.gen.nz
www.bnb.co.nz/redwood.html
Double $80 Single $45 (Full Breakfast)
Dinner $25 by arrangement
1 Queen 1 Double 1 Twin (3 bdrm)
1 Ensuite 1 Host share

Redwood is situated in the new Brookvale Estate Development. It is 3km from the Havelock North
village where there are a great variety of shops and restaurants. Hawkes Bay is a well-known tourist
resort with something for everyone. Having travelled extensively both within New Zealand and overseas
we have enjoyed the hospitality of many homestays and are pleased to be able to offer the same in
return. Not suitable for children.

Havelock North *B&B Homestay 5km N of Havelock North*

Totara Stables
Sharon A. Bellaart & John W. Hayes
324 Te Mata - Mangateretere Road, Havelock North,
RD 2, Hastings
Tel (06) 877 8882   Fax (06) 877 8891
Mob 025 863 910   totarastables@xtra.co.nz
www.geocities.com/totarastables
Double $95-$105 Single $75 (Continental Breakfast)
Credit cards accepted
1 King/Twin 1 Queen 1 Twin (3 bdrm)
1 Ensuite 1 Private

Offering a unique Bed & Breakfast experience in a lovingly restored 1910 villa. Take a peek into the
museum of early pioneer farming displayed in the century old stables or marvel at the simplicity of
early stationary motors. Feed the hand reared deer or arrange a ride in a classic 1951 Sunbeam Talbot
motor car. We are located in the heart of the Te Mata wine region only minutes from the pictureque
village of Havelock North. Non smoking and not suitable for children under 12 years.

HAWKES BAY

Waimarama Beach *Homestay 34km SE of Hastings*

Rita & Murray Webb
68 Harper Road, Waimarama, Hawkes Bay
Tel (06) 874 6795 rwebb@xtra.co.nz
www.bnb.co.nz/webb.html
Double $80 Single $45 (Full Breakfast) Dinner $25
2 Double (2 bdrm)
1 Guests share

Lovely beach for surfing, swimming, diving, boating,
fishing etc. Bushwalks and golf course nearby. Situated
only 5 minutes walk from beach with lovely views of
sea, local park and farmland. Nearest town is Havelock North - 20 minutes drive, with Napier 40
minutes. We have 2 double rooms available, a spa pool and separate toilet and bathroom for guests.
Cooked breakfast is offered and dinner is available if required. Please phone for reservations 06-874
6795. No smoking inside please. Pets: 1 cat, 1 dog.

Waipawa *Farmstay Country Home 2km E of Waipawa*

Haowhenua
Caroline & David Jefferd
77 Pourerere Road, RD 1, Waipawa 4170
Tel (06) 857 8241 Fax (06) 857 8261
Mob 025 2684 854 d.jefferd@xtra.co.nz
www.bnb.co.nz/haowhenua.html
Double $100 Single $75 (Full Breakfast)
Child 1/2 price Dinner $25pp Credit cards accepted
1 Queen (1 bdrm)
1 Ensuite

Come and enjoy an evening or two at "Haowhenua" with a farming family in a spacious and comfortable
old country home set in park like surrounds with lovely gardens and swimming pool, and share your
adventures with us. We have two cats and a labrador and only 2km off State Highway 2 and in close
proximity to all of Hawkes Bay's attractions. No smoking inside. Please phone for directions.

Waipawa *Homestay 2km N of Waipawa*

Corgarff Homestay
Judy & Neil McHardy
104 Great North Road, Waipawa, Hawkes Bay
Tel (06) 857 7828 Fax (06) 857 7055
corgarff@xtra.co.nz
www.bnb.co.nz/corgarffhomestay.html
Double $100 Single $50 (Full Breakfast)
Child $25 Dinner $25 Credit cards accepted
2 King/Twin 2 Twin 1 Single (3 bdrm)
1 Ensuite 1 Guests share 1 Host share

A warm welcome awaits you at Corgarff, our very sunny and comfortable home, set in 13 acres amongst
lovely old trees. We have a flock of Texel sheep and a Birman Cat 'Mollie'. Our guest wing has a
separate entrance and also a small private sitting room with TV. Our facilities are very suitable for
wheelchair or disabled persons. Children under 12 half price. Three hours easy run to ferry in Wellington.
Four challenging golf courses within easy reach. Five safe sandy beaches. Hastings and top NZ Wineries
less than 30 minutes. First class rivers for trout fishing. Directions: 2km North of Waipawa town clock.
An old Elm tree drive. Rapid number 1306 on SH2.

Waipawa *B&B 40km S of Hastings*

Abbotsford Oaks
Nicolette Brasell & Chris Davis
85 Abbotsford Road, Waipawa, Central Hawke's Bay
Tel 06 857 8960 Fax 06 857 8961
Mob 025 296 1160
nicolette@abbotsfordoaks.co.nz
www.abbotsfordoaks.co.nz

Double $120-$195 Single $95-$170 (Full Breakfast)
Dinner by arrangement
1 King 3 Queen (4 bdrm)
1 Ensuite 3 Private

Abbotsford Oaks is a substantial and unique historical property providing superior boutique accommodation. It is located in a picturesque setting, surrounded by 3.5 acres of garden. It has spacious, well appointed suites, most with their own lounge and bathroom. Enjoy breakfast in your private lounge, the dining room or garden. Ideal for that restful getaway (as our two cats have found), corporate retreat or as a base to visit the many attractions Hawke's Bay has to offer. Visit our website for more information.

Waipawa *B&B 1km NE of Waipawa*

Abbot Heights
Jacqui & Charlie Hutchison
47 Abbot Avenue, Waipawa,
Tel (06) 857 8585 Fax (06) 857 8580
Mob 0274 330 047   chipper@paradise.net.nz
www.bnb.co.nz/abbotheights.html

Double $130 Single $70 (Continental Breakfast)
2 Queen (2 bdrm)
1 Ensuite 1 Private

Abbot Heights is a comfortable new colonial style home
set in 18 tranquil acres. Our two guest bedrooms have goose down duvets, bathrobes, electric blankets and percale linen. One bathroom has a spa bath. Enjoy breakfast by a sunny window or sip your latte by the fire in a deep leather armchair. Indoor heated pool and tennis courts close. Jet boat tours and professional hunting or fishing guide; bookings essential. Five local golf courses, excellent restaurants, wineries and safe sandy beaches within half hours drive. Our friendly cat is Myrtle.

Waipukurau *Farmstay Self-contained 20km S of Waipukurau*

Hinerangi Station
Caroline & Dan von Dadelszen
615 Hinerangi Road, RD 1, Waipukurau
Tel (06) 855 8273 Fax (06) 855 8273
carovond@amcom.co.nz
www.hinerangi.co.nz

Double $100-$120 Single $80 (Full Breakfast)
Child $30 Dinner $30pp $110 Double
$40 each extra person S/C cottage Pets welcome
2 Queen 1 Double 5 Single (4 bdrm)
2 Private 2 Guests share

Hinerangi Station is an 1800 acre sheep, cattle and deer farm set in the rolling hills of Central Hawkes Bay. Our spacious 1920 homestead was designed by Louis Hay of Napier Art Deco fame. It has a full size billiard table and there is a tennis court and swimming pool in the garden. Guests have their own private entrance. "The Cookhouse",a recently renovated 100 yr old cottage offers self contained accommodation for couples and families. We have one terrier and a cat.

HAWKES BAY

Waipukurau *Farmstay 7km E of Waipukurau*

Mangatarata Country Estate
Judy & Donald Macdonald
415 Mangatarata Road, RD 5, Waipukurau
Tel (06) 858 8275 0800 858 857
Fax (06) 858 8270 Mob 021 480 769
mangatarata@xtra.co.nz
www.hawkesbaynz.com/pages/mangataratacountryestate
Double $150-$170 Single $85
(Full Breakfast) Dinner $35pp
2 Queen 1 Double 3 Single (3 bdrm)
1 Private 1 Guests share

Retreat to a beautiful historic homestead nestled in the heart of Hawkes Bay, Wine Country.

Unwind with uninterrupted farm views from the gracious Victorian verandah. Experience beef and sheep farming first hand or wander through the extensive gardens with swimming pool, pathways and a pond where birdlife prevails.

Enjoy a generous breakfast and good coffee in the private dining room or on the verandah, weather providing. Other sumptuous meals may be arranged by request. Gourmet lamb is Judy's speciality, complimented with fresh produce from the kitchen garden or grown locally.

Meet Mac the Scottish terrier and the two cats who arrived and stayed. Mangatarata is one of Hawkes Bay's most historic sheep stations and is still a working farm of 2,500 acres.

The perfect location for a memorable getaway with truly New Zealand uniqueness

Waipukurau *Farmstay   9km   W of Waipukurau*

Mynthurst
Annabelle & David   Hamilton
912 Lindsay Road , RD 3 , Waipukurau
Tel (06) 857 8093   Fax (06) 857 8093
Mob 025 232 2458   mynthurst@xtra.co.nz
www.bnb.co.nz/ .html

Double $150 Single $85 (Full Breakfast) Child $25
Dinner $35pp   Extra space avail for families
1 King/Twin 1 Double 1 Single (3   bdrm)
1 Ensuite 1 Private

Mynthurst, genuine working sheep and cattle farm 560 hectares. Guests from NZ and overseas welcomed for 19 years. The homestead is large, warm and comfortable. Observe farm activities, enjoy swimming, trout fishing, golf, tennis, wineries. Dinner available on request, using finest local produce. Whether travelling North or South, visiting beautiful Hawkes Bay, you'll find Mynthurst the perfect retreat. 1/2 hour from Hastings SH2. Booking avoids disappointment. Phone for directions. No smoking. Children welcome. Two Cats. Expect Excellence. Farm tour included. Superb Environment.

Waipukurau *Homestay Waipukurau Central*

Airlie Mount
Rashida & Aart van Saarloos
South Service Lane, off Porangahau Road,
PO Box 368, Waipukurau
Tel (06) 858 7601   Fax (06) 858 7609
Mob 025 249 9726   salos@xtra.co.nz
www.bnb.co.nz/airliemount.html

Double $90-$110 Single $60-$80 (Full Breakfast)
Child $30 under 12 Self contained lodge From $20 pp
1 King/Twin 1 Queen 1 Single (2 bdrm)   2 Ensuite

Historic fully restored "Airlie Mount", built in 1870, is situated in the exact centre of Waipukurau, a few steps away from shops and restaurants - yet it's an island of tranquillity, surrounded by cottage gardens and native bush. The comfortable (non-smoking) homestead offers verandahs, billiard room and swimming pool. The guest rooms are very private, have their own bathrooms, TV and outside courtyards. Your hosts have travelled extensively and have two children and a Labrador who all enjoy meeting new guests.   Historic Homestead walks arranged.

HAWKES BAY

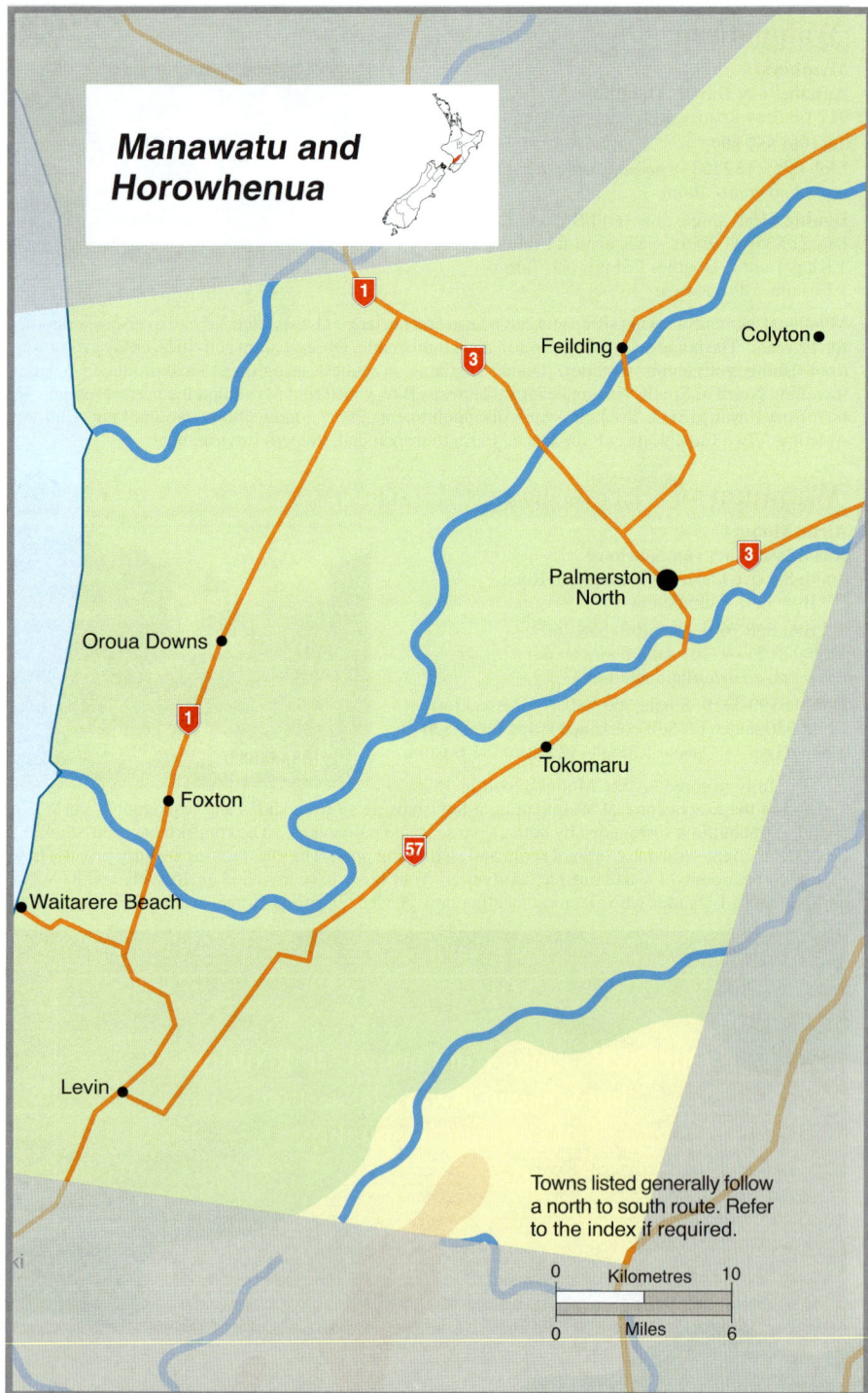

Manawatu and Horowhenua

Feilding

Colyton

Palmerston North

Oroua Downs

Foxton

Tokomaru

Waitarere Beach

Levin

Towns listed generally follow a north to south route. Refer to the index if required.

0   Kilometres   10

0   Miles   6

Colyton - Feilding
Farmstay 16km E of Feilding

Hiamoe
Toos and   John Cousins
Waiata, Colyton, Feilding
Tel (06) 328 7713   Fax (06) 328 7787
Mob 027 4100931   johnhiamoe@clear.net.nz.
www.bnb.co.nz/hiamoe.html
Double $80 Single $50 (Full Breakfast)
Child $20, preschool free Dinner $15 Pets welcome
1 Queen 1 Double 1 Single (2 bdrm)
1 Ensuite

Toos, John, Edmund (10yrs), Julius (9yrs) and Guido (9yrs) look forward to giving you a warm welcome to "Hiamoe" and during your stay, it is our aim that you experience a home away from home.Third generation, farming our deer, cattle,sheep and forestry property and live in a restored 100-year-old colonial home. We have many interests ,enjoy visitors and as Holland is Toos original homeland ,we are accustomed to travel.   Central heating ,open fires ,fenced pool.

Feilding
Homestay Feilding Central

Avoca Homestay
Margaret Hickmott
12 Freyberg Street, Feilding
Tel (06) 323 4699   margh-avoca@inspire.net.nz
www.bnb.co.nz/avocahomestay.html
Double $85 Single $50-$70 (Full Breakfast)
Dinner $25 by arrangement
1 Queen 2 Twin (2 bdrm)
1 Ensuite 1 Host share

Enjoy a break in friendly Feilding, twelve times winner
of New Zealand's Most Beautiful Town Award. You are assured of a warm welcome and an enjoyable stay in a comfortable smoke free home set in an attractive garden with mature trees and a spectacular shrubbery. Off street parking is provided for your vehicle. The main bedroom has a queensize bed, ensuite and an outside entrance for your convenience. We are within easy walking distance of the town centre and well situated for the Manfield Park complex.

Feilding - Palmerston North
Country 13km NE of Feilding

Puketawa B&B/Country Stay
Nelson & Phyllis Whitelock
987 Colyton Road, RD5, Feilding
Tel (06) 328 7819   Fax (06) 328 7919
Mob 021 046 2023   nelson.phyllis@xtra.co.nz
www.bnb.co.nz/puketawa.html
Double $90 Single $50 (Full Breakfast)
Child half price Dinner $25 Children welcome
1 Queen 1 Twin 1 Single (3 bdrm)
1 Ensuite 1 Private

Discover Puketawa for yourself. Experience friendly
Kiwi hospitality in our comfortable national award-winning home situated beside 10 acres of native bush, and surrounded by extensive gardens. Delicious meals are Phyl's speciality prepared from homegrown produce. We enjoy the great outdoors, gardening, travel, music, reading, etc, as well as meeting new friends from NZ and around the world. Four wheel drive tour of the farm is available. Situated handy to both Palmerston North and Feilding, 2 hours from Wellington and Napier.

MANAWATU, HOROWHENUA

Palmerston North - Hokowhitu   *Homestay Palmerston North Central*

Glenfyne
Jillian & Alex McRobert
413 Albert Street, Hokowhitu, Palmerston North

Tel (06) 358 1626   Fax (06) 358 1626
glenfyne@inspire.net.nz
www.bnb.co.nz/glenfyne.html

Double $80 Single $50 (Full Breakfast)
Credit cards accepted
1 Double 2 Single (2 bdrm)
1 Guests share

A warm welcome awaits you in our comfortable home. We are a retired, non-smoking couple with varied interests: meeting people, travel, cooking and golf. Our home is close to Massey University and the Manawatu Golf Club. There are some interesting walkways nearby, and two minutes will take you to the Hokowhitu Village (Post Office, Pharmacy, Restaurants etc). Jillian is a Kiwi Host, assuring you of great hospitality. Laundry facilities and covered off-street parking are available. We are happy to meet public transport.

Palmerston North   *B&B Separate/Suite Palmerston North Central*

The Gables
Monica & Paul Stichbury
179 Fitzherbert Avenue, Palmerston North

Tel (06) 358 3209   Fax (06) 358 3209
Thegables.pn.nz@xtra.co.nz
www.friars.co.nz/hosts/gables.html

Double $80-$110 Single $50-$80
(Continental Breakfast) Dinner $20 by arrangement
Credit cards accepted
3 Queen 1 Single (4 bdrm)
1 Private 2 Guests share

Our fully restored 1930's home in a mature garden with historic trees is only 10 minutes walk from the CBD and numerous restaurants and a few minutes by car or bus from Massey University. Our self contained cottage in the style of a New England Barn is very popular, and, like the house, furnished with antiques and decorated in the country style. We host children only by arrangement. Our delightful pomeranian Bobby "the fluffy doorbell" will announce your arrival.

Palmerston North   *B&B Homestay*

Karaka House
Lynn & David Whitburn
473 College Street, Hokowhitu, Palmerston North

Tel (06) 358 8684   Fax (06) 358 8685
Mob 025 245 2765   dave_lynn@xtra.co.nz
www.bnb.co.nz/karakahouse.html

Double $90-$110 Single $65 (Full Breakfast)
Dinner by arrangement
2 Queen 2 Single (3 bdrm)
1 Guests share

Lynn and David offer you a warm welcome to Karaka House. We are a friendly couple who enjoy meeting people in the relaxed atmosphere of our home which is within an easy walk of the city centre, restaurants and theatres. The College of Education, Polytech and Massey are within easy reach (on bus route). The tiled front entrance opens to a wide hall with a rimu staircase leading to the large sunny bedrooms which have been designed with your comfort in mind. We look forward to meeting you.

Palmerston North - Rongotea   *Farmstay 20km W of Palmerston North*

Andellen
Kay and Warren Nitschke
RD 3, Palmerston North

Tel (06) 324 8359   Fax (06) 324 8359
Mob 027 244 1393   kw@inspire.net.nz
www.bnb.co.nz/andellen.html

Double $80 Single $45 (Continental Breakfast)
Child 1/2 price Dinner B/A $25 pp
Credit cards accepted Children welcome Pets welcome
1 Queen 2 Single (2 bdrm) 1 Ensuite 1 Private

Kay, Warren and Libby (8 years old) welcome you to "Andellen", a lovely large 90 year old farm villa set on 42 acres with extensive lawn, garden and orchard. We offer guests the opportunity to relax in a lovely tranquil country setting. Seasonal farm activities available. Children very welcome. Beach 10 minutes away. We have a pet cat and dog. Directions: Situated 11 kms South of Sanson or 11 kms North of Himitangi intersection. Off State Highway 1, into Kaimatarau Road and travel across first intersection. Next gate on left - Farm no. 221. Our name is on the gate. Dinner by arrangement.

Palmerston North   *B&B 3.5km E of Palmerston North*

Clairemont
Joy & Dick Archer
10 James Line, RD 10, Palmerston North

Tel (06) 357 5508   Fax (06) 357 5501
clairemont@inspire.net.nz
www.bnb.co.nz/clairemont.html

Double $75 Single $50 (Full Breakfast)
1 Double 1 Twin (2 bdrm)
1 Guests share

Welcome to Clairemont. We are a rural spot within the city boundary, plenty of trees and a quite extensive garden.
On our 1¼ acres we keep a few sheep, silky bantams, and our little dog Toby. We are handy to river walks, golf course, and shops are a few minutes away. We have a cosy, spacious family home we would like to share with you. Our interests are walking, gardening, model engineering and barbershop singing. Good off street parking. Homebaked suppers provided.

Palmerston North   *B&B 4km E of Palmerston North*

Panorama B&B
Claire & Bill Sawers
30 Moonshine Valley Road, RD1,
Aokautere, Palmerston North

Tel (06) 354 8816   Fax (06) 356 2757
panorama.bb@paradise.net.nz
www.homepages.paradise.net.nz/sawers/

Double $80 Single $50 (Full Breakfast)
Child $20 Credit cards accepted
1 Double 1 Twin (2 bdrm)
1 Guests share

A warm welcome awaits you at our home in Moonshine Valley. We offer a private and peaceful stay in a rural-residential area. Situated only eight minutes drive to the Square, four minutes to Massey University and closer to the International Pacific College. Guests share a lounge/dining room with refreshments always available. The bathroom includes a bath and shower. Interesting walkways and gardens are nearby, or just relax on the terrace and enjoy the panoramic city, rural and mountain views with our cat Sophie.

Palmerston North *B&B Homestay 13km E of Palmerston North*

Country Lane Homestay
Fay and Allan Hutchinson
52 Orrs Road, RD1 Aokautere, Palmerston North
Tel (06) 326 8529 Fax (06) 326 9216
Mob 025 485 833 ashhurst.timber@xtra.co.nz
www.bnb.co.nz/user82.html
Double $90-$120 Single $50 (Full Breakfast)
Dinner $25 - $30
1 King/Twin 1 Queen 1 Double 1 Single (3 bdrm)
1 Ensuite 2 Private 1 Host share

Luxury Country living, a short distance from Palmerston North near the Manawatu Gorge and below the wind farm. Ten kilometres from the Pacific College and two kilometres from Equestrian Centre. Excellent stop over en route to/from Wellington or East Coast eg. Napier. Our large home is newly decorated, with some antiques in a country traditional style and is surrounded by our pleasant garden. We have our sawmill on the property as well as coloured sheep, horses, and raise a few calves. The Manawatu River borders our property. It is our pleasure to provide home cooked meals for you with some of our local produce.

Palmerston North *B&B Self-contained 5.5km SW of Central Palmerston North*

Udys on Anders
Glenda & Tim Udy
52 Anders Road, Palmerston North,
Tel (06) 354 1722 0800 157 981 Fax (06) 354 1711
Mob 0274 409 299 kiwitim@clear.net.nz
www.udysonanders.co.nz
Double $120 Single $90 (Full Breakfast) Child $20
Dinner neg. Children welcome
1 Queen 1 Double (1 bdrm)
1 Ensuite

We have a fully self-contained apartment attached to out home. We are in a quiet country location, four and a half acres of lawn, edge of town, seven minutes to CBD. We have a plexipave tennis court and a beautiful Mediterranean courtyard for our guest to make use of, also a games room with snooker table and table tennis. The apartment has a queen bed with ensuite, walk-in wardrobe, separate lounge with futon sofa bed, dining area and total cooking facilities - breakfast is included. Apartment is smoke-free.

Tokomaru *Self-contained 19km S of*

Hi-Da-Way Lodge
Sue & Trevor Palmer
21 Albert Road, RD 4, Palmerston North
Tel (06) 329 8731 Fax (06) 329 8732
Mob 021 119 4443 hi-da-way-lodge@xtra.co.nz
www.bnb.co.nz/hidawaylodge.html
Double $95 Single $70 (Full Breakfast) Child $25
Second Cabin $25per extra person
Dinner by arrangement
1 Double 2 Single (2 bdrm)
1 Private

Looking for something unique - then Hi-Da-Way lodge extends a warm welcome. The fully self contained rustic cabin is set in a peaceful garden setting surrounded by trees and has its own spa, TV, video and fridge/freezer. Guests may enjoy volley ball, shared swimming pool, BBQ or just meander around our 6.5 hectare property. Situated just 10 mins from Massey University and 1 1/2 hours from Wellington off State Highway 57. We have two boys still at home and two pet dogs who enjoy meeting people. Treat yourself.

Oroua Downs   *Farmstay 14km N of Foxton*

Oroua Downs Farmstay
Bev & Ian Wilson
Omanuka Road, RD 11, Foxton

Tel (06) 329 9859   Fax (06) 329 9859
Mob 0274 986 023   getwilsons@xtra.co.nz
www.bnb.co.nz/orouadownsfarmstay.html

Double $80 Single $40 (Full Breakfast)
Child $20 Dinner $20pp
2 Double 1 Twin (3 bdrm)
1 Guests share

Bev and Ian invite you to share their spacious 2 storey, smoke free home nestled amongst 1 1/2 acres of tree-lined gardens. Enjoy the opportunity to relax and leisurely walk with our cat amongst the garden listening to the bird song. We also operate a Building and Wooden Toy manufacturing business. Directions: turn off at Bed & Breakfast sign on State Highway 1, 14km north of Foxton and 16km south of Sanson. Travel 2 km down Omanuka Road.

Foxton   *Farmstay 1km E of Foxton*

Karnak Stud
Margaret Barbour
Ridge Road, Foxton

Tel (06) 363 7764   Fax (06) 363 8941
www.bnb.co.nz/karnakstud.html

Double $85 Single $60 (Full Breakfast)
Child Under six free Horse $5 per night
Credit cards accepted Children welcome Pets welcome
1 Double 1 Twin 1 Single (2 bdrm)
1 Ensuite 1 Private

Karnak Stud, mini farm, is an ideal quiet stopover one and a half hours from Wellington. Perfect for children to meet friendly farm dog Meg, cat Mousie, a thoroughbred horse and quiet cattle. Relaxing country living, healthy farmstay food. Enjoy table tennis, darts, pool and children's toys. Wander through our sixteen acres of pasture and woodland. Follow Farmstay arrow on State Highway One for one kilometre up Purcell Street to a white fence. Take the next wide gateway on your left. Ideal for the whole family. Bring your pets and horse too!

Waitarere Beach   *Homestay 14km W of Levin*

Dunes
Robyn & Grant Powell
10 Ngati Huia Place, Waitarere Beach,

Tel (06) 368 7957   Mob 025 285 3643
sand.dunes@xtra.co.nz
sand.dunes

Double $100-115 Single $75-90 (Continental Breakfast)
Dinner $30 Credit cards accepted
2 Queen (2 bdrm)
2 Ensuite

Robyn & Grant (formerly of Miranui Homestay, Palmerston North) welcome you to our new absolute beachfront retreat. Enjoy beach walks and magnificent view of Kapiti and Mounts Taranaki and Ruapehu. We offer two queen size bedrooms, ensuites, own living areas with TV, tea/coffee making facilities and continental breakfast provided. Situated 14 kilometres north west of Levin, approximately one and a half hours from Wellington and 35 minutes from Palmerston North. Laundry facilities, off-street parking, non-smoking. Dinner by arrangement.

Levin *Farmstay 3.4km E of Levin*

Lynn Beau Ley
Beverley & Peter Lynn
Queen Street East, RD 1, Levin

Tel (06) 368 0310 Fax (06) 368 0310
Mob 025 274 4564 lynnbeauley@paradise.net.nz
www.bnb.co.nz/lynnbeauley.html

Double $85 Single $60 (Full Breakfast)
Dinner $20 by arrangement Credit cards accepted
1 Double 2 Single (2 bdrm)
1 Ensuite 1 Private

A 10 acre pastoral retreat 4 minutes from town centre. Comfortable distance for ferry/air travel. We farm sheep and cattle, and enjoy entertaining. Our home is spacious, ranch-style with warm aspect, situated in one acre of lawns and gardens. Tastefully appointed guest rooms, delicious breakfasts and many extras. Beverley has many years experience in hospitality business. Peter a background in management and financial services. Turn east off SH1 at Post Office into Queen Street East. We are 3.4km on left. Sign at gate.

Levin *Farmstay 9km SE of Levin*

Buttercup Acres
Ivan & Pat Keating
55 Florida Road, RD 20, Levin

Tel (06) 368 0557 buttercupacres@xtra.co.nz
www.bnb.co.nz/buttercupacres.html

Double $90 Single $45 (Full Breakfast)
Dinner $20 Credit cards accepted
1 Double 2 Single (2 bdrm)
1 Ensuite 1 Private

Buttercup Acres is a small tranquil rural property at the foothills of the Tararua Ranges. We specialise in breeding Miniature Horses and Alpaca's. Our home is surrounded by 3 acres of gardens and a large pond. In the evenings you can relax in the lounge. Learn to spin or weave in our weaving studio or view the stars through our telescope. Our model railway will fascinate visitors. Free laundry facilities available. Directions: At Ohau turn into Muhunoa East Road. 5km to Florida Road.

Levin   *B&B Separate/Suite Self-contained 5min Levin*

Fantails
Heather Watson
40 MacArthur Street, Levin

Tel (06) 368 9011   Fax (06) 368 9279   fantails@xtra.co.nz   www.fantails.co.nz

Double $90-$120 Single $60-$80 (Full Breakfast) Child neg Dinner $45 S/C Cottages $100 - $140
Credit cards accepted Pets welcome Smoking area inside
1 King 2 Queen 1 Twin 4 Single (4 bdrm)
3 Ensuite 1 Private

Welcome to Fantails, a hidden oasis of native bush, mature trees, native birds and other species, all set
in two acres of park-like gardens only minutes from the town centre by car. Experience our garden
where you can pick fruit of the season from our trees, view our raised vegetable garden made of ponga
logs. Learn about worm farming and companion planting plus a little humour tossed in.
Our breakfasts are quite a treat with a lovely view of fantails, native pigeons and other bird life. Different
diets are catered for and all our meals are Certified Organic. We also have a treat for you with milking
our goat (Mayling) or you can have afternoon tea with our floppsy bunny (Annabella), excellent with
children.
If you require timeout for a few days take one of out two cottages; they sleep two - four people. They
are very private and have everything required. Then in the evening why not try our Sauna and natural
bush shower and then rest in our quiet and secure environment and very comfortable beds. If you
require wheelchair friendly accommodation we are happy to assist. We are also only one hour away
from the Wellington Ferry Terminal and are smoke free.

Levin   *Farmstay Separate/Suite Self-contained 2.5km S of Levin*

Range View Farmstay
Ann & Errol Quinn
112 Buller Rd, RD 1, Levin

Tel (06) 368 5530   Fax (06) 368 5810
Mob 025 494 533   farm.stay@xtra.co.nz
www.bnb.co.nz/rangeview.html

Double $90-$110 Single $90 (Full Breakfast)
Child under 10: $15.00 $20 pp extra person
Credit cards accepted Children welcome
2 Queen 1 Double 2 Single (3 bdrm)
2 Private

Errol and Ann welcome you to their private, quiet, fully self contained two bedroom cottage and separate bedsitter offering you all the comforts. Set on 8 acres of land with quiet animals including miniature horse and gig, 90 kilometres to Wellington, 35 minute drive to Palmerston North. The cottage has modern kitchen facilities, sleeps 6, has separate toilet, laundry, bathroom with shower and bath. Large verandah with view of Tararua Ranges. Walking distance to tranquil Lake Papatonga and Bush Walks.

Levin   *B&B Farmstay Homestay 1 km N of Levin*

Greenacres
Derek & Dorothy Burt
88 Avenue North, Levin,

Tel (06) 368 7062   Fax (06) 368 7062
plantagenet@paradise.net.nz
www.levinbb.com

Double $90 Single $60 (Continental/Full Breakfast)
Dinner $20
2 Queen (2 bdrm)
2 Ensuite

Quality accommodation in peaceful, relaxing rural surrounds, warm hospitality and every comfort considered. Spacious bedrooms with ensuite, TV, coffee & tea. Laundry, computer, fax/phone. Derek & Dorothy Burt your hosts, Somerset & Edward their cats. New house on 10 acres 2km north of Levin. Calves on paddocks. Dinner available on request and full English or continental breakfast. 100m off SH1 on Avenue North. Horses and floats accommodated. Camper vans.

If you need any information ask your hosts,
they are your own personal travel agent and guide.

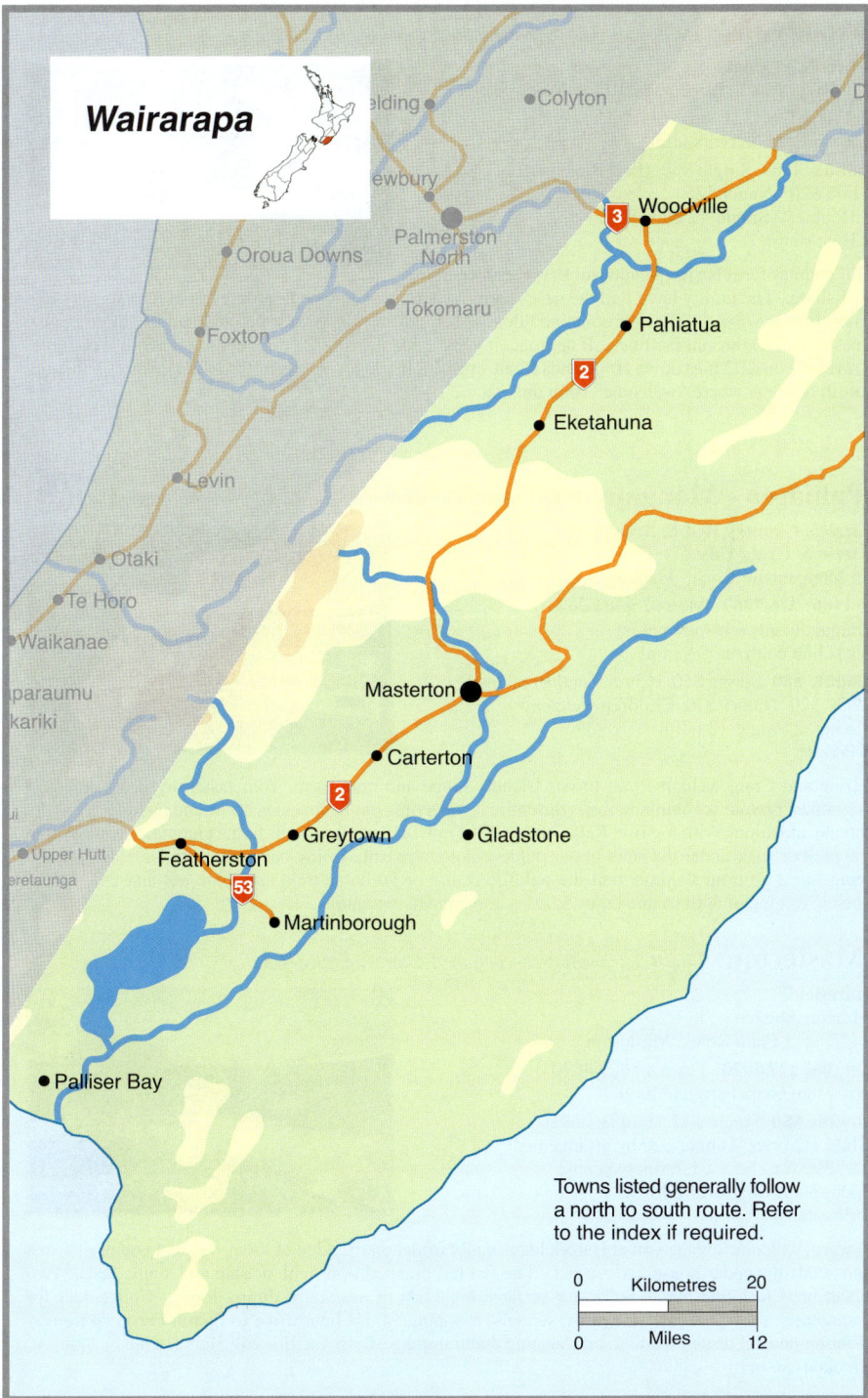

Wairarapa

Colyton

elding

ewbury

Oroua Downs

Palmerston
North

Woodville

Tokomaru

Pahiatua

Foxton

Eketahuna

Levin

Otaki

Te Horo

Waikanae

paraumu

kariki

Masterton

Carterton

Greytown

Gladstone

Upper Hutt

Featherston

eretaunga

Martinborough

Palliser Bay

Towns listed generally follow
a north to south route. Refer
to the index if required.

0   Kilometres   20

0   Miles   12

Woodville *B&B Farmstay Self-contained 13km NE of Woodville*

Chris & Jo Coats
370 River Road, Hopelands, RD 1, Woodville
Tel (06) 376 4521 jo.coats@clear.net.nz
www.bnb.co.nz/coats.html
Double $100 Single $50 (Full Breakfast)
Child $20 Dinner $25
1 Double 2 Single (2 bdrm)
1 Host share

Hill country farm beside Manawatu River renowned for
its fishing. The family have fled the nest. Farming activities may be in progress and tourists may like
to become involved. The self contained double bed unit has its own toilet and handbasin otherwise
guests share bathroom facilities. If approaching via Pahiatua, ring for directions and avoid Woodville.
Travellers on SH2 turn down Hopelands Road, cross high bridge over river, turn right towards Pahiatua,
fourth house is where "welcome" is on the mat.

Pahiatua - Mangamaire *B&B Farmstay Self-contained 8km S of Pahiatua*

Lizzie's Country Bed & Breakfast
Lizzie & Craig Udy
86 Mangamaire Road, Mangamaire, Pahiatua
Tel (06) 376 7367 Mob 025 204 2648
craigandlizudy@inspire.net.nz
www.bnb.co.nz/lizzies.html
Double $80 Single $50 (Continental Breakfast)
Child $20 Dinner $20 Children welcome
1 King 2 Single (2 bdrm)
1 Private

Lizzie and Craig welcome you to our friendly home and mini farm. Your tastefully decorated, self
contained, private accommodation is the entire lower storey of our spacious home and includes a private
lounge and dining with log fire. Relax and watch a movie in our luxurious home cinema, take a swim in
the pool or soak under the stars in our outdoor hot water bath. Enjoy our tame farm animals, tour the
wind farm, go trout fishing, visit the wildlife centre or go horse trekking. Dine out and enjoy local
cuisine or dine in with us and enjoy Lizzies home made specialties.

Masterton *B&B Farmstay Self-contained 3km W of Masterton*

Harefield
Marion Ahearn
147 Upper Plain Road, Masterton
Tel (06) 377 4070 Fax (06) 377 4070
www.bnb.co.nz/harefield.html
Double $80 Single $45 (Full Breakfast)
Child 1/2 price Dinner $20 by arrangement
S/C Flat for 2 $55 Children welcome
1 Double 1 Single (1 bdrm)
1 Private

A warm welcome awaits you at Harefield, a small farmlet on the edge of town. A quiet country garden
surrounds the cedar house and s/c flat. The flat has one bedroom with double and single beds. Two
divan beds in living area. Self-cater or have breakfast in our warm dining room. Convenient for
restaurants, showgrounds, vineyards, schools, tramping. 1 1/2 hour drive to Picton Ferry. We enjoy
meeting people, travel, reading, art, farming and tramping. Baby facilities available. One outside cat.
Smoke free.

Masterton   *B&B Farmstay Homestay Rural Homestay 10km W of Masterton*

Tidsfordriv
Glenys Hansen
4 Cootes Road, Matahiwi RD 8, Masterton
Tel (06) 378 9967 Fax (06) 378 9957
ghansen@contact.net.nz
www.bnb.co.nz/tidsfordriv.html

Double $80-$85 Single $50 (Full Breakfast)
Child 1/2 price Dinner $20 B/A Credit cards accepted
1 Queen 2 Single (2 bdrm)
1 Private

A warm welcome awaits you at 'Tidsfordriv' - a 64 acre
farmlet - seven kilometres off the main bypass route. A comfortable modern home set in park like
surroundings with large gardens, ponds and many species of wetland birds. Enjoy bird watching with
ease. Glenys has home-hosted for 16 years and invites you to join her for dinner. Conservation, gardening
and travel are her interests. A Labrador dog is the family pet. Local Wairarapa attractions - National
Wildlife Centre, gardens, vineyards, Tararua Forest Park.

Masterton   *Homestay 1km E of Masterton*

Mas des Saules
Mary & Steve Blakemore
9A Pokohiwi Road, Homebush, Masterton
Tel (06) 377 2577 Fax (06) 377 2578
Mob 025 620 8728   mas-des-saules@wise.net.nz
www.bnb.co.nz/masdessaules.html

Double $110 Single $65 (Full Breakfast) Child $40
Dinner $35 Credit cards accepted Children welcome
2 Queen (2 bdrm)
1 Guests share

Down a country lane, amongst apple orchards, discover our tranquil French Provencal farmhouse with
its stream, water fowl, and petanque court. Our children have departed, leaving us with a cat, small dog,
and cattle on our small farm. Guest lounge and bathroom with bath and shower. Open fire and central
heating. Enjoy farmhouse cooking with fresh vegetables from our large country garden. We can also
provide barbecues and picnic lunches. We are a well travelled couple who enjoy helping guests discover
the unspoilt Wairarapa.

Please let us know how you enjoyed your B&B.
There are comment forms at the end of the book.

Masterton *Farmstay 2km E of Masterton*

Apple Source Orchard Stay
Niel & Raewyn Groombridge
Te Ore Ore, RD 6, Masterton
Tel (06) 377 0820   Fax (06) 370 9401
Mob 021 667 092   raeg@wise.net.nz
www.bnb.co.nz/applesource.html

Double $100 Single $75 (Continental Breakfast)
Child 1/2 price Dinner $30
2 Queen 1 Single (2 bdrm)
2 Ensuite

Try an experience that's a little different! Our colonial
style homestead is set in an operating apple orchard and has a separate guest wing with lounge and two bedrooms with ensuites. You are welcome to share dinner or a country breakfast with us and enjoy the ambience of stanley range based cooking along with relaxing by the open fire or on the deck. There are orchard walks and a garden haven. Watch the daily orchard activities and pick some fruit in season. Ask us about the Model A tourer courtesy car.

Masterton *B&B Guesthouse Central Masterton*

Victoria House
Marion and Sara Monks and Mike Parker
15 Victoria Street, Masterton
Tel (06) 377 0186   Fax (06) 377 0186
parker.monks@xtra.co.nz
www.bnb.co.nz/victoriahouse.html

Double $80 Single $50 (Continental Breakfast)
Twin $80 Credit cards accepted
3 Double 1 Twin 2 Single (6 bdrm)
2 Guests share

Victoria House is a two storey house built pre 1886, renovated to retain the character of the period. The peaceful nature of the furnishings and outdoor area create a quiet, relaxing atmosphere, great for a "get away from it" weekend. We are also only a three minute walk from the town centre and Masterton's excellant restaurants. Bcing "wine friendly" hosts we enjoy discussing wines and freely offer advice on the Wairararapa's growing wine industry.

Masterton *B&B Self-contained Masterton Central*

Natusch Town House
Anne Bohm
55 Lincoln Road, Masterton,
Tel (06) 378 9252   Fax (06) 378 9330
Mob 027 436 3732   anne@natusch.co.nz
www.natusch.co.nz

Double $160 Single $100 (Continental Breakfast)
Credit cards accepted
4 Queen (4 bdrm)
1 Ensuite 1 Private

Self contained, hosts live off-site. Booking is for the whole house. You choose who, if any, are to share with you. A marvellous old two storied self-contained home built in 1893. Right in the centre of town within easy reach of great dining, bars, parks etc. Four double bedrooms each with a queen sized bed, two bathrooms, parlour, dining room and well appointed modern kitchen, off-street parking for up to four cars. Old style with luxury appointments. This is a Historic Places Trust listed home - a delight to stay in. A delicious breakfast is included on a self help basis.

Masterton - Whareama *Homestay Self-contained 32km E of Masterton*

Blairlogie Homestead
Barbara & Graham Ingram-Monk
Blairlogie-Langdale Rd, Masterton,
Tel (06) 372 3777   Fax (06) 372 3778
Mob 021 185 5309   blairlogie@wise.net.nz
www.wairarapa.co.nz/blairlogie
Double $100-$130 Single $65-$70 (Special Breakfast)
Child $25 - $35 Dinner $30 S/C cottage $90 - $110
Credit cards accepted Children welcome
2 Queen 2 Double 2 Twin 1 Single (5 bdrm)
2 Ensuite 1 Private 2 Guests share

Chill out in our historic homestead. Enjoy a luxury breakfast on the sunny verandah, take a picnic to Castlepoint beach, return to dinner in front of a log fire. Relax in our elegant sitting room, choose a video or book, or watch Sky TV. Swim in our solar-heated pool, walk the discovery trail set in 25 acres of woodland and gardens with many native birds, play pool or petanque. Children welcome. Come join us in our peaceful, country lifestyle!

Masterton *Homestay 1km S of Masterton*

Carrbridge House
Ross & Cushla Hollings
31 Andrew Street, Masterton,
Tel (06) 370 2999   Fax (06) 370 2950
hols@xtra.co.nz
www.carrbridge-house.co.nz
Double $100-$120 Single $90-$100
(Special Breakfast)
2 Queen (2 bdrm)
2 Ensuite

At Carrbridge House we offer you a relaxing stay in our comfortable home set in four parklike acres in rural Masterton. Unwind with afternoon tea before unpacking in one of our well-appointed rooms with flowers, complimentary port, bath robes, and hairdryers. Both have ensuites and one has its own private lounge and TV. Start the day with our special breakfast which can be enjoyed in the dining room or on our large verandah. For your added enjoyment we offer petanque, croquet and bicycles. Come visit us in the beautiful Wairarapa.

Ensuite or private bathroom is yours exclusively.
Guest share bathroom is shared with other guests.
Host share bathroom is shared with the family.

Masterton *B&B Farmstay Homestay Self-contained 3km E of Town*

Littleacres
Lynette Teahan
Homebush Road, R.D.5, Masterton

Tel (06) 3770236 Fax (06) 3770936
Mob 027 419 2856 lynette@littleacres.co.nz
www.littleacres.co.nz

Double $105 Single $90 (Full Breakfast)
Family Max. $120 Children welcome Pets welcome
2 Queen (2 bdrm)
2 Ensuite

Littleacres offers excellent accommodation in a lovely park like setting,close to Masterton, but still in the country.In the spring,the fields of daffodils is spectacular! Both the Orchard and Camelia suites have en-suites, separate lounges, and are private from the main house. The gardens and bush are restful and encourage you to wander. Littleacres is ideal for that restful weekend or time out for two, or as a base to enjoy the Wairarapa. Families and pets are welcome (kennels available).

Carterton *B&B 1km N of Carterton*

Homecroft
Christine & Neil Stewart
Somerset Road, RD 2, Carterton

Tel (06) 379 5959 homecroft@xtra.co.nz
www.bnb.co.nz/homecroft.html

Double $85 Single $50 (Full Breakfast)
Dinner $25pp by arr.
1 Queen 1 Double 1 Twin (3 bdrm)
1 Ensuite 1 Private 1 Guests share

Homecroft is surrounded by our country garden and farmland yet handy to the vineyards, crafts, antiques, and golf courses of the Wairarapa. Wellington and the inter-island ferry 90 minutes away. Accommodation, with own entrance, in a separate wing of the house with small lounge, the sunny bedrooms open onto a deck. The double room with ensuite is separate from the house. All bedrooms overlook the garden. A leisurely breakfast at Homecroft is an enjoyable experience. We look forward to making your stay with us happy and relaxing.

Carterton *B&B 3km S of Carterton*

Portland House
Judy Betts
Portland Road, State Highway 2, Carterton

Tel (06) 379 8809 Mob 025 602 8358
portlandhouse@paradise.net.nz
www.bnb.co.nz/portlandhouse.html

Double $80 Single $50 (Full Breakfast)
Dinner by prior arrangement Credit cards accepted
1 Double 1 Twin (2 bdrm)
1 Private 1 Host share

A warm and friendly welcome awaits you at Portland House, a 125 year old refurbished villa and home to Birmans Missy and George. You can rest, relax and enjoy the country air of the Wairarapa in our peaceful surroundings and comfortable home. We are just off the main highway (SH2) and within 5 to 10 minutes drive to Masterton, the cafes in Greytown, the vineyards in Martinborough, the scenic Waiohine Gorge, the Tararua Forest Park and many wonderful Wairarapa Gardens.

Gladstone *B&B Homestay 22km E of Carterton*

Hinana Cottage
Louise Walker
Fire No 15, Admiral Road, RD 3, Masterton
Tel (06) 372 7667   Mob 027 499 8928
hinanacottage@xtra.co.nz
www.bnb.co.nz/hinanacottage.html

Double $110-$135 (Special Breakfast)
Dinner By arrangement $45 pp Credit cards accepted
1 Queen 1 Double (2 bdrm)
1 Ensuite 1 Host share

Experience the peace and tranquillity of Hinana Cottage, a delightfully restored 1930's bungalow nestling in the Gladstone hills, with spectacular views of the Tararuas and Wairarapa Valley. Handy to Masterton, Carterton and Greytown and an easy 35 minutes from Martinborough. Ideally situated for the exploration of Wairarapa's vineyards, walkways, caves and rivers. Relax in the outdoor spa pool, play petanque, or laze by the open fire and enjoy Hinana's native timber floors, ornate plaster ceilings, fine china and beautiful linen - all reminders of a bygone era.

Gladstone *B&B Farmstay 15km SE of Masterton*

Cavelands Homestay
Belinda & Rod Cranswick
Fire No 10, Cavelands Road, RD 4, Masterton
Tel (06) 372 7733   Fax (06) 372 7773
Mob 027 436 5738   cranswick@wise.net.nz
www.bnb.co.nz/cavelands.html

Double $120-$135 Single $110 (Full Breakfast)
Dinner $50pp by arr. Credit cards accepted
1 Queen 1 Twin (2 bdrm)
1 Private

Country hospitality awaits in our homestead (1870s circa) on our 200 acre sheep and cattle stud. Queen bedroom opens on a sunny verandah, and twin bedroom nearby. Elegant private sitting room with open fire. Delicious hearty breakfasts and homemade panforte with coffee. Foxy Ollie and two cats share our home. Experience Caveland's beauty and explore glowworm caves, walks, sheep mustering demos, mountain biking and grass tennis. Central to Gladstone's attractions, gardens, vineyards, ostrich and cheese farms.

Greytown *B&B Homestay*

Westwood Country House
Jill Kemp
PO Box 34, 82 West Street, Greytown
Tel (06) 304 8510   Fax (06) 304 8610
Mob 027 471 6466   westwood.kemp@xtra.co.nz
www.westwood.greytown.co.nz

Double $175-$200 Single $75 (Full Breakfast)
Credit cards accepted
3 King/Twin 1 Single (4 bdrm)
3 Ensuite 1 Private 1 Guests share

A top category award winner in 'New Zealand House of the Year', Westwood has been designed to blend with its picturesque surroundings - nine acres of magnificent trees, with mountain views, a tranquil stream and formal Herb Garden. Just a short stroll to historic Greytown's cafes and specialty shops. Enjoy stylish comfort with an old fashioned ambience in your spacious ensuite room with private entrance, verandah, tea/coffee making facilities and SKY television. Breakfast poolside in summer or fireside in winter. Experience country hospitality at its best! King Beds are Super Kings.

Greytown *B&B Homestay 80km N of Wellington*

The Ambers
Marilla & Steve Davis
78 Kuratawhiti Street, Greytown
Tel (06) 304 8588 Fax (06) 304 8590
Mob 025 994 394
ambershomestay@xtra.co.nz
www.bnb.co.nz/theambers.html

Double $100-$120 Single $70
(Continental Breakfast)
Child $25 Self-contained cottage
Credit cards accepted
1 King 1 Queen 1 Double (3 bdrm)
1 Ensuite 1 Private 1 Guests share

Built in the 1800's The Ambers exudes the ambience of its era. The house is nestled in two acres of gardens with many beautiful old trees. Our guest wing is separate enough to provide privacy or the intimate atmosphere you desire without feeling isolated from us.

We offer guests secluded verandahs, a spa pool for those starry summer nights, lounge with open fire for winter. The Cherub Room has a queen bed and private bathroom. The Vintage Room has a king bed with ensuite bathroom. If two couples wish to share a bathroom we also have our Oak Aged Room with double bed.

Breakfast includes homemade muffins and fresh fruit in season. We are within walking distance of Greytown's Main Street with unique wooden Victorian architecture, cafes, and ten minutes drive to Martinborough's vineyards. If you desire the ultimate privacy or a 'romantic getaway' we offer a "Blissful" cottage set in its own private garden featuring lovely old trees. Country Bliss Cottage has two double bedrooms, with own amenities including fire and bath. For tariff please contact Marilla Davis at above numbers.

Within walking distance of Greytown's Main Street

Featherston   *B&B Separate/Suite*

Woodland Holt Bed & Breakfast
Judi Adams
47 Watt Street, Featherston

Tel (06) 308 9927   Mob 025 291 2774
woodland-holt@xtra.co.nz
www.bnb.co.nz/woodlandholtbedbreakfast.html

Double $100-$120 Single $65 (Continental Breakfast)
Dinner $35
1 Double 1 Twin 1 Single (3 bdrm)
1 Guests share

Providing friendly hospitality. Interests include travelling, gardening, books, music, cross-stitch and collecting. Secluded gardens contain native, exotic and rare plants. Warm, luxury accommodation with off street parking. Breakfast includes home made treats and preserves. Explore beautiful Wairarapa or relax in comfort. View Meakin-at-Woodland, an extensive private collection of china by Alfred Meakin, and J&G Meakin. Dine at a local restaurant or arrange to join me for an evening meal. Picnic hampers are available (additional charge). We look forward to your company and making your stay enjoyable.

Martinborough   *B&B Homestay 0.5km NW of Martinborough*

Oak House
Polly & Chris Buring
45 Kitchener Street, Martinborough

Tel (06) 306 9198   Fax (06) 306 8198
chrispolly.oakhouse@xtra.co.nz
www.bnb.co.nz/oakhouse.html

Double $100-$120 Single $55 (Special Breakfast)
Child By arrangement Dinner By arrangement
2 Queen 2 Single (3 bdrm)
1 Ensuite 1 Guests share

Our characterful eighty year old Californian bungalow offers gracious accommodation. Our spacious lounge provides a relaxed setting for sampling winemaker Chris's wonderful products. Our guest wing has its own entrance, bathroom (large bath and shower) and separate w.c. Our new bedroom has ensuite facilities. Bedrooms enjoy afternoon sun and garden views. Breakfast features fresh croissants, home preserved local fruits and conserves. Creative cook Polly matches delicious dishes (often local game) with Chris' great wines. Tour our onsite winery with Chris. Meet our multi-talented cats.

Martinborough   *Homestay gardens 1km SW of Martinborough*

Ross Glyn
Kenneth & Odette Trigg
1 Grey Street, Martinborough

Tel (06) 306 9967   Fax (06) 306 8267
rossglyn1@hotmail.com
www.bnb.co.nz/rossglyn.html

Double $90 Single $55 (Full Breakfast)
Dinner $25+ Children welcome
1 Double 2 Single (2 bdrm)
1 Private 1 Guests share

Our home nestles in over two acres of landscaped gardens which includes woodlands, rose garden, orchard, Japanese garden and we are surrounded by Vineyards. Both our guestrooms have french doors opening onto a sunny deck with private access. Guests are welcome to relax with us and our small spoilt dog and cat in our large cosy (woodburner heated) lounge. Breakfast includes fresh croissants, homemade jams, jellies and preserved fruit. Cooked breakfast on request and dinner by arrangement.

Martinborough - Wairarapa *B&B Self-contained Martinborough Central*

Beatson's of Martinborough
Karin Beatson & John Cooper
9A Cologne Street, Martinborough,
Wairarapa

Tel (06) 306 8242 Fax (06) 306 8243
Mob 0274 499 827
beatsons@wise.net.nz
www.beatsons.co.nz

Double $120-$150 Single $100
(Full Breakfast) Dinner by arrangement
Credit cards accepted
4 King/Twin 5 Queen (9 bdrm)
9 Ensuite

Hosts Karin Beatson and John Cooper offer you a friendly and relaxed stay in their 1905 houses "Harrington" and "Cologne", lovingly restored as boutique accommodation, to ensure your year-round comfort.

Furnishing includes some antiques and an interesting collection of New Zealand paintings and crafts. Polished matai floors, high ceilings and individually decorated, spacious bedrooms with ensuites feature. In the living areas, french doors open onto verandahs, with tables overlooking the garden with its cottage plantings, natives, fruits trees and herbs. Woodburners provide winter warmth.

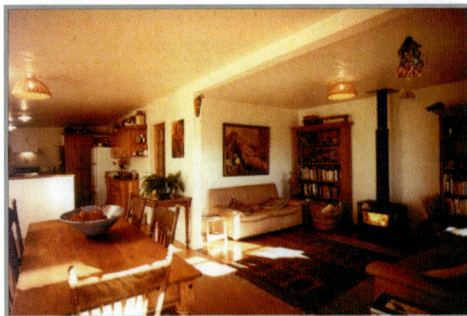

Great home cooking includes speciality country breakfasts using local products, homemade breads and preserves. (Dinners and functions by arrangement). "Heriot Cottage" is a one-bedroomed self-contained comfortable colonial garden cottage featuring an original clawfoot bath, and a verandah to sip wine on. Beatson's of Martinborough are just five minutes walk from Martinborough Square with its cafes, restaurants and speciality shops. Close to vineyards.

Just minutes walk from cafes, restaurants and speciality shops

Martinborough *B&B Country B&B 4km E of Martinborough*

Alder Hey
Sheryll & John Lett
Hinakura Road, RD 4, Martinborough
Tel (06) 306 9599   Fax (06) 306 9598
Mob 025 247 5012   bnb@alderhey.co.nz
www.alderhey.co.nz

Double $110-$120 Single $80 (Full Breakfast)
Credit cards accepted
2 Queen 1 Twin (2 bdrm)
1 Ensuite 1 Private

Nestled in a pretty valley five minutes drive east of
Martinborough, we are close to the golf course and vineyards. The spacious and comfortable guest
wing has its own entrance, with a lounge/library overlooking our olive grove which leads down to the
trout stream on our boundary. Great country breakfasts with farm fresh eggs in our farmhouse kitchen
or on the deck on a lovely Wairarapa morning. Walk in the country, visit a vineyard. We warmly
welcome you!

Martinborough *Homestay Separate/Suite 1km Martinborough*

The Old Manse
Sandra & John Hargrave
Cnr Grey & Roberts Streets, Martinborough,
Tel (06) 306 8599   0800 399 229   Fax (06) 306 8540
Mob 025 399 229   info@oldmanse.co.nz
www.bnb.co.nz/theoldmanse.html

Double $150-$170 (Full Breakfast)
Credit cards accepted
5 Queen 1 Twin (6 bdrm)   6 Ensuite

In the heart of the wine district, a beautifully restored
Presbyterian Manse, built in 1876, has been transformed
into a boutique homestay. Spacious, relaxed accommodation in a quiet and peaceful setting. One twin,
plus five queen size bedrooms all with their own ensuites. All day sun. Off-street parking and open
fireplace. Amenities include spa pool, petanque and billiards. Enjoy breakfast or wine overlooking
vineyard. Walking distance to Martinborough Square with a selection of excellent restaurants. Close to
vineyards, antique and craft shops, adventure quad bikes and golf courses. Qualmark 4+

Palliser Bay *Homestay Rural 35km S of Martinborough*

Tarawai
Maria Wallace & Ron Allan
Pounui Ridge, 2110 Western Lake Road, Palliser Bay
Tel (06) 307 7660   Fax (06) 307 7661
Mob 025 218 5889   tarawai@xtra.co.nz
www.bnb.co.nz/tarawai.html

Double $209 Single $165 (Full Breakfast)
Child Under 14 $66 Dinner $70 per person
Credit cards accepted Children welcome
2 King/Twin 1 Queen (3 bdrm)
3 Ensuite

The tranquil atmosphere at Tarawai is enhanced by the panoramic views of Palliser Bay and South
Wairarapa's farmlands, ranges, river and lakes. The two level contemporary home is designed for guest
comfort, with a sunny tiled atrium and quality fittings. Accommodation in this award winning home
comprises one queen and two king/twin bedrooms, all with ensuite bedrooms. There is a guest sitting
room between the two downstairs bedrooms, and another lounge with open fire upstairs. Dinner by
arrangement. Our varied menus feature fresh produce and home baking.

Wellington

Otaki

Te Horo

Waikanae

1

Paraparaumu

Raumati South

Paekakariki

Pukerua Bay

Wellington City

Wellington City
enlargement next page

Pimmerton

Mana

Paremata   Whitby   Pauatahanui

2

Upper Hutt

Heretaunga

Tawa

Korokoro   Lower Hutt

Johnsonville   Petone

Oharu Valley

Khandallah

Ngaio   Matiu/Somes Island

Wadestown

Thorndon   Wainuiomata

Karori   Wellington Central
Kelburn   Roseneath
Aro Valley   Mt Victoria   Eastbourne
Hataitai

Vogeltown   Karaka Bay

Melrose   Seatoun

Island Bay   Breaker Bay

Palmer Head

Wellington
International
Airport

Kilometres
0   10
Miles
0   6

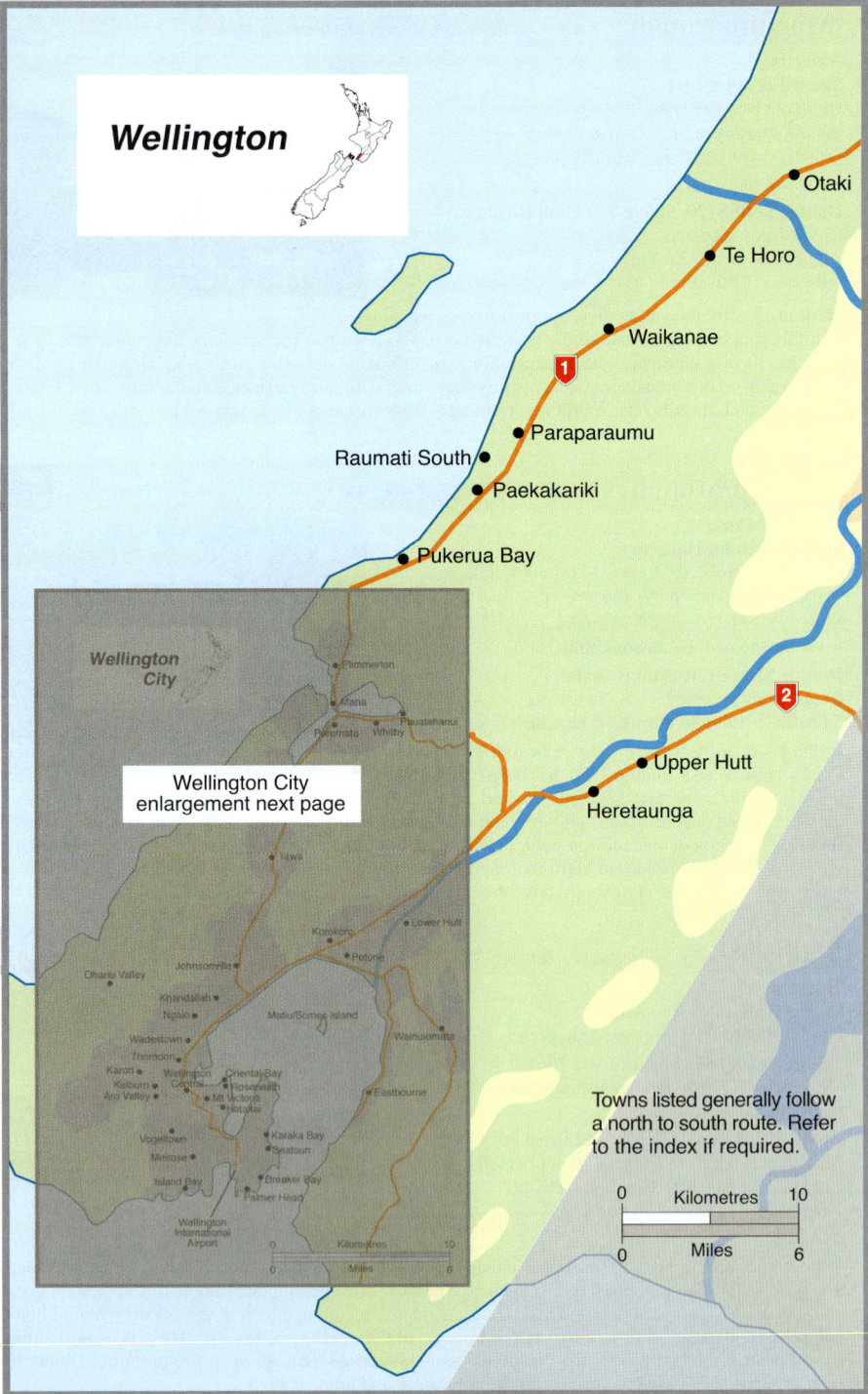

Towns listed generally follow
a north to south route. Refer
to the index if required.

0   Kilometres   10

0   Miles   6

Wellington City

Towns listed generally follow
a north to south route. Refer
to the index if required.

Plimmerton

Mana

Pauatahanui

Paremata   Whitby

Tawa

Korokoro

Lower Hutt

Petone

Johnsonville

Ohariu Valley

Khandallah

Matiu/Somes Island

Ngaio

Wadestown

Wainuiomata

Karori

Wellington
Central

Oriental Bay

Kelburn

Roseneath

Aro Valley

Mt Victoria

Eastbourne

Brooklyn

Hataitai

Mt. Cook

Vogeltown

Mornington

Karaka Bay

Melrose

Seatoun

Island Bay

Breaker Bay

Palmer Head

Wellington
International
Airport

| 0 | Kilometres | 5 |
| 0 | Miles | 3 |

Otaki *B&B & Art Studio 72km N of Wellington City*

Waitohu Lodge
Mary & Keith Oldham
294 Main Highway, Otaki, Wellington
Tel (06) 364 5389 0800 364 239
Fax (06) 364 5350 waitohulodge@xtra.co.nz
www.waitohulodge.homestead.com

Double $85-$95 Single $65 (Full Breakfast)
Child $30 Dinner $30 by arrangement
Credit cards accepted
1 Queen 4 Single (3 bdrm) 1 Private 1 Guests share

Waitohu Lodge, your "QUALITY AWARD" winning homestay is easy to find and only 50 mins drive to Wellington City and the Picton ferry. Set back from the highway in trees and gardens we offer you quality, spacious, quiet, smokefree accommodation and friendly country hospitality. Enjoy comfortable beds, garden views, spabath and showers, guest lounge with television, books and complimentary tea/coffee, delicious breakfasts. Keith taught Geography, Mary paints and sells her art.We enjoy people, travel, wines, our homegrown produce and Burmese cat Raj. WELCOME.

Te Horo *Homestay Separate/Suite Country 65km N of Wellington*

Te Horo Lodge
Craig Garner
109 Arcus Road, Te Horo, Kapiti Coast
Tel (06) 364 3393 0800 483 467
Fax (06) 364 3323 Mob 027 430 6009
reservations@tehorolodge.co.nz
www.tehorolodge.co.nz

Double $185-$265 Single $135-$185 (Full Breakfast)
Child n/a Dinner $50 b/a Credit cards accepted
4 King/Twin 1 Single (4 bdrm) 4 Ensuite

Our purpose-built lodge offers a relaxing tranquil environment set next to five acres of gardens and orchards and surrounded by another five acres of native bush. The downstairs guest rooms open on to a verandah and expansive lawns. The upstairs master suite features a large cathedral window looking into the tree tops and the serenity of the bush. A feature stone fireplace anchors the lounge. The grounds include a swimming pool, spa, gazebo and petanque court. Home cooked evening meals are available by prior arrangement. The Lodge is not suitable for children.

Te Horo *B&B Homestay 3km S of Otaki*

Cottle Bush
Roz White & Jon Allan
990a State Highway 1, Te Horo 5560,
Tel (06) 364 3566 Mob 021 254 3501
jonandroz@msn.com
www.bnb.co.nz/cottlebush.html

Double $90-$120 Single $65-$80 Dinner $30
2 Queen 1 Twin (3 bdrm)
1 Ensuite 1 Guests share

Roz and Jon invite you to share their spacious two storey, smoke free home, nestled among the mature native totara, matai and titoki trees of Cottle Bush. Join us and our friendly dogs for a relaxing stay in a secluded rural atmosphere, not far from local attractions and amenities and only an hour from Wellington. When you wake, enjoy your choice of cooked or continental breakfast. In the evening dine at a local restaurant or join us for dinner. Please make contact prior to arrival by letter, phone or e-mail

Te Horo *B&B Farmstay Homestay 7 km N of Waikanae*

Pateke Lagoons Wetlands
Peter & Adrienne Dale
152 Te Hapua Rd, Te Horo Otaki,
Tel 06 364 2222   Fax 06 364 2214
Mob 021 439661   peter@pateke-lagoons.co.nz
www.pateke-lagoons.co.nz
Double $195 Single $175 (Special Breakfast)
Dinner by arrangement
2 Queen 1 Single (2 bdrm)   2 Ensuite 1 Private

Pateke Lagoons is a purpose built lodge overlooking a
private 50 acre wetland and wildfowl refuge. It offers
peace and quiet in tranquil rural surroundings. Two guest
rooms,each with private courtyard. Large lounge with wildfowl and wetland ecology library. Beautiful
views of farmland, sea, and wetland. Easy 30 minute walking tracks through native bush and wetland,
with golf cart available. Fresh seafood is our specialty with garden fresh vegetables. Full breakfast
using local products. Feed the horses and pet the cat. Open wetlands are unsuitable for children.

Waikanae *B&B Homestay 5km w of Waikanae*

Shepreth Homestay
Lorraine & Warren Birch
12 Major Durie Place, Waikanae Beach 6010,
Tel 04 905 2130   Fax 04 905 2139   Mob 0274 441 088
shepreth@paradise.net.nz
www.bnb.co.nz/shepreth.html
Double $100-$120 Single $70-$80 (Full Breakfast)
Dinner $ Credit cards accepted
1 Queen 2 Twin (2 bdrm)
1 Private

You will find it easy to relax and enjoy your surroundings
in our comfortable modern home overlooking Kapiti Island and the beach. The spacious guest rooms
have their own sitting area and kitchenette. Breakfasts are delicious! We only take one party of guests at
a time,and enjoy spending time with both New Zealand and overseas guests. We're 50 minutes from
Wellington, easy to find with several cafes and restaurants close by. Our cat lives here too. You are
assured of a warm welcome.

Waikanae *Homestay 58km N of Wellington*

Millrest
Colleen & Gordon Butchers
57 Park Avenue, Waikanae, Kapiti Coast
Tel (04) 904 2424   Fax (04) 904 2424
topdog@paradise.net.nz
www.bnb.co.nz/millrest.html
Double $90 Single $65 (Full Breakfast)
Less 10% if prebooked by night before
Dinner by arrangement
1 Queen 1 Twin (2 bdrm)
1 Private

We invite you to share the informal lifestyle in our warm spacious home set in park like surroundings on
your next holiday. We are an active retired couple who enjoy welcoming new friends and helping them
to take advantage of the attractions of the Kapiti Coast and New Zealand. Alternatively if you feel like
peace and tranquillity this will suit you too as we host only one party at a time. Buffy, our beagle cross
dog shares our smoke free home. Not suitable for children under 10 years. Directions: Please phone,
write or fax.

Waikanae Beach *Self-contained 5km W of Waikanae*

Konini Cottage
Maggie & Bob Smith
26 Konini Crescent, Waikanae Beach
Tel (04) 904 6610   Fax (04) 904 6610
konini@paradise.net.nz
www.bnb.co.nz/koninicottage.html
Double $120 Single $100 (Full Breakfast) Child $25
Credit cards accepted Children welcome
1 Queen 2 Single (2 bdrm)
1 Private

Our tastefully furnished Lockwood cottage set in an acre of tranquil grounds, bordering the golf links and only 300 metres to the beach, offers peace and privacy. The fully equipped kitchen enables self-catering. Deduct $15 per person if you supply your own breakfast. Breakfast supplied by us may either be in our home or served in the cottage. Laundry facilities in cottage. Directions: turn off SH1 at traffic lights to beach, 4km to old service station, take right fork, then first right, 1km to Konini Crescent.

Waikanae *B&B Homestay 1km S of Post Office*

Karu Crescent Homestay
Pauline & Allan Jones
27b Karu Crescent, Waikanae,
Tel (04) 293 6532   Fax (04) 293 6532
Mob 025 300 785   albeach@paradise.net.nz
www.bnb.co.nz/karucrescent.html
Double $90-$110 Single $60 (Full Breakfast)
Credit cards accepted
1 Queen (1 bdrm)
1 Ensuite

Pauline and Allan invite you to our warm, relaxing new home which is ideally placed as a break in your journey to or from Wellington and the ferry. We are just two minutes drive off State Highway One. Our home is within easy walking distance of good restaurants and river walks. Guest tea and coffee making facilities and laundry are always available. We enjoy meeting visitors from home and overseas. Our interests include music, crafts, and overseas travel. Directions: please phone.

Waikanae *Self-contained 1km E of Waikanae*

Country Patch
Sue & Brian Wilson
18 Kea Street, Waikanae
Tel (04) 293 5165   Fax (04) 293 5164
Mob 027 457 8421   booking@countrypatch.co.nz
www.countrypatch.co.nz
Double $110-$185 Single $85-$130
(Continental Breakfast) Child $25
Dinner By arrangement Credit cards accepted
2 King/Twin 1 Queen 2 Single (3 bdrm)
3 Ensuite

Two delightful self contained accommodation sites. Country patch studio with its own entrance and deck has a queen bed with ensuite and twin beds on the mezzanine floor of the kitchen lounge. Country patch villa has an open fire and a large verandah with magic views. It is wheelchair accessible and the two bedrooms (each with ensuite) have king beds that unzip to twin. We warmly invite you to share our patch of the country with Kate (16), Simon (14) and Holly our labrador.

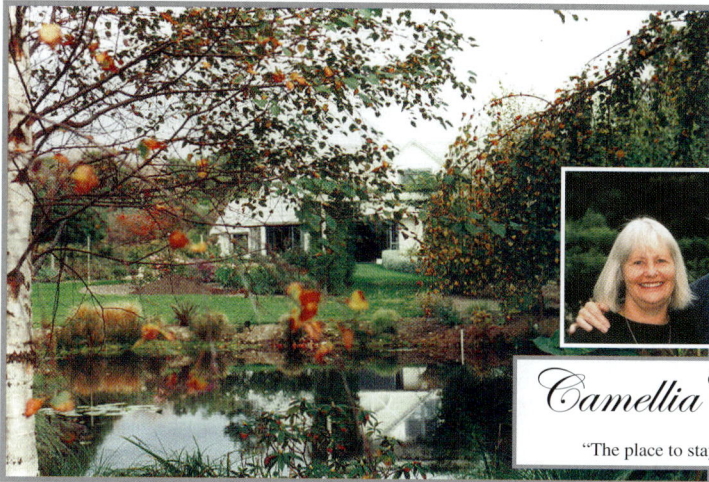

Camellia Cottage
@ Sudbury
"The place to stay in Kapiti"

Waikanae *Boutique Cottage & Homestay, 50 minutes from ferry*

Sudbury Homestay and Garden
Glenys and Brian Daw
39 Manu Grove, Waikanae 6010

Tel (04) 902 8530 Fax (04) 902 8531 Mob 021 129 6970
stay@sudbury.co.nz www.sudbury.co.nz

Double $120-$150 Single $100-$150
Special Continental Breakfast
Dinner by arrangement   Credit cards accepted
2 Queen (2 bdrm)
1 Private 1 Guests share

Camellia Cottage

If you are looking for genuine and sincere Kiwi hospitality then look no further. **Camellia Cottage** is nestled in a beautiful 2^1/2 acre garden with natural bush and native birds, rhododendrons, camellias, roses and a large lily pond. A romantic hideaway Camellia Cottage offers a quality queen-size bedroom, is charmingly furnished complete with a fully equipped kitchenette, TV, Hi-fi and many little luxuries for your comfort.

Alternatively, join us in our lovely home where Sudbury's **Frangipani** guest-room opens directly to the garden and pond.

Your comfort is always our priority

Awake to birdsong and enjoy a leisurely breakfast which includes fresh fruit platter, delicious freshly baked pastries, home-made jams/preserves, a choice of teas and freshly brewed coffee.
Waikanae is centrally located on the Kapiti Coast (State Highway 1) only 50 minutes from Wellington. Superb village restaurants are only 5 minutes away or by prior arrangement, dinner with wine from the cellar is available.
Guest email, fax, and telephone · ample off-street parking · laundry facilities · complimentary bicycles · directions provided when booking.

Kapiti Island · 4 golf courses · safe beaches · bush walks · horse riding · wildlife sanctuary · car and motorcycle museum · art galleries · antiques.

We can advise you on things to do while you are here, and also assist
with onward travel and accommodation requirements.

There are no pets at Sudbury.   We regret that Sudbury is unsuitable for children.

Arrive as strangers but leave as friends

Waikanae *B&B Self-contained Rural Cottage 6km E of Waikanae*

RiverStone
Paul & Eppie Murton
111 Ngatiawa Road, Waikanae
Tel (04) 293 1936 Fax (04) 293 1936
riverstone@paradise.net.nz
www.bnb.co.nz/riverstone.html
Double $100 Single $70 (Full Breakfast) Child $45
Credit cards accepted
1 Queen 1 Twin (2 bdrm)
1 Private

Birdsong, the sound of the river and complete privacy. Peace and quiet with a scrumptious breakfast and comfortable accommodation. Riverstone has five hectares of paddocks and garden with river walks and local pottery and cafe. Waikanae, Raumati and Paraparaumu have a variety of cafes, shops, boutiques, Lindale farm park, the Southward Car museum, Nga Manu bird sanctuary, golf courses and beautiful beaches. Pick up from train or bus. Laundry facilities. Smoke free. No pets.

Paraparaumu *Homestay   60km   N of Wellington*

Jude & Vic Young
72 Bluegum Road, Paraparaumu
Tel (04) 902 0199 Fax (04) 902 0199
www.bnb.co.nz/youngparaparaumu.html
Double $75 Single $45 (Full Breakfast)
Child 1/2 price   Dinner $20
1 Queen 1 Twin (2 bdrm)
1 Private 1 Host share

Our 1950's beach house has hill and island views and is situated two blocks back from Marine Parade. Shops, golf course, airport, cafes and excellent restaurants are 1-2km walk away. Off-street parking is provided and we will meet bus or train. Jude is, with prior notice, pleased to provide meals for those on special diets. We love walking, food, music, and Citroens. Non smokers preferred. We have a cat. Directions: watch for yellow letterbox on seaward corner of Bluegum and Rua Roads.

Paraparaumu *Self-contained 55km N of Wellington*

M & S Homestay
Sytske & Marius Kruiniger
60A Ratanui Road, Paraparaumu
Tel (04) 299 8098 Fax (04) 297 3447
Mob (04) 297 3447 mskapiti@xtra.co.nz
www.bnb.co.nz/mshomestay.html
Double $70 Single $60 (Continental Breakfast)
Child $5 under 5yrs extra persons $10
Credit cards accepted Children welcome
1 Queen 2 Single (2 bdrm)
1 Private

Our self-contained accommodation is peaceful and sunny. A view across small lake, full with wildlife. Beach, shopping centre and excellent restaurants close by. Sunny lounge with t.v., books and games; well equipped kitchen, bathroom and laundry facilities. Information about indoor and outdoor attractions available. No dogs please and guests are asked not to smoke indoors. Please phone or fax for bookings and directions. We look forward meeting you. Breakfast is optional and is $5.00 per person.

Paraparaumu Beach   *Homestay 5.5km NW of Paraparaumu*

Beachstay
Ernie & Rhoda Stevenson
17 Takahe Drive, Kotuku Park, Paraparaumu Beach
Tel (04) 902 6466   Fax (04) 902 6466
Mob 025 232 5106
www.bnb.co.nz/beachstayparaparaumu.html

Double $75 Single $50 (Continental Breakfast)
Child $20 Dinner $25 by arrangement
Credit cards accepted
1 Double 2 Single (2 bdrm)   1 Private

Enjoy warm friendly hospitality in the relaxing atmosphere of our modern new home. Peaceful surroundings next to river estuary and beach. Wonderful views of sea, lake and hills. Lovely coastal and river walks. Tourist attractions include trips to Kapiti Island Bird Sanctuary. Paraparaumu Beach world ranking Golf Course six minutes drive. South Island Ferry Terminal 45 minutes away. We are newly retired non smokers who enjoy meeting people. We love our NZ scenery and bush walking. Ernie paints landscapes. Enquiries welcome. NZAFFH members.

Raumati South - Kapiti Coast   *B&B Homestay 2km S of Paraparaumu*

Te Whare Rakau Lodge
Robert Gooch and Clive Rivers
246 State Highway, Raumati South, Kapiti Coast
Tel 04-9040064   Fax 04-9040064   Mob 021-1597690
tewharerakau@paradise.net.nz
www.bnb.co.nz/tewharerakau.html

Double $100-$135 Single $80-$95 (Special Breakfast)
Dinner By Request $30 +
1 Queen 2 Single (2 bdrm)
1 Ensuite

Te Whare Rakau Lodge. Hosts Clive & Rob Welcome You to enjoy Subtropical Gardens, set amongst Mature trees on a 3 acre established Lifestyle Block. A Spacious Comfortable Double Bedroom with Ensuite, Own Entrance opening to Extensive Decking. Private Lounge available. Cable Television, Fax and Internet facilities.   We enjoy People, Fine Wine, Tasty Food and Music. A Beautiful place to Sunbathe, Relax & Unwind. Non Smoking indoors. 2km from Shopping Centre & Beaches. 50km from Wellington City. Trains every Half hour. Not suitable children/pets.

Paekakariki   *Homestay Separate/Suite 10km S of Paraparaumu*

Killara Homestay
Carole & Don Boddie
70 Ames Street, Paekakariki
Tel (04) 905 5544   Fax (04) 905 5533
Mob 025 944 551   killara@paradise.net.nz
www.killarahomestay.co.nz

Double $110-$130 Single $100-$110
(Continental Breakfast) Credit cards accepted
1 Queen 1 Twin (2 bdrm)
1 Private

Relax, enjoy the sound of the sea, fabulous views and direct beach access from our absolute beachfront home. Spacious accommodation upstairs includes a guest lounge,with outstanding views from Kapiti Island to the South Island. Internet and laundry facilities available. We host one party at a time. Have a relaxing spa bath; enjoy beach activities (surf-casting gear available); walk to local cafes/restaurants; or explore the Kapiti Coast. 15 minutes to 5 golf courses, 30 minutes to Wellington. Close to shops/transport.

Pukerua Bay *Homestay Separate/Suite 32km N of Wellington*

Sheena's Homestay
Sheena Taylor
2 Gray Street, Pukerua Bay 6010, Kapiti Coast
Tel (04) 239 9947 Fax (04) 239 9942
Mob 025 602 1503 homestay@sheenas.co.nz
www.bnb.co.nz/sheenashomestay.html

Double $70 Single $45 (Full Breakfast) Child $20
Dinner by arrangement Credit cards accepted
1 Double 1 Twin 1 Single (2 bdrm)
1 Host share

Come share our warm, sunny refurbished smokefree home. Relax in the conservatory - enjoy the views. We have two friendly cats -Tabitha & Sienna. Pukerua Bay, home of creative people, has an interesting beach about 15 mins walk. Railway station closeby. Sheena is a keen spinner - spinning wheel/fibre available to use. Restaurants & cafes 5-15 mins drive. Most special diets catered for, lunches arranged. Smokers seating undercover; off-street parking; laundry facilities; garaging for bikes; powerpoint small campervans; cot & highchair. Personal care for people with disabilities.

Plimmerton *B&B Self-contained 6km N of Porirua*

Aquavilla
Graham & Carolyn Wallace
16 Steyne Ave, Plimmerton
Tel (04) 233 1146 Mob 027 231 0141
aquavilla@paradise.net.nz
www.bnb.co.nz/aquavilla.html

Double $140 Single $120 (Special Breakfast)
Child neg Dinner $40 Extra adults $50 neg
Credit cards accepted Children welcome
1 Queen 1 Single (1 bdrm) 1 Private

"An absolute gem. We'll never forget your hospitality and the fun we had". This is what others think of us, so come and unwind in our colourful self-contained cottage in a garden setting, crisp white cotton sheets, gourmet breakfasts, fresh flowers, homemade biscuits and Supreme coffee. Sip wine on the deck or down at the beach as the sun sets. Attached to our 1920's home, your accommodation has its own charming courtyards, lounge, bedroom, kitchenette, bathroom and parking at the door. In the centre of Plimmerton Village, with 6 cafes, beach only a few metres away.

Plimmerton *Farmstay Self-contained 20min N of Wellington*

Southridge Farm
Katrina and Andrew Smith
Southridge, 96 The Track, Plimmerton, Wellington
Tel (04) 233 1104 . Fax (04) 233 1112
aksmith@paradise.net.nz
www.bnb.co.nz/southrigefarm.html

Double $95 Single $75 (Continental Breakfast)
Child negotiable Children welcome Pets welcome
1 Queen 1 Single (1 bdrm)
1 Ensuite

We have it all at 'Southridge Farm'. Rural but residential. State Highway 1, beach, trains and restaurants all only 1km away. Major shopping centre 7km away. We have a lovely modern self-contained cottage with kitchen including washing machine if self-catering is preferred. Couch has a sofabed. Cot and foldaway bed also available. All outside animals including horses can be accommodated with notice. Andrew & Katrina, child Lachlan and farm dog Penny warmly invite you to share in our relaxing rural experience.

Mana   *B&B 13km N of WELLINGTON*

Le Solaire
Irene Denford
16A Mana View Road, Mana, Wellington
Tel (04) 233 8407   Fax (04) 233 8450
Mob 025 439 822   irene.denford@xtra.co.nz
http://www.lesolaire.co.nz
Double $110-$130 Single $80 (Special Breakfast)
Child free Credit cards accepted
1 King 1 Queen 1 Double (3 bdrm)   3 Ensuite

Dream away the evenings on one of the many decks whilst
listening to good music and watching the sun set over the South Island. Modern, sunny three level
home, with off street parking. Situated just 2 minutes walk from restaurants, train station, beaches and
beautiful Pauatahanui Inlet. Wellington CBD 20 minutes by car or train, and Porirua city 4 kilometres.
Home has spectacular sea views and spacious lounges. Guest rooms have lounge chairs, television, tea/
coffee facilities and internet lines. All have ensuite bathrooms, one with spa bath. Host is well travelled
and has many interests, including art, theatre, music and trout fishing.

Whitby   *Homestay 10km NE of Porirua*

Oldfields
Elaine & John Oldfield
22 Musket Lane, Whitby, Wellington
Tel (04) 234 1002   Mob 021 254 0869
oldfields@paradise.net.nz
www.bnb.co.nz/oldfield.html
Double $105 Single $85 (Full Breakfast)
Dinner $25 By arrangement
2 Queen (2 bdrm)
1 Guests share

Would you enjoy a stay in a tranquil home with bush views and overlooking a mature and well-tended
garden? Oldfields is situated in a quiet cul-de-sac in the suburb of Whitby, 10 minutes by car from
Paremata Station and 25 minutes from central Wellington. Having travelled and lived overseas we are
always interested in meeting people, whether they are from just up the road in New Zealand or further
a field. We welcome you to stay with us and our cats Tinker & Roxy.

Pauatahanui   *B&B Self-contained 5km E of Plimmerton*

Ration Point Country Cottage
Leigh Tuohy
485 Grays Road, Pauatahanui,
Tel (04)237 8349   Fax (04) 237 4797
Mob 021 427 629   rationpointbb@xtra.co.nz
www.rationpoint.com
Double $150 Single $80-$110 (Full Breakfast)
Child $25 Children welcome
1 Queen 1 Double 2 Single (1 bdrm)
1 Private

Our rural homestead and cottage is sited on ten acres
overlooking the picturesque Pauatahanui Harbour and surrounding countryside. The cottage features
open-plan living, dining and kitchenette. Fully equipped bathroom includes hairdryer, bathrobes,
toiletries, washing machine and clothes dryer. Full breakfast provisions are included plus many extra
features to enjoy. Our friendly farm animals include ponies, cows, sheep and hens. Our house pets are
two German Shepherds and a cat. We are handy to many restaurants and cafes. Twenty five minutes to
Wellington city; twenty minutes to Kapiti Coast.

Tawa   *Homestay 15km N of Wellington*

Tawa Homestay
Jeannette & Alf Levick
17 Mascot Street, Tawa, Wellington
Tel (04) 232 5989   Fax (04) 232 5987
milsom.family@xtra.co.nz
www.bnb.co.nz/tawahomestay.html
Double $90 Single $50 (Special Breakfast)
Dinner $20pp 3 course candlelit dinner
Credit cards accepted
1 Queen 1 Single (2 bdrm)
1 Host share

Our comfortable family home is in a quiet street in Tawa. We have a separate toilet, shower and spa bath. Freshly ground coffee a speciality, with breakfast of your choice. Jeannette's interests are: Japanese language, porcelain painting, knitting, dressmaking, playing tennis, learning to play golf and the piano and gardening. Alf's interests are: Amateur radio, woodwork, Toastmasters International - and being allowed to help in the garden. We are both members of Lions International.

Tawa   *Homestay 15km N of Wellington*

chaplin homestay
Joy & Bill Chaplin
3 Kiwi Place, Tawa, Wellington
Tel (04) 232 5547   Fax (04) 232 5547
Mob 025 6803599   chapta@xtra.co.nz
www.bnb.co.nz/chaplin.html
Double $90 Single $45 (Full Breakfast)
Dinner by arrangement
1 Double 1 Single (2 bdrm)
1 Guests share

No. 3 is situated in a quiet street seven minutes by car and rail to Porirua City and 15 minutes from Wellington and the InterIsland Ferry Terminal. Our house is wheelchair friendly and we have an extra bedroom downstairs with single bed or cot if required at reduced rate of $25. Spa, laundry facilities also available. Safe off-street parking. Tawa is close to beaches, ten-pin bowling, swimming pool and fine walks. Our house is 'smokefree'. Dinner by arrangement. Please phone for directions.

Tawa   *B&B Homestay 15km NW of Wellington CBD*

Jocelyn & David Perry
5 Fyvie Avenue, Linden, Tawa
Tel (04) 232 7664   djperry@actrix.co.nz
www.bnb.co.nz/perry.html
Double $80 Single $50 (Continental Breakfast)
Child $20 Dinner By arrangement Children welcome
1 Double 1 Twin 1 Single (3 bdrm)
1 Guests share 1 Host share

We are a retired couple. Together we welcome you to stay with us. There is a five minute walk to the suburban railway station with a half hourly service into the city (15 minutes) and north to the Kapiti Coast. Alternatively you can drive north to the Coast, enjoying sea and rural views before sampling tourist attractions in this area. We are happy to provide transport to and from the Interisland ferry. Laundry facilities available.

Upper Hutt - Te Marua   *Homestay Separate/Suite 7.4km N of Upper Hutt*

Te Marua Homestay
Sheryl & Lloyd Homer
108A Plateau Road, Te Marua, Upper Hutt
Tel (04) 526 7851   0800 110 851   Fax (04) 526 7866
Mob 025 501 679   sheryl.lloyd@clear.net.nz
www.bnb.co.nz/homer.html

Double $90 Single $50 (Continental Breakfast)
Dinner $25pp b/a Credit cards accepted
1 Queen 1 Double (2 bdrm)
1 Private

Our home is situated in a secluded bush setting. Guests
may relax on one of our private decks or read books from
our extensive library. For the more energetic there are bush walks, bike trails, trout fishing, swimming
and a golf course within walking distance. The guest wing has a kitchenette and television. Lloyd is a
landscape photographer with over 30 years experience photographing New Zealand. Sheryl is a teacher.
Travel, tramping, skiing, photography, music and meeting people are interests we enjoy.

Upper Hutt   *B&B Homestay 30mins Wellington*

Tranquility Homestay
Elaine & Alan
136 Akatarawa Road, Birchville, Upper Hutt
Tel (04) 526 6948   0800 270 787   Fax (04) 526 6968
Mob 025 405 962   tranquility@xtra.co.nz
www.bnb.co.nz/tranquility1.html

Double $98 Single $50-$98 (Continental Breakfast)
Child neg. Dinner $20 by prior arrangement
Children welcome Pets welcome
1 Queen 2 Single (3 bdrm)   1 Ensuite 2 Host share

Executive Timeout/Homestay. Escape from the stress of City Life just approx 30 minutes from Wellington
off SH2. Close to Upper Hutt - Restaurants, Cinema, Golf, Racecourse, leisure Centre (swimming),
Bush Walks etc. We are near the confluence of the Hutt and Akatarawa Rivers which is noted for its
fishing. 13km to Staglands. Country setting, relax and listen to the New Zealand Tuis and watch the
fantails or Wood Pigeons, or just simply relax and read. Comfortable and warm and friendly hospitality,
Good New Zealand style food.

Lower Hutt - Korokoro   *Homestay 12km N of Wellington*

Western Rise
Virginia & Maurice Gibbens
10 Stanhope Grove, Korokoro, Lower Hutt
Tel (04) 589 1872   Fax (04) 589 1873
Mob 0274 438 316   westernrise@paradise.net.nz
www.bnb.co.nz/westernrise.html

Double $85-$100 Single $55-$85 (Special Breakfast)
Dinner $15 Credit cards accepted
1 Queen 2 Single (2 bdrm)
1 Guests share

Just off State Highway 2, very quiet area, a warm, welcome awaits. Our Terrier/Cross dog Ben loves
guests. View Wellington's magnificent harbour relaxing over a meal in or out doors. Maurice is a
fingerprint expert with the New Zealand Police and Virginia enjoys the time spent with guests. Laundry
free if staying 2 consecutive nights. 10-13 minutes to Picton Ferry, handy to many restaurants. Of
street parking. Telephone for directions.

Lower Hutt *Homestay Separate/Suite*

Judy & Bob's Place
Judy & Bob Vine
11 Ngaio Crescent, Lower Hutt
Tel (04) 971 1192   Fax (04) 971 6192
Mob 021 510 682   bob.vine@paradise.net.nz
www.bnb.co.nz/judybobsplace.html
Single $50 (Full Breakfast) Dinner $25
Credit cards accepted
1 Queen 2 Single (2 bdrm)   1 Private 1 Guests share

Our home is situated plumb in the centre of Woburn, a picturesque and quiet central city suburb of Lower Hutt, known for its generous sized houses and beautiful gardens. Within walking distance of the Lower Hutt downtown, 15 minutes drive from central Wellington and its Railway Station and Ferry terminals; Airport 25 minutes; 3 minutes walk to Woburn Rail Station. Separate lounge and TV. Love to entertain and share hearty Kiwi style cooking with good New Zealand wine. Laundry facilities. Directions: Please phone, fax, email or write. Transfer transport available. High speed and dial up Internet connections available.

Lower Hutt *B&B Homestay 0.5km SE of Lower Hutt Central*

Rose Cottage
Maureen & Gordon Gellen
70A Hautana Street, Lower Hutt, Wellington
Tel (04) 566 7755   Fax (04) 566 0777
Mob 021 481 732   gellen@xtra.co.nz
www.bnb.co.nz/rosecottagelowerhutt.html
Double $105-$115 Single $75-$85 (Full Breakfast)
Dinner $30 by arrangement Credit cards accepted
1 Queen 1 Single (2 bdrm)
1 Ensuite 1 Host share

Relax in the comfort of our cosy home which is just a five minute walk to the Hutt City Centre. Originally built in 1910 the house has been fully renovated. We have travelled extensively Overseas and in NZ. Interests include Travel, Gardening, Sports and live Theatre. As well as TV in Guest room there's Coffee and Tea-making facilities. Breakfast will be served in our Dining room at your convenience. Unsuitable for children. We look forward to welcoming you into our smoke-free home which we share with Scuffin our cat.

Lower Hutt *Homestay 2km E of Lower Hutt*

Tyndall House
Paulene & Nigel Lyne
6/2 Tyndall Street, Lower Hutt, Wellington 6009
Tel (04) 569 1958   Fax (04) 569 1952
Mob 025 851 901   tyndallhouse@xtra.co.nz
www.bnb.co.nz/tyndallhouse.html
Double $110-$115 Single $80-$95 (Full Breakfast)
Dinner $30 Credit cards accepted
2 Queen (2 bdrm)
2 Private

Our home is situated beneath a bush reserve in a tranquil haven. Paulene and Nigel enjoy having people to stay. We offer secure parking, sunny elegant bedrooms with garden views, Sky TV and tea/coffee making facilities. We are 15 minutes from the ferry terminal and 20 minutes from Te Papa - the museum of New Zealand. Come and relax in our peaceful surroundings. We look forward to welcoming you into our home.

Lower Hutt - Korokoro   *B&B   12km N of Wellington*

Devenport Estate - *Vineyard Accommodation*
Alasdair, Christopher, Marlene
1 Korokoro Road, Korokoro, Petone, Lower Hutt

Tel (04) 586 6868   Fax (04) 586 6869
Mob 025 274 0394
devenport_estate@hotmail.com
homepages.paradise.net.nz/devenpor

Double **$120**   Single $80   (Continental Breakfast)
Credit cards accepted Children welcome
2 Queen 1 Single (2 bdrm)
1 Ensuite 1 Private

Stay at the closest vineyard to the capital. Only 15 minutes to Ferry/City & Stadium yet with the privacy and quietness of a country retreat. Devenport Estate is an Edwardian-styled homestead overlooking Wellington Harbour, built at the turn of the century (2000!) based upon the MacDonald family home in Scotland. Nestled amongst native bush we have carved out a colourful garden around the homestead and planted over 400 Pinot Gris grapevines in our hobby vineyard. Devenport was built for views comfort and peacefulness.

Guests enjoy stunning sea, bush and garden views from their bedrooms. Bedrooms contain queen-sized bed (1 also with single bed), writing desk, chairs, TV, tea-making services, hair dryer, electric blanket with either an en suite or private bathroom.   Relax in the guest living room or outside in the sun on the titanic deck chairs. Play petanque or deck quoits, admire the vines and water features or watch the yachts sail past on the harbour.

Avoid city stress and leave your car here, we are only a 15 minute train ride to central Wellington. We offer free arrival/departure transfers from Petone Station. Devenport provides free internet access, a free laundry service for guests stays over two or more nights and plenty of off street parking.

Breakfast in the formal Dining Room or alfresco, overlooking Somes Island. At night, enjoy the vast variety of restaurants of Petone's Jackson Street - only a 5 minute drive from Devenport. Alasdair, Christopher, Marlene and two cocker spaniels, welcome you to a comfortable stay in Wellington on our vineyard estate.

Devenport was built for views comfort and peacefulness.

Lower Hutt

Park Avenue B&B
Pam & Ray Ward
788 High Street, Lower Hutt

Tel (04) 567 4788 Mob 025 285 8709
pam.ray.ward@xtra.co.nz
Double $90-$130 Single $60-$90 Dinner B/A
1 Queen 1 Double 1 Twin (3 bdrm)
1 Ensuite 1 Private

A warm and friendly welcome awaits guests in this gracious home, recently refurbished. Conveniently situated - only 1500 metres off SH2 (Avalon exit), one kilometre to Hutt or Boulcott Hospitals, 20 minutes to the Ferry Terminal. All essential services and facilities available at nearby Park Avenue shops. Relax by the indoor heated plunge/spa pool or in the secluded gardens. Take a stroll to Avalon Park. Off-street parking. Full English breakfast available at small extra cost. Evening meals served by prior arrangement.

Petone - Korokoro   *2km W of Petone*

Matairangi
Kate & Barry Malcolm
29 Singers Road, Korokoro, Petone

Tel (04) 566 6010 barrym@actrix.co.nz
www.bnb.co.nz/malcolm.html

Double $80 Single $55 Child $30
Credit cards accepted
1 Twin (1 bdrm)
1 Private

Welcome to our hectare of peaceful natural bush and native birds, a hilltop perch with amazing views over Wellington Harbour and surrounding hills. Here you can enjoy your own private ground floor space including sitting room with tea/coffee facilities. Upstairs, Kate and Barry look forward to your company. Our interests are forest restoration, beekeeping, gardening and local history. New laid eggs and freshly baked bread are on the breakfast menu. The ferry terminal is a 15 minute drive away. Also email, laundry, parking.

Lower Hutt - Stokes Valley   *B&B Homestay 8km NE of Lower Hutt*

Kowhai B&B
Glenys & Peter Lockett
88a Manuka Street, Stokes Valley, Lower Hutt

Tel (04) 563 6671 Mob 0274 433341
p_g.lockett@xtra.co.nz
www.bnb.co.nz/kowhaibb.html

Double $85-$95 Single $70 (Full Breakfast)
1 Queen 1 Double (2 bdrm)
1 Private

We are surrounded by bush and gardens in a quiet street. Your rooms and large guest lounge are upstairs with private deck, Sky TV, stereo, tea/coffee facilities. We want you to feel relaxed, so take only one booking at a time. Lucy the cat shares our home. Nearby: golf, boutique cinema, racecourse, swimming pool, bush walks. Wellington CBD/Picton ferry 25 minutes. Lower/Upper Hutt, 15 minutes. We have travelled extensively and enjoy meeting people.

Petone   *Homestay 3km S of Lower Hutt*

Anne & Reg Cotter
1 Bolton Street, Petone, Wellington
Tel (04) 568 6960   Fax (04) 568 6956
www.bnb.co.nz/cotter.html
Double $80 Single $40 (Full Breakfast)
Child 1/2 price over 10yrs Dinner $15
Credit cards accepted Children welcome
1 Double 2 Single (2 bdrm)
1 Host share

We have a 100 year old home by the beach. We are two minutes from a Museum on beach, shop and bus route to the city. A restaurant is nearby. We are ten minutes from Picton Ferries. Off street parking available. Children are very welcome. Reg is a keen amateur ornithologist and goes to the Chatham Islands with an expedition trying to find the nestling place of the Taiko - a rare sea bird, on endangered list. Other interests are genealogy and conservation. Laundry facilities are available.

Petone - Korokoro   *Homestay 2km W of Petone*

Korokoro Homestay
Bridget & Jim Austin
100 Korokoro Road, Korokoro, Petone
Tel (04) 589 1678   0800 116 575   Fax (04) 589 2678
Mob 025 260 4948   jaustin@clear.net.nz
www.bnb.co.nz/korokorohomestay.html
Double $90-$150 Single $55 (Continental Breakfast)
Child by arrangement Dinner by arrangement
Credit cards accepted
1 Queen 1 Twin (2 bdrm)
1 Guests share

We have a large garden and Bush reserve, in a very quiet locality yet only 12 minutes to Wellington and Ferries. Easy to find. We came from England to New Zealand in 1957 and enjoy travel. Jim is a desultory woodworker with a background in machinery. Bridget teaches and is a weaver/feltmaker, working and selling from home. We enjoy visual arts, theatre, cinema, music, books and the outdoors. Your food will be home-cooked and mainly organic as we prefer an environmentally friendly lifestyle.

Wainuiomata   *B&B Homestay Self-contained 6km E of Lower Hutt*

Kaponga House
Hilary and Neville
22 Kaponga Street, Wainuiomata,
Tel (04) 564 3495 After 5pm   Fax (04) 564 3495
hilwha@xtra.co.nz
www.bnb.co.nz/kaponga.html
Double $80 Single $50
1 Queen (1 bdrm)
1 Private

Hilary and Neville offer you top quality accommodation in a quiet bush setting just 20 minutes drive from Wellington City. Our ground floor apartment includes one double bedroom, private bathroom with heated towel rail, laundry, spacious lounge/living room with gas heating, TV, tea/coffee making facilities and fridge. Nearby attractions include the Rimutaka Forest Park, seal colony, and 18 hole golf course. We enjoy gardening, golf, tennis and travel, and meeting new people. We look forward to welcoming you to our home. Genuine 'kiwi' hospitality guaranteed.

Eastbourne   *Homestay 3km N of Eastbourne*

Bush House
Belinda Cattermole
12 Waitohu Rd, York Bay, Eastbourne, Wellington
Tel (04) 568 5250   Fax (04) 568 5250
Mob 025 654 5433
www.bnb.co.nz/bushhouse.html
Double $100 Single $70 (Full Breakfast)
Dinner by arrangement
1 Double 1 Single (2 bdrm)
1 Private 1 Host share

Come and enjoy the peace and tranquility of the Eastern
Bays. You will be hosted in a beautifully restored 1920's settler cottage nestled amongst native bush
and looking towards the Kaikoura mountains of the South Island. My love of cordon-bleu cooking and
the pleasure of the table are satisfied through the use of my country kitchen and dining room. Other
attractions: A Devon Rex cat. Eastbourne is a small seaside village across the harbour from Wellington
city with a range of attractions.

Eastbourne   *B&B Self-contained 12km E of Wellington*

Treetops Romantic Hideaway
Robyn & Roger Cooper
7 Huia Road, Days Bay, Eastbourne
Tel (04) 562 7692   Fax (04) 562 7690
Mob 025 616 9826   bnb@treetops.net.nz
www.treetops.net.nz
Double $110-$130 Single $95-$105
(Continental Breakfast) Child $25
Sofabeds in lounge $30pp Credit cards accepted
1 Queen (1bdrm) 2 single divans in lounge   1 Private

Secluded retreat in stunning location above Wellington harbour. Ride our private cable car through
native bush to the front door, or walk up through ferns and beeches. Sparkling sea views from bedroom
and lounge; fully-equipped kitchenette, bath/shower/toilet. Wake to songs of the bellbird; breakfast on
your private garden patio; relax indoors with books, games, TV, radio. Phone, computer port. Portacot,
highchair, laundry available. 250 metres to picturesque beach, cafes, harbour ferry. Central Wellington
20 minutes by ferry or car. Ideal honeymoon location.

Eastbourne   *B&B Homestay 17km E of Wellington*

Lowry Bay Homestay
Pam & Forde Clarke
35 Cheviot Road, Lowry Bay, Eastbourne, Wellington
Tel (04) 568 4407   0508 266 546   Fax (04) 568 4408
homestay@lowrybay.co.nz
www.lowrybay.co.nz
Double $100-$130 Single $80-$110 (Full Breakfast)
Child Negotiable Credit cards accepted
1 King 1 Queen 1 Single (2 bdrm)
1 Private

Enjoy our hospitality. Welcome to our special home. Warm, restful, peaceful, yet close to Wellington
and Hutt Cities, transport, local restaurants and art galleries. Play tennis on our court, stroll to the
beach, walk in the bush, sail on our 28 foot yacht, or relax under a sun umbrella on the deck. Native
birds abound. Our sunny, elegant bedrooms have garden views, TV, tea/coffee and central heating. We
have two daughters, Isabella 20 and Kirsty 14, a cat and many interests. Laundry. Non-smoking
indoors. From SH2 follow Petone signs then Eastbourne.

Eastbourne   *B&B Homestay 17km NE of Wellington*

At The Bay
Jennifer & Ken
Marine Drive, Sorrento Bay, Eastbourne
Postal address - P.O.Box 3717 Wellington

Tel (04) 568 4817   0800 390 385   Fax (04) 568 4817
Mob +64 25 500 670   at.the.bay@ihug.co.nz
www.bnb.co.nz/jenniferkenshomestay.html

Double $90-$115 Single $70-$90 (Full Breakfast)
Child by arrangement Dinner by arrangement
Credit cards accepted
1 Double 1 Single (2 bdrm)   1 Private

Jennifer, Ken and our friendly cat Tuppence look forward to giving you a warm welcome to our home. It is nestled amongst native bush by the beach. Share with us the magical views of Wellington harbour and the city. You may wish to join us on a deck in summer, or in front of a cosy fire in winter. Please phone, fax or email us for directions. At any time we would be pleased to assist you with your stay. We hope to make your stay a memorable one.

Eastbourne - Wellington   *B&B Homestay 17km E of Wellington*

Frinton by the Sea
Wendy & Doug Stephenson
55 Rona Street, Eastbourne, Wellington

Tel (04) 562 7540   Fax (04) 562 7860
Mob 0274 417 365   frinton@xtra.co.nz
www.frintonbythesea.co.nz

Double $115-$130 Single $100-$115
(Special Breakfast) Child Not suitable
Dinner On request Credit cards accepted
2 Queen (2 bdrm)   1 Ensuite 1 Private

You are invited to share in the peace and tranquillity of our bush clad home overlooking Wellington Harbour. We offer cosy well appointed bedrooms with doors opening out onto a balcony. Enjoy the unique village atmosphere of Eastbourne with its restaurants, galleries, gift shops and beach, or take the harbour ferry to Wellington. Our interests are the arts, theatre and music. Wendy, Doug, our golden lab Max, JR Missy and two cuddly cats look forward to greeting you. Be assured of a warm welcome and an enjoyable stay.

Ohariu Valley - Wellington   *B&B Rural B&B 20km N of Wellington*

Tikara Cottage
Mary McCallum
995 Ohariu Valley Rd, R D Johnsonville, Wellington

Tel office: (04) 473 4086 lodge: (04) 477 4646
Fax (04) 473 4084   Mob 021 223 6405
tikaralodge@xtra.co.nz
www.tikaralodge.co.nz

Double $90-$120 Single $70 (Continental Breakfast)
Child neg Dinner B/A Luxury Lodge POA
3 Queen 1 Twin (4 bdrm)
1 Ensuite

Enjoy the comfort and tranquility of our 1900's cottage, nestled on a private section neighbouring our 370 acre property 'Tikara'. Stroll, pinic or barbeque in our beautiful six acre gardens. Communal kitchen, lounge and dining area with open fire. Ten mins from local shops/restaurants, 21 mins from CBD*. You will be welcomed by Mary and Bruce, our daughters and young grandsons. Meet Sally, Bessie and Jem our dogs. Laundry available. Dinner by arrangement. *golf and horseriding close by.

Johnsonville   *B&B Homestay 1km N of Johnsonville*

Cherswud
Marilyn and David McDonald
121 Helston Rd, Johnsonville, Wellington
Tel (04) 478 5017   Fax (04) 478 5516
Mob 025 84 12 15   marilyn@macmaz.co.nz
www.bnb.co.nz/cherswud.html
Double $95 Single $70 (Special Breakfast)
Child $40 Dinner $35
2 Queen 1 Single (3 bdrm)

We are delighted to welcome you to join us at Cherswud, our fully restored 1919 home with two cats, two lounges, conservatory, sunny deck, spacious bedrooms and luxurious guest-share bathroom with spa bath and massage shower. Bedrooms with comfortable beds, electric blankets, feather duvets, well-stocked bookcases, tea and coffee. We offer smokefree accommodation and warm hospitality with delicious meals. Dinner, with wine, by prior arrangement, although eight restaurants are within 12 minutes' walk. Two minutes off SH1 and 10 minutes from the ferry.

Khandallah - Wellington   *Homestay Separate/Suite 7km N of Wellington*

Sue & Ted Clothier
22 Lohia Street, Khandallah, Wellington
Tel (04) 479 1180   Fax (04) 479 2717
www.bnb.co.nz/clothier.html
Double $100 Single $70 (Full Breakfast)
Credit cards accepted
1 Twin (1 bdrm)
1 Ensuite

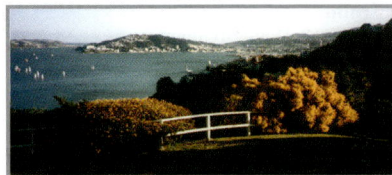

This is a lovely, sunny and warm open plan home with glorious harbour and city views. A quiet easily accessible street just ten minutes from the city and five minutes from the ferry. Close to Khandallah village where you can make use of the excellent local restaurant, cafe or English country pub. We are a non-smoking household. Another family member is an aristocratic white cat called Dali. We enjoy sharing our home with our guests.

Khandallah - Wellington   *B&B 7km N of Wellington Central*

Khandallah Bed & Breakfast
Margaret & Tim Fairhall
50 Clark Street, Khandallah, Wellington
Tel (04) 479 5578   fairhall@paradise.net.nz
www.bnb.co.nz/fairhall.html
Double $150 - $180 Single $150 (Full Breakfast)
Child Neg. Credit cards accepted
1 Queen 1 Twin (2 bdrm)
1 Ensuite 1 Private

A large home filled with antiques and New Zealand art. Large garden with heated pool and tennis court, guests welcome to use. We enjoy golf and can arrange a game. Lovely bush walks nearby. Walk to local pub or restaurant for dinner. Bedrooms includes TV, tea/coffee, home baking, electric blankets, heating. Laundry facilities available. Breakfasts continental or full, with homemade jams, muffins and preserved fruit. We love sports, Wellington and meeting people. Samantha, a tubby black cat in residence. Phone or e-mail for directions.

Ngaio - Wellington   *Homestay & Self-contained 7km NW of Wellington*

Ngaio Homestay
Jennifer & Christopher Timmings
56 Fox St, Ngaio, Wellington

Tel (04) 479 5325 Fax (04) 479 4325
jennifer.timmings@clear.net.nz
www.bnb.co.nz/ngaiohomestay.html

Double $110-$130 Single $80-$100
(Continental Breakfast) Child neg Dinner $25pp B/A
S/C $130 per dble, extra person $45 C/C accepted
1 Queen 2 Double 2 Twin 2 Single (5 bdrm)
3 Ensuite 1 Private 1 Host share

Our multi-level family home is in Ngaio, 5 mins to ferry terminal, 10 mins to CBD. We offer: views, sun, off street parking, quiet surroundings, 2 mins bush walk to local train station, homely atmosphere. Jennifer is a pianist and plays harp. Dinner with live music $40pp. Our 2 self contained units are adjacent to our property, 1 double, 1 twin, each unit can sleep up to 4 persons. Equipped kitchen, laundry facilities, phone, Cable TV, perfect for relocating or immigrating. Weekly rates offered. Internet facilities available.

Karori - Wellington   *Homestay 5km W of Wellington*

Campbell Homestay
Murray & Elaine Campbell
83 Campbell Street, Karori, Wellington

Tel (04) 476 6110 Fax (04) 476 6593
Mob 025 535 080 ctool@ihug.co.nz
www.bnb.co.nz/campbellhomestay.html

Double $95 Single $60 (Continental Breakfast)
Child 1/2 price Dinner $30 Credit cards accepted
Children welcome Pets welcome
1 Queen 1 Twin 3 Single (3 bdrm)
1 Guests share

Welcome to our home in the suburbs, easy to find from motorway or ferry terminal. Telephone and we will meet you at ferry, train, bus or air terminals. Join us for pre-dinner drinks, dine with us, or eat out at the local pub/cafe or licenced restaurant. We are close to the city on three bus routes. Make use of our laundry, large garden, spacious home, email/internet facilities. Meet Charlie our border collie dog and Honey the cat.

Karori - Wellington   *B&B 4 km W of Wellington CBD*

Bristow Place
Helen & Tony Thomson
8 Bristow Place, Karori, Wellington

Tel +64 4 476 6291 Fax +64 4 476 6293
Mob +64 21 656 825 h.t.thomson@xtra.co.nz
www.bnb.co.nz/bristowplace.html

Double $150 Single $110 (Full Breakfast)
Dinner by arrangement
1 Queen (1 bdrm)
1 Private

Quiet, sunny location 5 minutes drive from city centre.
Easy to find with parking available. We are happy to meet you at ferry, airport, etc. Close to transport or walk to local shops, restaurants. Guest bedroom provides Sky TV, tea / coffee facilities, electric blankets. Private bathroom with full bath, separate shower. Enjoy sole use of a lounge or join us for coffee and conversation. Our interests include sport, music, bridge, travel. German spoken. Gourmet dinner by arrangement. Internet, fax, laundry service at small charges.

Karori - Wellington   *Self-contained 5km W of Wellington*

Karori Cottage
Kaye & Peter Eady
11 Shirley Street, Karori, Wellington
Tel (04) 977 5104   Mob 025 609 9003
eady1@paradise.net.nz
www.bnb.co.nz/karoricottage.html
Double $100-$120 (Continental Breakfast) Child $10
1 Queen 1 Twin (2 bdrm)
1 Private

A cosy self-contained cottage at the rear of our section with drive on access. Queen and twin bedrooms and bathroom upstairs, lounge/dining area with open fire and kitchen downstairs opening onto a sunny courtyard. Children can play on the large front lawn, climb trees and share the trampoline with our three children (six, nine and 12 years). Laundry facilities. Close to bus route and great local deli/cafe.

Wadestown - Wellington   *Homestay 5km W of Wellingtom*

Ti Whanake
Julie Foley
72 Wilton Road, Wadestown, Wellington
Tel (04) 499 6602   Fax (04) 473 7332
Mob 025 203 2228 www.bnb.co.nz/foley.html
Single $60 (Continental Breakfast) Dinner By neg.
Credit cards accepted
1 Twin 1 Single (2 bdrm)
1 Private 1 Guests share

A short walk to Otari Native Botanic Gardens and bus from door to central city 10 minutes. Own bathroom, separate lounge if preferred, electric blankets and heaters. Share the fireside in the evening with the host and Persian cat or attend some of the varied activities in the 'Cultural Capital'. Gardening, embroidery, playing the cello and mahjong are some of the interests the host enjoys. Visitors can be collected from the ferry etc. Parking on the street. Phone for directions.

Wadestown - Wellington   *B&B 2.5km NW of Wellington*

The Nikau Palms Bed & Breakfast
Diane Boyd
95 Sar Street, Wadestown, Wellington
Tel 04 499 4513   Mob 025 674 0644
thenikaupalms@xtra.co.nz
www.thenikaupalms.co.nz
Double $150 Single $110 (Full Breakfast)
1 Queen (1 bdrm)
1 Ensuite

You are invited to share the spectacular views of Wellington Harbour overlooking the City, Ferry and Westpac Trust Stadium, all within walking distance. Our home is only a few minutes drive from Wellington's attractions and historic Thorndon with its restaurants, shops and heritage trails, and Katherine Mansfield's birthplace. The bedroom includes ensuite and private sitting room. Full cooked or continental breakfast provided. The guests' dining room includes tea and coffee making facilities and refrigerator. Off street parking provided. Not suitable for children.

Kelburn - Wellington   *B&B Boutique B&B 1km W of Wellington central*

'Rawhiti'
Annabel Leask
40 Rawhiti Terrace, Kelburn, Wellington
Tel (04) 934 4859 Fax (04) 972 4859
Mob 027 276 8240 rawhiti@paradise.net.nz
www.rawhiti.co.nz
Double $160-$200 Single $130-$160
(Special Breakfast) Credit cards accepted
1 King/Twin 1 King (2 bdrm)
1 Ensuite 1 Host share

ìRawhitiî is located in the prime suburb of Kelburn and within walking distance of the city centre. Magnificent views of harbour and city are seen from all rooms including the small private garden at the rear. A charming 1903 two-storeyed home furnished to create an elegant and tranquil ambience. Its historical features, wonderful outlook and quality chattels combine to offer guests a special stay in Wellington. Annabel has travelled widely with interests in the Arts and golf. A two minute walk to the Cable Car, Botanic Gardens and Victoria University.

Kelburn - Wellington   *B&B Homestay 2km W of Wellington*

Rangiora B&B
Lesley and Malcolm Shaw
177 Glenmore Street, Kelburn, Wellington 6005
Tel (04) 475 9888 rangiora.bnb@xtra.co.nz
www.bnb.co.nz/rangiora.html
Double $100 Single $90 (Continental Breakfast)
Child neg. Credit cards accepted Children welcome
1 Queen 1 Double (2 bdrm)
1 Guests share

LOCATION LOCATION LOCATION!!! We are very easy to find. Our modern hillside home is just 5 minutes drive from central Wellington, the Hawkestone Street motorway exit, the Stadium, and ferry terminals. Walking distance from several excellent restaurants. Cable Car, Botanic Gardens, Victoria University and Karori Sanctuary are also a short walk. Katherine Mansfield Birthplace and Thorndon Heritage Trail are a short drive. Tea/coffee making, TV, in rooms. Free E-mail access. Ample on-street parking. Courtesy car from/to ferry, bus, train. On city bus route. We have a small dog named Patsy.

Kelburn - Wellington   *B&B 1km W of Wellington*

Glenlodge
Brenda Leighs
5 Glen Road, Kelburn, Wellington
Tel (04) 973 7881 Fax (04) 802 5268
Mob 021 294 0747 glenlodge@paradise.net.nz
www.bnb.co.nz/glenlodge.html
Double $140-$165 (Full Breakfast)
Dinner by arrangement weekly rate available on request
1 Queen (1 bdrm)
1 Ensuite

There is no better location for your stay in Wellington than at Glenlodge. The Botanical Gardens and Cable Car, which will have you in downtown Wellington within minutes, are literally at our front door. There are excellent cafes, galleries and shops within walking distance. With your beautifully appointed bedroom, ensuite and private guest lounge a memorable visit is guaranteed. Start your day with a full breakfast before heading off for a days sightseeing. Dinner by arrangement. Meet and greet and laundry facilities available. Unsuitable for children. Smokefree. We have a miniature Schnauzer.

Aro Valley - Wellington   *B&B Self-contained 1km S of Wellington*

206 Aro Self-Contained Cottage
Russell and Shirley Martin
206 Aro St, Aro Valley,

Tel (04) 973 7008   Mob 021 177 1957
info-206aro@paradise.net.nz
www.bnb.co.nz/user184.html

Double $140 Single $140 (Continental Breakfast)
Child $10 Children welcome Pets welcome
1 Queen 1 Double (1 bdrm)
1 Private

206Aro is a self-contained cottage, with complete privacy in Aro Valley. Fully
fitted with quality accommodation touches - 100% cotton sheets, new futon sofa, etc. Native bush
behind cottage and over the road; Plus a deck for sunny weather. Wellington downtown city is a 5-10
minutes drive (Free parking), or a nice 20 minute walk. Complimentary breakfast materials, drinks and
daytime snacks, and free cable TV, range of videos, and use of stereo. Kids/pets welcome. Discounts
for stays more than 2 nights. Run by Russell and Shirley.

Mt Cook - Wellington   *B&B Homestay 1.2km from Courtenay Place*

Apartment One
Jim & Colleen Bargh
2 King Street, Mt Cook, Wellington

Tel (04) 385 1112   Mob Colleen 025 247 8145
Jim 027 275 0913   apartmentone@yahoo.co.nz
www.bnb.co.nz/apartmentone2.html

Double $150-$165 Single $130-$145 (Full Breakfast)
2 Queen (2 bdrm)
2 Ensuite

Experience apartment living in the city. We moved off
the farm into our converted warehouse to try city life.
We love its ever-changing beauty and the people are simply the best. Come try it for yourself. Buses
depart every few minutes. Two minutes walk to the Basin Reserve and 10/15 minutes walk to Courtenay
Place (Wellington's restaurant, cafe and theatre district). Less than 10 mins drive to the ferry terminal
and airport. We serve a deluxe breakfast to get you through your eventful day.

Oriental Bay - Wellington   *B&B 0.75km N of Wellington*

No 11
Virginia Barton-Chapple
11 Hay Street, Oriental Bay, Wellington

Tel (04) 801 9290   Fax (04) 801 9295
vbarton-chapple@nbpr.co.nz
www.bnb.co.nz/noorientalbay.html

Double $120 Single $95 (Special Breakfast)
Credit cards accepted
1 King/Twin (1 bdrm)
1 Guests share 1 Host share

Oriental Bay is perhaps the finest location in Wellington. No 11 has an intimate view of the city and is
an easy stroll to Te Papa: the Museum of New Zealand, the City Art Gallery, all the major theatres and
cinemas, great restaurants and cafes. Virginia has extensive knowledge of what's going on, and where
to go. The accommodation is in a comfortable room for two, with bathroom adjacent, electric blankets
and tea & coffee facilities. Breakfast will be an occasion. Cat in residence.

Mt Victoria - Wellington   *B&B Homestay 0.5km E of Central Wellington*

Villa Vittorio
Annette & Logan Russell
6 Hawker Street, Mt Victoria, Wellington

Tel (04) 801 5761 Fax (04) 801 5762 Mob 025 321 267
l&a@villavittorio.co.nz   www.villavittorio.co.nz

Double $150-$180 Single $115-$125 (Full Breakfast)
Dinner from $50 Credit cards accepted
1 Double (1 bdrm)   Separate/Suite
1 Private

WELCOME TO VILLA VITTORIO. Centrally located
close by Courtenay Place. Short walk to restaurants,
theatres, shopping, conference centres, Te Papa Museum,
Parliament and Stadium.
Guest bedroom with TV, tea and coffee facilities.
Adjoining sitting room with balcony overlooking city.
Bathroom with shower and bath.
Breakfast served in Italian styled dining room or outside
in courtyard. We enjoy having guests, having travelled
extensively ourselves. Transport and gourmet dinner by
arrangement. Garaging and laundry at small charge. No
children or pets. **Directions:** Phone, fax, email or write.

275

Mt Victoria - Wellington *B&B Homestay Wellington Central*

Dream Catcher - Arts & Accommodation
Taly & John Hoekman
56 Pirie Street, Mt Victoria, Wellington
Tel (04) 801 9363 Mob 021 210 6762
www.bnb.co.nz/dreamcatcher.html
Double $110-$130 Single $90-$110 (Special Breakfast)
Child $40 2nd child free Credit cards accepted
1 Queen 2 Double 2 Single (3 bdrm)
1 Ensuite 2 Private 1 Guests share

Dream Catcher is a renovated spacious Victorian house in central, picturesque historic Mount Victoria, only 5 minutes stroll from Wellington's day/night vibrant attractions. Quality accommodations available: 1) "VIP Suite" - private livingroom, double bedroom and ensuite. 2) "Upstairs" - a self contained 2nd storey includes two bedrooms, guests shared bathroom, deck, verandah, living/kitchen, sun, and city views. Taly, John, their teenage daughter and two cats, keen travellers themselves, welcome the city visitor to enjoy the relaxed comfort of home, and the fresh generous breakfasts in the main kitchen or the back garden.

Mt Victoria - Wellington *B&B Homestay Wellington Central*

Scarborough House
Sue Hiles & Miles Davidson
36 Scarborough Tce, Mt Victoria, Wellington
Tel + 64 4 801 8534 Fax + 64 4 801 8536
Mob 025 501 346 info@scarborough-house.co.nz
www.scarborough-house.co.nz
Double $135-$150 Single $120 (Full Breakfast)
Child $50 Credit cards accepted
1 King/Twin 1 Queen (2 bdrm)
2 Private

Welcome to Scarborough House, our modern centrally-heated home in a quiet, sunny Mt Vic street with views over the city, walk to Courtenay Place - the restaurant, cafe and theatre district, Te Papa Museum, and the waterfront. King, queen or twin accommodation. Private guest bathrooms. Breakfast of your choice. Tea/coffee facilities, hairdryer, bathrobes, Sky Digital TV, laundry and garaging available. Our interests include travel, skiing, golf and many of the activities our magnificent city offers. Children over 12 welcome; we are smokefree.

Mt Victoria - Wellington City *B&B Self-contained Wellington City*

Austinvilla
Averil & Ian
11 Austin Street, Mt Victoria, Wellington
Tel (04) 385 8334 Fax (04) 385 8336
Mob 027 273 7760 info@austinvilla.co.nz
www.austinvilla.co.nz
Double $140-$160 (Continental Breakfast)
Children welcome
2 Queen (2 bdrm)
2 Ensuite

A warm welcome to one of Mt Victoria's most elegant turn of the century villas. Set amongst beautiful gardens and only five minutes walk to theatres, restaurants, Oriental Bay and Te Papa museum. Very close to public transport and a seven minute drive to airport, ferries and Westpac Stadium. Two spacious, elegant apartments offer privacy and include kitchen, queen bed, ensuite with bath and shower, lounge, Sky TV, phone and CD player. Both apartments have French doors to private courtyard, and have their own entranceway. Laundry facilities and garaging available. Continental breakfast provided. Children over 10 years old welcome. Smokefree.

Roseneath - Wellington *B&B Homestay 3km E of Wellington*

Harbourview Homestay and B&B
Hilda & Geoff Stedman
125 Te Anau Road, Roseneath, Wellington
Tel (04) 386 1043 0800 0800 78
hildastedman@clear.net.nz
www.bnb.co.nz/harbourviewhomestayandbb.html
Double $120-$150 Single $95-$115 (Full Breakfast)
Dinner from $35 Credit cards accepted
Children welcome
1 Double 2 Single (2 bdrm) 2 Private

This boutique guesthouse is 5 minutes drive from Wellington city, 10 minutes drive from the airport and on the No. 14 bus route. The house offers comfortable hospitality and elegance. Each bedroom opens on to a wide deck, offering expansive views of Wellington harbour. Pleasantly decorated rooms feature quality beds and linen. There is a choice of a double bedroom and/or share twin room, separate guest's bathroom with shower and spa bath. Harbourview is situated in a peaceful setting close to the city, catering for Businesspeople, Tourists and Honeymooners. A surcharge will be added if paying by credit card.

Hataitai - Wellington *B&B Self-contained 3km E of Wellington CBD*

Top O' T'ill
Cathryn & Dennis Riley
2 Waitoa Rd, Hataitai, Wellington 6003
Tel (04) 976 2718 Fax (04) 976 2719
Mob 025 716 482 top.o.hill@xtra.co.nz
www.bnb.co.nz/topotill.html
Double $95-$120 Single $65-$110 (Full Breakfast)
Credit cards accepted
2 Queen 1 Twin 1 Single (4 bdrm)
2 Ensuite 1 Private 1 Guests share

Hataitai - 'breath of the ocean', is a popular suburb midway between the Airport and central Wellington. City attractions are 5-10 minutes by bus or car. Our comfortable family home of 60 years is a welcome retreat for guests. The quality studio is fully equipped, including cable television and phone. Long term rates available. We share a range of cultural interests, have travelled widely, and will be glad to help you make the most of your visit to Wellington. Not suitable for young children. Directions: www.wellingtonmap.co.nz(Accommodation/HataitaiHomestay)

Hataitai - Wellington *B&B Separate/Suite 1km E of Wellington City*

Matai House
Raema & Rex Collins
41 Matai Road, Hataitai, Wellington 6003
Tel (04) 934 6985 Fax (04) 934 6987
matai@paradise.net.nz
www.mataihouse.co.nz
Double $190-$250 Single $190-$250
(Special Breakfast)
Credit cards: Visa MasterCard Amex JCB Diners
2 King (2 bdrm)   2 Ensuite

Frommers Guide ìSpecial find- a place only insiders know aboutî. Qualmark 4 star ìExcellent. Consistently achieves high quality levels with a wide range of facilities and servicesî. Panoramic sea views, purpose-built guest floor, lounge, private entrance. Suites have cable TV, modems, bi-fold doors onto decking. Hairdryers, toiletries, robes, heated towel rails, fresh flowers, tea/coffee making, fridge, laundry, ironing. Telephone/fax/email access. Off-street parking. Flexitime breakfast, espresso coffee. City four minutes, ferry eight. Friendly, helpful hosts. Free instant confirmations on www.mataihouse.co.nz

Brooklyn (city end) - Wellington
Homestay 3km SW of City

Karepa
Ann and Tom Hodgson
56 Karepa Street, Brooklyn, Wellington
Tel (04) 384 4193   Fax (04) 384 4180
Mob 025 KAREPA (025 527 372)   golf@xtra.co.nz
www.holidayletting.co.nz/karepa

Double $130-$165 Single $95-$125 (Full Breakfast)
Child by arrangement Dinner $35 by arrangement
extra person $35 Credit cards accepted
2 King 1 Double 1 Single (3 bdrm)
1 Ensuite 1 Guests share

Stay at 'Karepa' our sunny, spacious home overlooking city, harbour and mountains. The secluded rear garden adjoins native bush. Private guest rooms have TV, and tea/coffee facilities. City 5 minutes, ferry 10 and airport 15. Residents of 21 years, ex UK, we have travelled widely, play golf and tennis, and enjoy Wellington's many attractions. Ann gardens and Tom watches from his deckchair. On-site parking. Bus at door. Laundry facilities. Sorry, no smokers or pets. Please phone/fax for directions.

Brooklyn City Side - Wellington
B&B Homestay 2km S of Wellington

Quintessential Wellington
Georgie Jones
2A Coolidge Street, Brooklyn, Wellington
Tel +64 4 380 1982   Fax +64 4 380 1985
Mob 025 243 5674   georgie.jones@xtra.co.nz
www.bnb.co.nz/quintessentialwellington.html

Double $100-$120 Single $80-$100 (Full Breakfast)
Child negotiable Credit cards accepted
1 Queen 2 Single (2 bdrm)
1 Private

Warm personal welcome to travellers and business visitors. Home features striking architecture, stunning harbour, city, sky and bush vistas. Relax or work in warm peaceful surroundings. City and bush walks, local and national transport handy. Front door parking; private luxurious guestrooms (shower and double bath); secluded deck. Guidance available on local and regional attractions and activities. Interests include travel, visual and performing arts, architecture, contemporary design, current affairs. Free laundry. email, TV, fridge, tea/coffee-making facilities.

Vogeltown - Wellington
Homestay 3km S of Wellington Central

Vogeltown Homestay
Valerie Tait
14 Krull Street, Vogeltown, Wellington
Tel (04) 934 2004   Fax (04) 934 2004
valerie.tait@paradise.net.nz
www.bnb.co.nz/vogeltownhomestay.html

Double $80 Single $50 (Continental Breakfast)
Credit cards accepted
1 Queen 2 Single (2 bdrm)
1 Guests share

Vogeltown is a quiet suburb 10-15 minutes from airport and ferry. The city's many attractions are easily reached by bus or car. Two comfortable rooms share a guest bathroom and look out onto a private, sunny deck. Originally from northern England, I've lived in Wellington for many years and enjoy sharing my home and knowledge of the city with visitors. I've travelled extensively around NZ and tramped most of the major tracks. The house is smoke-free. Well-behaved children and pets welcome. Laundry facilities.

Vogeltown - Wellington *B&B Homestay 3KM S of Wellington CBD*

Finnimore House
Willie and Kathleen Ryan
2 Dransfield St, Vogeltown, Wellington
Tel +64 4 389 9894 Fax +64 4 389 9894
w.f.ryan@xtra.co.nz
www.finnimorehouse.co.nz
Double $90-$115 Single $70-$85 (Full Breakfast)
Child $20 Children welcome
2 Queen 2 Single (2 bdrm)

Welcome to Finnimore House, a unique Victorian manor 5 minutes drive from downtown Wellington. Your hosts, Willie and Kathleen Ryan, offer a warm welcome, good conversation, large comfortable rooms and a hearty breakfast. We cater to a wide range of needs, from a traditional B&B experience, to a welcoming family homestay with a genuine Irish flavour. Finnimore House offers you a great location for your stay in Wellington, with ample, secure, off-street parking and handy public transport. We'd love to show you our magical city.

Mornington - Wellington *Homestay*

Ngahere House
Hilary & David Capper
147 The Ridgeway, Mornington, Wellington
Tel (04) 389 4501 h.capper@xtra.co.nz
www.bnb.co.nz/ngahere.html
Double $120 (Full Breakfast)
1 Queen (1 bdrm)
1 Private

Relax in our private, modern, sunny home with panoramic views of the city, harbour and mountains. We overlook a grove of native trees from our sunroom and deck. Garaging is available. Our private guestroom has tea and coffee facilities, a desk and seating. The private bathroom includes a bath and separate shower. City 10 minutes. Ferry and airport 15 minutes. On bus route. Restaurants and Art Deco cinema are nearby. We enjoy entertaining, travel, reading, films, walking and the arts.

Seatoun - Wellington *B&B Homestay 9km S of Wellington*

Francesca's
Frances Drewell
10 Monro Street, Seatoun, Wellington
Tel (04) 388 6719 Fax (04) 388 6719
francesdrewell@paradise.net.nz
www.bnb.co.nz/francescas.html
Double $90 Single $55 (Full Breakfast) Child $25
Dinner $25 by arrangement Credit cards accepted
1 Double 2 Single (2 bdrm)
1 Guests share

Although handy to Wellington Airport (3 kms away) our modern home is located in a quiet seaside village. A warm welcome awaits you in a home away from home. Choice of restaurants nearby. Flat off-street parking. Laundry facilities available. Directions: entering Wellington from the north follow the signs to the Airport then the signs to Seatoun. Monro Street is the second street on the left after the shops. From the Airport first turn right then as above. Bus stop one minute, frequent service.

Karaka Bay - Wellington   *B&B Homestay 5km S of Wellington*

Edge Water Boutique Homestay
Stella & Colin Lovering
459 Karaka Bay Road, Seatoun, Wellington
Tel (04) 388 4446   Fax (04) 388 4446
Mob (021) 613 357
edgewaterwellington@xtra.co.nz
www.edgewaterwellington.co.nz

Double $170-$270 Single $140-$240 (Full Breakfast)
Dinner $80 wines included Off Peak rates apply
Credit cards accepted Children welcome
2 SuperKing 1 King/Twin 1 Queen (4 bdrm) Separate/
Suite
4 Ensuite

Located at Karaka Bay, Edgewater is amongst the houses and homes of directors, producers, cast and crew of Peter Jackson's trilogy, Lord of the Rings.   Seatoun is a historic seaside village where waterfront houses were originally built as convalescent and holiday homes.

This award winning Mediterranean-style home features expansive ocean views of Wellington's outer harbour. Edgewater offers four airy guest suites with peaked cedar ceiling beneath separate roofs. All suites have private guest entrances, which open out to the sea or inner courtyard.

Stella serves fresh fruits, homemade breads, pancakes and egg dishes for breakfast in the dining room or alfresco in the inner courtyard or on the guest balcony in the morning

sun. Dinner is also offered, specialising in premium quality meats, seafood and game. As an ex owner/ chef of an award winning Wellington restaurant, Stella's motto is 'fresh is best'.

Edgewater has featured on CNN International 'Hot Spots' April 2000. 'Documentary NZ' August 2000. 'Gala Magazine' December 2002. We have a tabby cat and a small scruffy dog. Please phone, fax or email for directions. Only ten minutes to Wellington City Airport.

NZ Herald, 'NZ top must see B&B.'

Island Bay - Wellington

The Lighthouse and The Keep
Bruce Stokell
326 The Esplanade & 116 the Esplanade, Island Bay, Wellington

Tel (04) 472 4177   Fax (04) 472 4177   Mob 027-4425 555
bruce@sportwork.co.nz   www.bnb.co.nz/thelighthouse.html

Double $180-$200
1 Double (1 bdrm)
1 Private

Island Bay - 10 minutes city centre, 10 minutes airport, 20 minutes ferry terminal.
The Lighthouse is on the South coast and has views of the island, fishing boats in the bay, the beach and rocks, the far coastline, the open sea, the shipping and, on a clear day, the South Island. There are local shops and restaurants. The Lighthouse has a kitchen and bathroom on the first floor, the bedroom/sitting room on the middle floor and the lookout/bedroom on the top. Romantic.
The Keep is a stone tower just two minutes from the lighthouse. It has a lounge/kitchen on one level and a bed with ensuite on the next level. Also a spa bath in the bedroom. It is very cosy and has excellent views of the seas especially in a storm. Stairs from the bedroom lead to a hatch which opens on to the roof.

The Lighthouse

The Keep

Island Bay/Melrose - Wellington   *B&B Self-contained 8 km S of City*

Buckley Homestay
Mrs Willy Muller
51 Buckley Road, Melrose, Island Bay, Wellington
Tel (04) 934 7151   Mob 025 607 1853
kandwmuller@paradise.net.nz
www.bnb.co.nz/buckley.html
Double $95-$130 (Full Breakfast)
Dinner by arrangement Credit cards accepted
Children welcome Pets welcome Smoking area inside
1 King/Twin 1 Double 2 Single (3 bdrm)
1 Private 1 Host share

Large sunny home with spectacular scenery and beautiful views over Wellington, Cook Strait and Mountains. New tastefully decorated, private entrance, 1 Bedroom, self contained, double flat with private balcony, T.V, tiled Conservatory, fridge and microwave. Surf or swim at our safe local beach. Close to hospitals. We are interested in food, wine, travel, relaxing and meeting people. Willy is a nurse, enjoys cooking, gardening and speaks Dutch. No pets or children at home. Off street parking is provided.

Island Bay - Wellington   *B&B Homestay 3km S of Wellington*

Ma Maison
Margo Frost
9 Tamar Street, Island Bay, Wellington
Tel (04) 383 4018   Fax (04) 383 4018
Mob 025 242 9827   bedandbreakfast@paradise.net.nz
www.nzwellingtonhomestay.co.nz
Double $110 Single $90 (Full Breakfast)
2 Queen (2 bdrm)
1 Ensuite 1 Private

Comfort and quality, our 1920's boutique homestay is decorated with a French flavour. Set in a peaceful, picturesque garden, up a lavendar lined drive. Romantic rooms, both have posturepaedic Queen beds, equipped to ensure total comfort. One bedroom has an ensuite, the other a private bathroom with shower and claw-foot bath. Easy walking to local restaurants, eight minutes drive to city, very close to excellent bus service that will take you to Te Papa, theatres, shopping, stadium, ferries, airport, public and private hospitals. A sweet timid cat called Chloe.

Island Bay - Wellington   *B&B*

Maurice Burnett
392 The Esplande, Island Bay, Wellington
Tel (04) 383 6128   Fax (04) 383 6128
www.bnb.co.nz/islandbaybb.html
Double $120 Single $65 (Continental Breakfast)
1 Double 1 Twin (2 bdrm)
2 Ensuite

Comfortable home on the south coast offering extensive views of Cook Strait and the South Island, from Red Rocks to the harbour entrance. Sit back and relax, enjoy the magnificent sunsets and watch the Interislander ferries go past the front door. Both rooms are ensuite, have Sky TV, fridge, tea and coffee making facilities. Excellent restaurants and takeaway meals are available nearby. We are situation 10 minutes from the central city and 10 minutes from the airport. We will meet public transport by arrangement.

Chatham Islands *Farmstay*

Te Matarae
Wendy & Pat Smith
PO Box 63, Te Matarae, Chatham Islands
Tel (03) 305 0144   Fax (03) 305 0144
www.bnb.co.nz/smithchathamislands.html
Double $100 Single $85 (Special Breakfast)
Dinner $30 Children welcome
2 Queen 2 Single (3 bdrm)
2 Ensuite 1 Host share

Relax in our natural wood home which is situated in eighty acres of bush on lagoon edge with mown walkways throughout. The lagoon is ideal for swimming and fishing and has nice sandy beaches. Farm activities and kayaks available. Farm is eleven hundred acres and includes four other bush reserves. Guests may meal with family or in separate dining room. Bedrooms are separated from main house by covered swimming pool. We are a non smoking household; so request guests to refrain from doing so in our home. Most meal ingredients are home produced. We have two cats and a host of domestic farm animals. Air travel exit points are Christchurch and Wellington. Rental car with guide available. Pick up and deliver to airport. The Chatham Islands situated 800km east of Mainland New Zealand, are Islands of Mystery. A place where volcanic cones rise from the mist and sea. Due to isolation and recent history of colonisation, many plants and animals are unique.

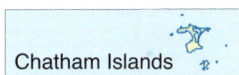

Chatham Islands

Ensuite or private bathroom is yours exclusively.
Guest share bathroom is shared with other guests.
Hosts share bathroom is shared with the family.

Marlborough

French Pass

Pelorus Sound

6

Rai Valley

Mahau Sound Anakiwa
Canvastown
Havelock Queen Charlotte Sound
Pelorus Bridge Linkwater Picton
Koromiko Port Underwood

Able Bay

Tuamarina

Rapaura

63 Renwick Blenheim
Wairau Valley

1

Towns listed generally follow
a north to south route. Refer
to the index if required.

0   Kilometres   20

0   Miles   12

Awatere Valley

French Pass   *B&B Homestay 110km NE of Nelson*

Ngaio Bay Homestay, B&B, and Retreat
Jude and Roger Sonneland
Ngaio Bay, French Pass, RD3 Rai Valley

Tel (03) 576 5287   homestay@ngaiobay.co.nz
www.ngaiobay.co.nz

Double $200   Single $125   (Full Breakfast)   Child $70
Dinner included in rate children under two $30
Children welcome
2 Queen 3 Single (2 bdrm)
1 Ensuite 1 Private

Ngaio Bay, 2 hours scenic drive from Nelson or Blenheim, is our own wilderness beach paradise, close to the awesome waters of French Pass. The Garden Cottage and Rose and Dolphin offer comfortable private accommodation overlooking beach, garden and bush. A honeymoon favourite.Guests linger at our table enjoying scrumptious food and good conversation, open fire for cool evenings. Organic vegetable garden and orchard, colourful flower garden. Swimming, walking, boating. Private fireheated bath on beach a speciality. Children welcome. 3 loveable labradors.Dinner in tariff.

Picton - Anakiwa   *Homestay Separate/Suite Self-contained 22km W of Picton*

Crafters Homestay & Gallery
Leslie & Ross Close
Anakiwa Road, RD 1, Picton

Tel (03) 574 2547   Fax (03) 574 2947
Mob 025 231 2245
crafters@actrix.gen.nz
www.bnb.co.nz/craftershomestaygallery.html

Double $95 Single $60 (Continental Breakfast)
Dinner $30 by arrangement Credit cards accepted
1 Twin (1 bdrm)
1 Private

Our home at the head of Queen Charlotte Sound has a magnificent view, this tranquil and peaceful area is noted for bush walks, bird life, boating and kayaking. Our warm and comfortable self-contained guest area has twin bedroom, sunny lounge, private bathroom and fully equipped kitchen. Ross is a wood turner and Leslie a potter, both are happy to demonstrate their skills and their Gallery is open every day. Perfect for a longer stay. Not suitable for children.

Picton - Waikawa Bay   *B&B 4km NE of Picton*

Bayside
Pam & John
33 Beach Road, Waikawa Bay, Picton

Tel (03) 573 7783   Fax (03) 573 7783
Mob 021 104 4011
pamjohn@xtra.co.nz
www.bnb.co.nz/seaviewpicton.html

Double $90 Single $50 (Full Breakfast)
1 Queen 2 Single (2 bdrm)
1 Ensuite 1 Private

We offer you warm hospitality in our new home only 4 kms from the Ferry Terminal, minutes from the South Island's largest marina where there is a cafe/restaurant for an evening meal and 20 minutes from the wine country. With Picton being the gateway to the South Island, we are able to advise on all activities in the area. We enjoy meeting people and our interests include sailing, walking, gardening and travel. We look forward to meeting you Laundry available.

Picton   *B&B Homestay 1km E of Picton Central*

Retreat Inn
Alison & Geoff
20 Lincoln Street, Picton

Tel (03) 573 8160   Fax (03) 573 7799
elliott.orchard@xtra.co.nz
www.retreat-inn.co.nz

Double $100 Single $70 (Special Breakfast)
Enquire re. private facilities $115 Credit cards accepted
1 Queen 2 Single (2 bdrm)
2 Guests share

'Retreat Inn' is an ideal spot to relax and ponder! Nestled on a hillside, surrounded by natural vegetation (& native birds), it is quiet and restful ... and only 1km from the quaint waterside village of Picton. Cosy guest bedrooms are upstairs, facing the sun ... very comfortable beds all have electric blankets. Breakfast at 'Retreat Inn' is special. Transport provided locally. Laundry facilities. Flat off-street parking. Sorry, no smoking indoors. We are a 2 person/2 cat household!

Port Underwood Sound   *B&B Self-contained 35km SE of Picton*

Ocean Ridge
Sara & Ken Roush
Ocean Bay, Private Bag, Blenheim

Tel (03) 579 9474   Fax (03) 579 9474
roush@nmb.quik.co.nz
www.nmb.quik.co.nz/roush

Double $150 (Continental Breakfast)
Credit cards accepted
2 Queen 1 Double 1 Single (3 bdrm)
3 Ensuite

Majestic views of Port Underwood Sound's rocky shoreline and sandy beaches, the open Pacific Ocean and distant snowcapped mountains. Magnificent sunrises and sunsets. All this from our self-catered apartment containing kitchen, lounge, dining area, gamesroom and 3 bedrooms (each with seaviews and ensuite bathroom). Experience nature on our walking tracks or just relax on the decks and in the hot spa pool. Purchase food provisions in Picton or Blenheim before taking the scenic and historic Port Underwood Road (part gravel) to a secluded coastal paradise.

Picton   *B&B Homestay 200mtr S of Picton*

Rivenhall
Nan & Malcolm Laurenson
118 Wellington Street, Picton,

Tel (03) 573 7692   Fax (03) 573 7692
rivenhall.picton@xtra.co.nz
www.bnb.co.nz/rivenhall.html

Double $110 Single $70 (Full Breakfast)
}Dinner $30pp B/A Credit cards accepted
Children welcome
1 Queen 1 Double (2 bdrm)
2 Private

Up the rise, on the left, at the top of Wellington Street, is Rivenhall. A gracious home with all the warmth, comfort and charm of days gone by, overlooking the town of Picton with its background of surrounding hills. Yet it is an easy walk to the centre of town or the ferry's beyond. Evening meal on request, courtesy car pick up from the ferry, bus or train. Laundry facilities. The Marlborough Sounds start at the bottom of our street.

Picton *B&B Self-contained Picton Central*

Grandvue
Rosalie & Russell Mathews
19 Otago Street, Picton

Tel (03) 573 8553   Fax (03) 573 8556
grandvue-mathews@clear.net.nz
www.nzhomestay.co.nz/mathews.htm
Double $90 Single $60 (Full Breakfast) Child $25
Credit cards accepted
1 Queen (1 bdrm)
1 Ensuite

Situated on the hills overlooking Picton, Grandvue offers panoramic views of Queen Charlotte Sound. At the end of a cul-de-sac Grandvue is a quiet haven in a secluded garden, five minutes walk to town and its assortment of restaurants. Accommodation is a comfortable, warm self-contained apartment with TV, video, and access to a barbecue. Feast on scenic views from our upstairs conservatory, while enjoying a delicious and satisfying breakfast. A portable cot and highchair are available. Courtesy transport & laundry facilities available.

Picton *B&B Homestay 800m N of Picton*

Echo Lodge
Lyn & Eddie Thoroughgood
5 Rutland Street, Picton

Tel (03) 573 6367   Fax (03) 573 6387
www.bnb.co.nz/echolodge.html
Double $70-$80 Single $55
(Full Breakfast) (Special Breakfast)
1 Double 1 Twin 1 Single (3 bdrm)
2 Ensuite 1 Private

Lyn and Eddie and our little dog Osca welcome you to a relaxed atmosphere at Echo Lodge. Breakfast is our speciality. Come and experience our home-made bread, jams, omelettes and treats. Comfortable bedrooms with ensuites. Also tea and coffee-making facilitie ensure a good nights sleep. We are five minutes walk to shops, restaurants, ferries, busses and bush walks. Make yourself comfortable in our large lounge with a cosy wood fire for those chilly nights. A courtesy car is available, as is off-street parking.

Picton - Kenepuru Sounds *B&B Farmstay 80km NE of Havelock*

The Nikaus
Alison & Robin Bowron
Waitaria Bay, RD 2, Picton

Tel (03) 573 4432   Fax (03) 573 4432
Mob 025 544 712   www.bnb.co.nz/thenikaus.html
Double $100 Single $50 (Full Breakfast) Dinner $30
Credit cards accepted
1 Double 2 Single (2 bdrm)   1 Guests share

The Nikaus is a Sounds sheep & cattle farm situated in Waitaria Bay, Kenepuru Sound, 2 hours drive from Blenheim or Picton. We offer friendly personal service in our comfortable spacious home. The large gardens (in AA Garden Book) contain many rhododendrons, roses, Camellia, lilies and perennials with big sloping lawns and views out to sea. We have three adult children. A non-smoking household with interests in farming, boating, fishing and gardening. We have a dog, Minny (Jack Russel x). Other animals include the farm dogs, donkeys, pet wild pigs, turkeys, hens and peacocks.   Good hearty country meals, home grown produce, home made ice-cream a speciality thanks to 'Muggies' our friendly hose cow. There are local operators available for fishing trips, launch charters and water and land taxis.

Picton *Homestay Picton Central*

The White House
Gwen Stevenson
114 High Street, Picton
Tel **(03) 573 6767** Fax (03) 573 8871
thewhitehousepicton@xtra.co.nz
www.bnb.co.nz/thewhitehousepicton.html
Double $60 Single $40
(Continental Breakfast)
Twin $60
2 Double 3 Single (4 bdrm)
2 Guests share

The White House in Picton's main street offers affordable luxury 'just ask any previous guest' a minute's walk to Picton's fabulous cafes and restaurants for your evening meal. Bedrooms and lounge are upstairs and guests are welcome to make tea/coffee in the kitchen. Laundry available at small charge. Non smoking. Not suitable for children.

Picton *B&B Homestay Picton central*

Palm Haven
Dae & Peter Robertson
15A Otago Street, Picton
Tel **(03) 573 5644** Fax (03) 573 5645
palmhaven@xtra.co.nz
www.bnb.co.nz/palmhaven.html
Double $70-$85 Single $50-$65 (Continental Breakfast)
Child $25 Dinner B/A Children welcome Pets welcome
2 Queen 2 Twin 2 Single (4 bdrm)
2 Ensuite 1 Guests share

Couples, families and singles are welcome in our modern, spacious home, designed for your comfort and convenience. It's just a few minutes walk from the centre of town and all leisure activities. Our guest rooms - two with full ensuite facilities and two with ensuite vanities and guest-only shared shower and separate toilet - can be easily adapted to your needs. We provide cot, highchair, offer a laundry service and courtesy pick-up. We're keen lawn bowlers, and we share our home with Toby the red tabby cat.

Picton - Queen Charlotte Sounds *Homestay Self-contained 11km Picton*

Ngakuta Bay Homestay
Eve & Scott Dawson
Manuka Drive, RD 1, Ngakuta Bay
Tel **(03) 573 8853** Fax (03) 573 8353
Mob 025 237 3300 ngakutabayhouse@xtra.co.nz
www.picton.co.nz/ngakuta
Double $100-$120 Single $80 (Continental Breakfast)
Self-contained unit $100 - $150 weekly rates from $500
1 King 1 Double 2 Twin (4 bdrm)
2 Ensuite 2 Private

Ngakuta Bay Homestay is on the scenic Queen Charlotte Drive set in an acre of bush, the Homestay is built of NZ beach with large verandahs giving magnificent views over Ngakuta Bay. Each room has French doors onto the verandah with fridge, complimentary tea & coffee. Large lounge area with Sky TV. Also available from the Homestay are sailing dinghys, windsurfers and kayaks. The Bay has landscaped recreational area with safe swimming and barbecue facilities making it an ideal holiday resort for water sports, walking and fishing.

Picton - Ngakuta Bay *B&B Homestay Self-contained 11km W of Picton*

Bayswater
Paul & Judy Mann
25 Manuka Drive, Ngakuta Bay, Queen Charlotte Drive,
RD 1, Picton

Tel (03) 573 5966   Fax (03) 573 5966
www.bnb.co.nz/bayswater.html

Double $90 Single $50 (Continental Breakfast)
1 Queen 1 Twin (2 bdrm)
1 Ensuite 1 Private

Welcome to Bayswater B&B in Ngakuta Bay, situated
11km from Picton and 24km from Havelock on Queen Charlotte Drive in the beautiful Marlborough
Sounds. Your accommodation consists of a self-contained apartment with two double bedrooms, two
bathrooms, kitchen, dining and lounge. Spectacular views over Ngakuta Bay and surrounding bush.
The Bay has a picnic area and safe swimming; the Queen Charlotte Track is close by. Remember to
bring food if self-catering. Suitable for longer stays. Come relax in paradise. Complimentary transport
available.

Picton - Queen Charlotte Sounds *B&B 16km W of Picton*

Tanglewood
Linda & Stephen Hearn
Queen Charlotte Drive, The Grove, RD 1, Picton

Tel (03) 574 2080   Fax (03) 574 2044
Mob 027 481 4388 tanglewood.hearn@xtra.co.nz
www.bnb.co.nz/tanglewoodpicton.html

Double $95-$105 Single $80 (Full Breakfast)
Dinner $35 S/C Unit $150 Credit cards accepted
2 King/Twin (2 bdrm)
2 Ensuite

Nestled amongst the native ferns overlooking Queen Charlotte Sounds. Our private guest wing includes
spacious rooms with ensuites, lounge, kitchenette and barbeque area.   Guests may choose to self-cater
or home cooked meal available by arrangement. Relax in our new spa surrounded by our beautiful
native garden, listen to the birds or take a walk with us to view the glow-worms. For privacy, swimming,
fishing, kayaking or walking the Queen Charlotte Track. We look forward to making you welcome.

Picton - Anakiwa *Homestay Self-contained 22km W of Picton*

Tirimoana House
Stephanie & Peter Bonser
257 Anakiwa Road, RD 1, Picton

Tel 0064-3-574 2627   Fax 0064-3-574 2627
Mob 0064-27-2247260 enquiries@tirimoanahouse.com
www.tirimoanahouse.com

Double $95-$140 Single $70-$90 (Continental Full
Breakfast) Dinner $35 S/C Flat $85 - 95, $15 each extra
1 King/Twin 2 Queen 2 Double 2 Single (4 bdrm)
3 Ensuite 1 Private

Every room in our long-established waterfront homestay
commands spectacular views of Queen Charlotte Sound. Our great reputation has been built on creating
a warm and friendly environment for our guests. Dinners are available with local cuisine a speciality.
All bedrooms and our stunning 'Sunrise Suite' have own bathrooms and s/c flat has own private deck.
After kayaking, walking, boating, mountain biking or visiting local wineries, relax in our swimming
and hot spa pools. 'Arrive as guests and leave as friends' is our maxim. Stephanie. Peter and Digby the
Pointer would love to meet you.

Port Underwood Sound   *B&B Homestay 20km E of Picton*

Oyster Bay Lodge
Jim & Lynnette Mark
Oyster Bay, PO Box 146, Picton

Tel (03) 579 9644   Fax (03) 579 9645
Mob 025 316 630   jimlynnemark@xtra.co.nz
www.bnb.co.nz/oysterbaylodge.html

Double $85 Single $55 (Full Breakfast) Dinner $30
2 Double 1 Single (2 bdrm)
1 Guests share

Our home/lodge is set in beautiful Oyster Bay where the
first white man born in the South Island lived for many years. Oyster Bay Lodge has an uninterrupted
view over the Bay in a charming historical part of Marlbourgh Sounds. We share this delightful spot
with our lovely Bichon Frise Tammy. Lynnette is an avid patchwork and quilter, while Jim is a semi-
retired bulider. We both enjoy music and look foward to your company. Directions - follow Port
Underwood Drive east from Picton, through Waikawa Bay, Whatamonga Bay, over the hill, don't turn
off, the next Bay on your right is Oyster Bay and we're on the far side of the Bay.

Picton   *B&B Self-contained Picton Central*

Lincoln Cottage
Laurel & Bruce Sisson
19 Lincoln Street, Picton

Tel (03) 573 5285   Fax (03) 573 5286
Mob 021 658 140   lincolncottage@xtra.co.nz
pictonstay.com

Double $90-$100 Single $75 (Continental Breakfast)
Child $15 Credit cards accepted Children welcome
Smoking area inside
1 King/Twin 2 Queen 1 Twin 1 Single (4 bdrm)
2 Ensuite 1 Guests share

A warm welcome awaits you at our completely refurbished self contained cottage, set in a peaceful
location within walking distance of town. We are surrounded by beautiful bush and delightful walkways.
Enjoy a delicious breakfast - panoramic views from the dining room, the ambience (including a cosy
fire in the winter), or just relax on the sundeck. A fully equipped kitchen, off-street parking, laundry
facilities and courtesy transport are available for your convenience. We look forward to meeting you.

Picton - Karaka Point   *B&B Homestay 8km E of Picton*

Karaka Point Lodge
Juliet & Brian Kirke
Karaka Heights, 312 Port Underwood Road, Picton

Tel (03) 573 7700   Fax (03) 573 5444
Mob 021 103 1689
jb@karakapointlodge.co.nz
www.karakapointlodge.co.nz

Room Rate $175-$250 (Continental Breakfast)
Dinner $55pp B/A   Credit cards accepted
2 King (2 bdrm)   2 Ensuite

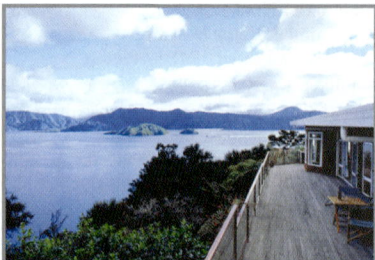

Luxury Boutique Accommodation in Picton's magical Marlborough Sounds, 10 minutes drive from
Picton Village. The secure, tranquil, romantic guest rooms have private entrances from the spacious
furnished deck   and spectacular panoramic marine views. Best beds, CD players, TV, Tea making, air-
conditioning, guest computer, BBQ & secluded spa. Generous breakfasts included- cooked extra. Gourmet
dinners featuring Marlborough's finest produce are available & served either in the dining alcove or on
the deck.   Multiple night discounts. Stay 2 + nights & receive a free bottle of Marlborough wine.

Picton - Whatamango Bay *B&B Homestay 10km E of Picton*

Whatamango Lodge
Ralph and Wendy Cass
17 McCormicks Road, Whatamango Bay, Picton

Tel (03) 573 5110 Fax (03) 573 5110
whatamango.lodge@paradise.net.nz
www.picton.co.nz/whatamango

Double $90-$120 Single $75
(Full Breakfast) Dinner $30
2 Queen (2 bdrm)   Self-contained
2 Ensuite

Welcome to Whatamango Lodge, situated at the head of Whatamango Bay, looking out towards Queen Charlotte Sound. We invite you to share our modern, waterfront home and enjoy total peace and tranquillity. Relax on your own private balcony and watch the magnificent birdlife. Take a stroll around the beach or swim in the crystal clear water. There are also numerous bush walks. You may like to use our dinghy or fish off the rocks.

Kayaks are available to paddle round the bay. We are situated 10 mins on a sealed road from Picton. Follow the Port Underwood Road from Waikawa to Whatamango Bay, turn left into McCormicks Rd, waterfront location, no 17. A courtesy car is also available for transport to or from the ferry.

Guest accommodation comprises
1. A self contained unit (sleeps 4), Queen sized bedroom, lounge (sofa bed), full kitchen facilities, large deck.
2. Queen sized bedroom with ensuite. Use of spacious lounge and balcony. Laundry facilities available.
Dinner is available by arrangement and features traditional New Zealand cuisine, served with complimentary wine. For breakfast choose either a full country style cooked breakfast, or a light continental breakfast, or if you prefer a delectable combination of both. We are a non-smoking household. Not suitable for children.

Pelorus - Mahau Sound   *B&B Homestay 33km W of Picton*

Ramona
Phyl & Ken Illes
460 Moetapu Bay Road, Mahau Sound, Marlborough

Tel (03) 574 2215   Fax (03) 574 2915
Mob 025 247 6668
www.bnb.co.nz/ramona.html

Double $95 Single $75 (Continental Breakfast)
Lunch & dinner by arrangement
2 Double 2 Twin (2 bdrm)

Our new beachfront home on the beautiful Mahau Sound
has been designed for you to share. Our guest floor has
its own conservatory, here you can view the passing water traffic. Awake to the call of Bellbirds and
Tuis, and after breakfast stroll around our rhododendron garden, or fossick on the beach. In the evening,
see our glowworms. Phyl, a quilter and keen gardener, and Ken, a retired builder, will arrange visits to
local art and craft studios, at your request.

Picton   *B&B Self-contained N of Blenheim*

Milton Cottage
Jenny & Derick Foss
27B Milton Tce, Picton,

Tel (03) 573 5466   0800 11 33 76   Fax (03) 573 5188
Mob 0800 287 267   fosshome@ihug.co.nz
www.bnb.co.nz/miltoncottage.html

Double $150 Single $150 (Continental Full Breakfast)
Child $30.00 (max 2)10yrs and older Children welcome
1 Queen 1 Twin (2 bdrm)

"Milton Cottage" is a luxury, self-contained holiday home, with provisions for self-catering breakfasts supplied.
An easy 10-minute-walk to the centre of Picton; 25 minutes to Blenheim by car. Sleeps maximum four
guests with shared bathroom. One double room with queen-size bed and one twin room with two single beds.
Comfortable and cosy living area with TV and music centre. Fully equipped kitchen and laundry. Sun decks
off main bedroom and living areas. The latter furnished with outdoor dinning and BBQ facilities. Covered
carport and additional parking for boat/car. Ferry terminal pick-up. Honeymoon and special occasion packages
available. Rates on request. Note: Single party bookings only. Regret, no pets. No children under 10 years.

Picton   *B&B*

St Catherine's
Paul & Gill Macdonald
123 Wellington Street, Picton,

Tel (03) 573 8580   Fax (03) 573 8580
Mob 021 180 2469   stcatherines@paradise.net.nz
www.stcatherines.co.nz

Double $90-$120 Single $60 (Full Breakfast)
Child Free under 12 Dinner N/A Children welcome
1 King 1 Queen 1 Single (2 bdrm)
1 Ensuite 1 Host share

Spacious, historic former convent built in 1880's and still
retaining much of its original character & charm. Set in
secluded grounds yet only a short walk to the foreshore and Picton's many cafes and restaurants. Our
main room offers guests a magnificent super-king four poster bed with ensuite shower/toilet and private
balcony with views to the sea and hills, relax and watch the sunset. Continental and/or cooked breakfast
is provided to suit. Sample our home baking! Children welcome (we have 2 boys ourselves).

Picton - Mahau Sound *B&B Homestay 33km W of Picton*

The Rock Sound Stay ™
Melvyn & Denyse Goodall
464 Moetapu Bay Road, RD2, Picton 7372

Tel (03) 574 2672   Fax (03) 574 2672
Mob 025 952024
soundstay@therock.org.nz
www.bnb.co.nz/therock.html

Double $125-$150 Single $75 (Full Breakfast)
Dinner & lunch by arrangement
1 Queen 1 Double (2 bdrm)
2 Ensuite

The Rock Sound Stay is a unique accommodation experience where you can relax in a bygone era, with your hosts and their three dogs. Offering full en-suite facilities with claw footed baths and rooms overlooking the Water or the Garden. The original Homestead built by a Timber Baron at the turn of the century, is set in almost three acres of native bush on the Side of Mount Cawte only 20 metres from the sea, with gentle sloping paths to over 100 metres of sea fontage.

Picton - Waikawa Bay *B&B Homestay 4km Picton*

Sunny Corner
Dorothy & Joe Brewer
4 Whitby Close, Waikawa Bay, Picton

Tel (03) 573 8238 jodobrewer@xtra.co.nz
www.bnb.co.nz/sunnycorner.html

Double $90 Single $60
(Full Breakfast)
2 Double (2 bdrm)
1 Ensuite

Our new home overlooks hills covered in native bush - a haven for bird life. We would love to make you welcome. A lounge with Sky TV and video is available for guests' use and also free Internet access. Laundry available. Tea and coffee making facilities in rooms. Courtesy collection from ferries, train or bus and we offer lifts to local restaurants in the evenings. Enjoy the peaceful surrounding only four kilometres from the ferry and minutes from Waikawa Marina.

Picton *B&B Self-contained Cottage in Waikawa Bay - 2 bedrooms Picton Central*

The Gables
Ian & Paula Allen
20 Waikawa Road, Picton,

Tel (03) 573 6772   Fax (03) 573 6772
Mob 021 158 5974   info@thegables.co.nz
www.thegables.co.nz

Double $110-$135 Single $90 (Full Breakfast)
Child $25 Self contained cottage $150
4 Queen 1 Double 2 Single (5 bdrm)
4 Ensuite 1 Private

'The Gables' is a charming and historic homestead situated close to all of Picton's attractions and amenities. A leisurely amble takes you to the splendid foreshore area, or a selection of restaurants, pubs, shops and supermarkets. Likewise, close to hand are the boating marina, water taxis, train station, and the ferry terminal. Magnificent walks overlooking the sounds and the harbour are literally on our doorstep. 'The Gables' offers three spacious comfortable rooms and a private guest lounge for your ease and relaxation, as well as two separate, self contained cottages behind the homestead, affording privacy and casual elegance.

Picton *B&B 3km NE of Picton*

Michiru
Rosemary & Paul Royer
247B Waikawa Road, Waikawa, Picton

Tel (03) 573 6793 Fax (03) 573 6793
Mob 021 117 5155
royer@xtra.co.nz
www.bnb.co.nz/michiru.html

Double $95 - $130 Single $70 (Full Breakfast)
Dinner $30 B/A Children welcome
1 King 1 Single (2 bdrm)
2 Private

Your base for exploring the wonderful Marlborough Sounds and wineries. Spend two nights or more with us and enjoy a complimentary bottle of best local wine. Overlooking Waikawa Bay and marina, only three kilometres from Picton. The bright and sunny rooms are all located on the ground floor with a lovely private guest lounge and garden patio shared with 'Puss' our cat. Use of laundry, bikes and fun kayaks. Enjoy Rosemary's delightful cuisine by arrangement. We will pick up / drop off at ferry terminal.

Picton - Little Ngakuta Bay *B&B 11km W of Picton*

Waterfront Bed & Breakfast
Vicki & David Bendell
Queen Charlotte Drive, 2383 Little Ngakuta Bay RD1

Tel (03) 573 8584 bendell@xtra.co.nz
www.picton.co.nz/for/kotare

Double $145-$165 Single $125 (Full Breakfast)
Child $35 Dinner B/A Off season rates May - Sep
Children welcome
1 Queen 1 Double 2 Single (2 bdrm)
1 Ensuite 1 Private 1 Host share

If staying on the waterfront is your accommodation requirement then our seaside cottage will exceed that expectation. It is as close to the water's edge as you can get. The aptly named "Boatshed" and "Pacific" rooms are separate from the cottage and offer ensuite private bathrooms, comfortable beds with Italian cotton linen, writing bureau, toiletries, tea/coffee (no TV in the room here). We consider accommodation an integral part of your holiday itinerary. Our young family (and dog) welcome you for a break from the ordinary.

Blenheim *Homestay 3km S of Blenheim*

Hillsview
Adrienne & Rex Handley
Please Phone

Tel (03) 578 9562 Fax (03) 578 9562
Mob 025 627 6727 aidrex@xtra.co.nz
www.bnb.co.nz/hillsview.html

Double $75-$85 Single $50 Less 10% if booked by the
night before.   (Full Breakfast)
Dinner by arrangement
1 King/Twin 1 Double 2 Twin 1 Single (4 bdrm)
2 Private

Welcome to our warm, spacious, non-smoking home in a quiet suburb with outdoor pool, off-street parking, and no pets. All beds have quality mattresses, electric blankets and wool underlays. Interests: Rex's (retired airline pilot) - are aviation oriented - models, microlights, homebuilts and gliding. Builds miniature steam locomotives, has 1930 Model A soft top tourer vintage car and enjoys barbershop singing. Adrienne's - cooking, spinning, woolcraft. Let us share these hobbies, plus our caring personal attention, complimentary beverages and all the comforts of home with you.

Blenheim *Farmstay 1.5km S of Blenheim*

Rhododendron Lodge
Audrey & Charlie Chambers
St Andrews, RD 4, State Highway 1, Blenheim
Tel (03) 578 1145   Fax (03) 578 1145
www.bnb.co.nz/rhododendronlodge.html
Double $80 Single $60 (Full Breakfast)
Suite $100   10% discount 3 days or more
2 Queen 2 Single (3 bdrm)
1 Ensuite 1 Private

Welcome to our small farm in Blenheim for quality accommodation in our spacious home with excellent beds. Bacon, eggs and tomatoes from our farm make a delicious breakfast. Our executive suite has a "Bechstein" piano. Tree ferns and gardens surround a large swimming pool. Spacious lawns with rhododendrons, roses and trees. We are close to Gourmet restaurants and have a selection of their menus. Marlborough has beautiful parks, wine trails, and scenic Marlborough sounds. Laundry available and courtesy phone call for next homestay. Happy Holidays.

Blenheim - Rapaura *Vineyard Homestay 12km NW of Blenheim*

Thainstone
Vivienne & Jim Murray
120 Giffords Rd, RD 3, Rapaura
Tel (03) 572 8823   Fax (03) 572 8623
Mob 021 283 1484   thainstone@xtra.co.nz
www.marlborough.co.nz/thainstone
Double $120 Single $70 (Full Breakfast) Dinner $30
S/C House $120 - $180, 2-4 people Credit cards accepted
1 King 2 Queen 1 Double 1 Twin 1 Single (5 bdrm)
1 Ensuite 1 Private 1 Guests share

Our large home is surrounded by vineyards and within walking distance of the Wairau River and several wineries. In our home there are three upstairs bedrooms and a guest lounge which opens onto a swimming pool courtyard. The self-catering house has two bedrooms and is fully equipped for longer stays. We are widely travelled and some interests are bird watching, trout fishing, woodworking and cards. Evening meals, by prior arrangement, are served with Marlborough wines. Unsuitable for children.

Blenheim *Homestay Self-contained 500m W of Blenheim Central*

Beaver B&B
Jen & Russell Hopkins
60 Beaver Road, Blenheim
Tel (03) 578 8401   Fax (03) 578 8401
Mob 021 626 151
rdhopkins@xtra.co.nz
www.bnb.co.nz/beaverbb.html
Double $80 Single $60 (Continental Breakfast)
Credit cards accepted
1 Queen (1 bdrm)
1 Ensuite

Our self-contained unit can accommodate one couple or a single. Features include your own entrance, queensize bed, mini kitchen, bathroom - large bath, shower and separate toilet. Use of our laundry can be made upon request. Two cats and a bird live with us. We have off-street parking and are within ten minutes walk from central Blenheim. Please phone before 8 am or after 4.30 pm during the working week. If no response, Jennie can be contacted via her cell-phone. Fax us anytime.

Blenheim *B&B Homestay 2km N of Blenheim*

Philmar
Wynnis & Lex Phillips
63 Colemans Road, Blenheim
Tel (03) 577 7788 Fax (03) 577 7788
www.bnb.co.nz/philmar.html
Double $70 Single $50
(Continental Breakfast)
Dinner $20pp
2 Queen 1 Twin (3 bdrm)
1 Guests share

Welcome to our home 2kms from the town centre. Guests can join us in our spacious sunny living areas. We both enjoy all TV sports and our other interests include wood turning, handcrafts and the Lions organisation. Blenheim is an ideal place to visit Picton, Nelson, whale watch and the many wineries, parks and craft shops in the area . Smoking is not encouraged. Just phone to be picked up at airport, train or bus. Dinner on request.

Awatere Valley - Blenheim *Farmstay 63km S of Blenheim*

Duntroon
Trish & Robert Oswald
Awatere Valley, Private Bag, Blenheim
Tel (03) 575 7374 Fax (03) 575 7281
Mob 0274 865 223 oswald@xtra.co.nz
www.bnb.co.nz/duntroon.html
Double $110-$130 Single $70-$90 (Full Breakfast)
Child $70 Dinner B/A Backpacker accommodation $20
Credit cards accepted
1 Double 4 Single (3 bdrm)   1 Guests share 1 Host share

Come and enjoy the peaceful surroundings of our 3500 acre high country Merino property in the beautiful Awatere Valley. The large homestead set in established grounds with tennis court and swimming pool offers warm spacious bedrooms with comfortable beds. Lunch and dinner served with local wines by arrangement. Farm tours on request. Our interests include clay-target shooting, travel, flying, tennis, boating and handcrafts. Over the summer the Awatere Valley Road is open through Molesworth Station to Hamner Springs.

Blenheim *B&B Homestay Vineyard Homestay 12km W of Blenheim*

Black Birch Lodge
Margaret & David Barnsley
Jeffries Road, RD 3, Blenheim
Tel (03) 572 8876 Fax (03) 572 8806
barnsley@ihug.co.nz
www.bnb.co.nz/blackbirchlodge.html
Double $140-$150 Single $85-$100 (Full Breakfast)
Child 1/2 price Dinner $40 by arrangement
Credit cards accepted Children welcome
2 Queen 3 Single (3 bdrm)
2 Ensuite

Black Birch Lodge is ideally situated for exploring Marlborough's wine trail. Your hosts have been involved in the wine industry since 1981 both as growers and David as editor of Winepress. Most Marlborough wineries are only a matter of minutes away, the closest being the prestigious Herzog Winery and Restaurant situated at the bottom of Black Birch's vineyard. Other features include tennis court, pool, bikes, library, laundry, wine trail advice, vineyard walks and trout fishing in nearby Wairau River. We have a small friendly dog, "Perro".

Blenheim   *B&B Homestay Family Blenheim Central*

Grove Bank
Pauline & Peter Pickering
2652 State Highway 1, Grovetown, Blenheim
Tel (03) 578 8407   0800 422 632   Fax (03) 578 8407
grovebank@xtra.co.nz
www.grovebank.co.nz
Double $70-$85 Single $50-$55
(Full Breakfast) Dinner $20 - $35
Groups $75 - $180 Credit cards accepted
3 King/Twin 4 Queen 2 Single (8 bdrm)
6 Ensuite 1 Private 1 Spa bath

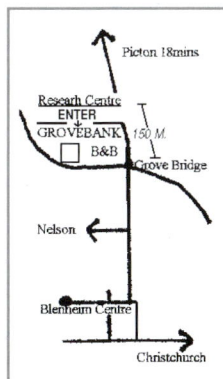

Pauline and Peter invite you to stay at our 8 acre olive grove and vineyard, which is located conveniently on SH1 on the northern boundary of Blenheim. We offer 8 double bedrooms with ensuites plus bedroom and bathroom appliances. Our home is designed especially with homestay guests in mind. Spacious guest lounges (with televisions) opening onto large balconies, offer panoramic views of the plains ranges and river.

After a day of sightseeing and enjoying the delights of the "Gourmet Province", cool off in the swimming pool, relax in the spa, take a stroll in Pauline's gardens the olive grove/vineyard. Some courtesy transport is available for evening dining.

We offer continental and cooked breakfast and meals as requested. A former restaurateur and butcher, Peter's breakfasts are legendary. Evening meals may consist of meats and fresh grown vegetables or fish caught by Peter from the Marlborough Sounds, rivers and lakes. If you feel like dining out, Marlborough's finest Italian Restaurant (Best pasta in the world - "Cuisine"), the Whitehaven winery and cafe and local bar and bistro are within 5 minutes walking distance.

We are happy to share our extensive local knowledge and contacts which will enable you to personalise and optimise your stay in the "Gourmet Province"/ Free laundry facilities.

Directions: On Blenheim's north boundary definitely 100 metres north of narrow concrete bridge, on state highway 1, turn into multi signed entrance shared by the Research Centre. Then immediately turn left into gravel drive and follow to house.

Blenheim
B&B Homestay Country Homestay 1.5km S of Blenheim

Green Gables
Jeannine & Benjamin Van Straaten
RD4, St Andrews, Gate 3011, Blenheim

Tel (03) 577 9205 0800 273 050
Fax (03) 577 9206 Mob 02 111 588 11
green_gables_blenheim@xtra.co.nz
www.bnb.co.nz/greengables.html

Double $85-$120 Single $40-$60
(Continental Breakfast) Dinner $25
Cooked breakfast $5 extra
2 Queen 2 Double (3 bdrm)
3 Ensuite

Enjoy your stay at our luxurious and exceptionally spacious two storey home located in rural Blenheim. Only 2km from the town centre, Green Gables is set in a tranquil, one acre landscaped garden and offers quiet, luxurious surroundings, although close to State Highway 1 and to town.

Guest accommodation comprises of three large bedrooms, all with en suite bathrooms. Two of our rooms have queen - sized beds and the third has a double bed. All rooms are fully equipped with electric blankets, radio clocks, hair dryers and room heating and two rooms have glass doors that open onto private balconies affording panoramic views of Blenheim. An adjoining guest lounge has a small library and television set and there are additional TV sets in the queen rooms. Coffee and tea making facilities are available and you are invited to use the laundry, fax and email facilities if required.

For breakfast choose either a full, country-style cooked breakfast or a light continental breakfast or if you prefer a delectable combination of both, served with delicious home-made jams and preserves. Dinner is available by arrangement and features traditional New Zealand cuisine served with a complimentary drink. We are horticulturists and grow cut flowers. Our ginger cat Sharky is visitor friendly and lives outside. Green Gables backs onto the picturesque Opawa river. In season this gentle river offers trout fishing, eeling and whitebaiting. A small rowing boat is available for your use at no extra charge. As an additional courtesy we would be pleased to help you with the on-booking of your B&B accommodation. Let us phone ahead for you and you'll make valuable savings on your phone card.

Directions: On SH1, 1/2 km south of Blenheim town, gate number 3011. 20 minutes form Picton ferry. Green Gables sign at drive entrance.

Blenheim *Farmstay 5km S of Blenheim*

Windmill Farm
Millie Amos
3516 Main Road, Riverlands, Blenheim
Tel (03) 577 7853   Fax (03) 577 7853
www.bnb.co.nz/windmillfarm.html
Double $80 Single $50
(Continental Breakfast)
1 Double 2 Twin (2 bdrm)
1 Ensuite 1 Private

Only 5km south of Blenheim on SH1, you will find Windmill Farm, a spacious and modern home in close proximity to the golf driving range and to Montana Winery. Comfortably appointed spacious twin bedroom with private ensuite and one double bedroom with private bathroom and spa. We have travelled to many countries overseas and aim to make our guests feel welcome and relaxed. We are non smokers who enjoy gardens, travel and meeting people. We welcome you to our home. Please phone first.

Blenheim *Homestay Blenheim Central*

Maxwell House
John and Barbara Ryan
82 Maxwell Road, Blenheim
Tel (03) 577 7545   Fax (03) 577 7545
Mob 025 234 9977   mt.olympus@xtra.co.nz
www.bnb.co.nz/maxwellhouse.html
Double $125 Single $100 (Full Breakfast)
Credit cards accepted Children welcome
1 Queen 1 Twin (2 bdrm)
2 Ensuite

Welcome to Marlborough. We invite you to stay at Maxwell House, a grand old Victorian residence. Built in 1880 our home has been elegantly restored and is classified with the Historic Places Trust. Our large guest rooms are individually appointed with ensuite, lounge area, television and tea and coffee making facilities. Breakfast will be a memorable experience, served around the original 1880's Kauri table. Set on a large established property Maxwell House is an easy ten minute walk to the town centre. Non Smoking.

Blenheim - Rapaura *B&B Self-contained 15km SW of Blenheim*

Tamar Vineyard
Clive & Yvonne Dasler
67 Rapaura Road, RD 3, Blenheim
Tel (03) 572 8408   0800 429 922   Fax (03) 572 8405
tamar.vineyard@xtra.co.nz
www.tamarvineyard.co.nz
Double $150-$175 Single $130 (Special Breakfast)
Child negotiable Credit cards accepted
1 Queen 1 Single (1 bdrm)
1 Private

Situated in the heart of the wine region, Tamar is one of Marlborough's oldest vineyards. Our newly built cottage is a romantic retreat with breathtaking views through the vines to the Richmond Ranges. Luxuriate in an ornately carved four poster bed under a feather down duvet, then enjoy a gourmet breakfast before taking a leisurely stroll to nearby wineries and restaurants. Or let us help organise your wine trail, skifield, or Marlborough Sounds experience. Our secluded, smoke free cottage is self-contained and a warm welcome and memorable stay is assured.

Blenheim *B&B Homestay 3km Blenheim Centre*

Richmond View
Allan & Jan Graham
25 Elmwood Avenue, Blenheim,
Tel (03) 578 8001   Fax (03) 578 8001
Mob 025 458 074   a.w.graham@xtra.co.nz
http://nzhomestay/graham.html
Double $90 Single $70 (Continental Breakfast)
Children welcome
1 Queen 1 Twin (2 bdrm)
1 Guests share

We welcome you to our new home built on the slopes of
Wither Hills situated to the South side of Blenheim, having panoramic views of town, Richmond ranges
and Cook Strait in the distance. Offering Queen and Twin rooms with electric blankets and heating.
Complimetary spa available. Bathroom and toilet are separate and private. Our interests comprise
boating,four wheel driving, vintage cars, flying and enjoying Marlborough's fantastic waterways and
wineries which you can share by arrangement. Local pickup available on request.

Blenheim *B&B Homestay Self-contained 6min N of Blenheim*

Chardonnay Lodge
George and Ellenor Mayo
1048 Rapaura Road, Rapaura, Blenheim
Tel (03) 570 5194   Fax (03) 570 5196
info@chardonnaylodge.co.nz
www.chardonnaylodge.co.nz
Double $110-$130 (Special Breakfast) Child $20
(5 yrs - 13yrs) extra persons in villa $30 pp
Credit cards accepted
3 Queen 3 Single (3 bdrm)   3 Ensuite

We offer excellent accommodation and facilities, including secluded solar heated swimming pool, private
spa, sun lounges, barbecue and a full sized tennis court. Central to the superb vineyards and restaurants,
with Blenheim just 6 minutes away we provide homestay with own ensuite or high standard self-contained
villas. You will find everything you and your family need for a comfortable and relaxing stay. Our fluffy
persian cats will welcome you to the lawns and garden. We are 2.2km from the Spring Creek turn off on
SH1. Courtesy vehicle to ferry, bus and rail. Location map, pictures and information on web site.

Blenheim *B&B 100m W of Blenheim*

Henry Maxwell's Central B&B
Rae Woodman
28 Henry Street, Blenheim,
Tel (03) 578 8086   0800 436 796   Fax (03) 578 8086
Mob 025 200 9862
stay@henrymaxwells.co.nz
www.henrymaxwells.co.nz
Double $90-$120 Single $65 (Continental Breakfast)
(Full Breakfast)
3 Queen 4 Twin 3 Single (4 bdrm)
2 Ensuite 1 Private

Welcome to 'Henrys', a gracious 75 year old home. Guests have spacious quiet rooms, 2 with ensuites,
2 share bathroom. TV, tea, coffee, cookies and complimentary port. Queen size beds and large comfortable
arm chairs. All overlook gardens. Breakfast in the unique dining room (maps and charts) is something
to remember. Three minutes stroll to town, many excellent restaurants, shops, theatre, movies, etc.
Find 'Henrys', corner of Henry and Munro Streets between High Street and Maxwell Road. Offstreet
parking. Relax and enjoy the garden and sun.

Blenheim   *B&B Homestay 7km N of Blenheim*

Blue Ridge Estate
Lesley & Brian Avery
50 O'Dwyers Road, RD 3, Blenheim

Tel (03) 570 2198   Fax (03) 570 2199
lavery@clear.net.nz
www.blueridge.co.nz

Double $150-$195 Single $120-$165 (Continental Full
Breakfast) Dinner By arrangement
2 Queen 2 Twin (3 bdrm)
1 Ensuite 2 Private

Set on a 20-acre purpose-designed homestay property,
Blue Ridge Estate, 2002 Marlborough Master Builders' "House of the Year", enjoys a rural setting with
stunning views across vineyards to the Richmond Range and is close to many of Marlborough's fine
wineries, restaurants and gardens. Our home has proven most popular with both international and New
Zealand visitors. Come share our home with Bella our friendly young labrador, where comfort and
privacy will ensure your Marlborough visit is indeed a memorable one.

Blenheim - Wairau Valley   *Farmstay 35km W of Blenheim*

Lansdowne Farm Park
Margaret & David Dillon
Wairua Valley, RD 1, Blenheim

Tel (03) 572 2838   Fax (03) 572 2828
lansdowne.farm@xtra.co.nz
www.lansdowne.co.nz

Double $120 Single $70 (Continental Full Special
Breakfast) Child $35 Dinner $35 Children welcome
1 King/Twin 2 Double 2 Twin 1 Single (6 bdrm)
3 Ensuite 1 Private

Happy Days - The classic 1960's family farm. We'll make
certain you're snug whenever you check in at Lansdowne. We'll see you're comfortable in the farmhouse
or Woodland Cottage and serve you seasonal farm style meals. We'll provide total rest and relaxation or
a choice of daily activities. Get into it all or take time out to mediate. Heaps of farm fun for all the
family. Take in Wairua Valley's scenic wineries to wilderness experience. There are no strangers here
- just friends we haven't met!

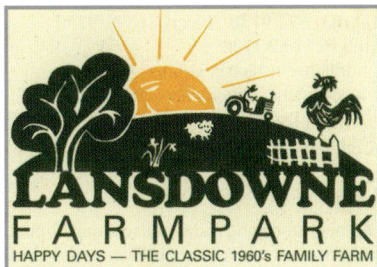

Blenheim   *B&B   Blenheim Central*

Rose Villa
Richard Grylls
63 Main Street, Blenheim,

Tel (03) 577 5112   Fax (03) 577 5112
richardgrylls@hotmail.com
www.bnb.co.nz/rosevillablenheim.html

Double $80-$110 Single $50-$60
(Special Breakfast)
Child $15 - $25 four bed family room $40 pp
2 Queen (3 bdrm)
1 Ensuite 1 Private

Friendly, welcoming bed and breakfast. Off-road secure parking. Priced to suit all budgets with discounts
for extended stays. Restaurant and bar all close to accommodation.   Wine trails and tasting tours.
Fishing trips. Great walks. Experienced host, ex. English Country House Hotel. Good local knowledge,
experience in wine industry. Breakfasts our speciality - enjoyed on the deck. Two minutes walk to town
centre.

Blenheim   *B&B Homestay 9km NW of Blenheim*

Stonehaven Vineyard Homestay
Paulette & John Hansen
414 Rapaura Road, Blenheim,
Tel (03) 572 9730   Fax (03) 572 9730
Mob 025 682 1120
jandphansen@actrix.gen.nz
www.stonehavenhomestay.co.nz

Double $160-$200 Single $90-$120
(Continental Full Breakfast) Dinner $50pp wine included
1 King 1 Queen 2 Single (3 bdrm)
2 Ensuite 1 Private

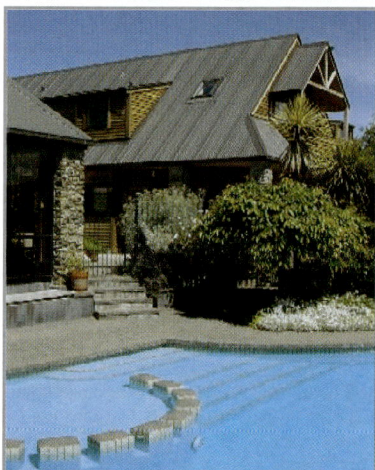

Our new stone and cedar house is surrounded by gardens and 18 acres of Sauvignon Blanc vines in the premium grape growing area of Marlborough.
The house, which reflects the warmth, space and comfort to make your stay relaxing and memorable, commands exquisite views over the vineyards to the craggy Richmond Ranges beyond. Close by are some of New Zealand's most outstanding wineries.
Start the day with a delicious breakfast of your choice served in the summerhouse overlooking the swimming pool. Complimentary wines are served to match the 3 course evening meal which features our home grown vegetables and locally produced seasonal ingredients. Occasionally wild game such as venison or trout may be included.
Marlborough offers many activities to occupy your day and a picnic lunch can be provided. You may like us to organise and book some of these attractions or, if you plan to stay with us for 2 or more nights, we can offer scenic tours, winery tours, 4 wheel drive tours such as

Pelorus to Nelson over old gold trails or we can take you to more out of the way locations for trout fishing or tramping in our beautiful backcountry where we can introduce you to our native flora and fauna.   The snowfields are an hour's drive away and offer good skiing in winter. We can meet you or drop you off at either the airport at Blenheim or the ferry terminal at Picton. We look forward to making your stay with us as relaxing or as active as you choose. We are non smokers and our interests include native flora and fauna, hunting, fishing, tramping, cooking and New Zealand history.

Skiing, fishing, tramping and old gold trails

Renwick   *Homestay Self-contained Vineyard Lodge 15km W of Blenheim*

LeGrys Vineyard
Jennifer & John Joslin
Conders Bend Road, Renwick, Marlborough

Tel (03) 572 9490   Fax (03) 572 9491
Mob 021 313 208   stay@legrys.co.nz
www.legrys.co.nz

Double $140 (Full Breakfast) S/C double + max 4 $225
+ $45 pp Credit cards accepted
2 Queen 2 Single (3 bdrm)   2 Private

Waterfall Lodge - self-contained, vineyard setting. Two beds. Queen, two single. Kitchen facilities, dining, lounge area, gas BBQ. Main house - queen room, private bathroom. Both offer unique mud-brick construction and offer rustic charm combined with stylish furnishings. Breakfast hamper with full provisions daily. Ideal base for winery visits, golf, Sounds cruising, walking, Trout fishing. Blenheim Town 10 minutes drive. Solar heated indoor pool. LeGrys & Mudhouse wines available, complimentary tasting and tray of nibbles to welcome you. John and Jennifer cruised the world in their yacht. We have a Springer Spaniel, Pippin and Airedale Alice.

Renwick   *Homestay 10km W of Blenheim*

Clovelly
Don & Sue Clifford
2a Nelson Place, Renwick, Marlborough 7352

Tel (03) 572 9593   Fax (03) 572 7293
Mob 025 986 917   clifford@actrix.gen.nz
www.clovelly.co.nz

Double $110 Single $80 (Full Breakfast)
1 Queen 1 Twin (2 bdrm)
2 Private

Our colonial style home is set in 1/2 an acre of lovely private grounds in the heart of vineyard country. We overlook orchards and out to the Richmond Range. Relax under the trees with refreshments or by a glowing fire in winter. Visit our quaint local English pub - dine in the village or vineyard restaurants. We are within 'stroll and taste' distance of a number of prestigious vineyards. Rest and unwind with Don and Sue and our two little Scottish terriers Chloe and Phoebe, who will welcome you warmly.

Renwick   *B&B Homestay 10km W of Blenheim*

Rimu Guest House
David & Elizabeth Eastman
9 Wilson St, Renwick,

Tel 03 572 7575   Fax 03 572 7575
Mob 025 298 0764
rimuguesthouse@xtra.co.nz
www.bnb.co.nz/rimuguesthouse.html

Double $90 Single $70 (Continental Breakfast)
Dinner B/A Party of four $160
1 Queen 1 Double (2 bdrm)

When you want a special place to call home base while you explore Marlborough's food, wine and arts trails, Liz and Dave's Rimu Guest House offers you everything you need 'as you like it'. Savour the views of the Richmond Ranges, the peace and tranquility of our character home and gardens in the heart of Marlborough's wine region. Enjoy home baking, fresh beverages, e-mail facilities and complimentary use of bicycles. A warm welcome awaits you.

Havelock   *B&B   40km W of Picton*

Carnlough
Margaret & Reg Williams
101 Main Road, Havelock, Marlborough
Tel (03) 574 1444   Paregma@clear.net.nz
www.bnb.co.nz/carnlough.html
Double $80-$90   Single $80
(Continental Breakfast) (Full Breakfast)
Child $20 Credit cards accepted
1 Queen (1 bdrm)
1 Ensuite

For space and comfort, stay at our modernised 1930's villa located at Havelock on the main road between Nelson and Blenheim, about 40 minutes from the Picton Ferry and 20 minutes from Marlborough wine trail. We have travelled widely abroad and are members of the local Lions Club. Our friendly West Highland Terrier loves to greet our guests. Havelock is the hub of many outdoor activities on and off the water. The town is well served with excellent restaurants within walking distance of our home.

Canvastown   *Homestay 10km W of Havelock*

Woodchester
Judy & Ted Tomlinson
84 Te Hora Pa Road, Canvastown
Tel (03) 574 1123   Fax (03) 574 1123
woodchesterlodge@woodchesterlodge.co.nz
www.woodchesterlodge.co.nz
Double $90   Single $55 (Full Breakfast)
Child From $18 Dinner From $20
Children welcome
1 Queen/Single divan 1 Twin (2 bdrm)

We are a friendly retired couple and have a Jack Russell dog called Mr Fox to say hello. Our home is lodge style with country atmosphere. We look forward to enjoying your company and sharing meals and conversation in our dining room and lounge. BBQ's in the Summer available. Consider more than one night's stay, as fishing and sightseeing trips are only minutes away. Walking and tramping tracks are prolific or cruise the fabulous sounds in comfort. Welcome to Woodchester Lodge and enjoy.

Pelorus Bridge   *Self-contained Guest House 45mins Blenheim & Nelson*

Lord Lionel
Lionel & Monika Neilands
SH6 Pelorus, RD 2, Rai Valley, Marlborough
Tel (03) 574 2770   Fax (03) 574 2770
www.bnb.co.nz/lordlionel.html
Double $90-$100   Single $50 (Full Breakfast)
Child $20 (12 & under) Credit cards accepted
1 King 3 Double 2 Single (6 bdrm)
1 Private 2 Guests share

We wish to invite you to our riverbank lodge. A fishing paradise in the heart of the Pelorus River Country with excellent fishing for Rainbow, brown trout and some salmon. We are situated 45 minutes from Nelson and Blenheim on State Highway 6 in the midst of 1 1/2 acre of native forest with prolific bird life. We are in the heart of great walking tracks. We are 1 1/2km from Pelorus Bridge Scenic Reserve, which is one of the finest reserves in New Zealand. As we have our own private dwelling, the guests have the run of the house with excellent cooking facilities. Entire house available. Directions: 1.5km on Blenheim side of Pelorus Bridge, LH side, just before Bowns Creek Bridge.

Nelson, Golden Bay

- Pakawau
- Collingwood
- Parapara
- Patons Rock
- Tata Beach
- Takaka
- Abel Tasman National Park
- **60**
- Marahau
- Kaiteriteri
- Riwaka
- Motueka
- Tasman
- Cable Bay
- Ruby Bay
- Thorpe
- Mapua
- Nelson
- **6**
- Richmond
- Wakefield
- Golden Downs

Towns listed generally follow
a north to south route. Refer
to the index if required.

| 0 | Kilometres | 20 |
| 0 | Miles | 12 |

- **6**
- **63**
- Mangles Valley
- Tophouse
- Murchison
- St Arnaud
- Nelson Lakes
- **65**
- Maruia Valley

Nelson - Cable Bay   *B&B 20km N of Nelson*

Quail Ridge
Ken and Gerrie Young
Cable Bay Rd, Hira, RD1, Nelson
Tel (03) 545 1899   Fax (03) 545 1890
quailridge@clear.net.nz
www.quailridge.co.nz
Double $135 Single $120 (Continental Breakfast)
Child $25 Dinner $40 pp Barbecue $25.00pp
2 Queen 2 Single (2 bdrm)
2 Ensuite

Quail Ridge offers a very special, memorable experience. The Cable Bay location is quiet and beautiful with wonderful water, island and farmland views. The two attractive separately located guest studios are designed for privacy and relaxation. Terraces provide socialising, barbecuing and outdoor dining areas. A quiet swimming beach, national walkway, and fishing are nearby with 4WD bikes, kayaking, and horse trekking locally. Restaurants and activities of Nelson city are 20 minutes away. Always a friendly welcome - our dog and cat enjoy sharing the moment.

Nelson   *B&B Homestay 6km NE of Nelson*

Mike's B&B
Mike Cooper & Lennane Kent
4 Seaton Street, Nelson
Tel (03) 545 1671   Fax (03) 545 1671
cooperkent@actrix.gen.nz
www.bnb.co.nz/kent.html
Double $65-$70 (Full Breakfast) Child neg
Dinner $30 with prior notice Credit cards accepted
1 Queen 1 Double 1 Single (2 bdrm)
2 Ensuite

Five minutes from Nelson City centre we give you a warm welcome to our comfortable home in a safe quiet neighbourhood with superb views over Tasman Bay and out to the Tasman mountains. Our guest accommodation is almost self-contained and is well equipped with a small lounge, fridge, TV, tea and coffee making facilities and a microwave. Laundry facilities are available for your use. Our interests include our large collection of books which you are welcome to use, sea fishing, education and our lively schnauzer dog.

Nelson   *B&B Homestay or Self Contained Apartment 2km SW of Nelson*

Harbour View Homestay
Judy Black
11 Fifeshire Crescent, Nelson
Tel (03) 548 8567 Fax (03) 548 8667
Mob 025 247 4445
www.harbourviewaccommodation.co.nz
Double $120-$140 Single $90-$125
(Continental Breakfast) Full breakfast $5pp extra
Credit cards accepted
2 Queen 2 Single (3 bdrm)   2 Ensuite 1 Private

Harbour View Homestay
Nelson NZ

Our home is above the harbour entrance. Huge windows capture spectacular views of beautiful Tasman Bay, Haulashore Island, Tahunanui Beach, across the sea to Abel Tasman National Park and mountains. Observe from the bedrooms, dining room and decks, ships and pleasure craft cruising by as they enter and leave the harbour. If you can tear yourself away from our magnificent view, within walking distance along the waterfront there are excellent cafes and restaurants. Your hosts, Judy and David and Possum the cat, offer you a warm welcome and a memorable stay.

Nelson *B&B Nelson Central*

Borogove
Judy & Bill Hiener
27 Grove Street, Nelson

Tel (03) 548 9442   0800 379 308   Fax (03) 548 9443
hihiener@xtra.co.nz
www.bnb.co.nz/borogove.html

Double $100-$115
(Full Breakfast)
2 Queen (2 bdrm)
2 Ensuite

Behind a high laurel hedge you will discover Borogove, our century-old heritage home set in a fragrant garden. Characteristic high ceilings, period furniture and antiques contribute to its unique charm. Bedrooms are elegantly decorated and have en-suite bathrooms. Relaxing armchairs, tea/coffee, heaters, electric blankets, reading-lights and TV ensure your comfort. Generous cooked breakfasts are served in our Victorian dining room. It is a three minute walk to the Visitors' Centre, the shops and restaurants. Abel Tasman bus collection. Off-street parking.

Nelson *B&B Self-contained Homestay Units 5km SW of Nelson*

Arapiki
Kay & Geoff Gudsell
21 Arapiki Road, Stoke, Nelson

Tel (03) 547 3741   Fax (03) 547 3742
bnb@nelsonparadise.co.nz
www.nelsonparadise.co.nz

Double $75-$110 Single $70-$90
(Continental Breakfast - optional $7.50pp)
Credit cards accepted
1 Queen 1 Double 1 Single (2 bdrm)
2 Ensuite

Enjoy a relaxing holiday in the midst of your trip. The two quality smokefree units in our large home offer comfort, privacy and offstreet parking in a central location. The larger Unit 1 is in a private garden setting. A ranchslider opens on to a deck with outdoor furniture. It has an electric stove, microwave, TV, auto washing machine & phone. Unit 2 has a balcony with seating to enjoy sea and mountain views. It has a microwave, hotplate, TV & phone. We have a Tonkinese cat.

Nelson *B&B Homestay 6km S of Nelson*

Tarata Homestay
John & Mercia Hoskin
5 Tarata Street, Stoke, Nelson

Tel (03) 547 3426   0800 107 308   Fax (03) 547 3640
hosts@taratahomestay.co.nz
www.taratahomestay.co.nz

Double $90-$95 Single $65-$70 (Continental Breakfast)
Child $25 Credit cards accepted
1 Queen 1 Twin (2 bdrm)
1 Private

In a quiet street surrounded by gardens and mature trees,
we offer quality accommodation for only one party of guests at a time giving them exclusive use of all facilities. These include a comfortable lounge with a range of complimentary teas and coffee. We have a comprehensive selection of local information so that you can plan your stay, and we are always available to help you with ideas, expecially if time is limited. Our elderly Golden Labrador loves the opportunity to socialise with guests.

Nelson   *Homestay 2km W of Nelson Central*

Jubilee House
Patsy & Sheridan Parris
107 Quebec Road, Nelson

Tel **(03) 54 88 5 11**   0800 11 88 91
Fax (03) 54 88 5 11
Mob 027 44 8 7 7 67
info@jubileehouse.co.nz
www.jubileehouse.co.nz

Double $95-$105 Single $65-$75
(Full Breakfast) (Special Breakfast)
Credit cards accepted
2 Double 2 Single (4 bdrm)
1 Bathroom, guest shared

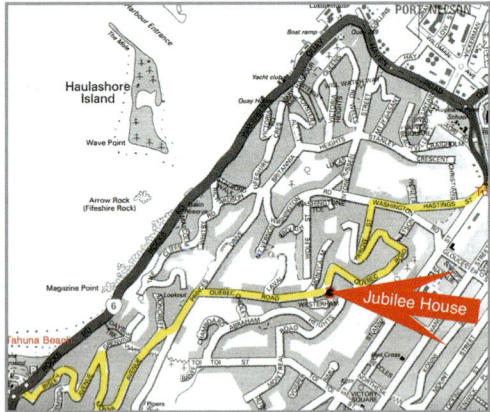

Many of our guests have told us we have some of the finest views of any Bed & Breakfast in New Zealand. High on a ridge overlooking the whole of Nelson City, beautiful Tasman Bay, mountains and harbour entrance. Drive downtown in three minutes, or try our new walkway from the top of Quebec Road to the valley below.

Breakfast is special, our own Muesli made with Beech honey and cinnamon, homemade yoghurt, breads, muffins and scones. Taste our local Pomeroy's fruit or spiced teas, or Sheridan's special blend of coffee beans. Waffles are our specialities, topped with seasonal fruit and real Canadian maple syrup. You might like to go savoury with salami, tasty bacon and Bratwurst sausage. We can serve something traditional or different, or cater for your special diet, with adequate notice.

As Nelson leads the rest of the country in sunshine hours stay a while in this beautiful region. You may even get to see one of our spectacular sunsets. We are happy to help or advise you on places of interest and things to do, or on the many great restaurants and cafes we have in our city.   We provide a smoke free environment, courtesy pick-up from the visitor centre or bus depot, and offer off street parking. KJ our Devon Rex cat may grace you with his presence; he is non-allergenic as his coat is wool.

Visit our website: www.jubileehouse.co.nz

Nelson *B&B Homestay 2km E of Nelson*

Brooklands
Lorraine & Barry Signal
106 Brooklands Rd, Atawhai, Nelson

Tel (03) 545 1423 Fax (03)5451423
bsignal@paradise.net.nz
www.bnb.co.nz/brooklands.html

Double $100-$125 Single $65 (Full Breakfast)
Child B/A Dinner $35 Credit cards accepted
1 Queen 2 Double 2 Single (3 bdrm)
1 Ensuite 1 Guests share   Children welcome

Brooklands is a spacious, luxurious 4 level home with superb sea views. Guests have exclusive use of 2 levels. The large bathroom has a spa bath for two. One bedroom has a private balcony. There are spacious indoor/outdoor living areas. We enjoy sports, running, travel and outdoors. Lorraine makes dolls and bears and enjoys crafts, gardening and cooking. We are close to Nelson's attractions - beaches, crafts, wine trails, national parks, lakes and mountains. We enjoy making new friends. Smoke free. Courtesy transport available.

Nelson *B&B Nelson Central*

The Baywick Inn
Tim Bayley & Janet Southwick
51 Domett Street, Nelson

Tel (03) 545 6514 Fax (03) 545 6517
Mob 0274 545 823 baywicks@iconz.co.nz
www.baywicks.com

Double $125-$155 Single $95-$120 (Special Breakfast)
Dinner $40pp Credit cards accepted
3 Queen 1 Single (3 bdrm)
2 Ensuite 1 Private

Overlooking the Maitai River, Brook Stream and Centre of New Zealand this elegantly restored 1885 Victorian, offers spacious and luxuriously appointed rooms. Each has its own character and charm with antique furnishings, comfortable beds and modern amenities. Enjoy afternoon tea or cappuccino in the cozy guest lounge, sunroom or garden and chat with Tim about his classic MG's. Janet, a cook by profession, makes breakfast to order, healthy or indulgent, cooked or continental. This Canadian/New Zealand ambiance is enhanced by their lively fox terrier.

Nelson Central *B&B 0.8km E of Nelson*

Sunflower Cottage
Marion & Chris Burton
70 Tasman Street, Nelson

Tel (03) 548 1588 Fax (03) 548 1588
marion@sunfloweraccommodation.co.nz
www.sunfloweraccommodation.co.nz

Double $95 Single $75
(Continental Breakfast)
2 King/Twin 2 Twin 2 Single (2 bdrm)
2 Ensuite

Welcome to our home on the banks of the Maitai River. Our large bedrooms, with ensuite bathrooms, are serviced daily with fresh flowers, complimentary basket of fruit and contain TV, microwave, fridge, tea/coffee making facilities, and toaster. Breakfast is self-service. We are very close to Queen's Gardens, Suter Art Gallery and the Botanical Hill, where after an easy walk to the centre of New Zealand, you experience wonderful views over Tasman Bay and Nelson township. Courtesy car to airport or bus depot.

Nelson - Tahunanui   *B&B 3km SW of Nelson*

Somerset House
Nicki & Richard Harden
33 Chamberlain Street, Tahunanui, Nelson

Tel (03) 548 5998   Fax (03) 548 5436
Mob 0272 101 475   R.Harden@xtra.co.nz
www.bnb.co.nz/somersethouse.html

Double $110 Single $75 (Continental & Full Breakfast)
Child Neg Credit cards accepted Children welcome
1 Queen 1 Single (2 bdrm)
1 Ensuite

Our quiet hillside home, nestled in ¹/₂ acre of gardens,
enjoys panoramic 180 degrees views - including Tasman Bay and Tahunanui Beach, with the distant
mountain backdrop affording us glorious sunsets. The guest rooms,situated at the south western wing
of house offer own access, tea/coffee facilities, elec blankets and outdoor spa. We invite you to enjoy a
drink and chat on our large deck before going on to the fabulous waterfront restaurants just minutes
away. A well travelled social family - including one son and two cats.

Nelson   *B&B 2km S of Nelson*

Beach Front B&B
Oriel & Peter Phillips
581 Rocks Road, Nelson

Tel (03) 548 5299   Fax (03) 548 5299
Mob 025 216 5237   peterp@tasman.net
www.bnb.co.nz/beachfrontbb.html

Double $95-$105 Single $85 (Continental Full
Breakfast) Credit cards accepted
1 Queen 1 Double (2 bdrm)
1 Ensuite 1 Private

Our home is situated overlooking Tahunanui Beach, Haulashore Island and Nelson waterfront with
amazing daytime mountain views and magnificent sunsets. Enjoy a wine out on the deck with your
hosts. Excellent restaurants and cafes within walking distance, stroll to beach or a five-minute drive to
the city or World of Wearable Art. Golf course, tennis courts and airport nearby. One hour drive to Abel
Tasman. Both rooms have ensuite/private bathrooms, quality beds, electric blankets, fridge, TV, tea &
coffee making facilities, heaters, iron and hairdryers. Kiwi Host.

Nelson   *B&B 5km S of Nelson*

Cherry Trees Bed and Breakfast
Ann & John Connor
537 Waimea Road, Wakatu, Nelson

Tel (03) 547 3735   Mob 025 266 7579
caz.overton@xtra.co.nz
www.bnb.co.nz/cherrytrees.html

Double $90 (Full Breakfast) Credit cards accepted
1 King 1 Double (2 bdrm)
1 Ensuite 1 Private 1 Guests share

Imagine beautiful sunsets and magnificent views of
Mount Arthur Range and Tasman Bay. Private colourful
garden to enjoy great breakfasts and evening drinks or
just relax. Situated 5 minutes drive to fine restaurants/cafes, Honest Lawyer Pub, Suburban Club, World
of WearableArts and Collectible Cars complex, Tahunanui Beach, Nelson City. In our home you will
find a warm, friendly atmosphere, good comfortable beds, small guest lounge, TV, tea/coffee, hairdryer
etc. Most of all, great hospitality and sensitivity to your needs. Don't imagine,come,relax enjoy.

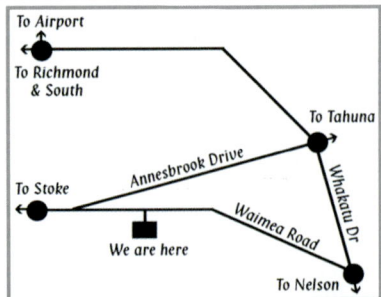

310

Nelson   *Nelson Central*

Peppertree B&B
Richard Savill & Carolyn Sygrove
31 Seymour Ave, Nelson

Tel (03) 546 9881   Fax (03) 546 9881
c.sygrove@clear.net.nz
www.bnb.co.nz/peppertreebb.html

Double $100   Child $15   Dinner $20 by arrangement
each extra adult $30   Credit cards accepted
1 Queen 1 Double 1 Single (1 bdrm)
1 Ensuite

Enjoy space and privacy in our Heritage Villa, only ten minutes riverside walk from Nelson's city centre. The master bedroom has an ensuite bathroom and walk in wardrobe. Your private adjoining rooms include a large lounge with double innersprung sofabed, single bed, log fire, Sky TV, fridge, kettle, toaster etc. and sunroom with cane setting and private entrance. Email/internet/fax facilities and off-street parking available. Children are welcome. We have two daughters aged nine and seven and a friendly cat called Chocolate.

Nelson - Stoke   *B&B 7KM SW of Nelson city centre*

Sakura Bed & Breakfast
Fumio & Sayuri Noguchi
604 Main Road, Stoke, Nelson

Tel (03) 547 0229   Fax (03) 547 0229
Mob 021 547 022
fumio.noguchi@paradise.net.nz
www.sakura-nelson.co.nz

Double $140   Single $75   (Full Breakfast)   Child $20
Children welcome
1 King 4 Single (3 bdrm)
1 Ensuite 1 Host share

We offer delicious Japanese Breakfast (We are friendly Japanese hosts). Also we serve cooked breakfast with Muffins & Scones (just baked). The choice is yours. Only 5 minutes drive from Nelson Airport and 10 minutes from Nelson city centre. Modern, sunny and comfortable house with peaceful garden area. Situated in a quiet cul-de-sac off the Main Road. Complimentary Japanese Green Tea, coffee, tea, biscuits, fruits at all times. Complimentary transport from Airport and Central Nelson.

Nelson - Tahunanui   *B&B Self-contained 8km W of Nelson*

Parkside Bed & Breakfast
Diane & Brent Williams
16 Centennial Road, Tahunanui, Nelson

Tel (03) 548 6629   0800 548 662   Fax (03) 548 6621
Mob 021 548 663
parkside.nelson@xtra.co.nz
www.bnb.co.nz/parkside.html

Double $95-$130   Single $75-$110   (Continental
Breakfast)   Credit cards accepted   Children welcome
1 King 4 Queen 2 Single (4 bdrm)
3 Ensuite 1 Private

Welcome to our friendly atmosphere at Parkside. In our separate large modern bedrooms and guest lounge there are TV, fridge, tea/coffee facilities. Close to restaurants, golf course, sporting grounds, beach and airport. Shopping from Nelson City is only eight minutes drive. Enjoy a deluxe breakfast and a stroll in our garden. All rooms have quality fittings for your comfort. You can be sure of a warm friendly stay in our smoke free home with our two daughters aged 16 and 8 and friendly cat Mickey.

Nelson *B&B Separate/Suite 0.5km Nelson*

Grampian Villa
John & Jo Fitzwater
209 Collingwood St, Nelson, Nelson

Tel (03) 545 8209 Fax (03) 548 5783
Mob 021 459736 (Jo) or 021 969 071 (John)
Jo@GrampianVilla.co.nz
www.GrampianVilla.co.nz

Double $150-$295 Single $150-$280
(Continental Full Special Breakfast) Child POA
Credit cards accepted
1 SuperKing/Twin 2 SuperKing 1 Queen (4 bdrm)

Located in the mature tree-lined streets on the lower
slopes of The Grampians, overlooking Nelson City,
historic 115 year old Grampian Villa is a pleasant 5
minute walk to Nelson's City Centre.
Four spacious ensuited rooms (3 SuperKing, 1 Queen
with clawfoot bath and shower) each have French
doors opening onto the spacious verandahs with views
of Nelson City and the sea.
Facilities: • Spacious tiled showers with heated floors
and large heated towel rails • Wireless DSL Internet
access • Writing desk in all rooms • Fax and computer
available. • Toiletries, robes and hairdryer in all bathrooms • Heated tile flooring in tiled bathrooms •
Clawfoot baths in some suites • Quality Sheridan linen in all rooms • TV, DVD, In-House movies etc.
available in all bedrooms • Complimentary tea/coffee, port, local chocolates, cookies • Enjoy a Latte or
gourmet coffee from our professional espresso coffee machine • Gourmet cooked and continental breakfast
• Off road under cover parking. • TV, VCR, CD, DVD, Stereo and SKY available in Lounge • Central
heating for your comfort • We regret we cannot accommodate children under the age of twelve years.

Spacious verandahs with views of city and sea

Nelson *B&B Central*

Mikonui
Elizabeth Osborne
7 Grove Street, Nelson

Tel (03) 548 3623 0800 4 MIKONUI
bess.osborne@xtra.co.nz
www.bnb.co.nz/mikonui.html

Double $100 Single $70 (Full Breakfast)
1 Queen 1 Double 1 Twin (3 bdrm)
3 Ensuite

100 metres from the Visitor Information Centre in the heart of Nelson City is the Mikonui. This delightful family home, built in the 1920's features a lovely rimu staircase which leads to three tastefully appointed guest rooms all with ensuites. A short stroll to restaurants, cafes, the cinema and the beautiful Queens Gardens. Nelson, gateway to the Abel Tasman National Park and home to the World of Wearable Art. Come and enjoy this wonderful region, you won't be disappointed.

Nelson *Self-contained Nelson*

The Little Manor
Angela Higgins
12 Nile St West, Nelson

Tel (03) 545 1411 Fax (03) 545 1417
Mob 021 247 1891 the.little.manor@xtra.co.nz
www.bnb.co.nz/thelittlemanor.html

Double $195-$240 Single $185 (Full Breakfast)
Child $15 Children welcome
1 King/Twin 1 Double (2 bdrm)
1 Private

Fully self-contained in historic inner city. This two storey uniquely designed cottage dates back to the 1860s. The ambience is quiet and tranquil with antiques throughout, open fire, claw foot bath with luxury comforts of today. Its quaintness unfolds with many rooms including upstairs spacious reading room, two bedrooms and deck. Front and back couryard. Moments away from art and pottery galleries, award winning restaurants, cafes, gardens and shopping district. Generous pantry of condiments and breakfast basket of bread, croissants, eggs, fresh fruit and much more.

Nelson Central *B&B Central*

About Time B&B
Martina Utz & Toby Pugno
13 Wainui Street, Nelson

Tel (03) 546 7841 Fax (03) 546 7841
aboutime@ihug.co.nz
www.bnb.co.nz/user64.html

Double $95-$115 Single $75
1 King/Twin 1 Queen 1 Single (3 bdrm)
2 Ensuite 1 Host share

About Time B&B is a beautifully restored character villa. It's situated within walking distance to award-winning restaurants, cafes and many tourist attractions. We are a Swiss/Italian couple recently moved to New Zealand, much travelled and enjoy meeting people. Our home combines charm with modern facilities and offers a warm, friendly relaxed atmosphere. Relax in our cosy guest lounge or large, sunny veranda. Pleasantly decorated rooms feature quality beds and bedding. Free tea and coffee are available at all times. We have two Weimaraner dogs which are people-friendly. No children under 12.

Nelson *B&B 4.5km S of Nelson*

Annesbrook House
Kath and Tony Charlton
201 Annesbrook Drive, Tahunanui, Nelson

Tel (03) 548 5868 Fax (03) 548 5802
tony.kath@paradise.net.nz
www.bnb.co.nz/annesbrook.html

Double $75-$90 Single $65
(Continental Breakfast)
1 Queen 1 Double (2 bdrm)
2 Ensuite 1 Host share

Drive up our private drive from Highway 6 to our peaceful home in a quiet sunny bush setting, with lovely views of the sea and mountains. Each bedsit has its own separate entrance, safe parking (some covered), ensuite, TV, fridge, electric blanket, hairdryer, heating, table and chairs, T+T facilities, microwave. Telephone available. We can book you in to many of the area's tourist attractions including boat trips and walks in the Abel Tasman National Park. We are centrally situated near Tahuna Beach, golf, airport, clubs, restaurants. Look for the lime green letterbox.

Nelson *B&B Self-contained 7km SW of Nelson*

Ariki Lodge
Sylvie & Herve Laparra de Salgues
3 Ardilea Ave, Stoke, Nelson

Tel (03) 547 3900 Fax (03) 547 6751
sylvie@arikilodge.net.nz
arikilodge.net.nz

Double $180 Single $140 (Special Breakfast)
Dinner $45 Cottage $200
2 King 1 Queen 1 Twin (4 bdrm)
3 Ensuite

Ariki Lodge is a unique house built in schist-rock with native rimu panelled ceilings. Artist's residence, pleasant, private, quiet and sunny. We invite you to enjoy our comfortable and charming full self-contained cottage or luxurious, independent, ground floor ensuite rooms furnished with super king beds - gardens, barbecue, terraces, conservatory, spa-pool, private off-street parking. French cuisine is a speciality: scrumptious breakfasts, lunches, evening meals. Visit Herve's Studio Gallery, palette-knife oil paintings and watercolours. No pets - children by arrangement.

Nelson *B&B Historic Bed & Breakfast Hotel 500m E of Nelson Central*

Sussex House Bed & Breakfast
Val & Wayne Ballantyne
238 Bridge Street, Nelson
Tel (03) 548 9972   0800 868 687   Fax (03) 548 9975
Mob 027 447 4186
reservations@sussex.co.nz   www.sussex.co.nz

Double $120-$150 Single $100-$130
(Continental Breakfast) Credit cards accepted
5 Queen 3 Twin 3 Single (5 bdrm) Separate/Suite
4 Ensuite 1 Private

Experience the peace and charm of yesteryear in our fully
restored c1880's B&B, one of Nelson's original family
homes. Situated beside the beautiful Maitai River, Sussex
House has retained all the original character and romantic
ambience of the era.
It is only minutes walk from central Nelson's award
winning restaurants and cafes, the Queens Gardens, Suter
Art Gallery and Botanical Hill (The Centre Of NZ) and
many good walks, river and bush.
The five sunny bedrooms all have TV's and are spacious
and charmingly furnished. All rooms have access to the
verandahs and complimentary tea & coffee facilities are
provided.

Breakfast includes lots of fresh and preserved fruits, homemade muffins baked fresh every morning, hot
croissants, homemade yoghurts, cheeses and a large variety of cereals, bagels, rolls, breads and crumpets.
Sussex House provides a smoke free environment and all foods, to the best of our knowledge, are free
from genetically modified ingredients. We regret that we are not suited to children. Other facilities
include: Wheelchair suite; Email/Internet station; fax; courtesy phone; laundry facilities; separate lounge
for guest entertaining; complimentary port; tea & coffee facilities; very sociable cat (Riley); bread to
feed the ducks.

Nelson *B&B*

Lamont B&B
Pam & Rex Lucas
167a Tahunanui Drive, Nelson,
Tel 03 548 5551   Fax 03 548 5501   Mob 025 351 678
rexpam@xtra.co.nz
www.bnb.co.nz/lamont.html
Double $90 Single $65 (Full Breakfast) Child B/A
Dinner $30 Children welcome
1 Queen 1 Double (2 bdrm)
1 Private

We are in a position to offer high standard accommodation
having two double-bed rooms with own toilet and bathroom facilities. Our house is on a private property
in Tahunanui Drive opposite the Nelson Surburban Club where it is possible to get an evening meal
every night except Monday. A two minute drive to Tahuna Beach and five minutes to a number of
waterfront restaurants gives plenty of variety and choice. We look forward to discussing your
accommodation requirements with you. 'Kiri' is the much loved family cat.

Nelson *B&B 500m S of Nelson central*

Haven Guesthouse B&B
Kathy Perkins
89 Haven Road, Nelson
Tel (03) 545 9321   0800 446 783   Fax (03) 545 9320
havengh@xtra.co.nz
www.havenguesthouse.co.nz
Double $89-$160 Single $75-$90 (Continental
Breakfast) Child $10 Children welcome
Family Room 1 King & Single   2 King   4 Queen
1 King twin 1 Twin (9 bdrm)
9 Ensuite

Recent extensive renovations to the Haven Guest House, one of Nelson's oldest homes, now provides
9 bedrooms all with en-suite TV & phone. Originally built circa 1860 for the first collector of customs,
it is situated opposite the Wearable Arts venue, just a 5 minute walk to town and a 5 minute drive to the
beach. A delicious continental breakfast is served and tea/coffee making facilities are available in the
dining room. Internet/fax/laundry facilities are also available.

Nelson - Howard Valley *B&B Farmstay 21km W of St Arnaud*

Whareatea Farmstay
Beavan and Honora Undrill
Howard Valley, RD 2, Nelson
Tel (03) 521 1135   Fax (03) 521 1136
Mob 021 463 925
info@whareatea.co.nz
www.whareatea.co.nz
Double $110 Single $55 (Continental Breakfast)
(Full Breakfast) Dinner $30 per person
1 Double (1 bdrm)
1 Private

Whareatea Farmstay offers you peace and relaxation in
the mountains. 100 acres of alpine meadow with bush walks and waterfalls, gold panning, trout fishing
nearby. Craft studio on property. Large modern home, outdoor spa available at no extra charge. Your
comfort and enjoyment is our aim. Household pets include a dog, cat and rainbow lorikeet. Not suitable
for children under 12.

Nelson Central   *B&B 400m NE of Nelson Central*

Grove Villa
Gerry & Christine
36 Grove Street, Nelson

Tel (03) 548 8895   0800 488 900
Fax (03) 548 8856   gerry@grovevilla.co.nz
www.grovevilla.co.nz

Double $85-$140 Single $70-$115
(Continental Breakfast) Credit cards accepted
Children welcome
1 King/Twin 2 Queen 1 Double 2 Twin 2 Single
(6 bdrm)
3 Ensuite 1 Private 1 Guests share

Welcome to Grove Villa, our character Victorian home, furnished for comfort in period style. Our relaxed hospitality, with its emphasis on personal service, aims to enhance your enjoyment of this beautiful city. Delicious breakfasts feature homemade breads, muffins and jams, with freshly made yoghurt and fresh fruit salads using local produce.
Grove Villa is ideally situated just five minutes' walk from the heart of Nelson and its many attractions. Intercity bus routes can drop you at our door. We will be happy to share our knowledge of the area to help you to plan your activities or to select from Nelson's excellent range of restaurants. You can begin your Abel Tasman National Park excursions with pick-ups from our door.

- 100 year-old villa with period furnishings
- Sunny verandahs and courtyard
- Delicious homemade breakfasts
- Baggage storage available
- Comfortable rooms with ensuite, private or shared bathrooms
- Pick up and drop-off point for Abel Tasman National Park and other tours
- Knowledgeable advice on local attractions
- All day refreshments
- Five-minute walk to city centre

Nelson *B&B 7 km N of Nelson*

Avonbank Homestay
Dale & Clive Cook
3 Seaton Street, Marybank, Nelson

Tel 03 5450056   Fax 03 5450056   Mob 025 200 2530
clivecook@ts.co.nz
www.bnb.co.nz/avonbank.html

Double $80 Single $55 (Continental Breakfast)
Child $25 Dinner $20 by arrangement Children welcome
1 King/Twin 1 Queen (2 bdrm)
1 Host Share

Welcome to our sunny non-smoking home.   We are only five minutes from Central Nelson on the Blenheim side.   Relax in our spa pool and enjoy spectacular sunsets across Tasman Bay or read from our many books. We have travelled extensively both overseas and in New Zealand and enjoy sharing our special area of Nelson with others.   Children are welcome.   Electric blankets on beds.   Off street parking. Bus at gate. Laundry facilities available. Quiet safe neighbourhood. Taz, our cat, will welcome you with rolly pollys.

Nelson Central *B&B Homestay 3mins Nelson Central*

Trafalgar Square
Janine Fisher & Dennis Shacklady
368A Trafalgar Square, Nelson,

Tel 03 54 66659 Homestay-Nelson@xtra.co.nz
www.homestay-nelson.co.nz

Double $90 (Full Breakfast)
2 Queen (2 bdrm)
2 Ensuite

Nestled alongside the Nelson Cathedral in a quiet cul-de-sac, our classic 1932 home offers you a relaxed atmosphere only minutes walking distance to central city shopping, restaurants and other attractions. Off street parking is provided. Our two comfortable guest rooms feature queen sized beds, en-suite bathrooms, couch and television. Your choice of breakfast, continental or cooked, using fresh local produce where possible. At Trafalgar Square we offer you a warm welcome to our home, which is non-smoking.

Nelson Central *B&B Self-contained Cottage 400m S of Town*

The Garden Cottage
Randi Westphal
194 Collingwood Street, Nelson,

Tel (03) 547 3762   Fax (03) 547 3762
Mob 027 824 9911   info@gardencottage.co.nz
www.gardencottage.co.nz

Double $140 Single $110 Child $20 10% discount
for stays over 6 days 3rd child free Children welcome
1 Queen 2 Twin 1 Single (2 bdrm)
1 Private

Experience the best Nelson has to offer! Only a 5-minute stroll to Nelson's city centre, your private hideaway is fully fitted out as a home with full kitchen, washer/dryer, refrigerator, microwave, bath, shower, TV, VCR, stereo, quality beds and linen, clock radios, hair dryer, library, and comfortable period furniture. A sunny deck with patio furniture is hidden behind trees and flowers. Located on a beautiful, safe, tree-lined street uptown from the cathedral, this beautifully refurbished cottage is perfect for couples or families!

Nelson *B&B Nelson Central*

Lyell House B & B
Sue Mangos
6 Collingwood Street, Nelson,
Tel (03) 548 9290   0800 89 47 83   Fax (03) 548 9296
Mob 027 448 6373   info@LyellHouse.co.nz
www.LyellHouse.co.nz
Double $80-$175   Single $70-$160   (Continental
Breakfast)
1 King 1 Queen 1 Twin 1 Single (3 bdrm)
1 Ensuite

"Home Away From Home", we're easily found, 5 minutes walk to Nelson City and Restaurants, perfect for guests with/without their own transport. Separate guest access, locks on all rooms. Free "Anytime" tea/coffee. Filtered drinking water, Air Filtration System. Guest Comments: "Friendly, Sunny, Warm, Clean, Fresh, Great showers, Comfy beds, Quiet, Relaxing, Love the colours, Beautiful gardens, Feel safe..." Sorry, not suitable pets or young children. Off street parking. Relax in your room or join us in our family lounge - wonderfully comfy recliners!

Nelson - Central *Self-contained 500m S of Nelson Central*

Kowhai Cottage
Marion & Andrew
272 Rutherford Street, Nelson,
Tel (03) 548 1272   Mob 025 400 216
marion@kowhaicottage.co.nz
www.kowhaicottage.co.nz
Double $110   Single $90 (Continental Breakfast)
Child $25 Children welcome
1 King 1 Double (1 bdrm)   1 Private

Come and enjoy our well-presented character accommodation located in the premier residential area of Nelson. Our delightful 1930's bungalow is situated in

a quiet street, ten minutes walk from the heart of the city, yet right on the doorstep of fabulous walking tracks, parks and historic houses. Our warm and comfortable self-contained area has a double king bedroom, attractive sun room with comfortable double sofa bed, private bathroom and elegantly appointed private lounge, kitchen facilities and secure garage parking. Cat and one child in residence.

Richmond *Homestay 0.5km E of Richmond*

Hunterville
Cecile & Alan Strang
30 Hunter Avenue, Richmond, Nelson
Tel (03) 544 5852   0800 372 220   Fax (03) 544 5852
strangsa@clear.net.nz.
www.bnb.co.nz/hunterville.html
Double $100   Single $60 (Full Breakfast)
Child 1/2 price Dinner $20 B/A Children welcome
1 King 1 Twin 1 Single (3 bdrm)
1 Private 1 Host share   Pets welcome

A welcome with complimentary drinks poolside in summer, fireside in winter awaits you when you stay in our peaceful home where birdsongs greet you from surrounding bush. We are on the route to Golden Bay, Abel Tasman Park Region but just 15 minutes from Nelson. We travel frequently overseas so appreciate travellers' needs. With firm comfortable beds, good laundry, dinner with local food, wine, and with travellers tales your stay with us will be memorable. Our other interests are music, reading, bridge and 'Coco', Dalmation, and 'Waldo' - both very friendly dogs.

Richmond *Homestay 0.5km E of Richmond*

Anderson Homestay
Jean & Jack Anderson
46 Rochfort Drive, Richmond, Nelson
Tel (03) 544 2175   Fax (03) 544 2175
Mob 0274 440 530
www.bnb.co.nz/andersonhomestay.html
Double $60 Single $35 (Full Breakfast) Child $15
Dinner $12.50 Credit cards accepted
1 Double 2 Single (2 bdrm)
1 Guests share

We are a couple who like meeting people. Near by are lovely gardens, crafts, such as Pottery, Glass Blowing, Dried Flowers and Wood Turning. Beaches at Tahuna and Rabbit Island are only 10 minutes away by car. We are situated in an area very central for travellers going South, North or to Golden Bay and Tasman area. Buses and planes met. Enjoy Kiwi hospitality in Richmond. Directions: Above round-about in Queen Street turn into Wasbourn Drive, Farnham Drive and Rochfort Drive.

Richmond *B&B Homestay Country Homestay B&B 2km S of Richmond*

Nicholls Country Homestay B&B
Alison & Murray Nicholls
87 Main Road, Hope, Nelson
Tel (03) 544 8026   Fax (03) 544 8026
m_a.nicholls@xtra.co.nz
www.bnb.co.nz/nicholls.html
Double $80 Single $40 (Full Breakfast) Child $25
Dinner $12.50 Children welcome
1 Queen 1 Double 2 Single (3 bdrm)
1 Guests share 1 Host share

We are situated on a kiwifruit orchard on State Highway 6, 2km south of Richmond. A lengthy driveway ensures quiet surroundings in a lovely garden setting, with a pool. We are centrally situated, placing Nelson's many attractions within easy reach. We will happily provide information about these and make arrangements as required. Complimentary tea or coffee is offered to guests upon arrival and dinner may be provided by arrangement. A phonecall before arrival would be appreciated. Ours is a non smoking home.

Richmond *B&B Homestay Self-contained 10km W of Nelson*

Chester Le House
Noelene & Michael Smith
39 Washbourn Drive, Richmond, Nelson
Tel (03) 544 7279   Fax (03) 544 7279
Mob 025 213 5335 n.smith@xtra.co.nz
www.bnb.co.nz/chesterlehouse.html
Double $85 Single $50 (Full Breakfast)
Dinner $25 by arrangement Flat $90
Credit cards accepted
1 Double 4 Single (3 bdrm)
1 Ensuite 1 Guests share 1 Host share

We live in a fantastic part of New Zealand in a lovely modern home that we enjoy sharing with many people. Lovely views and all the comforts of home await you. Two twin rooms and queen suite with ensuite available. Lock your car in our garage and enjoy a barbecue or evening meal with us. Laundry and drier available. Pick up from terminals available. Only 10 minutes from Nelson city, Richmond is close to wineries and a scenic 40 minutes drive to Abel Tasman National Park.

Richmond *B&B Self-contained 10km S of Nelson*

Bay View
Janice & Ray O'Loughlin
37 Kihilla Road, Richmond
Tel (03) 544 6541   Fax (03) 544 6541
Mob 025 623 0252
bayview@ts.co.nz
www.bnb.co.nz/bayviewrichmond.html

Double $80-$100 Single $65 (Full Breakfast)
Dinner by arrangement Credit cards accepted
2 Queen 1 Twin (3 bdrm)
1 Ensuite 1 Guests share

Bayview is a modern, spacious home built on the hills
above Richmond township, with spectacular views of
Tasman Bay and mountain ranges.
We offer rooms that are quiet, private and
immaculately furnished with your complete comfort
in mind. A large guest bathroom has shower and spa
bath. The lounge opens onto a sheltered deck where
you can relax, enjoy a drink or sit and chat. The self-
contained suite with private entrance, off-street
parking, kitchen, bathroom/laundry, lounge area and
Queen bed offers privacy and all home comforts.
We have two miniature Schnauzer dogs, a variety of
birds in a large aviary, tend our colourful garden and
enjoy meeting people from new Zealand and overseas.
By car Bayview is 15 minutes from Nelson, 2 minutes
from Richmond and award-winning restaurants, close
to National parks, beaches, vineyards and crafts. Be
assured of warm, friendly hospitality and a happy stay
in our smokefree home.

By car Bayview is 15 minutes from Nelson, 2 minutes from Richmond

Richmond *B&B Guesthouse 1km E of Richmond*

Antiquarian Guest House
Robert & Joanne Such
12A Surrey Road, Richmond, Nelson

Tel (03) 544 0253 Fax (03) 544 0253
Mob 025 417 504 souchjoanne@hotmail.com
www.bnb.co.nz/antiquarian.html

Double $95 Single $75 (Full Breakfast)
Credit cards accepted Children welcome Pets welcome
1 King 1 Queen 1 Twin (3 bdrm)
1 Ensuite 1 Guests share

Bob and Joanne Such welcome you to their peaceful home only 2 minutes from Richmond (15 minutes drive south of Nelson) - excellent base for exploring National Parks, beaches, arts/crafts, skifields etc. Relax in the garden, beside the swimming pool or in our large TV/Guest lounge. Tea/coffee facilities, home baking and memorable breakfasts. Our family pet is Gemma (friendly border collie). As local antique shop owners we know the area well.

Richmond *B&B Homestay 12km SW of Nelson*

Idesia
Jenny & Barry McKee
14 Idesia Grove, Richmond, Nelson

Tel (03) 544 0409 0800 361 845 Fax (03) 544 0402
Mob 025 604 0869
idesian@xtra.co.nz
www.idesia.co.nz

Double $85-$105 (Full Breakfast)
Dinner $30 by arrangement Credit cards accepted
1 King/Twin 1 Queen 1 Twin (3 bdrm)
1 Ensuite 1 Private

A warm welcome to our home centrally located to explore the Nelson/Tasman region. 2km from Highway 6, in a quiet grove neighbouring the country. Our modern house is elevated to catch the sun and views. For your comfort the bedrooms, recently furnished, have superior beds. Breakfast includes a continental selection and/or a cooked breakfast. Join us for dinner, by prior arrangement, and relax with us in the lounge over coffee. Our aim is to provide a home away from home and to offer tasty meals.

Richmond *B&B Self-contained 6km N of Richmond*

Best Island Retreat
Chris & Lynn Hawkins
Best Island, RD 1 Richmond, Nelson

Tel (03) 544 9985 Fax (03) 544 9985
Mob 025 470 242 feedback@clear.net.nz
bestislandretreat.com

Double $160 Single $120 (Continental Breakfast)
1 Queen (1 bdrm)
1 Ensuite 1 Private

Nestled on the banks of the Waimea estuary, absolute waterfront, no road noise. Luxury for two only, enjoy the peace and quiet of the area, use our kayaks to explore the estuary. Only six minutes from some of the finest wineries and cafes in the district. A golf course is on the island. Fishing for flounder and snapper is improving in the area. Central to all of the beautiful areas around Nelson and Richmond. And our two Bichons Basil and Claud will always be pleased to see you.

Brightwater *Farmstay 17km S of Nelson*

Teapot Valley Farmstay & Vineyard
Liz & Roy Brown
Bell Road, Teapot Valley, Brightwater, Nelson

Tel (03) 542 3570 Fax (03) 542 3570 rcb@clear.net.nz
www.bnb.co.nz/teapotfarmstayvineyard.html

Double $95 Single $75 (Full Breakfast) Dinner B/A
Credit cards accepted   Pets welcome   Horse facilities
1 Queen (1 bdrm)
1 Guests share 1 Host share

Welcome to our 20 acre mini-farm and pinot-noir
vineyard. We are 20 minutes drive south of Nelson, centrally sited to the region's many attractions and
only 10 minutes drive to the nearest cafe, bars and restaurants. Experience the feeling of tranquility that
surrounds our comfortable home. Meet our friendly pets which include a NZ wild pony, wild sheep and
be entertained by our two little Belgium Barge dogs. Go fo a magic beach ride on our special horse
Rocco. Enjoy a farm style or continental breakfast. Smoke free home, we look forward to meeting you.

Thorpe *Homestay Rural Homestay 55km W of Nelson*

Rerenga Farm
Robert & Joan Panzer
Dovedale Road, Thorpe, Nelson

Tel (03) 543 3825 Fax (03) 543 3640
Mob 025 243 1284 Robert@Customtours.co.nz
www.customtours.co.nz

Double $95 Single $75 (Full Breakfast)
(Special Breakfast) Dinner $30 Credit cards accepted
Children welcome
1 Queen (1 bdrm)
1 Ensuite

You are offered a peaceful, rural retreat with international hosts (Dutch and North American). Our two
children are real 'Kiwis'. The homestead is surrounded by rolling hills, forests and situated along the
Dove River. We have a variety of trees, chickens, pigs, sheep, and an outdoor cat and dog. Note: our
main business is 'Tailored Travel', personalized New Zealand Custom Tours (2-4 pax), tailored to your
specific requirements and dates.

Mapua *Self-contained Country Accomodation 10km N of Richmond*

Atholwood Country Accommodation
Robyn & Grahame Williams
Bronte Road East, off Coastal Highway 60, near Mapua

Tel (03) 540 2925 Fax (03) 540 3258
Mob 025 310 309 atholwood@xtra.co.nz
www.atholwood.co.nz

Double $150-$170 Single $120-$150
(Special Breakfast) Child by arrangement
Dinner $40 by arrangement Self contained $200
Credit cards accepted Children welcome
1 King/Twin 2 Queen 3 Single (3 bdrm)
3 Ensuite

Beauty, Seclusion and Tranquillity. We welcome you to share our home situated on the shores of the
Waimea Inlet with 2 acres of garden and bush. The guest wing is upstairs within the main house and has
two rooms, each with ensuites and a guest lounge. "The Gatehouse" is self-contained with full amenities,
opening out to a private terrace. Start your day with a special breakfast and to finish - award-winning
Restaurants are close by in Mapua. Our beautiful cat "Carlos" completes the family.

Mapua Village *B&B Homestay 30km W of Nelson*

Mapua Seaview B&B
Murray & Diana Brown
40 Langford Drive, Mapua Village, Nelson
Tel (03) 540 2006 Fax (03) 540 2036
Mob 025 839 634
seaview@mapua.co.nz   www.mapua.co.nz

Double $95-$110
Choice of cooked and continental breakfast
Credit cards accepted
2 Queen (2 bdrm)
2 Ensuite

Seaview B&B is nestled overlooking the delightful seaside village of 'Port Mapua' on the shores of Tasman Bay.Great views of the 'Waimea Estuary' and Mountains (see our photo).
Observe also the busy daily spectacle of migratory bird life. Swimming beaches and walking trails, plus a choice of water-front cafe's and restaurants all within a few minutes walking distance from "Seaview" Bed and Breakfast. We are central to districts Vineyards and Craft studios and only a 25 min scenic drive to Kaiteriteri and the "Able Tasman" Park, now famous worldwide for walking trails and golden sandy beaches. We strive to offer a homely and relaxed peaceful atmosphere, with our home being on a elevated garden setting location that offers fantastic view's. Comfortable (queen-size) beds, private bathrooms, TV etc.

Relaxed peaceful atmosphere

324

Mapua   *B&B Self-contained 4km S of Mapua*

Kimeret Place Boutique B&B
Clare & Peter Jones
Bronte Road East (off SH60), RD 1, Upper Moutere,
Nelson

Tel (03) 540 2727   Fax (03) 540 2726
stay@kimeretplace.co.nz   www.kimeretplace.co.nz

Double $155-$185 Single $115-$145 (Special Breakfast)
Child $5 - $20 Cottage - 2 bdr $220 - $290
Credit cards accepted Children welcome
3 King/Twin 1 Queen (4 bdrm)   4 Ensuite

A tranquil setting in the heart of the wine & craft region: with stunning views, heated pool & spa. Just 4km to award-winning restaurants and 30 minutes from the Abel Tasman National Park. A range of accommodation: all with ensuite facilities, TV, Hi-fi, video/DVD, tea/coffee, fridge, sitting area and views from either balcony or deck. The self-contained accommodation also has a kitchenette and dining area. Light meals, local wines, laundry facilities and Internet are also available. Dog-lovers may wish to meet our two friendly Labradors.

Ruby Bay   *B&B 20km W of Nelson*

Broadsea B&B
Rae & John Robinson
42 Broadsea Avenue, Ruby Bay, Nelson

Tel (03) 540 3511 Fax (03) 540 3511
www.bnb.co.nz/broadseabb.html

Double $110 Single $90 (Continental Breakfast)
(Full Breakfast) Child not suitable
1 Queen (1 bdrm)
1 Ensuite 1 Private

Beach front accommodation, double room with own bathroom and toilet. Lovely walks on beach and reserve, cafes, Tavern, wineries, restaurants, in close vicinity. Fifteen minutes from Richmond & Motueka. Beaches, Rabbit Island, Kaiteriteri, Tahuna in close proximity. Near gateway to Abel Tasman National Park. Plenty of places to see, or 2 minutes to the beach with no maddening crowds. We want guests to feel at home and have their privacy. A continental and full cooked breakfast is served, and cups of coffee, tea and biscuits available. Birman cat and Labrador Sally will greet you outside.

Ruby Bay   *B&B 16km S of Motueka*

Tasman View
Gerald B & Jenny E Allsopp
106 Brabant Drive, Pine Hill Heights, Ruby Bay,
Mapua 7155

Tel (03) 540 2966 Fax (03) 540 2965
Mob 027 439 0041 jg.allsopp@xtra.co.nz
www.tasmanview.co.nz

Double $175 Single $150 (Full Breakfast) Queen $110
2 King/Twin 1 Queen (3 bdrm)
2 Private

Extensive views of Tasman Bay from our new Mediterranean/Kiwi style home. Peaceful surroundings with native bush walks in adjoining reserve. Upstairs private wing. Take in the atmosphere while enjoying a meal or coffee at the excellent restaurants and patisserie/cafe at nearby Mapua village. 15 minutes to Motueka or Richmond, 30 minutes to Nelson or Marahau, gateway to Abel Tasman National Park. Transport by arrangement. Our spoilt Burmese cats have their own quarters but on request will be happy to socialise. Check out our website for further details.

Ruby Bay *B&B 32km W of Nelson*

Sandstone House
John and Jenny Marchbanks
30 Korepo Rd, Ruby Bay, Nelson
Tel (03) 540 3251   Fax (03) 540 3251
Mob 025 246 0444
sandstone@rubybay.net.nz
www.rubybay.net.nz
Double $190 Single $170 (Full Breakfast)
2 Queen (2 bdrm)
2 Ensuite

Welcome to Sandstone House - we enjoy a maritime and
semi-rural situation, ideally situated midway between Nelson and Motueka. We are handy to all the fine
attractions that this region has to offer - National Parks, wineries, award winning restaurants, beaches,
arts and crafts, the famous Mapua Wharf and lots lots more. We are happy to assist you to make the most
of your holiday. Please feel free to relax and enjoy our quality, comfortable facilities.

Tasman - Nelson *B&B Self-contained Boutique B&B 8km S of Motueka*

Aporo Pondsiders
Marian & Mike Day
Permin Road, Tasman, Nelson
Tel (03) 526 6858   Fax (03) 526 6258
Mob 025 240 3757   marian@aporo.co.nz
www.aporo.co.nz
Double $220 (Full Breakfast) Credit cards accepted
4 King/Twin (4 bdrm)
2 Ensuite 2 Guests share

Secluded, peaceful, three stylish yet relaxed spacious
cottages, staggered for privacy, overlooking a large ornamental pond, countryside and mountains. Includes
delicious hamper full breakfast. Two have large sitting/dining room, kitchen galley, king bedroom,
ensuite (one with bath), balcony. The third has two bedrooms, bathroom, full kitchen and balcony.
Centrally situated off Coastal Highway 60, between Nelson/Motueka enabling travellers to explore the
best of the province; Abel Tasman, Kahurangi National Parks, Golden Bay. Beautiful safe swimming
beaches, walks, golf courses, trout rivers, arts, wineries are nearby.

Tasman - Upper Moutere *B&B Self-contained 10mins Mouteka*

Maple Grove
Judy Stratford & George Page
72 Flaxmore Road, RD 2, Upper Moutere, Nelson
Tel (03) 543 2267   Fax (03) 543 2267
Mob 025 623 8631   george1judy@xtra.co.nz
www.maplegrove.co.nz
Double $140-$185 (Continental Full Special Breakfast)
Child Neg Children welcome Pets welcome
1 Queen 1 Double 1 Twin (2 bdrm)   1 Private

Purpose built boutique self contained cottage giving a private hideaway . Enjoy it as your secluded
base in the heart of Nelson countryside. Graced with ambiance and care, a mix of the charm of yesteryear
and the convenience of today. Situated on four acres with pond and large old trees. Not far from many
well known vineyards and cafes. If you’re into tramping you are at the gateway of the Abel
Tasman And Kahurangi National Parks, in fact you can watch the sun go down behind Mt Arthur while
you enjoy your evening wine on the veranda. We have colourful hens, some sheep and calves. Also lots
of bird life. Peace for the soul with the beauty of each season.Just magic Autamn colours and spring
blossoms. Let us make your holiday one to remember.

Motueka Valley *B&B Homestay 28km S of Motueka*

Doone Cottage Country Homestay
Glen & Stan Davenport
2455 Motueka Valley Highway, RD 1, Motueka
Tel (03) 526 8740 Fax (03) 526 8740
Mob 021 258 7389
doone-cottage@xtra.co.nz www.doonecottage.co.nz
Double $130-$175 Single $110-$155 (Full Breakfast)
Dinner by arrangement Credit cards accepted
2 King/Twin 1 Queen (3 bdrm)
3 Ensuite

Overlooking Motueka River Valley and the Mt Arthur range, this charming 130 year old cottage has welcomed homestay guests for over 20 years.
Situated in 4 acres of secluded native trees, ferns and flower gardens on a natural river terrace neighbouring a 1000-acre deer farm, it offers homely hospitality, peace and tranquillity, friendly, helpful, experienced hosts, **very comfortable beds,** full ensuites, all home cooked meals, homemade breads, preserves, homegrown produce, free range eggs, etc. Comfortably furnished cottage style, guest rooms and private garden chalet have extensive garden/valley views. Native birds abound, sheep, chickens, ducks and donkeys. Your hostess spins wool from the raw fleece, her weaving studio offers sweaters, blankets, wall hangings, rugs, etc. which she has produced. A chuckling steam runs through the property, flowing into the Motueka, famous for its **brown trout,** with five more trout streams close by. Guiding & licences available.
Our central location offers **short distances** to excellent day trips/activities in **Abel Tasman, Kahurangi** and **Nelson Lakes National Parks.** Nelson and Golden Bay - mountain and coastal bush walks, wilderness fishing, golf etc. (Bookings handled for cruising, water taxis, kayaking, horse trekking). Award winning wineries, arts and crafts. Or simply relax and soak up the country atmosphere of yesteryear in this special place.

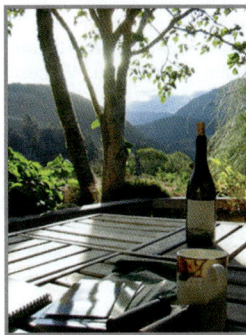

Directions: 45 minutes to Nelson; 2.5 hours to Picton; 3 hours to the West Coast; 5 hours to Christchurch.

Motueka Valley *Farmstay Self-contained 18km S of Motueka*

Mountain View Cottage/Dexter Farmstay
A & V Hall
Waiwhero Road, RD 1, Motueka

Tel (03) 526 8857 ajandvhall@xtra.co.nz
www.bnb.co.nz/mountainviewcottage.html

Double $95 Single $60 (Special Breakfast)
Dinner $25 Cottage $95 Credit cards accepted
1 King/Twin 1 Double (2 bdrm)
1 Ensuite 1 Private

Your hosts Alan and Veronica offer B&B Farmstay and
separate cottage accommodation on our 35 acre organic
property complete with unique Dexter cows and Native Bush Covenanted Area. Perfectly situated for
anglers, close to 3 National Parks and art/craft/garden trails. Mountain View Cottage is completely
self-contained while our homestead offers spacious bedroom with own ensuite, tea/coffee & TV facilities.
Meals are cooked on our wood-fired range and breakfast comprises choice of homemade muesli, bread,
yoghurt, pancakes and organic eggs. Mitzi the cat completes the picture.

Motueka Valley *Homestay 25km S of Motueka*

The Kahurangi Brown Trout
David Davies & Heather Lindsay
Westbank Road, Pokororo, RD 1, Motueka

Tel (03) 526 8736 0800 460 421
enquiries@kbtrout.co.nz
www.kbtrout.co.nz

Double $95-$125 Single $75-$105 (Full Breakfast)
Child $25 Dinner $18 - $35 Credit cards accepted
Children welcome Pets welcome
2 King/Twin 1 Single (2 bdrm)   2 Ensuite

Comments from last season's visitors say it all. "Everything
was wonderful! This was a superb place to stay. The food was
awesome. The beds and shower outstanding! The coffee, atmosphere, gardens and company: wonderful.
What a find late at night. An amazing place and great food; such a peaceful place; wonderful food, fun
and fellowship; great beds! We'll be back. The walk on Mt Arthur was outstanding as were the meals
and gardens. Great blueberries to great beds! Hope to come back some day."

Motueka Valley *Farmstay Self-contained 34km S of Motueka*

River Island Lodge
Carol Mckeever & Alistair Webber
Baton Valley Road, Woodstock, RD 1, Motueka

Tel (03) 543 3844 Fax (03) 543 3802
relax@riverislandlodge.co.nz
www.riverislandlodge.co.nz

Double $140-$180 Single $120 (Continental Breakfast)
Dinner $35 Reduced rates for 2 or more rooms
Credit cards accepted Children welcome
5 Queen 3 Twin (5 bdrm)
5 Ensuite

River Island Lodge offers stylish, self contained accommodation with a relaxed country feel. Fish for
trout, swim in clear river pools, go horse trekking or kayaking or relax and enjoy the remote, rural
atmosphere. Our farming family includes two school age children,farm dogs, horses,cattle and hens.
Prepare your favourite meals in your own well equipped kitchen or have delicious meals prepared for
you. The lodge is ideal for families, groups or individuals. Perfectly located to enjoy Nelson's wine and
craft trails and The Abel Tasman National Park.

Motueka   *B&B 0.5km S of Motueka*

Rosewood
Barbara & Jerry Leary
48 Woodlands Avenue, Motueka

Tel (03) 528 6750   Fax (03) 528 6718
Mob 021 251 0131
Barbara.Leary.Rosewood@xtra.co.nz
accommodation-new-zealand.co.nz/rosewood

Double $90 Single $55 (Full Breakfast)
Child 1/2 price Credit cards accepted
1 Double 2 Single (2 bdrm)
1 Private 1 Host share

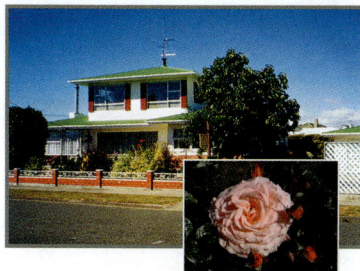

Enjoy a relaxed, friendly, atmosphere in our comfortable spacious home. A 5 minute walk to shops and cafes.   We offer a private lounge for relaxation together with Sky TV. Nearby is the scenic Motueka River with plenty of bountiful trout or a round of golf on the picturesque golf links are local attractions. Interests include golf, fishing, and roses. Barbara is always available to give helpful advice on your day excursions. She also prepares a delicious country-style breakfast. Love to see you as will Jasper our cat.

Motueka   *B&B Homestay 1.4km E of Motueka*

Rebecca & Ian Williams
186 Thorp Street, Motueka

Tel (03) 528 9385   Fax (03) 528 9385
Mob 0274 480 466
B&B@motueka-homestay.co.nz
www.motueka-homestay.co.nz

Double $100 Single $50
(Continental Breakfast) (Full Breakfast)
Child $20 Dinner by arrangement
1 Queen 2 Single (2 bdrm)
2 Ensuite

We only look expensive. We are 1.4 km to Motueka shopping centre and 1.2 km to 18 hole golf course. Each bedroom has own ensuite. The guest lounge has tea and coffee making facilities and fridge. Motueka is the stop-over place for visitors to explore Abel Tasman and Kahurangi National Parks. Golden Bay and Kaiteriteri golden sands beach is 10km away. We have a Jack Russell dog. Visa and M/C.

Motueka   *B&B Separate/Suite Self-contained 1km S of Motueka*

Ashley Troubadour
Coral & John Horton
430 High Street, Motueka

Tel (03) 528 7318   0800 222 046
Fax (03) 528 7318
www.bnb.co.nz/ashleytroubadour.html

Double $75 Single $52 (Continental Breakfast)
Child $10 S/C $85 - $110
Credit cards accepted
2 Queen 2 Double 2 Single (4 bdrm)
2 Ensuite 2 Guests share

Ashley Troubadour used to be a nunnery. Nowadays it is an adventure base for the Abel Tasman National Park and all other outdoor pursuits available in this area. You name it, we've got it and John and Coral Horton, your friendly Ashley Troubadour hosts, will gladly arrange all bookings to make your stay a pleasure. Laundry facilities, security room and ample off-street parking are available for your peace of mind. Our ensuite rooms are near new and fully self contained in quiet garden setting.

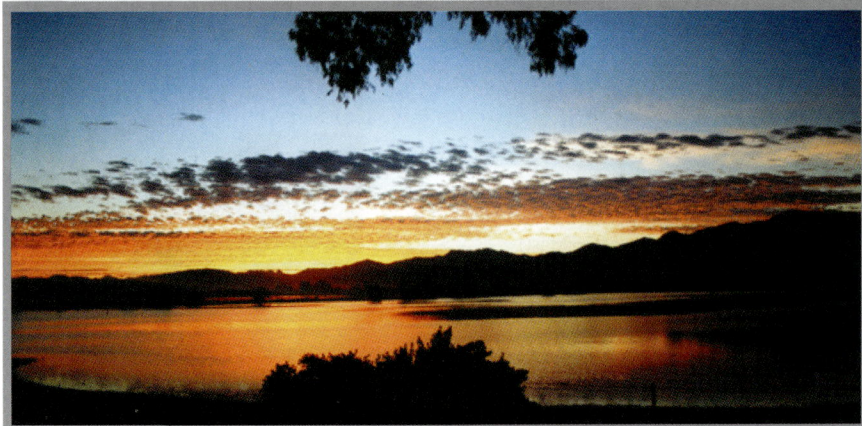

Motueka *B&B Homestay 2km S of Motueka*

Grey Heron - The Italian Organic Homestay
Sandro Lionello & Laura Totis
110 Trewavas Street, Motueka 7161
Tel (03) 528 0472   Fax (03) 528 0472
Mob 021 266 0345
sandro@greyheron.co.nz   www.greyheron.co.nz
Double $85-$110 Single $50-$80
(Full Breakfast) Dinner $30
1 Single-king 3 Queen (4 bdrm)
1 Ensuite 1 Guests share

We are a couple recently moved from the North of Italy to the South of New Zealand, much travelled and keen on tramping and mountaineering.
Our beautiful garden faces the Moutere River Estuary: you will enjoy our breakfast (Continental plus Italian specialities including organic home-made bread and jams) overlooking a super tidal view of the estuary and of the Kahurangi National Park mountain range. You will appreciate our Mediterranean atmosphere in the heart of New Zealand nature, among native trees and lovely singing birds. Depending on the season, you will have the chance to see the spectacular White Herons and Royal Spoonbills feeding in the estuary.
Plan a longer holiday in this Region and **profit** by Sandro's experience in Geology, Outdoor Activities and Italian Language Teaching. **Book** with us:
* 1-day botanical/geological guided walks along the tracks of the surrounding National Parks. For those on a **tight schedule** we have a special half-day walking option in the beautiful Kahurangi National Park. * Rock-climbing lessons by special arrangements. * Italian Language lessons for beginners and advanced.
Our house is close to the beach: you can have a jog or a quiet walk along the Quay, safe wind-surfing and swimming just across the road. The 18 hole golf course is 15 min. walking. The Ensuite bedroom is small and cosy and includes a private driveway and ground-floor entrance.
On request we prepare delicious recipes of our Italian Cuisine, famous all around the world, using fresh herbs from our garden. You can enjoy dinner with us, overlooking wonderful sunsets beyond the mountains. Coffee, tea, laundry facilities. Secure off-street parking. Links with kayaking and trout fishing companies for booking tours. BENVENUTI TUTTI GLI AMICI ITALIANI.

Directions: From Nelson, at the Southern roundabout in High street, turn right towards Port Motueka, then turn left into Trewavas Street. From the West Coast, at the Clock Tower in High Street, go straight and then turn right into Trewavas Street. Look for our sign.

Motueka *B&B 2km S of Motueka*

Estuary
Bonnie & Eric Stretton
543 High St South, Motueka

Tel (03) 528 6391
b.stretton@xtra.co.nz
www.bnb.co.nz/estuary.html

Double $110 Single $90 (Full Breakfast)
1 Queen (1 bdrm)
1 Ensuite

Comfortable, private guestroom with queen size bed,
ensuite, Sky TV, fridge, home comforts and views through olive trees to the estuary. We offer full
breakfast on the balcony overlooking our peaceful garden or at our family dining table. Guests are
welcome to use the swimming pool, laundry and internet facilities. Close to Motueka and happy to
offer advice/make bookings for the many delightful local attractions. One teenager, friendly spaniel
and two kittens complete the family and we have a small craft gallery. Across from the coastal highway
into Motueka, turn left at roundabout.

Motueka *B&B Homestay 52km W of Nelson*

Time Out
Valerie Rae & Ian McLauchlan
41 King Edward Street, Motueka 7161,

Tel (03) 528 4696 0800 005 097
rae.mclauchlan@xtra.co.nz
www.bnb.co.nz/timeout.html

Double $60-$95 Single $45-$85 (Continental Breakfast)
Child upon application   Children welcome
1 Queen 1 Double 2 Twin 3 Single (4 bdrm)
1 Guests share 1 Host share   Credit cards accepted

Character villa c1901. Park-like garden, beautiful trees. The upstairs guest bedrooms are spacious and
quiet with comfortable beds and lovely views of the surrounding mountain ranges. Rooms serviced
daily. Our kitchen, laundry and internet are available for your use. Log fires heat the house during
cooler months. Motueka township is 2kms from the villa. We offer you a friendly home with excellent
service to use as a base whilst you enjoy the many attractions of this region. We have a small dog called
'Rocky'.

Motueka *B&B and Self Contained Apartment 500m E of Motueka*

Golf View Chalet
Kathleen & Neil Holder
20A Teece Drive, Motueka,

Tel (03) 528 8353 info@GolfViewChalet.co.nz
www.GolfViewChalet.co.nz

Double $85-$95 Single $70
(Continental Full Special Breakfast) Child $20
S.C Apartment $95 double $15 extra adult
3 Queen 1 Double 4 Single (4 bdrm)
1 Ensuite 2 Private   Children welcome

Welcome to our sunny home "on 18 hole golf course", beside the sea. Close to restaurants, National
Parks and golden beaches nearby - your choice of the regions attractions. Then sleep well in our
comfortable beds. Generous flexitime breakfast is served in hosts dining room. Breakfast option available
for self-cater apartment (extra). Complimentary laundry, tea, coffee making facilities, guest fridge,
BBQ. Directions: from High Street (main street), State Highway 60, turn into Tudor Street, left Thorp
Street, right Krammer Street, left into Teece Drive.

Takaka Hill - Motueka *B&B Homestay 18km NW of Motueka*

home

Marble Park B&B Countrystay
Evelyn Dalzell
State Highway 60,, Kairuru. Takaka Hill, Motueka

Tel (03) 528 6068   Fax (03) 528 6068
Mob 025 228 0336 marbleparkhs@xtra.co.nz
www.bnb.co.nz/user140.html

Double $120-$140 Single $100 (Full Breakfast)
Child $30 under 12 Dinner B/A 2 course $25pp
Children welcome
2 Queen 1 Twin (3 bdrm)   3 Ensuite

En route to Golden Bay, a few minutes drive from the summit of Marble Mountain (Takaka Hill) Marble Park B&B, Countrystay, is ideally situated to explore the Motueka, Golden Bay areas.Spectacular views, Unique Karst Marble formations.Close to Ngarua Caves featuring skeletal remains of N.Z's extinct Moa. Harwoods Hole, twelfth largest tomo (sinkhole) in the world, and largest in Southern Hemisphere. Trout Fishing nearby.Pets on property. Bark Art. Quotes from guestbook."Beautiful family atmosphere", "Astonishing Place", "We could stay forever".

Riwaka Valley *Self-contained 15km NW of Motueka*

Kaiweka Farm
Reginald & Pauline Dysart
RD 3, Riwaka Valley, Motueka

Tel (03) 528 9267   Fax (03) 528 9267
Mob 025 605 2753
rdysart@xtra.co.nz
www.bnb.co.nz/kaiwekafarm.html

Double $100 Single $85 (Continental Breakfast)
Child $10 Dinner by arrangement Credit cards accepted
1 Double 1 Single (1 bdrm)
1 Private

Kaiweka Farm is situated in the north branch of the Riwaka Valley adjacent to the national park and scenic reserve at the Riwaka River source. We are close to the Abel Tasman National Park, Kaiteriteri Beach and beautiful walks. We offer accommodation in a modern self contained flat. This is truly a unique place to relax away from the bustle of the cities. We have four children and enjoy the company of our dogs and two cats. Smoking outside please.

Kaiteriteri *B&B 9km N of Motueka*

Seaview B&B
Jackie & Tig McNab
259 Riwaka-Kaiteriteri Road, RD 2, Motueka

Tel (03) 528 9341   Fax (03) 528 9341
www.bnb.co.nz/seaviewbb.html

Double $100 Single $85 (Continental Breakfast)
Credit cards accepted
2 Queen (2 bdrm)
1 Guests share

Jackie and Tig welcome you to our peaceful and ideally located coastal property just 5 minutes to Kaiteriteri beach and handy to Abel Tasman and Kahurangi National Parks. Nearby attractions include sea kayaking, water taxi trips, beach and bush walks, golden sands and safe swimming beaches. Set against a large area of private native bush with abundant birdlife we offer panoramic views of Tasman Bay with breathtaking sunrises and sunsets. Large continental breakfast with homemade jams. Guest lounge with tea/coffee making facilities. Bar and restaurant 4 minutes.

Kaiteriteri   *B&B 16km N of Motueka*

@ home NEW ZEALAND

Bayview
Aileen & Tim Rich
Kaiteriteri Heights, RD 2, Motueka

Tel (03) 527 8090   Fax (03) 527 8090
Mob 027 4545 835   book@kaiteriteribandb.co.nz
www.kaiteriteribandb.co.nz

Double $150-$180   (Full Breakfast)
Dinner by arrangement Credit cards accepted
1 King/Twin 1 King 1 Twin (2 bdrm)
2 Ensuite

We welcome you to paradise and real New Zealand hospitality. Kaiteriteri Beach, the gateway to the Abel Tasman National Park with the most beautiful coastline in New Zealand and the sunniest weather.

Here we provide Bed and Breakfast at its very best. Your rooms are large, beautifully furnished with extensive views of the bay. You have a comfortable sitting area, outside terrace, ensuite with heated towel rail and hair dryer, fridge, and tea/coffee making facilities, radio and TV. Laundry, phone, fax and email are available. You are welcome to share our living area, terraces, extensive collection of books, or be as private as you wish.

A full breakfast is served at your convenience, on your terrace or in the dining room. Dinner (fresh New Zealand fish, meat and produce) is available by prior arrangement. There are two restaurants (seasonal) within walking distance and a variety of cafes and hotels within five to 10 minutes drive.

From Bayview enjoy coastal and bush walks, see plenty of bird-life, or relax and swim at one of three beautiful beaches. Stay an extra day and explore the Abel Tasman National Park. We can book your trip by launch, water-taxi or kayak. They all operate from Kaiteriteri Beach. There is excellent trout fishing in the Riwaka River, five minutes away. Visit craft people or wineries; take a day trip over the Takaka Hill to Golden Bay.

Our location is quiet and peaceful. Turn off four kilometres along the Kaiteriteri Road at the blue B&B sign on Cederman Drive corner. Our name is on the gate. Map on homepage.

What our guests say! *"Everything has a touch of class." "Wonderful stay in fabulous home, thanks for hospitality." "Absolutely delightful. Wonderful views and hospitality." "Wonderful place, excellent hospitality, enjoyed our stay and time in Abel Tasman immensely." "Our best stay in every way. Many, many thanks."*

Kaiteriteri *B&B 13km N of Motueka*

Everton B&B
Martin & Diane Everton
Kotare Place, Little Kaiteriteri, RD 2 Motueka

Tel (03) 527 8301   Fax (03) 527 8301
Mob 027 450 5944   everton@xtra.co.nz
www.evertonbandb.co.nz

Double $100 Single $80 (Full Breakfast)
Credit cards accepted
1 Queen 1 Twin (2 bdrm)   1 Guests share

We live 3 minutes walk from the golden sands of Little
Kaiteriteri Beach with wonderful sea views. Full breakfast includes fresh home baked bread or muffins. Our interests include golf, music, travel, walking, conversation and reading. The Abel Tasman National Park starts here where you can kayak, walk and take boat trips. Nearby there are good restaurants, wineries and craft shopping. Trout and sea fishing can be arranged. We are licensed to take you on a personalised trip in our boat if you choose. Email is offered and even a piano to play! We have no pets and are non-smokers, but guests are welcome to smoke outside.

Kaiteriteri *B&B Homestay 15km N of Motueka*

Bellbird Lodge
Anthea & Brian Harvey
Sandy Bay Road, Kaiteriteri, RD2, Motueka

Tel (03) 527 8555   Fax (03) 527 8556
Mob 0256 788 441   stay@bellbirdlodge.com
www.bellbirdlodge.com

Double $140-$175 Single $100-$120
(Special Breakfast) Dinner B/A (May - Sept.)
1 King/Twin 1 Queen 1 Twin (3 bdrm)
1 Ensuite 1 Private

Situated in a tranquil hillside setting with panoramic sea
views, Bellbird Lodge is close to Kaiteriteri Beach and Abel Tasman National Park. The tastefully furnished guest rooms are on the ground floor and have tea/coffee making facilities. Enjoy a buffet breakfast with sumptuous hot course of the day served in the dining room or alfresco on the terrace with its stunning view, accompanied by songs of bellbirds and tuis. Welcome to our modern home where warm, friendly hospitality and quality food and accommodation await you.

Kaiteriteri *Self-contained 13km N of Motueka*

The Haven
Tom & Alison Rowling
Kaiteriteri, RD2, Motueka

Tel (03) 527 8085   Fax (03) 527 8065
thehaven@internet.co.nz
www.thehaven.co.nz

Double $150 extra couple $50
1 King 2 Twin (2 bdrm)
1 Ensuite 1 Private

The Haven - the name says it all. Just the sound of the
waves, bird song, and the occasional haunting cry of the big back back gulls as they soar overhead. A retreat from the stress of everyday life with a nautical theme reflecting Tom's lifetime association with ships and the sea. Self-contained, two bedrooms, the Captain's Cabin with king size bed and ensuite, the Crew's quarters with 2 large single beds and private bathroom. The galley kitchen has generous breakfast provisions and two decks provide outdoor living. Not suitable for small children. We are smokefree.

Kaiteriteri   *15km N of Motueka*

Ngaiomi
Julie & Allan Hunter
Kaiteriteri / Sandy Bay, Motueka RD 2, Nelson

Tel (03) 527 8274   Fax (03) 527 8309
Mob 025 543 009
homes@goldensands.co.nz
www.bnb.co.nz/ngaiomi.html

Double $85-$135 (Continental Breakfast)
1 Queen 1 Double (1 bdrm)
1 Ensuite

Welcome to Ngaiomi. Your private villa set in our garden
has ensuite facilities, kitchenette and TV. You will wake to the song of the Bellbird and Tui. Partake of breakfast on your deck while enjoying the sea views. We are just minutes away from the golden sands of Kaiteriteri Beach and start of the Abel Tasman National Park. This area offers kayaking, bush walks and marvellous boat trips. Top rated wineries, restaurants and craft shopping beckon. Hosts Julie and Allan and cats Middy and Ben.

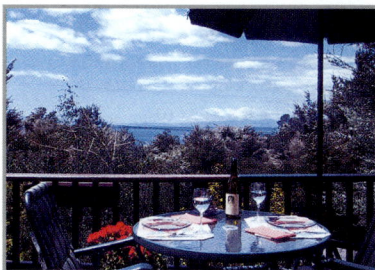

Kaiteriteri   *B&B Self-contained 13km N of Motueka*

Robyn's Nest B & B
Robyn & Mike O'Donnell
1 Rowling Road, Kaiteriteri,

Tel (03) 527 8466   Mob 021 431 735
robynod@ihug.co.nz
www.bnb.co.nz/robynsnestbandb.html

Double $130 Single $100 (Continental Breakfast)
Child neg. Children welcome
1 King/Twin 1 Queen 1 Single (2 bdrm)
2 Ensuite

Welcome to Kaiteriteri, Robyn's Nest offers warm hospitality in an ideal situation. Two minutes walk to beaches, around the corner to Abel Tasman National Park, 30min drive to Kahurangi National Park, 1hr drive to Nelson, Golden Bay or Nelson Lakes National Park. One self contained studio unit with Queen and single pull-out, plus King/Twin with ensuite. Both have private entry, off street parking. Continental breakfast includes homemade muesli and preserves. Children welcome. We look forward to hosting you and providing local information.

Abel Tasman National Park - Marahau   *B&B Homestay Self-contained*
Motels 18km NW of Motueka

Abel Tasman Bed & Breakfast
George Bloomfield
Abel Tasman National Park, Marahau,

Tel (03) 527 8181   Fax (03) 527 8181
abel.tasman.stables.accom@xtra.co.nz
www.abletasmanstables.co.nz

Double $95-$120 Single $65   Self contained motels $120
(Continental Special Breakfast)   Credit cards accepted
5 Queen 2 Double 3 Single (6 bdrm)
5 Ensuite 1 Private 1 Host share

Great views, hospitality, peaceful garden setting are yours at Abel Tasman Stables accommodation. Closest ensuite facility to Abel Tasman National park. Guests comments include 'I know now that hospitality is not just a word', TH, Germany. 'Wonderful place, friendly hospitality. The best things for really special holidays. We leave a piece of our hearts', P&M, Italy. 'The creme-de-la-creme of our holiday. What a view', MN & JW, England. Homestay bed & breakfast or self-contained options. Cafe close by.

Abel Tasman National Park - Marahau *B&B 17km NW of Motueka*

Sandspit
Paul & Marieann Kennedy
Lady Barkly Grove off Tokongawa Drive,
Split Apple Rock, RD 2, Motueka

Tel (03) 527 8388   Fax (03) 527 8388
Mob 025 240 4370   kennedy.keenan@xtra.co.nz
www.ozpal.com/sandspit

Double $130 Single $100 (Full Breakfast)
2 Queen (2 bdrm)   2 Ensuite

Sandspit is set in the Split Apple Rock sanctuary overlooking Marahau and the tranquil waters of Abel Tasman National Park. Sit on the deck and enjoy our freshly prepared delicious breakfast while looking out over the bay. Take a leisurely, stroll to Split Apple Beach or a dip in the pool. Kayak, walk and swim in the park or just sit on the deck and take in the magnificent view. Swimming pool, private entrance, TV, fridge, tea/coffee and home baking. Internet access. Directions: On the Marahau - Kaiteriteri Road, take the Tokongawa Drive turnoff. 0.6km up Tokongawa Drive turn left into Lady Barlky Grove. Sandspit is 100m on your left.

Abel Tasman National Park *B&B 17km NW of Motueka*

Twin Views
Ellenor & Les King
Tokongawa Drive, Split Apple Rock, RD 2, Motueka

Tel (03) 527 8475   Fax (03) 527 8479
Mob 025 318 937   twinviews@xtra.co.nz
www.twinviews.co.nz

Double $135-$145 (Special Breakfast)
Credit cards accepted
1 King/Twin 1 Queen (2 bdrm)
2 Ensuite

Wake to the sound of waves breaking on the beach below in this new architect designed home with magnificent sea views overlooking Tasman Bay. Each room has panoramic sea views, ensuite, fridge, tea/coffee making facilities, TV, hair dryer, heated towel rails, comfortable seating. We are only minutes away from two beaches, bush walks and five minutes drive to start of Abel Tasman Track. Directions: Go past Kaiteriteri Beach towards Marahau for 4km. Turn right onto Tokongawa Drive and go right to the top.

Abel Tasman National Park *B&B Homestay 17km NW of Motueka*

Split Apple Rock Homestay
Thelma & Rodger Boys
Tokongawa Drive, Split Apple Rock, RD 2, Motueka

Tel (03) 527 8182   Fax (03) 527 8172
www.bnb.co.nz/splitapple.html

Double $130 Single $115 (Full Breakfast)
Dinner $30 B/A
1 Queen 1 Twin (2 bdrm)
2 Ensuite

Turn your head through 180 degrees to drink in the panoramic sea views of Tasman Bay and Abel Tasman National Park. In our Eco-log home, rooms have private entrances and decking. We are within short walking distance of two golden beaches, five minutes drive to Marahau and the start of the Abel Tasman National Park where walking, kayaking, boating, swimming and more are available. Two cats in residence. Directions: on the Marahau/Kaiteriteri Road take the Tokongawa Drive turnoff, 1.2km up Tokongawa Drive the 'Split Apple Rock Homestay' sign is on your right.

Takaka - Patons Rock Beach   *Farmstay Self-contained 4 villas 10km W of Takaka*

Patondale
Vicki & David James
Patons Rock, RD 2, Takaka

Tel (03) 525 8262 Res.0800306697 Fax (03) 525 8262
Mob 025 936 891
patondale@xtra.co.nz
www.bnb.co.nz/patondale.html

Double $120 Single $70 (Continental Full Breakfast)
Child $20 $120 dbl. Villas Credit cards accepted
4 King 1 Queen 10 Single (10 bdrm)
5 Private

Farmstay: A "Bay Beauty" awake to the sound of the sea below and enjoy with us a hearty breakfast.Our lovely home has "simply magic" views,pretty gardens and is very peaceful "above the rest" surrounded by our 200 acre dairy farm. Villas: four new, spacious, deluxe self-contained units, own attached carports. Two bedrooms. Peaceful rural setting a few minutes walk to the beach.Central location. "Simply the Best" Your kiwi hosts David & Vicki invite you to be our guests.

Takaka - Tata Beach   *B&B Homestay 15km NE of Takaka*

The Devonshires
Brian & Susan Devonshire
Tata Heights Drive, Tata Beach, R. D. 1, Takaka

Tel (03) 525 7987 Fax (03) 525 7987 Mob 025 463 118
devs.1@xtra.co.nz
www.bnb.co.nz/thedevonshires.html

Double $90 Single $55 (Full Breakfast)
Child not suitable Dinner $25 -$30 by arrangement
1 Queen (1 bdrm)   Credit cards accepted
1 Ensuite 1 Guests share

The Devonshires have moved to Tata Beach and invite you to enjoy their newly built home and stroll to the beautiful golden beach. A tranquil base for exploring the truly sc enic Golden Bay, the Abel Tasman walkway, Kahurangi National Park, Farewell Spit, amazing coastal scenery, fishing the rivers or visiting interesting craftspeople. Brian, an educator, wine and American Football buff is a keen fisherman. Susan enjoys crafts, painting, gardening and practising her culinary skills. Charlie Brown is the resident cat. Longer visits welcomed.

Takaka   *B&B Self-contained 5km S of Takaka*

Rose Cottage
Margaret & Phil Baker
Hamama Road, RD 1, Takaka

Tel (03) 525 9048 Fax (03) 525 9043
www.bnb.co.nz/rosecottage.html

Double $75-$85 Single $55-$65 (Continental Breakfast)
Self contained units $95 - $125
Credit cards accepted
1 Queen 2 Single (2 bdrm)
1 Guests share

Rose cottage, much loved home of Phil and Margaret situated in the beautiful Takaka valley, in 2 1/2 acres of garden amongst 300 year old Totara trees, is ideally situated to explore Golden Bay's many attractions. Our 3 self contained units have full kitchens, private sun decks and quality furniture made by Phil in his craft workshop. The 12 metre indoor solar-heated swimming pool is available to our guests. Our interests are travel, photography, gardening, arts and crafts and helping to make our guests' stay a memorable one.

Takaka   *Homestay Takaka Township*

Haven House
Pam Peacock
177 Commercial Street, Takaka, Golden Bay
Tel (03) 525 9554 Fax (03) 525 8720
www.bnb.co.nz/havenhouse.html
Double $85 Single $65 (Continental Breakfast)
Child neg Triple $110 Credit cards accepted
Children welcome
1 Queen 1 Twin 2 Single (3 bdrm)
1 Guests share 1 Host share

A relaxed 'home away form home' atmosphere, happy echoes from the past in furnishings and character. Guest lounge, 24 hour tea/coffee. A large secluded, tranquil garden, to enjoy afternoon tea, picnic, barbecue. Your Haven. 'Home' goodies and orchard fruits complement the breakfast, served in sunny conservatory or outside on terrace overlooking rose garden. Central to all tourist attractions, 10 minutes stroll to shops and cafes. Our aim is friendly personal service and hospitality endeavouring to make your stay a memorable one. Looking forward to meeting you.

Takaka   *Homestay   2km S of Takaka*

Croxfords Homestay
Pam & John   Croxford
Dodson Road, RD 1, Takaka, Golden Bay
Tel (03) 525 7177 0800 26 41 56 Fax (03) 525 7177
croxfords@xtra.co.nz
www.kahurangiwalks.co.nz
Double $100 Single $70 (Full Breakfast) Child $10
Dinner $25 Credit cards accepted Children welcome
1 Double 3 Single (2 bdrm)
2 Ensuite

You are welcome to our spacious home in a peaceful rural setting close to Takaka. Views of Kahurangi National Park are spectacular. Pam loves cooking evening meals, including special diets, using home grown produce. Breakfasts include home made bread, muesli, yoghurt and preserves. We enjoy assisting visitors make the most of their visit. We are near beaches and national parks. We have many New Zealand books. No children at home, or pets. Non smokers preferred. We offer guided walks in the Abel Tasman and Kahurangi national parks.

Takaka - Ligar Bay   *B&B Homestay 12km NE of Takaka*

Amethyst House
Les and Trish Tregoning
Nyhane Drive, Ligar Bay RD1, Takaka
Tel (03) 525 7337 0800 525 733   Fax (03) 525 7337
Mob 021 182 4217
enquiries@amethystaccommodation.co.nz
www.amethystaccommodation.co.nz
Double $150-$170 Single $130-$150 (Full Breakfast)
1 SuperKing 1 Queen (2 bdrm)
1 Ensuite 1 Private

Amethyst House invites guests to experience the best of Golden Bay. Relax in the luxury and comfort of our spacious new home. Two luxurious and comfortable double guests suites with private patios/ entrances and ensuite/bathroom facilities, TV, electric blankets and coffee/tea making facilities. Located at the gateway to the Abel Tasman National Park, explore the beautiful beaches and spectacular scenery. Close to cafes, bowling green, golf course, kayaking and local crafts people. Four minute stroll to where the golden sands meet the crystal clear waters of Golden Bay. Burmese pet cat 'Mishka'.

Parapara *B&B 20km NW of Takaka*

Hakea Hill House
Vic & Liza Eastman
PO Box 35, Collingwood 7171

Tel (03) 524 8487   Fax (03) 524 8487
vic.eastman@clear.net.nz
www.bnb.co.nz/hakeahillhouse.html

Double $120 Single $80 (Full Breakfast) Child $40
Dinner by arrangement Credit cards accepted
Children welcome
2 Double 6 Single (3 bdrm)
1 Guests share

Hakea Hill House at Parapara has views from its hilltop of all Golden Bay. The two story house is modern and spacious. Two guest rooms have large balconies; the third for children has four bunk beds and a cot. American and New Zealand electric outlets are installed. Television, tea or coffee, and telephone lines are available in rooms. Vic is a practicing physician with an interest in astronomy. Liza is a quilter and cares for two outdoor dogs. Please contact us personally for reservations and directions.

Collingwood *B&B Self-contained 25km N of Takaka*

Skara Brae Garden Motels & Bed and Breakfast
Joanne & Pax Northover
Elizabeth Street, Collingwood

Tel (03) 524 8464   0800 752 722   Fax (03) 524 8474
skarabrae@xtra.co.nz
www.accommodationcollingwood.co.nz

Double $120 Single $90 (Continental Breakfast)
2 self-contained units $90 Credit cards accepted
2 Queen 1 Double 1 Twin 2 Single (4 bdrm)
1 Ensuite 3 Private

Skara Brae, the original police residence in Collingwood built in 1908, has been tastefully renovated over the years.
Our historic home is in a quiet, peaceful garden setting. Join us in the house for bed and breakfast or our two self contained motel units. Either way you will experience a warm welcoming atmosphere and individual attention. We are a minute away from the excellent Courthouse Cafe and local tavern bistro bar and it is a short stroll to the beach. Farewell Spit trips depart close by.

Collingwood *B&B Homestay 3km SE of Takaka*

Win's B&B
Heather Margaret Win
State Highway 60, Plain Road, RD 1

Tel (03) 524 8381
www.bnb.co.nz/wins.html

Double $60 Single $35 (Full Breakfast)
Child $20
Dinner by arrangement
Children welcome
1 Queen 2 Double 1 Twin (4 bdrm)
1 Guests share 1 Host share

A warm welcome to Win's Bed & Breakfast. Win's backs onto a sheep and cattle farm with mountain range in the background, close to walking tracks and beach. Three kilometres from Collingwood where there are two excellent cafes and a tavern bistro bar; also bookings for Farewell Spit trips. I have a cat called Bibbee.

Pakawau Beach - Collingwood *Homestay Self-contained 12km N of Collingwood*

Pakawau Homestay
Val & Graham Williams
Pakawau Beach, RD, Collingwood

Tel (03) 524 8168 Fax (03) 524 8168
www.bnb.co.nz/pakawauhomestay.html

Double $90-$100 Single $80
(Continental Breakfast)
Dinner $25 S/C $80
1 Queen 2 Double 1 Single (2 bdrm)
1 Ensuite 1 Host share

We are the northern most homestay in the South Island,
9km from Farewell Spit. We offer self-contained accommodation from $80 per night. The Farewell Spit Tours will pick you up from our gate. You only have to walk a few metres through our garden to a safe swimming beach. Local seafoods available, eg. whitebait, scallops, or you can walk across the road to a licensed cafe. We are non smokers, have two cats and look forward to sharing our lifestyle with you.

Golden Downs *Lodge 20km SW of Wakefield*

Golden Downs Lodge
William Cameron
Cnr Valley Road and Kerr Hill Road, Kohatu, SH6,
Wakefield

Tel (03) 522 4175 Fax (03) 522 4611
goldendowns@clear.net.nz
www.bnb.co.nz/goldendownslodge.html

Double $95 Single $50 (Full Breakfast)
Child $20 Dinner $25 - $35
Children welcome Pets welcome
2 Double 6 Single (3 bdrm)
3 Private

Golden Downs lodge is a quirky, homely retreat at the heart of Golden Downs forest. Set on thirty acres of tree covered grounds, the lodge occupies the old Golden Downs village hall. We are proud of our fine food prepared from local produce, and an atmosphere of intelligent and entertaining hospitality.

Nelson Lakes - St Arnaud *Homestay 85km S of Nelson*

Nelson Lakes Homestay
Gay & Merv Patch
RD 2, State Highway 63, Nelson

Tel (03) 521 1191 Fax (03) 521 1191
Mob 021 261 8529 Home@Tasman.net
www.bnb.co.nz/nelsonlakeshomestay.html

Double $125 Single $90 (Full Breakfast)
Dinner $35 pp by arrangement Credit cards accepted
2 King/Twin 1 Queen (2 bdrm)
2 Ensuite

We invite you to enjoy the luxury and comfort of our spacious modern home, just four kilometres east of St Arnaud, Lake Rotoiti and Nelson Lakes National Park - a year around adventure playground. Relax in our comfortable lounge; enjoy coffee or tea and cookies and the magnificent views from every window. There is garaging for your vehicle and laundry facilities for your use. Enjoy our delicious meals and friendly relaxed atmosphere. We are a non smoking household with one cat. Directions: State Highway 63; four kilometres east of St Arnaud.

Tophouse - Nelson Lakes *Farmstay Self-contained 9km N of St Arnaud*

Tophouse
Gladys & Mac Hollick
Nelson Lakes, RD 2, Nelson
Tel (03) 521 1848 0800 867 468
Fax (03) 521 1848
tophouse@clear.net.nz
www.tophouse.co.nz

Double $80 Single $40 (Continental Breakfast)
Child $20 Dinner $20
Credit cards accepted Children welcome
1 Queen 5 Double 19 Single (13 bdrm)
4 Private 2 Guests share

*Come, see and feel
the living history
of this unique
place*

We, Gladys and Mac Hollick together with our two cats, invite you to share our unique home with huge open fires, lovely setting and homely atmosphere. Tophouse, a cob (mud) building, dating from the 1880's when it was a hotel, and reopened in 1989 as a Farm Guest House, has that 'good old days' feel about it.

Situated on a 300 ha (730 acre) picturesque high country farm running cattle, with much native bush and an abundance of bird life also a unique 9 hole golf course. A popular holiday spot for its peace and beauty, bush walks, fishing and in the winter serves the two local ski fields.

Tophouse is only 9km from St Arnaud, gateway to Nelson Lakes National Park.

A typical farmhouse dinner is taken with family and since the fire's going 'real' toast for breakfast. Cottages are 2 bedroom, fully self contained including kitchen, with great views of the surrounding mountains.

Directions:
Just off State Highway 63 between Blenheim and Murchison and 9km from St Arnaud is Tophouse, that's us. The area took its name from the building. If travelling from Nelson, leave State Highway 6 at Belgrove and travel towards St Arnaud, we're signposted from the main road and looking forward to your visit.

Murchison *B&B Homestay Cottage 0.5km N of Murchison*

Coch-y-bondhu Lodge
Noela & Mike Buchanan
15 Grey Street, Murchison,
Tel (03) 523 9196 Fax (03) 523 9196
Mob 027 415 1019
cochybondhu@xtra.co.nz
www.homestays.net.nz/cochybondhu.htm
Double $100-$150 (Full Breakfast)
Dinner By Arrangement Credit cards accepted
2 Queen 1 Double 1 Twin 1 Single (4 bdrm)
2 Ensuite 1 Private 1 Guests share 1 Host share

We pride ourselves on our warm Kiwi hospitality, good wholesome food and comfortable beds. Our large, uniquely crafted home is set on 3 acres, secluded, quiet, surrounded by mature trees and overlooking the Buller River. We are 10 minutes walk from the town centre but you get the feeling you are in the middle of the wilderness. We encourage native birds and see many varieties. We have a friendly dog, several cows and hens. Mike is a professional fishing guide, a member of the NZPFGA.

Murchison *Farmstay 16km S of Murchison*

Awapiriti Farmstay
Jean Hayward & Andrew Motte-Harrison
Highway 65, Maruia Valley, Murchison
Tel (03) 523 9466 Fax (03) 523 9777
awapiriti@ihug.co.nz   www.bnb.co.nz/awapiriti.html
Double $110-$130 Single $100 (Full Breakfast)
Dinner by arrangement Pets welcome
1 King/Twin 1 Queen 2 Single (3 bdrm)
2 Ensuite 1 Private

Experience something different: visit Awapiriti, nestled between the Maruia River and bush-clad hills in the beautiful Maruia Valley. Share our home and enjoy good food and company. Breathe the clean country air, admire clear night skies. Enjoy walks in the native bush, take a farm tour to see the elk, cattle, sheep, etc. Meet the dogs and cats. Fishing and hunting guides can be arranged, and other activities such as white-water rafting, kayaking and therapeutic massage. Three hours approx. from Picton/Christchurch/Hokitika and 1.5 hours from Nelson, Awapiriti is a haven for adults, unsuitable for children.

The difference between a B&B and a hotel
is that you don't hug the hotel staff when you leave.

West Coast

Towns listed generally follow a north to south route. Refer to the index if required.

Karamea

Hector

67

Cape Foulwind Westport

6

69

Punakaiki Reefton

Barrytown

7

Nine Mile Creek

Greymouth

Moana

Lake Brunner

Hokitika Inchbonnie

Lake Kaniere

6

Harihari Castle Hill Village

Whataroa

Lake Coleridge Darfield

Franz Josef Mt Hutt Aylesbury

Fox Glacier Methven

Bruce Bay Staveley

Paringa Rakaia

Mount Cook

Ashburton

Haast

6 Lake Tekapo Kimbell Fairlie Geraldine

Burkes Pass Fairlie

0	Kilometres	60

| 0 | Miles | 36 |

WEST COAST

Karamea   *Self-contained lodge 100km NW of Westport*

Karamea Lodge
Jenny and Mark Roumieu
4589 Karamea Highway, Karamea,

Tel (03) 782 6033 or 782 6034 roumieu@xtra.co.nz
www.bnb.co.nz/karamealodge.html

Double $130-$150 (Continental Breakfast)
Child By arrangement
1 King 1 Queen 1 Queen/Single (Twin) (3 bdrm)
3 Ensuite

Discover our new spectacularly located lodge, situated
on the Otumahana Estuary, Karamea. Each room has its
own private deck, ensuite and tea/coffee making facilities.
The lodge provides a stylish self catering kitchen, viewing lounge, television room and guest laundry.
Karamea with its year round mild climate, is gateway to the Kahurangi National Park, and is renowned
for its trout fishing, whitebaiting, limestones arches, caves and bird watching. We can assist with
arrangements for whatever adventure beckons and welcome you to our part of paradise.

Karamea   *B&B Farmstay 84km N of Westport*

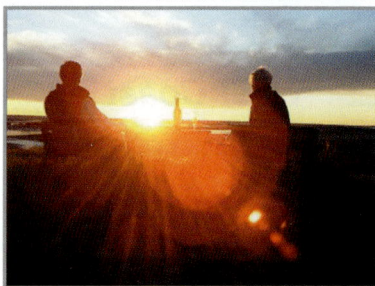

Beachfront Farmstay
Dianne & Russell Anderson
Karamea, SH 67, Karamea

Tel (03) 782 6762   Fax (03) 782 6762
Mob 021 782676 farmstay@xtra.co.nz
www.WestCoastBeachAccommodation.co.nz

Double $110-$145 Single $80-$100 (Special Breakfast)
Child $35 Dinner $40 Credit cards accepted
1 King 1 Queen 1 Twin (3 bdrm)
2 Ensuite 1 Host share

Welcome to a spectacular area of the West Coast.Our home
is 2 mins walk to a beautiful sandy beach with awesome views and amazing sunsets, great for walking
or jogging. Relax in our spacious home and garden. We milk 330 friesian cows on our undulating
pasture. Join us for delicious country cuisine, organic vegetables, homemade desserts, NZ wine also
generous cooked breakfasts. Our area offers scenic walks, guided tours in limestone caves with extinct
birds, unique limestone arches, 9 hole golf course, horse riding, bird watching, fishing, guides available.

Karamea   *Farmstay Self-contained 0.5km Karamea*

Bridge Farm
Rosalie & Peter Sampson
Bridge Street, Karamea, RD 1, Westport

Tel (03) 782 6955   0800 KARAMEA
Fax (03) 782 6748   Enquires@karameamotels.co.nz
karameamotels.co.nz

Double $85-$120 (Continental Breakfast) Child $10
Extra adult $20   Credit cards accepted
6 Queen 8 Single (10 bdrm)
8 Private

Since relinquishing their dairy farm to daughter Caroline and son-in-law Bevan, Rosalie and Peter have
purpose-built on the property accommodation that neatly bridges the gap between motel and farm stay.
Both are happy to share their extensive knowledge of their district, its people and environment and
introduce guests to the many short walks that Karamea offers. Each quality suite is self contained and
has a private lounge that overlooks the farm to Kahurangi National Park beyond. A small mob of deer
and alpaca graze nearby.

Westport - Cape Foulwind *B&B Homestay Self-contained 11km SW of Westport*

Steeples Homestay
Pauline & Bruce Cargill
Lighthouse Road, Cape Foulwind, RD 2, Westport

Tel (03) 789 7876 Mob 021 663 687
Steepleshomestay@xtra.co.nz
www.bnb.co.nz/steepleshomestay.html

Double $80 Single $50 (Full Breakfast) Child $15
Separate self contained unit $120 Credit cards accepted
1 Queen 2 Single (2 bdrm) 1 Private

Enjoy our peaceful rural home, magnificent views of
Tasman Sea, rugged coastline beaches, great swimming, surfing, fishing, walking. Within five minutes
walk the very popular seal colony walkway, great dining at Bay House Restaurant and friendly local
Star Tavern, or play a round of golf at Carters Beach Golf links. Other local attractions include Coaltown
Museum, horse riding, underworld and white water rafting, bush walks, Punakaiki National Park. We
are keen gardeners and enjoy all sports and have a Jack Russell dog and a cat. All laundry facilities
available and off street parking. Self contained unit can be B&B by arrangement.

Westport *Homestay Westport Central*

Havenlee Homestay
Jan & Ian Stevenson
76 Queen Street, Westport

Tel (03) 789 8543 0800 673 619 Fax (03) 789 8502
Mob 025 627 2702 info@havenlee.co.nz
www.havenlee.co.nz

Double $90-$99 Single $60-$75 (Continental Plus)
Child neg Credit cards accepted
1 Queen 1 Double 1 Twin (3 bdrm)
1 Guests share suite

Peace in Paradise - this is Havenlee, offering tranquil location 300 metres from town centre. Born and
bred West Coasters - hospitality is part of our heritage. Share our spacious home set amongst native and
exotic trees and shrubs, idyllic for exploring our environmental wonderland. Check out the Seal Colony,
Punakaiki Pancake Rocks, awesome adventure experiences, nature walks or just rest and recharge.
Enjoy a generous continental-plus breakfast. Bathroom (with tub), shower room and toilet each separate.
Laundry facilities, local knowledge in a friendly relaxed, smoke free environment.

Westport *2km N of Westport*

Chrystal Lodge
Ann & Bill Blythe
PO Box 128, Westport

Tel (03) 789 8617 0800 259 953 Fax (03) 789 8617
blythea@xtra.co.nz
www.bnb.co.nz/chrystallodge.html

Double $65-$75 Single $60-$65 Child neg
Continental breakfast $7.50 pp optional Separate / Suite
Credit cards accepted Children welcome
2 Queen 1 Single (2 bdrm)
2 Ensuite 1 Guests share

Ann and Bill would like to welcome you to Chrystal Lodge. We are established on 20 acres beside a
beach ideal for walking, surfing and fishing. Our separate self-contained units have a fully equipped
kitchen/lounge with ensuite bedrooms. The garden setting has ample off street parking. Free guest
laundry. Pony available for children. We have one shy cat. Seasonal rates. Directions: Turn right at the
Post Office, continue down Brougham Street, turn left at Derby Street until at the beach.

Westport - Cape Foulwind *Homestay 11km W of Westport*

Clifftop Homestay
Paddy & Gail Alexander
Clifftop Lane, Cape Foulwind, RD 2, Westport
Tel (03) 789 5472 clifftophomestay@yahoo.com
www.bnb.co.nz/clifftophomestay.html
Double $90-$120 Single $80 (Continental Breakfast)
Child $15 Twin Bed/Sit $120 Children welcome
2 Double 1 Single (2 bdrm)
1 Private 1 Host share

We and 'Murphy the Beagle' invite you to discover the
magic of the Cape. Our boutique clifftop homestay offers two private, stylish rooms, one with spacious
bed/lounge room with breathtaking sea views and Sky TV. The upmarket bathroom has spa bath, heated
towel rails, hairdryer and separate toilet. Enjoy complimentary tea/coffee/biscuits or a locally brewed beer
on our balcony or in our garden courtyard. Whether you stroll the beach, explore coastal walks, visit the
seal colony, watch spectacular sunsets from the lighthouse - you will find 'the Cape' restorative to body
and soul. Restaurant and country pub nearby. First right past Star Tavern, right at beach carpark.

Westport - Cape Foulwind *B&B Farmstay Self-contained 10km W of Westport*

Lighthouse Homestay
Derek Parsons & Helen Jenkins
32 Lighthouse Road, Cape Foulwind, Westport
Tel (03) 789 7942 0800 227 322 Fax (03) 789 7942
Mob 025 857 583 derek.parsons@xtra.co.nz
www.bnb.co.nz/
lighthousehomestay.html
Double $90-$150 Single $80 (Continental Breakfast)
1 King/Twin 2 Queen 1 Double 2 Single (3 bdrm)
2 Ensuite 1 Private

Enjoy the soothing tranquillity of amazing sea views from your bedroom/patio. Walk the impressive
Cape Foulwind Walkway with its seals and captivating coastline, ending at the magic Bay House
Restaurant overlooking Tauranga Bay. Numerous outdoor activities and attractions nearby. Helen and
Derek can take you out on the farm shifting cattle or walking through native rainforest. Let 'Poppy' our
fox terrier take you beachwalking below the cliffs. Self-contained cottage option. Short walk to friendly
country pub. Smokefree inside.

Westport *B&B Homestay Self-contained 3km S of Westport*

Bellaville Homestay
Marlene & Ross Burrow
No 10 on SH 67, Carters Beach
Po Box 157, Westport
Tel (03) 789 8457 0800 789 845 Mob 025 6131 689
fairhalls@xtra.co.nz
www.bnb.co.nz/bellaville.html
Double $80 Single $60 (Full Breakfast)
Child $15 Children welcome
1 Queen 1 Single (1 bdrm)
1 Ensuite 1 Private

We promise you arrive as strangers and leave as friends. Wake to the sound of waves pounding our safe
walking and swimming beach. Minutes from fully licensed café bar, golf course, seal colony, airport.
Off street parking. Easy access to very large, sunny, quiet accommodation with private entrance, own
patio, ensuite, private bathroom, spa, shower and separate toilet. Sky TV, hair dryer, laundry, tea &
coffee facilities with home baking. Having travelled extensively overseas and in New Zealand we look
forward to chatting with you.

Westport   *B&B Separate/Suite*

Archer House
Kerrie Fairhall
75 Queen Street, Westport,
Tel (03) 789 8778   Fax (03) 789 8763
Mob 025 260 3677   accom@archerhouse.co.nz
www.archerhouse.co.nz
Double $120-$150 Single $110-$140 (Full Breakfast)
Credit cards accepted
3 Queen 2 Single (3 bdrm)
2 Ensuite 1 Private

3 large bedrooms, 2 with ensuites, 1 with private facilities. All bedrooms have TVs and tea/coffee facilities. Bathrooms have a hair dryer, heated towel rail and toiletries. Sunny balconies and relax in a sheltered private conservatory or one of the two guest lounges. New Zealand Heritage Home, with outstanding historic significance to the West Coast created by leadlighting masterpieces, fireplaces and antique furniture. Short stroll to all town amenities including Victoria Square and heated swimming pool. Whole home is available for rental for those who prefer privacy

Westport - Carters Beach   *B&B 5km S of Westport*

Carters Beach B&B
Sue & John Bennett
McIntyres Road, On SH67A, Westport
Tel (03) 789 8056
www.bnb.co.nz/cartersbeachbb.html
Double $80-$90 Single $60-$70
(Continental Breakfast)
2 Queen 1 Twin (3 bdrm)
1 Ensuite 1 Private

Welcome to our lovely relaxed atmosphere at Carters Beach. Situated only 5km from the village of Westport. We are within a three minute walk to our very clean and safe beach and fully licensed bar/café and bakery. Golf course and the famous seal colony within a few minutes drive. Our rooms are very spacious with own private entrance and decking. Ideal accommodation for couples or families travelling together. We look forward to listening to your travel tales and sharing our local knowledge with you.

Westport   *Self-contained 14km S of Westport*

Okari Lake Hideaway
Marie Dickson
Virgin Flat Road, Westport,
Tel (03) 789 6841   0800 H D AWAY Fax (03) 789 6841
Mob 0274 452 410   marie.greg@xtra.co.nz
www.hideaway.com
Double $180 (Full Breakfast) Children welcome
1 Queen (1 bdrm)
1 Private

If you are looking for peace and tranquillity this private exclusive cottage, which is built over a private lake, is the perfect place for you. There is a boat moored on the cottage jetty for your use. The location of the lake allows for all-weather trout fishing. This is a bird watches paradise - there are many varieties of native birds and water foul. A book on native birds and binoculars are to help identify them. We are only 35 minutes from Punakaiki and 30 minutes from the Bay House.

Westport   *B&B 4km SW of Westport Central*

Lakeside Terrace B&B
Anne & Wynne Goldie
Lakeside Terrace, Alma Road, Westport

Tel (03) 789 7438 wa.goldie@xtra.co.nz
www.bnb.co.nz/lakeside.html

Double $90-$100 Single $65-$75
(Continental Breakfast)
1 Queen 1 Double 1 Single (3 bdrm)
1 Private

We offer quality accommodation for one party of guests
at a time in our modern sunny home, set in a peaceful
rural area, surrounded by native trees and shrubs and the
native ducks on nearby lakes. Experience the amazing outdoor activities and attractions the West Coast/
Buller has to offer, or just relax and enjoy the tranquillity of your'back to nature’ surrounds
with magical panoramic views. Hospitality is our heritage – you can be assured of a warm
welcome and a memorable stay. Cat on property.

Reefton   *B&B*

Quartz Lodge
Toni and Ian Walker
78 Sheil Street, Reefton, West Coast

Tel (03) 732 8383   0800 302 725   Fax (03) 732 8083
Mob 025 619 4520   quartz-lodge@xtra.co.nz
www.bnb.co.nz/quartzlodge.html

Double $100-$130 Single $75-$95 (Full Breakfast)
Child $35 Credit cards accepted Children welcome
1 King 1 Queen 1 Twin 1 Single (3 bdrm)
1 Ensuite 1 Private 1 Guests share

Toni and Ian invite you to experience "Quartz Lodge" in Reefton, the town nestled within Victoria
Forest Park and in the heart of the West Coast quartz gold/coal mining country. Let this be your home
away from home - but with all the extras. Huge picture windows in every room offer best views in
town. Guests only entrance, lounge/dining area. Luxurious beds-rooms serviced daily. Country style
breakfast, tea/coffee facilities, laundry service and phone/fax. Centrally heated. Arriving late? Not a
problem. Your comfort is our priority.

Reefton   *B&B Separate/Suite Self-contained Reefton Central*

Historic Reef Cottage B&B and Cafe
Susan & Ronnie Standfield
51-55 Broadway, Reefton

Tel (03) 732 8440   0800 770 440   Fax (03) 732 8440
reefton@clear.net.nz   www.reefcottage.co.nz

Double $78-$130 Single $58-$105 (Full Breakfast)
Child 1/2 price Dinner $10 - $35 Credit cards accepted
1 King/Twin 1 Queen 2 Double (4 bdrm)
2 Ensuite 2 Private

Built in 1887 from native timbers for a local barrister.
This historical Edwardian home has been carefully
renovated to add light and space without losing its olde
world charm. Elegantly decorated the house features
charming character rooms serviced daily. Reefton is
nestled in Historic Gold/Coal mining country between native beech forests and the Inangahua River,
Reef Cottage is unrivalled as the finest accommodation in Reefton. Reef Café next door offers casual
dining, specialist coffees and decadent desserts. Trout fishing, hiking, 4WD and tours available.

Punakaiki *B&B Homestay 45km N of Greymouth*

The Rocks Homestay
Peg & Kevin Piper
No. 33 Hartmount Place, PO Box 16, Punakaiki 7850

Tel (03) 731 1141 0800 272 164 Fax (03) 731 1142
therocks@minidata.co.nz www.therockshomestay.com

Double $110-$165 Single $95-$110
(Special Breakfast) Child $40 - $60
Dinner $35- $45 by arrangement
S/C House $140 - $180 Credit cards accepted
2 Queen 2 Twin (3 bdrm)
3 Ensuite

Huge windows and astounding views in all directions - coast, sea, cliffs, rainforest, National Park. The Rocks Homestay sits above the forest - comfortable, modern, warm, friendly - unique in its wilderness location. Healthy breakfasts with home baking. Home-cooked evening meals may be arranged. Visit the Pancake Rocks and Blowholes, walk Truman Track to the beach, photograph the limestone gorges. Stay a while and experience unspoiled New Zealand. Enjoy the reference library.

Punakaiki - Barrytown *B&B Homestay Self-contained 30km N of Greymouth*

Kathleen & Alister Schroeder
13A Cargill Road, Barrytown RD 1, Westland

Tel (03) 731 1006 Fax (03) 731 1106
www.bnb.co.nz/schroeder.html

Double $85-$95 Single $50 (Continental Breakfast)
3 Queen 1 Twin (4 bdrm)

We have a new spacious home on a quiet rear section, a garden setting, with native bush backdrop and sea views. We offer a self-contained flat downstairs, with queen size waterbed, twin beds in spacious living area, full kitchen, washing machine, parking and separate entrance. We also have two queen rooms upstairs. Breakfast with host. Punakaiki pancake rocks and adventure activities in Paparoa National Park, 15 minutes north. Greymouth is 20 minutes south. Turn at Barrytown Hotel corner, past three houses on left, up the lane, house on left.

Nine Mile Bay *Self-contained 15km N of Greymouth*

Tasman Beach B&B
Jill Cotton
9 Mile Coast Road, RD 1, Runanga,
Highway 6, Westland

Tel (03) 762 7117 Fax (03) 762 7161
tasbeach@xtra.co.nz
www.bnb.co.nz/tasmanbeachbb.html

Double $110 Single $90 (Continental Breakfast)
Child $5
1 Queen 1 Twin (2 bdrm)
1 Private

Dramatic location, stunning views and sunsets are yours from this absolute beachfront cottage 15 min north Greymouth. The bushed landscape provides healthy sea air and quality water for the refurbished holiday cottage with new facilities. Our home adjoins. We are wildlife enthusiasts so please excuse the little blue penguins who choose to visit us. Heaps of adventures await you at the Blow Holes Punakaiki 20 mins north. Breakfast always included. Full kitchen and laundry. Children enjoyed and welcome.

Nine Mile Creek *B&B Homestay 14km N of Greymouth*

The Breakers
Frank & Barbara Ash
PO Box 188, Greymouth, Westland
Tel (03) 762 7743 0800 350 590 Fax (03) 762 7733
stay@breakers.co.nz
www.breakers.co.nz
Double $145-$225 (Full Breakfast) Child N/A
Dinner $55 Credit cards accepted
1 King 3 Queen 2 Twin (4 bdrm)
4 Ensuite

One of the West Coast's most spectacularly located B&B's, with stunning views over the ocean. Private beach access allows you to fossick for jade and beautiful stones. All rooms are 'en-suite' with TV and hot beverage making facilities. A gourmet dinner is available, with 24 hours notice, includes NZ wines and is constantly accompanied by the crashing waves! The Breakers is a wonderful base to visit the Pancake Rocks, the Paparoa National Park and the best stretch of coastline in NZ. Sorry, unsuitable for children.

Greymouth *Homestay 4km S of Greymouth*

Tides
Ib Pupich
5 Stanton Crescent, Greymouth,
Tel (03) 768 4348 Fax (03) 768 4348
IbPupich@xtra.co.nz
www.bnb.co.nz/pupich.html
Double $100-$110 Single $90-$95 (Full Breakfast)
1 King/Twin (1 bdrm)
1 Ensuite

We offer warm hospitality in our lovely home overlooking the Tasman Sea and South to Mount Cook and Tasman. You can be assured of a relaxed stay in this quiet street only five minutes walk from the beach. Your room, with its private deck is spacious and comfortable with lovely sea views. There is much to do and see in the area; lakes, rivers, wonderful bush and coastline walks. Trout fishing and golf or just laze on the deck and watch the sun go down.

Greymouth *Homestay Greymouth Central*

Ardwyn House
Mary Owen
48 Chapel Street, Greymouth
Tel (03) 768 6107 Fax (03) 768 5177
Mob 025 376 027 ardwynhouse@hotmail.com
www.bnb.co.nz/ardwynhouse.html
Double $80-$85 Single $50 (Full Breakfast)
Child 1/2 price Credit cards accepted
2 Queen 3 Single (3 bdrm)
1 Guests share

Ardwyn House is three minutes walk from the town centre in a quiet garden setting offering sea, river and town views. The house was built in the 1920's and is a fine example of an imposing residence with fine woodwork and leadlight windows, whilst being a comfortable and friendly home. Greymouths ideally situated for travellers touring the West Coast being central with good choice of restaurants. We offer a courtesy car service to and from local travel centres and also provide off street parking.

Greymouth *Homestay 4km S of Greymouth*

Piners Homestay
Bev & Graham Piner
75 Main South Road, Karoro, Greymouth

Tel (03) 768 5397   Fax (03) 768 5396
tpiner@paradise.net.nz
www.bnb.co.nz/pinershomestay.html

Double $85-$90 Single $60-$65 (Full Breakfast)
Child Neg Dinner $30 Credit cards accepted
Children welcome
1 Double 1 Twin (2 bdrm)
1 Guests share

We have been welcoming guests to our home for over eleven years and look forward to sharing it with you. You will be near the beach and will see amazing sunsets. There is off road parking. Your hostess enjoys creating delicious food using home grown and local produce. Dinner $30pp. We take a maximum of four guests. There is a second toilet adjacent to the bedrooms. We have two spoilt cats. Courtesy pick up from Tranz Alpine or bus. We are four kilometers south of town centre. See you soon.

Greymouth *Homestay 6km S of Greymouth*

Paroa Homestay (formerly Pam's Homestay)
Pam Sutherland
345 Main South Road, Greymouth

Tel (03) 762 6769   Fax (03) 762 6765
Mob 025 685 6280 paroahomestay@xtra.co.nz
www.coast-comforts.co.nz

Double $99-$115 Single $79-$99 (Special Breakfast)
Child neg. Credit cards accepted
1 King/Twin 1 King 1 Double (3 bdrm)
1 Ensuite 1 Private 1 Guests share

Relax on terraces overlooking the sea and watch incredible sunsets. Three minutes walk to the beach. Towering trees, native bush surrounds spacious classic home with luxurious guest lounge. Excellent restaurants within 3-6 minutes drive. Experience superb continental breakfast as baking and cooking is Pam's forté (previously owning Greymouth's busiest Cafe/Bar). Pam has NZQA Food Hygiene qualifications. West Coast born, Pam's local knowledge is invaluable. Pam enjoys hospitality, antiques, china, organic gardening and bus walking. Courtesy transport from train/bus. Off-street parking. Children over five years welcome.

Greymouth *B&B 1km S of Greymouth*

Rosewood
Rhonda & Stephan Palten
20 High St, Greymouth

Tel (03) 768 4674 0800 185 748 Fax (03) 768 4694
Mob 027 242 7080 rosewoodnz@xtra.co.nz
www.rosewoodnz.co.nz

Double $110-$150 Single $85-$110 (Full Breakfast)
Child $20 Credit cards accepted Children welcome
1 King/Twin 4 Queen 1 Twin 2 Single (5 bdrm)
3 Ensuite 1 Private 1 Guests share

Rosewood is one of Greymouth's finest old restored homes, a few minutes walk from the town centre with its restaurants & cafés. Rooms are well appointed & feature quality king and queen beds with modern ensuites or bathroom. Separate guest lounge/dining room with complimentary tea/coffee and homemade biscuits. Hosts Rhonda, her German husband Stephan & their 2 children allow you to recover from your journey or activities of the day and offer a superb breakfast making a perfect start to your day.

Greymouth *Homestay 3km S of Greymouth*

Maryglen Homestay
Allison & Glen Palmer
20 Weenink Road, Karoro, Greymouth
Tel (03) 768 0706 0800 627 945 Fax (03) 768 0599
Mob 027 4380 479 mary@bandb.co.nz
www.bandb.co.nz
Double $95-$115 Single $75-$85
(Continental Breakfast) Child neg Dinner $25pp
Credit cards accepted Children welcome
2 King/Twin 1 Queen 1 Single (3 bdrm)
3 Ensuite 1 Host share

"What a view!" "Such a quiet location." Guests comments about our home set in bush overlooking the sea. Downstairs rooms have own entrance onto larger deck where you can enjoy the bush and amazing sunsets. Each bedroom has TV and hot drink facilities. Our dog Lady and cat Misty enjoy visitors company. Allison enjoys gardening, hospitality and playing bridge (games can be arranged). Glen is a jigsaw fan. Off main road, level access, parking. Complimentary pick up from bus/train. Transport to scenic spots (small charge).

Greymouth *Homestay 6km S of Greymouth*

Sunsetview
Russell & Jill Fairhall
335 Main South Road, Greymouth 7801
Tel (03) 762 6616 Fax (03) 762 6616
sunsetview@xtra.co.nz
www.bnb.co.nz/sunsetview.html
Double $100-$140 Single $90 (Full Breakfast)
1 King/Twin 1 King 1 Queen (3 bdrm)
2 Ensuite 1 Private

Russell and Jill welcome you to our sunny modern home with amazing sea and mountain views. We offer well-appointed superior bedrooms. TV in rooms. Home cooked meals available on request. Tea, coffee and laundry facilities available. Outdoor areas with pool and barbecue. Short walk to beach. Trips arranged to visit modern and old gold mining sites. Fishing trips can be arranged. We offer a courtesy car service to and from local travel centres and provide off-street parking.

Greymouth - Runanga *Homestay 27km N of Greymouth*

Golden Sands Homestay
Sue & Tom Costelloe
4 Golden Sands Road, Barrytown, Runanga
Tel (03) 731 1115 Fax (03) 731 1116
goldensands@paradise.net.nz
www.bnb.co.nz/goldensandshomestay.html
Double $85-$95 Single $50 (Continental Breakfast)
Child by arrangement Dinner by arrangement
2 Queen 1 Twin (3 bdrm)
1 Ensuite 2 Private

Nestled between the Paparoa Range and the Tasman Sea on the Greymouth to Westport Scenic Highway, Golden Sands Homestay offers a friendly atmosphere and comfortable rooms. It is handy to Punakaiki, the Pancake Rocks, and the Paparoa National Park to the north, with Greymouth a twenty-five minute drive to the south. As well as stunning views and wonderful sunsets, Golden Sands Homestay has Sky television, Internet facilities, a cosy fire in winter and a contented cat. Access and facilities for disabled people. Nearby restaurants.

Greymouth *Homestay 12km N of Greymouth*

Westway
John Best & Wayne Margison
58 Herd Street, Dunollie, Greymouth
Tel (03) 762 7077 Fax (03) 762 7377
Mob 0274 952 844 westway@xtra.co.nz
www.bnb.co.nz/westway.html
Double $100-$120 Single $85-$95
(Continental Breakfast) Dinner $20 - $40
Twin $85 - $95 Children welcome
2 Queen 1 Twin (3 bdrm)
1 Ensuite 1 Private

Westway is situated in a sleepy valley at the end of the road. A wonderful location from which to explore areas of significant history and natural beauty. Walk the bush and coastal tracks - visit gold and coal mining sites - fish the lakes, rivers and sea. Enjoy the West Coast's unique attractions. Guests arriving or departing Greymouth by train or bus can be provided with complimentary transport. All meals are available with prior notice. Off-peak and concession rates are available.

Greymouth *B&B Self-contained 28km N of Greymouth*

Pininoa Country Chalet
Pat & Lew Ferris
SH 7. Matai, Grey Valley, Westland
Tel (03) 732 3408 Fax (03) 732 3409
pininoa@hyper.net.nz
www.bnb.co.nz/pininoa.html
(Continental Breakfast) Dinner B/A
Single party bookings $150 - $220
2 King/Twin 1 Queen (2 bdrm)
1 Private

Welcome to the peace and tranquility of our country retreat. Enjoy private bush walks or just relaxing in our large organic garden. Warm, two bedroom self contained Chalet where everything is provided for your comfort. Easy driving distance to great fishing rivers, so stay an extra night or two, relax, catch a fish, watch the stars and join us for a wine on the terrace. We are semi retired, have two spoilt but obedient dogs. Not suitable for children. Smoking OK on the verandah.

Greymouth *B&B 15km S of Greymouth*

Chapel Hill
Gay Sweeney
783 Rutherglen Road, Paroa, Greymouth
Tel (03) 762 6662 Fax (03) 762 6664
Mob 025 816 736
gsweeney@clear.net.nz OR gay@chapelhill.co.nz
www.chapelhill.co.nz
Double $95-$120 Single $85 (Continental Breakfast)
Dinner $25
2 Queen 1 Double 1 Twin 1 Single (5 bdrm)
1 Ensuite

Chapel Hill is an architect designed lodge set in ten acres of gardens and native rain forest, minutes from the historic goldfield atttractions of Shantytown and Woods Creek. Because of our forest birds and wildlife we cannot accept pets - and the lodge with its lofts and balconies is not child-safe. The lodge features amazing rain forest views from every room and three sitting rooms to relax in including an enormous log fire,and a TV snug. Owner, Gay Sweeney, makes sure there are no timetables for her guests - you breakfast when you want, and do what you want.

Greymouth *B&B Homestay 3km N of Greymouth*

Oak Lodge
Colette and Brian MacKenzie
Coal Creek, State Highway 6, Greymouth
Tel (03) 768 6832 0800 351 000 Fax (03) 768 4362
oaklodgenz@xtra.co.nz
www.oaklodge.co.nz
Double $100-$150 Single $90 (Full Breakfast)
Children welcome
1 Queen 1 Double 1 Twin 2 Single (3 bdrm)
3 Ensuite

This 100 year old farmhouse is full of character, and only 3 minutes from Greymouth. It is surrounded by extensive gardens, has a spa/jacuzzi, swimming pool, sauna, tennis court, billiard room, guest lounge and laundry facilities. This 20 acre hobby farm has an unusual collection of black sheep, hens, and a very friendly donkey called Finias. Colette and Brian, who have travelled themselves, extend a very warm welcome to you. A generous farmhouse breakfast is served. "We came as guests and leave as friends"

Moana - Lake Brunner *B&B Homestay 35km E of Greymouth*

Lancewood
Jan & Simon Wilkins
2177 Arnold Valley Road, Moana, Lake Brunner
Tel (03) 738 0844
lancewood.upon.moana@paradise.net.nz
www.bnb.co.nz/lancewood.html
Double $120-$140 Single $120
(Continental Breakfast) Child B/A Children welcome
1 Queen (1 bdrm)
1 Ensuite

A very warm welcome awaits you at 'Lancewood'. Relax with us enjoying captivating views of Lake Brunner, amidst a scenic backdrop of the Southern Alps. Spend time enjoying bush walks, gold planning trout fishing or a scenic launch trip. Your accommodation has an ensuite, double queen bed, complimentary tea and coffee facilities plus TV and fridge. A continental breakfast will be provided at your door. Don't be disappointed by not booking ahead. We look forward to sharing our piece of paradise with you.

Moana - Lake Brunner *Self-contained Moana*

Lake View B&B
Brent & Madeline Beadle
18 Johns Road, Moana, Westland
Tel (03) 738 0886 Fax (03) 738 0887
Mob 0274 318 022 browntrout@minidata.co.nz
www.fishnhunt.co.nz/guides/brunner/index.htm
Double $110 Single $90 (Continental Breakfast)
Child $30 Children welcome
1 King 2 Single (2 bdrm)
1 Private

Lake View B&B offers guets fantastic views of Lake Brunner from the lounge, the decking or while lying in bed. Accommodation is a very private self-contained cottage adjacent to our house only five minutes walk to the village centre, cafe or hotel. The lake is famous for its trout fishing. Brent is a fishing guide. Lake tours, canoe hire, bush walks, pottery, and gold panning are all close. The Tranzalpine stops at Moana. Christchurch is three hours away by road.

Hokitika Central *B&B Separate/Suite Hokitika*

Teichelmann's Bed & Breakfast
Frances & Brian Ward
20 Hamilton Street, Hokitika

Tel (03) 755 8232 0800 743 742 Fax (03) 755 8239
teichel@xtra.co.nz
www.teichelmanns.co.nz

Double $165-$180 Single $120-$135 (Full Breakfast)
Credit cards accepted
2 King/Twin 2 King 1 Double 2 Twin 1 Single
(6 bdrm)
5 Ensuite 1 Private

Frances and Brian welcome you to 'Catch your Breath and Breakfast' staying in our centrally situated, character home in the heritage area of Hokitika. Located opposite the information centre and museum, Teichelmann's is a short walk away from interesting craft galleries, shops, restaurants and cafes. Stroll on the beach in the evening and experience a West Coast sunset...the wild, romantic West Coast at its best. We look forward to your visit.

Hokitika *B&B Homestay 0.5km N of Hokitika*

Terrace View Homestays
Dianne & Chris Ward
24 Whitcombe Terrace, Hokitika

Tel (03) 755 7357 0800 261 949 Fax (03) 755 8760
Mob 0274 371 254 wardc@xtra.co.nz
www.bnb.co.nz/terraceviewhomestays.html

Double $110-$125 Single $90-$100 (Full Breakfast)
Dinner by arrangement Credit cards accepted
2 Queen 2 Single (3 bdrm)
1 Ensuite 1 Private 1 Guests share

Welcome to our home. Bedrooms have ensuite or private bathrooms. Views of Hokitika, mountains, sea and sunsets can be experienced from our upstairs lounge. Enjoy genuine NZ hospitality. Complimentary tours to glow worms are offered. Chris (Property Consultant and Rotarian) enjoys travel, golf and fishing; Dianne (Reading Teacher) enjoys travel, crafts, ceramic dolls and cooking. From the main highway, turn into Tudor Street (airport signed), next left into Bonar Drive, continue up to hilltop (Whitcombe Terrace) taking left turns.

Hokitika *Homestay 1km N of Hokitika*

Alpine Vista Homestay
Rayleine & Jon Olson
38 Bonar Drive, Hokitika

Tel (03) 755 8732 Fax (03) 755 8732
Mob 025 202 2401 jolson@minidata.co.nz
www.alpinevistahomestay.freeservers.com

Double $110 Single $80 (Full Breakfast)
Credit cards accepted
1 Queen 1 Twin (2 bdrm)
1 Ensuite

Our comfortable home is on a terrace overlooking Hokitika with unsurpassed views of the Southern Alps, Tasman Sea and brilliant sunsets. The guest rooms have a private entrance and are connected by a small sitting room with TV. You are welcomed with home baking, tea/coffee making facilities available. We invite you to join us for a drink in the evening. Jon, a 4th generation Coaster, has abundant local knowledge. From main highway turn into Tudor Street signed Airport. Left into Bonar Drive, up into cul-de-sac.

Hokitika   *Homestay Semi-rural B&B 4km E of Hokitika*

Prospect House
Danielle & Lindsay Smith
Blue Spur, RD 2, Hokitika
Tel (03) 755 8043 0800 377 969   Fax (03) 755 6787
Mob 025 221 2779
prospect@minidata.co.nz
www.prospecthouse.co.nz

Double **$160-$180** (Full Breakfast) Dinner by arrangement
Credit cards accepted
1 King 1 Queen 1 Double 1 Single (3 bdrm)
2 Ensuite 1 Private

Prospect House is situated on the outskirts of Hokitika on an ancient river terrace property of some 10 acres. This lovely colonial style family home commands sweeping views of the Southern Alps, has beautiful gardens and trees and is owned by a caring, friendly family.

Our guest books are full of accolades as to the space and luxurious comfort of our home and the friendliness of the host family.All say that they wish they had arranged their trip so that they could stay longer.

This spacious home features native rimu timbers, central heating, large deck and BBQ facilities, piped music throughout and full office facilities too. The main suite contains a King size double bed and full ensuite plus tea and coffee making facilities as well. Adjoining this is a separate bedroom with a double and single bed. The second suite has a Queen size bed and ensuite. Breakfast can be either continental or a full cooked breakfast.

Our interests vary from the garden to music, current affairs, sport flying and yes ... catering for guests. We can arrange scenic flights for you to the Glaciers or to the historic goldtown port of Okarito or to other interesting destinations. We can also assist to arrange other adventures for you. We have two dogs, a Westie and a Scotty. We also have two cats.

To find us, if travelling from North turn left into
Hampden Street, continue on for 3km without turning again.

Hokitika   *Rural Homestay 3km S of Hokitika*

Meadowbank
Alison & Tom Muir
Takutai, RD 3, Hokitika

Tel (03) 755 6723   Fax (03) 755 6723
www.bnb.co.nz/meadowbank.html

Double $80 Single $50 (Full Breakfast)
Child 1/2 price Dinner by arrangement
1 Double 2 Single (2 bdrm)
1 Guests share

Tom and Alison welcome you to their lifestyle property,
situated just minutes south of Hokitika. Our large home, which we share with 2 cats, is modern, sunny
and warm, and has a large garden. Nearby we have the beach, excellent golf-links, an old gold mine,
river, and of course Hokitika, with all its attractions. Directions: Travel south 2kms from south end of
Hokitika Bridge on SH6, turn right - 200 metres on right. North-bound traffic - look for sign 1km north
of Golf-links and Paddleboat.

Hokitika   *Homestay 1km N of Hokitika*

Montezuma
Russell & Alison Alldridge
261 Revell Street, Hokitika, Westland

Tel (03) 755 7025
www.bnb.co.nz/montezuma.html

Double $90 Single $65 (Continental Breakfast)
1 Queen 1 Double (2 bdrm)
1 Ensuite 1 Guests share 1 Host share

Welcome to Montezuma by the sea. So named after a
ship that was wrecked here in 1865. Alison a
Queenslander, Russell a genuine West Coaster. Enjoy a
leisurely walk along the beach, watch the breathtaking
sunset, visit the nearby Glow Worm Dell and take time out to enjoy our West Coast hospitality. Directions:
When travelling to Hokitika from North take first turn to your right (Richards Drive). Our house is the
last on the street. When travelling from South turn left at the last street out of town.

Hokitika   *B&B Homestay Self-contained 0.9km E of Hokitika*

Larry's Rest
Linda & Paul Hewson
188 Rolleston Street, Hokitika,

Tel (03) 755 7636   Mob 021 220 3295
info@larrysrest.co.nz
www.larrysrest.co.nz

Double $110-$130 Single $100-$125
(Continental Breakfast) Cottage from $115 double
Credit cards accepted Children welcome
2 Queen 2 Twin (4 bdrm)
1 Ensuite 2 Private

Receive a warm welcome at Larry's Rest where outdoor enthusiasts Linda and Paul will willingly share
their extensive knowledge of South Island walks, activities and attractions, enabling you to make the
most of your holiday. Choose from our Queen room (ensuite), Twin room (own bathroom) or Self-
Contained Cottage with Twin room and Queen room, opening onto a secluded garden/outdoor living
area. Spacious living area, kitchen/dining, laundry. Wheelchair friendly bathroom. Families welcome.
Signposted from the main highway opposite the "Four Square" store.

Hokitika   *B&B Separate/Suite 2km E of Hokitika*

Craidenlie Lodge
Jenny & Bruce Smith
Blue Spur, Hokitika

Tel (03) 755 5063   0800 361 361   Fax (03) 755 8497
bruce@craidenlielodge.co.nz
www.craidenlielodge.co.nz

Double $180-$280 Single $180-$280
(Full Breakfast) Credit cards accepted
4 Queen 2 Twin (6 bdrm)
4 Ensuite 1 Private 1 Guests share

Our visitor's book has interesting entries: Roger and Jane Somers from the UK, "We have travelled to NZ five times. This is the best B&B we have every stayed at."
We converted our 6500 square foot family home into a lodge in 1999 located on a 40 acre section our home provides complete quiet and privacy. The native Kahikatea trees that surround the lodge are unique.
Bruce is a tennis nut, a born and bred fourth generation Coaster and entrepreneur; he will delight you with his local knowledge.
Hokitika is the centre of the West Coast, most guests base themselves here for visits to the glaciers and the Punakaiki Pancake rocks, allow two nights.
If you choose to join us the quiet and private setting with beautiful grounds will not disappoint you.

Hokitika - Lake Kaniere *B&B Self-contained 15min E of Hokitika*

Serenity
Kay & Dave Clausen
6 Stuart Street, Hans Bay, Lake Kaniere,
Postal: PO Box 133, Hokitika

Tel (03) 755 5038 Mob 025 372 666
dmkeclausen@xtra.co.nz
www.bnb.co.nz/serenity.html

Double $80 Single $60 (Continental Breakfast)
Child $20 under 15 years extra adults (over dbl) $40
1 Queen 2 Single (1 bdrm)   1 Private

Lake Kaniere is set amongst beautiful New Zealand native
bush. The scenery is breathtaking. There are many bush-walks around the lake, and Dorothy Falls is just a short drive from 'Serenity'. Our studio apartment is self-catering and has full kitchen and bathroom facilities. All linen is provided. Restaurants and cafe-bars are just a shortdrive away, at Hokitika, or it's great to just relax and enjoy the surroundings at Lake Kaniere - a very unspoilt place! 'Serenity' is two minutes walk from the Lake. Separate access, studio apartment.

Hokitika - Upper Kokatahi *Farmstay Self-contained 28km E of Hokitika*

Trish & Terry Sheridan
Middle Branch Road, Upper Kokatahi RD1, Hokitika

Tel (03) 755 7967
www.bnb.co.nz/sheridan.html

Double $90-$100 Single $50 (Full Breakfast)
Child Neg. Dinner $30 B/A S/C Unit From $60
Children welcome Pets welcome
1 Queen 2 Double 3 Twin (6 bdrm)
1 Ensuite

Welcome to our 1000-acre dairy farm at the top of Kokatahi Valley 28km East of Hokitika. Numerous day walks, three rives with trout fishing and kayaking and Lake Kaniere are all minutes away. Share our newly renovated home or stay in our fully serviced self-contained unit. We enjoy meeting people and love travelling. Terry enjoys current affairs and all sports while Trish is happy in the kitchen or garden. Enjoy dining with us in peaceful surroundings.

Ruatapu *B&B Country Stay 12km S of Hokitika*

Berwick's Hill
Eileen & Roger Berwick
Ruatapu, Ruatapu-Ross Road,
State Highway 6, RD 3, Hokitika

Tel (03) 755 7876 Fax (03) 755 7870
Mob 025 673 7387 berwicks@xtra.co.nz
www.bnb.co.nz/berwickshill.html

Double $90-$100 Single $60 (Full Breakfast)
Dinner $35 by arrangement Credit cards accepted
1 Queen 2 Single (2 bdrm)
1 Ensuite 1 Private

Welcome to Berwick's Hill. We offer you a warm and relaxed stay in our comfortable home. Magnificent views of the Tasman Sea and the Southern Alps are seen from the main living areas.Experience the sunsets and sunrises. We are close to Lake Mahinapua,bush walks, the beach and Golf course. We run sheep and cattle and grow pine trees on our hobby farm. We have one farm dog and we share our home with our two cats and our house dog.

Harihari *Farmstay Luxury Farmstay / Country Lodge 0.5km S of Hari Hari*

Wapiti Park Homestead
Bev & Grant Muir
RD 1, Hari Hari 7953, South Westland

Tel (03) 753 3074   0800 WAPITI   Fax (03) 753 3074
wapitipark@xtra.co.nz   www.wapitipark.co.nz

Double $165-$345 Single $125-$275
(Special Breakfast) Dinner $60 - 5 course Credit cards accepted
6 King 1 Twin 4 Single (7 bdrm)
6 Ensuite 1 Private

Hosts Grant and Beverleigh invite you to join them and discover the unique experience of staying at Wapiti Park Homestead. Enjoy a special combination of elegance, informal sophistication, and warm hospitality. Relax in complete comfort and affordable luxury.
Set in tranquil surroundings amid extensive gardens, our modern colonial style Lodge is built on the site of the original Hari Hari accommodation house, coaching stop and Post Office, and overlooks its own small farm which specialises in the breeding of Wapiti (Rocky Mountain Elk).
Join Grant on the 6pm tour to handfeed the Wapiti, meet the farm pet "Vicki" and learn about the Elk Antler Velvet Extract and its significant potential health benefits. Enjoy spacious indoor/outdoor areas; large bedrooms with superior comfort beds and ensuites or private facilities; 2 lounges and a trophy games room; a well stocked bar fridge and selection of NZ wines; and our renowned "All you can eat" Country style 5 course dinners. Special diets catered for by prior arrangement.
Our location on State Highway 6 makes us the ideal stopover between the Nelson/Christchurch - Wanaka/ Queenstown areas. However to explore this scenic wonderland of rainforests, glaciers, lakes and National Parks; to pursue the challenges of our renowned brown trout fishery, to hunt or to simply catch your breath and relax, you really need at least a 2 night stay. Guided hunting and fishing available and other activities arranged on request.
Unsuitable for children under 12. Direct booking, multi-night and off season discounts available. Advance booking recommended. *Spoil Yourself!*

"Outstanding - five star at its best." (E&L Australia)
"Well above expectations. Fantastic food and hospitality." (M&J UK)
"We loved it. Best stay of our whole trip. Super food, wonderful Elk and Hosts." (S&J USA)

Whataroa   *Farmstay 35km N of Franz Josef*

Matai Lodge
Glenice & Jim Purcell
Whataroa, South Westland

Tel (03) 753 4156   0800 787 235
Fax (03) 753 4156   Mob 021 155 2506
jpurcell@xtra.co.nz
www.bnb.co.nz/matailodgewhataroa.html

Double $120-$180   Single $100
(Continental Full Breakfast) Dinner $40pp
1 King/Twin 1 King 2 Single (3 bdrm)
1 Ensuite 1 Private

Matai Lodge rests in the tranquil valley 20 minutes north of Franz Josef Glacier in the small farming community of Whataroa. You are welcome to share with us our modern spacious home on the 400 acre farm of sheep, cows, and farm dog. Upstairs is a suite of a king-size room and twin room with conservatory and private bathroom and downstairs a king-size ensuite you are welcome to join us for a home cooked dinner with NZ wine, over which we enjoy hearing tales from your home, and we will help you discover ours, with local advice and activity bookings available our motto is 'A STRANGER is a FRIEND we have yet to meet'.

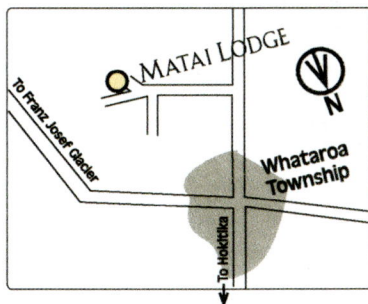

You will need at least two days to see the Glaciers, walk in the World Heritage Park, kayak on the Okirito Lagoon, or visit the White Heron Bird Sanctuary by jet boat and see the spectacular scenery, or go horse trekking. Glenice and Jim play golf at the scenic golf course in Whataroa, green fees $10, clubs available.

Glenice has travelled to Japan teaching felting, weaving and spinning and enjoyed Japanese customs and language and being hosted by her many friends there. Jim and Glenice look forward to sharing their home and tranquil scenic paradise with you. Also available: Tel/Fax, Email, Sky TV, Laundry.

Driving Time from Matai Lodge to: Christchurch 5 hours, Picton 6 hours, Nelson 6 hours, Queenstown 6 hours, Wanaka 4 hours, Greymouth 2 hours, Whataroa 3km, and Franz Josef 20 minutes.

Whataroa - South Westland   *B&B Farmstay 13km N of Whataroa/10 mins*

Mt Adam Lodge
Elsa & Mac MacRae
State Highway 6, Whataroa, South Westland
Tel (03) 753 4030   0800 675 137   Fax (03) 753 4264
mtadamlodge@paradise.net.nz
www.mountadamlodge.co.nz

Double $90-$120 Single $75-$90
(Continental Breakfast) Credit cards accepted
2 Queen 1 Double 4 Twin (7 bdrm)
5 Ensuite 2 Guests share

If you're wanting to escape the crowds in the busy tourist centres then we are an ideal place for you to stay. Just a short 35 minute drive north of Franz Josef Glacier. We are situated on our farm at the foot of Mt Adam surrounded by farmlands and beautiful native bush. Our lodge is just newly established and offers comfortable accommodation and a fully licensed restaurant. You can stroll along the river bank and the farm tracks meeting our variety of animals along the way.

Franz Josef Glacier   *Self-contained 3km N of Franz Josef*

Franz Josef Glacier B&B
Marie & Glenn Coburn
Stoney Creek, State Highway 6, Franz Josef Glacier
Tel (03) 752 0171   Fax (03) 752 0213
mcoburn@paradise.net.nz
www.bnb.co.nz/franzjosefglacierbb.html

Double $100-$150 Single $95-$125 (Full Breakfast)
Dinner by arrangement Credit cards accepted
  Children welcome
2 Queen (2 bdrm)   1 Ensuite 1 Private

Marie, Glenn, Sophie-Rose(5yrs) & cat Tigger, invite you
to come experience West Coast hospitality in the privacy of our unit. Separate from the house, our room is surrounded with gardens, farmland, rainforest, native birds and mountain views. Also avaiable a self-contained unit with cooking facilities on a separtate property near Lake Mapourika - a perfect country retreat. Marie's family have lived in Franz Josef over 100 years, so has lots of local knowledge and is able to assist with bookings on Helicopter Flights, Glacier Walks, Fishing, etc.

Franz Josef Glacier   *B&B Homestay 1.5km N of Franz Josef Glacier*

Holly Homestead
Gerard & Bernie Oudemans
State Highway 6, Franz Josef Glacier, South Westland
Tel (03) 752 0299   Fax (03) 752 0298
stay@hollyhomestead.co.nz
www.hollyhomestead.co.nz

Double $150-$220 Single $130-$190 (Full Breakfast)
Child N/A Credit cards accepted
2 King/Twin 2 Queen (4 bdrm)
2 Ensuite 1 Private 1 Guests share

Gerard and Bernie invite you to share their character 1920's home. Located on "The Glacier Highway", Holly Homestead offers the peace and quiet of the country with the convenience of the township nearby. We happily provide local information and bookings for various activities for you to enjoy our magnificent region. There's plenty to do, or you can have a rest by relaxing in our comfortable guest lounge. Spectacular view from breakfast table, clouds permitting! Reservations recommended November to March (inclusive). Children aged 12+ welcome.

Franz Josef   *B&B 4km N of Franz Josef Glacier*

Lacebark Bed and Breakfast
Julie Wolbers and Jo Crofton
26 Greens Road, Franz Josef Glacier,
Tel (03) 752 0072   Fax (03) 752 0272
jojulie@xtra.co.nz
www.bnb.co.nz/lacebark.html

Double $130 Single $100 (Continental Breakfast)
1 Queen (1 bdrm)
1 Private

Welcome to our world heritage rainforest and West Coast
glacier country. Enjoy a relaxing bath and a comfortable
night's sleep in our new home after taking in the regions
scenic attractions. We are located centrally to the glacier, Okarito and the white heron sanctuary. We
can offer expert advice on local bush walks and tramping opportunities of the region. Enjoy stunning
alpine views from your bedroom window. Our home is situated in a quiet rural location 5 minutes drive
from Franz Josef township.

Franz Josef   *B&B 3km S of Franz Josef*

Knightswood B&B
Sheryl Pearson & Gerry Findlay
State Highway 6, Franz Josef Glacier,
Tel (03) 752 0059   Fax (03) 752 0061
knightswood@xtra.co.nz
www.knightswood.co.nz

Double $140-$180 Single $120-$150 (Full Breakfast)
Child Price dependent on age Dinner By arrangement
1 King/Twin 1 King 1 Queen 1 Single (3 bdrm)
2 Ensuite 1 Host share

Enjoy our modern home on 24 acres, with spectacular
alpine views. Although minutes from the town and glacier, we assure you peace and tranquility. Gerry,
a helicopter pilot and former wildlife ranger, and Sheryl enjoy convivial conversation and sharing
experiences. Enjoy an interpretive guided walk through our own native bush, view the prolific bird life
or venture further for a scenic glacial flight, hike the glaciers, forests or wild coastline, or kayak and fish
on our lakes and rivers.

Fox Glacier   *Homestay 0 km N of Fox Glacier*

Roaring Billy Lodge
Billy & Kathy
PO Box 16, 21 State Highway 6, Fox Glacier
Tel (03) 751 0815   Fax (03) 751 0085
kathynz@xtra.co.nz
www.bnb.co.nz/roaringbillylodge.html

Double $85-$100 Single $70-$85 (Special Breakfast)
Credit cards accepted
1 King/Twin 1 Double 1 Twin (2 bdrm)
1 Guests share

Welcome to the comfort, warmth and hospitality of our
two-story home. Our livingroom, kitchen, diningroom and veranda are upstairs and lined with local
timbers, with 360-degree views of glacier valley, mountains, farms and the township. We're the closest
homestay to the glacier and 2 minutes walk to all eating and tourist facilities. We are happy to book
your local activities. The bus goes past our home. We offer a special cooked vegetarian breakfast. We
have one cat, Koko and one dog, Angel.

Fox Glacier   *B&B Farmstay 0.5km W of Fox Glacier*

The Homestead
Noeleen & Kevin Williams
PO Box 25, Cook Flat Road, Fox Glacier
Tel (03) 751 0835   Fax (03) 751 0805
foxhmstd@xtra.co.nz
www.bnb.co.nz/thehomestead.html

Double $125-$155
(Continental Breakfast)
Cooked Breakfast $7pp
1 King/Twin 2 Queen (3 bdrm)
2 Ensuite 1 Private

Kevin, Noeleen and Chancey our friendly
Corgi, welcome you to our 2,200 acre beef
cattle and sheep farm. Beautiful native
bush-clad mountains surround on three sides, and we enjoy a view of Mt Cook.
Our spacious 105 year old character home, built for Kevin's grandparents has fine stained glass windows.
The breakfast room overlooks peaceful pastures to the hills, and you are served homemade yoghurt,
jams, marmalade, scones etc, with a cooked breakfast if desired.
The guest lounge, with its beautiful wooden panelled ceiling, has an open plan fire for cool autumn
nights.
A rural retreat within walking distance of village facilities, with Matheson (Mirror Lake) and glacier
nearby. It is our pleasure to help you with helihikes, helicopter scenic flights and glacier walks. Unsuitable
for small children. Bookings recommended. Smoke-free.

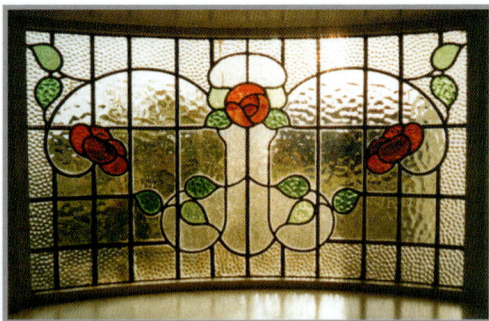

Directions: On Cook Flat Road, 5th house on right, 400m back off road before Church.

Fox Glacier   *Homestay Fox Glacier Central*

Reflection Lodge
Raelene Tuck
PO Box 46, Cook Flat Road, Fox Glacier

Tel (03) 751 0707   Fax (03) 751 0707
raelene@reflectionlodge.co.nz
www.reflectionlodge.co.nz

Double $130-$155 (Continental Breakfast)
Child $35 Twin $130 Children welcome
2 Queen 1 Single (3 bdrm)
1 Ensuite

Welcome to the Glacier region. Reflection Lodge offers
panoramic views of Mt Cook and Mt Tasman, New Zealand's two highest peaks reflecting in our own
private lake. Myself and Colin (a local helicopter pilot), are fourth generation West Coasters and have
lived in the Glacier region for 12 years. We invite you to share the comfort of our home and gardens.
We are more than happy to assist you with any activities in our picturesque region. We enjoy meeting
people and look forward to sharing our wonderful piece of paradise.

Fox Glacier   *Homestay*

Fox Glacier Homestay
Eunice & Michael Sullivan
64 Cook Flat Road, Fox Glacier,

Tel (03) 751 0817   Fax (03) 751 0817
euni@xtra.co.nz
www.bnb.co.nz/foxglacier.html

Double $90-$110 Single $70-$90
(Continental Breakfast) Children welcome
Pets welcome
1 Queen 1 Double 1 Single (3 bdrm)
1 Host share

Eunice and Michael are third generation farming and tourism family. We have three grown children, 1
dog (Ruff), 1 cat (Black Cat). Our grandparents were founders of the Fox Glacier Hotel. We are a
couple who enjoy meeting people and would like to share the joys of living in our little paradise (rain
and all). Our home is surrounded by a large garden and have views of the mountains and Mt Cook. A
five minute walk from township.

Fox Glacier   *B&B Self-contained 2km W of Fox Glacier*

Mountain View
Julene & Phil Silcock
Williams Drive, Fox Glacier,

Tel (03) 751 0770   Fax (03) 751 0774
gingephil@actrix.co.nz
www.bnb.co.nz/user104.html

Double $120-$140 (Continental Breakfast)
1 King 1 Double 1 Twin (3 bdrm)
3 Ensuite

Our family welcomes you to Mountain View B&B. Set
on 10 acres of farmland surrounded by bush clad hills with spectacular views of Mt Cook and Mt
Tasman. Situated 2km from Fox Village our 5 year old country home has it all, peaceful surroundings
and friendly hospitality. We have extensive knowledge of the area and can organise Glacier flights and
walks. We are just 2 minutes drive to restaurants and cafes. We have 2 school age children Harry 9 and
Katie 7, 1 cat, 1 toy poodle and 2 horses. Children welcome. Smoke free.

WEST COAST

Fox Glacier   *B&B Homestay Fox Glacier town centre*

Pekanga Homestay
Mike and Nicole Hall
Glacier Lane, Pekanga Drive, Fox Glacier

Tel (03) 751 0016   0800 10 26 25
Fax (03) 751 0740
info@fox-glacier.co.nz
www.bnb.co.nz/pekangahomestay.html

Double $90-$130 Single $70-$110
(Continental Breakfast) Dinner by prior arrangement
Children by arrangement
1 King/Twin 1 Queen 1 Twin (3 bdrm)

Nicole and Mike welcome you to their Bed and Breakfast built new in 2001.

We are set agains the native bush with off street parking. Relax in the lounge with warm fire, huge selection of books and Sky TV.

We are located in the centre of Fox Glacier, some 500 metres from Cafes, Restaraunts, Helicopter Flights and Guided Glacier walking companies.

Mike is a local helicopter pilot and has a host of information on the area. Nicole has previously worked in tourist infomation and can help make your stay a well organised one.

www.bnb.co.nz/pekangahomestay.html

Fox Glacier *B&B Boutique Accommodation 160km S of Hokitika*

Lea & Dave Bentley
Cook Flat Road, Fox Glacier, South Westland
Tel (03) 751 0849 Fax (03) 751 0849
davidbentley@xtra.co.nz
mistypeaks.co.nz

Double $250
4 King/Twin 4 King (4 bdrm)
4 Ensuite 4 Private

Lea & Dave Bentley welcome you to 'Misty Peaks' our new purpose-built Boutique Accommodation offering you the very best in quality, comfort and genuine Kiwi hospitality.'Misty Peaks' offers four private guest suites each with luxurious bedding, private ensuites, hairdryers, telephone, tv and complimentary gift basket to enjoy. Each suite has double-opening doors to veranda, double glazing and individual guest access.The veranda around "Misty Peaks" provides a comfortable setting to take in breathtaking views of Mt Cook and Mt Tasman, stunning sunsets and the delightful ever-changing rural setting.

A well appointed guest lounge with wood fire provides a quality atmosphere to relax in and enjoy a complimentary drink with other guests. An A La Carte dinner offering quality fresh New Zealand produce and wines is available every evening with all guests dining together.

Breakfast is available at a time to suit your plans for the day. Fresh fruit hot muffins and bread, a delicious full cooked or continental. Complimentary tea and coffee available at all times.

Our aim is to make your stay at *Misty Peaks* one to rememeber, and hopefully one day you will return to our little part of paradise to share it with us again.

Bruce Bay *Farmstay 50km S of Fox Glacier*

Mulvaney Farmstay
Peter & Malai Millar
PO Box 117, Bruce Bay, South Westland
Tel (03) 751 0865 0800 393 297 Fax (03) 751 0865
mulvaney@xtra.co.nz
www.bnb.co.nz/millar.html
Double $80-$95 Single $65 (Continental Breakfast)
Child n/a Dinner $30
1 Queen 1 Double 1 Twin (3 bdrm)
1 Guests share 1 Host share

Welcome to Mulvaney Farmstays! We run a beef farm
consisting mainly of Hereford and Limosin cattle. Our house was built in the 1920's by my Great Uncle
Jack Mulvaney, for his bride to be but she never arrived. Jack Mulvaney was of Irish descent, just as the
rest of his family was who settled in this valley 130 years ago. So he lived here by himself until 1971
raising Hereford cattle. We have now lived her for 20 years with our children (who are all grown up and
studying away from home).

Paringa *Farmstay Homestay 70km S of Fox Glacier*

Condon Farmstays
Glynis & Tony Condon
NZ Post Ltd, Lake Paringa, South Westland
Tel (03) 751 0895 Fax (03) 751 0001
Mob 025 647 4965 condonfarms@xtra.co.nz
www.bnb.co.nz/condonfarmstays.html
Double $85 Single $50 (Full Breakfast) Child $20
Dinner $30 by arrangement Children welcome
1 Double 4 Single (3 bdrm)
1 Host share

We run a 4th generation working beef farm, with a few sheep. We enjoy meeting people and have
travelled to America, England, Kenya, Australia and some parts of Europe. Our farm is nestled beneath
the bush clad foothills of the Southern Alps, close to Lake Paringa and the Paringa River. We have three
adult children and three grandchildren. Two children live in New Zealand and one overseas. Our
interests include hunting, jet boating, fishing, spinning, knitting and reading.Tony is a civil marriage
celebrant. We have one house cat and a small dog.

Haast *B&B Homestay Self-contained 16km S of Haast*

Okuru Beach
Marian & Derek Beynon
Okuru, Haast, South Westland
Tel (03) 750 0719 Fax (03) 750 0722
okurubeach@xtra.co.nz www.okurubeach.co.nz
Double $75-$80 Single $50 (Continental Breakfast)
Child $20 Dinner $20 by arrangement
Self-contained $85 Credit cards accepted
3 Double 4 Single (5 bdrm)
1 Ensuite 1 Private 1 Guests share

Okuru Beach gives you the opportunity to stay in a unique part
of our country, in a friendly relaxed environment. Enjoy coastal
beaches with driftwood, shells and penguins in season. Walk in
the rainforest and view the native birds. We and our friendly Labrador dog enjoy sharing our comfortable
home and local knowledge. Dinner served with prior notice. Our interests are our handcraft shop, coin
collecting, fishing and tramping. Also available - Seaview Cottage, self-contained sleeps 4 persons.
Directions - turn into Jacksons Bay Road, drive 14km turn into Okuru.

Canterbury

Reefton

Kaikoura

Hanmer Springs

7

Waiau

1

Inchbonnie

Culverden

Gore Bay

Waikari

Waipara

Castle Hill Village

Amberley

73

Lake Coleridge

Rangiora

Waikuku Beach

Oxford

Mt Hutt

Darfield

72

West Melton

Chch. City enlargement next page

Methven

Lincoln

Staveley

Okains Bay

Rakaia

Akaroa

Akaroa Harbour

Ashburton

1

Ealing

0 Kilometres 40

0 Miles 24

Towns listed generally follow
a north to south route. Refer
to the index if required.

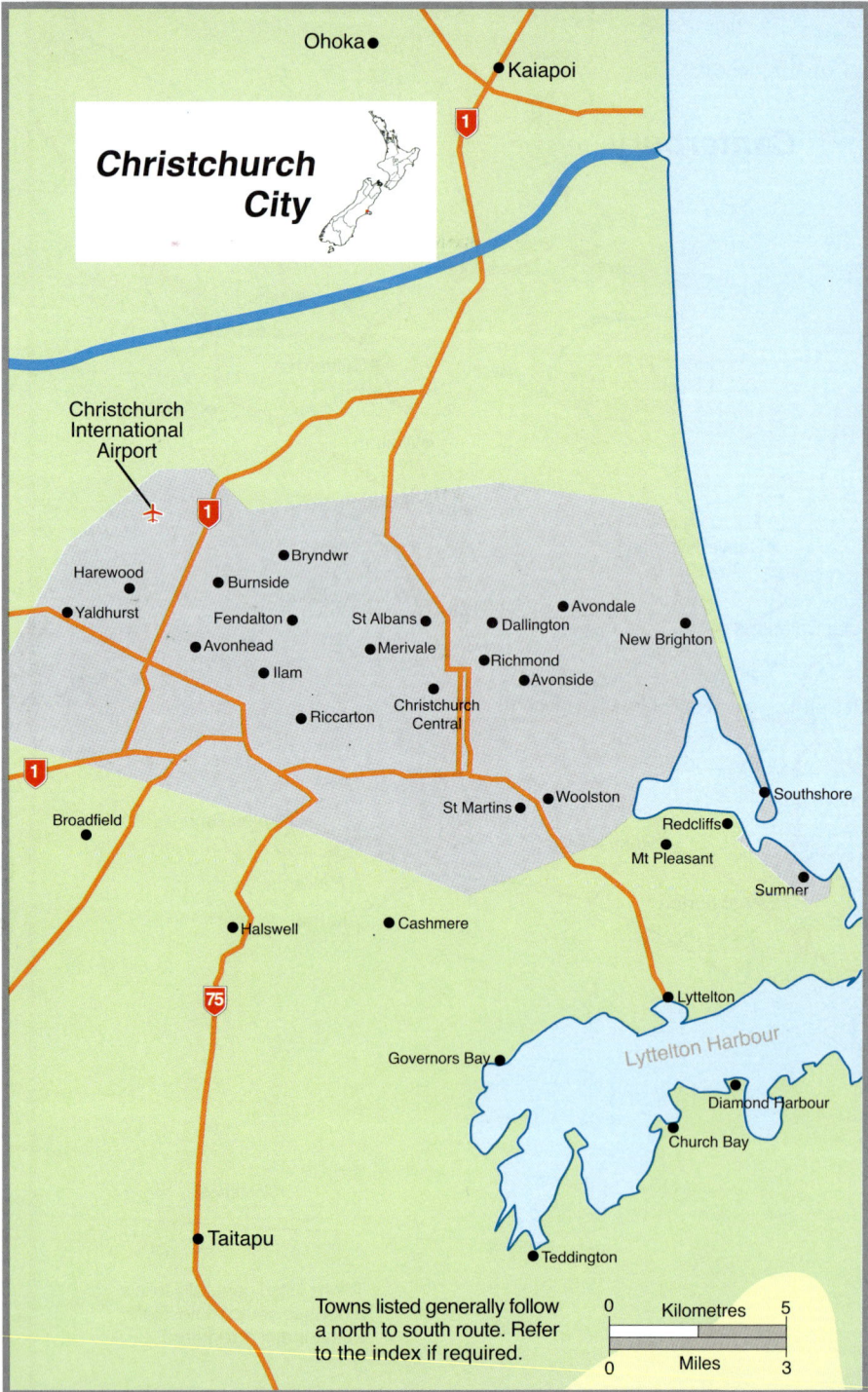

Christchurch City

Ohoka

Kaiapoi

1

Christchurch International Airport

1

Harewood

Yaldhurst

Bryndwr

Burnside

Fendalton

Avonhead

Ilam

St Albans

Merivale

Dallington

Richmond

Avonside

Avondale

New Brighton

Riccarton

Christchurch Central

Woolston

Southshore

St Martins

Redcliffs

Mt Pleasant

Sumner

Broadfield

Halswell

Cashmere

Lyttelton

75

Governors Bay

Lyttelton Harbour

Diamond Harbour

Church Bay

Taitapu

Teddington

Towns listed generally follow a north to south route. Refer to the index if required.

| 0 | Kilometres | 5 |
| 0 | Miles | 3 |

Kaikoura   *Homestay Back packers   130km   S of Blenheim*

Bay-View
Margaret Woodill
296 Scarborough Street, Kaikoura
Tel (03) 319 5480   Fax (03) 319 7480
MSBSDH@xtra.co.nz
www.bnb.co.nz/bayviewkaikoura.html

Double $75 Single $45 (Full Breakfast)
Child $15 under 14   Dinner $25   Queen ensuite $85
Children welcome Pets welcome
2 Queen 1 Twin 1 Single (4 bdrm)
1 Ensuite 1 Private 1 Guests share 1 Host share

Our spacious family home on Kaikoura Peninsula has splendid mountain and sea views and is exceptionally quiet. Only five minutes from the Kaikoura township, off the main highway south. The house nestles in an acre of colourful garden and there is plenty of off-street parking. A guest lounge is available or you are more than welcome to socialise with the host. Laundry facilities and tea/coffee with homemade baking available.

Traditional breakfast with home baked bread, muesli, home preserves, available early as required for whale/dolphin watching guests. Enjoy breakfast in the dining area or out on the sunny deck whilst taking in the magnificent mountain view.   We book local activities and happily meet bus or train.

Margaret, your friendly host, has lived in the area for most of her life. She has a grown family of four and seven grandchildren.   Margaret enjoys gardening, golf, bowls, sewing, choir and her amusing Burmese cat. She especially enjoys warmly welcoming guests into her home.

Guests comments: *"This B&B is an unforgettable memory for me in NZ five weeks travel"* (Japan). *"Beautiful place, beautiful food, fabulous hospitality, Margaret. Thank you for opening up your home and welcoming us. Be back again"* (Wellington). *"Thank you for meeting the train and showing us the area. You were highly recommended and we absolutely endorse this"* (UK). *"Many thanks for your generous hospitality. You and your lovely home are a credit to B&B Homestays"* (UK). *"The most amazing breakfast in all of New Zealand. The views are amazing too and so is Margaret's hospitality"* (Australia). *"We felt like family! Thank you for such a lovely visit and wonderful, delicious meals. We thank you a million!"* (USA).

"Let Our Home be Your Home"

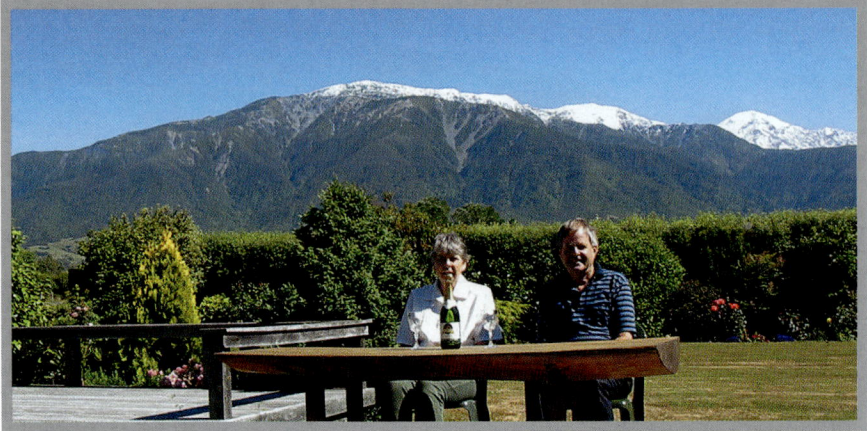

Kaikoura *B&B Self-contained 5km N of Kaikoura*

Ardara Lodge
Alison & Ian Boyd
233 Schoolhouse Road, RD1, Kaikoura
Tel (03) 319 5736   0800 226 164   Fax (03) 319 5732
aemboyd@xtra.co.nz   www.ardaralodge.com
Double $95-$100 Single $70-$80
(Continental Breakfast) Child $15   Children welcome
Cottage, 2 - 6 persons $120 - $200   Credit cards accepted
6 Queen 2 Twin 3 Single (6 bdrm)
5 Ensuite

You will enjoy a relaxed and peaceful stay in a beautiful rural setting near the magnificent Kaikoura mountains. Relax on our deck and enjoy Alison's colourful garden which completes the panoramic view. Enjoy our outdoor hot tub (spa), view the Kaikoura mountains by day and the stars by night.   Ian's Great, Great, Uncle Jim, left "Ardara", Ireland in 1876. He bought our land here in Kaikoura in 1883 and milked cows. He established an orchard and planted macrocarpa trees for shelter   One macrocarpa tree was milled and used to build the cottage which was designed and built by Ian in 1998.

The cottage has an upstairs bedroom with a queen and two single beds. Downstairs there is a bedroom with a queen bed, a bathroom with a shower, and a lounge, kitchen, dining room. The deck is private with a great view of the mountains. It has been very popular with groups, families and honeymoon couples.

The house has ensuite bathrooms with queen beds, TV, fridge, settee and coffee/tea facilities. You have your own private entrance and you can come and go as you please. We offer laundry facilities, off street parking, courtesy car from bus/train.

Bookings for local tourist attractions, restaurants and farm tours can be arranged. Ian's brother Murray, has Donegal House, an Irish Garden Bar and Restaurant, which is within walking distance. Ian is a retired teacher and Alison a librarian. Our hobbies are tennis, golf, designing and building houses, gardening, handcrafts, spinning and we like to travel. No smoking indoors please. We look forward to your company.   Directions: Driving north, 4km from Kaikoura on SH1, turn left, 1.5km along Schoolhouse Road.

TERRACE ON THE PARK APARTMENT
Our one and two bedroom upmarket apartments are in central Christchurch and within walking distance to all amenities such as the Arts Centre, Museum, Casino and Hagley Park. The third level apartments are in a quiet area and have good views. Double queen bed, single bed, television, video, etc. Tariff: ($110-$120 per night (min. 3 nights) or $665 per week. Serviced weekly. For more information: http://ardaralodge.com/flat.htm

Kaikoura *B&B Homestay Kaikoura Central*

Bevron
Bev & Ron Barr
196 Esplanade, Kaikoura
Tel (03) 319 5432   Fax (03) 319 5432
bevronhouse@hotmail.com
www.bnb.co.nz/bevron.html
Double $90 Single $80 (Continental Breakfast)
Child 1/2 price
2 Double 2 Twin (2 bdrm)
2 Ensuite

We are a friendly active retired couple who enjoy meeting new people and sharing the delights of our home on the beachfront. The view from our balcony is breathtaking, giving an unobstructed panorama of sea and mountains. We have guest TV lounge and games room. There is a swimming beach opposite, with children's play area and BBQ. Kaikoura has many tourist attractions, we are happy to help with bookings. Our home is centrally located, being a short walk to restaurants, galleries and scenic attractions.

Kaikoura *Farmstay 20km SW of Kaikoura*

The Kahutara Homestead
Nikki & John Smith
PO Box 9, Kaikoura
Tel (03) 319 5580   0800 27 33 51   Fax (03) 319 5580
kahutarahomestead@xtra.co.nz
www.bnb.co.nz/thekahutara.html
Double $190-$210 Single $150 (Full Breakfast)
Dinner $50 - $70 Credit cards accepted
2 Queen 3 Single (3 bdrm)
1 Ensuite 1 Private 1 Guests share

The Kahutara - a haven in the hills. An award-winning homestay situated on the Inland Kaikoura Route. The Alpine Pacific Triangle linking Kaikoura with the Hamner Springs thermal pool resort or fish the Clarence River for trout: one and a half hours drive. We operate a 2600-acre beef cattle and sheep farm with a small thoroughbred stud. Enjoy quality homestead accommodation in well-appointed rooms, and experience country hospitality. Complimentary pre dinner drinks and local Marlborough/Canterbury wines served with dinner. Walk the surrounding valley or enjoy lawn croquet.

Kaikoura *B&B Farmstay Self-contained motel 20km N of Kaikoura*

Clematis Grove Retreat
Margaret & Ken Hamilton
Blue Duck Valley, RD 1, Kaikoura
Tel (03) 319 5264   0800 319 525   Fax (03) 319 5278
clematisgrove@xtra.co.nz
www.virtual-kaikoura.com/clematis grove
Double $80-$120 Single $70 (Continental Breakfast)
Child 1/2 price Dinner $30 Full breakfast b/a
Credit cards accepted
2 King/Twin 1 Queen 1 Double 1 Twin 2 Single
(4 bdrm)
2 Ensuite 1 Private 1 Host share

Coming to Kaikoura? Come and stay at Clematis Grove. Experience real NZ hospitality on a high country farm. Luxury accommodation at an affordable price, extremely private. Why stay in town? Come away from the crowds. At your door walk through our native forest, trees estimated up to 1100 years old. Listen to our native birds: watch our incredible native pigeons. You will be amazed at the stars at night, a Morepork calls. Farm tours can be arranged. Incredible views of Kaikoura and the mountains.

Kaikoura *B&B 130km S of Blenheim*

Churchill Park Lodge
Moira & Stan Paul
34 Churchill Street, Kaikoura, Marlborough

Tel (03) 319 5526 0800 363 690
Fax (03) 319 5526 cplodge@ihug.co.nz
www.churchillparklodge.co.nz

Double $90-$95 Single $75-$80
(Continental Breakfast)
Child $20 Children welcome
Credit cards accepted
1 Queen 1 Double 1 Single (2 bdrm)
2 Ensuite

We proudly offer you the choice of two separate upstairs suites with ensuite bathrooms, TV, fridge, lounge settee, dining suite, and tea/coffee making facilities including coffee percolator, heater and electric blankets. We have designed your room to guarantee your stay with us is comfortable and enjoyable. Our rooms are smoke free. We offer laundry facilities and off-street parking.

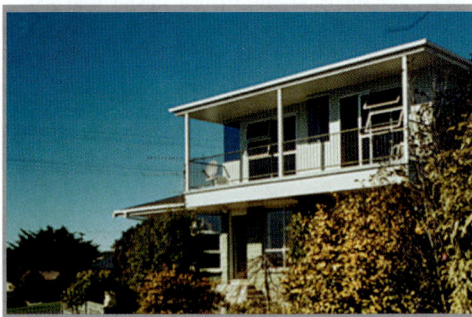

We believe the sea and mountain views we offer from your room and balcony is unbeatable in Kaikoura. Take time to relax and enjoy your continental breakfast while watching the sun rise out of the sea.

Our home is only five minutes walk through Churchill Park to the town centre where you will find a restaurant that will suit your taste buds, souvenir shops, Visitor Information Centre and a walk along the beach. We are in close walking distance to Whalewatch and Dolphin Encounter Tour Departure Stations and are happy to book local tours and offer a courtesy pick up from train or bus stations.

We are a Christian couple and like Muffy, our cat, are friendly and welcoming and look forward to making your stay a time to remember.

Unbeatable sea and mountain views

Kaikoura   *B&B Lodge 3km N of Kaikoura*

Carrickfin Lodge
Roger Boyd
Mill Road, Kaikoura

Tel (03) 319 5165   0800 265 963
Fax (03) 319 5162
www.bnb.co.nz/carrickfinlodge.html

Double $100 Single $80 (Full Breakfast)
Child Not Suitable
Carrickfin Cottage, fully S/C
Sleeps 8 $100 - $120
5 Queen 2 Single (6 bdrm)
6 Ensuite

Welcome to Kaikoura (Kai = food   Koura = Crayfish).
My name is Roger and I'm the fourth generation "Boyd" to live and farm "Carrickfin". It is an ancient Irish name from where my Great Gran father emigrated. Dongal is still the home of the "Boyds". He bought and settled this land in 1867 for 100 gold sovereigns which he got prospecting.
The Lodge is built on 100 acres adjoining the Kairkoura township. It is a large and spacious place with an open fire and a guests' bar. It was built well back from the road amidst two acres of lawns and shrubs to give complete privacy and security.
There are breathtaking views from all rooms looking directly at the "Seaward Kaikouras" a spectacular mountain range which rises to 8,500ft. These mountains are home to a unique and variety of wild life. Our sea and coastline is also unique for the Whales, Dolphins, Seals and many ocean going birds including the Wandering Albatros. It is one place in the world where Whales are found all the year round. As well as fattening heifers I am a professional Wool Classer by trade and have worked in shearing sheds throughout the South Island high Country. Another feature of "Carrickfin Lodge" is the big English Breakfast which is legendary. I am 3km from Whale Watch, Dolphin Encounter and some of the best restaurants.
Carrickfin Cottage, fully self-contained, sleeps 8. Tariff $100 - $120

Directions: At the north end of town turn west into Mill Road. I am up on the left (Easy to find - hard to leave).

Kaikoura *B&B, Farmstay, Licenced Rest & Accommodation   5km N of Kaikoura*

Donegal House
Murray Boyd
Schoolhouse Road, Kaikoura

Tel (03) 319 5083   Fax (03) 319 5083
donegalhouse@xtra.co.nz   www.donegalhouse.co.nz

Double $120 Single $100   (Continental Breakfast)
Child $15 Dinner $24.50 Credit cards accepted
12 queen 3 single (13 bedrooms)
13 ensuite

"Donegal House"
The little Irish Pub in the country, brimming with warmth
and hospitality, open fires and accordion music.

Set on an historical dairy farm which has been farmed by the Boyd family since their arrival from Donegal, Ireland in 1865, "Donegal House" offers, accommodation, full bar facilities and a public licensed restaurant.

The a-la-carte menu, specialising in Kaikoura's famous crayfish and seafood, plus locally farmed beef. NZ beers, Kilkenny and Guinness are on tap along with a good selection of Marlborough wines.

Two spring fed lakes, home to Chinook salmon, Mute and Black Swans, Blue Teal, Paradise and Mallard ducks, are feature in the extensive lawns and gardens which surround "Donegal House". the towering Kaikoura Mountains make a perfect backdrop to this unique setting. The Restaurant and Bar facilities at "Donegal House" have become a very popular place for visitors staying at the nearby Carrick-finn Lodge, Ardara Lodge, The Old Convent and Dylans Country Stay, to meet the Kaikoura locals and enjoy the rural hospitality in a unique Irish atmosphere.

We book whale watching, dolphin and seal swimming and horse trekking etc. "Even if you're not Irish-this is the place for you!" "A home away from home!"

Directions:
Driving North 4kms from Kaikoura on SH1 turn left at Large transit signs, 1.6km along Schoolhouse Road.

Kaikoura *Separate/Suite B&B Inn 3.6km N of Kaikoura*

Old Convent
Gordon, Judith, Jenny
Mt Fyffe Road, Kaikoura
Tel (03) 319 6603 0800 365 603   Fax (03) 319 6690
o.convent@xtra.co.nz   www.theoldconvent.co.nz
Double $110-$175 Single $75 (Full Breakfast)
Family Suites $205 Credit cards accepted
Children welcome Pets welcome
3 King/Twin 3 Queen 6 Double 3 Twin 2 Single
(17 bdrm) 14 Ensuite 2 Private

One of Kaikoura's few historic buildings, the Old Convent, built to a French design in 1911, offers unique accommodation in a tranquil setting just minutes from town. Your hosts, a journalist, home restorer and human rights lawyer are Kiwis whose families came to Kaikoura and Central Otago in the 1850s. They have many connections with Australia. The Old Convent offers delicious dinners (crayfish), cooked or light breakfast, internet, the travellers' bar, laundry, bikes, swimming pool and a special guest lounge, the beautiful old chapel.

Kaikoura *B&B Homestay*

Bendamere House
Ellen & Peter Smith   37 Adelphi Tce, Kaikoura
Tel (03) 319 5830 Fax (03) 319 7337
bendamerehouse@xtra.co.nz
www.bnb.co.nz/bendamere.html
Double $80-$110 Single $60-$70 (Full Breakfast)
Child $15 Children welcome
2 Queen 1 Twin 4 Single (3 bdrm)
2 Ensuite 1 Private

We are retired dairy farmers and fourth generation Kaikourians with extensive knowledge of the area. Our 1930's restored home and large garden are just minutes from the township, beach, Whale Watch and other attractions. Incredible views of the Pacific Ocean and Seaward Kaikoura Mountains. Well appointed rooms offer electric blankets, heaters, hairdryers, television and tea-making facilities. Fax and laundry available. We enjoy helping visitors get the most of our their stay in our lovely seaside town. True country breakfast and other homemade treats. Courtesy car available to meet buses and trains.

Conway Flat - Kaikoura *B&B Homestay Self-contained 45km S of Kaikoura*

Rafa Point Retreat
Geoff & Shirley Cant
509 Conway Flat Road, Conway Flat, RD Cheviot
Tel (03) 319 2740 0800 002 822   Fax (03) 319 2749
Mob 021 949 116 rafapoint@paradise.net.nz
homepages.paradise.net.nz/thecantz
Double $75-$85 Single $60 (Full Breakfast)
Child $15 Dinner $25 (optional) Children welcome
2 Queen 3 Single (3 bdrm)
1 Private 1 Guests share 1 Host share

Our place is located in a farming area on the coast with extensive sea views. Our home is a restored 1920 villa surrounded by 2 acres of extensive gardens with exotic plants and fruit trees. We are 40 minutes from Kaikoura for whale watching and central to Marlborough and North Canterbury wine areas. Hanmer Springs is 1 hour away for hot baths and winter skiing. Children welcome. Breakfast includes homemade bread, jams and preserves. Your hosts are semi-retired with a hospitality background.

Kaikoura *B&B Separate/Suite Central Kaikoura*

Lemon Tree Lodge
Tricia & Andy Pike
31 Adelphi Terrace, Kaikoura
Tel (03) 319 7464   0800 108 951   Fax (03) 319 7467
Mob 025 648 0670   info@lemontree.co.nz
www.lemontree.co.nz
Double $100-$220 Single $90-$165 (Special Breakfast)
Credit cards accepted
1 King/Twin 3 Queen 1 Twin (4 bdrm)
4 Ensuite

Overlooking Kaikoura with spectacular views of the ocean and mountains.
Our four well appointed rooms all have en-suite facilities. Two rooms have
striking elevated views and private balconies; two are situated in a tranquil garden setting with their own
private decks. All rooms have colour TV, hairdryers, bathrobes, mini fridges, tea and fresh ground coffee
facilities, iron and ironing boards, drinking water, fresh flowers and complimentary chocolates. There is
a viewing deck with a luxury 5 - 6 person hot tub for our guest to enjoy and relax in.

Kaikoura *B&B 4km Kaikoura town centre*

The Point
Peter & Gwenda Smith
Fyffe Quay, Kaikoura
Tel (03) 319 5422   Fax (03) 319 7422
pointsmith@xtra.co.nz
www.bnb.co.nz/thepoint.html
Double $90 Single $75 (Continental Breakfast)
1 Queen 1 Double (2 bdrm)
2 Ensuite

We offer you a warm and friendly welcome to our family
home, which we share with our two daughters. Enjoy
the quietness and unique location of this beautiful 125 year old farmhouse. On the waterfront and
surrounded by 90 acres of farmland (part of Kaikoura Peninsula). Spectacular views of the sea and
mountains. Ideally situated for walks around the Kaikoura peninsula and seal colony. Five minutes
walk to one of Kaikoura's top restaurants. We run daily sheep shearing shows, have farm dogs and one
cat.

Kaikoura *B&B*

Shambala B&B
Owen & Trish Jellyman
191 Beach Rd, Kaikoura
Tel 03 319 7111   0800 7426 2252   Fax 03 319 7111
shambala@xtra.co.nz
www.bnb.co.nz/shambala.html
Double $95-$125 Single $70 (Full Breakfast)
Child B/A Children welcome
4 Queen 1 Twin (5 bdrm)
3 Ensuite 2 Private

Shambala B&B is set in a tranquil and peaceful atmosphere with a country
outlook and mountain views with stream boundary. We are 2km from the
town centre and two minutes from the closest restaurant. We provide
complimentary Devonshire tea and spacious indoor and outdoor living with
a lovely BBQ area. There is a courtesy car available and safe lockup for motorbikes. Enjoy a continental
and fully cooked breakfast in our lovely dining room. Help yourself to tea and coffee all day. All
bedrooms have either an ensuite or private bathroom.

Kaikoura *B&B 6km S of Kaikoura*

Fyffe Country Lodge
Chris Rye
State Highway One, Kaikoura,
Tel 03 319 6869   Fax 03 319 6865
Mob 021 161 162 5   fyffe@xtra.co.nz   fyffecountrylodge.com
Double $240 Single $160   (Full Breakfast)   Dinner $32.00
4 King 2 Queen 1 Twin (7 bdrm)
7 Ensuite

Fyffe Country Lodge is a small luxury lodge with an award winning restaurant close to whalewatching in Kaikoura. The lodge is beautifully created of rammed earth with Canadian cedar shakes on the roof, its rustic charm gives the property a timeless atmosphere. At Fyffe you can expect to find the finest of linens, individually decor'd rooms/suites, a superb menu sporting fresh local delicacies. Excellent service and gracious hosts. Fyffe has a class all of its own. Not suitable for young Children or Pets

Kaikoura *B&B Boutique/Deluxe B&B 0km Kaikoura*

Nikau Lodge
John & Lilla Fitzwater   53 Deal Street, Kaikoura
Tel +64 (0)3-319- 6973 Fax +64 (0)3-319- 69
Mob +64 (0)21-682-076   johnfitz@gotournz.com
www.NikauLodge.com
Double $100-$175 Single $90-$175
(Full Special Breakfast)   Credit cards accepted
1 King/Twin 5 Queen (6 bdrm)
5 Ensuite 1 Private

Conveniently located in the heart of Kaikoura on SH1
with magnificent hilltop views of sea & mountains, Nikau
offers high quality affordable B&B accommodation. Five
minutes walk takes you to Kaikoura's main street where you can enjoy local Rock Lobster. Relax in the
hot-tub or garden with a glass of wine and gaze at the stars and snow-capped mountains. Internet access,
SkyTV, complimentary tea/coffee, laundry, in-room TV/movies etc. Friendly new owners John & Lilla
Fitzwater welcome the opportunity to make your stay enjoyable and memorable.

Waiau - Mt Lyford   *Farmstay Homestay 21km N of Waiau*

Mason Hills
Averil & Robert Leckey
Inland Kaikoura Road, Waiau, RD, North Canterbury
Tel (03) 315 6611   0800 101 961   Fax (03) 315 6611
Mob 025 285 1333 mason_hills@xtra.co.nz
www.bnb.co.nz/masonhills.html
Double $120 Single $100 (Full Breakfast)
Dinner $30 by arrangement Credit cards accepted
Children welcome
1 Queen 2 Single (2 bdrm) 1 Ensuite 1 Private

Conveniently situated midway between Kaikoura and Hanmer Springs on the "Alpine Pacific Triangle"
(SH70), Mason Hills Station offers a real New Zealand rural experience: * Fourth generation New
Zealanders. * Commercial Sheep and Beef Hill Country Station. * Large character Homestead in a
genuine alpine setting. * 21 kms north of Waiau, 1km south of Mt Lyford ski field turn off. * 4WD
Farm Tour encompassing spectacular Alpine to Pacific views available as an extra. Averil, Robert and
Gracie the Labrador look forward to welcoming you.

Hanmer Springs   *Country Homestay 5km SW of Hanmer Springs*

Mira Monte
Anna & Theo van de Wiel
324 Woodbank Road, Hanmer Springs
Tel (03) 315 7604   Fax (03) 315 7604
Mob 021 043 1218 vdwiel@xtra.co.nz
www.bnb.co.nz/miramonte.html
Double $110-$130 Single $85-$100
(Special Breakfast) Child neg.
Dinner $35 By arrangement Credit cards accepted
2 King 1 Single (2 bdrm)
2 Ensuite

Close to the thrills of Hanmer Springs, at the foot of the mountains, lies our peaceful home. Our guest
rooms have been tastefully decorated to make your stay special. Relax in your own sittingroom or join
us. We make a great espresso! Years in the hospitality trade have taught us how to pamper you. There
is a piano and our large garden has a swimming pool. 'Bella' our Labrador and 'Mindy' our Jack
Russell are part of the family. Come as a Stranger! Leave as a Friend!

Hanmer Springs   *B&B Self-contained*

Cheltenham House
Maree & Len Earl
13 Cheltenham Street, Hanmer Springs
Tel (03) 315 7545 Fax (03) 315 7645
cheltenham@xtra.co.nz www.cheltenham.co.nz
Double $140-$180 Single $115-$150
(Special Breakfast) Child by arrangement
Extra person $30 Credit cards accepted
2 King/Twin 4 Queen 2 Single (6 bdrm)
5 Ensuite 1 Private

Cheltenham House offers luxury B&B accommodation, 200 metres from the Thermal Pools, restaurants and forest walks. This gracious 1930's home was renovated with the guests comfort paramount. The four spacious, sunny suites in the house and two cottage suites in the extensive garden, are all centrally heated. Enjoy breakfast of your choice, served in your suite, and local wine in the original rimu panelled billiard room in the evening. Together with our gentle labrador and sociable siamese, we look forward to meeting you.

Hanmer Springs   *B&B Hanmer Springs*

Hanmer View
Will & Helen Lawson
8 Oregon Heights, Hanmer Springs, 8273
Tel (03) 315 7947 0800 92 0800 Fax (03) 315 7958
hanmerview@xtra.co.nz
www.hanmerview.co.nz
Double $110-$150 Single $90-$120 (Full Breakfast)
Dinner by arrangement Credit cards accepted
1 King/Twin 2 Queen (3 bdrm)
3 Ensuite

Hanmer View is surrounded by beautiful forest and adjoins Conical Hill track. Breathtaking alpine views. Purpose built to ensure guests enjoy a quiet, relaxing stay in warm, spacious luxury rooms. Each individually decorated room has ensuite, TV, wool duvets and hand made quilts. Tea, coffee and cake is always available and your hosts, Will and Helen delight in serving you a generous scrumptious breakfast. No-one goes away hungry. Short stroll to village, thermal pools and tourist attractions. See letterbox sign, on right, end Oregon Heights. Garden café on site.

Hanmer Springs   *B&B Hanmer Springs*

Free Bs Bed & Breakfast
Pamela Shearing
164c Hanmer Springs Rd, Hanmer Springs
Tel (03) 3155 100 0800 337 332 Mob 025 626 4866
pam_gary@xtra.co.nz
www.bnb.co.nz/freebs.html
Double $69-$89 Single $50 (Full Breakfast)
Child $30
2 Queen 1 Twin (3 bdrm)
3 Ensuite

Free Bs Bed and Breakfast is located one minute drive from the Hanmer township, in a quiet relaxing stressfree atmosphere. With beautiful views of the mountains, located next to a deer farm, come and enjoy the quiet of Free Bs, away from the hustle and bustle of town. Pam and Gary will do there utmost to insure your stay in Hanmer Springs is complete, with its 12 natural thermal pools, forest walks, & hunting, fishing, tramping, jet boating, bungy jumping. We have three cats.

Hanmer Springs   *B&B & Self-contained 130km N of Christchurch*

Albergo Hanmer
Fine Accommodation

Bascha & Beat Blattner
88 Rippingale Road, Hanmer Springs
Tel (03) 315 7428 Fax (03) 315 7428
Tollfree 0800 342 313
albergohanmer@hotmail.com
www.albergohanmer.com
Check our website for special packages!

Cost	Double $120 - $220, Single $100 - $160
	S/C .Villa: $250 - $350, Dinner by prior
	arrangement
	All major credit cards accepted
Beds	2 Super King/Twin, 1 Cali-King/Twin, 1 King
Baths	**3 Ensuites (SPA)/ HOT TUB**

BREAKFASTS – WELLNESS – CUISINE

RENOWNED 3-course gourmet breakfasts, the wafting smell of freshly baked Swiss miniloaves & superb Italian coffee! Dine by candle light – tailormade menu features Pacific Rim & European cuisine, surprise Swiss desserts. Set in a magic mountain arena with views from all windows, Albergo Hanmer offers PEACE, PRIVACY and ALL DAY SUN, yet only 2 mins drive from the Thermal Pools/cafes/shops and 18 hole golf.
The interior styling is modern, creating a fresh, light & comfortable feel (u/floor heating).
CHOOSE from the spacious suites in the main lodge guest wing: In-room TV/tea&coffee/fridges with large ensuites/ Spa, (great water pressure!). Two guest lounge areas provide internet facilities, latest mags, and CD's. Chef's kitchen & laundry available.
OR for ultra decadence, experience our new stand alone 2-room ALPINE VILLA: Self-contained with PRIVATE OUTDOOR HOT TUB and includes: Californian King/ Twin, marbled ensuite with panorama window (views while you shower!), bidet, IN-ROOM CINEMA, air con. Dedicated hosts, Bascha & Beat Blattner are a young couple (NZ & Swiss origins) with 18 years experience in hospitality & tourism. Bascha's background is in Fashion & Design. Beat is a Tourism Expert. We speak English, Swiss/German, French, Spanish and Italian. WE CAN ARRANGE YOUR HUNTING & FISHING TOURS, ON SITE MASSAGES/FACIALS.
Guest comments: *'Wow – Rejuvenated, refreshed & rearing to go again. Thanks for a wonderful experience!'* Jo Baker, NZ. *'......your incredible breakfasts will linger in our memories long after the taste has gone – magnific!'* V & M Henderson, NSW AU. *'Thank you for creating such an artistic, stimulating, get-comfortable environment.'* Bob Streeter, Fort Collins, USA.

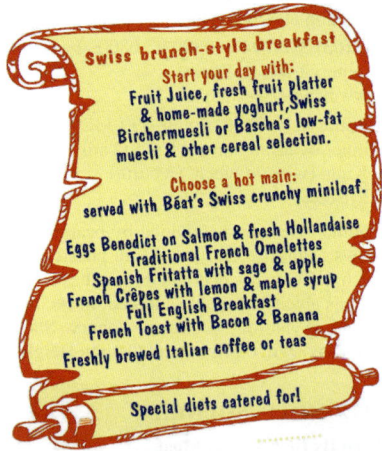

Swiss brunch-style breakfast
Start your day with:
Fruit Juice, fresh fruit platter
& home-made yoghurt, Swiss
Birchermuesli or Bascha's low-fat
muesli & other cereal selection.

Choose a hot main:
served with Beat's Swiss crunchy miniloaf.

Eggs Benedict on Salmon & fresh Hollandaise
Traditional French Omelettes
Spanish Fritatta with sage & apple
French Crêpes with lemon & maple syrup
Full English Breakfast
French Toast with Bacon & Banana
Freshly brewed Italian coffee or teas

Special diets catered for!

DIRECTIONS: At junction before main village, 300m past Shell Garage, take ARGELINS ROAD (Centre branch), go past Hanmer Golf Club, take first road on left RIPPINGALE RD (no exit). Albergo Hanmer is 900m down at the end of this country lane.

Hanmer Springs *B&B 130km N of Christchurch*

Spring Valley B&B
Rose & Jim van Beek
166B Hanmer Springs Road, Hanmer Springs

Tel (03) 315 7174 Fax (03) 315 7174
Mob 025 278 4862   contact@springvalley.co.nz
www.springvalley.co.nz

Double $120-$150 Single $90 (Full Breakfast)
1 Superking (1 bdrm)
1 Ensuite 1 Private

Spring Valley is a brand new spacious home one minutes
drive from Hanmer's Thermal Pools, restaurants and bars.
We offer one large guest room that is quiet, private and immaculately furnished with stunning rural and
mountain views. (Deer farm ten metres from your patio.) Unwind and relax in your double spa bath
and enjoy the view. Large ensuite with under-tile heating, heated towel rails complete with walk in
wardrobe make this suite spacious and comfortable. A full breakfast is served in the privacy of your
room. Free courtesy transport to and from restaurants and bars. Jim, Rose and Boots the cat look
forward to meeting you.

Hanmer Springs *Homestay 8km S of Hanmer*

Charwell
Judy & Bill Clarkson
74P Medway Road, Hanmer Springs

Tel (03) 315 5070 Fax (03) 315 5071
Mob 021 347 905   charwell.countrystay@xtra.co.nz
www.bnb.co.nz/charwell.html

Double $120-$150 (Continental /Full Breakfast)
1 King 2 Queen (3 bdrm)
3 Ensuite

A new home, built with our homestay guests' comfort in
mind. A secluded elevated site giving full panoramic
views of the Hanmer basin and Waiau River. Nestled among wilding pines with an abundance of bird
life. Your hosts have travelled extensively overseas and throughout NZ and enjoy company whether
local or overseas. Seven kilometres from the Hamner Thermal Pools and on the Alpine Pacific Triangle
with opportunities for a wide range of activities within an easy days' drive. We have a venerable Jack
Russell aged 14.

Culverden *Farmstay 3km S of Culverden*

Ballindalloch
Diane & Dougal Norrie
Culverden, North Canterbury

Tel (03) 315 8220 Fax (03) 315 8220
Mob 0274 373 184
www.bnb.co.nz/ballindalloch.html

Double $110 Single $60 (Full Breakfast)
Child $30 Dinner $30
1 Queen 2 Single (2 bdrm)
1 Guests share

Welcome to 'Ballindalloch' a 2090 acre irrigated farm three kilometres south of Culverden. We milk
1100 cows through two floating rotary dairies at present but are in the process of building a 70 rotary
dairy which will be in operation this year. We have 1000 Corriedale sheep stud. Our home is centrally
heated in winter and has a log fire. We are just over one hour north of Christchurch and Hanmer Springs
half an hour to the north and Kaikoura whales one and a half hour's drive. We have travelled extensively
overseas and appreciate relaxing in a homely atmosphere - we extend this to all guests. We have one cat
Thomas, guests are welcome to smoke outdoors.

Gore Bay *B&B Homestay 8km E of Cheviot*

Gore Bay B&B
Valerie & Peter McClatchy
6 Cathedral Road, Gore Bay, Cheviot RD 3

Tel (03) 319 8535 gorebay.bnb@xtra.co.nz
www.bnb.co.nz/gorebaybb.html

Double $80-$100 Single $60 (Continental Breakfast)
Credit cards accepted Children welcome
1 Double 2 Twin (2 bdrm)
1 Ensuite 1 Host share

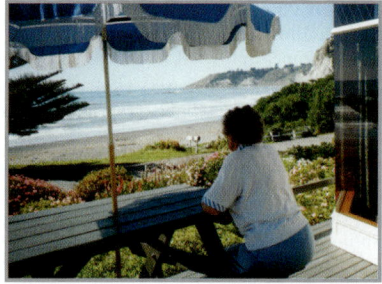

We invite you to the natural beauty and peaceful tranquillity of Gore Bay. Enjoy panoramic sea-views from our beach-front home and our sun and sea paradise provides bush and beach walks, tennis, swimming, surfing, gardens and the spectacular Cathedral Cliffs. Golf and good restaurants nearby. Just 60 minutes drive from Hanmer Springs Thermal Resort and Kaikoura Whale Watch, 90 minutes north of Christchurch and 3 1/2 hours from Inter-island ferry. We are a retired couple enjoying sport, art and travel.

Waikari *B&B Homestay Self-contained 28km NW of Amberley*

Tullach Glas Motel B&B
Patsy & Ivor McMillan
38 Princes St, Waikari, North Canterbury

Tel (03) 314 4931 0800 37 30 30 Fax (03) 314 4936
info@countrystay.co.nz
www.countrystay.co.nz

Double $75 Single $45 (Continental Breakfast)
Child $10 Dinner $20pp B/A
2 Queen 1 Twin 1 Single (3 bdrm)
2 Ensuite 1 Private

Welcome to our country home. We are 50min from Christchurch International Airport and and ideal stop off point to major tourist attractions nearby. We have our own small farm, Biddy the sheep dog and BC our very aloof black cat. Rest awhile with us, lunch at local wineries, fish in our lakes and river, walk, horse trek, play golf or just admire the view.

Waipara *B&B 10km N of Amberley*

Winery Cottage
Julian Ball
RD 3, Amberley, North Canterbury

Tel (03) 314 6909 Fax (03) 314 6909
winery.cottage@xtra.co.nz www.winerycottage.co.nz

Double $130 (Full Breakfast) Dinner $40
Self Contained $90 Credit cards accepted
2 Queen (2 bdrm)
2 Ensuite

Situated on the northern edge of Waipara village, Winery Cottage offers you the ideal location to experience the many attractions that make our area unique. Base yourself in a cosy cottage with warm, spacious bedrooms and your very own modern ensuite bathroom. In the morning take a relaxed hearty breakfast with freshly baked breads, home-made muesli, fruit juice, hot porridge and filling cooked breakfast. Evening meal available upon request.Also now on offer is a modern self-contained house on it's own section with a fully equiped kitchen and laundry facilities.

Amberley   *Rural homestay 1km S of Amberley*

Tullamore
Joanna & David Cameron
231 Carters Road, Amberley, North Canterbury
Tel (03) 314 7454 Fax (03) 314 7454
Mob 021 236 3196 waituna.waikari@xtra.co.nz
www.bnb.co.nz/waituna.html
Double $130-$150 Single $75 ((Full Breakfast)
Dinner $40 by arrangement Credit cards accepted
1 Queen 3 Single (3 bdrm)
1 Ensuite 1 Private 1 Guests share

"Tullamore" is a modern home situated on 10 acres in a quiet rural setting, 400 metres off SH1 just south of Amberley. Waipara wineries and Amberley Golf Club are five minutes away. Christchurch airport is half an hour, Hanmer Springs one hour, Kaikoura whales 100km, Blenheim wineries and Picton ferry 3-4 hours. We have travelled extensively and lived in Ireland until 1972 (David is English). We enjoy sports, travelling, our growing family and meeting people. We now look forward to welcoming you to our new home.

Amberley   *Farmstay Homestay 1km S of Amberley*

Bredon Downs Homestay
Bob & Veronica Lucy
Bredon Downs, Amberley, RD 1, North Canterbury
Tel (03) 314 9356 or (03) 314 8018 Fax (03) 314 8994
Mob 025 494 517 lucy.lucy@xtra.co.nz
www.bnb.co.nz/bredondownshomestay.html
Double $100-$110 Single $60 (Full Breakfast)
Dinner $35 by arr. (incl. wine) Credit cards accepted
1 Queen 1 Twin 1 Single (3 bdrm)
1 Ensuite 1 Private

Our drive goes off SH1 and so we are conveniently en route to and from the inter-island ferry, just 48km north of Christchurch and 100km south of the Kaikoura whales, and easy to find. The house is surrounded by an English style garden with swimming pool, and close to the Waipara wineries, beach and attractive golf course. We breed ostriches which we are pleased to show visitors, have travelled extensively and lived abroad, and now share our lives with a Newfoundland and a Labrador, two geriatric donkeys and Rupert the cat!

Waikuku Beach   *B&B Homestay 30km N of Christchurch*

Emmanuel House
Graham and Mary Dacombe
20 Allin Drive, Waikuku Beach, North Canterbury
Tel (03) 312 7782 Fax (03) 312 7783
emmanuel.house@xtra.co.nz
www.bnb.co.nz/emmanuelhouse.html
Double $75 Single $50 (Continental Breakfast)
Dinner $20 B/A Child under 12 - 1/2 price, under 5 free
1 Double 1 Twin (2 bdrm)
1 Private

We warmly invite you to our new one-level purpose-built home in its tranquil rural setting with wheelchair access throughout. Emmanual House is 2km from the main highway, within walking distance of the beach and 30km north of Christchurch. Close by is the thriving rural township of Rangiora. Amateur radio (ZL3NZ) music, correspondence, and people are our interests. Dine privately for our real 'Kiwi' continental breakfast, or with family if you desire an evening meal. Complimentary tea/coffee/home baking always available.

Waikuku Beach *B&B Farmstay 20km N of Christchurch*

Waikuku Beach Bed and Breakfast
Vicki and Wayne Freeth
14 Collins drive, Waikuku Beach,
Tel (03) 310 0463   0800 945 569   Fax (03) 310 0453
info@waikuku.com   www.waikuku.com
Double $75-$105 Single $45-$85
(Continental Breakfast) Dinner $20
cooked breakfast $8 Children welcome
3 Queen (3 bdrm)
1 Ensuite

Waikuku Beach Bed and Breakfast offers you a relaxed
noise free nights sleep away from the hustle of the city yet with in easy access to all the attractions our
region has to offer. Our family home is within easy walking distance of the picturesque Waikuku Beach
where you can swim, walk fish or just take in the fresh air and spectacular scenery. Our rooms are large
and open onto garden rooms. You may choose to have a spa, read or soak up the sun, a favourite
pastime of our cat Lucky.

Kaiapoi *B&B 15km N of Christchurch*

Morichele
Helen & Richard Moore
25 Hilton Street, Kaiapoi
Tel (03) 327 5247   Fax (03) 327 5247
morichele@xtra.co.nz
www.bnb.co.nz/morichele.html
Double $85 Single $60 (Full Breakfast) Child neg.
Dinner by arrangement
1 Double 1 Twin (2 bdrm)

Kaiapoi is a riverside town close to the Waimakariri and
Cam rivers, for fishing. It's within a 2 hour drive of skifields, Hanmer Springs, Akaroa and Kaikoura,
each with their own attractions. We offer comfortable accommodation, with offstreet parking, and your
own entrance, sitting/dining area with fridge, tea and coffee making facilities, TV and video. There are
cafes and restaurants within walking distance, or you are welcome to bring back takeaways. Extra bed,
fax, email and laundry available.

Rangiora *B&B 30km N of Christchurch*

Willow Glen
Glenda & Malcolm Ross
419 High Street, Rangiora
Tel (03) 313 9940   Fax (03) 313 9946
Mob 025 984 893   rosshighway@xtra.co.nz
www.willowglenrangiora.co.nz
Double $110 Single $75 (Full Breakfast)
1 Queen 1 Double (2 bdrm)
1 Ensuite 1 Private 1 Guests share

Nestled on the northern side of Rangiora township on
Highway 72, heading towards Oxford 30 minutes from Christchurch, roughly one hour to Mt Hutt.
Walking distance to cafes and restaurants. Malcolm and I invite you to share our enchanting English
style home for some Kiwi hospitality. Off street parking available. Warm comfortable beds, electric
blankets, quality linen, and a hearty home style continental or cooked breakfast. Bedrooms overlook
the garden with views of surrounding countryside. Meet Lucy our Foxy and Ralph our elderly cat.
Email facilities available.

Rangiora *B&B 7km W of Rangiora Town*

Springbank Vineyard
Daphne Robinson
1035 Oxford Road, RD1, Rangiora

Tel (03) 312 5653   Fax (03) 312 5623
springbankvineyard@hotmail.com
www.bnb.co.nz/springbankvineyard.html

Double $100 Single $50 (Full Breakfast)
2 Queen 2 Twin 1 Single (5 bdrm)
1 Ensuite 1 Host share

Historic Springbank Homestead, originally one of Canterbury's great estates, is encircled by spacious grounds and vineyards, with sheep, cattle, deer and horses grazing nearby. Exquisite lavender fields are also being established. Lovely large sunny bedrooms overlook the grounds, and many colonial antiques and paintings grace the 140 year old homestead. Situated just 30 minutes from Christchurch between Rangiora and Cust on AA's Scenic Highway 72, Springbank is close to golf courses and many famous tourist attractions. International skifield Mt Hutt is an hour's drive away. Relax, enjoy, unwind. It's a truly New Zealand experience.

Oxford *Homestay Oxford Central*

Glenariff
Beth & John Minns
136 High Street, Oxford, Canterbury

Tel (03) 312 4678
www.bnb.co.nz/glenariff.html

Double $80 Single $40 (Full Breakfast) Child $15
Dinner $25 by arrangement
1 Double 2 Single (2 bdrm)
1 Guests share

'Glenariff' is a character home (circa 1886) operated as a Devonshire tea rooms set in a large country garden with mature trees. Oxford is a friendly country town with most leisure activities catered for. It will be our pleasure to welcome you to our home to relax and share our hospitality. A leisurely breakfast, candle light dinner or perhaps Devonshire tea served on the verandah. We have a pet cat and are smoke free. Directions: High Street is off Main Street - sign on gate.

Oxford *B&B Homestay 40mins W of Christchurch Airport*

Hielan' House
Shirley & John Farrell
74 Bush Road, Oxford, North Canterbury

Tel (03) 312 4382   0800 279 382   Fax (03) 312 4382
Mob 025 359 435   meg29@ihug.co.nz
www.bnb.co.nz/hielanhouse.html

Double $110-$130 Single $80 (Special Breakfast)
Child price on application Dinner by arrangement
Credit cards accepted Children welcome Pets welcome
1 King/Twin 1 Queen (2 bdrm)
1 Ensuite 1 Private

Nestled on six acres in peaceful rural surroundings with the Oxford foothills as a backdrop, we have two quality upstairs guest rooms with their own relaxing areas, ensuites and a separate entrance. TV, tea/coffee making facilities. Inground swimming pool, laundry, fax/internet facilities. On Inland Scenic Route 72 in the South Island. Christchurch 45 mins away. Delicious menu breakfasts, lunch and dinners, organic meat and home grown vegetables in season. Your warm welcome includes home baking and that inviting cup of coffee/tea. Friendly farm animals.

West Melton - Christchurch   *Rural Homestay 15km W of Christchurch*

Shettleston Farm
Cherry & Donald Moffat
Bells Road, West Melton, RD 1, Christchurch

Tel (03) 347 8311   Fax (03) 347 8391
Mob 029 234 7831   shettlestonfarm@xtra.co.nz
www.bnb.co.nz/shettlestonfarm.html

Double $85 Single $65 (Continental Breakfast)
Dinner $25pp Credit cards accepted
1 Double 1 Twin (2 bdrm)
1 Private 1 Guests share

Enjoy the best of both worlds, 15 minutes from Christchurch Airport, 25 minutes from City Centre, yet a world away on our 10 acre country retreat. Our modern home is furnished with colonial furniture and our grounds display a collection of vintage farm machinery to complete the nostalgic atmosphere. We share our paradise with a flock of black and coloured sheep, "Poppyseed" our cow, goats, two donkeys, a collection of waterfowl on our pond, our faithful Golden Retriever and one spoilt cat. Smoke free home.

West Melton   *B&B Farmstay 25km W of Christchurch*

Hopesgate
Yvonne & Robert Overton
Hoskyns Road, RD 5, Christchurch

Tel (03) 347 8330   Fax (03) 347 8330
Mob 025 311 234   robove@free.net.nz
www.bnb.co.nz/hopesgate .html

Double $90 Single $60 (Full Breakfast)
Dinner $20 B/A Credit cards accepted
1 Queen 2 Single (2 bdrm)
1 Guests share

We have a 30 hectare property where we farm sheep and grow lavender. Close to all amenities, in a quiet rural setting with magnificent views of the mountains. Countless day trips can be taken from our home. We have enjoyed entertaining folk from different parts of the world and look forward to meeting and caring for many more. Relax with us and enjoy a farmhouse dinner. Begin or end a memorable holiday with us. 15 minutes from Christchurch Airport. Smoke free home. Friendly cat.

West Coast Road - Christchurch   *Homestay 10km W of Christchurch*

GP's Place
Gwenda & Peter Bickley
164 Old West Coast Road, RD 6, Christchurch

Tel (03) 342 9196   Fax (03) 342 4196
Mob 021 158 6208 gpsplace_@hotmail.com
www.bnb.co.nz/gpsplace.html

Double $90 Single $50 (Full Breakfast) Dinner $25
1 Queen 1 Twin (2 bdrm)
1 Private

Gwenda and Peter invite you to come and enjoy the ambience of our warm and spacious home set in a large garden with magnificent views of the Southern Alps. Our home is situated on 7.5 acres where we farm ostriches and various other farm animals. We are ideally located just 7 minutes from the airport and 10 minutes from the city. A full sized tennis court is available for guests use.

Yaldhurst - Christchurch *B&B Homestay 10km W of Christchurch*

Cherry Grove
Jan & Kirwan Berry
431 Old West Coast Road, RD 6, Christchurch

Tel (03) 342 8629 Fax (03) 342 4321
cherrygrove@netaccess.co.nz
users.netaccess.co.nz/cherrygrove/

Double $80-$90 Single $65 (Continental Breakfast)
Children welcome
1 Queen 1 Twin (2 bdrm)
1 Ensuite 1 Private

Relax, enjoy the best of both worlds in a lovely rural setting just 20 minutes to the city centre. You are welcome to wander in our spacious gardens, feed the ducks and breathe our clear country air. We offer an Airport pickup only 10 minutes away, as is the Antarctic Centre. We are on the direct route to the West Coast and to many ski fields. Close by are several vineyards and golf courses. You are assured of a very warm welcome at Cherry Grove.

Yaldhurst - Christchurch *B&B Separate suite 8km W of City*

Gladsome Lodge
Stuart & Sue Barr
314 Yaldhurst Road, Avonhead, Christchurch 4

Tel (03) 342 7414 0800 222 617 Fax (03) 342 3414
Mob 025 299 1684 sue@gladsomelodge.com
www.gladsomelodge.com

Double $80-$90 Single $60 (Continental Breakfast)
Child neg Dinner $25 Credit cards accepted
2 Queen 2 Double 2 Twin 3 Single (5 bdrm)
1 Ensuite 3 Guests share

Located close to Airport with easy access to key attractions. Be assured of professional, attentive hosting in a friendly environment. Enjoy our property which has a tennis court, swimming pool, spa and sauna available. We are able to accommodate couples travelling together as a group. Have knowledge of Maori history and culture. We are centrally heated. On bus route to City. On route to ski fields and West Coast Highway. Hosts Sue and Stuart, New Zealanders who have travelled and have a wide variety of interests.

CANTERBURY

Our B&Bs range from homely to luxurious,
but you can always be assured of superior hospitality.

Avonhead - Christchurch *B&B 10 kms W of City Centre*

home
NEW ZEALAND

Russley 302

Sally & Brian Carpenter
302 Russley Road,
Avonhead, Christchurch 8004

Tel (03) 358 6543
Fax (03) 358 6553
Mob 025 224 3752
carpsrussley302@clear.net.nz
www.bnb.co.nz/russley.html

Double $110-$120
Single $70-$110
(Full Breakfast)
Credit cards accepted
1 Queen 1 Twin 1 Single (3 bdrm)
1 Ensuite 1 Private 1 Host share

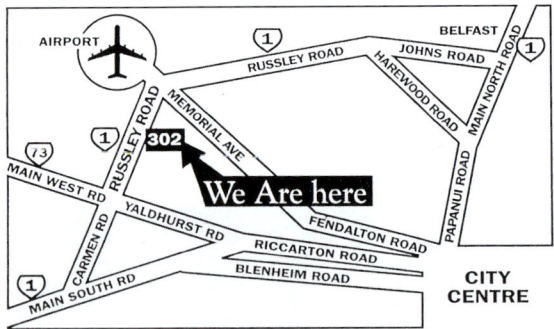

Situated 2 minutes from Christchurch Airport "Russley 302" is an ideal first or last night stay.

We are retired sheep farmers living in a rural setting farming, black/coloured sheep.

Wool from these sheep form the basis of Sally's involvement in the handcraft industry. Brian's interests include Rotary & sport.

Our modern home offers electric blankets, hairdryers, refrigerators, tea/coffee, laundry facilities and excellent off-street parking.

We have enjoyed many years of farm hosting and invite you to share this experience with us.

Avonhead - Christchurch *Self-contained 10 min W of Christchurch*

Ash Croft
Sky & Raewyn Williams
6 Fovant Street, Avonhead, Christchurch

Tel (03) 342 3416 Fax (03) 342 3415
Mob 0275 663 724 bookings@ashcroftgroup.com
www.ashcroftgroup.com

Double $100-$120 Child under 5 free
$10 each additional person Credit cards accepted
2 Queen 2 Twin (3 bdrm)
1 Private

Quality accommodation for the visitor to Christchurch, offering privacy and comfort, off-street parking and a child-friendly environment. Modern facilities, full kitchen, dining area, lounge with comfortable furnishings, TV, VCR, CD/Radio/Tapeplayer, collection of videotapes, book library and childrens games/toys. Bathroom includes full bath and separate shower. Laundry with washing machine and dryer. Easy access to airport, city centre, local shopping centres and tourist attractions. Contact us or see our website for details of either of our two holiday homes.

Burnside - Christchurch *B&B 8km NW of Christchurch*

Burnside Bed & Breakfast
Elaine & Neil Roberts
31 O'Connor Place, Burnside 8005, Christchurch

Tel (03) 358 7671 Fax (03) 358 7761
elaine.neil.roberts@xtra.co.nz
www.bnb.co.nz/burnside.html

Double $90 Single $65 (Continental Breakfast)
1 Queen 1 Twin (2 bdrm)
1 Guests share

Welcome to our comfortable, modern home in a quiet street, five minutes from the airport and fifteen minutes to the city centre. You are greeted with fresh flowers and sweets in your bedroom. Relax in the garden with tea or coffee and freshly baked muffins. Enjoy a generous continental breakfast. Off street parking and laundry facilities are available. We have travelled in New Zealand and overseas. Our interests include sport, walks, gardening and local history. We enjoy sharing our home with guests and look forward to meeting you.

Ilam - Christchurch *Homestay 7.5km NW of Christchurch*

Anne & Tony Fogarty Homestay
Anne & Tony Fogarty
7 Westmont Street, Ilam, Christchurch 8004

Tel (03) 358 2762 Fax (03) 358 2767
tony.fogarty@xtra.co.nz
www.bnb.co.nz/annetonyfogartyhomestay.html

Double $80 Single $50 (Continental Breakfast)
Dinner $30 by arrangement Credit cards accepted
4 Single (2 bdrm)
1 Guests share

Our home is in the beautiful suburb of Ilam, ideally situated close to Christchurch Airport (7 mins by car), the Railway Station (10 mins), and the central City with its many attractions (10mins). We are adjacent to the city bus route. Guests are welcome to use our Laundry. We have a wide range of interests which include, our four adult children, Sport, Travel, Politics, and Gardening. We are able to provide conversational English classes for speakers of other languages (fee would apply).

Harewood - Christchurch   *B&B Homestay 7.5km N of City Centre*

Highsted Homestead
Peter & Sherryn
132B Highsted Road, Christchurch,
Tel (03) 359 6486   Fax (03) 359 6490
Mob 025 676 4625   h.h@xtra.co.nz
www.bnb.co.nz/highstedhomestay.html
Double $120-$140 Single $90-$110 (Full Breakfast)
Credit cards accepted
1 Queen 1 Twin 1 Single (2 bdrm)
1 Ensuite 1 Private 1 Guests share

Located 5 minutes from Christchurch Airport & 10 minutes from City. A great location from which to start & finish your trip around the South Island. Situated amidst a 1/2 acre quiet, secluded garden setting. Lovely guest rooms include tea/coffee facilities,fridge & TV. We invite you to spend time with our family and get a real glimpse of NZ life. We have 2 teenage children. Close by is the Antarctic Centre and NZ's best Kiwi viewing area at Willowbank Wildlife Reserve. Excellent local restaurants, courtesy airport pick-up and guests rental car available.

Riccarton - Christchurch   *Homestay 4km W of City Centre*

Riccarton Homestay
Caroline & Keith Curry
70A Puriri Street, Riccarton, Christchurch
Tel (03) 348 4081   Fax (03) 348 4081
curryc@xtra.co.nz
www.bnb.co.nz/riccartonhomestay.html
Double $90 Single $60 (Continental Breakfast)
Credit cards accepted
4 Single (2 bdrm)
1 Guests share

Our home is a comfortable, modern two storied townhouse in a quiet street near the University. Facilities for guests are two spacious upstairs twin bedrooms, a bathroom and separate toilet. The laundry is available for guest use. We are a pet and smoke free home. We offer a pick up service from the airport, railway station or city centre. Keith enjoys the outdoors and Caroline is a part time tourist guide interested in local history and embroidery and we both travel frequently locally and overseas.

Bryndwr - Christchurch   *B&B Homestay 5km NW of City Centre*

Bryndwr Homestay
Patricia & Win Clancey
89A Aorangi Road, Bryndwr, Christchurch
Tel (03) 351 6092   Fax (03) 351 6092
wclancey@xtra.co.nz
www.bnb.co.nz/bryndwrbb.html
Double $100-$110 Single $80-$85 (Full Breakfast)
Child by arrangement Credit cards accepted
1 Queen 2 Single (2 bdrm)
1 Ensuite 1 Host share

We warmly welcome you to our spacious and comfortable
home set in quiet attractive gardens. The en-suite room opens onto a balcony overlooking a secluded outdoor swimming pool. A sun room/TV room is ideal as a second (private) lounge. Tea/coffee, juice, home baking always available. Generous breakfasts. We have both travelled, have wide ranges of interest and enjoy talking to people. If needed, we are happy to help with travel plans. Courtesy pick-up, off street parking and laundry facilities are available.

Bryndwr - Christchurch *B&B Homestay NW of Christchurch*

Bryndwr B&B
Kathy & Brian Moore
108 Aorangi Road, Christchurch,
Tel (03) 351 6299 eroom.b@clear.net.nz
www.bnb.co.nz/bryndwrbb2.html
Double $85 Single $65 (Full Breakfast)
1 Double 1 Single (2 bdrm)
1 Guests share

Welcome to share our comfortable family home with
relaxing outdoor garden area. Located in the Northwest
corner of Christchurch 5 km from the Airport off Wairakei Road or via Memorial Avenue, left onto Ilam
Road, past Aqualand and on to Aorangi Road. Easy walking distances to local area shops and restaurants.
Welcome to bring home takeaways. Complimentary tea or coffee any time. Laundry and ironing
facilities available. Short 3 minutes walk to Bus route, only 10 minutes ride to the City Centre, passing
Botanical Gardens, Museum and Art Centre. Inspection welcomed. Feel free to ring if you have any
questions, we may be able to help.

Fendalton - Christchurch *B&B Separate/Suite 10 min NW of City*

Ambience on Avon
Lawson & Helen Little
9 Kotare Street, Fendalton, Christchurch
Tel (03) 348 4537 0800 22 66 28 Fax (03) 348 4837
Mob 025 333 627 lawsonh@amcom.co.nz
www.ambience-on-avon.co.nz
Double $150-$190 Single $140-$180
(Special Breakfast) Credit cards accepted
1 Queen 1 Double (2 bdrm)
1 Ensuite 1 Private

Ambience on Avon in a private, picturesque garden on the Avon. Helen & Lawson, your gracious hosts
enjoy welcoming guests into their home with its elegant comfortable understated furnishings, guest
lounge with a large open fire, TV. Enjoy homebaking, complimentary wine & refreshments antipasto
under the large elm tree or in the river garden , or relax in leather therapeutic chairs in family room
opening into garden. Art, comfortable beds, fine linen, electric blankets, room heaters and all modern
conveniences for a relaxing friendly-hosted stay. Courtesy pick up.

Fendalton - Christchurch *B&B Boutique B&B Central Christchurch*

Anselm House
Jan & Leigh Webber
34 Kahu Road, Fendalton, Christchurch
Tel (03) 343 4260 0800 267 356 Fax (03) 343 4261
Mob 025 272 6260 anselm@paradise.net.nz
www.anselmhouse.co.nz
Double $120-$150 Single $100-$120 (Full Breakfast)
Dinner $30 each
2 Queen (2 bdrm)
2 Ensuite

Anselm House is a lovely fifty-year-old home, built of
pink Hanmer marble, and designed by the famous
architect Heathcote Helmore. One boundary runs alongside the Avon River. Special attractions include:
safe off-street parking; courtesy airport transport; only a four minute walk to the Riccarton Mall for
shops, restaurants and banks; adjacent to historic Riccarton House and Deans Bush; close to the
University; within easy walking distance of Hagley Park, Art Galleries, city centre. Not suitable for
pets or children under 12.

Dallington - Christchurch   *B&B 4km NE of Christchurch*

Killarney
Lynne & Russell Haigh
27 Dallington Terrace, Dallington, Christchurch
Tel (03) 381 7449   Fax (03) 381 7449
Mob 025 235 2409   haigh.killarney@xtra.co.nz
www.bnb.co.nz/killarney.html
Double $90   Single $70 (Full Breakfast) Child neg
2 Double (2 bdrm)
1 Ensuite 1 Private 1 Host share

Peace, tranquillity and a cottage garden on the banks of
the river Avon. Detached double (ensuite) accommodation is warm and cosy with fridge, microwave,
TV, extra single couch-bed and a private garden. Double accommodation, lounge and private bathroom
available inside. Tea/coffee, home baking and laundry service always available. Scenic river walks or
borrow our dinghy and row! Six minutes drive to city centre. Buses stop nearby. Phone for directions
(courtesy pickup occasionally available). Both of us and our two cats look forward to meeting you.

Merivale - Christchurch   *B&B 3min Christchurch*

Melrose
Elaine & David Baxter
39 Holly Road, Merivale, Christchurch
Tel (03) 355 1929   Fax (03) 355 1927
Mob 025 647 5564   BaxterMelrose@xtra.co.nz
www.melrose-bb.co.nz
Double $105   Single $75 (Full Breakfast)
Credit cards accepted
3 Queen (3 bdrm)
1 Private 2 Guests share

A warm welcome awaits you at Melrose, a charming
character home (1910) located in a small quiet street, just
off Papanui Road only minutes away from the city and all the shops, restaurants and cafes of Merivale.
Our house is spacious, we offer large rooms with tea and coffee making facilities and a private dining
room/lounge. We have many interests and having travelled extensively, are keen to accommodate your
needs. Our family comprises of two daughters and a boxer Milly. Off street parking. Children are welcome.

St Albans - Christchurch   *B&B Homestay 1.5km N of Christchurch Central*

Barrich House
Barbara & Richard Harman
82 Caledonian Road, St Albans, Christchurch 8001
Tel (03) 365 3985   Mob 025 659 5787
r.harman@ext.canterbury.ac.nz
www.bnb.co.nz/barrichhouse.html
Double $80-$120   Single $50-$90 (Special Breakfast)
Child negotiable Dinner by arrangement
1 Queen 1 Twin (2 bdrm)
1 Ensuite 1 Private

Our welcoming home, startlingly alive and furnished with strong but tasteful interior colours, is in a
quiet street within easy walking distance of the city and tourist amenities. Both rooms are well appointed
and have very comfortable beds. The spacious queen room has arm chairs and overlooks a lovely
courtyard. Excellent breakfast menu. Friendly hosts willing to help you plan your visit for best value.
Complementary pick-up transport and use of laundry. Tea, coffee and biscuits are always available.
Please contact us in advance.

Avondale - Christchurch *B&B 8km NE of Christchurch Central*

Hulverstone Lodge
Diane & Ian Ross
18 Hulverstone Drive, Avondale, Christchurch

Tel (03) 388 6505   0800 388 6505   Fax (03) 388 6025
Mob 025 433 830   hulverstone@caverock.net.nz
www.canterburypages.co.nz/hulverstone

Double $80-$120 Single $70-$100 (Full Breakfast)
Credit cards accepted
3 King/Twin 1 Single (4 bdrm)
1 Ensuite 1 Private 1 Guests share

Gracing the bank of the Avon River in a quiet suburb, yet only 10 minutes from the city centre, stands picturesque Hulverstone Lodge. From our charming guest rooms watch the sun rise over the river, catch glimpses of the Southern Alps or enjoy views of the Port Hills.
Delightful riverside walks pass the door. A pleasant stroll along the riverbank leads to New Brighton with its sandy Pacific Ocean beach and pier. Numerous golf courses and the QEII leisure complex are close at hand.
Located just off Christchurch's Ring Road system, Hulverstone Lodge offers easy access to all major tourist attractions, while frequent buses provide convenient transport to the city.
An ideal base for holidays year-round, Hulverstone Lodge is only a couple of hours from quaint Akaroa, Hanmer Hot Springs thermal attraction, Kaikoura's Whale Watch, and several ski-fields.
You are guaranteed warm hospitality and quality accommodation at Hulverstone Lodge. All our rooms are decorated with fresh flowers from our garden.
We offer: Complimentary pick-up; Fax and email facilities; King or twin beds; Advice on onward travel planning; French and German languages spoken; A delicious breakfast. Come and experience the ambience of Hulverstone Lodge.

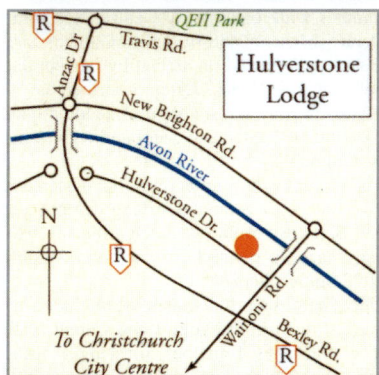

Follow the Ring Road (marked with an Ⓡ on the big blue/green road signs) clockwise until it crosses the Avon River. Turn left then left again.

Christchurch City *Private Hotel* *Christchurch Central*

Windsor B&B Hotel
Carol Healey & Don Evans
52 Armagh Street, Christchurch 1

Tel (03) 366 1503   0800 366 1503
Fax (03) 366 9796
reservations@windsorhotel.co.nz
www.windsorhotel.co.nz

Double $108   Single $75 (Full Breakfast)
Child $15 under 12 yrs with Adult
Quad/Family $150   Triple $132
(40 bdrm)   Credit cards accepted
24 Guests share

Looking for Bed & Breakfast accommodation in Christchurch, then try "The Windsor". Built at the turn of the century this inner city residence is located on the Tourist Tram Route and is within 5-10 minutes walk of the City Centre, Restaurants, Banks, Town Hall, Convention Centre, Casino, Arts Centre, Museum and Botanical Gardens.

Guests are greeted on arrival by our pet dachshund "Miss Winnie" and shown around our charming colonial style home. Often described as "Traditional" this family operated Bed and Breakfast Hotel prides itself on the standard of accommodation that it offers. The nicely furnished bedrooms are all individually heated and decorated with a small posy of flowers and a watercolour by local artist Denise McCulloch.

The shared bathroom facilities have been conveniently appointed with bathrobes provided, giving warmth and comfort in the Bed and Breakfast tradition. Such things as "Hotties" and "Brollies" add charm to the style of accommodation offered, as does our 1928 Studebaker sedan.

Our generous morning breakfast (included in the tariff) offers Fruit Juice, Fresh Fruits, Yogurt and Cereals followed by Bacon and Eggs, Sausages, Tomatoes, Toast and Marmalade, and is served in the dining room each morning between 6.30 and 9.00 am. The complimentary Tea and Coffee making facilities allow guests to help themselves at their own convenience and we serve "Supper" (Tea, Coffee and Biscuits) each evening in the lounge at 9.00 pm. As part of our service the Hotel offers Laundry Facilities, off Street Parking for the motorist and bicycle and baggage storage.

Quote this book for 10% discount.

Christchurch City *B&B Separate/Suite*

Turret House
Justine & Paddy Dougherty
435 Durham Street North, Christchurch

Tel (03) 365 3900   0800 48 87 73
Fax (03) 365 5601
turretb.bchch@xtra.co.nz
www.turrethouse.co.nz

Double $95-$130   Single $75-$130
(Continental Breakfast)
Credit cards accepted
3 King/Twin 3 Queen 1 Twin 1 Single (8 bdrm)
8 Ensuite

'Céad Míle Fáilte' *(One hundred thousand welcomes)*
Turret House is a gracious superior Bed & Breakfast accommodation located in downtown Christchurch.
It is within easy walking distance of Cathedral Square, the Botanical Gardens, Museum, Art Gallery, the
Arts Centre and Hagley Park 18 hole golf course. Also Casino, new Convention Centre, Town Hall.

Built around 1900 this historic residence is one of only three in the area protected by the New Zealand
Historic Places Trust. It has been restored to capture the original character and charm. Situated within
the grounds is one of Christchurch's best examples of our native kauri tree. Attractively decorated
bedrooms with heaters and electric blankets combine comfort and old world elegance, with private
bathrooms, some with bath and shower, all offering a totally relaxed and comfortable environment.

Tea, coffee and biscuits available 24 hrs. Cots and highchairs are also available. Family room sleeps 4.
If you're looking for a place to stay where the accommodation is superior and the atmosphere friendly
- experience Turret House. Non smoking policy.

Directions:
Just 15 minutes from Christchurch Airport. Situated on the corner of Bealey Ave and Durham
Street. (Off-street parking).

Christchurch City *B&B Self-contained Christchurch Central*

Riverview Lodge
Ernst and Sabine Wipperfuerth
361 Cambridge Terrace, Christchurch 1

Tel (03) 365 2860 Fax (03) 365 2845
riverview.lodge@xtra.co.nz
www.riverview.net.nz

Double $150-$190 Single $95-$135
(Full Breakfast) (Special Breakfast)
S/C suites $220 Credit cards accepted
Children welcome
3 Queen 1 Double 1 Twin 1 Single (5 bdrm)
4 Ensuite 1 Private

If you like quality accommodation in a relaxed
and quiet atmosphere, still just minutes walking
away from the centre of an exciting city: this is
the place to stay.
Riverview Lodge is a restored Edwardian
residence that reflects the grace and style of the
period with some fine Kauri carvings.
Guest rooms are elegant combining modern
facilities with colonial furnishings. Balconies
provide wonderfull river views.
The Edwardian townhouse next door has two
very spacious (80m2) apartments (one/two
bedrooms) for a private stay.
Guests find antiques and quality furniture, a
fully equipped kitchen, lounge, bathroom, TV
and private telephone.

For full breakfast we invite guests into the lodge or if requested supply a continental breakfast in the suite.
As ex-tour operators we'll be happy to help you with planning and bookings. Kayaks, bicycles and golf
clubs are for guests to use. We are multilingual.

For information on our two inner city holiday cottages please look up: www.moacottages.co.nz

Christchurch City *B&B B&B Hotel*

Croydon House
Nita Herbst
63 Armagh Street, Christchurch
Tel (03) 366 5111   0800 276 936   Fax (03) 377 6110
welcome@croydon.co.nz   www.croydon.co.nz
Double $120-$145 Single $90-$105 (Full Breakfast)
Child $20 under 12 years Children welcome
Self-contained apartment $170 - $190
Credit cards accepted
1 King 4 Queen 2 Double 3 Twin 2 Single (12 bdrm)
10 Ensuite

'Community Pride'
Garden Award
- last three
consecutive years

Croydon House is a charming Hotel offering fine *accommodation* in the *heart* of New Zealand's Garden City. All Bedrooms are tastefully refurbished with private or ensuite bathroom.
Start your day with our scrumptious buffet and indulge yourself in a deliciously cooked breakfast prepared especially for you.
Historic tram, art gallery, casino, art centre. Explore the city's major attractions, great restaurants, conference venues and the famous Botanical Gardens are within easy walking distance.
We provide Internet access. For more information visit our Home Page on the Internet with on-line booking form.
Croydon House has received the 'Community Pride' Garden Award for the last three consecutive years.

Christchurch City *B&B Christchurch Central*

Home Lea B&B
Pauline & Gerald Oliver
195 Bealey Avenue, Christchurch
Tel (03) 379 9977   0800 355 321   Fax (03) 379 4099
homelea@xtra.co.nz   www.homelea.co.nz
Double $90-$115 Single $65-$90 Child $15
Dinner By arrangement Children welcome
1 King 3 Queen 3 Single (5 bdrm)
2 Ensuite 1 Private 1 Guests share

Home Lea offers the traveller a comfortable and enjoyable
stay. Built in the early 1900's, Home Lea has the charm
and character of a large New Zealand home of that era: Rimu panelling, leadlight windows, and a large
lounge with a log fire. Tea, coffee, biscuits and fruit are available at all times. Off street parking, and
email/fax facilities available for guests. Pauline and Gerald are happy to share there knowledge of local
attractions and their special interests are travel, sailing and music.

Christchurch City *B&B Separate/Suite Christchurch Central*

Orari B&B
Ashton Owen
42 Gloucester St, Christchurch 1,
Tel (03) 365 6569   Fax (03) 365 2525
orari.bb@xtra.co.nz   www.orari.net.nz
Double $160-$190 Single $130-$150
(Special Breakfast) Credit cards accepted
1 King/Twin 9 Queen 5 Single (10 bdrm)
8 Ensuite 2 Private

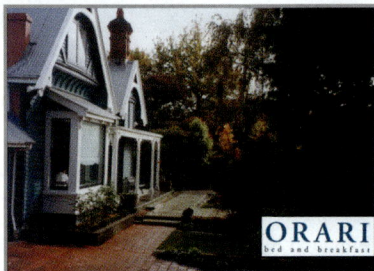

Orari was built in 1893. Of Kauri construction with
beautifully proportioned rooms, Orari is located in the
heart of the city directly opposite Christchurch's new Art Gallery. Orari is within easy walking distance
of the Art Centre, the Botanic Gardens, Museum, Hagley Park, Town Hall, Casino, Convention Centre
and Cathedral Square. Featuring 10 bedrooms with private bathrooms, off street parking and wheel
chair access, it provides comfortable, friendly accommodation for travellers, business people and small
group conferences. Enjoy the convenience of the inner city in an elegant heritage home.

Christchurch City *B&B Christchurch Central*

Apartment 37
Lynne & David
Apartment 37, PO Box 177, Old Government Buildings,
Cathedral Square, Christchurch
Tel (03) 377 7473   Fax (03) 377 7863
Mob 025 622 0849 apartment37@xtra.co.nz
www.bnb.co.nz/apartment.html
Double $135-$165 Single $135-$150
(Special Breakfast) Credit cards accepted
1 Queen 1 Twin (2 bdrm) 2 Ensuite

In the heart of Christchurch (Cathedral Square), Apartment 37 is
unique offering warm friendly hospitality and elegant accommodation
in a grand historic building with central city convenience. In addition
enjoy many extras including Sky TV, tea/coffee making facilities, and access to in-building facilities
(lap pool, gymnasium, spa, sauna, restaurant). Walk to Christchurch's vibrant attractions - Arts Centre,
museum, botanic gardens, Hagley park, shops, cafes, conference centre, and entertainment or use transport
right on door step. Perfect for holidays or business. Please phone for directions.

Christchurch City *B&B Separate/Suite Christchurch Central*

The Manor
Alison & Ross Ruddenklau
82 Bealey Avenue, City Central, Christchurch
Tel (03) 366 8584   0800 366 859   Fax (03) 366 4946
info@themanor.co.nz
www.themanor.co.nz
Double $187 - $347 Single $167 - $347 (Full Breakfast)
Credit cards accepted Children welcome
5 King/Twin 4 Queen (9 bdrm)
9 Ensuite

The Manor is a beautifully restored Victorian mansion, built in 1860.

The original architecture includes a magnificent entrance foyer, lead light windows and wood panelling.

The tariff includes a scrumptious breakfast with a hot dish.

We are a short drive from the airport and conveniently situated 10 - 15 mins level walk to Art centre, Botanical gardens, Art galleries, City centre, golf course, museums, restaurants.

Free parking and internet access is available to guests.

The Manor Cafe is open daily from 7am catering to guests and the public.

Christchurch City *B&B Separate/Suite B&B Guesthouse*

Devon Bed & Breakfast Hotel
Sandra & Benjamin Humphrey
69 Armagh Street, Christchurch

Tel (03) 366 0398 0800 283 386 Fax (03) 366 0398
bandbdevonhotel@xtra.co.nz
www.devonbandbhotel.co.nz

Double $95-$150 Single $80-$99 (Full Breakfast)
Child Under 15, $1 per year of age $20 Extra Adults
Credit cards accepted
6 Queen 3 Twin 2 Single (11 bdrm)
6 Ensuite 1 Private 2 Guests share

The Devon is a personal guest house located in the heart of beautiful Christchurch city, which offers elegance and comfort in the style of an olde worlde English manor. Just five minutes' walk to Christchurch Cathedral, Town Hall, and Convention Centre, casino, museum, art gallery, hospital and botanical gardens in Hagley Park. TV lounge, tea & coffee making facilities. Off street parking.

Christchurch City *B&B*

Holly House
Erica & Allister Stewart
1/337 Cambridge Terrace, Inner City, Christchurch

Tel (03) 371 7337 a.e.stewart@xtra.co.nz
www.bnb.co.nz/hollyhouse.html

Double $120 Single $110 (Special Breakfast)
1 King/Twin (1 bdrm)
1 Private

We would be pleased to welcome you to our home which is within walking distance to anywhere in the inner city. We have one lovely bedroom which can be arranged as twin beds or one king size bed. The guests' bathroom is adjacent to the bedroom. The sitting room overlooks the beautiful tree-lined Avon River. A comment from our visitors' book: "Holly House is an absolute gem." Erica is an artist working with stained glass, and clay sculpture. Allister is a retired school teacher.

Christchurch - City East *B&B Homestay Self-contained 1.5km E of Christchurch*

Lanslow Lodge
Lance Ching & Dennis Munslow
564 Cashel Street, City East, Christchurch

Tel (03) 942 9842 Fax (03) 942 9842
Mob 021 262 4377 lanslowlodge@xtra.co.nz
www.bnb.co.nz/lanslow.html

Double $70-$80 Single $40-$45
(Continental Breakfast) Dinner $20 video hire $5
Smoking area inside
3 Queen 1 Twin 2 Single (4 bdrm) 1 Private

Lanslow Lodge (House) character 1930's villa home-away-from-home, atmosphere, where you can relax, read or just stroll around garden with Amy our friendly westhightland terrier. Join us for a chat over pre-dinner drinks by the fire. Ten minutes to city center. Bus at gate. Five minutes walk to Eastgate Mall. We do our best to suit everyone and if we don't offer a service please ask and we will endeavor to provide it. Not suitable for children. The house is smoke free.

Christchurch - Central *Homestay*

Summers House
Jackie & Kieran
76 Park Terrace, Christchurch 1,
Tel (03) 374 2320 Fax (03) 377 8623
stay@summers.net.nz
www.summers.net.nz
Double $120-$150 (Special Breakfast)
1 King/Twin (1 bdrm)
1 Ensuite

Large warm comfortable suite looking out over Hagley
Park and the Avon River and just a few minutes walk
from the city centre, new Art Gallery, Arts Centre, the Square and Botanic Gardens. Our facilities
include superking/twin beds with electric blankets, private bathroom, fridge, TV, video and phone, with
tea, coffee and refreshments available in room, and onsite parking. Breakfast is selected from our menu
and served in your room. Check out up to midday. We offer affordable luxury with one party at a time.

Avonside - Christchurch *B&B Garden Studio 4km E of Christchurch*

Avon Park Lodge
Murray & Richeena Bullard
144A Kerrs Road, Avonside, Christchurch
Tel (03) 389 1904 Fax (03) 389 1904
Mob 025 641 9692 avonparklodge@clear.net.nz
www.bnb.co.nz/avonparklodge.html
Double $85 Single $60 (Full Breakfast)
Child by arrangement Garden Studio $95
Credit cards accepted
2 Queen 2 Twin (3 bdrm)
1 Ensuite 1 Guests share

Enjoy quiet, peaceful surroundings in our beautiful garden and two storey home close to parks and the
Avon river. The two upstairs guest bedrooms are comfortably furnished and include tea and coffee
making facilities, etc. Our garden studio with ensuite is complete with fridge and microwave. Close to
frequent public transport (including bus to the railway station). Five min drive to the city. Your hosts
and their lovable boxer dog Gus assure you of a warm, friendly welcome. Complimentary pick-up.

Southshore - Christchurch *B&B Homestay 10km E of Christchurch*

Southshore Homestay
Jan & Graham Pluck
71A Rockinghorse Road, South Shore, Christchurch 7
Tel (03) 388 4067 Fax (03) 365 3775
grahamandjan@xtra.co.nz
www.bnb.co.nz/southshorehomestay.html
Double $90-$120 (Full Breakfast) Dinner $35pp
Credit cards accepted
1 Queen (1 bdrm)
1 Ensuite

Twenty minutes from the city, Southshore lies between the ocean and the Avon Estuary. Sheltered by
the dunes wilderness, our comfortable home is a quiet retreat set in an interesting seaside garden from
where a private track over the dunes provides easy access to miles of safe, sandy beach. Nearby, the
Estuary walkway offers expansive views and varied bird life. We are non-smokers, semi-retired with
interests in gardening, vintage cars, embroidery and our cat. Please phone for reservations. Airport
pickup available.

CANTERBURY

Christchurch City - Richmond   *B&B 1.5km E of Christchurch centre*   home NEW ZEALAND

Willow Lodge
Grania McKenzie
71 River Road, Avonside, Christchurch 1
Tel (03) 389 9395   Fax (03) 381 5395
willow@inet.net.nz
www.willowlodge.co.nz

Double $100-$150 Single $70-$100
(Special Breakfast) Child $25 Children welcome
Homestay   Separate/Suite   Credit cards accepted
1 King/Twin 2 Queen 1 Single (3 bdrm)
1 Ensuite 2 Private

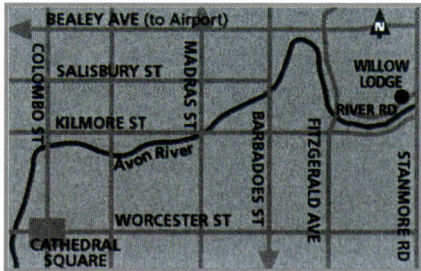

• Beautiful river setting   • Family suite   • 1928 Art Deco house   • Stroll into town.
Relax and unwind, read or chat, make yourself at home here at Willow Lodge. Enjoy our house with its
1920's architecture and style, and contemporary N.Z. art and books. The views over the river are
unsurpassed, and lovely in all seasons. Excellent large, firm beds.
Our generous breakfasts include organic bread, cereals, fresh fruit, eggs, good coffee & teas.
Christchurch with a population of nearly 400,000 people, boasts excellent food & wine, bookshops,
fashion, antiques and a lively arts scene. We have a wonderful brand new Art Gallery and over 20
cinemas. Christchurch is also well located for day trips - Akaroa and Banks Peninsula, Arthurs Pass,
Hanmer Springs, Kaikoura and several ski fields.
We welcome your questions and are happy to share our local knowledge. Shuttle or taxi service to the
gate from air/rail/coach. Also available: mountain bike, off street parking and laundry.

Times: Central city is 5 minutes by car, and 20 minutes walk. Airport or rail is 20 minutes by car.

Woolston - Christchurch *B&B Homestay 4km E of Christchurch*

Treeview
Kathy & Laurence Carr
6 Lomond Place, Woolston, Christchurch 6
Tel (03) 384 2352
www.bnb.co.nz/treeview.html

Double $80 Single $45 (Continental Breakfast)
Child $20 Dinner $20
1 Double 2 Single (2 bdrm)
1 Guests share

Welcome. Kiwi hospitality. Smoke free sunny home in quiet cul-de-sac. Garden with seating. Guests carport. Comfortable beds, electric blankets, hair drier. Generous breakfast in dining room with cathedral ceilings. 10 mins by car to city and beaches. Bus handy. Courtesy transport from Railway Station. Airport shuttle service. From Cathedral Square take Gloucester Street to roundabout at Linwood Avenue. turn right. Pass Eastgate Mall to traffic lights end of avenue of trees. Right into Hargood Street. First left into Clydesdale, first left Lomond Place.

St Martins - Christchurch *B&B Self-contained 4km S of Christchurch City Centre*

Kleynbos B&B
Gerda De Kleyne & Hans van den Bos
59 Ngaio Street, Christchurch
Tel (03) 332 2896 Fax (03) 332 2896
KLEYNBOS@xtra.co.nz
www.bnb.co.nz/kleynbosbb.html

Double $85 Single $75 (Continental Breakfast)
Credit cards accepted
1 Queen 1 Double 1 Single (2 bdrm)
2 Ensuite 1 Guests share

Especially for you, quality accommodation with a personal touch. Close, 4km, to the city centre, in an easy to find, friendly, tree-lined, residential street. That's us! Your large room with ensuite bathroom is $85 and has its own microwave, fridge, water boiler etc. Our children are 11 and 14. Gerda works in Mental Health. Having guests is like family who have come to stay. Directions: SH74 Barbadoes Street, Waltham Road, Wilsons Road, Right into Gamblins Road, first left. Do you need your own kitchen, private entrance or a full house?

St Martins - Christchurch *B&B Self-catering apartments City Centre*

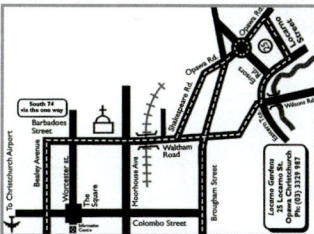

Locarno Gardens
Aileen & David Davies 25 Locarno Street, St Martins, Christchurch 8002
Tel (03) 332 9987 Fax (03) 332 9687 Mob 025 399 747 locarno@xtra.co.nz
www.cottagestays.co.nz/begonia/cottage.htm

Double $85-$110 Single $85-$110 Extra person $25 Continental Breakfast extra
1 King 1 Queen 1 Twin (3 bdrm) 2 Ensuite 1 Private

Mt Pleasant - Christchurch   *Homestay 8km E of Christchurch*

Plains View
Robyn & Peter Fleury
2 Plains View, Mt Pleasant, Christchurch 8
Tel (03) 384 5558   Fax (03) 384 5558
Mob 025 211 3606   Fleury@inet.net.nz
www.bnb.co.nz/fleury.html

Double $70-$85 Single $45 (Continental Breakfast)
1 Queen 1 Double 1 Single (3 bdrm)
1 Guests share

Enjoy our warm hospitality in the comfort of our modern home, spacious and sunny with wonderful views of the city and Southern Alps. Close by sumner beach, Ferrymead historical Park, Mt Cavendish Gondola and a variety of restaurants. Our interests include 4 wheel driving the outdoors, tapestry and gardening. our travels have taken us throughout New Zealand and overseas. We provide complimentary tea and coffee and are a non smoking household. Please phone for directions. Complimentary pickup available by arrangement (conditions apply).

Mt Pleasant - Christchurch   *B&B Homestay 7km E of City Centre*

The Cotterage
Jennifer Cotter
24B Soleares Avenue, Mt Pleasant, Christchurch 8008
Tel (03) 384 2898   Fax (03) 384 2898   jen@e3.net.nz
www.bnb.co.nz/thecotterage.html

Double $110 Single $65 (Continental Breakfast)
Child neg Dinner $20 B/A Twin $95
Credit cards accepted
1 Queen 1 Twin 1 Single (3 bdrm)
1 Ensuite 1 Host share

Away from the city smog. Quiet secluded comfort in homely cottage down private lane. Charming tranquil garden. Sunny bedrooms opening on to covered terrace (for breakfast al fresco!) Tea and coffee always available. Many cafes, pubs, good restaurants 5 minutes drive. Estuary where bird life abounds 2 minutes walk. Nearby scenic attractions include Sumner beach, hills, walks, gondola, Lyttelton Harbour. City centre is 15 minutes. We enjoy company, have travelled extensively, enjoy creative pursuits, gardening, books. Two resident cats. Laundry facilities. Smoking outdoors. Please phone for directions.

Mt Pleasant - Christchurch   *B&B Separate/Suite 7km E of City Centre*

The Nest on Mount Pleasant
Kathryn & Kai Tovgaard
24 Toledo Place, Christchurch 8
Tel 0064 3 3 849 485   Fax 0064 3 3 848 385
thenestonMP@xtra.co.nz
www.PlacesToStay.co.nz/places/5011.asp

Double $85-$115 Single $75-$100 (Full Breakfast)
Child discounted Dinner b/a Credit cards accepted
2 Queen 2 Twin (3 bdrm)
1 Ensuite 1 Guests share

Unique self-contained home (including full kitchen and laundry facilities) yet with all the service of a homestay: This is the promise of THE NEST. Warm hospitality guaranteed with hosts next door. Situated in one of Christchurch's most exclusive Hill suburbs set in native bush. Views of Estuary, Sea and Mountains beyond. Tranquil and secure, with garage parking. TV, Stereo and BBQ. Very close to Chistchurch's best beaches with excellent cafes and restaurants, Ferrymead Historic Park, Lyttelton Harbour, and hillside walks with breathtaking views to the Southern Alps.

Redcliffs - Christchurch *B&B Homestay 8km E of Christchurch*

Redcliffs on Sea
Cynthia & Lyndsey Ebert
125 Main Road, Redcliffs, Christchurch 8
Tel (03) 384 9792 Fax (03) 384 9703
redcliffs@nzhomestay.co.nz
www.nzhomestay.co.nz/ebert.htm
Double $120 Single $75 (Continental Breakfast)
Credit cards accepted
1 Queen 1 Single (1 bdrm)
1 Ensuite

Relax and enjoy our comfortable home by the sea, situated
approximately 15 minutes from the city, our home is "absolute water front ", on the Avon-Heathcote
Estuary with magnificent views of the sea, birds and boating. We are non smoking and our guest
facilities include a sunny queen and single bedroom with its own ensuite and TV. Local restaurants
offer a choice of cuisine, continental breakfast is included in the tariff, laundry facilities and off street
parking. What more could you wish for?

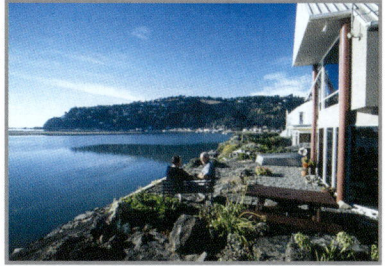

New Brighton - Christchurch *B&B Self-contained 9km E of City*

The Sculpture House
Bon Suter
411 Pine Avenue, Christchurch,
Tel (03) 388 3359 bonsuter@value.net.nz
www.bnb.co.nz/sculpturehouse.html
Double $120-$190 (Continental Breakfast) Child $20
Pets welcome
2 Queen 1 Double 1 Single (2 bdrm)
2 Private

Fifteen minutes from the city Marine parade runs along
the coastline and is close to the avon estury. Across the
road is a sculpture garden sheltering in a wilderness of sand dunes. An artists retreat with a beautiful
garden and romantic outdoor bath in sub-tropical settings. Easy access to miles of safe sandy beaches
unique bird life dune and estury walkways. We offer two self contained studio apartments one up one
down.

Sumner - Christchurch *B&B Self-contained 10km E of Christchurch*

Villa Alexandra
Wendy & Bob Perry
1 Kinsey Terrace, Christchurch 8
Tel (03) 326 6291 Fax (03) 326 6096
villa_alexandra@xtra.co.nz
www.villaalexandra.co.nz
Double $85-$110 Single $70 (Full Breakfast)
Child $15 over 12yrs. Dinner $35 by arrangement.
1 Queen 1 Double 1 Twin 1 Single (4 bdrm)
2 Ensuite 2 Private

Enjoy the warmest hospitality in our spacious turn of
the century villa overlooking Sumner Bay. Our home retains the graciousness of a bygone era while
offering all modern comforts. In winter enjoy open fires, cosy farmhouse kitchen and on sunny days the
verandah and turret. Spectacular sea views from Sumner to the Kaikouras. We enjoy food, wine,
music, gardening, tramping, travel. The children have flown, but we still have three hens. 5 mins walk
to beach; off street parking; laundry. Also self-contained beach front apartment, 2 double bedrooms,
$135 per night, min. three nights.

Sumner Beach - Christchurch *B&B Guesthouse 8km E of Christchurch*

Cave Rock Guest House
Gayle & Norm Eade
16 Esplanade, Sumner, Christchurch
Tel (03) 326 6844 Fax (03) 326 5600
Mob 025 360 212 eade@chch.planet.org.nz
www.caverockguesthouse.co.nz
Double $95-$110 Single $80 (Continental Breakfast)
Child $15 Credit cards accepted
4 Queen (4 bdrm)
4 Ensuite

The Cave Rock Guest House is Christchurch's only seafront accommodation directly opposite Sumner's famous "Cave Rock". Your hosts Gayle and Norm Eade have been in the hospitality industry for 15 years and enjoy meeting people from overseas and within NZ. Our large double rooms have seaviews and are self contained. All have colour TV, heating and ensuite bathrooms, and can sleep up to 4. Kitchen facilities available. Sumner Village is an ideal location, 15 minutes from Christchurch city. We have a very friendly Dalmatian dog.

Sumner - Christchurch *B&B 8kms E of Christchurch*

Ocean View
Anna & Christian van Uden
65 Ocean View Terrace, Sumner, Christchurch
Tel (03) 326 4888 Fax (03) 326 4888
oceanview@clear.net.nz
www.bnb.co.nz/user5.html
Double $95-$130 Single $65-$90
(Continental Breakfast) Child neg
Credit cards accepted
1 Queen 1 Twin (2 bdrm) 2 Private

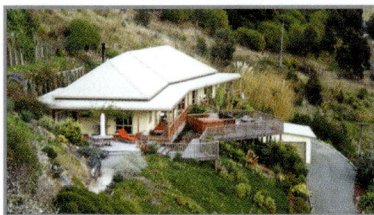

Chris, Anna and Dominic welcome you to Ocean View B&B. Fifteen minutes from Christchurch city and is set in the popular seaside suburb of Sumner. Sumner's relaxing village atmosphere has much to offer the traveller. Take advantage of the views up the coast and out to sea from the guest rooms that have direct access to expansive verandas and decking positioned to capture the sun. Guest lounge has television tea and coffee facilities. Set on three acres of land providing a rural flavour. Directions: Please telephone, e-mail or visit our brochure.

Sumner - Christchurch *B&B Self-contained 15km E of Central Christchurch*

Abbott House Sumner Bed & Breakfast
Janet & Chris Abbott
104 Nayland Street, Sumner, Christchurch
Tel (03) 326 6111 Mob 0800 020 654 Fax (03) 326 6111
info@abbotthouse.co.nz www.abbotthouse.co.nz
Double $70-$120 Single $70-$120 (Continental Breakfast)
Children welcome Child $10 Credit cards
2 King 1 Double 1 Single (2 bdrm) 2 Private

Your hosts, Chris and Janet Abbott welcome you to our historic restored 1870's villa in Christchurch's unique seaside village. Our home is oneblock from the beach, and an easy 10-minute walk along the beach to Sumner's many cafés, restaurants, boutique shops and cinema. The studio and 3-room suite are separate and individually self-contained. Both have king-sized beds, TV and video, en-suite bathrooms, and kitchen areas. Our rambling garden is patrolled by Levi the cat, and hens who provide wonderful fresh eggs. Laundry facilities available.

Sumner - Christchurch *B&B 8km E of Christchurch*

Tiro Moana
Helen Mackay
89 Richmond Hill Road, Sumner, Christchurch
Tel (03) 326 6209 Fax (03) 326 6203
enquiries@tiromoana.co.nz
www.tiromoana.co.nz
Double $100-$140 Single $60-$80 (Full Breakfast)
Child $15 Dinner B/A Children welcome
1 King/Twin 1 Queen 1 Double (3 bdrm)
1 Ensuite 1 Private

Sumner, only 15 minutes from the city, with interesting cafes, movies, theatres and walks. Tiro Moana - built 1904 in a splendid position overlooking the beach. A perfect spot to relax, wander the garden have a bath outside under the stars and sleep to the sound of the sea. The atmosphere is friendly, relaxed and informal providing guests' lounge, tea and coffee facilities, a fresh and generous breakfast. Laundry facilities are available. We look forward to welcoming you.

Lower Cashmere - Christchurch *B&B*

Teresa & Dave Hughes
4 Piper Lane, Beckenham, Christchurch
Tel (03) 337 3581 teresahughes@paradise.net.nz
www.bnb.co.nz/hughes.html
Double $95 Single $80 (Continental Breakfast)
2 Single (1 bdrm)
1 Private

A warm welcome awaits you at my new home and garden, situated in a quiet lane at the foot of the Cashmere hills, handily situated to bus routes and only 10 minutes ride to the city centre. Various restaurants are close by, or you are welcome to bring home take-aways. Your room has either a double or two single beds, with electric blankets. Tea, coffee. and biscuits are always available. Secure off-street parking.

Cashmere - Christchurch *B&B 5km S of Christchurch*

Janet Milne
12A Hackthorne Road, Cashmere, Christchurch
Tel (03) 337 1423
www.bnb.co.nz/milne.html
Single $50 (Continental Breakfast)
1 Queen 1 Single (1 bdrm)
1 Ensuite 1 Host share

Two storeyed home in quiet back section on Cashmere Hills. Lower storey is an independent suite comprising two hand basins, shower, lavatory, kingsize bed with electric blanket, two single bunks, television, telephone, heaters, and table and chairs. Tea/coffee making facilities.
Non smokers only. I am a registered general nurse; obstetrics nurse; a university student studying for a degree in linguistics; and an English language teacher. The piano loves attention. Spanish and English are my favourite languages. 'Explorer' of foreign countries.

Cashmere - Christchurch *B&B Homestay 5km S of Christchurch*

City Lights
Jan & Bob Thayer
34 Harry Ell Drive, Cashmere, Christchurch
Tel (03) 332 5566   Fax (03) 337 0038
Mob 021 105 8593   jancitylights@xtra.co.nz
www.bnb.co.nz/citylightschristchurch.html

Double $120-$150 Single $100 (Full Breakfast)
Dinner by arrangement
1 King/Twin 1 Queen 1 Twin (3 bdrm)
1 Private

Stunning panoramic views and a warm welcome await you in our spacious modern Mediterranean style home nestled in the Cashmere Hills.
Enjoy the quiet and private gardens, beautiful heated saltwater swimming pool (Oct-April), piano, home gym, and the nearby Port Hills walkways. Relax in any of the sundrenched outdoor areas and enjoy the million dollar views from the mountains to the sea or curl up with a book in the spacious warm and well appointed living areas or private lounge.
Bedrooms have comfortable excellent quality beds and linen including cosy luxurious robes in which to relax.
Delicious full breakfasts with fresh locally grown produce, great coffee and freshly baked bread. Superb dinners available by arrangement and special diets catered for. Alternatively we can tell you about some great Christchurch restaurants in this area.
Our home is smokefree inside and we share it with our lovely old cat Che. Our interests include sports (arm chair), walking, gardening, kayaking, rotary, travel, good food and wine, and most importantly our two little grandchildren.
We prefer to host one couple or group of people at a time. This ensures your privacy and enables us to focus on your requirements.
Bob and Jan have travelled a lot and really appreciate our beautiful country. It would be our privilege to help you plan to get the very best out of your time here whether you are on holidays or business.
We look forward to welcoming you to our home with tea/coffee and fresh baking or a cool drink.
Directions will be given at time of booking.

Modern Mediterranean style home nestled in the Cashmere Hills

Halswell - Christchurch *B&B Self-contained 6km SE of City Centre*

Overton
Judi & Joe Brizzell
241 Kennedys Bush Road, Halswell, Christchurch 3
Tel (03) 322 8326   Fax (03) 322 8350
Mob 025 623 0831   brizzell.accom@xtra.co.nz
www.canterburypages.co.nz/overton
Double $85-$110 Single $60-$85 (Full Breakfast)
Child Neg Dinner $30 Credit cards accepted
1 Queen 4 Twin (3 bdrm)
1 Private 1 Host share

Tranquil, cosy and convenient. Only 20 minutes from the city and near the Akaroa highway, our extensive garden on the Port Hills overlooks the rural Canterbury Plains to the Southern Alps. Enjoy a warm hosted experience. The self-contained, exclusive-to-you ìGarden Lodgeî is fully equipped - two bedrooms (one queen, one twin), private bathroom, kitchen and TV. Twin bedroom in our home. New Zealand cuisine, featuring seasonal home-grown produce. Interests include our garden, fishing, fibre-arts, walking in the adjacent park and our friendly dog.

Broadfield - Christchurch *B&B Farmstay Self-contained*

Huntingdon Grange   *16km SW of Christchurch Central*
Gaye & Lindsay Johnson
Shands Road, RD6, Broadfield, Christchurch
Tel (03) 344 5899   Fax (03) 344 5533
Mob 027 446 6144   stay@huntingdongrange.co.nz
www.huntingdongrange.co.nz
Double $150-$260 Single $150 (Full Breakfast)
2 King/Twin 1 King 3 Queen (5 bdrm)
3 Ensuite

Just minutes from Christchurch city or airport, enjoy the ambience of our small country estate. Nestled amongst established trees and gardens, Huntingdon Grange is the ideal place to stay while visiting Christchurch or on your journey around the South Island. Quality furnishings and tasteful decor enhance your relaxation and enjoyment. Unwind in our stylish lounge with open fire in winter or on our barbeque terrance or in the heated swimming pool in summer. Enjoy tennis, petanque, croquet or visit the wineries, golf courses and country cafes close by.

CANTERBURY

Lincoln - Christchurch *Country 20km S of Christchurch Central*

Menteith Country Homestay
Fay & Stephen Graham
Springs Road, RD 6, Christchurch 8021
Tel (03) 325 2395   Fax (03) 325 2396
menteith@paradise.net.nz
www.bnb.co.nz/menteithcountryhomestay.html
Double $135 - $150 Single $110 - $125 Child negotiable
2 King/Twin 1 Queen (3 bdrm)
3 Ensuite

Our tranquil farmlet supports a small sheep flock for Fay's spinning - try your hand! and 7 beehives. Guest rooms with well equipped ensuite bathrooms surround the heated spa and swimming pool conservatory - a great place to relax after a busy day sightseeing. Robes provided. Be pampered with crisp linen, large fluffy towels, refrigerator, tea and coffee facilities, TV, phone, hairdryer, plenty of heat and warm cosy beds. Smoking welcome outside. Hearty breakfasts are served in our sunny dining room. Delightful reasonably-priced restaurants nearby. Golf course and university 3km. Resident cat.

Tai Tapu - Christchurch *B&B Homestay 15km S of Christchurch*

Pear Drop Inn
Erik & Paula Gray
Akaroa Highway 75, Tai Tapu, RD 2, Christchurch
Tel (03) 329 6778   Fax (03) 329 6661
Mob 021 1266 873   peardropinn@clear.net.nz
www.bnb.co.nz/peardropinn.html
Double $100 Single $50 (Special Breakfast)
Child 1/2 price Dinner $25 Credit cards accepted
1 King 1 Queen 1 Twin 6 Single (3 bdrm)
1 Ensuite 1 Guests share 1 Host share

Welcome to our comfortable country home, nestled in 2 1/2 acres of trees, garden/orchard. Superbly located for City and Country activities. We offer you warm relaxed Kiwi hospitality and home cooked meals.[if required] Sprayfree vegetables/produce from our garden. Meal times flexible. Our rooms are spacious, and comfortably appointed. We include fresh fruit and goodies in each room. Local wineries, restaurants, walking tracks, golf, all within 5 minutes. Christchurch City centre 15 mins. Akaroa Village 1 hour drive.

Cass Bay - Lyttelton *B&B Homestay Self-contained 6km SE of Christchurch*

Harbour View Homestay
Susi & Hank Boots
3 Mariners Cove, Cass Bay, Lyttelton, Christchurch
Tel (03) 328 7250   Fax (03) 328 7251
Mob 027 226 2633
harbourview.homestay@clear.net.nz
www.harbourviewhomestay.co.nz
Double $110-$130 Single $95 (Full Breakfast)
s/c from $160 Credit cards accepted Children welcome
1 King 1 Twin (2 bdrm) 2 Ensuite 1 Guests share

Cass Bay, nestled in the beautiful Lyttelton harbour basin with swimming beaches and walking tracks, offers easy access to all city amenities. It is an ideal base for day-trips to many tourist attractions. Our new home incorporates warmth, luxury and comfort, has a relaxed atmosphere, a lovely garden-setting with a petanque area and outdoor chessgame and breath-taking views. Our beds are very comfortable and extra long. Our s/c accommodation offers microwave-cooking. Wir sprechen Deutsch, Schweizerdeutsch en spreken Nederlands. 10% discount from 3 days.

Lyttelton *B&B 9km E of Christchurch*

Shonagh O'Hagan's Guest House
Shonagh O'Hagan
Dalcroy House, 16 Godley Quay, Lyttelton
Tel (03) 328 8577   Mob (025) 346 351
shonagh.ohagan@xtra.co.nz
www.bnb.co.nz/shonaghohagans.html
Double $115 Single $85 (Full Breakfast) Child $25
Dinner $35 Credit cards accepted Children welcome
1 King/Twin 2 Queen 1 Double (4 bdrm)
1 Guests share 2 Host share

Dalcory House built 1859, has been a Boarding School, private residents, rental property, and hostel for naval rating's in WW2. Shonagh your hostess is a Cook, Nurse, Educator, Health manager and mother. Have a comfortable nights sleep in pleasant surroundings with a clear view of Lyttelton Port and Harbour, 5 minutes walk from the centre of Lyttelton and 1 minutes drive to the centre of Christchurch. Shonagh and her son will ensure your stay is comfortable and memorable.

Church Bay - Lyttelton   *Homestay 25km SE of Christchurch*

'The Priory'
Anne Prior
177 Marine Drive, Main Road, Church Bay,
RD1, Lyttelton

Tel (03) 329 4441 Mob 025 644 9641
thepriory@xtra.co.nz   www.bnb.co.nz/thepriory.html

Double $85 Single $60 (Full Breakfast)
Child $10 Dinner $20 by arrangement
1 Queen 1 Double 2 Single (1 bdrm)   1 Host share

ìThe Prioryî at Church Bay is just 30 minutes from Christchurch city, located on the southern edge of Lyttelton Harbour. Upstairs studio sleeps six, with great elevated views overlooking Church Bay and the harbour. Pretty cottage garden. Shared bathroom, cooked & continental breakfast available, evening meals on request (complimentary ìThe Prioryî homemade fruit wines). Be playing golf in just 5 minutes, with good swimming just a short walk away and other activities close by. Close boat ramp makes it ideal for sailing holidays. (Shy cat).

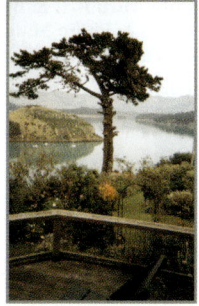

Governors Bay   *B&B 13km SE of Christchurch*

Governors Bay Bed & Breakfast
Karen & Kevin McGrath
14 Hays Rise, Governors Bay, Lyttelton RD1

Tel (03) 329 9930 Mob 021 622 657
karenkev@xtra.co.nz   www.brochures.co.nz/gbb&b

Double $110 Single $95 (Continental Breakfast)
Credit cards accepted Pets welcome
1 Queen (2 bdrm)   1 Private

Unique timber home designed to accommodate our B&B private guest wing. Separate entrance with sunny morning deck. Enjoy brekky in your room or on the deck. Queen room with picture window has panoramic views of Lyttelton Harbour. TV, fridge, and CD player. Private guest lounge optional extra, or convert for more sleeping. Rural walking tracks start at back of our 3 acre property. Karen operates Earth Healer Aromatherapy and offers complimentary aromatherapy baths. Full treatments and Reiki by appointment. We and our lab X "Bella-Brae" look forward to welcoming you soon.

Teddington - Lyttelton Harbour   *Farmstay*

Bergli Hill Farmstay   *20km S of Christchurch*
Rowena & Max Dorfliger
265 Charteris Bay Road, Teddington, R.D.1 Lyttelton

Tel (03) 329 9118 Fax (03) 329 9118
Mob 025 829 410 bergli@ihug.co.nz
www.vmacgill.net/bergli

Double $105-$125 Single $70-$90 (Full Breakfast)
Child $5 less Dinner $25 B/A Credit cards accepted
2 Queen 1 Double 3 Single (3 bdrm)
2 Ensuite 1 Host share

Lyttelton Harbour and the Port Hills create a dynamic panorama you can enjoy from our custom-built log chalet. Rowena speaks Japanese (but is a Kiwi) and Max speaks German. We are both self-employed (woodworker and shadow puppeteer) and enjoy sharing a sail on Max's yacht. Our pet cat and sheep welcome guests enthusiastically. Whether relaxing on the veranda at Max's hand-crafted table or sipping wine in the spa bath, we are sure you will make good memories.

CANTERBURY

Church Bay - Diamond Harbour *B&B Self-contained 35km S of Christchurch*

Kai-o-ruru Bed & Breakfast
Robin & Philip Manger
32 James Drive, Church Bay, RD 1, Lyttelton

Tel (03) 329 4788 Fax (03) 329 4788
manger@xtra.co.nz
www.bnb.co.nz/kaiorurubedbreakfast.html

Double $90 Single $50 (Full Breakfast) Dinner $25
2 Single (1 bdrm)
1 Ensuite

Explore Banks Peninsula from Church Bay. Our cosy,
ensuite unit overlooks Quail Island and our coastal garden.
The room has a tea/coffee tray, home-made biscuits, books, TV, fridge. We are a non-smoking household
with an unobtrusive cat. Philip and I are travelled, retired teachers who enjoy welcoming travellers to
our wonderful area. Languages: German, Dutch (some Italian, Spanish).

Purau - Lyttelton Harbour *B&B 35km SE of Chrsitchurch*

Mt Evans B&B
Pauline Croft & Barry Kendall
53 Purau-Port Levy Rd,
RD 2 Diamond Harbour, Lyttelton

Tel (03) 329 4414 Fax (03) 329 4414
kendallcroft@hyper.net.nz
www.bnb.co.nz/mtevans.html

Double $75-$95 Single $70-$90
(Continental Breakfast) Child $15
Dinner 'By arrangement' Two separate cottages
2 Queen 2 Single (2 bdrm) 2 Private

Our home is situated on 1.5 hectares, amongst mature trees on the gentle slopes of Mt Evans. Just 500 metres
from the beach, we offer tranquil rural accommodation in two separate and sunny modern cottages. A perfect
base for exploring Banks Peninsular and Christchurch (ferry seven minutes to Lyttelton) or to relax and
unwind. Local attractions include swimming, boating etc, wildlife cruises, Mountain biking, tramping (we
are experienced outdoor people happy to share our knowledge) abundant bird life and wonderful views.

Akaroa - Paua Bay *B&B Farmstay 12km E of Akaroa*

Paua Bay Farmstay
Murray & Sue Johns
Postal - c/o 113 Beach Road, Akaroa, Banks Peninsula

Tel (03) 304 8511 Fax (03) 304 8511
Mob 021 133 8194 info@pauabay.com
www.pauabay.com

Double $90 Single $60 (Full Breakfast) Child neg
Dinner $25 Children welcome
1 Queen 1 Twin (2 bdrm)
1 Guests share

Set in a private bay, our 900 acre sheep, deer and cattle farm is surrounded by coast-line, native bush
and streams. You are spoilt for choice - Walk to the beach, enjoy seals and extensive bird life, join in
seasonal farming activities or horse-riding. Swim in the pool, laze in the hammock and don't miss the
secluded moonlit bath under the stars overlooking the pacific ... In the evening share a meal of fresh
farm produce with relaxed conversation gathered around the large kitchen table.

Akaroa - Barry's Bay   *B&B Farmstay Homestay 12km before Akaroa*

Rosslyn Estate
Ross, Lynette, Kirsty (11) & Matt (9) Curry
Barry's Bay, RD 2, Akaroa
Tel (03) 304 5804 Fax (03) 304 5804
Rosslyn@xtra.co.nz
www.bnb.co.nz/rosslynestate.html
Double $115-$130 Single $100
(Full Breakfast) Dinner $30pp
Child negotiable Laundry no charge
Credit cards accepted
2 Queen (2 bdrm)
2 Ensuite

Experience the tranquility of farm life while conveniently situated on the main road between Christchurch and Akaroa, allowing you to explore this intriguing volcanic peninsula with ease. Our home is set amid rolling hills 400m from the road, overlooking the Akaroa Harbour. Rosslyn is a large historic homestead built in the 1860's. The estate is rich in history and has been our family home for four generations.

We take pride in offering quality home grown and prepared produce from vegetables and fruit to preserves and baking. It is a pleasure for us to share our evening meal, served in the farm style kitchen at the family table. Breakfast ranges from fresh fruit to full cooked with smoke cured bacon and home-made bread toasted on the embers.

Two large ground floor rooms have been refurbished to accommodate you in comfort. Each room has ensuite bathroom, firm queen bed, central heating, screened windows and antiques of the period. A spa room, pool, laundry, email and ph/fax are also available. French doors leading to expansive verandahs and informal gardens make the most of serene harbour views.

Our 160 cow-working dairy farm also runs deer and many pets, most of whom live outside. The streams are lined with bush attracting an abundance of native birds. We look forward to welcoming you with a fresh pot of tea, coffee or cool drink served with home baking, hearing of your adventures and helping you to plan new ones for the remainder of your holiday.

Directions:
Main Christchurch-Akaroa road (SH75), 'Rosslyn Estate' sign behind red picket fence (left traveling to Akaroa) at French Farm/Wainui turn off.

Okains Bay - Banks Peninsula *Farmstay 20km N of Akaroa*

Kawatea
Judy & Kerry Thacker
Okains Bay, Banks Peninsula
Tel (03) 304 8621   Fax (03) 304 8621
kawatea@xtra.co.nz   www.nzfarmstay.co.nz/thacker.htm

Double $90-$130 Single $65-$90 (Full Breakfast)
Child B/A Dinner $25 - $30 Credit cards accepted
3 Queen 2 Single (3 bdrm)
1 Ensuite 1 Private 1 Guests share

Experience the grace and charm of yesteryear, while enjoying the fine food and wine of NZ today. Revel in the peace of country life, but still be close to sights and activities. Escape to 'Kawatea', an historic Edwardian homestead set in spacious gardens, and surrounded by land farmed by our Irish ancestors since the 1850s. Built in 1900 from native timbers, it features stained glass windows and handcrafted furniture, and has been carefully renovated to add light and space without losing its old world charm.

Linger over your choice of breakfast in the sunny conservatory. Join us for barbeques on the expansive verandahs, savouring seafood from the Bay, and creative country fare from our garden and farm. Gather around the dining table by the fire, sharing experiences with fellow travellers.

Participate in farm activities such as moving stock, feeding pet sheep, lambing, calving or shearing. Wander our 1400-acre hillside farm, climbing to enjoy a panoramic view of Banks Peninsula. Relax or swim at Okains Bay, observe the birdlife on the estuary, or walk along the scenic coastline to secluded beaches and a seal

colony with excellent photographic opportunities. Learn about Maori Culture and the life of early settlers at the acclaimed Okains Bay Museum.

Explore Akaroa, with its strong French influence, visit art galleries and craft shops. Play golf, go horse riding, sample local wines and watch traditional cheeses being made. Take a harbour cruise or swim with the rare Hector's dolphin. We have been providing farmstays since 1988, and pride ourselves on thoughtful personal service. Romantic weekends and special occasion dinners are also catered for. We hope you come as a visitor but leave as a friend.

Directions: Take Highway 75 from Christchurch through Duvauchelle. Turn left at signpost marked Okains Bay. Drive to the top of the Bay - we are 6km downhill on the right.

Akaroa Harbour   *Farmstay 20km E of Akaroa*

Bossu
Rana & Garry Simes
Wainui, Akaroa, RD 2, Banks Peninsula
Tel (03) 304 8421   Fax (03) 304 8421
bossu@xtra.co.nz
www.bossufarmstay.co.nz
Double $130 Single $80 (Full Breakfast) Dinner $30
1 Queen 3 Single (3 bdrm)
1 Private 1 Guests share

"Bossu" farm of 100 acres is on 2 kms of the harbour
foreshore offering panoramic views of Akaroa and the surrounding countryside. Our farm tours are a specialty with sheep, cattle, forestry and a small vineyard. We also have a Jack Russell dog. We offer fishing, sightings of dolphin, penguin and nesting sea birds. A well used grass tennis court is a feature of our extensive garden. We enjoy golf, bridge, tennis and travel. Directions: first property on seaward side after Wainui.

Akaroa   *Farmstay 5km N of Akaroa*

Hanne & Paul LeLievre
Box 4, Akaroa, Banks Peninsula
Tel (03) 304 7255   Fax (03) 304 7255
Mob 025 942 070   Double.L@Xtra.co.nz
www.bnb.co.nz/lelievre.html
Double $95 Single $50 (Full Breakfast)
Dinner $25 Credit cards accepted
1 Queen 1 Single (1 bdrm)
1 Ensuite

Our home is situated 1.5km up the Takamatua valley and
only 5km from Akaroa. We farm sheep, cattle and deer, and usually have a menagerie of dogs, cats and orphaned pets around.   Hanne is Danish and speaks that language fluently. We have both worked in Australia for 10 years. We offer spacious accommodation in a sheltered position and invite you to enjoy some good old fashioned country hospitality. A trip to the "Akaroa Seal Colony Safari" should be considered a must.

Akaroa   *Self-contained self-contained individual cottages 1km N of Akaroa*

Loch Hill Country Cottages
Jill and Murray Gibb (resident managers)
PO Box 21, Main Highway, Akaroa
Tel (03) 304 7195   0800 456 244   Fax (03) 304 7672
lochhill@xtra.co.nz   www.lochhill.co.nz
Double $120-$165 Single $100
(Continental Breakfast) Child $15 under 12 yrs
Breakfast $10pp Credit cards accepted
2 King/Twin 2 King 8 Queen 4 Single (11 bdrm)
5 Ensuite 3 Private

'Loch-Hill' with magnificent sea-views overlooking Akaroa,
and cluster of fully self-contained luxurious cottages, nestled
in surrounding bush, park and garden setting, offers privacy and tranquillity. Some large cottages have air-conditioning. Try our romantic honeymoon cottages with cozy log-fires and double spa-baths. Enjoy wonderful views form your balcony. Experience the hospitality of 'Loch-Hill' "Caid Mile Failte" (One hundred thousand welcomes). Explore or relax in these idyllic, secluded surroundings. Perfect for your holiday retreat, smaller business conference, or wedding group. Special rates available.

Akaroa Harbour   *Country B&B 7km N of Akaroa*

Cabbage Tree Corner
Prue Billings & Ben Kennard
RD 1, Akaroa
Tel (03) 304 5155 Mob 021 655 862
prueb@xtra.co.nz
www.breakfast.co.nz
Double $100-$120 Single $75 (Full Breakfast)
Dinner $30 B/A Credit cards accepted
Children welcome
1 Queen 2 Single (2 bdrm)
2 Ensuite

Superbly sited in a commanding position above the north end of Akaroa harbour, this newly-restored 1920's farmhouse offers peace, comfort and views to die for. On the main highway it's close to all the Peninsula's attractions. Go walking, cycling or boating, see the dolphins, or enjoy the fine restaurants. Then relax in the peaceful atmosphere of our smoke free home. Expect a generous breakfast of fine fresh foods. Please phone for directions. The Akaroa/Christchurch bus stops at our gate.

Akaroa   *B&B Homestay Separate/Suite 80km SE of Christchurch*

Lavaud House
Mary Farrell
83 Rue Lavaud, Akaroa
Tel (03) 304 7121   Fax (03) 304 7121
lavaudhouse@xtra.co.nz
www.nzhomestay.co.nz/lavaudhouse.html
Double $120-$155 Single $90-$125
(Continental Breakfast) Credit cards accepted
1 King 2 Queen 1 Twin (4 bdrm)
3 Ensuite 1 Private

'Lavaud House' is a gracious, historic home which overlooks the beach and harbour. Being centrally located, you are only five minutes walking distance from restaurants, galleries and shops. Relax in the comfort of elegant furnishings, listen to beautiful music (Bluthner grand piano), or wander in our peaceful garden with its magnificent harbour views and enchanting native birds. In the evening I invite you to enjoy a complimentary glass of wine with me and, in the morning, a delicious continental breakfast.

Akaroa   *B&B 80km SE of Christchurch*

The Maples
Lesley & Peter Keppel
158 Rue Jolie, Akaroa
Tel (03) 304 8767   Fax (03) 304 8767
maplesakaroa@xtra.co.nz
www.themaplesakaroa.co.nz
Double $110-$120 Single $80-$85 (Full Breakfast)
Credit cards accepted
3 Queen 1 Single (3 bdrm)
3 Ensuite

The Maples is a charming historic two storey home built in 1877. It is situated in a delightful garden setting, three minutes walk from the cafes and waterfront. We offer two queen bedrooms with ensuites upstairs and a separate garden room with a queen and single bed also ensuited. You can relax in the separate guests lounge were tea and coffee is available. Our delicious continental and cooked breakfasts usually include freshly baked brioche and croissants.

Akaroa   *B&B Farmstay 5km S of Akaroa*

home
NEW ZEALAND

Onuku Heights - Historic Farmstay
Eckhard Keppler
Onuku Heights, Akaroa,

Tel (03) 304 7112   Fax (03) 304 7116
onuku.heights@paradise.net.nz   www.onuku-heights.co.nz

Double $140-$240 (Full Breakfast) Dinner $40 - $60 by prior arrangement Credit cards accepted
3 King (3 bdrm)
3 Ensuite

Onuku Heights is a charming, carefully restored 1860's homestead overlooking the Akaroa Harbour. Nestled in orchard and tranquil gardens with an abundance of bird life, it is surrounded by native bush reserves, streams and waterfalls on a 309 hectare working sheep farm.

Enjoy spacious rooms furnished with antiques, comfortable firm king size beds and exquisite ensuite bathrooms. The two guest rooms in the homestead have majestic sea views and the sunny cottage room has quaint garden views. There is a separate well-appointed guest lounge with an open fire and veranda. Explore the beautiful scenery on well maintained walking tracks, going up to 700m altitude with breathtaking panoramic views of the Akaroa Harbour, the ocean and the Alps. Our property is part of the Banks Peninsula Track. Join us in the farm activities, recline in a sun-lounger, or just dream the day away under an apple tree. Indulge yourself at the heated pool; soak up the sun, listening to the trickling fountain and basking in the stunning views.

In the morning we prepare you a delicious breakfast with freshly baked bread, homemade jam, cereals, fruits from the orchard; bacon and eggs if you like. In the evening you may choose one of Akaroa's fine restaurants, a mere 15 minute drive away or we can spoil you with a three course candle lit dinner by prior arrangement. Then relax on the veranda with a glass of wine, enjoy the sunset and beautiful birdsong.

CANTERBURY

Akaroa *B&B Homestay 80km SE of Christchurch*

Maison de la Mer
Laurice & Alan Bradford
1 Rue Benoit, Akaroa, Banks Peninsula
Tel (03) 304 8907   Fax (03) 304 8907
Mob 025 376 982   maisondelamer@xtra.co.nz
www.maisondelamer.co.nz
Double $140-$185 Single $110 (Full Breakfast)
Credit cards accepted
3 Queen 1 Single (3 bdrm)
3 Ensuite

Maisondelamer is a 1910 two-storey villa sited directly
opposite the beach. Guests can easily walk to the shops, restaurants, and cafes. Two rooms have harbour views, and one has a double spa bath, and one has a private sitting room. All rooms are elegantly furnished and have television and tea/coffee facilities. Enjoy a complimentary glass of wine with us in our lounge or on the verandah in summer. It is our aim to provide a warm welcome, and we can assure you of an enjoyable stay.

Akaroa *Boutique B&B 80KM SE of Christchurch*

Wilderness House
Jim & Liz Coubrough
42 Rue Grehan, Akaroa
Tel (03) 304 7517   Fax (03) 304 7518
Mob 021 669 381   info@wildernesshouse.co.nz
www.wildernesshouse.co.nz
Double $195-$220 Single $160-$180 (Full Breakfast)
Dinner by arrangement Credit cards accepted
1 King/Twin 3 Queen (4 bdrm)
3 Ensuite 1 Private

Wilderness House is a beautiful historic home set in a
large traditional garden containing protected trees, old roses and a private vineyard. Charming bedrooms, with their own character, feature fine linen, fresh flowers, tea/coffee and home baking. Elegant lounge opens to verandah and garden. Delicious continental and cooked breakfasts. We take particular care to make you feel comfortable, relaxed and welcome in our home. Join us for a glass of wine in the evening. Short stroll to harbour, restaurants and shops. Resident cats, Beethoven and Harry.

French Farm - Akaroa Harbour *B&B 70km SE of Christchurch*

Bantry Lodge
Dolina & David Barker
French Farm, RD2, Akaroa
Tel (03) 304 5161   Fax (03) 304 5162
Mob 025 284 8260 barker.d@xtra.co.nz
www.bantrylodge.co.nz
Double $110-$120 Single $80-$90 (Full Breakfast)
Dinner $40, by arrangement
1 Queen 1 Double (2 bdrm)

Bantry Lodge occupies a prominent site in French Farm
with views of the Akaroa hills and harbour. The 1995 guest wing, added to our 1880's home, has a spacious sitting room, two bedrooms, bathroom and servery. A full breakfast is served in the kitchen, dining room, or on the verandah overlooking the harbour. We have one shy cat. Our home is non-smoking. Surrounded by developing gardens amongst established trees, our home is an ideal place for guests to relax.

Akaroa   *B&B Self-contained   3km   N of Akaroa*

Akaroa Country Lodge
David & Sue Thurston
18 Bells Road, Takamatua, Akaroa
Tel (03) 304 7499   0800 492 568   Fax (03) 304 7499
Mob 025 370 664   takamatua@xtra.co.nz
www.bnb.co.nz/ .html

Double $160 Single $150 (Continental Breakfast)
Children welcome
3 Queen (3 bdrm)
3 Ensuite

This is New Zealand and its best! A picturesque and easy 1.5 hour drive from Christchurch brings you to this spacious colonial home set amongst century-old walnut trees, bounded by creeks and bush teeming with wildlife. Enjoy the tranquil garden with its roses, croquet lawn and swimming pool or the seaside resort of Akaroa is three minutes away. Guest rooms are situated in a separate wing with rooms opening on to the verandah and are centrally heated by radiators from a wood-burning range, complemented by two open fires.

Akaroa   *B&B 80km SE of Christchurch*

La Belle Villa
Maureen and Barry
113 Rue Jolie, Akaroa
Tel (03) 304 7084   Fax (03) 304 7084
Mob 021 339 304   mbdewar@xtra.co.nz
www.bnb.co.nz/labellevillaakaroa.html

Double $100-$120 Single $75-$85 Winter rates apply
1 King 2 Queen 1 Twin (4 bdrm)
1 Ensuite 2 Private

A warm welcome awaits you. Relax in the comfort of a bygone era, and appreciate the antiques in our picturesque historic villa with separate guest lounge. Built in the 1870's as one of the first doctor's surgeries in Akaroa and is now established on approx. 1/2 acre of beautiful, mature grounds. Enjoy the indoor/outdoor living, private swimming pool and gently trickling stream. We offer to make your stay with us special. Being centrally situated, restaurants, cafes, wine bars and beach are all walking distance.

Castle Hill - Highcountry Canterbury   *B&B Homestay 33km W of Springfield*

The Burn Alpine B&B
Bob Edge & Phil Stephenson
11 Torlesse Place, Castle Hill Village, Canterbury
Tel (03) 318 7559   Fax (03) 318 7558
theburn@xtra.co.nz
www.theburn.co.nz

Double $100 Single $60 (Continental Breakfast)
Child 1/2 price Dinner $25 dinner b&b $85 p/p
Credit cards accepted Children welcome
3 Double 2 Single (4 bdrm)
2 Guests share

One hour west of Christchurch a carefree atmosphere prevails at "The Burn". Nestled in the heart of the Southern Alps, it's arguably New Zealand's highest B&B. We designed and built our alpine lodge to maximise mountain vistas. Centered in the mystic Castlehill basin, surrounded by native forest, this is a fantastic place to return after a days activity or just kick back and relax on the sunny deck. A host of outdoor sports include ski/snowboarding, hiking, mountain biking, and flyfishing. Professional flyfishing guiding available in house.

Darfield *B&B Homestay boutique accommodation 4km W of Darfield*

The Oaks Historic Homestead
Madeleine de Jong
State Highway 73, Cnr Clintons Rd, Darfield

Tel (03) 3187 232 Fax (03) 3187 236
Mob 021 046 0840 theoaks@quicksilver.net.nz
www.bnb.co.nz/oakshistoric.html

Double $150-$275 Single $125 (Continental Breakfast)
Dinner $38 pp on request Children welcome
3 Queen 1 Single (4 bdrm)
1 Ensuite 2 Private

One of Canterbury's oldest and most beautiful homesteads, lovingly restored to its former glory. Located amidst the stunning scenery of the Southern Alps on State highway 73 to the westcoast,with all major Canterbury ski fields , golf courses and tourist attractions on its doorstep The Oaks features; 4 guest rooms with ensuite/private bathrooms; a guest dining and living room featuring stunning open fires; a traditional large homestead kitchen; beautiful verandas for outdoor seating/entertaining; large grounds/ ample of parking. Children welcome, cot, highchair,stroller availbale at no cost. Pets on request.

Darfield *B&B Homestay 40km W of Christchurch*

Oakden Manor
Pam & Alister Duncan
33 Oakden Drive, Darfield, Canterbury

Tel (03) 317 9226 Fax (03) 317 9246
Mob 025 931 642 pamandal@actrix.co.nz
www.bnb.co.nz/oakden.html

Double $90-$110 Single $60 (Full Breakfast)
Child $45 Dinner B/A Children welcome
1 King 1 Double 2 Single (3 bdrm)
1 Private 1 Host share

Genuine Kiwi hospitality waits you in our modern home where you can enjoy our tranquil garden, lawn games and our friendly Cairn Terrier. Take in local activities such as jet boating, skiing, fishing, golf or take a trip on the Tranz Alpine to the West Coast from Darfield. Complete our day with a prearranged meal either with us or at one of the superb local restaurants. Guests have comfortable lounge with tea/ coffee and TV facilities.

Mt Hutt - Methven *Farmstay 4km NW of Methven - Mt Hutt Village*

Green Gables Deer Farm
Colleen & Roger Mehrtens
185 Waimarama Rd, Mt Hutt Village, Methven

Tel (03) 302 8308 0800 466 093 Fax (03) 302 8309
greengables@xtra.co.nz
www.nzfarmstay.com

Double $140-$155 Single $100-$110
(Special Breakfast) Child $55 Dinner $45pp
All beds - Superkings Credit cards accepted
2 King 2 Twin (3 bdrm)
2 Ensuite 1 Private

Relax at Green Gables, tranquil surroundings, private entrances, superking beds, electric blankets, ensuites, toiletries, sumptuous breakfasts, tea & coffee facilities. Complimentry pre dinner drinks when dining in. Restaurants nearby. Enjoy a cup of tea on arrival, meet pet deer & Labrador. 1hr Christchurch Airport. Five hours Queenstown. Attractions: 18 hole Golf courses Methven & Terrace Downs. Hot Air Ballooning, Bush & Mountain walks, Fishing, Jet Boating, Horse Riding, Skiing Mt Hutt. Green Gables on S/H77 4kms NW Methven. Inland 72 Scenic-Route turn S/H77 5kms on right.

Mt Hutt - Methven   *Farmstay 8km N of Methven*

Tyrone Deer Farm
Pam & Roger Callaghan
Mt Hutt Station Road, RD 12, Rakaia,
Methven/Rakaia Gorge Alternative Route

Tel (03) 302 8096   Fax (03) 302 8099
tyronedeerfarm@xtra.co.nz
www.bnb.co.nz/tyronedeerfarm.html

Double $120-$130 Single $85
(Full Breakfast) Dinner $35pp B/A   S/C $130 double
1 Queen 1 Double 1 Twin (3 bdrm)
2 Ensuite 1 Private

Welcome to **Tyrone Deer Farm**, centrally situated in the Mount Hutt, Rakaia Gorge, Methven area in the middle of the South Island, 5km from the Inland Tourist Route (Highway 72) and one hour from Christchurch International Airport, making **Tyrone** an ideal stopover heading south to Queenstown.

Our home is positioned with mountain views (Mt Hutt) and deer grazing a few metres away, and has ensuite bedrooms with electric blankets, wool underlays and duvets on the beds, also heater and hair dryers. The lounge has open fire, TV, tea & coffee making facilities and guest fridge.

Come meet Guz, our pet deer, her daughter $$s, 10.30 our cat. Laze in the garden, swim in the pool, relax. Evening meal served with New Zealand wine by arrangement.

We are able to arrange professional guides for fishing (salmon and trout) and for hunting; especially Tahr, Red Deer, and Chamois. Skiing at Mt Hutt, hot-air ballooning, jet-boating, golf on nearby 18 hole courses. Numerous walks - scenic, bush, garden alpine.
Directions: please refer to map.

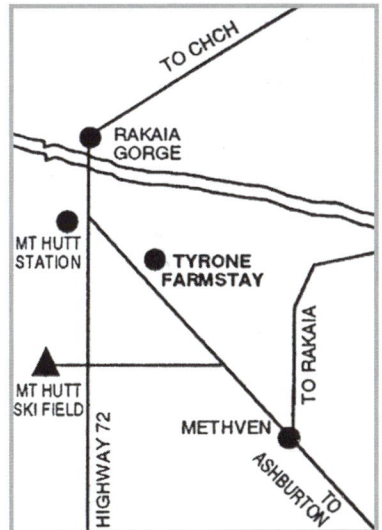

In the Mt. Hutt village of Methven we have two full equipped self contained units. Self catering $130 per night for two; extra person $40 per night or $20 extra child.

423

Mt Hutt - Methven *B&B Farmstay Separate/Suite 11km W of Methven*

Glenview Farmstay
Helen & Mike Johnstone
142 Hart Road, Methven,

Tel (03) 302 8620   Fax (03) 302 8620
helenmikejohnstone@yahoo.com
www.bnb.co.nz/glenviewfarmstay.html

Double $100 Single $60
(Full Breakfast) Dinner $25
Child $25   Children welcome
2 Queen 1 Double 2 Twin 1 Single (5 bdrm)

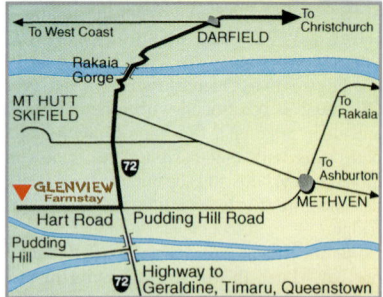

Glenview farmstay is situated at the base of Mt Hutt Ski Field with superb views of both the mountains and the Canterbury plains.

Our 1,200 acre farm consists of mainly cattle with a few sheep. There is a unit in the garden with ensuite queen and single beds, TV, and tea/coffee-making facilities.

All rooms have separate access, good heating, and are non-smoking. Meals and farm tours on request.

Methven provides skiing, golf, ballooning, tramping, fishing and jet boating.

Glenview is on the inland scenic highway 72, we are just 10 mins out of Methven and one hour from Christchurch airport.

Mt Hutt - Methven   *Farmstay 6km E of Methven*

Pagey's Farmstay
Shirley & Gene Pagey
Chertsey Road, Methven Mt-Hutt Village, Methven

Tel (03) 302 1713   Fax (03) 302 1714
pageysfarmstay@wave.co.nz
www.bnb.co.nz/pageysfarmstay.html

Double $90 Single $60 (Full Breakfast)
Child 1/2 price under 12yrs Dinner $25pp
1 King 1 Queen 4 Single (3 bdrm)
1 Guests share

Come as guests and leave as friends who have enjoyed our hospitality and beautiful 4500 sq ft home set amidst aged trees, 1.5 acres of rose garden and lawn. Enjoy pre dinner drinks, home grown cuisine and wine.   Experience farm activities, clean air, peace, tranquility and mountain views. Surrounding activities include bush walks, 2 golf courses, ballooning, skiing and horse riding. Transport can be arranged. YOU MAY NEVER WANT TO LEAVE. Directions: From Methven town centre, turn down Methven Chertsey Road, 6 km on left.

Staveley - Mt. Somers   *B&B Homestay 20km SW of Methven*

Korobahn Lodge
Caroline & John Lartice
Burgess Rd, Staveley,

Tel (03) 303 0828   Mob 021 183 4418
carolinel@xtra.co.nz
www.korobahnlodge.co.nz

Double $100-$130 Single $80-$90 (Full Breakfast)
Dinner $35
2 Queen (2 bdrm)
1 Ensuite 1 Private

Welcome to our unique North American barn style homestead. Korobahn is tucked into the foot of Mt Somers and stands in several acres of gardens, surrounded by farmland. The property is on Inland Scenic Highway 72, approximatly 110 kilometres SW of Christchurch Airport and on the way to Mt. Cook and Queenstown. Methven, 22 kilometres away, has a variety of cafes and restaurants. Local activites inculde bush walking, horse treks, jet boating, fishing, eco tours and skiing. (Close to Mt Hutt ski field.)

Rakaia   *B&B Homestay Guesthouse 50km S of Christchurch*

St Ita's Guesthouse
Miriam & Ken Cutforth
11 Barrhill/Methven Road, Rakaia Village, Canterbury

Tel (03) 302 7546   Fax (03) 302 7546
Mob 0274 371 459   stitas@xtra.co.nz
www.stitas.co.nz

Double $110-$120 Single $70 (Full Breakfast)
Child $30 Dinner $30 pp Credit cards accepted
1 Queen 1 Double 4 Single (3 bdrm)
3 Ensuite

Relax in our elegant and comfortable historic former convent, 600 metres from SH1 in small town New Zealand. Excellent base for exploring Ashburton District. Excellent first and last stop from Christchurch International Airport. All bedrooms have ensuites and garden views. Walking distance to local shops, hotels, crafts and winery. Close to golf and salmon fishing, 30 minutes to skiing, jet boating and more. Dinner based on local produce served with wine. Full breakfasts. Share the open fire with our cat and golden retriever.

Ashburton   *B&B Farmstay 8km W of Ashburton*

Carradale Farm
Karen & Jim McIntyre
Ferriman's Rd (Rapid no. 200), RD 8, Ashburton

Tel (03) 308 6577   Fax (03) 308 6548
Mob 025 338 044
carradale@ashburton.co.nz.
www.ashburton.co.nz/carradale

Double $90-$100 Single $60
(Continental Breakfast) (Full Breakfast)
Child 1/2 price under 12yrs Dinner $30 B/A
Caravan powerpoint $25   Credit cards accepted
1 Double 2 Twin (3 bdrm)
1 Ensuite 2 Private

Our homestead which captures the sun in all rooms is cosy and inviting. It is situated in a sheltered garden where you can enjoy peace, tranquillity and fresh country air or indulge in a game of tennis. All guest rooms have comfortable beds, electric blankets, reading lamps and tea/coffee making facilities. Laundry and ironing facilities available. Dinner is by arrangement and features traditional New Zealand cuisine including home grown meat and vegetables. Breakfast is served with delicious home made jams and preserves.

We have a 220 acre irrigated sheep and cattle farm. You may like to join in farm activities or be taken for a farm tour.

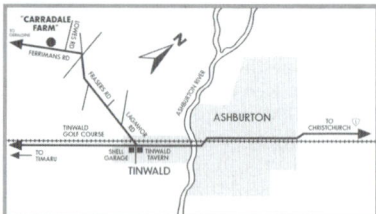

As we have both travelled extensively in New Zealand, Australia, United Kingdom, Europe, North America and Zimbabwe. We would like to offer hospitality to fellow travellers. Our hobbies include meeting people, travel, reading, photography, gardening, sewing, cake decorating, rugby, cricket, Jim belongs to the Masonic Lodge and Karen is involved in Community Affairs.

For the weary traveller a spa pool is available. For young children we have a cot and high chair. There is a power point for camper vans.

> *Carradale Farm "Where people come*
> *as strangers and leave as friends"*

Ashburton *Homestay*

Pat & Dave Weir
1 Sudbury Street, Ashburton Central
Tel (03) 308 3534 d&pweir@xtra.co.nz
www.bnb.co.nz/weir.html

Double $70 Single $40 (Full Breakfast) Dinner $20
Credit cards accepted
1 Double 2 Single (2 bdrm)
1 Host share

Our comfortable home is situated in a quiet street with
the added pleasure of looking onto a rural scene. We are
10-15 mins walk from town or 3-5 mins to riding for the disabled grounds or river walkway. Guest
rooms have comfortable beds with electric blankets. We welcome the opportunity to meet and greet
visitors and wish to make your stay a happy one. Your hosts are semi-retired, hobbies general/varied
from meeting people to walking etc. Request visitors no smoking inside home. Laundry facilities
available.

Ashburton *B&B Homestay 1km S of Ashburton Centre*

A Welcome Inn
Betty & Bruce Arnst
13 Thomson Street, Tinwald, Ashburton
Tel (03) 308 7297 Fax (03) 308 7297
bb_arnst@xtra.co.nz
www.bnb.co.nz/awelcomeinn.html

Double $100-$120 Single $60-$70 (Full Breakfast)
Child Negotiable by age Dinner $30 pp.
1 Double 1 Twin (2 bdrm)

We are a retired couple who have travelled overseas and
in New Zealand and love sharing experiences with travellers. We provide a warm friendly stay in our
comfortable modern home with an opportunity for travellers to meet New Zealanders in a family setting.
We have two elderly pets, both living outdoors. We have a small private lounge for guests, but join us
in our large lounge, or in our pleasant garden. Located five minutes from Lake Hood. One hour south
from International Airport. Near sports facilities.

Ashburton *B&B Ashburton*

Falcutt House
Nola & Stuart Lovett
23 Falcon Drive, Ashburton,
Tel (03) 308 9253 Mob 025 474 438
www.bnb.co.nz/falcutthouse.html

Double $90 Single $50 (Full Breakfast)
Child $30 under 12 Dinner $25 By arrangement
2 Twin (2 bdrm)
1 Private

A new house situated in a quiet cul-de-sac surrounded by
pleasant garden, with private areas. Two comfortable twin
bedrooms. Guests' private bathroom with separate toilet. Visit farm upon request. Close to town and
restaurants. Off street parking available.

South Canterbury, North Otago

Fox Glacier

e Bay

Mount Cook

80

Lake Tekapo

Burkes Pass

Kimbell

Fairlie

Geraldine

Ealing

ley

1

79

8

8

Lake Pukaki

Twizel

Temuka

Seadown

Timaru

8

Omarama

Kingsdown

Makihikihi

Kurow

Waimate

82

1

Danseys Pass

85

Oamaru

Waianakarua

Moeraki

Palmerston

Towns listed generally follow
a north to south route. Refer
to the index if required.

0   Kilometres   30

0   Miles   18

Geraldine   *Guest Lodge   3km N of Geraldine*

The Crossing
Richard & Barbara Sahlie
124 Woodbury Road, RD 21, Geraldine

Tel (03) 693 9689   Fax (03) 693 9789
srelax@xtra.co.nz
www.bnb.co.nz/thecrossing.html

Double $160-$190 Single $140-$170
(Continental Breakfast) (Full Breakfast) Dinner B/A
Extra Person $30   Credit cards accepted
3 Queen 1 Single (3 bdrm)
3 Ensuite

Experience New Zealand history on thirty seven tranquil acres near the base of the Four Peaks Range.

The Crossing is a beautifully restored and furnished English style manor house built in 1908. Our spacious lounges have open fires and comfortable seating. A shaded verandah overlooks the lovely gardens, where you can relax and read or enjoy a leisurely game of croquet or petanque.

Enjoy dinner and your choice of beverages in our fully licensed restaurant. Dinners by prior arrangement.

The Crossing is your perfect base for exploring the central South Island. Local attractions include fishing for salmon and trout, white water rafting, nature treks in Peel Forest, and ski fields are nearby. Golfers, spend a week and play fourteen uncrowded courses each within one hours drive. All have low green fees and welcome visitors. We are located on the main route between Christchurch and Queenstown or Mount Cook.

Directions: Signposted on SH 72/79 approx 3 km north of Geraldine, turn into Woodbury Road, then 1 km on right hand side. Children over 12 welcome. We are members of the Heritage and Character Inns of NZ.

Geraldine *B&B 1Km S of Geraldine*

Victoria Villa
Leigh & Jerry Basinger
55 Cox Street, Geraldine,
Tel (03) 693 8605 Fax (03) 693 8609
Mob 025 821 842 jbasinger@xtra.co.nz
www.bnb.co.nz/aoteavilla.html

Double $100-$125 Single $80 (Full Breakfast)
Child $15 Dinner by arrangement Credit cards accepted
2 Queen 1 Double 2 Single (4 bdrm)
2 Ensuite 1 Guests share

Welcome to our historical villa, completely refurbished -
spacious double bedrooms with ensuites and guest bathroom. Off street parking. On Highway 79 to Mt.
Cook and Queenstown. 7 minutes walk to Geraldine Village. Adjacent to domain and swimming pool,
bowling green, tennis, netball courts, childrens play area, and picnic area. Gourmet meals by arrangement.
Personality pet dog and cat. Well travelled hosts who will assist you with your interests in this area, to
maximise an enjoyable stay.

Geraldine *B&B 0.2km S of Geraldine*

Lilymay
Lois & Les Gillum
29 Cox Street, Geraldine
Tel (03) 693 8838 0800 545 9629
0800 Lilymay elgillum@chc.quik.co.nz
www.bnb.co.nz/lilymay.html

Double $80-$95 Single $55-$60 (Full Breakfast)
Child $15 - 20 Dinner n/a Children welcome
2 Queen 1 Double 3 Twin 3 Single (3 bdrm)

A charming character home set in a large garden where Sammy the cat plays. A friendly, warm welcome
is assured with tea/coffee and Lois' homebaked cookies. Ample offstreet parking and separate guest
entrance. Teas, coffee, etc available at all times in the guestlounge with cosy open fire. The Village,
shops, cafes, restaurants, crafts a short stroll away. We are on the main highway to the Southern Lakes
and mountains and the ideal stopover from Christchurch (137km).

Geraldine *B&B Separate/Suite Sleep out 0.5km S of Geraldine*

Forest View
Joyce & John Leverno
128 Talbot Street, Geraldine
Tel (03) 693 9928 0800 572 740 Fax (03) 693 9928
Mob 021 440 349 forest.view@xtra.co.nz
www.bnb.co.nz/forestview.html

Double $80-$120 Single $55-$75 (Full Breakfast)
Child Neg Dinner $35 by arrangement Sleep out $45
Credit cards accepted Children welcome
1 King 1 Queen 1 Double 1 Twin 1 Single (4 bdrm)
1 Ensuite 1 Private 1 Guests share

We have a charming two storey, character home set in a cottage garden where our dog and Oscar and
Emmy love to play. You will be warmly welcomed on arrival and a refreshing cup of tea or coffee is
available in the guest lounge at all times. We are a short stroll to the cafes and restaurants in the
charming village of Geraldine which is the ideal first stop from Christchurch (137km) as you travel
towards the Southern Lakes and mountains.

Temuka   *B&B Homestay Separate/Suite 20km N of Timaru*

Ashfield B&B
Ann & Martin Bosman
71 Cass Street, Temuka

Tel (03) 615 6157   Fax (03) 615 9062
ashfield@paradise.net.nz
www.bnb.co.nz/ashfieldbb.html

Double $90-$110 Single $55-$65 (Special Breakfast)
Child neg Credit cards accepted Children welcome
1 King 2 Queen 1 Double (4 bdrm)
1 Ensuite 1 Guests share

Ashfield is set on 4 acres of woodlands, 10 minutes walk from shops and restaurants. Built in in 1883 Ashfield features marble fireplaces and gilt mirrors, and a full size snooker table. Two of our upstairs bedrooms open up to a balcony with lovely views of the mountains. We enjoy spending the evening with guests by the open fire. In close proximity are skifields. salmon and trout fishing. So join us for a wonderful stay in a lovely setting. One cat and one outside dog. Guests welcome to use laundry.

Timaru Central   *Homestay*

Margaret & Nevis Jones
16 Selwyn Street, Timaru

Tel (03) 688 1400   Fax (03) 688 1400
www.bnb.co.nz/jonestimaru.html

Double $90 Single $55 (Full Breakfast)
Child 1/2 price Dinner $25 Credit cards accepted
2 Double 1 Twin (3 bdrm)
2 Ensuite 1 Guests share

Welcome to our spacious character brick home built in the 1920's and situated in a beautiful garden with a grass tennis court. A secluded property with off street parking and views of the surrounding sea and mountains. Centrally situated, only 5 minutes from the beach and town with an excellent choice of cafes and restaurants. On arrival tea is served on our sunny verandah. Hosts have lived and worked extensively overseas, namely South Africa, U.K and the Middle East, and enjoy music, theatre, tennis and golf. Dinner by arrangement.

Timaru - Seadown   *Homestay Separate/Suite Country Homestay 4.8km N of Timaru*

Country Homestay
Margaret and Ross Paterson
491 Seadown Road, Seadown, RD 3, Timaru

Tel (03) 688 2468   Fax (03) 688 2468
www.bnb.co.nz/countryhomestay.html

Double $80 Single $50 (Full Breakfast)
Child 1/2 price Dinner $20 Credit cards accepted
1 Double 2 Single (3 bdrm)
1 Guests share

Our Homestay is approximately 10 minutes north of Timaru, situated 4.8 kms on Seadown Road off State Highway 1 at Washdyke - second house on left past Pharlap Statue. We have hosted on our farm for 11 years - now retired and have a country farmlet with some farm animals, with views of farmland and mountains. Day trips to Mt Cook, Hydro Lakes and ski fields, fishing, golf course few minutes away. Electric blankets on all beds - laundry facilities available. Interests are farming, gardening, spinning and overseas travel.

Timaru   *Homestay Timaru Central*

Bidwill House
Dorothy & Ron White
15 Bidwill Street, Timaru
Tel (03) 688 5856   Fax (03) 688 5870
Mob 025 238 8122   bidwillhouse@xtra.co.nz
www.bnb.co.nz/bidwillhouse.html
Double $100 Single $80 (Full Breakfast)
Child 1/2 price Dinner $15 - $25by arrangement
Credit cards accepted
1 King/Twin 2 Single (2 bdrm)
1 Ensuite

Bidwill House offers superior personalised homestay in a classic two storeyed home with a delightful garden in a quiet street in central Timaru - five minutes walk to the town centre, restaurants and Caroline Bay. The guest bedroom has a super-king/twin with a smaller bedroom with two single beds. The two rooms are only available to the one booking. Laundry facilities and a courtesy car are available. We look forward to welcoming guests to our home, and offer our hospitality to those who prefer a homestay.

Timaru   *B&B Homestay*

Okare Boutique Accommodation
Malcolm Smith
11 Wai-iti Road, Timaru
Tel (03) 688 0316   Fax (03) 688 0368
Mob 027 229 7301   okare@xtra.co.nz okare.co.nz
Double $95-$125 Single $85 (Full Breakfast)
Child $40 Credit cards accepted Children welcome
1 King/Twin 1 Queen 1 Double 1 Twin 4 Single (5 bdrm)
1 Ensuite 1 Private 1 Guests share 1 Host share

Okare is a substantial Edwardian brick residence built in 1909 and offers discerning travellers and small families visiting the region comfortable accommodation with warm welcoming hospitality. Okare offers substantial sunny living spaces for our guests, upstairs there is a super King/twin and one twin room with share bathroom and a Double with twin spa-bath ensuite, downstairs a queen room with private facilities. We are situated only five minutes walk from a selection of restaurants, Boudicca's our own, offers a charge back facility. We have a baby and two huskies for your entertainment.

Timaru   *B&B Homestay 5km N of Pleasant Point*

Ballyagan
Gail & Bill Clarke
State Highway 8 Levels, RD 4, Timaru
Tel (03) 614 8221   Fax (03) 614 8221
Mob 025 653 7663
www.bnb.co.nz/ballyagan.html
Double $90-$120 Single $55 (Full Breakfast)
Child 1/2 price Dinner $25 by arrangement
Credit cards accepted Children welcome
1 Queen 1 Double 4 Single (4 bdrm)
1 Ensuite 1 Private 1 Guests share

Welcome to Ballyagan. Our home is among trees and gardens with native birds, small farm walk, pet sheep, cat. Bedrooms have electric blankets and bedside lamps. Restaurants five minutes to Pleasant Point vintage trains and golf course. We serve Devonshire afternoon tea, herbal-tea and fresh percolated coffee. Samlpe our local wine. Mount Cook ski fields and fishing within reasonable distance. Tea making, laundry facilities available. We enjoy meeting and hosting guests. Directions: SH8 7km from Washdyke. 5km from Pleasant Point. B&B Homestay sign at gate.

Timaru *B&B Farmstay Homestay 3.5km NW of Central/City Timaru*

Ranui
Margaret & Kevin Cosgrove
5 Kellands Hill, Timaru

Tel (03) 686 1288   Fax (03) 686 1285
Mob 025 321 458 / 025 2919311 ranui@timaru.com
www.bnb.co.nz/ranui.html

Double $95-$120 Single $75 (Full Breakfast)
Child $^1/_2$ price Dinner $30 Separate/Suite $150.00
Credit cards accepted Children welcome
3 Queen 2 Single (4 bdrm)
1 Ensuite 1 Private 2 Guests share

Our spacious home on 9 acres enjoys the best of both worlds - country living only $3^1/_2$ kms from the centre of Timaru. Set in $1^1/_2$ acres of established gardens with a magnificent view of Mt Cook we offer a relaxed atmosphere, heated swimming pool (summer), private spa pool, Sky TV in bedroom, dinner by arrangement. We run coloured sheep, the wool of which Margaret spins and knits. We enjoy golfing, boating and meeting people. Our family are all away. Children welcome. Phone for directions.

Timaru *Farmstay 26km SW of Timaru*

Craigmore Farmhouse
Raewyn & Kerry Swann
Craigmore Hill Road, Maungati District, 2RD, Timaru

Tel (03) 612 9822   Fax (03) 612 9822
Mob 025 337 718 farmstaytimaru@xtra.co.nz
www.craigmore.com

Double $110-$120 Single $70 (Continental Breakfast)
Dinner $30 2 Campervan sites
1 King 1 Queen 1 Single (3 bdrm)
2 Private 1 Guests share

Craigmore Farmhouse is designed to catch the sunshine and amazing views of the countryside. Sheep, deer and cattle are farmed on this limestone hill property. Farm tours optional. A popular nine hole golf course adjoins Craigmore. You can enjoy tramping to view ancient Rock Art or just relax in true country style. Craigmore Farmstay accommodation is within the Manager's Residence. Please phone, fax or email to make a reservation. Raewyn and Kerry look forward to meeting you. Directions and map on website.

Timaru *B&B Homestay 8km town centre*

Rosebrook Lodge
Alastair & Janice Rowley
336 Gleniti Road, Hadlow, 4RD, Timaru

Tel (03) 686 2771   Fax (03) 686 2771
Mob 025 264 9777 ajrowley@xtra.co.nz
www.bnb.co.nz/rosebrooklodge.html

Double $110 Single $70 (Full Breakfast)
Child $30 Dinner $30
2 Double 1 Twin 1 Single (4 bdrm)
1 Private

A warm welcome awaits you at Rosebrook Lodge. Our very comfortable home is nestled amongst 3 acres of mature trees, Rhododendrons, Azaleas and Roses - a mini park. Relax on one of the two patios and view the mountains with complimentary tea and coffee and homemade baking. Enjoy a walk in the surrounding countryside or mountain bikes available for further exploring. Mt. Nimrod, a 3 hr walk - a 'mini Milford', just half an hour away. Golf course close by. Evening meals by arrangement.

Timaru   *B&B Farmstay Homestay 3km S of Timaru*

Mountain View B&B
Marlene & Norman McIntosh
23 Talbot Rd, RD1 Kingsdown, Timaru
Tel 03 688 1070   Fax 03 688 1069   Mob 021 113 8517
mvhomestay@xtra.co.nz
www.bnb.co.nz/mtview.html

Double $80 Single $55 (Full Breakfast) Child $20
Dinner $25.00 BA Children welcome Pets welcome
1 Queen 1 Double 1 Twin (3 bdrm)
2 Private

'Mountain View'is a farmlet on Talbot Rd, 200 metres from State Highway 1. Blue and white Bed & Breakfast signs on highway 3km from Timaru. Semi-retired farmers - pet deer and sheep. Home is situated in tranquil garden over-looking farmland with views of mountains. Private bathrooms - laundry facilities available. Tea, Coffee. Nearby fishing, golf courses, swimming and walk to sea coast. Day trips comfortably taken to Mt Cook, Hydro lakes and Ski Fields.   We enjoy meeting people and look forward to offering our hospitality.

Makikihi - Waimate   *Farmstay 37km S of Timaru*

Alford Farm
June & Ken McAuley
Lower Hook Road, RD 8, Waimate
Tel (03) 689 5778   Fax (03) 689 5779
Mob 025 267 6008   alfordfarmstays@paradise.net.nz
www.bnb.co.nz/alfordfarm.html

Double $80 Single $50 (Continental Breakfast)
Dinner $25 Credit cards accepted
1 Double 2 Single (2 bdrm)
1 Host share

Halfway between Dunedin and Christchurch: stop over to enjoy the peaceful surroundings on out deer and cattle farm. Guests are offered a farm tour or can participate in farm activities if time permits. Hosting since 1985 we enjoy sharing our home, farm, attractive garden and native birds with visitors. Attractions: trout and salmon fishing, penguin colony, two golf courses, bush walks and day trips to Mount Cook. Directions: four kilometres south of Makikihi, turn inland into Lower Hook Road. Second on the right (two kilometres). Rapid No. 202.

Fairlie   *Farmstay Homestay 3km W of Fairlie*

Fontmell
Anne & Norman McConnell
Nixons Road 169, RD 17, Fairlie
Tel (03) 685 8379   Fax (03) 685 8379
www.bnb.co.nz/fontmell.html

Double $90-$110 Single $55 (Full Breakfast)
Child $25 Dinner $25
1 Queen 1 Double 2 Twin 1 Single (4 bdrm)
1 Private 1 Guests share

Our farm consists of 400 acres producing fat lambs, cattle and deer, with numerous other animals and bird life. The house is situated in a large English style garden with many mature trees in a tranquil setting. In the area are two skifields, golf courses, walkways and scenic drives. Informative farm tours available. Our interests include golf, gardening and music. Directions: Travel 1 km from town centre, along Tekapo highway, then turn left into Nixon's Road when two more kilometers will bring you to the "Fontmell" entrance.

Fairlie *B&B 1.5km NW of Fairlie*

Ashgrove
Maria & Stewart Evans
Mt Cook Rd, Fairlie, Mt Cook Rd, Fairlie,

Tel 03 6858797   Fax 03 6858795   Mob 025 2895323
maria@ashgrove.co.nz
www.bnb.co.nz/ashgrove.html

Double $120-$150 Single $80 (Continental Breakfast)
Child Neg Children welcome
1 King/Twin (1 bdrm)
1 Private

Enjoy a restful stopover on your South Island journey at
our 3-acre farmlet.. The house is set amongst established
trees and gardens. Guest facilities include a private sunny sitting room. Microwave, Fridge, TV, Tea &
Coffee are available. We also offer refreshments for sale. Only 10 minutes walk to award winning
restaurants. We are happy to share our knowledge of the South Island, especially to trampers and those
keen to fish the clear lakes & rivers of the region.

Kimbell *Country Homestay 8km W of Fairlie*

Rivendell Lodge
Joan Gill
15 Stanton Road, Kimbell, RD 17, Fairlie

Tel (03) 685 8833   Fax (03) 685 8825
Mob 027 481 9189   Rivendell.lodge@xtra.co.nz
www.fairlie.co.nz/rivendell

Double $105 Single $65 (Full Breakfast) Child neg
Dinner $35 Credit cards accepted Children welcome
2 Queen 3 Single (3 bdrm)
2 Private 1 Host share

Welcome to my one acre paradise; a haven of peace and tranquility offering quality country comfort and
hospitality. I am a well travelled writer with a passion for mountains, literature and good conversation.
I enjoy cooking and gardening and use home grown produce wherever possible. Take time out for
fishing, skiing, walking, golf or water sports. Relax in the garden, complete with stream and cat, or
come with us to some of our favourite places. Complimentary refreshments on arrival. Laundry facilities
and internet access available

Burkes Pass *B&B Country Homestay 23km E of Lake Tekapo*

Dobson Lodge
Margaret & Keith Walter
Dobson Lodge, RD 17,
Burkes Pass, Mackenzie Country

Tel (03) 685 8316   Fax (03) 685 8316
dobson_lodge@xtra.co.nz
www.mtcook.org.nz/dobsonlodge/

Double $110130152 Single $70-$100
(Continental Breakfast) Child neg Dinner $25pp
S/C railway carriage $40 - $60 Credit cards accepted
2 Queen 1 Double 1 Single (3 bdrm)
2 Ensuite 1 Host share

Come and share our unique glacier stone cottage with exceptional character set in 17 acres. We are
nestled in a picturesque valley, with views on Mount Dobson and are close to Lake Tekapo. We are on
the main tourist route, approximately halfway between Christchurch and Queenstown or Dunedin. There
are small restaurants close by. Our interests include photography, crafts and animals. We have one cat,
a friendly Collie and pet sheep. As well as the lodge, self contained railway accommodation is available.

Lake Tekapo *B&B Homestay 40km W of Fairlie*

Freda Du Faur House
Dawn & Barry Clark
1 Esther Hope Street, Lake Tekapo
Tel (03) 680 6513
www.bnb.co.nz/fredadufaurhouse.html
Double $100-$105 Single $65
(Continental Breakfast) Child neg.
Credit cards accepted
1 Queen 1 Double 2 Single (3 bdrm) 1 Guests share

Experience tranquillity and a touch of mountain magic. A warm and friendly welcome. Comfortable home, mountain and lake views. Rimu panelling, heart timber furniture, attractive decor, blending with the McKenzie Country. Bedrooms in private wing overlooking garden, two opening onto balcony. Refreshments on patio surrounded by roses or view ever changing panorama from lounge. Walkways nearby. Mt Cook one hour away. Views of skifield. Our cat "Missy" welcomes you. Five minutes to shops and restaurants. From SH8 turn into Lakeview Heights and follow green B&B sign into Barbara Hay Street. Then right and see our Freda Du Faur sign.

Lake Tekapo *B&B 43km W of Fairlie*

Creel House
Grant & Rosemary Brown
36 Murray Place, Lake Tekapo,
Tel (03) 680 6516 Fax (03) 680 6659
creelhouse.l.tek@xtra.co.nz
www.bnb.co.nz/creelhouse.html
Double $140-$150 Single $75 (Special Breakfast)
$110 double/twin Off-season tariff
Credit cards accepted Children welcome
2 Queen 1 Twin (3 bdrm)
1 Ensuite 2 Private

Built by Grant, our three storied home with expansive balconies offers panoramic views of the Southern Alps, Mt John, Lake Tekapo and surrounding mountains. All rooms are spacious and comfortable, with guest lounge and separate guest entrance. A NZ native garden adds an attractive feature. Restaurants in township. Our two daughters are 13 & 15 years, we live on the ground floor with two cats thus separate from our guest accommodation. Grant is a professional flyfishing guide (NZPFGA) and offers guided tours.

Lake Pukaki - Mt Cook *Homestay 12km N of Twizel*

Rhoborough Downs
Roberta Preston
Lake Pukaki, PB, Fairlie
Tel (03) 435 0509 0800 420 007 Fax (03) 435 0509
ra.preston@xtra.co.nz
www.bnb.co.nz/rhoboroughdowns.html
Double $100 Single $50 (Continental Breakfast)
Child $30 Dinner $30
1 Double 3 Single (3 bdrm)
1 Guests share

A quiet place to stop, halfway between Christchurch and Queenstown or Christchurch and Dunedin via Waitaki Valley. 40 minutes to Mt Cook. The 18,000 acre property has been in the family 80 years. Merino sheep graze to 6,000 feet, Hereford cattle. Views of the Southern sky the homestead is set in tranquil gardens afternoon tea/drinks served on the veranda, have a cat and dog. Twizel has a bank, doctor, restaurants, shops. Dinner by arrangement. Please phone for bookings and directions. Cot available.

Lake Pukaki *Farmstay 27km Lake Tekapo*

Tasman Downs Station
Linda, Bruce & Ian Hayman
Lake Tekapo
Tel **(03) 680 6841**   Fax (03) 680 6851
samjane@xtra.co.nz
www.bnb.co.nz/tasmandownsstation.html
Double $110-$130 Single $80 (Full Breakfast)
Dinner $35pp
1 Queen 2 Single (2 bdrm)
1 Private 1 Host share

"A place of unsurpassed beauty" located on the shores of Lake Pukaki with magnificent views of Mount Cook and the Southern Alps. Our local stone home blends in with the natural peaceful surrounds. Bruce, an ex-RAF pilot, has rich pioneering and surprisingly wide experiences. This high country farm in the family since 1914, runs mainly cattle with crops grown for self-sufficiency. This is your great opportunity to experience true farm life with friendly hosts and a good natured corgi.

Twizel - Mt Cook *B&B*

Artemis B&B
Jan & Bob Wilson
33 North West Arch, Twizel
Tel **(03) 435 0388**   Fax (03) 435 0377
artemistwizel@paradise.net.nz
www.bnb.co.nz/user188.html
Double $115 Single $80 (Special Breakfast)
2 Queen 1 Single (2 bdrm)
1 Ensuite 1 Private

Welcome to the magnificent Mackenzie basin. Our modern home has stunning mountain views along with peace and tranquility. We are only 45 minutes from Mount Cook and three minutes drive to nearby restaurants. A guest sitting room with balcony - tea, coffee and complimentary snack and television. Our special continental breakfast includes a choice of juices, fruits, cereals, cheeses and homemade croissants, toast and jams. A selection of teas and coffees. We look forward to sharing our home with you.

Twizel   *Homestay Separate/Suite Self-contained Loft 2km W of Twizel*

Heartland Lodge
Jenny & Dave Pullen
19 North West Arch, Twizel, South Canterbury
Tel **(03) 435 0008**   0800 164 666   Fax (03) 435 0387
Mob 0274 927 778   european@xtra.co.nz
www.heartland-lodge.co.nz
Double $160 Single $120 (Full Breakfast)
Child Neg Dinner $45 by arrangement
Loft From $100 Credit cards accepted
2 King/Twin (2 bdrm)
2 Ensuite

Welcome to our lovely, large Homestay Lodge, only 45 minutes from Mt Cook. Luxuriously appointed guest rooms feature ensuites with spa baths. Guests are invited to join us for a complimentary pre-dinner drink before sharing a delicious three course dinner complemented by New Zealand wine (by prior arrangement) or dining at one of several nearby restaurants. Our black Labrador, Megan and donkey, Monty, will extend a warm welcome. 'The Loft' - a large self-service apartment above our garage sleeps up to six. Directions: Please phone 0800 164 666.

437

Twizel

Aoraki Lodge
Oksana & Vlad Fomin
32 Mackenzie Drive, Twizel/Mt Cook 8773
Tel (03) 435 0300   Fax (03) 435 0305
Mob 027 414 9646   aorakilodge@xtra.co.nz
www.bnb.co.nz/aorakilodge.html

Double $145-$150 Single $90 (Full Breakfast)
Child $30 Credit cards accepted
1 Queen 2 Double 4 Single (4 bdrm)
4 Ensuite 1 Private 1 Host share

Haere Mai ki Aoraki (Welcome to Aoraki Lodge). If you prefer a casual informal atmosphere with friendly hosts then Aoraki Lodge is the place for you. Relax in our warm, sunny home and enjoy our private garden. Native birds can be seen and heard. Vlad is a well known fishing guide and can offer helpful advice and information on all the attractions in the area. We look forward to meeting you.

Twizel - Lake Ruataniwha   *Homestay 4km SW of Twizel*

Lake Ruataniwha Homestay
Robin & Lester Baikie
9 Max Smith Drive, Twizel,
Tel (03) 435 0532   Fax (03) 435 0522
Mob 025 321 532   robinandlester@xtra.co.nz
www.bnb.co.nz/lakeruatniwhahomestay.html

Double $120-$140 Single $70-$90 Child neg.
Dinner $30 pp Children welcome
2 Queen 1 Twin (3 bdrm)
1 Ensuite

Welcome to our new home, built on four hectares overlooking Lake Ruataniwha with 360-degree views of the lake and mountains. We have traveled overseas and enjoy meeting people. Kitchen/living areas are opening onto large decks to relax on and enjoy the view. We have a variety of farm animals close to our house: which our grandchildren delight in feeding when they visit. Our interests are farming, horse trekking, sport and CWI. Email and fax facilities available. An ideal stopover between Christchurch and Queenstown.

Twizel   *B&B Self-contained*

Anne & Matt Hunter
58 Tekapo Drive, Twizel
Tel (03) 435 0038   Fax (03) 435 0038
annehunter@xtra.co.nz
www.bnb.co.nz/amhunter.html

Double $140 Single $90 (Full Breakfast) Child $45
Dinner $40 Self contained cottage $90
2 King/Twin (2 bdrm)
2 Ensuite

Hunters House was built in 2003. It is architecturally designed for guests and features every comfort and a warm welcoming environment. It overlooks the native tussocks and trees of the Green Belt. Guest privacy is assured. All rooms are sited for sun and views. The unique attractions of the Mackenzie Country and Aoraki Mt Cook are well known to the Hunters, and they are always happy to share their knowledge. Cead mille fuilte.

Omarama   *Farmstay 1km S of Omarama*

Omarama Station
Beth & Dick Wardell
Omarama, North Otago

Tel (03) 438 9821   Fax (03) 438 9822
wardell@paradise.net.nz   www.omaramastation.co.nz

Double $100-$120   Single $60   (Full Breakfast)
Child $20 - $50   Dinner $35
2 Queen 2 Single (3 bdrm)   1 Ensuite 1 Private

Omarama Station is a merino sheep and cattle property
adjacent to the Omarama township. The 100 year old
homestead is nestled in a small valley in a tranquil
parklike setting of willows, poplars and a fast flowing
stream (good fly fishing), pleasant walking environs, and
interesting historical perspective to the high country as
this was the original station in the area. Swimming pool and a pleasant garden. An opportunity to
experience day to day farming activities. Dinner by arrangement.

Kurow   *Farmstay Self-contained Campervans or tents 60km W of Oamaru*

Glenmac
Kaye & Keith Dennison
RD 7K, Oamaru

Tel (03) 436 0200   Fax (03) 436 0202
Mob 027 222 1119
glenmac@farmstaynewzealand.co.nz
www.farmstaynewzealand.co.nz

Double $80-$100   Single $40-$50   (Full Breakfast)
Child under 13 yrs $1/2$ price   Dinner $25 $16pp
S/C POA   Credit cards accepted   Smoking area inside
1 Queen 2 Double 2 Twin (4 bdrm)
1 Ensuite 1 Guests share 1 Host share

The perfect place to get away from traffic noises, enjoy home cooked meals, have a comfortable bed, relax
and be treated as one of the family. Explore our 4000 acre high country farm. See merino sheep and beef
cattle. Either on farm or nearby enjoy horse riding, four wheel drive farm tour, walking/tramping, fishing
(guide available), golf or explore the NEW Fossil Trail. Also available - Self-contained Cottage.

Kurow   *B&B Self-contained Homestyle 2.7km E of Kurow*

Western House
Bernadette & Michael Parish
Highway 83, Kurow, North Oago

Tel (03) 436 0876   Fax (03) 436 0872
mbparish@xtra.co.nz
www.westernhouse.co.nz

Double $100-$120   Single $90-$120   (Full Breakfast)
Dinner $40   Credit cards accepted
2 Queen 1 Double 1 Twin (4 bdrm)
1 Ensuite 1 Private 1 Guests share

Western House, built in 1871, as an accomodation house
is surrounded by extensive garden and orchard with mountain views. Enjoy wood fires, fresh flowers,
hearty breakfasts and wholesome dinners. A warm welcome awaits guests for an enjoyable stay with us
and our cat simba. Attractions: Trout and salmon fishing (guide available), golf (clubs on-site), tennis,
squash, walks, mountain biking, 4WD, swimming pool, beehive tours, and historic water wheel built
1899.

Oamaru   *B&B Homestay 1.3km N of Oamaru town centre*

Highway House Boutique B&B
Stephanie & Norman Slater
43 Lynn Street (Cnr Thames Highway and Lynn St),
Orana Park, Oamaru
Tel (03) 437 1066   0800 003 319   Fax (03) 437 1066
Mob 025 200 2976   cns@ihug.co.nz
www.bnb.co.nz/highway.html
Double $100-$120 Single $80-$100 (Full Breakfast)
Child Neg. Dinner B/A Children welcome
2 King 1 Twin (3 bdrm)   1 Host share

Our character residence on Thames Highway, the main north road (1.3km from Town centre), has been entirely refurbished to the highest standard. We provide a full cooked breakfast and other refreshments as required. We can assist with tours of historic Oamaru or visit to the nature sites. Our courtesy car can collect or take you to nearby dining establishments. If you appreciate a quality ambiance and particular assistance from Stephanie and Norman who have travelled widely overseas, Highway House will be ideal for you.

Oamaru   *Homestay*

Wallfield
Pat & Bill Bews
126 Reservoir Road, Oamaru
Tel (03) 437 0368   Mob 025 284 7303
b&pbews@xtra.co.nz
www.bnb.co.nz/wallfield.html
Double $80 Single $45 (Continental Breakfast)
1 Double 2 Single (2 bdrm)
1 Guests share

Our modern home is situated high above the North end
of Oamaru with superb views to the east and the mountains in the west. We have four children, all happily married, and an ever increasing number of grand children. We have been home hosting for the last twelve years and although recently retired from farming, still enjoy the buzz of meeting new friends. Our interests include gardening and tramping.

Oamaru   *Homestay 8km SW of Oamaru*

Tara
Marianne & Baxter Smith
Springhill Road, 3 ORD, Oamaru
Tel (03) 434 8187   Fax (03) 434 8187
smith.tara@xtra.co.nz
www.tarahomestay.com
Double $95 Single $55 (Full Breakfast)
Dinner $30 by arrangement
2 Single (1 bdrm)
1 Private

Want to be pampered? "Tara" is the place for you. Enjoy
the comfort and luxuries of our character Oamaru stone home. "Tara" boasts all day sun and the privacy to soak up the country atmosphere. Nestled amongst eleven acres of roses, mature trees and rural farmland "Tara" is the perfect place to unwind. Our livestock include Alpacas, coloured sheep, donkeys and an aviary. We also have a Burmese cat and a Lassie Collie. My husband Baxter and I will ensure your visit is an enjoyable experience. Please phone for directions.

Oamaru   *Homestay Oamaru Central*

Jenny & Gerald Lynch-Blosse
11 Stour Street, South Hill, Oamaru, North Otago
Tel (03) 434 9628 geraldlb@clear.net.nz
www.bnb.co.nz/lynchblosse.html
Double **$120** Single $75 (Continental Breakfast)
Dinner $35
1 Double 2 Single (2 bdrm)
1 Ensuite 1 Private 1 Host share

We have a charming, character home surrounded by
gardens, in a quiet street near the main highway. Our
guest bedrooms are well appointed. Tea or coffee is
available. Dinner by arrangement is preceded by drinks
beside the fire. We have travelled, and enjoy meeting people, especially visitors to New Zealand.
Oamaru has many fine, stone, Victorian buildings. Enjoy one of Oamaru's many lovely walks, the
attractive public gardens, or visit our art gallery, museum or penguin colony. A warm welcome awaits
you. Family cat.

Oamaru - Waianakarua   *Homestay 25km S of Oamaru*

Glen Foulis
Margaret & John Munro
39 Middle Ridge Road, Waianakarua, ORD 9, Oamaru
Tel (03) 439 5559   Fax (03) 439 5220
Mob 021 940 777   hjm@wxc.net.nz
www.glenhomestays.co.nz
Double **$95** Single $60 (Full Breakfast) Child $35
Dinner $12 - $30 by arrangement Campervans $25
Credit cards accepted
1 King/Twin 2 Single (2 bdrm)
1 Private 1 Guests share 1 Host share

Set in farm and forest country we enjoy a quiet, beauty. Open fires on cold nights and sunny terraces.
Acres of green lawns and tall trees present a foreground for views of the forested river valley. Three-
course dinner including wine $30 (24 hour prior notice necessary). Golden retrievers, Adam and McDuff
are gentle and well trained; Caolila is our playful Abyssinnian cat. Scottish highland cattle graze nearby.
Five minutes on SH1 to North Otago's many attractions. Just ask us. Second nights stay 10% discount.

If you would like dinner
most hosts require 24 hours' notice.

441

Waianakarua - Oamaru *B&B Farmstay 30km S of Oamaru*

Glen Dendron
Anne & John Mackay
284 Breakneck Road, 9 - O R D, Waianakarua, Oamaru
Tel (03) 439 5288 Fax (03) 439 5288
Mob 021 615 287
anne.john.mackay@xtra.co.nz
www.bnb.co.nz/glendendron.html

Double $100-$130 Single $60-$70 (Full Breakfast)
Child $35 Children welcome
Dinner $30 with wine Credit cards accepted
2 King/Twin 1 Queen 1 Double (4 bdrm)
2 Ensuite 1 Guests share

Whitestone Waitaki Tourism Award Winner 2003.
Enjoy tranquility and beauty when you stay in our stylish modern home, spectacularly sited on a hilltop overlooking the picturesque Waianakarua river and surrounded by five acres of garden, containing hundreds of different plants. After a sumptuous farm cooked breakfast, feed the sheep and alpacas. Then take a stroll through the forest, native bush complete with waterfalls and birds or beside the river. Play a round on the private family golf course. Later, watch the seals and penguins nearby. Then, complete a perfect day with our gourmet three-course dinner with fine NZ wine before snuggling down for a peaceful sleep in the fresh country air.

After a lifetime spent in farming and forestry we relish the opportunity to share our home and semi-retired lifestyle with guests. Our adult family lives overseas so we travel frequently and have a great interest in other countries and cultures. We are very keen gardeners, read widely and enjoy antiques. Anne is a floral artist and John is involved with the Lions organization.

An overnight stay is not enough to do justice to this lovely area - with so much to see, why not stay awhile! Use us as a base for day visits to Oamaru, Dunedin, Waitaki Valley and Mt Cook. Christchurch International Airport - 3.5 hours.
We don't mind short notice!

We can plan customised itineraries of the area's many attractions
- Oamaru's historic architecture
- Beaches, fishing, seals and penguins
- Famous Moeraki Boulders and other interesting geological features
- Garden, heritage and fossil trails

Oamaru *B&B Homestay Victorian B&B Hotel/Homestay 1 min Oamaru Central*

Criterion B&B Victorian Hotel
Wenda & John Eason
3 Tyne St   Harbourside, P.O. Box 238   Oamaru,
Tel (03) 434 6247 0800 259 334   Mob 027 6031363
bnb@criterion.net.nz www.criterion.net.nz
Double $145 Single $95 ((Special Breakfast)
Child $25 Dinner on site facilities
Credit cards accepted Children welcome
3 Queen 2 Double 4 Twin 1 Single (6 bdrm)
1 Ensuite 1 Guests share

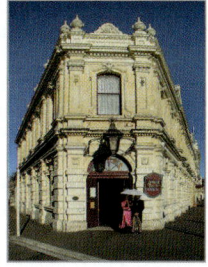

Our B&B accommodation is themed in the Victorian style; double, queen and
single beds with Battenburg lace duvets, quality linens and towels reflecting the ambiance of the period.
The beds are furnished with electric blankets and feather duvets for your comfort. Victorian furbishments
compliment all areas of the hotel. Built in 1877, Set in the Historic area close to penguins. Cooked
breakfast in the old NZ fashion.   We would like guests to feel at home with us, for this is our home as
well, and like the old hotels of yesteryear, We share our living areas with you.

Oamaru *Homestay Self-contained full kitchen 3km S of Oamaru, just of SH1*

Springbank
Joan & Stan Taylor
60 Weston Road, Oamaru,
Tel (03) 434 6602   Fax (03) 434 6602
Mob 025 669 2902
www.bnb.co.nz/springbank.html
Double $85 Single $50 (Continental Breakfast)
Child $10
1 Double 1 Twin (1 bdrm)
1 Private

We look forward to sharing our retirement haven with visitors from overseas and New Zealand. Our
modern home and separate guest flat are set in a peaceful and private large garden. Feed the gold fish
and pamper Oscar our cat. Our guest flat is sunny, warm, spacious and comfortable. We enjoy helping
visitors discover our district's best kept secrets! Penguins, gardens, Moeraki Boulders, beaches, pool,
fishing and golf. Our interests - travel, gardening, grandchildren. Stan, Lions and follows sports. Joan
all handcrafts, patchwork, floral design.

Oamaru *B&B 10km S of Omaru*

Sunnyside B&B
Andrina Butcher
3 Kakanui Road, Kakanui, Oamaru
Tel (03) 439 5442 Fax (03) 439 5442
Mob 025 285 3342   tonyandrina@xtra.co.nz
www.bnb.co.nz/sunnyside.html
Double $70 Single $50 (Continental Breakfast)
Child $20
1 Queen (1 bdrm)
1 Ensuite

Kakanui is a pretty coastal township on the Vanished World Fossil Trail. You can walk, swim, surf, fish,
kayak on the river or fossick for interesting minerals. There is a shop and café nearby. We are centrally
located for historic Oamaru, Moeraki Boulders, Central Otago Goldfields, Waitaki Valley Hydro-lakes,
penguins and much more. We are semi-retired from forestry and urban tree management. You can be
assured of a warm welcome from our two tabby cats, Stan and Ollie and us.

Oamaru   *B&B Self-contained Semi-rural Cottage 2km N of Oamaru Central*

Coral Sea Cottage & Ocean View
Nicola & Peter Mountain
34 Harlech Street, Oamaru,

Tel (03) 437 1422   Fax (03) 437 1422
Mob 021 659 757 or 021 042 6997
nmountainnz@hotmail.com
www.bnb.co.nz/coralsea.html

Double $75-$112 Single $30-$65 (Special Breakfast)
Child (5 - 16) $23 Children welcome Pets welcome
3 King/Twin 1 Single (4 bdrm)   1 Ensuite 1 Private

Come and relax in our delightful, newly equipped, cosy
cottage with secluded garden or in new self-contained accommodation in our home, Ocean View, with
magnificent panoramic views. In a five acre hillside setting with sheep, chickens, pheasants, pet cow,
dogs (small), cats and teenage boys. Breakfast provisions include eggs. Near local shops and restaurants
and only five minutes drive to historic town centre, art galleries and famous blue penguin colony. We
look forward to welcoming you and offering help with planning your visit to our area.

Moeraki - Oamaru   *B&B Farmstay 38km S of Oamaru*

Moeraki Boulder Downs Farmstay & B&B
Jan & Ken Wheeler
State Highway 1, Moeraki, RD 2,
Palmerston, North Otago

Tel (03) 439 4855   Fax (03) 439 4355
Mob 025 614 6396 farmstay@moerakiboulders.co.nz
www.moerakiboulders.co.nz

Double $90-$120 Single $70 (Full Breakfast)
Child $40 Dinner B/A Credit cards accepted
1 Queen 2 Twin (2 bdrm)   1 Guests share

Indulge yourself and enjoy warm hospitality at our country retreat by the sea. We invite you to join us
for a traditional New Zealand dinner - then relax by the fire in our charming 1920?s homestead. Breakfast
with the bellbirds - then stroll along the beautiful beach to Moeraki Boulders and quaint fishing village.
Sheep farm tours available. Stay two nights and experience the Moeraki penguins, seals, historic Oamaru,
golf courses and antique shops nearby. We are enroute to Christchurch, Dunedin, Queenstown and Mt
Cook.

All our B&Bs are non-smoking
unless stated otherwise in the text.

Otago and North Catlins

Towns listed generally follow a north to south route. Refer to the index if required.

Mount Cook

Lake Tekapo
Kim
Burkes Pass

Makarora

Lake Pukaki
Twizel

Omarama

Lake Hawea
Albert Town
Wanaka

Kurow

6

Glenorchy
Arrowtown

Danseys Pass

Queenstown Gibbston Cromwell

Earnscleugh Alexandra

85

Kingston

Palmerston

Garston

6

Roxburgh

1

Ettrick Millers Flat

Portobello

Wendonside

Blueskin Bay

den

Port Chalmers

Balfour

Mosgiel

8

Waikaka

Lawrence **1** Dunedin Broad Bay

Gore Pukerau

Waihola

Winton Mataura

Milton

Vaianiwa Wyndham

Clinton Balclutha

cargill

Kaka Point

Mokotua

Owaka Nuggets

| 0 | Kilometres | 40 |
| 0 | Miles | 24 |

Makarora   *Homestay Self-contained Cottage 65km N of Wanaka*

Larrivee Homestay
Andrea and Paul
Makarora, via Wanaka

Tel (03) 443 9177   andipaul@xtra.co.nz
www.larriveehomestay.co.nz

Double $120 Single $80 (Continental /Full Breakfast)
Child 1/2 price under 12yrs Dinner $35 BYO
2 Double 2 Single (3 bdrm)
1 Ensuite 1 Private 1 Guests share

Nestled in native bush bordering Mt Aspiring National
Park, our unique home and cottage are secluded, quiet
and comfortable. Originally from the USA, we have lived in Makarora for over 25 years and like
sharing our mountain retreat and enjoying good food and conversation. Many activities are available
locally, including fishing, bird watching, jet boating, scenic flights and bush walks - including the
wonderful 'Siberia Experience', fly/walk/boat trip. We are happy to help make arrangements for activities.

Makarora   *B&B Self-contained 65km N of Wanaka*

Makarora Homestead
Kenna Fraser
53 Rata Road, Makarora

Tel (03) 443 1532   bnb@makarora.com
www.makarora.com

Double $95-$105 (Continental Breakfast)
Children welcome
7 Queen 1 Double 4 Twin (8 bdrm)
2 Ensuite

Makarora Homestead offers a secluded retreat in the
midst of the Southern Alps and is perfect for travellers looking for the warmth & ambience of a home.
A selfcontained comfortable house with a private sunny deck leads into the open plan kitchen/dining/
living area. Two new detached bedrooms have queen beds, ensuite bathrooms & verandah. With pet
farm animals to feed, our friendly border collie & ducks & chickens Makarora Homestead provides a
fun rural experience for any age.

Lake Hawea   *Homestay 15km N of Wanaka*

Sylvan Chalet
Lyall Campbell
4 Bodkin Street, Lake Hawea, RD 2, Wanaka

Tel (03) 443 1343   Mob 025 224 9192
lyallc@xtra.co.nz
www.inow.co.nz/sylvanchalet

Double $80 Single $40 (Continental Breakfast)
Child $30
1 Double 2 Single (2 bdrm)
1 Ensuite 1 Host share

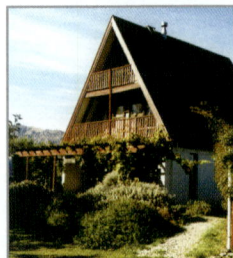

I am a retired school teacher - now a craft dyer of silk, a spinner and cross-country skier. My three-
storied A-frame is in a sheltered compound with many specimen trees. One guest room has an ensuite,
the other opens to a balcony; both have mountain views. Access via a circular staircase. Washing
machine available. Lake Hawea two minutes walk away. I have a cat and small dog. Directions: From
Wanaka-Haast Rd turn off to Lake Hawea - past hotel to store - see A-frame through Archway.

Wanaka   *Homestay Wanaka Central*

Lake Wanaka Homestay
Gailie & Peter Cooke
85 Warren Street, Wanaka
Tel (03) 443 7995   0800 443 799   Fax (03) 443 7945
wanakahomestay@xtra.co.nz
www.lakewanakahomestay.co.nz
Double $90-$100 Single $60 (Full Breakfast)
Child neg
1 Double 1 Twin 1 Single (3 bdrm)
1 Guests share 1 Host share

Friendly, welcoming Bed and Breakfast Homestay. Relax with us and enjoy breath-taking views of the lake and mountains. Three minutes walk to central Wanaka shops and restaurants. Peter is a keen fly fisherman and is happy to show guests where to find "the big ones". 'Kim' our Labrador is everyone's friend. Comfortable beds, electric blankets, heaters and hairdryers. Tea, coffee, biscuits and muffins anytime. Gaille and Peter have shared their home with guests for many years making wonderful friendships. We both enjoy meeting and helping people.

Wanaka   *Homestay Wanaka*

Aspiring Images
Betty & George Russell
26 Norman Terrace, Wanaka
Tel (03) 443 8358   Fax (03) 443 8327
grussell@xtra.co.nz   www.aspiringimages.co.nz
Double $120-$140 Single $75-$100 (Full Breakfast)
Child B/A Dinner $35 B/A Credit cards accepted
1 King/Twin 1 Queen (2 bdrm)
1 Ensuite 1 Private 1 Guests share

The challenge - portray Wanaka and our homestay in 85 words! Wanaka is: magical; tranquil; dramatic; refreshing; exhilarating; captivatingly beautiful. Wanaka has: activities both challenging and restful, fascinating history, distinctive micro-climate, ecological diversity, mountain light ever changing. Our homestay offers: informative welcoming hosts, warmth and comfort, lake and mountain views, adjacent park with lake access, mountain bikes to ride. We are: ex-teachers with musical, sporting, photographic and Rotary interests; well travelled both nationally and internationally, qualified to help with NZ itineraries.

Lake Wanaka   *B&B Homestay Self-contained Wanaka*

Beacon Point
Diana & Dan Pinckney
302 Beacon Point Road, PO Box 6, Lake Wanaka
Tel (03) 443 1253   Fax (03) 443 1254
Mob Di 025 246 0222 / Dan 025 354 847
dan.di@lakewanaka.co.nz   www.beaconpoint.co.nz
Double $90-$120 (Continental Breakfast) Child $30
Dinner $30 Children welcome
1 Queen 1 Twin (2 bdrm)
2 Private

Our new home "Beacon Point" B & B is surrounded by 1 acre of lawn and garden for your enjoyment. It leads to a walking track to the village around the edge of the lake with snow capped mountains in winter. Private spacious studio with ensuite, Queen and single beds (2 rooms), kitchen, T.V, sundeck and BBQ area. Studio equiped with every need for a perfect stay. We are very flexable and enjoy planning your days with you. Our intrests include farming, forestry, fly fishing, real estate, boating, gardening and our grandchildren. Turn right at lake - Lakeside Road - then to Beacon Point Road 302.

OTAGO, NORTH CATLINS

Wanaka   *B&B Self-contained 10km N of Wanaka*

The Stone Cottage
Belinda Wilson
Wanaka, RD 2, Central Otago

Tel (03) 443 1878   Fax (03) 443 1276
stonecottage@xtra.co.nz
www.stonecottage.co.nz

Double $220-$240 Single $200 (Full Breakfast)
Child 1/2 price under 12yrs Dinner $65
Credit cards accepted
1 King 1 Queen 1 Double 2 Single (2 bdrm)
1 Ensuite 1 Private

Fifty years ago, a spectacular garden was created at Dublin Bay on the tranquil shores of Lake Wanaka. Its beauty still blooms today against a backdrop of the majestic Southern Alps. Accommodation is private, comfortable and elegantly decorated.

The Stone Cottage offers two self-contained loft apartments with breathtaking views over lake Wanaka to snow clad alps beyond. Featuring your own bathroom, bedroom, kitchen, living room and balcony. Television, fax and email available. Private entrance.

Enjoy breakfast at leisure, made from fresh ingredients from your well stocked fully equipped kitchen, Pre dinner drinks, delicious 3 course dinner and NZ wines or a gourmet picnic hamper is available by arrangement.

Walk along the beach just 4 minutes from The Stone Cottage or wander in the enchanting garden. Guests can experience trout fishing, nature walks, golf, boating, horse riding, wine tasting and ski fields nearby.

Only 10 minutes from Wanaka, this is the perfect retreat for those who value privacy and the unique beauty of this area.

Relax in the magic atmosphere at The Stone Cottage and awake to the dawn bird chorus of native bellbirds and fantails.

Wanaka *B&B Homestay Wanaka*

Harpers
Jo & Ian Harper
95 McDougall Street, Wanaka
Tel (03) 443 8894   Fax (03) 443 8834
harpers@xtra.co.nz
www.bnb.co.nz/harpers.html
Double $110 Single $70 (Continental Breakfast)
Credit cards accepted
1 King/Twin 2 Twin (2 bdrm)
1 Ensuite 1 Private 1 Guests share

We take pride in offering a friendly, comfortable home. Share breakfast and awesome lake and mountain views with us. Also explore our extensive garden, which provides a tranquil environment for relaxing. We offer a drink and muffins on your arrival. This is a smoke-free home. Recent guests' comments: "A wonderful stay - hot bath, hot pancakes, hot view and such a welcome. The best yet." "Thanks for your warm and friendly hospitality, very high standard of service and lovely pancakes." "Lovely stay, wonderful views, pancakes delicious."

Wanaka *Homestay Rural 4km S of Wanaka*

Stonehaven
Deirdre & Dennis
Halliday Lane, RD 2, Wanaka
Tel (03) 443 9516   Fax (03) 443 9513
moghul@xtra.co.nz
www.stonehaven.co.nz
Double $95 Single $75 (Full Breakfast)
Child $20 neg portacots & high chairs avail.
Credit cards accepted Children welcome
1 Queen 1 Double 2 Single (2 bdrm)
1 Ensuite 1 Private

Our home is set in a developing two acres about five minutes drive from Wanaka. All beds have electric blankets, tea and coffee is freely available. We have extensive views of surrounding mountains. Children are welcome. Child care by arrangement. Our nearby tree collection has an accent on autumn colour. Local walks a speciality. Organic fruit both in season and preserved. We have twin fourteen year old girls, a small dog, and two cats. No smoking inside please. Please phone for directions.

Wanaka *Homestay 2min N of Wanaka*

Hunt's Homestay
Bill & Ruth Hunt
56 Manuka Crescent, Wanaka 9192, Central Otago
Tel (03) 443 1053   Fax (03) 443 1355
Mob 025 265 0114   relax@huntshomestay.co.nz
www.huntshomestay.co.nz
Double $110 Single $70 (Continental Breakfast)
Child by arrangement Credit cards accepted
1 Queen 2 Single (2 bdrm)
1 Guests share

Welcome to our modern home in Wanaka where we will greet you with tea or coffee in our smoke-free house and settle you in your spacious ground-floor accommodation. After farming near Wanaka, we built this house over looking the mountains and lake, and so have a good knowledge of the area. Through our membership of Lake Wanaka Tourism we are kept informed of all tourist activities in the area. Our interests are golf, gardening, travel and meeting people. We have no resident children or pets.

Wanaka *Homestay Lodge 2.8km N of Wanaka Central*

Anubis Lodge
Bobbie & Michele Mercer
264 Beacon Point Road, Wanaka
Tel (03) 443 7807 Fax (03) 443 7803 Mob 025 407 816
m.b.mercer@xtra.co.nz www.anubis.co.nz or
www.wanakahomestay.co.nz/anubris
Double $185-$225 Single $150-$175
(Full Special Breakfast) Credit cards accepted
2 King 1 Queen (3 bdrm)
3 Ensuite

Our stone house is purpose built for bed & breakfast accommodation, rooms are large with own dressing rooms and ensuite bathrooms and for your comfort we have included tea and coffee facilities and televisions in every room. Beds are luxuriously fitted with quality linen, feather duvets and electric blankets. Décor accented with native timber, fresh flowers, Italian art, Belgian rugs, Scottish leather and English lines, central heating plus two fireplaces keep us cosy. Breakfast is varied and generous, with a sumptuous selection of homemade breads, yoghurts, preserves with fresh fruit and cereals. As breakfast is the most important meal of the day, choose a popular favourite from our full cooked menu.

You can enjoy our wide open views to lake and mountains, while playing a game of tennis on our astro-turf court or take a short walk to the lake edge for fishing, swimming or secluded relaxation.

We certainly look forward to meeting you. But don't take our recommendation, here's what one of our guests thought.

"If you're lucky enough to have the opportunity to book here, do! We started with two nights and stayed five. This home and the bedrooms take your breath away. Bobbie-Jean (owner's daughter) and Bernie have the youthful energy to cater to their guests starting with a breakfast menu that includes eggs Benedict to afternoon drinks and nibbles.

The B&B is so crisp, clean and well decorated that you will return home after your travels with a whole new level of appreciation of how life can be. The beautiful house is equipped with French doors along the whole back of the house that brings the outdoors in with stunning views of Lake Wanaka and the surrounding mountains. The backyard is a great place to sample the fabulous NZ wines and enjoy the end of the day." *December 2002, Tom Wolf.*

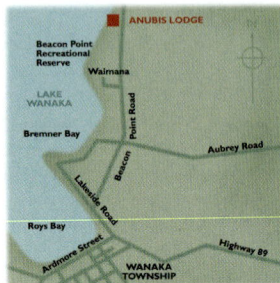

Wanaka *B&B Homestay 2km N of Wanaka Central*

Lake Wanaka Home Hosting
Joyce & Lex Turnbull
19 Bill's Way, Wanaka
Tel (03) 443 9060 Fax (03) 443 1626
Mob 025 228 9160 lex.joy@xtra.co.nz
www.lakewanakahomehosting.co.nz
Double $100-$135 Single $65 (Full Breakfast)
Child under 10 years $25 Dinner $35
1 King/Twin 1 Double 1 Twin (3 bdrm)
2 Private

We welcome visitors to Wanaka, enjoy sharing our natural surroundings with others. We have a large peaceful home where our guests can experience not only the austerity of the lake and mountains around them, but also experience the ambience of Wanaka itself. Guest room with super king bed has adjoining TV lounge with TV, tea coffee facilities, private bathroom. Good laundry facilities. We wish your stay in Wanaka will be a very happy one. Directions: please ring for directions. We enjoy your company.

Wanaka *B&B Homestay*

Northridge
Richie & Sue Heathfield / Atkinson
11 Botting Place, PO Box 376, Wanaka
Tel (03) 443 8835 Fax (03) 443 1835
Mob 025 950 436 stay@northridgewanaka.co.nz
www.northridgewanaka.co.nz
Double $130-$160 Single $100 (Full Breakfast)
Credit cards accepted
2 Queen 2 Single (3 bdrm)
1 Ensuite 2 Private 1 Guests share

Looking for quality accommodation with spectacular views Northridge is the place for you. Situated in a prime location on a ridge overlooking Lake Wanaka,the Mountains and within walking distance to restaurants, shops and the lakefront. Our quality 2 storey Native Timber and Schist stone home lends itself to indoor/outdoor living, where you can wander through the garden or sit on the patio with refreshments and take in the everchanging scenery. Northridge is centrally heated to keep us all cosy in winter.

Wanaka *Separate/Suite Boutique B&B Lodge Wanaka Central*

Wanaka Springs Boutique B&B Lodge
Lynne & Murray Dalziell
21 Warren Street, Wanaka 9192, Central Otago
Tel (03) 443 8421 Fax (03) 443 8429
Mob 027 223 2512 relax@wanakasprings.com
www.wanakasprings.com
Double $230-$275 (Special Breakfast)
Honeymoon Room Credit cards accepted
6 Queen 2 Twin (8 bdrm)
8 Ensuite

This 2001/2002 New Zealand Tourism Award Finalist for hosted accommodation offers a unique experience of 'informal sophistication' for the discerning traveller. In its intimate yet private setting, the Lodge's reputation as Wanaka's 'in-town retreat' is more than justified by its high standards of comfort, hospitality and facilities. Savour our special breakfast buffet and afternoon tea while you enjoy the stunning views and enjoy the services and facilities of a small hotel but retains the warmth, personality and charm of a boutique lodge just a three minute stroll from town centre.

Wanaka *B&B Separate/Suite Boutique Accommodation Wanaka Central*

Te Wanaka Lodge
Graeme & Andy Oxley
23 Brownston Street, Wanaka
Tel (03) 443 9224 0800 WANAKA (926252)
Fax (03) 443 9246
tewanakalodge@xtra.co.nz
www.tewanaka.co.nz
Double $145-$180 Single $135-$170
(Full Breakfast) Self contained Cottage $195
Credit cards accepted
9 Queen 4 Twin (13 bdrm)
13 Ensuite

Nestled in the heart of Wanaka, Te Wanaka Lodge is a two minute walk to the lake, restaurants, shops and golf course. Tastefully decorated with fishing and skiing memorabilia, Te Wanaka Lodge has a distinctive Alpine ambience.

On a hot summer's day laze under our walnut tree with a cool drink from the House Bar, or in winter relax by the warmth of our log fire after enjoying a soak in our secluded garden hot tub.

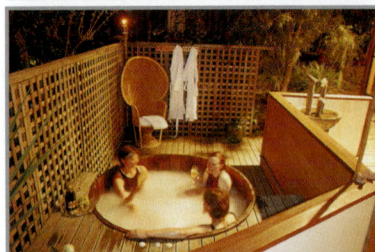

• All bedrooms with ensuite and private balcony
• Full cooked breakfast included
• House Bar specialising in local beers and wines
• Sky TV, video, CD and book library
• Off street parking
• Ski drying room and laundry service
• Full business facilities
• In-house massage therapy
• Mountain bikes & equipment available

Wanaka   *B&B Homestay 2.5km E of Wanaka*

Riverside
Lesley & Norman West
11 Riverbank Road, RD 2, Wanaka

Tel (03) 443 1522   Fax (03) 443 1522
Mob 025 601 4640   n.l.west@paradise.net.nz
www.bnb.co.nz/riverside.html

Double $100-$110 Single $70 (Full Breakfast)
Dinner By arrangement
1 Queen 2 Twin (2 bdrm)
1 Guests share

We welcome guests to the tranquility of our private home set on six acres overlooking the Cardrona River. Just 100 metres from S.H.,84 and 5 mins (2.5km) from Lake Wanaka we offer you a friendly and peaceful environment with extensive mountain and rural views. Guests are welcome to relax by the open fire in winter, or enjoy the shady terraces in summer. Just two well-appointed guest rooms with quality linen and central heating ensures your stay will be relaxing and enjoyable. Fishing, a lake cruise in our boat and dinner available by arrangement. We have two cats and a small friendly dog (outdoors).

Wanaka - Albert Town   *B&B Homestay 6km N of Wanaka*

Riversong
Ann Horrax
5 Wicklow Terrace, Albert Town, RD 2, Wanaka

Tel (03) 443 8567   info@happyhomestay.co.nz
www.happyhomestay.co.nz

Double $110-$130 Single $85-$90 (Full Breakfast)
Child $25 Dinner $30pp by arrangement
Springwater Apartment $200 - $250
Credit cards accepted Children welcome
1 King/Twin 1 Queen 1 Single (3 bdrm)
1 Ensuite 1 Private 1 Guests share

'Riversong' - situated at historic Albert Town, on the banks of the magnificent Clutha River, with uninterrupted river and mountain views, five minutes from Wanaka. Lies at the heart of Central Otago's natural and scenic beauty; trout fishing, three ski fields, Mt Aspiring National Park and much more. My background is healthcare and Ian's law. We invite you to share the comfort of our home and garden and Ian's knowledge of the region's fishing. We are committed to providing a friendly and relaxed atmosphere. We have two outside lab dogs.

Wanaka   *B&B Homestay 4KM So of Wanaka*

The Tin Shed
Boyd & Nan Ottrey
431 Riverbank Road, RD 2, Wanaka

Tel 03 4437449 Mob 021 462 654 ottrey@xtra.co.nz
www.bnb.co.nz/thetinshed.html

Double $100 Single $80 (Continental Breakfast)
Child B/A Dinner B/A Children welcome Pets welcome
2 Queen 1 Twin (3 bdrm)
1 Ensuite 1 Host share

We share our home with (sometimes) adult children, and Samoyed (dog) Nikita who welcomes guests as much as we do. Our home is very close to Wanaka, renowned for it's lake, beautiful mountain vistas, and marvellous restaurants and emerging vineyards. We have close proximity to lakes, fishing, mountains, golf, climbing, walking and other outdoor pursuits. Cardrona and Treble Cone are 15 minutes away, Queenstown 1 hour.

Lake Wanaka   *B&B Self-contained 2.3km NW of Wanaka Centre*

Peak-Sportchalet
Alex and Christine Schafer
36 Hunter Crescent, Lake Wanaka
Tel 0064 3 443 6990   Fax 0064 3 443 4969
stay@peak-sportchalet.co.nz
www.Peak-Sportchalet.co.nz
Double $90-$120 Single $65-$70 (Full Breakfast)
Children welcome
1 King/Twin 1 King 1 Twin (3 bdrm)
2 Ensuite 1 Private

PEAK-Sportchalet - Life the way it should be. All rooms are different in design and colour. We have two options. Stay at our luxury Chalet with its own lounge, fireplace and bathroom, with underfloor heating or choose a double ensuite in the main house. Start your day with a delicious cooked Breakfastbuffet. Relax after your adventures on the sunny verandah, enjoying great mountain views, or in the Wintertime in front of a cosy logfire. We speak german. We welcome you together with our two children.

Wanaka   *Luxury Boutique Retreat 2km N of Wanaka Central*

Minaret Lodge
Gary Tate
34 Eely Point Road, Wanaka
Tel (03) 443 1856   Fax (03) 443 1846
Mob 021 644 406   info@minaretlodge.co.nz
www.minaretlodge.co.nz
Double $350 Single $330 (Special Breakfast)
Dinner B/A
5 King/Twin (5 bdrm)
5 Ensuite

Wanaka's luxury boutique retreat, bed & breakfast lodge, set in park-like setting, located within 10 minute walk to Wanaka town centre. The Lodge features a mud brick (adobe) construction with plastered finish, incoorporating local schist stone. The separate guest room chalets have ensuites with heated tiled floor, fine furniture and linen, deck, sauna, spa, mountain bikes, ski storage and drying room included in facilities. Gourmet breakfast and aperitifs included in the tariff.

Wanaka   *B&B Boutique B&B 2km S of Wanaka*

Mountain Range
Lindsey and Matthew Brady
Heritage Park, Cardrona Valley Road, PO Box 451
Tel (03) 443 7400   Fax (03) 443 7450
Mob (021) 443 741   stay@mountainrange.co.nz
www.mountainrange.co.nz
Double $225-$260 Single $195 (Full Breakfast)
Child under 5's free
2 King/Twin 1 King 4 Queen (7 bdrm)
7 Ensuite

Set on 10 acres of private parkland, Mountain Range draws its name and inspiration from the breathtaking mountain views that provide a unique backdrop for this peaceful and relaxing retreat. The lodge benefits from total seclusion and privacy, yet is only 2 minutes from the local amenities and restaurants.   7 spacious guestrooms with luxury ensuite bathrooms. Delicious continental and cooked breakfast. Sumptuous guest lounge with elegant furnishings and log fire. Complimentary teas, coffees, snacks and aperitifs. Laundry service. No pets. Children under 12 by arrangement.

Wanaka *B&B Homestay*

Temasek House
Vivien Reid & Mandy Madin
7 Huchan Lane, Wanaka 9192,

Tel (03) 443 1655 Fax (03) 443 1655
temasek.house@xtra.co.nz
www.bnb.co.nz/temasek.html

Double $90-$105 Single $60 (Full Breakfast)
twin $90 Children welcome
1 Queen 1 Twin 1 Single (3 bdrm)
1 Ensuite

Under new management. Only 1.5km from the town centre, Temasek House offers guests a friendly, 'homely' atmosphere. Our home is ideally situated for the local skifields and Mount Aspiring National Park. A large comfortable lounge opens on to a balcony with mountain views. A gentle stroll to local restaurants and lakeside. Tea and coffee complimentary with homemade treats. Use of washing machine and dryer available for a small additional charge. One small dog on property.

Wanaka *B&B Homestay*

Harris Mountain View
Ross and Chris Greenwood
30 Mataraki Place, Wanaka

Tel (03) 443 5115 Fax (03) 443 5116
Mob 021 030 2278 rcgreenwood@xtra.co.nz
www.harrismountainview.co.nz

Double $100-$130 Single $80-$90
(Continental Breakfast) Child $80 - $100
4 King/Twin 2 King (2 bdrm)

Newly built home, best views in Wanaka! Lookig across the lake and up to the Harris Mountain Ranges.Large and spacious house with natural wood being a feature throughout. Large guest bedrooms have super king sized double or single beds with tea and coffee-making facilities and own external access. Rooms share a large bathroom with a double shower, spa bath and two separate WCs. We can arrange all activities and cater especially for skiers in the winter months.2 tame children and a dog !

Wanaka *B&B Self-contained 2km E of Wanaka*

Oregon Hollow
Robyn & Gene Clements
149 Anderson Road, RD 2, Wanaka, Otago

Tel (03) 443 4086 Fax (03) 443 4086
Mob 021 418 878 gene.c@clear.net.nz
www.bnb.co.nz/oregonhollow.html

Double $160-$185 Single $140 (Special Breakfast)
1 Queen (1 bdrm)
1 Private

Oregon Hollow is a luxury one bedroom apartment (renovated 2003) attached to our house. Set in a peaceful location yet less than two kilometres to Wanaka?s restaurants and amenities. The apartment has a separate entrance, private bathroom, and large living area with a kitchenette and log burner, TV, DVD and stereo. Quality bed linen, furnishings are fitted throughout. A private patio is set in our one acre of country garden. A speciality breakfast hamper is provided. We have a son, Oliver, two Jack Russell Terriers and a cat.

Wanaka   *B&B Homestay 2.4km E of Wanaka*

The Cedars
Mary & Graham Dowdall
7 Riverbank Road, RD 2, Wanaka 9192

Tel (03) 443 1544   Fax (03) 443 1544
Mob 021 120 8960   thecedarswanaka@xtra.co.nz
www.bnb.co.nz/cedars.html

Double $110-$150 Single $70-$100 (Full Breakfast)
Dinner B/A Children welcome Smoking area inside
2 Queen 1 Single (2 bdrm)
1 Private 1 Guests share

Céad Míle Fáilte - One hundred thousand welcomes. A warm Irish/Kiwi welcome awaits at 'The Cedars', by Mary, Graham and pet English Collie, Flipper. Our stone home set on 11 acres includes panoramic views, expansive gardens, guest lounge with large open fire. Nearby attractions include The Maze, The Warbirds Museum (both internationally acclaimed), golf, ski-fields, walking tracks, paragliding, lakes and rivers for water pursuits: shops and restaurants. Full breakfast is served with fresh and homemade produce. We offer evening meals or BBQ by prior arrangement.

Cromwell   *Homestay*

Stuart's Homestay
Elaine & Ian Stuart
5 Mansor Court, Cromwell,

Tel (03) 445 3636   Fax (03) 445 3636
Mob 025 203 3825   ian.elaine@xtra.co.nz
www.bnb.co.nz/stuart.html

Double $100-$120 Single $60 (Full Breakfast)
Dinner $15 - $20 by arrangement Credit cards accepted
2 Queen 2 Single (3 bdrm)
1 Ensuite 1 Private

Welcome to our home which is situated within walking distance to most of Cromwell's amenities. We are semi-retired Southland farmers who have been home hosting for over ten years. Now enjoying living in the stone fruit and wine region of Central Otago. Cromwell is a quiet and relaxed tourist town which is known for historic gold diggings, vineyards, orchards, trout fishing, boating, walks and close to ski fields. Share dinner with us or just Bed and Breakfast. We enjoy sharing our home with visitors and a friendly stay is assured.

Cromwell   *B&B Homestay 1km N of Cromwell*

Cottage Gardens
Jill & Colin McColl
3 Alpha Street, cnr State Highway 8B, Cromwell

Tel (03) 445 0628   Fax (03) 445 0628 eco@xtra.co.nz
www.bnb.co.nz/cottagegardens.html

Double $85 Single $40-$55 (Continental Breakfast)
Dinner $20 Credit cards accepted
1 Twin 2 Single (3 bdrm)
1 Ensuite 2 Hosts share

Hospitality is our specialty. For nine years we have offered travellers good food and company, and welcome you to join us. Our spacious guest room has ensuite, TV, fridge, tea making facilities, private entrance with verandah overlooking garden and Lake Dunstan. Cromwell is surrounded by orchards, vineyards, ever-changing scenery and has excellent sporting facilities. Accompany Labrador Jessica May on lakeside walks. Fritter is a retired pre-school cat. Members of Lion International: retired orchardists. Free laundry. Queenstown and Wanaka 45 minutes, Te Anau 2 to $2^{1}/_{2}$ hours drive.

Cromwell - Northburn   *B&B Self-contained 4km N of Cromwell*

Quartz Reef Creek Bed and Breakfast
June Boulton
Quartz Reef Creek, RD 3, Northburn,
State Highway 8, Cromwell

Tel (03) 445 0404   Fax (03) 445 0404
june-boulton@xtra.co.nz
www.bnb.co.nz/boulton.html

Double $100-$110 Single $70-$80
(Continental Breakfast) Twin Room/single $100
Credit cards accepted
1 Queen 1 Twin 1 Single (3 bdrm) 1 Ensuite 1 Private

You are invited to stay at my peaceful and modern lakeside home located in Central Otago, a rapidly expanding wine growing region. Panoramic views from your sunny room include Lake Dunstan and surrounding mountains. Both rooms have total privacy with their own entrances. One has its own deck, tea making facilities, fridge, microwave and TV. Another room has twin beds, TV and sitting room with another single bed. I enjoy making pottery in my studio and supply local galleries. I have a dog Guinness and cat, Tom.

Cromwell   *Homestay Separate/Suite Lodge 5km N of Cromwell*

Lake Dunstan Lodge
Judy & Bill Thornbury
Northburn, RD 3, Cromwell

Tel (03) 445 1107 Fax (03) 445 3062
Mob 025 311 415 william.t@xtra.co.nz
www.lakedunstanlodge.co.nz

Double $100-$120 Single $70 (Full Breakfast)
Child neg Dinner $25pp by arrangement
Credit cards accepted
2 Queen 3 Single (3 bdrm) 1 Ensuite 1 Guests share

Friendly hospitality awaits you at our home privately situated beside Lake Dunstan. We are ex-Southland farmers and have a cat "Ollie". Our interests include "Lions", fishing, boating, gardening and crafts. Bedrooms have attached balconies, fridge, tea and coffee facilities. Guests share our living areas, spa pool and laundry. Local attractions: orchards, vineyards, gold diggings, fishing, boating, walks, 4 ski fields nearby. Enjoy dinner with us or just relax in the peaceful surroundings. No smoking indoors please. Directions: 5km north of Cromwell Bridge on SH8.

Cromwell - Lowburn   *B&B Homestay 1.5km N of Cromwell*

Walnut Grove
Adrian & Olivia Somerville
State Highway 6, Lowburn, RD 2,
Cromwell, Rapid No 67

Tel (03) 445 1112 Fax (03) 445 1115
Mob 027 477 4695 walnut.grove@xtra.co.nz
www.walnutgrove.co.nz

Double $135 Single $120 (Special Breakfast)
Credit cards accepted
1 King/Twin 1 Queen (2 bdrm)
2 Ensuite

Let our home be your home for your visit to Central Otago - beautiful in all seasons! Our spacious home is on 4 acres, almost surrounded by a working orchard and with mountain views and glimpse of Lake Dunstan. Each comfortable guestroom has ensuite, TV, telephone and tea/coffee-making facilities. Breakfast is served when it suits you. We have two Siamese cats, two dogs (one a Labrador) and our interests include meeting people, Rotary, travel, fishing and exploring Central Otago. Please ring ahead to make a reservation.

Cromwell - Bannockburn   *B&B Homestay Self-contained 6km Cromwell*

Aurum
Janette & Maurice Middleditch
RD 2, Bannockburn, Lawrence Street - Short Street
Tel (03) 445 2024   Fax (03) 445 2027
aurumgallery@xtra.co.nz
www.nzsouth.co.nz/aurumhomestay
Double $95-$110 Single $60-$75
(Continental Breakfast) Child neg.
Dinner by arrangement Credit cards accepted
1 Queen 1 Double (3 bdrm)
1 Private 1 Guests share

Situated in Bannockburn and surrounded by local wineries and historic gold mining sites, Aurum provides private guest living. Maurice is a scenic artist who exhibits throughout the country and Janette speaks Dutch and loves meeting people. Two bedrooms and bedsitting room with big bathroom and bath, hairdryer, TV, tea and coffee, and laundry facilities available. A continental breakfast will be served at a time suitable to you. Reservations essential.

Arrowtown   *Homestay Self-contained 18km NE of Queenstown*

Bains Homestay
Ann & Barry Bain
R32 Butel Road, Arrowtown, Otago
Tel (03) 442 1270   Fax (03) 442 1271
Mob 027 274 3360   bainshomestay@ihug.co.nz
www.dotco.co.nz/bainshomestay
Double $100-$120 (Full Breakfast) Child neg
Credit cards accepted Children welcome Pets welcome
1 Queen 4 Single (2 bdrm)
1 Ensuite 1 Private

We are a retired business couple who have travelled extensively. We welcome our guests to a peaceful, spacious, sunny self-contained upstairs suite complete with kitchen, and a balcony with panoramic views of surrounding mountains and the famous Millbrook golf resort. Meet our friendly Cocker Spaniel. Extra continental breakfast with freshly baked bread, jams etc is provided in your suite; or join us for a cooked starter. Complimentary laundry, road bikes, gold mining gear, BBQ etc. Our courtesy car is an Archbishop's 1924 Austin drophead coupe.

Arrowtown   *B&B Self-contained 20km N of Queenstown*

Polly-Anna Cottage
Daphne & Bill MacLaren
43 Bedford Street, Arrowtown
Tel (03) 442 1347   Fax (03) 442 1307
Mob 027 220 3974
www.bnb.co.nz/pollyannacottage.html
Double $95-$100 Single $70 (Continental Breakfast)
Dinner $30 by arrangement Credit cards accepted
Children welcome
1 Double 2 Single (2 bdrm)
1 Ensuite 1 Private

Daphne and Bill, retired business couple, have restored and renovated their quaint cute and cosy 100 year old cottage, nestled in an attractive garden, surrounded by spectacular mountains. Bill retired from Ford Dealer Industry; Have both travelled widely; Can inform on all local attractions and offer our warm hospitality, completely private ensuite facilities. 3 minutes from historic Arrowtown, 15 minutes to Queenstown. Try Daph's home preserves. Comments: "Highlight of our trip". "Thanks for Memory". Cat named Maggie. Come in, be surprised. Directions: Polly-Anna sign at front gate.

Arrowtown   *Homestay 19km E of Queenstown*

Rowan Cottage
Elizabeth & Michael Bushell
9 Thomson Street, Arrowtown

Tel (03) 442 0443   Mob 025 622 8105
www.bnb.co.nz/rowancottage.html

Double $90 Single $60 (Continental Breakfast)
Dinner $25pp
1 Double 2 Single (2 bdrm)
1 Guests share

Rowan Cottage is situated in a quiet tree lined street
with views to the mountains and hills. We are 10 minutes
walk to the town and 20 minutes drive to Queenstown. We have a lovely cottage garden to relax and
have coffee and homemade goodies. We are well travelled and can advise you on things to see and do
in our beautiful part of the country. Guests comments: Wonderful Hospitality - Very Comfortable -
Excellent Breakfasts.

Arrowtown   *Homestay Arrowtown*

Arrowtown Homestay
Anne & Arthur Gormack
18 Stafford Street, Arrowtown,

Tel (03) 442 1747   0800 184 990   Fax (03) 442 1787
agormack@xtra.co.nz
www.bnb.co.nz/arrowtownhomestay.html

Double $100 (Continental Breakfast)
1 King 2 Single (2 bdrm)
2 Ensuite

Our spacious home overlooking Millbrook Country Club
and the Wakatipu Basin, offers spectacular views from every window. Although only 5 minutes walk
from the town centre, our outlook is totally rural. We have a warm and comfortable home, and during
the Summer hope you will join us for a glass of wine beside our heated swimming pool.   Free use of
laundry. Freephone: 0800 184 990 PS In September 2003 we will have a new home on the same
property. Details as above.

Arrowtown   *B&B Separate/Suite B&B Lodge Arrowtown Central*

Arrowtown Lodge & Hiking Co
John & Margaret Wilson
7 Anglesea Street, Arrowtown

Tel (03) 442 1101   0800 258 802   Fax (03) 442 1108
hiking@queenstown.co.nz
www.arrowtownlodge.co.nz

Double $130-$180 Single $80-$120 (Full Breakfast)
Credit cards accepted Children welcome
2 King/Twin 2 Queen (4 bdrm)
4 Ensuite

Located in the historic part of Arrowtown. Arrowtown Lodge and Hiking Company is only 200 metres
from the centre of the village where guests can enjoy a good selection of restaurants, cafes and pubs.
Arrowtown Lodge is built in the old style using schist and mud brick. The four cottage style suites have
king or queen size beds, TV, tea and coffee making facilities, hair driers, heated floors, guest phones,
private guest entrance and off street car parking. Children welcome. Ancient Labrador resident. Guided
walks available.

Arrowtown *B&B Self-contained 2min Central Arrowtown*

Arrowtown Old Nick
Marie & Steve Waterhouse
70 Buckingham Street, Arrowtown,
Tel (03) 442 0066   0800 653 642   Fax (03) 442 0066
Mob 021 2585545
host@oldnick.co.nz   www.oldnick.co.nz

Double $120-$150   Single $90-$120   (Full Breakfast)
Child on application Children welcome Pets welcome
3 SuperKing/Twin 1 King (4 bdrm)
3 Ensuite 1 Private   Credit cards accepted

The Old Nick' was built in 1902 as the original residence & office of Arrowtown's police. By the late 1950s the residence was retired from active duty.

In 1995, transformation to lodgings of a more luxurious and inviting kind began, and today the original historic house set amidst Oak and Sycamore trees on a large lawn and gardens has become a place where people escape to (rather than from)!

Inside the main residence is one room with King bed that has a private bathroom across the hallway complete with spa bath, fluffy towels, toiletries and hair dryers. Adjoining the main house on the site where the police horses were once housed is 'The Stables', with a choice of three Super King/Twin rooms, all with ensuites.

They say the heart of any home is the kitchen and The Old Nick has a huge, warm heart indeed. Its sumptuous breakfasts are reason alone to stay here.

You could forego all the activities this region offers and head straight for the lounge. Surrounded by local artwork, it's here that you can sink into a deep leather sofa in front of the open fire with a good book or good friend.

If the lure of the great outdoors is too much, you can throw yourself into activities that have made this part of the world famous or you can explore historic sites like the disused jail that stands on the adjoining property or spend time strolling through Arrowtown or Queenstown sampling various shopping & restaurants/cafes.

Share our hospitality with our 6 year old son Daniel and our outside dog - Halifax.

Arrowtown *Self-contained Arrowtown Central*

Pam Miller
23 Berkshire Street,
Arrowtown
Tel (03) 442 1126
www.bnb.co.nz/miller.html
Double $95 Single $80 (Full Breakfast)
1 Queen (1 bdrm)
1 Private

You will be made very welcome at my home which is centrally located on the main road, entering Arrowtown from Queenstown. I am three blocks from the Arrowtown village centre. My accommodation for guests has a private entrance, double bedroom, small sitting room with TV and tea/coffee making facilities. Also a private bathroom with laundry facilities. Delicious continental or full breakfast is served in the dining room upstairs. Off street parking. Only 20 minutes drive to Queenstown.

Arrowtown - Queenstown *B&B Homestay 11km N of Queenstown*

Birchwood
Richard and Lynne Farrar
78 Lower Shotover Road, RD 1, Queenstown
Tel (03) 442 3499 0800 36 45 50 Fax (03) 442 3498
bnb@birchwood.net.nz
www.birchwood.net.nz
Double $125-$155 Single $100 (Full Breakfast)
Child 1/2 price Credit cards accepted
1 King 1 Double 2 Single (3 bdrm)
1 Ensuite 1 Private

You are warmly invited to stay with us in our modern, classic style country home set in a sunny, sheltered two acre garden. Relax in a private, tranquil setting or enjoy a game of tennis on our court. The house is single storeyed with good access and easy parking. There is a spacious, elegant guest room (ensuite) with its own entrance, and a choice of twin or double bedroom. Located halfway between Arrowtown and Queenstown. Nearby attractions include cafes, restaurants, wineries, skifields and golf courses. Come and enjoy this unique area.

Queenstown *B&B Self-contained 1.5km E of Queenstown Central*

Braemar House
Ann & Duncan Wilson
56 Panorama Terrace, Queenstown
Tel (03) 442 7385 Fax (03) 442 4385
Mob 025 651 1035
www.bnb.co.nz/braemarhouse.html
Double $105 Single $70 (Full Breakfast)
Child 1/2 price
1 Double 1 Single (1 bdrm)
1 Private

Our apartment is fully self-contained and occupies the middle floor of our home. A full breakfast is supplied if requested for $105 (double) or for the apartment only the tariff is $90. We have other beds available for groups of more than two people. There is a panoramic view of Lake Wakatipu and the surrounding mountains from the visitor's balcony and all rooms. Directions: Turn up Suburb Street off Frankton Road, then first right into Panorama Tce.

Arrowtown - Queenstown   *B&B Separate/Suite S/C 4km W of Arrowtown*

Willowbrook
Tamaki & Roy Llewellyn
Malaghan Road, RD 1, Queenstown

Tel (03) 442 1773   Fax (03) 442 1773   Mob 025 516 739
info@willowbrook.net.nz   www.willowbrook.net.nz

Double $130-$150 Single $105-$125
(Continental Breakfast) Credit cards accepted
2 King 2 Queen 3 Twin (7 bdrm)
5 Ensuite 1 Private

Willowbrook is a 1914 homestead at the foot of Coronet Peak in the beautiful Wakatipu Basin. The setting is rural, historical and distinctly peaceful, and with the attractions of Queenstown and Arrowtown only 15 and 5 minutes away respectively, Willowbrook can truly claim to offer the best of both worlds.   Four acres of mature garden contain a tennis court, luxurious spa pool and several outhouses.

The former 'Shearers Quarters' have been rebuilt and a hay barn renovated allowing Willowbrook to offer varied styles of accommodation. Bed and Breakfast in the *Old Farmhouse:* centrally heated double rooms, ensuite bathrooms, guest lounge with open fires and Sky TV.
The Barn: offers spacious ensuite accommodation separate from the main house. Super king bed (bunks for children), gas heating, fridge, TV. Annex available for extra members of same party. *The Cottage:* is a delightfully cosy two bedroom cottage with full kitchen

and laundry facilities. Ensuite bathrooms, underfloor heating, spacious sundecks and private lawn. Willowbrook is within easy reach of four ski fields and three picturesque golf courses. Kate and Allan are your hosts. Expect a warm welcome, friendly advice and traditional South Island hospitality.

Directions: We are on Malaghan Road (the 'back road' between Queenstown and Arrowtown). From Queenstown, take Gorge Road out through Arthurs Point, make no turns and after about 15 minutes, look for our sign on your right. From the north, turn right at Lake Hayes, go five kilometres and turn left into Malaghan Road (the sign says "Queenstown via Coronet Peak"). Millbrook Resort is on your left and we are three and a half kilometres further along the road, also on the left.

Queenstown   *Semi self contained 8km NE of Queenstown*

Collins Homestay
Pat & Ron Collins
Grant Road, RD 1, Queenstown

Tel (03) 442 3801 rcollins@queenstown.co.nz
www.bnb.co.nz/collins.html

Double $100-$120 Single $80 Credit cards accepted
2 Queen 2 Single (3 bdrm)
1 Ensuite 1 Private

Relaxed kiwi hospitality in rural environment with
mountain views , lovely gardens. Accommodation:
GARDEN COTTAGE with queen bed, ensuite, patio; GUEST WING, queen or twin, private bathroom.
Laundry facilities. Able to help with sightseeing arrangements. Our interests are golf, gardening,
family, fishing and walking our dog Meg   Directions: Grant Rd sign on Mailbox on S.H. 6 from North
2 km before Frankton. From South right at Frankton on S.H. 6 to Grant Rd 2 km on gravel Rd left turn.
2nd house end of lane.

Queenstown   *B&B Self-contained Queenstown Central*

Birchall House
Joan & John Blomfield
118 Panorama Terrace, Larchwood Heights,
Queenstown

Tel (03) 442 9985 Fax (03) 442 9980
birchall.house@xtra.co.nz   www.zqn.co.nz/birchall

Double $130-$145 Single $100-$110 (Full Breakfast)
Child $40 Children welcome
1 King/Twin 1 Queen (2 bdrm) 1 Private

Welcome to our new home in Queenstown, purpose
built to accommodate guests in a beautiful setting. At Birchall House, you enjoy a magnificent 200
degree view of Lake Wakatipu and surrounding mountains, and are within walking distance of town
centre. Our guest accommodation is spacious, private with separate entrance, centrally heated, smoke-
free, electric blankets on all beds. A continental or cooked breakfast is available. From Frankton Road,
turn up Hensman Road, then left into Sunset Lane. Or from Frankton Road, turn up Suburb Street, then
first right into Panorama Terrace. Access via Sunset Lane. Off street parking. We invite you to visit our
website at: www.zqn.co.nz/birchall

Queenstown   *Guesthouse 0.8km*

Scallywags Guesthouse
Evan Jenkins
27 Lomond Cresent, Queenstown

Tel (03) 442 7083 Fax (03) 442 5885
www.bnb.co.nz/scallywagsguesthouse.html

Double $58 Single $55 Children welcome
3 Queen 3 Twin (6 bdrm)
2 Guests share

A unique New Zealand home for you to share. We are a "B&B with no B". However bring your own
food and use the excellent kitchen and great BBQ area. Tea, coffee and milk are complimentary. Linen,
towels, duvets and electric blankets are on all beds. Share excellent new bathroom facilities. Fantastic
views - 180 degrees panorama - sunrise to sunset - lake, mountains, valleys. The ambience is casual and
informal. Enjoy company and conversation with other travellers. The house is situated adjacent to a
bush reserve with native bird life and song abundant. A peaceful haven just 10 minutes pleasant walk to
village centre.

Queenstown
Bed & Breakfast
NUMBER 12
.... a quiet convenient location

Queenstown   *B&B Homestay Self-contained Queenstown Central*

Number Twelve
Barbara & Murray Hercus
12 Brisbane Street, Queenstown
Tel (03) 442 9511 Fax (03) 442 9755
hercusbb@queenstown.co.nz
www.number12bb.co.nz
Double $120-$130 Single $90-$100
Credit cards accepted
2 King 2 Twin (2 bdrm)
1 Ensuite 1 Private

We would like you to come and share our conveniently situated house in a no exit street. You only have a 5 minute stroll to the town centre.

Our home has mountain and lake views. Our home is warm and sunny, windows double glazed and we have central heating for the winter months. Our bedrooms have TVs, coffee/tea making facilities, hair dryers and instant heaters. Our studio apartment has full kitchen facilities. Email & laundry is available.

We have a solar heated swimming pool (Dec/March) the sun deck and BBQ are for your use. Our sun room is available for your comfort.

Guests have the choice of either a full or continental breakfast in our dining room with its panoramic views. Once settled in you will seldom need to use your car again. There are several easy walking routes into the town centre, restaurants, shops and tourist centres. We are very close to the lake and our botanical gardens.

Whilst you are with us we will be happy to advise on tourist activities and sightseeing and make any arrangements you would wish. Barbara has a nursing/social work background and Murray is a retired chartered accountant. We have travelled extensively within our country and overseas. We have an interest in classical/choral music.

Directions:
Highway 6a into Queenstown - the Millennium Hotel will be on your right, do NOT turn right at the sign Town Centre but continue straight ahead Brisbane St is second on the left and we are on the left.

464

Queenstown   *Homestay   Queenstown Central*

The Stable
Isobel & Gordon McIntyre
17 Brisbane Street, Queenstown

Tel (03) 442 9251   Fax (03) 442 8293

gimac@queenstown.co.nz
www.thestablebb.com

Double $160-$180 Single $120
(Full Breakfast) Credit cards accepted
1 king/twin 1 double (2 bedrooms)
1 ensuite 1 private

A 130 year old stone stable, converted for guest accommodation, and listed by the New Zealand Historic Places Trust, shares a private courtyard with our home.

The **"Garden Room"** is in the house, providing convenience and comfort with lake and mountain views. Our home is in a quiet cul-de-sac and set in a garden abundant with rhododendrons and native birds. It is less than 100 metres from the beach where a small boat and canoe are available for guests' use.

The famous Kelvin Heights Golf Course is close and tennis courts, bowling greens and ice skating rink are in the adjacent park. All tourist facilities, shops and restaurants are within easy walking distance, less than 5 minutes stroll on well lit footpaths. Both rooms are well heated with views of garden, lake or mountains. Tea and coffee making facilities are available at all times.

Guests share our spacious living areas and make free use of our library and laundry. A courtesy car is available to and from the bus depots. We can advise about and are booking agents for all sightseeing tours. Do allow an extra day or two for all the activities in the Queenstown region.

No smoking indoors. Your hosts, with a farming background, have bred Welsh ponies and now enjoy weaving, cooking, gardening, sailing and the outdoors.

We have an interest in a successful vineyard and enjoy drinking and talking about wine. We enjoy meeting people and have travelled extensively overseas.

Directions:
Follow State Highway 6a (Frankton Road) to where it veers right at the Millenium Hotel. Continue straight ahead. Brisbane Street ("no exit") is 2nd on left. Phone for help if necessary.

OTAGO, NORTH CATLINS

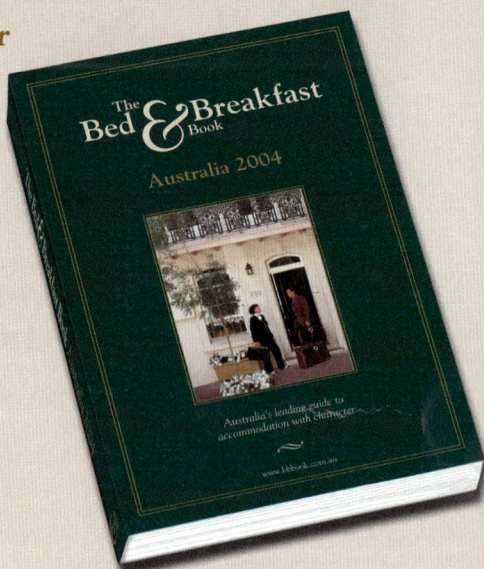

Queenstown Central   *Separate/Suite Boutique Hotel 200m N of Queenstown*

Queenstown House
69 Hallenstein Street, Queenstown
Tel (03) 442 9043   Fax (03) 442 8755
queenstown.house@xtra.co.nz
www.queenstownhouse.co.nz

Double $250-$595 Single $225 (Special Breakfast)
Credit cards accepted
10 King/Twin 4 Queen (14 bdrm)
14 Ensuite

Our unique B&B Hotel is celebrating 21 years, with further refurbishment in 2002 and the addition of 4 new rooms plus two luxurious suites.Magestic lake and mountain views.Delux breakfast menu and pre dinner hospitality is included.Relax in the fireside sitting rooms or outdoor patios enjoying our beautiful roses.Guest laundry,bag and car storage available. Hospitality and ambience specialists. 'Your memories make us famous'.

Queenstown   *B&B 800m Queenstown*

Monaghans
Elsie & Pat Monaghan
4 Panorama Terrace, Queenstown
Tel (03) 442 8690   Fax (03) 442 8620
patmonaghan@xtra.co.nz
www.bnb.co.nz/monaghans.html

Double $100 Single $85 (Continental Breakfast)
1 Queen (1 bdrm)
1 Ensuite

Welcome to our home in a quiet location, walking distance to town. Enjoy this panoramic view while you breakfast. One couple - personal attention. Spacious comfortable room with separate entrance and garden patio. Queen bed, own bathroom, TV, fridge and tea/coffee biscuits. Interests - music, gardening, sport, travel. We will enjoy your company but respect your privacy. Off street parking. Airport and bus transfers. Directions: turn right up Suburb Street off Frankton Road which is the main road into Queenstown then first right into Panorama Terrace.

Queenstown   *B&B 3km W of Queenstown*

Haus Helga
Helga & Ed Coolman
107 Wynyard Crescent, Fernhill, Queenstown
Tel (03) 442 6077   Fax (03) 442 4957
haushelga@xtra.co.nz
www.bnb.co.nz/haushelga.html

Double $225-$330 (Special Breakfast) Child $30
Extra adult $60 Credit cards accepted
2 King/Twin 2 Queen 2 Single (4 bdrm)
4 Ensuite 4 Private

Haus Helga overlooks Lake Wakatipu and the Remarkables Mountains and provides the "best view in all of New Zealand". Our luxurious home has extra large tastefully furnished guest rooms, each with a private deck or terrace. The self-contained suite includes a large kitchen/living/dining room. Our Voglauer guest room includes hand painted Austrian furniture and an ensuite with corner spa bath. We are now in our eighth year in operation and feel truly fortunate to have made so many great new friends, our wonderful guests.

Queenstown   *Self-contained Queenstown Central*

Anna's Cottage & Rose Suite
Myrna & Ken Sangster
67 Thompson Street, Queenstown

Tel (03) 442 8994   Fax (03) 441 8994
Mob 025 693 3025
www.bnb.co.nz/annascottage.html

Double $120-$145 Single $90
Continental breakfast available $10
Credit cards accepted
1 King/Twin 2 Queen (2 bdrm) 2 Private

A warm welcome to Anna's Cottage. Myrna a keen gardener and golfer, Ken with a love of fishing. Enjoy the peaceful garden setting and mountain views. Full kitchen facilities and living room combined. Washing machine. Tastefully decorated throughout, the bedroom is furnished with Sheridan linen. Only a few minutes from the centre of Queenstown. Private drive and parking at cottage. Attached to the end of our home The Rose Suite, self-contained, 1 Queen bed with ensuite, small kitchen, washing machine, furnished with Sheridan linen.

Queenstown   *B&B & Self-contained 1.5km NE of Queenstown*

Campbells B&B
Ruth Campbell
10 Wakatipu Heights, Queenstown

Tel (03) 442 9190   Fax (03) 442 4404
Mob 021 116 8801   roosterretreat@xtra.co.nz
www.bnb.co.nz/campbell.html

Double $120 Single $80 (Continental Breakfast)
S/C unit $250 Credit cards accepted Children welcome
1 King/Twin 1 Queen 1 Double 1 Single (3 bdrm)
2 Private 1 Guests share

Our two girls, cat, bantams and doves welcome other children to share their playground. This tranquil home with off street parking has outstanding views over Lake Wakatipu and Queenstown. The fully self-contained two bedroom cottage garden unit with full kitchen and laundry facilities has proved immensely popular with guests - especially those with children. Includes breakfast. A super king or twin room with private bathroom is in the house. Enjoy a generous continental breakfast including fresh baked bread and real coffee at your leisure. Complimentary tea/coffee and also laundry facilities. Guests say "Excellent value for money!"

Queenstown   *B&B Homestay Queenstown Central*

Larch Hill Home-stay B&B
Maria & Chris Lamens
16 Panners Way, Goldfields, Queenstown

Tel (03) 442 4811   Fax (03) 441 8882
info@larchhill.com www.larchhill.com

Double $110-$150 Single $100 (Special Breakfast)
Dinner $55 Apartment (twin share) $170 - $240
Credit cards Visa/MC
2 King 1 Queen 1 Twin 2 Single (4 bdrm)
2 Ensuite 2 Private

A warm welcome awaits you at Larch Hill. Our comfortable and relaxing homestay is just three minutes drive from the centre of town. Public transport stops at the drive way. All rooms have lake and mountain views. In winter there is a roaring log-fire awaiting your return from a days skiing or sightseeing. Maria provides three course dinners by prior arrangement. We have pleasure in organising any Queenstown experiences. We speak Italian, German and Dutch. Directions: from HW6a turn into Goldfield Heights at Sherwood Manor. Second left is Panners Way.

Queenstown   *B&B 500m N of Queenstown*

Chalet Queenstown
Gillian & Kel Frame
1 Dublin Street, Queenstown,

Tel (03) 442 7117   0800 222 457   Fax (03) 442 7508
chalet.queenstown@xtra.co.nz
www.chalet.co.nz

Double $125-$185 Single $89-$149
(Continental Breakfast) Triple $150 - $210
5 King/Twin 1 Queen 1 Single (6 bdrm)
6 Ensuite

You will love the location of Chalet Queenstown, a sunny site 500m from the Central PO and Botanical Gardens. An easy stroll will bring you to the lakeside walking track, and the Millenium walk on Queenstown Hill is also on our doorstep.

Gillian and Kel have been involved in the tourism industry for many years and have a thorough knowledge of Queenstown and surrounds. We enjoy meeting people, golf, scrabble, yoga and books.

Our well appointed rooms all have views of lake and/or mountains, ensuite facilities(shower), T.V, refrigerator, tea and coffee, hair dryer, oil heating, electric blankets, lovely linen and and super comfortable beds where a good nights sleep is assured.

We endeavour to provide guests with wholesome organic and preservative-free food and beverages. You will enjoy the hearty continental breakfast consisting of lots of fresh fruit, organic and flavoured yoghurts, your choice of milk, home made muesli, seeds, nuts and dried fruits, 100% juices, fresh baked croissants, cereals, toast, tea, good quality coffee and herbal teas.

Other features of our home:
- Complimentary mountain bike use
- Off-street parking
- Relaxed and friendly atmosphere
- Second hand book shop on site
- Laundry facilities (charge)
- Filtered water

We are happy to assist with all your reservations for activities and onward bookings through the NZ B&B book. Seasonal rates apply.

Queenstown *B&B & Homestay Apartments 0.8km NW of Central Queenstown*

Coronet View Homestay Apartments and B&B
Karen, Neil, Dawn & Warrick
28-30 Huff Street
Apartments 1, 2, 3, 4, 19a Adelaide Street
Tel (03) 442 6766 Fax (03) 442 6767
Mob 0274 320 895
stay@coronetview.com
www.coronetview.com

Double $100-$260
Child POA Children welcome
(Continental Full Special Breakfast)
Dinner $25 - $70
Apartment bedroom From $130 - $600
Credit cards accepted
Smoking area inside
8 King/Twin 1 Queen 1 Twin (10 bdrm)
9 Ensuite 1 Private

We warmly welcome you to both our Luxury Homestay and B&B located in the heart of Queenstown, with panoramic views over Queenstown, Lake Wakatipu, Coronet Peak and The Remarkables Mountain Range.

Let us help organise your day's activities so you can get the most out of Queenstown, New Zealand's adventure capital.

Have a spa/jacuzzi, swim in the pool or just relax. Enjoy the bakery breakfast freshly baked from our own bakery. Friendly Persian cats on property.

Directions: Less than 1km from central Queenstown, 10 minutes walk, 2 minutes by car.

Queenstown - Glenorchy *B&B Homestay 40mins Queenstown*

Lake Haven
Ronda & John
Benmore Place, Glenorchy

Tel (03) 442 9091   Fax (03) 442 9801
lakehaven@xtra.co.nz
www.bnb.co.nz/lakehaven.html

Double $120 Single $80 (Full Breakfast)
Child by arrangement Dinner by arrangement
Credit cards accepted Children welcome
2 King 1 Twin (3 bdrm)
3 Ensuite

Lake Haven offers quality accommodation and warm hospitality at our secluded Lakefront property with stunning lake and bush clad mountain views. Glenorchy is the base for several world famous walking tracks eg, Routeburn, renowned for its Trout fishing and a large range of activities. Ronda and John are longtime locals and are happy to assist you in exploring and enjoying our unique and beautiful area. Children welcome. Laundry facilities. Fishing guide available. Glenorchy - Gateway to paradise.

Queenstown *B&B Separate/Suite Boutique Hotel 300m NW of Queenstown*

Browns Boutique Hotel
Bridget & Nigel Brown
26 Isle Street, Queenstown

Tel (03) 441 2050   Fax (03) 441 2060
Mob 025 222 0681   stay@brownshotel.co.nz
www.brownshotel.co.nz

Double $220-$240 Single $180-$200
(Continental Breakfast) Credit cards accepted
10 King/Twin (10 bdrm) 10 Ensuite

Browns Boutique Hotel was opened in August 2000.
Located only two blocks walk from downtown
Queenstown with views over Queenstown Bay to the
Remarkables. Every guest room is well appointed, spacious and boasts a super king size bed along with French doors opening onto balconies over the courtyard. All rooms have their own generous sized ensuite including showers and baths. The bathrooms are fully tiled and feature Italian and German fittings.

Queenstown *Homestay*

Delfshaven
Irene Mertz
11 Salmond Place (off Kent Street), Queenstown,

Tel (03) 441 1447   Fax (03) 441 1383
Mob 025 659 2609   www.bnb.co.nz/mertz.html

Double $165 Single $150 (Special Breakfast)
Credit cards accepted
1 Double (1 bdrm)
1 Private

Nestled at the base of Queenstown is my sunny warm
modern home, offering magnificent unobstructed 180
degree views over town, lake and mountains. The comfortable guest room, with its own TV and tea-making facilities, opens out to the garden and those beautiful views. It is only a five minute downhill walk to the town. I am a retired teacher, widely travelled, enjoy good food and wine, love art, music and enjoy meeting people. A piano is waiting to be played. Welcome to Salmond Place.

Queenstown *B&B Homestay Country Stay, Dinners 10km W of Queenstown*

Saxony Downs High Country Stay
Sandra & Ray Drayton
Moke Lake Road, Queenstown
Tel (03) 442 5389 Fax (03) 442 5322
mail@saxonydowns.co.nz
www.saxonydowns.co.nz

Double $130 Single $80 (Special Breakfast)
Child N/A Dinner from $45 pp
1 Queen 1 Twin (2 bdrm)
1 Private

A world of mountain walks amidst alpine flora, birdlife, native beech forest and stunning mountain views. Relaxed seclusion on 23 acres bordering two high country farm stations, 10 minutes from town. Seven walking tracks, trout fishing on three alpine lakes nearby. Mountain bikes and fishing tackle available for guests' use. Guided walks available. Gourmet dinners with wine. Our valley contains one of 'Lord of the Rings' film sites. Ray, Sandra and our country cat Eric assure guests of a quality relaxing Alpine experience.

Queenstown *B&B 800m Queenstown central*

Balmoral Lodge
Les Walker
24 York Street, Queenstown,
Tel (03) 442 7209 Fax (03) 442 6499
balmoral.lodge@xtra.co.nz
www.zqnbalmoral.co.nz

Double $250 Single $195-$225 (Full Breakfast)
two bedroom suite $295 Children welcome
10 King/Twin 2 King 2 Queen (4 bdrm)
4 Ensuite

Balmoral Lodge provides luxury bed & breakfast. It is situated on Queenstown Hill just 800 metres from the town centre. Spectacular panoramic lake, mountain and township views from all rooms including exterior decks. Lavishly decorated. All rooms have ensuite bathrooms, baths with showers. Some have spa baths. Family suite shower only. Fridge and coffee-making. Full breakfast. Off-street parking. Laundry facilities. Honeymoon suite. Gracious hospitality.

Queenstown *B&B Homestay self contained guest wing 14km 14 of Queenstown*

Kahu Rise
Angela & Bill Dolan
455 Littles Road, RD1, Queenstown
Tel (03) 441 2077 0800 436 111 Fax (03) 441 2078
info@kahurise.co.nz
www.kahurise.co.nz

Double $170 (Full Breakfast)
1 Queen 2 Twin (2 bdrm)
1 Private

In the country, yet close to Queenstown, Arrowtown and local attractions, Kahu Rise offers both tranquility and convenience. We cater only for single party bookings (1-4). Our guest wing has a private bathroom, underfloor heating, tea and coffee facilities, refrigerator, TV, hairdryer, etc. Both rooms have mountain views and open directly on to the lawn. We prepare you a delicious home-cooked breakfast each morning and will advise on and book activities. Bill, Angela and Tess, our friendly dog, warmly welcome you.

Queenstown *B&B Self-contained Queenstown Central*

Cameo Cottage
John and Jean Lindsay
41 Goldfield Heights Road, Queenstown,

Tel (03) 442 5649   Fax (03) 442 5684
cameo_cottage@hotmail.com
www.bnb.co.nz/cameocottage.html

Double $120-$160 Single $90 (Continental Breakfast)
Child $30 self contained cottage $180 - $240
2 King 1 Single (2 bdrm)

Welcome to Cameo Cottage where you will experience real home comforts, with warm friendly atmosphere. Just 10 minutes from central Queenstown with an idealic view of Deer Park Heights and the Remarkable Mountains. We are close to all amenities and tourist attractions. We offer good hearty breakfasts, child safe facilities and equipment, complimentary laundry, ample off street parking. Rooms are serviced daily. John and I have been involved in the tourism industry for over 27 years and really love sharing our home and meeting people from all walks of life.

Queenstown *B&B Homestay 1.3km Queenstown*

Matterhorn Chalet
Maria & Joe Arnold
20 Wakatipu Heights, Queenstown,

Tel (03) 441 3935   Fax (03) 441 3935
Mob 021 951 577   dutch.swiss.kiwi@xtra.co.nz
www.matterhornchalet.com

Double $170-$190 (Special Breakfast)
2 King 2 Queen 2 Single (4 bdrm)
1 Ensuite

Imagine a European alpine lodge magically moved to the shores of Lake Wakatipu. Matterhorn Chalet is a luxury B&B with views as breath-taking as any in Europe (all rooms have lake views). Only 12 minutes walk to the bustling heart of downtown Queenstown. For peace and tranquility stay; this is the place for you. Great breakfasts. Maria and Joe speak English, Swiss, German and Dutch. For the most panorama views over Remarkables and Lake Wakatipu We provide a courtesy shuttle to Queenstown Airport.

Queenstown *Separate/Suite Boutique Accommodation 100m Queenstown*

The Dairy Guest House
Andrew & Claire Brinsley
10 Isle Street, Queenstown

Tel (03) 442 5164   0800 33 33 93   Fax (03) 442 5164
Mob 025 204 2585   info@thedairy.co.nz
www.bnb.co.nz/hosts/thedairy.html

Double $270-$325 (Full Breakfast)
Credit cards accepted
9 King/Twin 2 Queen (11 bdrm)   11 Ensuite

Discover a luxury Bed & Breakfast that offers the relaxed and comfortable hospitality of the Southern Alps of NZ, just 150 metres form the historic centre of Queenstown. The Dairy Guesthouse has 11 private rooms with en-suite, two lounge rooms, one with wood fire, separate TV lounge, ski storage, 6-seater hydrotherapy spa, and parking. Its focus is an original 1920's general store - from which the guesthouse takes its name. Begin each day with a sumptuous breakfast served in the Old Dairy from where you can view the beautiful surrounding mountains. NZ Tourism Awards Finalist 2001 and 2002. No children under 12 please.

Queenstown   *B&B Self-contained 10km E of Queenstown*

Milestone
Betty & John Turnbull
Ladies Mile, RD1, SH6, Queenstown

Tel (03) 441 4460   Fax (03) 441 4460
  jcturnbull@xtra.co.nz
www.themilestone.co.nz

Double $165-$225 Single $125-$165
(Special Breakfast) Dinner B/A Children welcome
3 Queen (3 bdrm)
2 Ensuite 1 Private

Milestone is an architecturally designed quality home built in 2001 of local Queenstown schist and set in three acres of informal gardens. Situated on the main highway - SH6 - it is just 10 minutes from either historic Arrowtown or Queenstown and nestles in the Wakatipu basin. The views or Coronet Peak, the Remarkables and the Crown Range are spectacular, and it is close to three ski fields and four golf courses.

Visitors can opt for relaxing pursuits or serious adventure activities, including rafting, jetboating, ballooning, paragliding, horse trekking, etc. As an experienced tramper and climber, John can suggest a gentle walk or a more energetic tramp or climb, or a good fishing river. Flights and rides can be arranged - it is no problem.

Guests are equally as welcome to spend time in the garden, and to share the passion Betty and John have for their trees, shrubs, roses and ponds. They may relax in the summer house or gazebo, or watch the deer and sheep grazing over the fence. Or they are welcome to take the two elderly dogs - labrador Kali and Dalmation Kachina, for a stroll.

Milestone is a four minute drive from the airport, the closest tavern and restaurant and the supermarket, and 10 minutes from award-winning eating establishments, two casinos, boutique shopping and Queenstown's nightlife.

The rooms are warm and well appointed with antique furniture, televisions, tea and coffee making facilities, robes and fresh flowers. The schist cottage is adjacent to the house - beside the orchard, and is self-contained with a divan couch in the living room for an extra guest. This is a great honeymoon hideaway - most appropriate as Betty is a marriage celebrant and has married couples amongst the roses and beside the waterfall. She is also a craft teacher and has been teaching porcelain doll making for 25 years. At Milestone guests are offered luxury, romance, privacy and peace along with southern hospitality.

Garston *B&B Homestay Self-contained 50km S of Queenstown*

Bev & Matt Menlove
17 Blackmore Road, Private Bag, Garston 9660
Tel (03) 248 8516 mattmenlove@xtra.co.nz
www.bnb.co.nz/menlove.html

Double $80 Single $50 (Continental Breakfast)
Dinner $25 by arrangement
1 Double 1 Single (1 bdrm)
1 Ensuite

We are organic gardeners and our other interests include lawn bowls, sailing, gliding and alternative energy. Garston is New Zealand's most inland village with the Mataura River (famous for its fly fishing) flowing through the valley, surrounded by the Hector Range and the Eyre Mountains. A fishing guide is available with advance notice. For day trips, Garston is central to Queenstown, Te Anau, Milford Sound or Invercargill. We look forward to meeting you.

Alexandra - Earnscleugh *Orchardstay 6km W of Alexandra*

Iversen
Robyn & Roger Marshall
47 Blackman Road, RD 1 Alexandra, Central Otago
Tel (03) 449 2520 Fax (03) 449 2519
Mob 025 384 348 r.r.marshall@xtra.co.nz
www.bnb.co.nz/iversen.html

Double $110 Single $70 (Continental Breakfast)
Child by arrangement Dinner $25 by arrangement
Credit cards accepted
2 Queen (2 bdrm)
1 Guests share

Our self-contained guest accommodation offers you privacy and comfort. Combined with a warm welcome into our home, you can share with us, the peaceful and relaxing setting our our cherry orchard. While at Iversen , you can experience the grandeur and contrasts of the Central Otago landscape, walk the thyme covered hills, visit local wineries or just relax. Directions: From Alexandra or Clyde, travel on Earnscleugh Road, turn into Blackman Road and look for our sign on the left. Advanced bookings preferred.

Alexandra *B&B Vineyard Homestay 6km N of Alexandra*

Hawkdun Rise Vineyard Stay
Judy & Roy Faris
Hawkdun Rise, Letts Gully Road,
Alexandra, Central Otago
Tel (03) 448 7782 Fax (03) 448 7752
Mob 025 337 072 rfaris@clear.net.nz
www.vineyardstay.co.nz

Double $125 Single $90 (Full Breakfast)
Credit cards accepted
2 Queen 1 Double (3 bdrm)
2 Ensuite 1 Guests share

Welcome to our new home set in a small productive vineyard with commanding views of the surrounding hills. Accommodation is semi-detached and we are a professional couple with grown family now sharing our home with a Burmese cat. We can assist with wine trail tours, rail trail adventure, golf, fishing and 4WD overland trips. Visit us if you are looking for privacy, tranquillity and executive accommodation.

Alexandra - Central Otago   *Homestay 3.5km N of Alexandra*

Duart
Mary & Keith McLean
Bruce's Hill Lane, Rapid No. 356,
Highway 85, RD 3, Alexandra
Tel (03) 448 9190   Fax (03) 448 9190
duart.homestay@xtra.co.nz   www.duarthomestay.co.nz

Double $90 Single $70 (Continental Breakfast)
Child $50 Dinner $25 b/a Smoking area inside
1 Double 1 Twin 1 Single (3 bdrm)
1 Ensuite

Your accredited Kiwi hosts, Mary and Keith, welcome you to our secluded home, 5 minutes from Alexandra. Your privacy is assured, but we enjoy company and conversation if that is your wish. Relish the spectacular views from our extensive stone terraced garden, or relax on the verandahs, sitting room or library. Revel in the myriad activities and experiences Alexander offers; we pick you up from the Rail Trail, bus depot, Grape Escape. Laundry, Sky TV, complimentary tea, coffee, biscuits, fruit anytime. Complimentary pre-dinner drink and nibbles. Children and pets welcome.

Alexandra   *B&B 1km Alexandra*

Evelyn & Hugh Smith
22 Craig Place, Alexandra
Tel (03) 448 9268   Mob 025 614 9161
www.bnb.co.nz/alexandra.html

Double $75 Single $35 (Continental Breakfast)
Child $15
1 Double 1 Twin (2 bdrm)
1 Ensuite

We would like to welcome you to our modern sunny home Bridgehill. We are the closest B&B to Alexandra only one kilometre away. Hugh and I had a B&B in Clyde for many years and we enjoy meeting people.
Beautiful garden, unique scenery, orchards and vineyards nearby. One hour's drive from Queenstown, Wanaka. There are many restaurants locally. A warm welcome awaits you from our small dachshund called Bradley. We would all like to meet you.

Roxburgh - Millers Flat   *B&B 16km S of Roxburgh*

The Studio
Sheena & Wallace Boag
Millers Flat, RD 2, Roxburgh, Central Otago
Tel (03) 446 6872   Fax (03) 446 6872
www.bnb.co.nz/thestudio.html

Double $75 Single $45 (Continental Breakfast)
Child $20 Dinner $20 by arrangement
double bed settee (upstairs)   Credit cards accepted
2 Single (1 bdrm)
1 Ensuite

An easy 2-hour drive from Dunedin, Wanaka, Queenstown and Invercargill, Millers Flat is an attractive village in farming and fruitgrowing country, well-equipped with recreational facilities, easy access to fishing, walking tracks, gardens to visit, and the well-known community-owned store, "Faigan's". We live on 10 acres in a 110 year old house of rammed-earth construction. Our guest accommodation is a 2-storey building of more recent vintage, formerly Wallace's architectural studio, an interesting composition of space and light, comfortably-heated, with tea/coffee making facilities. Please phone ahead for directions.

Roxburgh - Ettrick *B&B Farmstay Self-contained 10km S of Roxburgh*

Clearburn Station
Margaret & Ian Lambeth
Dalmuir Road, RD 2, Roxburgh

Tel (03) 446 6712   Fax (03) 446 6774
JL.Lambeth@xtra.co.nz
www.bnb.co.nz/clearburnstation.html

Double $85 Single $50 (Continental Breakfast)
Child by arrangement Dinner $20 by arrangement
2 Single (1 bdrm)
1 Ensuite

Clearburn Station is a 5000 acre property with a Homestead Block and Hill Country Run stocked with sheep and cattle and operated as a family partnership with son John and his wife Linda and children. Guest accommodation is a detached self-contained unit with electric blankets, heaters, fridge, TV and tea making facilities. Guests are very welcome to join in the farm activities during their stay. Golf course and fishing are within five minutes drive. Directions: Please phone. An hour and three quarters drive from Dunedin.

Roxburgh   *Country Inn 9km S of Roxburgh*

The Seed Farm
Elaine & John Buchan
4760 Roxburgh-Ettrick Road, RD 2, Roxburgh

Tel (03) 446 6824   Fax (03) 446 6024
elaine@theseedfarm.co.nz
www.theseedfarm.co.nz

Double $110 Single $95 (Continental Breakfast)
Dinner by arrangement Credit cards accepted
3 Queen 2 Single (4 bdrm)
4 Ensuite

Nestled in the Teviot Valley centre of NZ's cherry and apricot growing region, the Seed Farm comprises a two storeyed cottage and separate stables set amidst two acres of cottage garden. The buildings all carry Historic Places Trust 2 classification reflecting their historic significance to the district. The stables have been converted and offer four self-contained bedrooms with TV, tea making facilities etc. The cottage contains a restaurant offering an eclectic menu in an olde world ambience.

Lawrence   *B&B 45 min Balclutha*

The Ark
Frieda Betman
8 Harrington Place (Main Road),

Tel (03) 485 9328   Fax (03) 485 9222
lawrence.infocentre@xtra.co.nz
www.thearknz.homestead.com

Double $90 Single $50 (Full Breakfast) Child $15
2 Double 1 Twin 1 Single (4 bdrm)
1 Host share

My home is situated on the main road near the picnic ground with its avenue of poplars. My garden is special to me, the home is 100 years old, has character, charm and a lived in feeling. It's home to Ambrose Pumpkin my cats and Holly a miniature Foxie. Guestrooms are restful with fresh flowers, fruit and breakfast includes hot bread, croissants, home-made jams. Free-range eggs. There is a lovely peaceful atmosphere in our early gold mining town. Approx. 45 mins to Dunedin airport, just over an hour to Dunedin. Please refer to "The Ark" when you contact us.

Dunedin *B&B 2km W of Dunedin*

Magnolia House
Joan & George Sutherland
18 Grendon Street, Maori Hill, Dunedin 9001
Tel (03) 467 5999 Fax (03) 467 5999
mrsuth@paradise.net.nz
www.bnb.co.nz/magnoliahouse.html
Double $95 Single $70 (Special Breakfast)
1 Queen 1 Double 2 Single (3 bdrm)
1 Private 2 Guests share

Our quiet turn-of-the-century villa sits in broad, flower-
bordered lawns backed by native bush with beautiful,
tuneful birds. All rooms have electric heating, comfortable beds with electric blanket, and antiques,
while the Queen room has an adjoining balcony. Close by is Moana Pool, the glorious Edwardian
house, "Olveston", and Otago Golf Course. Our special breakfast will set you up for the day. We have
a courtesy car, a Burmese and a Siamese cat. It is NOT SUITABLE FOR CHILDREN OR SMOKERS.

Dunedin *B&B Homestay 7km NE of Dunedin*

Harbourside B&B
Shirley & Don Parsons
6 Kiwi Street, St Leonards, Dunedin
Tel (03) 471 0690 Fax (03) 471 0063
harboursidebb@xtra.co.nz
www.bnb.co.nz/harboursidebb.html
Double $75-$90 Single $55 (Full Breakfast)
Child $15 Dinner $25 Credit cards accepted
2 Queen 1 Double 3 Single (3 bdrm)
1 Ensuite 1 Host share

We are situated in a quiet suburb overlooking Otago Harbour and surrounding hills. Within easy reach
of all local attractions. Lovely garden or harbour views from all rooms. Children very welcome.
Directions: Drive into city on one-way system watch for Highway 88 sign follow Anzac Avenue onto
Ravensbourne Rd. Continue approx 5 kms to St Leonards turn left at Playcentre opposite Boatshed into
Pukeko St then left into Kaka Rd, straight ahead to Kiwi St turn left into No. 6. Pets outside.

Dunedin *B&B Dunedin Central*

Deacons Court
Keith Heggie & Gail Marmont
342 High Street, Dunedin
Tel (03) 477 9053 0800 268 252 Fax (03) 477 9058
Deacons@es.co.nz
www.deaconscourt.co.nz
Double $100-$130 Single $60-$80 (Full Breakfast)
Child $20 - $30 Credit cards accepted
1 King 2 Queen 3 Single (3 bdrm)
2 Ensuite 1 Private

Deacons Court is a charming superior spacious Victorian Villa 1km walking distance from the city
centre and on a bus route. We offer you friendly but unobtrusive hospitality in a quiet secure haven.
Guests can relax in our delightful sheltered back garden and conservatory. All our bedrooms are large,
have ensuite or private bathrooms, heaters, TV & electric blankets. Complimentary 24hr tea or coffee,
free parking and laundry service available. We cater for non-smokers and have an unobtrusive cat.
Family groups welcome.

Dunedin   *800m W of Dunedin Central*

Castlewood
Donna & Peter Mitchell
240 York Place, Dunedin

Tel (03) 477 0526   Fax (03) 477 0526
relax@castlewood.co.nz
www.castlewood.co.nz

Double $145 Single $100 Twin $125 Ensuite $155
Credit cards accepted
2 Queen 1 Twin 1 Single (3 bdrm)
1 Ensuite 1 Private 1 Guests share

Recommeded by Lonely Planet, Frommers, Fodors and Lets Go guides, Castlewood provides superior accommodation in a gracious restored 1912 Tudor residence located a mere 10 minutes walk from Dunedin's best cafes, bars, galleries, museums, theatres and shopping. Relax with extensive views of Dunedin, sumptuous breafasts, guests sauna, and library. Your hosts, Peter & Donna appreciate the requirements of discerning travellers. Peter is a watercolour artist and author of 'Great Escapes' (a guide to NZ). For more information, references and maps view www.castlewood.co.nz.

Dunedin   *Separate/Suite Bed & Breakfast Inn 2km SW of Dunedin Central*

Glenfield House
Cal Johnstone & Wendy Gunn
3 Peel St, Mornington, Dunedin

Tel (03) 453 5923   Fax (03) 453 5984
glenfieldhouse@xtra.co.nz
www.bnb.co.nz/glenfieldhouse.html

Double $135-$175 Single $110-$135 (Full Breakfast)
Credit cards accepted
2 Queen 2 Double (4 bdrm)
2 Ensuite 1 Guests share

We welcome you to our restored Victorian residence on the edge of the green belt. We offer you warmth, elegance and informality. In all bedrooms we provide heating, cotton and feather bedding, TV, telephone and freshly ground coffee. Our blue suite incorporates an ensuite, a sun room and the opportunity for intimate dining overlooking the city and harbour. With notice, a sumptuous three course meal prepared from Otago produce will be served in the guest dining room. We thank you for not smoking.

Broad Bay - Otago Peninsula   *B&B 16km E of Dunedin*

Chy-an-Dowr
Susan & Herman van Velthoven
687 Portobello Road, Broad Bay, Dunedin

Tel (03) 478 0306 Fax (03) 478 0306
Mob 025 270 5533 hermanvv@xtra.co.nz
www.city-of-dunedin.co.nz/chy-an-dowr.html

Double $125-$160 (Full Breakfast)
Credit cards accepted
1 King/Twin 1 Queen 1 Double 1 Single (3 bdrm)
1 Ensuite 1 Private 2 Guests share

ìChy~an~Dowrî (ìHouse by the Waterî), our character 1920s harbourside home is located midway on the Otago Peninsula, central to all attractions and the Albatross & Penguin Colonies. We offer quality accommodation with panoramic harbour views. The upstairs guest area is spacious and private with comfortable rooms, bathrobes, tea/coffee, TV, fridge, ensuite/private facilities and sunroom. Enjoy a delicious breakfast at your leisure. Originally from Holland, we enjoy welcoming people into our home and sharing our wonderful location with them. We have a cat.

Dunedin *B&B Separate/Suite Dunedin Central*

Hulmes Court
Norman Wood
52 Tennyson street, Dunedin
Tel (03) 477 5319   0800 448 563   Fax (03) 477 5310
Mob 025 351 075
reservations@hulmes.co.nz   www.hulmes.co.nz

Double $100-$160 Single $65-$160
(Continental Breakfast) Credit cards accepted
Child please enquire   Children welcome
3 King 10 Queen 4 Twin 1 Single (14 bdrm)
8 Ensuite 3 Guests share

Hulmes Court and Hulmes Too are two beautiful homes situated right in the heart of Dunedin, only a few minutes walk from the Visitor Centre, restaurants, shops and theatres.

Your host Norman owns an advertising business, is interested in history, philosophy, geography and has stood for parliament twice. At the same time Norman at 37 and his staff are youthful and full of energy. We have journeyed widely and know what travellers need: peace, relaxation, comfortable beds, warmth, continental breakfasts, friendly service and good information. In addition, we provide complimentary laundry, internet & email, mountain bikes and off-street parking. We have a cute black cat called Solstice and we enjoy children staying with us.

Tennyson Street is a quiet side Street and the property has private gardens, trees, decks and sitting areas, a tranquil retreat from the hustle and bustle so near by.

The Victorian Hulmes Court is one of the oldest and most historic homes in Dunedin. It was built in the 1860's by the first provincial surgeon Edward Hulme who helped found the Otago Medical School. Hulmes Too is a large Edwardian home built next to Hulmes Court on the grounds of the original estate. For the first time in over a century the properties are back together again.

Hulmes Court & Too have a variety of rooms which cater for all tastes from the economical cute single Rose room at $65 per night to our large and grand en suite rooms in Hulmes Too at $160 per night.

Dunedin - Otago Peninsula   *Homestay & Self-contained 8km Dunedin City*

Captains Cottage
Christine & Robert Brown
422 Portobello Road, RD 2, Dunedin

Tel (03) 476 1431   Fax (03) 476 1431
Mob 0274 352 734   wildfilm@actrix.co.nz
www.wildfilm.co.nz

Double $145   Single $100   (Special Breakfast)
Dinner $30 $125 self contained
1 Queen/Twin 2 Double (3 bdrm)
1 Ensuite 1 Private 1 Guests share

Captains Cottage is on the waterfront set in bush with spectacular views. Enroute to Albatross, Penguin and Seal Colonies. Christine and Robert are wildlife film makers, Robert having filmed for BBC, National Geographic and Discovery. Our local and wildlife knowledge can help plan your stay. Come in our boat fishing or view the unique bird and marine life. Great food, hospitality, BBQ's, relaxing by our fire - come and share our comfortable, character-filled home or the "Captain's Retreat" a rustic, romantic, self-contained boathouse over the water.

Dunedin   *B&B Homestay 3.2km N of Dunedin Central*

home
NEW ZEALAND

Dalmore Lodge
Loraine & Mike Allpress
9 Falkirk Street, Dalmore, Dunedin

Tel (03) 473 6513   Fax (03) 473 6512
Mob 025 287 1517   bookings@dalmorelodge.co.nz
www.dalmorelodge.co.nz

Double $100-$120   Single $75-$95 (Special Breakfast)
Child neg. Credit cards accepted Children welcome
1 King/Twin 1 Queen 1 Double 2 Single (4 bdrm)
1 Private 1 Guests share

In its peaceful setting, just two minutes off the Northern Motorway you'll find Dalmore Lodge. Our Larchwood home offers views of the harbour, Pacific Ocean, city lights, Botanical Gardens and hills. A three minute drive or 20 minute walk takes you into the main business/shopping area. Public transport is available at the end of the driveway. We will take you to/from airport or bus by prior arrangement (extra minimal cost). Off street parking. We look forward to meeting you and sharing knowledge of Dunedin and its local attractions.

Portobello - Otago Peninsula   *B&B Self-contained 25min NE of Dunedin*

Lavender House
Rachel & Mike Kerr
4 Allans Beach Road, Portobello, Otago Peninsula

Tel (03) 478 0909   Fax (03) 478 0909
lavenderhousenz@hotmail.com
www.lavenderhouse.co.nz

Double $95-$145   Single $85-$135 (Special Breakfast)
Child P.O.A. Credit cards accepted Children welcome
3 Queen 2 Twin (4 bdrm)
2 Ensuite 1 Private 1 Guests share

Our B&B is a spacious 4 bdrm. historic (1880's) villa and is adjacent to our home. Set in 1/2 acre of beautiful gardens, sea views, rural outlook. Overlooking Lathum Bay, opposite 1908 Cafe. We are a sixth generation Peninsula family with two children, Jackson (5) Reuben (3). Luxuriously decorated, ensuites, lounge, dining area, return verandahs, off-street parking, Tea/Coffee, Laundry included! We are most central to Albatross, penguin & seal colonies, bird watching, Larnach Castle, golf course, scenic walks & drives. Kiwi hosts, excellent local knowledge.

OTAGO, NORTH CATLINS

Dunedin *B&B Homestay 4.5km SE of Dunedin Central*

Alloway
Lorraine & Stewart Harvey
65 Every Street, Andersons Bay, Dunedin
Tel (03) 454 5384   0800 387 245   Fax (03) 454 5364
alloway@xtra.co.nz   www.alloway.co.nz
Double $100-$160 Single $90-$120
(Continental Breakfast) Child neg.
Credit cards accepted
2 Queen 2 Single (2 bdrm)
1 Private 1 Guests share

We are situated on the gateway to the Otago Peninsula, which features wildlife, walking tracks, Taiaroa Head Albatross Colony, Disappearing Gun, Seal Colonies, Yellow Eyed Penguins, Glenfalloch Gardens and much more. We are seven minutes to town centre. Our home is a modern interpretation of a traditional Scottish house, and set in one acre of gardens and lawns, with indoor/outdoor living. Awake to the sound of abundant bird life in a quiet and secure neighbourhood. We serve delicious healthy breakfasts. Two luxury bedrooms complete with one queen and one single bed.

Port Chalmers - Dunedin   *Farmstay Homestay 20km NE of Dunedin*

Atanui
Betty & Bob Melville
Heywards Point Road, RD 1, Port Chalmers, Dunedin
Tel (03) 482 1107   Fax (03) 482 1107
atanui@actrix.gen.nz
www.bnb.co.nz/atanui.html
Double $100-$120 Single $80-$100
(Continental Breakfast) Child 1/2 price Dinner $25
Credit cards accepted
1 King/Twin 1 Queen 1 Twin (2 bdrm)
1 Ensuite 1 Guests share

Betty & Bob welcome you to our spacious stonehouse in a peaceful rural setting, 30 mins from Dunedin, with a spectacular view across the Otago harbour. Feed the Emu's, Aplaca's, peacocks etc. Good surfing beach and walking tracks. Relax in our spa pool. Three friendly cats. Three course farm-style meals available. Morning and afternoon teas complimentary. Children and campervans welcome. We look forward to meeting you.

Portobello - Otago Peninsula   *Self Contained Cottage 15km E of Dunedin*

Fern Grove Garden
Bill & Christine Strang
741 Portobello Road, Portobello, Dunedin
Tel (03) 478 0321   Mob 027 298 3110
strang@southnet.co.nz
www.inmark.co.nz/fgg/
Double $105-$135 (Continental Breakfast)
Credit cards accepted Children welcome
1 Queen 1 Single (1 bdrm)
1 Private

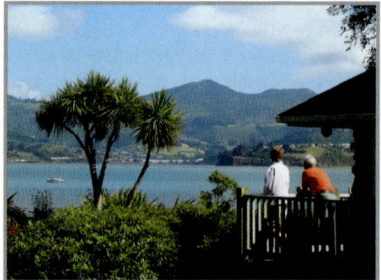

Harbourside frontage with panoramic water and peninsula views from comfortable three roomed private self-contained cottage including bedroom, kitchen-dining room, bathroom, and sundeck. Off-street parking. Laundry available. Tui and bellbirds in fern garden. We have a cat called Mikka. Albatross, penguins, seals, bird-watching launch trips, Larnach castle and scenic walks all nearby. 15 minutes from Dunedin: 5 minutes from Portobello. ìGreat cosy and comfortable place. Fabulous views in a beautiful spot.î World Travel Inc, Hamburg.

Dunedin   *B&B Homestay 2km N of central*

arden st bnb dunedin central
Joyce Lepperd
36 Arden Street, North East Valley, Dunedin central

Tel (03) 473 8860   Fax (03) 473 8861
Mob 0274046550 joyce-l@clear.net.nz
www.ardenstreethouse.co.nz

Double $65-$95 Single $45-$65 (Special Breakfast)
Child $10-15 Dinner $10 - $25 Credit cards accepted
3 Double 2 Twin 3 Single (5 bdrm)
1 Ensuite 1 Private

Comfortable warm 1930s character homestay, stained glass
themes. Close Botanical Gardens, University, Knox
college, city centre and community hospice. Arty decor, sunny, great views, birdsong, garden. Good modern
bathrooms, ensuite. Your host Joyce hosts social evening dinners - great way to meet 'the locals' using
organic produce from her garden. Good paino for guests use. Children welcome. We practice recycling!
Look out for QT the cat!

Dunedin   *B&B Homestay Separate/Suite 1 km Dunedin Central*

Highbrae Guesthouse
Fienie & Stephen Clark
376 High Street, City Rise, Dunedin

Tel (03) 479 2070   Fax (03) 479 2100
Mob 025 328 470 highbrae@xtra.co.nz
www.highbrae.co.nz

Double $85-$110 Single $65-$85 (Full Breakfast)
Child $10- $20 Credit cards accepted
1 King 1 Queen 1 Twin (3 bdrm)
1 Guests share 1 Host share

Experience a taste of early Dunedin. This heritage home in the centre of the city was built on the High
Street Cable Car route in 1908 to provide first class accommodation to its residents. Today it is still an
impressive home with spectacular views of the city and harbour. The three upstairs guest rooms are
carefully restored to preserve their character for visitors, who delight in the many features in the home.
A courtesy van can meet you at the bus or train if required.

Macandrew Bay - Otago Peninsula   *B&B Self-contained 11km E of Dunedin*

Mac Bay Retreat
Jeff & Helen Hall
38 Bayne Terrace, Macandrew Bay, Dunedin 9003

Tel (03) 476 1475   Fax (03) 476 1975
Mob 021 897 243 jhall9@ihug.co.nz
www.bnb.co.nz/macbayretreat.html

Double $95 Single $65 (Continental Breakfast)
1 King 1 Double (2 bdrm)
1 Ensuite

Mac Bay Retreat - Otago Peninsula. Welcome to your
private self-contained smoke-free retreat, 15 min from
Dunedin centre on the Otago Peninsula. Relax with the spectacular view overlooking the harbour from
Dunedin city to Port Chalmers. Your cosy retreat is separate from the host's house and gives you a
choice of either a super/king or double bed plus an ensuite, modern kitchen and TV. Suitable for one
couple, possibly two couples, travelling together. Only minutes from Dunedin's most popular attractions,
Larnach Castle, albatross and penguin colonies, etc.

OTAGO, NORTH CATLINS

Dunedin *B&B Dunedin Central*

Albatross Inn
Glynis Rees
770 George Street, Dunedin
Tel (03) 477 2727   0800 441 441   Fax (03) 477 2108
albatross.inn@xtra.co.nz
www.bnb.co.nz/albatrossinn1.html
Double $75-$125 Single $65-$85
(Continental Breakfast) Child $15
1 King 4 Queen 3 Double 5 Single (8 bdrm)
8 Ensuite

Welcome to Dunedin & Albatross Inn!
Our beautiful late Victorian House is ideally located on the main street close to the University, gardens, museum, shops and restaurants.
Our attractive rooms have ensuite bathrooms, telephone, TV, radio, tea/coffee, warm duvets and electric blankets on modern beds. Extra firm beds upon request. Very quiet rooms at rear of house. Several rooms have kitchenette and fridge. Enjoy your breakfast in front of the open fire in our lounge. We serve freshly baked bread and muffins, fresh fruit salad, yoghurt, juices, cereals, teas, freshly brewed coffee.

We are happy to recommend and book tours for you. All wildlife tours pick up and drop off here. We can recommend many great places to eat, most just a short walk down George Street. Nearby laundry, non-smoking, cot and highchair.
Our visitor book says! *"The convenience of your location is wonderful, you can walk everywhere! Combined with a gorgeous house, such friendly hosts"* Joe & Cathy Wallace, Georgia, USA. *"This is everything a B&B ought to be... our only regret is leaving..."* Dianna & William McDowey, England.
Winter special $69 Double - special conditions apply. Complimentary e-mail and internet.

Homepage: www.albatross.inn.co.nz.

Dunedin *B&B*

Highview Lodge
Diane & Graeme Connolly
70 Heriot Row, Dunedin

Tel (03) 477 0997   0800 244 664   Fax (03) 477 6036
Mob 025 611 4382   highviewlodgedunedin@xtra.co.nz
www.bnb.co.nz/highviewlodge.html

Double $85-$135 Single $65-$95
(Continental Breakfast) Child $20 Dinner $30
Full breakfast by arrangement   Children welcome
1 King 3 Queen 1 Single (4 bdrm)   2 Ensuite

Highview Lodge offers superior accommodation in a restored 1910 Edwardian home with all the comforts of modern living combined with the elegance of a bygone era. Lovely city and harbour views, and a garden with native birds. The city shops, university, hospital and many restaurants and attractions are within a five minute walk. City bus stop nearby. Well heated private rooms, guest lounge, kitchenettes, off-street parking, laundry, phone/fax, Sky TV. Cooked breakfast, dinner, city tours,optional extras. Pick up and deliver within city. Please phone for directions.

Broad Bay - Otago Peninsula   *B&B Homestay 16km E of Dunedin*

Broad Bay White House
Chris & Margaret Marshall
11 Clearwater Street, Broad Bay, Dunedin

Tel (03) 478 1160   Fax (03) 478 1159
maheno@paradise.net.nz
www.visit-dunedin.co.nz/bbwhitehouse.html

Double $120-$145 (Full Breakfast)
Dinner $25 by arrangement
2 Queen 1 Twin (3 bdrm)
2 Ensuite 1 Private

Looking for peace and quiet, privacy, panoramic views over the harbour, superb meals with silver service? Look no further. We are a 3.5 ha tranquil rural hideaway located on the Otago Peninsula. Handy to Albatross, Penguin and Seal colonies. All bedrooms enjoy spacious decks and panoramic views over the harbour. Relax and wander through gardens and enjoy the abundant bird life. Have fun with a game of petanque (no experience required).

Dunedin   *B&B Homestay 4km S of Dunedin*

Aberdeen B&B
Robert O'Shea
43A Aberdeen Road, St Clair, Dunedin

Tel (03) 487 8217 or (03) 479 7617
43AAR@bigfoot.com
www.bnb.co.nz/aberdeenbb.html

Double $115-$135 Single $80-$110
(Continental Breakfast) Child $25 Children welcome
1 Queen 1 Double 1 Single (2 bdrm)
2 Ensuite

Aberdeen B&B is a large, warm house, set in a quiet, sunny enclave on St Clair headland with spectacular views of beach and peninsula. It's two minutes' drive from St Clair Beach and about eight minutes' drive from the Visitors' Centre. There are two large en-suite rooms, one with a large spa bath. My son Joel (11) and I enjoy meeting people; we've travelled in USA, Canada, Europe, and Australia. We offer peace and privacy with the comforts of home.

Dunedin   *B&B Homestay Dunedin Central*

Grandview
Steve Scott
360 High Street, Dunedin 9001
Tel (03) 474 9472   0800 749 472   Fax (03) 474 9473
Mob 021 101 9857
nzgrandview@msn.com
www.bnb.co.nz/grandview2.html

Double $75-$195 Single $60-$125
(Continental Breakfast) (Special Breakfast)
Child $10 under 13 Children welcome
2 King 4 Queen 4 Double 10 Single (10 bdrm)
5 Ensuite

Grandview is centrally located! The Casino, Restaurants, Shops, Cafés and Bars are only a short stroll away!

Relax in luxury in this charming 1901 heritage listed edwardian mansion. Featuring magnificent panoramic views from our viewing platforms and spa area

Also 152cm big screen satellite TV, Video's, Internet, Laundry facilities, Mountainbikes and scrumptious continental breakfasts are all a complimentary part of the Grandview experience.

Ten rooms to suit all budgets! From $30pp share accomodation to our First Class Luxury Suites for your pleasure.

484

Broad Bay - Otago Peninsula *Self-contained 18Km E of Dunedin*

The Cottage
Julz Asher & Lutz Ritter
Broad Bay, Dunedin,
(contact only: 14 Howard St, Macandrew Bay)

Tel (03) 476 1877   Fax (03) 476 1873
Mob 027 228 3380   thecottage@xtra.co.nz
www.bnb.co.nz/cottagebroadbay.html

Double $120   Breakfast hamper $35 for two
1 Double (1 bdrm)
1 Ensuite

Private cottage. Built 1905 as a fisherman's retreat. Right on Otago Harbour. Picket-fence, mature bush gardens. Vignettes of harbour from verandah. Full of old-world nostalgia, original matai floors, interesting collectibles, a Bakelite phone (but no TV!) With luxurious towels, fresh linen, a comfortable bed - it's a real travellers oasis. Generous hamper breakfasts are a speciality. "The owners have thought of just about everything" Gourmet Travellers Magazine. "If you spend only one night at The Cottage, you'll be sorry... a few days is best" Grace Magazine.

Portobello - Otago Peninsula *Self-contained   15km E of Dunedin*

Ty yr Mor
Fiona Owens
34 Allan's Beach Road, Portobello, Dunedin

Tel (03) 478 1089   Mob 021 174 1089
Ty_yr_mor@hotmail.com
www.bnb.co.nz/tyyrmor.html

Double $120 Single $110 (Continental Breakfast)
Child $10 Children welcome Pets welcome
2 Queen (2 bdrm)
1 Private

Gaze at the stars in your 'fire bath' nestled between the native bush. Stroll along the golden sands; admire the yellow-eyed penguins, seal lions and seals. Visit the only land based Albatross colony. Have a professional massage and enjoy your own private cottage. For the energetic, mountain bikes and kayaks are for hire. Pets and children are very welcome. Book library. Full equipped kitchen, cot available. Futon sofa bed in lounge. BBQ available. Babysitting available.

Dunedin - Harington Point *B&B Self-contained 30km NE of Dunedin*

Harington Point Accommodation
Dave and Marie Rodger
932 Harington Point Road, RD2, Dunedin

Tel (03) 478 0287   Fax (03) 478 0089
mdrodger@ihug.co.nz
www.bnb.co.nz/haringtondunedin.html

Double $85 - $120 (Continental Breakfast)
S/C cottages From $85
3 Queen 1 Double 2 Twin 2 Single (5 bdrm)
5 Ensuite

Enjoy very comfortable self-contained cottages or B&B rooms, looking out to Otago Harbour. Local wildlife includes Albatross, Penguins, Seals, Shags and Sealions. The area has many historic features including 'the disappearing gun' and 'Larnach Castle'. Two minutes walk to the beach for a leisurely stroll - spectacular sunsets. Golf course, restaurants and cafes close by. The Otago Peninsula offers many scenic walks and drives. Let our local knowledge enhance your stay on the Peninsula.

Mosgiel   *Homestay 14km S of Dunedin*

The Old Vicarage
Lois & Lance Woodfield
14 Mure Street, Mosgiel, Otago
Tel (03) 489 8236 Fax (03) 489 8236
l.l.woodfield@clear.net.nz
www.bnb.co.nz/theoldvicarage.html

Double $65-$85 Single $45 (Continental Breakfast)
Credit cards accepted Children welcome
1 Queen 2 Single (2 bdrm)
1 Private 1 Guests share

Welcome to our English-style cottage home. Built in 1913 and used as the Vicarage for 46 years, before passing to private owners who made sympathetic restorations. The outstanding feature is the exquisitely balanced garden, laid out in 'rooms'. Two upstairs guest rooms and bathroom enjoy a commanding view of the garden. Warm Oregan panelling and leadlight windows enhance the atmosphere. Situated in Mosgiel, close to the Airport, just 15 minutes from Dunedin. We are a retired Christian couple who enjoy gardening, architecture, tramping and history.

Waihola   *B&B Homestay Self-contained 40km S of Dunedin*

Lillian & Trevor Robinson
Sandown Street, Rapid No 13, Waihola, South Otago
Tel (03) 417 8218 Fax (03) 417 8287
Mob 025 545 935 www.bnb.co.nz/robinson.html

Double $75 Single $50 (Full Breakfast)
Dinner $25 by arrangement Credit cards accepted
1 Queen 2 Single (2 bdrm)
1 Ensuite 1 Host share

We have a very comfortable home situated in a quiet street, only 15 minutes drive to Dunedin Airport. Our double room has Queen sized bed with ensuite, teamaking facilities, TV, fridge and heater. Lake Waihola is popular for boating, fishing and swimming. We enjoy meeting people and ensure a very pleasant stay. Please phone.

Waihola   *B&B Homestay Lakeside Cottage 40km S of Dunedin*

Lakeside Cottage
Robin & Bryan Leckie
Rapid No. 7, State Highway 1, Waihola, Otago 9057
Tel (03) 417 8946 0800 112 996 Fax (03) 417 8966
ivycottage@xtra.co.nz
www.bnb.co.nz/ivycottagelakewaihola.html

Double $80-$90 Single $60-$65 (Full Breakfast)
Child POA Dinner $25 B/A Long stay discount
Credit cards accepted
1 Double 3 Single (2 bdrm) 2 Ensuite

Our 'Lakeside' property is on SH1 near Dunedin Airport (15km). Guests enjoy unobstructed scenic views of Lake Waihola, farmlands and forests. Excellent base for day trips. North - Dunedin's albatross colony, heritage. South - The Catlins, scenic beauty, wild life. West - Central Otago orchards and vineyards. East - Taieri Mouth and Pacific beaches. Waihola features wetlands, whale fossils, walkways, and aquatic recreation. We have many interests. Our detached accommodation 'The Shed' has ensuites, tea facilities, TV, laundry, etc. Dining options include our cuisine with wine or Waihola restaurants. Bud is our friendly gold retriever.

Balclutha   *Farmstay 26km W of Balclutha*

Argyll Farmstay
Trish & Alan May
Clutha River Road, Clydevale, RD 4, Balclutha
Tel (03) 415 9268   Fax (03) 415 9268
Mob 0274 318 241   argyllfm@ihug.co.nz
www.bnb.co.nz/argyllfarmstay.html
Double $100 Single $50 (Full Breakfast) Child neg
Dinner $25 Credit cards accepted
1 Queen 1 Twin 2 Single (2 bdrm)
1 Private 1 Guests share

We welcome guests to our comfortable country home with large garden, and beautiful views of green pasture and river flats. We farm 710 acres running 2000 deer, 150 cattle and 1000 sheep. Alan is a experienced fisherman who is happy to share his knowledge of our local rivers. We are centrally located for people travelling to the Catlins, Queenstown or Te Anau. Directions: please telephone.

Balclutha   *B&B Boutique accommodation 4km N of Balclutha*

Lesmahagow
Noel & Kate O'Malley
Main Road, Benhar, RD 2, Balclutha
Tel (03) 418 2507   0800 301 224   Mob 025 578 465
lesmahagow@xtra.co.nz   www.lesmahagow.co.nz
Double $85-$110 (Special Breakfast) Dinner $30
Lunches on request   Children welcome
2 Queen 2 Double 1 Single (4 bdrm)
2 Guests share

Experience the peace and charm of yesteryear in historic Benhar. We offer quality and comfort in our character home and extensive gardens. Our guestrooms are spacious and attractively furnished, complete with electric blankets, robes and hairdryers. A continental breakfast with homemade baking can be enjoyed in our dining room or garden. Situated at the gateway to the Catlins, 40 mins. from Dunedin airport, your comfort is our objective. Your hosts, Noel and Kate and Thomas(cat), welcome you to Lesmahagow. Come as strangers, leave as friends.

Clinton   *B&B Farmstay Separate/Suite Self-contained 8.2km W of Clinton*

Strathearn Cottage Farmstay
Ngaire & Warwick Taylor
Strathearn Road, Wairuna RD, Clinton
Tel (03) 415 7444   Mob 0274 392 938
wf_na_taylor@xtra.co.nz
www.bnb.co.nz/strathearn.html
Double $85 Single $55 (Full Breakfast)
Child 6-12 $10, under 5 free Credit cards accepted
1 Double 1 Twin (1 bdrm)
1 Private

Introducing Strathearn's cosy self-contained cottage, "Grandma's House". Strathearn is an established 3000ac family operated sheep and beef farm. Join with us, our two kids, pets - kunekunes, alpacas, hens, ducks, cats & dog - and unwind whilst experiencing farm activities and hill vistas, or fishing the renowned Waipahi and Mataura Rivers. Breakfast at your leisure from our full breakfast hamper (sugar-free if required). Children welcome, cot available. "Grandma's House" overlooks SH1 between Clinton and Waipahi, making Strathearn halfway to everywhere Southern - Catlins, Fiordland, Invercargill, Dunedin and Central Otago.

OTAGO, NORTH CATLINS

Nuggets - The Catlins *Self-contained 24km Balclutha&Owaka*

Nugget Lodge
Kath & Noel Widdowson
Nugget Road 367, RD 1, Balclutha, South Otago

Tel (03) 412 8783   Fax (03) 412 8784
lighthouse@nuggetlodge.co.nz
www.bnb.co.nz/nuggetlodge.html

Double $95 (Continental Breakfast)
$25pp extra person $15pp breakfast
Credit cards accepted
1 King/Twin 1 Double 1 Single (2 bdrm) 2 Ensuite

A unique position above the incoming tide on a deserted beach. Sleep to the roar of the waves, breathe the sea air from modern, private ,centrally heated units. Guests may choose to rest and rejuvenate the soul or the eco-enthusiasts can experience seals, sealions, penguins, birds, walk tracks and magnificant unspoilt scenery. Stay a while as one day is not enought to experience all the Catlins magic. Host: wildlife Ranger/Photographer. Pets not welcome, not suitable for children. Restaurants nearby. OUR MOTTO: EDUCATE/INFORM/PROTECT

Kaka Point - The Catlins *B&B Self-contained 21km S of Balclutha*

Rata Cottage
Jean Schreuder
31 Rata Street, Kaka Point, South Otago

Tel (03) 412 8779
www.bnb.co.nz/ratacottage.html

Double $65 Single $60 (Continental Breakfast)
Child $7
1 Twin (1 bdrm)
1 Ensuite

A fully self contained sunny Bed & Breakfast unit in a tranquil bush garden setting, with sea view, bell birds and tuis. Bedroom with twin beds, plus double divan in lounge. Wheelchair facilities. Five minutes from a beautiful sandy beach for swimming or long walks. next door to scenic reserve and bush walks. You can have breakfast in the garden with the birds, or a visit from Baxter the cat if you wish. Non smoking. Laundry facilities available. Cooking facilities.

Kaka Point - The Catlins *B&B Self-contained 19kms SE of Balclutha*

Cardno's Accommodation
Lyn & Selwyn Cardno
8 Marine Tce, Kaka Point - The Catlins,
RD1, Balclutha

Tel (03) 412 8181   Fax (03) 412 8101
cardnos@xtra.co.nz
www.cardnosaccommodation.co.nz

Double $95-$120 Single $80 (Continental Breakfast)
2 Queen 1 Single (2 bdrm)
2 Ensuite

From our Luxury Fully Self Contained Unit and B&B accommodation, you have magnificient views of the sea and Nugget Point Lighthouse. Complimentry Chocolates, Tea/Coffee, water filter, television & stereo. The Restaurant/bar/shop and beach are 1 minute walk and the Lighthouse, Yellow Eyed Penguins along with many other wildlife and native birds are 15 minutes drive along the coastline. We share our home with two family pets, Otto a Minature Schnauzer and Nika a Birman Seal Point cat. Not suitable for children

Owaka - The Catlins *Farmstay Self-contained 16 S of Owaka*

Tarara Downs
Ida & John Burgess
857 Puaho Road, RD 2, Owaka, South Otago
Tel (03) 415 8293   Fax (03) 415 8293
Mob 025 215 1428   tarara@ihug.co.nz
www.bnb.co.nz/tararadowns.html
Double $55-$75 Single $45 (Full Breakfast)
Child 1/2 price Dinner $25 (2 course)
1 King/Twin 1 Double (2 bdrm)
1 Ensuite 1 Host share

Our 2000-acre farm is situated in an area renowned for its bush and coastal scenery, within walking distance of the beautiful Purakaunui Falls. Our farm runs sheep, cattle, deer and horses. As well as seeing normal farm activities, horse riding, bush walks and fishing trips are available in the district. We live in a comfortable farmhouse, our family have all left home, and enjoy eating our own local produce. Children very welcome. Directions: Follow signs to Purakaunui Falls - we are the closest house to them. We also have a self contained cottage at Pounawea 15km away, price on application.

Owaka - The Catlins *Farmstay Self-contained 15km S of Owaka*

Greenwood
Helen-May & Alan Burgess
739 Purakaunui Falls Road, Owaka, South Otago
Tel (03) 415 8259   Fax (03) 415 8259
Mob 025 384 538   greenwoodfarm@xtra.co.nz
www.bnb.co.nz/greenwood.html
Double $95-$100 Single $65 (Full Breakfast)
Child $35 Dinner $40
S/C Papatowai Beach house $70Dbl, $10 extra person
1 Queen 3 Single (3 bdrm)
1 Ensuite 1 Private 1 Host share

Welcome ... Situated within walking distance to the beautiful Purakaunui Falls, Alan enjoys taking people around our 1900 acre sheep, cattle and deer farm. Our home offers warm, comfortable accommodation. One guest bedroom has an ensuite, and day-room opening to a large garden. A private bathroom services other guest rooms. We enjoy dining with our guests. The Catlins area features the yellow-eyed penguin.

Owaka *B&B Farmstay Self-contained 6km N of Owaka*

Hillview
Kate & Bruce McLachlan
Rapid 161 Hunt Road, Katea, RD 2, Owaka
Tel (03) 415 8457   Fax (03) 415 8650
Mob 025 334 759   hillviewcatlins@xtra.co.nz
www.bnb.co.nz/hillview.html
Double $85 Single $60 (Continental Breakfast)
Child $40 Dinner from $20 Credit cards accepted
2 Queen 4 Single (4 bdrm)
2 Guests share

Our 450 acre cattle grazing unit is situated 15 min from Nugget Point, 10 mins from Cannibal Bay. Relax in our cosy private cottage set in a large developing garden, or enjoy the relaxed atmosphere of our home. Our Burmese cat and miniature poodle live outside. Occassionally we host foreign students. Our interests are varied. Bruce is a shepherd and enjoys working with horses and training sheepdogs. Kate is a librarian who enjoys reading, gardening, spinning wool, and glass art. We enjoy our grandchildren and meeting people. Breakfast with us or in private. Meals by arrangement. Bookings essential. Please phone after 4 pm.

Owaka - The Catlins *B&B Homestay 1/2 km N of Owaka*

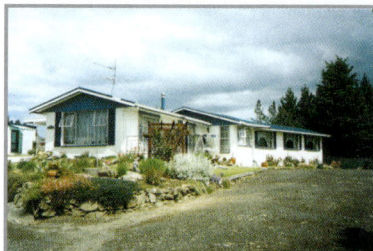

J T's Catlins B&B
John & Thelma Turnbull
Main Road, Owaka

Tel (03) 415 8127   Fax (03) 415 8129
Mob 025 649 7693   jtowaka@ihug.co.nz
www.bnb.co.nz/jts.html

Double $75-$90 Single $60 (Full Breakfast)
Child half price Dinner By arrangement
1 Queen 1 Twin (2 bdrm)
1 Guests share

Welcome to our warm and comfortable home, which is situated on a 25 acre farmlet, surrounded by colourful, peaceful gardens with splendid unspoilt views. Located in the heart of the Catlins, renowned for its wildlife and spectacular scenery, we are within walking distance of Owaka township with its restaurants, museum and other amenities. Our guests are encouraged to dine with us for the evening meal when we enjoy quality local food and wine. We look forward to meeting you. Travel safely.

Owaka - The Catlins *B&B Homestay 6km E of Owaka*

Kepplestone by the Sea
Esther & Jack Johnson
9 Surat Bay Road, Newhaven, The Catlins, Owaka

Tel (03) 415 8134   0800 105 134   Fax (03) 415 8137
kepplestone@xtra.co.nz
www.bnb.co.nz/kepplestone1.html

Double $95-$110 Single $65 (Special Breakfast)
Dinner by arrangement
1 King/Twin 1 Queen 2 Twin (3 bdrm)
2 Ensuite

There are no strangers here, only friends we haven't met.
Situated metres from Surat Bay, with Hooker sealions basking. Close to Catlins scenery, waterfalls, Royal Spoonbills, Golf. "Private Yelloweyed penguin viewing with Catlins Natural Wonders." Delicious homemade breakfasts. Fabulous meals served with Organically grown vegetables from garden. Alergy diets catered for, every care taken. Directions: Owaka, (Royal Terrace) Follow signs "towards" Pounawea, at golf course go "across" bridge, right to Newhaven, go 3km on metal road, at Suratbay Road, right first house on left.

A homestay is a B&B
where you share the family's living area.

Southland and South Catlins

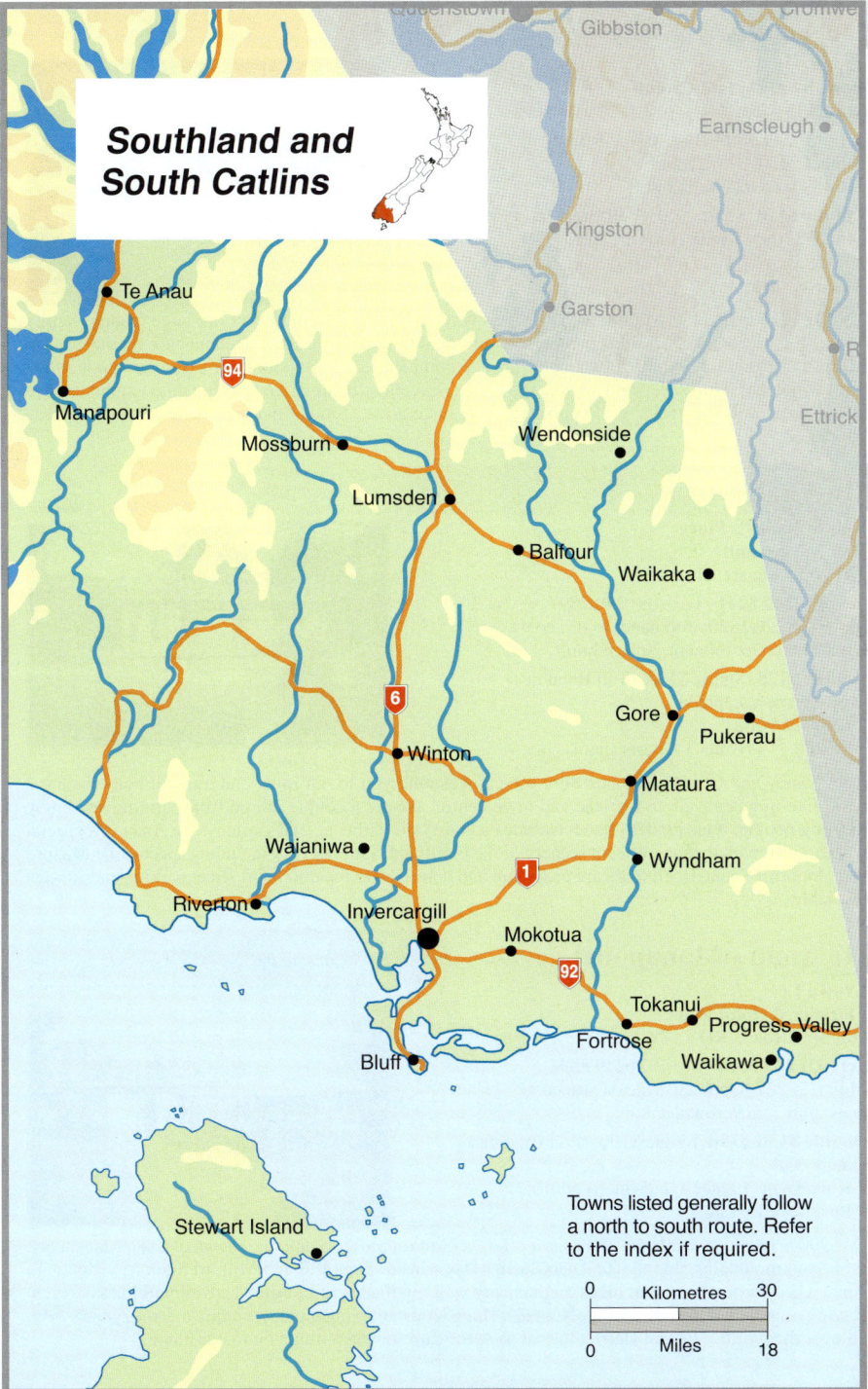

Queenstown · Gibbston
Cromwell
Earnscleugh ·
Te Anau
94
Kingston ·
Manapouri
Garston ·
Mossburn ·
Ettrick
Lumsden
Wendonside ·
Balfour ·
Waikaka ·
6
Gore ·
Pukerau ·
Winton ·
Mataura ·
Waianiwa ·
Wyndham ·
1
Riverton ·
Invercargill
Mokotua ·
92
Tokanui ·
Progress Valley ·
Fortrose ·
Bluff ·
Waikawa ·

Stewart Island

Towns listed generally follow a north to south route. Refer to the index if required.

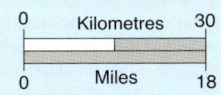

0 Kilometres 30
0 Miles 18

Te Anau   *Farmstay 20km E of Te Anau*

Tapua
Dorothy & Donald Cromb
RD 2, Te Anau
Tel (03) 249 5805   Fax (03) 249 5805
Tapua.Cromb@xtra.co.nz
www.bnb.co.nz/cromb.html

Double $110 Single $70 (Full Breakfast)
Dinner $30pp Credit cards accepted
1 King/Twin 1 Twin (2 bdrm)
1 Guests share

You are surrounded by "Million Dollar" views while enjoying the comfort of our large modern family home. Electric blankets, heaters in rooms. Traditional farm style meals. Excellent base for day trips to Milford or Doubtful Sound. A two night stay is recommended. Farm tour prior to dinner of our 348ha farm which has 3700 sheep and approx 100 cattle. Excellent fishing rivers within a few minutes drive as are great walking tracks, golf course etc. We have a cat. Smoke free home. Directions: Please phone.

Te Anau   *Homestay Self-contained*

Rob & Nancy's Place
R & N Marshall
13 Fergus Square, Te Anau
Tel (03) 249 8241   Fax (03) 249 7397
Mob 025 226 1820 rob.nancy@xtra.co.nz
www.bnb.co.nz/robnancysplace.html

Double $125 Single $125 (Full Breakfast)
Credit cards accepted
2 King (2 bdrm)
1 Ensuite 1 Private 1 Guests share

Rob, Nancy and Chardonnay our Burmese cat welcome you to our quiet and tranquil home facing a park, five minutes walk to the lake and town centre. We are a couple retired from farming and enjoy meeting people. Our modern home includes a courtyard barbecue and gardens. Te Anau is a special place to visit with the magnificent scenery of the Fiordland National Park including spectacular Milford and Doubtful Sounds. All tours are picked up and delivered to the door. Off street parking and storage available.

Te Anau - Manapouri   *Farmstay 20 min E of Manapouri*

Crown Lea
Florence & John Pine
Gillespie Road, RD 1, Te Anau
Tel (03) 249 8598   Fax (03) 249 8598
Mob 025 227 8366 crownlea@xtra.co.nz
www.bnb.co.nz/crownlea.html

Double $130-$150 Single $100 (Full Breakfast)
Dinner $30
1 King/Twin 1 Queen 1 Twin (3 bdrm)
1 Ensuite 2 Private

Our 900 acre sheep, cattle and deer farm offers a farm tour after 6 pm, and views of Lake Manapouri, Fiordland mountains, and the Te Anau Basin. Day trips to Doubtful and Milford Sounds, visits to Te Anau, Glow-worm Caves, or hikes on the many walking tracks, in Fiordland are all within easy reach. Having travelled in the UK, Europe, Canada, Hong Kong and Singapore, we enjoy meeting guests from all over the world. We and Harriet the cat look forward to welcoming you to our home.

Manapouri   *B&B Homestay 20km S of Te Anau*

The Cottage
Don & Joy MacDuff
Waiau St, Te Anau - Manapouri
Tel (03) 249 6838   Fax (03) 249 6839
don.joymacduff@xtra.co.nz
www.thecottagefiordland.co.nz
Double $95-$110 Single $75-$90 (Special Breakfast)
Credit cards accepted
2 Queen 1 Single (2 bdrm)
2 Ensuite

Gateway To The Scenic Wonders of Doubtful Sound. A 2min bush walk to where the boat departs for Doubtful Sound. We are happy to look after your car while you visit the Sound. Cozy Homestay B&B in tranquil bush setting, with lovely views. Warm ensuite rooms, cottage décor. French doors to cottage gardens. Tea & coffee facilities. Shared lounge with TV. Cooked full breakfast and laundry (extra charge). We, with Rosie our Skye Terrier, extend a warm welcome to all who choose to stay with us. Come as strangers, leave as friends.

Te Anau   *Homestay Country Homestay 3km S of Te Anau*

The Farmyard
Helen & Ray Willett
Charles Nairn Road -24, Te Anau 9681
Tel (03) 249 7833   Fax (03) 249 7830
Mob 025 289 0939
www.bnb.co.nz/thefarmyard.html
Double $90-$100 (Continental Breakfast)
1 Double 1 Single (1 bdrm)
1 Ensuite

Our country homestay, 3km from Te Anau, has detached, self contained cottage, privacy assured, peaceful rural setting and spectacular views of surrounding mountains. We are ideally situated for your Fiordland experience. Having for many years both worked on the Milford track and driven visitors to Milford Sound we are able to offer the very best advice for your Te Anau-Fiordland visit. Our pets - donkey, pony, sheep, pig, goats, terriers (2) are waiting to greet you!! Welcome to Te Anau-Fiordland. Please contact us for reservations.

Te Anau   *Homestay Te Anau Central*

House of Wood
Elaine & Trevor Lett
44 Moana Crescent, Te Anau

Tel (03) 249 8404   Fax (03) 249 7676
Mob 021 127 2978   houseofwood@xtra.co.nz
www.bnb.co.nz/houseofwood.html

Double $95-$120 Single $95 (Continental Breakfast)
1 King/Twin 1 Queen 1 Double (3 bdrm)
1 Ensuite 1 Guests share

"House of Wood" with natural timber throughout interior is a uniquely designed two storey wooden house with outside balconies and beautiful views. We know the Otago/Southland area extremely well and can help you make the most of your time here. When not greeting our guests we spend our time woodturning, walking, spinning, and exploring spectacular Fiordland. Along with Kaidy our Westhighland Terrier, we welcome you to our smokefree home which is in a quiet residential area. Please phone for directions.

Te Anau   *B&B 1km S of Te Anau*

The Cats Whiskers
Irene & Terry Maher
2 Lakefront Drive, Te Anau

Tel (03) 249 8112   Fax (03) 249 8112
i.t.maher@paradise.net.nz
www.webnz/bbnz/catwh.htm

Double $135-$145 Single $95 (Full Breakfast)
Child 1/2 price Credit cards accepted
1 King 2 Queen 4 Single (3 bdrm)
3 Ensuite

Situated opposite Department of Conservation headquarters, 10 min. walk to shops and restaurants. Comfortable pleasant rooms feature Queen or Twin. Family room - 1 King plus Twin. All ensuite, TV and tea making. Courtesy car to restaurants or meeting coaches. Off street parking and luggage storage for track walks or overnight kayaking. Agents for excursions to Milford and Doubtful Sounds. We have one Burmese cat. Directions: as you approach town, turn left where sign posted off Highway 94. First house on right. Off season rates. Guests laundry.

Te Anau   *B&B Farmstay Homestay Country Homestay 5km S of Te Anau*

Kepler Cottage
Jan & Jeff Ludemann
William Stephen Road, Te Anau

Tel (03) 249 7185   Fax (03) 249 7186
Mob 027 431 4076   kepler@teanau.co.nz
www.fiordlandaccommodation.co.nz

Double $130-$150 Single $100 (Full Breakfast)
Credit cards accepted
1 Queen 3 Single (3 bdrm)
1 Ensuite 1 Private

Jeff, an aircraft engineer, and Jan, who works from
home as a freelance journalist and marketing consultant, welcome you to their small farmlet on the edge of Fiordland, just five minutes drive from Te Anau. Relax outdoors in the garden and enjoy the peace and comfort of our rural location between visiting Milford or Doubtful Sounds, or walking one of the many nearby tracks. Our family includes a Cairn Terrier, and two cats. We can advise tours and sightseeing and make bookings where needed.

Te Anau   *Farmstay Self-contained 26km E of Te Anau*

Country Cottage
Carolyn & John Klein
The Key, RD 2, Te Anau
Tel (03) 249 5807   Fax (03) 249 5807
kleinbnb@ihug.co.nz
www.fishfiordland.com
Double $95   Single $75   (Continental Breakfast)
Child neg Credit cards accepted Pets welcome
1 Queen 3 Single (2 bdrm)
1 Private

We live at 'The Key', a tiny village on the main Queenstown-Te Anau highway, nestled under the Takitimu mountains, just 15 minutes drive from Te Anau. Our modern self-contained cottage is exclusively yours, well-equipped, very warm and comfortable with a 'beautiful' country view. We all enjoy meeting people and sharing our extensive knowledge of the region with you. John offers guided fishing on many of our local rivers. If you're looking for a real country experience, come and see us, we'd love to see you!

Te Anau   *B&B Self-contained Guesthouse 1km N of Te Anau Centre*

Shakespeare House
Margaret & Jeff Henderson
10 Dusky Street, PO Box 32, Te Anau
Tel (03) 249 7349   0800 249 349   Fax (03) 249 7629
marg.shakespeare.house@xtra.co.nz
www.shakespearehouse.co.nz
Double $80-$112   Single $60-$80   (Full Breakfast)
Child $5 - $15 S/C, 2 bedrooms, sleeps 5
Credit cards accepted Children welcome
4 King 3 Queen 4 Single (8 bdrm) 8 Ensuite

Shakespeare House is a well established Bed & Breakfast where we keep a home atmosphere with personal service. We are situated in a quiet residential area yet are within walking distance of shops, lake and restaurants. Our rooms are ground floor and with the choice of King, Double or Twin beds. Each room has private facilities, TV, tea/coffee making. Tariff includes continental or delicious cooked breakfast. Guest laundry available. Winter rates May to September. Along with Brothersoul our pussy we welcome you to Te Anau.

Te Anau   *B&B Farmstay Homestay 8km S of Te Anau*

Lynwood Park
Trina & Daniella Baker
State Highway 94, Te Anau
Tel (03) 249 7990   Fax (03) 249 7990
Mob 021 129 5626   lynwood.park@xtra.co.nz
www.bnb.co.nz/lynwoodpark.html
Double $70-$120   Single $50-$80   (Full Breakfast)
Child $30 Winter rates, May - Oct.
Credit cards accepted Children welcome
2 Queen 1 Double 3 Single (3 bdrm)
2 Ensuite 1 Private

Lynwood Park is a developing garden set amidst my families 450 acre sheep, cattle and deer farm. Each guest room has a private entrance, TV and tea/coffee making facilities. We offer free the use of our laundry facilities and childrens play area which Daniella my 5yr old,looks forward to sharing with you. We have two pet sheep, and a cat on the property. I am able to advise or arrange most activities to make your holiday a memorable experience.

SOUTHLAND, SOUTH CATLINS

Te Anau *B&B Farmstay Self-contained 2km E of Te Anau*

Rose 'n' Reel
Lyn & Lex Lawrence
Benloch Lane, RD 2, Te Anau
Tel (03) 249 7582 Fax (03) 249 7582
Mob 025 545 723 rosenreel@xtra.co.nz
www.rosenreel.co.nz

Double $90 Single $60 (Continental Breakfast)
Credit cards accepted
1 Queen 1 Double 1 Single (3 bdrm)
1 Private 1 Guests share

Genuine Kiwi hospitality in a magic setting 5 minutes from Te Anau. Hand feed tame fallow deer, meet two friendly cats. Sit on the veranda of our fully self contained cabin and enjoy watching deer with a lake and mountain view. The two room cabin has cooking facilities, fridge, microwave, TV, 1 Queen, 1 double plus bathroom. Our modern two storey smoke-free home is set in an extensive garden. Two downstairs guest bedrooms. Lex is a keen fly fisherman and average golfer, while I love to garden. Directions: Please phone.

Te Anau *B&B Te Anau Central*

Cosy Kiwi
Virginia and Gerhard Hirner
186 Milford Road, Te Anau 9681
Tel (03) 249 7475 0800 249 700
Fax 0064 3 249 8471 info@cosykiwi.com
www.cosykiwi.com

Double $95-$140 Single $70-$100
(Special Breakfast) Child neg Triple $135 - 160
Credit cards accepted Children welcome
4 King/Twin 3 Queen 9 Single (7 bdrm) 7 Ensuite

Virginia an Gerhard and our two children welcome you to our new Bed & Breakfast (20 years experience in hospitality, we speak German). Privacy with comfort, quiet spacious, ensuited bedrooms, quality beds, individual heating and television. Gourmet breakfast buffet of home-made breads, jams, fresh fruits, home-bottled fruits, yoghurt, brewed coffee, special teas, mouthwatering pancakes with maple syrup and more. Centrally located, bookings arranged for all tours, pick-up at gate. Guest lounge with Internet access, laundry, off-street parking and luggage storage.

Te Anau *Self-contained 5km N of Te Anau*

Fiordland Lodge
Robynne & Ron Peacock
472 Te Anau, Milford Highway RD 1, Te Anau
Tel (03) 249 7832 Fax (03) 249 7449
fiordlandguidesltd@xtra.co.nz
www.fiordlandlodge.co.nz

Double $220 Single $200 (Full Breakfast) Child $60
Dinner Availabe Extra adult $80 Credit cards accepted
2 Queen 5 Single (4 bdrm)
2 Private

Two self-contained log cabins, situated on our 40 acre farm overlooking Lake Te Anau, sit separate and private from the main Fiordland Lodge. The cabins are built in the traditional method with sundried logs. The interior is completed with recycled New Zealand native timbers. There is a queen-sized bed downstairs, and two/three single beds upstairs. Guests are welcome to relax in our new lodge and enjoy the convenience of dining in if they wish. Ron, a National Park Ranger for over 25 years, is a licensed fishing and nature guide.

Te Anau *B&B Self-contained Rural Lifestyle 1.5km N of Te Anau*

The Croft
Jane & Ross McEwan
Te Anau Milford Sound Road, RD 1, Te Anau
Tel (03) 249 7393   Fax (03) 249 7393
jane@thecroft.co.nz
www.thecroft.co.nz
Double $130 (Continental Breakfast)
Credit cards accepted
2 Queen 1 Single (2 bdrm) 2 Ensuite

Warm hospitality and quality accommodation are
guaranteed at 'The Croft', a small lifestyle farm only
minutes from Te Anau. Our two new self contained
cottages are set in private gardens and enjoy magnificent lake and mountain views. Timber ceilings,
large ensuite bathrooms, window seats and elegant furnishings are some of the highlights. Microwaves,
fridges, sinks & TV's. Enjoy breakfast with Jane & Ross or have it served in your cottage. Pets include
Dolly & Molly the sheep, Mac the Jack Russell, and Kitty. Lake and river access from our farm.

Te Anau *Farmstay Self-contained 26km E of Te Anau*

Davaar Country Cottage
Fiona & James Macdonald
RD 2, Te Anau,
Tel (03) 249 5838   Fax (03) 249 5839
davaar@xtra.co.nz
www.bnb.co.nz/davaarcountrycottage.html
Double $95 Single $65 (Continental Breakfast)
Child $15
2 Queen 2 Single (2 bdrm)
1 Private

'Davaar' is a 2800 acre sheep and cattle station, nestled under the Takitimu Mountains on the main
Queenstown-Te Anau Highway just before The Key. Exclusively yours, fully self-contained, comfortable
and spacious with excellent kitchen and laundry facilities, electric blankets, wood burning log fire and
TV. Located on the Mararoa River, with the Oreti River and Mavora lakes nearby ensures great fishing
opportunities, great scenery and a great base in which to explore Fiordland from. Your hosts James and
Fiona Macdonald look forward to welcoming you. Please phone for directions.

Te Anau *B&B Self-contained*

Edgewater XL B&B
Mark Excell
52 Lakefront Drive, Te Anau,
Tel (03) 249 7258   0800 433 439   Fax (03) 249 8099
edgewater.xl.motels@xtra.co.nz
www.bnb.co.nz/edgewaterxl.html
Double $185 (Continental Breakfast)
Children welcome
1 Queen 2 Single (2 bdrm)
1 Ensuite 1 Private

Situated on the lakefront, Edgewater XL B&B provides unobstructed views of the lake and Fiordland
National World Heritage Park. From your bedroom and private lounge, sliding doors open on to a
balcony. Your unit has coffee and tea-making facilities and ensuite with spa bath. Tariff includes
continental breakfast. We are a booking agent for all activities. Ian has good local knowledge of trout
fishing areas. This magic setting is only three minutes from the town centre. Off-season rates apply.

Te Anau   *B&B Self-contained 5km E of Te Anau*

Stonewall Cottage
Nicky Harrison & Jim Huntington
36 Kakapo Road, RD2, Te Anau
Tel (03) 249 8686 Fax (03) 249 8686
Mob 025 260 3414 hprojects@xtra.co.nz.
www.bnb.co.nz/stonewallcottage.html
Double $130 Single $100 (Continental Breakfast)
Child $20 neg. Children welcome
1 Queen (1 bdrm)
1 Ensuite

We welcome you to our new guest studio offering quality accommodation in a real rural retreat. Enjoy expansive mountain views from your own private courtyard. Our studio is self-contained with ensuite bathroom and full cooking facilities. A feature of our small deer farm is the dry stone walls which are ever increasing. You are invited to share in our daily farming and gardening activities or sit back and enjoy the tranquility after exploring the wonders of Fiordland.

Te Anau - Manapouri   *B&B Self-contained 19km S of Te Anau*

Rose Cottage B&B
Mary & Rennie McRae
1809 Te Anau, Manapouri Highway, RD1 Te Anau
Tel 03 249 6691 Fax 03 249 6690
Mob 0274 359512 025 6560404 renniemac@xtra.co.nz
www.bnb.co.nz/rosecottagebb.html
Double $105 Single $85 (Continental Breakfast)
Child $15
1 Queen 2 Twin (2 bdrm)
1 Private

Rose Cottage is a fully self-contained two bedroom house with washing and cooking facilities that sleeps up to six people. The cottage has one queen,two singles and a fold out double sofa in the lounge. We are located on a deer/sheep farm overlooking Fiordland National Park and the beautiful Lake Manapouri. We offer a place for people to chill out or as a base for exploring the surrounding area. We enjoy meeting people and sharing with them our local knowledge of the Fiordland area. Private parking is available and there's always a warm welcome from Biddy the Jack Russell.

Te Anau   *Homestay Self-contained 3km S of Te Anau*

The Coachhouse
Barry Eaton
11 Charles Nairn Road, Te Anau, Southland
Tel (03) 249 7078 barrye2000@xtra.co.nz
www.bnb.co.nz/coachhouse.html
Double $95 Single $70 (Full Breakfast)
Children welcome
1 Queen 1 Double 1 Twin (3 bdrm)
1 Ensuite 2 Private

The Coachhouse is a quiet area on 15 acres surrounded by trees next to a lovely golf course. Stay in 'Rose Cottage' or the main house. Barry has lived and worked in Fiordland for 38 years and knows the area intimately. We are easy to find. As you enter Te Anau, take the first left, first left again, second right into Charles Nairn Road, under the archway at the end of the road.

Te Anau   *B&B 1 km N of Te Anau Town*

Te Anau Lodge
Kerry Carey
52 Howden Street,

Tel (03) 249 7477 Fax (03) 249 7477
info@teanaulodge.com
www.teanaulodge.com

Double $150-$190 Single $120
(Full Breakfast)
Child $50 Children welcome
5 Queen 2 Twin 2 Single (7 bdrm)
6 Ensuite 1 Private

Step into a charming jewel of Southland
history and a really warm Fiordland welcome in one of the most beautiful corners of the country.
Te Anau Lodge began its existence as a convent in 1936 at the small nearby mining town of Nightcaps,
on the road to Invercargill. As the focus of the church changed, it passed into private hands in 1987 but
there are still plenty of traces of its clerical past, such as the magnificent chapel, where today the
delicious breakfast is served, using ingredients from our own gardens and a touch of Kiwi culinary
creativity. It was shifted to Te Anau, near the tranquil lake in 2003. A beautiful Rimu wood interior
awaits you and each of the 7 rooms has furniture in native woods.
Kerry, your host, is on hand to help you discover the multitude of wonders in the region including some
of New Zealand's finest guided and independent walks in the Fiordland National Park, the fjords at
Milford and Manapouri and the living water caves across Lake Te Anau. Not to forget the excellent
fishing to be organised in the area. Being of Maori descent, Kerry would like to share with you her
knowledge of the Maori culture and history.
You may just prefer to relax in our retreat, be it down in the gardens, out on the verandah or in front of
the open fire on cooler evenings. Time to relax before your next adventure!

Directions: After leaving the town centre towards Milford, Howden Street is the 2nd on the
left off Milford Road.

Mossburn *Farmstay 25km S of Mossburn*

Joyce & Murray Turner
RD 1, Otautau, Southland
Tel (03) 225 7602   Fax (03) 225 7602
murray.joyce@xtra.co.nz
www.innz.co.nz/host/e/etalcreek.html

Double $80 Single $50 (Full Breakfast)
Child $20 under 12 years Dinner $30
1 Queen 4 Single (3 bdrm)
1 Private 1 Guests share

Our modern home on 301 hectares, 3000 sheep 200 beef cattle is situated half-way between Invercargill and Te Anau, which can be reached in 1 hour. We enjoy meeting people, will provide quality accommodation, farm fresh food in a welcoming friendly atmosphere. You can join in farm activities, farm tour or just relax. The Aparima River is adjacent to the property. Murray's a keen fly fisherman. Guiding available. Pet Bichon Frise. Evening meal on request. Directions please phone/fax. 24 hours notice to avoid disappointment.

Mossburn *B&B Farmstay Self-contained 1km W of Mossburn*

Kowhai Lodge
Ailsa Broughton
5665 Highway 94, Mossburn,
Tel (03) 248 6137   Fax (03) 248 6137
kowhailodge@xtra.co.nz
www.nzhomestay.co.nz/broughton.html

Double $120 Single $100 (Special Breakfast)
Child $25
1 King/Twin 1 Queen (2 bdrm)
1 Private

Our beautifully restored cottage features a hand-built stone chimney and large open fire, with comfortable beds and cosy atmosphere. It is surrounded by red deer including a pet hind to feed. The Oreti River on our boundary provides top fishing. You can join us on the farm with the sheep, or plan some hunting, fishing or tramping. We offer a wonderful family atmosphere to enrich any child's holiday. We look forward to meeting you and sharing our 100% pure New Zealand Hospitality.

Lumsden *Farmstay self-contained room available 9km S of Lumsden*

Josephville Gardens
Annette & Bob Menlove
Rapid sign 824, State Highway 6, RD 4, Lumsden
Tel (03) 248 7114   Fax (03) 248 7114
Mob 025 204 9753 bobannette@menlove.net
www.bnb.co.nz/josephvillegardens.html

Double $100 Single $80 (Full Breakfast) Dinner $25
1 King/Twin 2 Double 1 Twin (4 bdrm)
1 Ensuite 1 Private 1 Host share

We have a 480 hectare farm which runs sheep, cattle and deer. Surrounding our comfortable warm home, we have a large garden with a selection of specimen trees, rhododendrons, roses, peonys and perennials. The golf course is 3km away - golf clubs are available- a good fishing river nearby. We have hiked in our mountains a lot and can give advise on where and what to see. If you wish a four wheel drive trip is available.

Winton *Farmstay Self-contained 10mins N of Winton*

Nethershiel Farm Cottage
Mrs Henderson & staff
710 Riverside No 3 Rd, Winton 9662
Tel (03) 236 0791 Fax (03) 236 0101
Mob 0274 434 0598 nethershiel.farm@xtra.co.nz
www.nethershielfarm.co.nz
Double $105 Single $55 (Full Breakfast)
Child $20 under 12yrs Credit cards accepted
Children welcome Pets welcome
2 Queen 4 Single (4 bdrm)
1 Private

Enjoy your own comfortable fully equipped three bedroom house plus separate bunkhouse for energetic children. Set in own garden on a sheep and flower farm, in the heart of Southland. Flowers bloom from October to May. Tennis court on property, trout river, excellent golf course nearby, only $15 per round. Plenty of trips, walks, tramps and adventure tours to do. Fishing guides available. Good central location for day trips everywhere in Fiordland and Stewart Island. Weekly discounts.

Balfour *Farmstay 3km N of Balfour*

Hillcrest
Liz & Ritchie Clark
206 Old Balfour Road, RD 1, Balfour
Tel (03) 201 6165 Fax (03) 201 6165   clarkrl@esi.co.nz
www.bnb.co.nz/hillcrestbalfour.html
Double $100-$120 Single $70 (Full Breakfast)
Dinner $25 pp Children welcome
2 King/Twin (2 bdrm) 1 Private 1 Host share

Welcome to our 650-acre sheep and deer farm. Relax in our garden; enjoy a farm tour with mountain views or a game of tennis. Trout fishing in the Mataura, Oreti and Waikaia rivers. Fishing guide can be arranged on request. Enjoy a relaxing dinner with fine food, wine and conversation. Breakfast is served with fresh baked bread, homemade yoghurt, muesli, jams and preserves. Interests include handcrafts, tennis, photography and fishing. We have three children attending boarding school and two cats. Directions: at Balfour crossroads, take the road to Waikaia, then first left Old Balfour Road and travel two and a half kilometres, we are on right.

Wendonside *Farmstay 15km N of Riversdale*

Ardlamont Farm
Dale & Lindsay Wright
110 Wendonside Church Road North,
Wendonside, RD 7, Gore
Tel (03) 202 7774 Fax (03) 202 7774
ardlamont@xtra.co.nz
www.bnb.co.nz/ardlamontfarm.html
Double $100 Single $70 (Full Breakfast) Dinner $30
1 Double 2 Single (2 bdrm)
1 Private

Experience "Ardlamont", a 4th generation 1200 acre sheep and beef farm offering panoramic views of Northern Southland. Gourmet meals a specialty, served with fine New Zealand wines. Tour the farm, then return to the renovated comforts of our 90 year old homestead. Having travelled widely we enjoy welcoming visitors into our home. Our 3 teenage children attend university/boarding school in Dunedin. Two of New Zealand's best trout rivers only five minutes away. 15 minutes off SH94 (Queenstown - Gore - Dunedin route) Well worth the detour.

SOUTHLAND,
SOUTH CATLINS

Waikaka   *B&B Farmstay 30km N of Gore*

Blackhills Farmstay
Dorothy & Tom Affleck
192 Robertson Road, RD 3, Gore, Southland
Tel (03) 207 2865   Fax (03) 207 2865
Mob 025 2091 563   afflecks@ispnz.co.nz
www.bnb.co.nz/blackhillsfarmstay.html
Double $100 Single $50 (Full Breakfast) Child $25
Dinner $25 by arrangement Children welcome
2 King/Twin 1 Queen (3 bdrm)
1 Private 1 Guests share 1 Host share

Venture off HW1 for the refreshment of a quiet rural visit. Turn off HW90 on to the Waikaka Road.
Drive approx. 10km, turn left at the T junction then first right on to Nicholson Road. Veer right to
Robertson Road. Our 800 acre sheep and beef farm on a ridge above the Waikaka River offers superb
views, a farm tour, sports facilities in nearby Waikaka and warm hospitality, midway between Dunedin
and Fiordland. Both in our 50s, our interests include travel, golf, gardening, cooking and music. We
appreciate guests of all ages.

Pukerau - Gore   *Country Homestay 12km E of Gore*

Connor Orchids
Dawn & David Connor
1158 State Highway 1, Pukerau, Southland
Tel (03) 205 3896   0800 372 484   Fax (03) 205 3896
Mob 025 669 1362   ddconnor@esi.co.nz
www.bnb.co.nz/connororchids.html
Double $80-$100 Single $45 (Full Breakfast)
Dinner by arrangement Credit cards accepted
1 King/Twin 1 Queen (2 bdrm)
1 Private 1 Guests share

Relax with us in our warm comfortable home set in a mature garden with a rural outlook. We are just
minutes away from several rivers including the Mataura which is well known for Brown Trout fishing.
Fishing guide available on request. Growing a variety of orchids is our main interest, we run a few pet
sheep. We enjoy meeting people and have travelled extensively ourselves. Complimentary tea &
coffee available. Smokefree accommodation.

Gore   *Farmstay Homestay 6km W of Gore*

Irwin's Farmstay
Sandy & Trish Irwin
Croydon Bush, RD 7, Gore, Southland
Tel (03) 208 6260
www.bnb.co.nz/irwinsfarmstay.html
Double $80 Single $50 (Full Breakfast)
Child neg Dinner $25pp by arrangement
1 Queen 4 Single (3 bdrm)
1 Guests share

Sandy and Tricia are semi-retired farmers living on 43 acres where we have sheep, farm dog and hens.
We are 10 minutes from Gore on the road to Dolamore Park where there are several bush walking
tracks. Golf course and fishing rivers a short drive away. We enjoy meeting people, sport, reading and
gardening. Laundry facilities, cot and highchair available. A Bichon Frise dog and a cat share our
home. No smoking indoors please. Please phone for directions.

Gore *B&B 1km S of Gore*

Charlton Lodge
Judy & Jim Milne
Cnr Charlton Road & Main St, Gore,

Tel (03) 208 9279   0800 95 63 43   Fax (03) 208 0161
Mob 025 228 9189   info@charltonlodge.co.nz
www.charltonlodge.co.nz

Double $75-$85 Single $55-$60 Child Neg
Children welcome
2 King/Twin 1 Queen 8 Single (11 bdrm)
1 Ensuite 3 Guests share

Charlton Lodge B&B Hotel offers southern hospitality in a smoke-free centrally heated environment with complimentary tea and coffee, providing off street parking, laundry services, a full cooked breakfast in our cosy dining room. We are situated on State Highway 1 close to the heart of Gore. On site cafe caters for day and evening meals from a traditional roast to lighter meals. Fish the world renowned Mataura River and have your catch cooked by your able host or peruse the arts, sport or gardens.

Mataura - Gore *Farmstay 12km S of Gore*

Kowhai Place
Helen & John Williams
291 Glendhu Road, RD 4, Gore

Tel (03) 203 8774   Fax (03) 203 8774
kowhaiplace@hotmail.com
www.bnb.co.nz/kowhaiplace.html

Double $80-$95 Single $45 (Full Breakfast)
Child 1/2 price Dinner $20 by arrangement
2 Queen 4 Single (4 bdrm)
1 Private 1 Guests share 1 Host share

John & Helen farm sheep and deer, on our 50 acre farmlet. We live 5 minutes, from one of the best brown trout fishing rivers in the world. Drive 1 hour south to the sea side and 1 1/2 hours northwest to lakes and ski fields. We both play golf, and enjoy gardening. Fishing guide, and garden tours can be arranged with prior notice. Over the past years, we have enjoyed sharing our spacious home and garden with lots of overseas guests. Enjoy the South.

Progress Valley - South Catlins *Farmstay Self-contained*

Catlins Farmstay B&B   *6km N of Waikawa*
June & Murray Stratford
174 Progress Valley Road, South Catlins, Southland

Tel (03) 246 8843   Fax (03) 246 8844
catlinsfarmstay@xtra.co.nz
www.catlinsfarmstay.co.nz

Double $160-$220 Single $100 (Special Breakfast)
Child neg. Dinner $40 S/C Credit cards accepted
1 King 2 Queen 2 Single (3 bdrm)
3 Ensuite 1 Private 1 Guests share 1 Host share

Ours is a great location close to fossil forest at Curio Bay. Superior new guest rooms plus king s/c suite available with private entrances. I specialise in dinners using local fish, our homegrown venison, beef or lamb, and organic vegetables, followed by delicious desserts and breakfasts. We farm 1000 acres running, 2500 sheep, 500 deer, 150 cattle with 3 sheepdogs. Farm tours by arrangement. Directions: turn off at Niagara Falls into Manse Road, drive 2kms. Ask about our s/c cottages at Waikawa and Curio Bay(www.cottagestays.co.nz/governors/cottage.htm)

Wyndham *Farmstay 3.65km E of Wyndham*

Smiths Farmstay
Beverly and Doug Smith
365 Wyndham - Mokoreta Road, RD 2, Wyndham, Southland
Tel (03) 206 4840 Fax (03) 206 4847 Mob 025 286 6920
beverly@smithsfarmstay.co.nz   www.smithsfarmstay.co.nz
Double $100-$120 Single $75 (Full Breakfast) Child Neg
Dinner $40 Credit cards accepted Smoking area inside
2 King/Twin 1 Queen 1 Twin (4 bdrm)
1 Ensuite 1 Private 1 Guests share

Beverly and Doug assure you of a warm welcome to the Modern Farm house set in 265 hectare sheep farm. We are situated on the hills above Wyndham only 3.65 km, set in quiet and peaceful surroundings.
Farm tour included in tarif. Feeding the animals and sheep shearing when in season. Doug will demonstrate his sheep dogs working. Beverly a registered nurse enjoys cooking, floral art, knitting, gardening and travel. We enjoy meeting people and both are of a friendly deposition, with a sense of humour.
"Each bedroom has a View and is tastefully furnished to meet your needs." "Genuine home cooking" "Special Diets on request." "Packed Lunches if required" you are most welcome to join us for the evening meal, which is $40pp. We love sharing Christmas Day with guests, enquiries welcome.
Fishermans Retreat; The Mataura, Wyndham and Mimihau Rivers are renowned for its abundance of Brown trout. Each of these Rivers are only a short 5Km away. Doug, a keen experienced fisherman is only too happy to share his knowledge of these rivers with you. Enjoy the Mad Mataura evening Rise a site to experience.
Gateway to Catlins, Only two hours from Queenstown, Te Anau and Dunedin. Laundry, Fax and email facilities available.

Direction: Come to Wyndham, follow signs to Mokoreta.

Fortrose - The Catlins *B&B Farmstay 50km SE of Invercargill*

Greenbush
Ann & Donald McKenzie
298 Fortrose - Otara Road, Fortrose, RD 5, Invercargill
Tel (03) 246 9506 Fax (03) 246 9505
Mob 025 239 5196 info@greenbush.co.nz
www.greenbush.co.nz
Double $120 Single $80 (Full Breakfast) Child neg
Dinner $40 by arrangement
1 King/Twin 1 Double 1 Twin (3 bdrm)
2 Ensuite

Greenbush Bed and Breakfast is ideally located off the Southern Scenic Route from Fortrose. Within 30 minutes drive from Greenbush you can enjoy Curio Bay, Waipapa Point and Slope Point the southern most point in the South Island. Greenbush is nestled in two acres of garden. You will wake to the song of birds and magnificent views of green rolling countryside. Enjoy our private beach access, lake and farm tour. Directions at Fortrose take "Coastal Route" drive 4kms.

Waikawa Harbour - South Catlins *Farmstay Self-cont*

Bay Farm *80km SE of Invercargill*
Alison & Bruce Yorke
595 Yorke Road, Progress Valley, RD 1, Tokanui
Tel (03) 246 8833 Fax (03) 246 8833
BAYFARM@xtra.co.nz
www.bayfarm.co.nz
Double $120 Single $80 (Full Breakfast) Dinner $30
Self Catering $120 Credit cards accepted
2 Queen 2 Single (3 bdrm)
1 Ensuite 1 Private 1 Host share

Bayfarm is a tranquil retreat situated in native forest overlooking Waikawa Harbour South Catlins. We farm sheep and cattle on 1200 acres. Dinner-fresh home grown produce. Non smokers preferred. Our interests include tramping, sailing, golf and meeting people. Fantail cottage is a modern self catering cottage for two adults, it has an extensive kitchen, queen bed, TV and ensuite. It is 150 metres from the homestead and completely private.

Mokotua *B&B Farmstay Self-contained cottage 20km NE of Invercargill*

Fernlea
Anne & Brian Perkins
Mokotua, RD 1, Invercargill on Southern Scenic Route
Tel (03) 239 5432 Fax (03) 239-5432
Mob 025 313 432 fernlea@southnet.co.nz
www.fernlea.co.nz
Double $100-$110 Single $60 (Full Breakfast)
Child $10 Dinner $30 by arrangement
2 Double (1 bdrm)
1 Private

Fernlea Bed and Breakfast was the SOUTHLAND SUPREME TOURISM AWARD WINNER 2000-2002. Anne's cottage is nestled in its own private olde world garden, is completely s/c and can sleep 4. Our dairy farm of 300 acres is home to 300 Holstein Friesian cows - farm tour included. Interests include golf, travel, tramping, fishing and people. Relax and enjoy a taste of real NZ farm life on your journey to discover the Catlins, or enroute to Stewart Island, Te Anau or Queenstown. Directions: From Invercargill on SH92, 20 mins from Invercargill turn left at Mokotua Garage.

Invercargill *B&B Homestay 5km N of Invercargill city*

Glenroy Park Homestay
Margaret & Alan Thomson
23 Glenroy Park Drive, Invercargill

Tel (03) 215 8464   Fax (03) 215 8464
home_hosp@actrix.co.nz
www.bnb.co.nz/glenroypark.html

Double $95-$110 Single $60-$70
(Continental Breakfast) Child $12 Dinner $30
1 Queen 1 Twin 1 Single (3 bdrm)
1 Private 1 Guests share

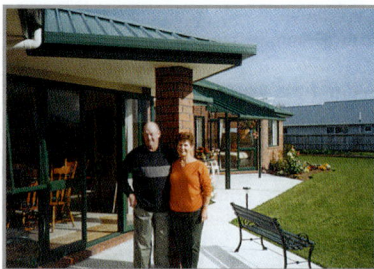

ìExclusively yours - in a quiet retreat with restaurants
and parks nearby. Be our special guests and share an evening of relaxation and friendship. Our interests
are golfing, meeting people travel and cooking. We look forward to having you visit us. Invercargill is
the gateway to Queenstown, Fiordland, Catlins and Stewart Island. Directions: from Queenstown turn
left at first traffic lights (Bainfield Road), take first left, third house on left. From Dunedin turn right at
first traffic lights (Queens Drive), travel to end, turn left, first street right, third house on left.

Invercargill *Farmstay Country stay and Garden 15km N of Invercargill*

Tudor Park
Joyce & John Robins
21 Lawrence Road, RD 6, Invercargill

Tel (03) 221 7150   Fax (03) 221 7150
Mob 025 310 031 tudorparksouth@hotmail.com
www.tudorpark.co.nz

Double $150 Single $90 (Full Breakfast) Child neg
Dinner $40 Twin $130 Credit cards accepted
1 King/Twin 1 King 1 Double (3 bdrm)
2 Ensuite 1 Private

When travelling in the Scenic South enjoy the peace and
tranquility of a comfortable country home set in a large four-acre garden, which was placed first in the
"2000 Southern Pride Beautification Award " for a large garden. Peonies and Hellebores are also being
grown. Fresh flowers, cotton sheets, private facilities and the 'best beds in NZ'. Close to Invercargill,
Stewart Island, SH6 to Te Anau and Queenstown. We enjoy overseas travel. Please book ahead if
possible. We also have a house available at Riverton, please enquire.

Invercargill *B&B*

The Oak Door
Lisa & Bill Stuart
22 Taiepa Road, Otatara, RD 9, Invercargill 9521

Tel 64 3 213 0633   Fax 64 3 213 0633
blstuart@xtra.co.nz
www.bnb.co.nz/theoakdoor.html

Double $80 Single $70 (Full Breakfast) Child POA
2 Queen 2 Twin 1 Single (3 bdrm)
2 Guests share

Bill (Kiwi) & Lisa (Canadian) invite you to stay in a unique restful home built by them. Relax - enjoy
the native bush setting and attractive gardens, just a five minute drive from Invercargill City Centre and
two minutes from the airport. Meet us at The Oak Door. Visit the area, enjoy sports (golf), scenery,
gardens, shops, restaurants, walking, area events. (No smoking/no pets.)**DIRECTIONS:** Drive past the
airport entrance. Take first left (Marama Ave South). Take first right Taiepa Road second drive on right
(#22).

Invercargill *B&B Farmstay 1km E of Invercargill*

The Grove Deer Farm
Alex & Eileen Henderson
154 Oteramika Road, RD 1, Invercargill
Tel (03) 216 6492   Fax (03) 216 6492
the_grove@xtra.co.nz
www.bnb.co.nz/thegrovedeerfarm.html
Double $90 Single $60 (Full Breakfast) Child neg
Credit cards accepted
1 Queen 4 Single (3 bdrm)
1 Guests share 1 Host share

Enjoy Bed & Breakfast on a deer farm. Situated in a unique rural setting only 1 kilometre from city boundary. See farmed deer and sheep. Guests welcome to tour of the farm.   Ideal stopover on Southern Scenic/Catlins Route and Stewart Island National Park Easy access to Fiordland walking tracks. Alex is a vintage car & machinery enthusiast and can arrange good viewing. Famous trout fishing rivers. Directions: Find Tweed Street - travel East. Cross Rockdale Road. We are 1 kilometer on right. Look for "The Grove" sign.

Invercargill *Farmstay Self-cont 10km E of Invercargill on Southern Scenic Rte*

Long Acres Farmstay
Helen & Graeme Spain
Waimatua, RD 11, Invercargill
Tel (03) 216 4470   Fax (03) 216 4470
Mob 025 228 1308   longacres@xtra.co.nz
www.bnb.co.nz/longacres.html
Double $100-$120 Single $80 (Full Breakfast)
Child neg Dinner $30 S/C $120 - $140
1 Queen 1 Double 1 Twin 2 Single (4 bdrm)
1 Private 1 Host share

Southland hospitality at its best awaits you at our warm and friendly home. Our farm is 850 acres carrying 3000 sheep and 80 cattle. We are a farming and shearing family. Shearing videos available to watch. Farm Tour available. Our farm is 30 minutes from Bluff. Transport to Stewart Island can be arranged. Our home and garden is relaxing and very peaceful. Being travellers ourselves we enjoy meeting visitors. A home cooked meal is always available. A welcome assured. Directions: From Invercargill east on Southern Scenic Route approx 15 mins. Look for Long Acres sign.

Invercargill - Waianiwa *B&B Homestay 18km W of Invercargill*

Annfield Flowers
Margaret & Mike Cockeram
126 Argyle-Otahuti Road, Waianiwa,
RD 4, Invercargill
Tel (03) 235 2690   Fax (03) 235 2745
Mob 021 385 134   annfield@ihug.co.nz
www.bnb.co.nz/annfieldflowers.html
Double $90-$105 (Full Breakfast)
Dinner $30, $20 - light meal Credit cards accepted
1 King/Twin (1 bdrm) 1 Ensuite

We are 1 km from the Southern Scenic Route (signposted Waianiwa/Drummound) and well placed for sightseeing, fishing and golf. Dating from 1866, Annfield has been renovated to retain character and include modern facilities. Our sunny guest room opens into the garden. Two cats and two dogs have limited access inside. We are semi-retired, grow flowers for export, keep coloured sheep and Dexter cattle. We enjoy meeting people and love to share dinner or a light meal, including our own produce. Complimentary laundry facilities.

SOUTHLAND,
SOUTH CATLINS

Invercargill
B&B Homestay Invercargill Central

Gala Lodge
Jeanette & Charlie Ireland
177 Gala Street, Invercargill
Tel (03) 218 8884 Fax (03) 218 9148
charlie.ireland@xtra.co.nz
www.bnb.co.nz/galalodge.html
Double $100 Single $60 (Full Breakfast) Child neg.
Dinner $25 by arrangement Budget backpackers room
1 Queen 2 Twin 1 Single (3 bdrm)
2 Ensuite 1 Guests share 1 Host share

Gala Lodge, ideally situated for visitors to Invercargill, overlooks beautiful Queens Park, City centre, Museum and Information centre. The home has well appointed, upstairs bedrooms (electric blankets provided). Downstairs, kitchen and two guest lounges. Spacious gardens, ample car parking. Hosts background - Farming, Police work, Education & Training, Gardening. Interests - Reading, Genealogy, handcrafts, travel. Many years hosting students of many nationalities including Japan and China. We provide a relaxing, friendly base, support in travel arrangements. Courtesy car available. Most buses stop here. You are very welcome.

Invercargill
B&B Homestay 4km N of Invercargill Central

Stoneleigh Homestay
Joan & Neville Milne
15 Stoneleigh Lane, Invercargill
Tel (03) 215 8921 Fax (03) 215 8491
www.bnb.co.nz/stoneleighhomestay.html
Double $90-$110 Single $65-$75 (Full Breakfast)
Dinner $30
1 Queen 3 Single (3 bdrm)
1 Guests share

We welcome guests to share our warm comfortable new home, which has underfloor heating. Neville owns a wholesale fruit and vegetable market and Joan enjoys cooking so we would love to share an evening meal with you. We are keen golfers and members of the Invercargill Golf Club; rated in the top 10 courses in NZ. Our home is five minutes drive from the city centre, on the main highway to Queenstown and Te Anau. City and airport pick-ups can be arranged.

Invercargill
B&B Homestay 6km NE of Invercargill

The Manor
Pat & Frank Forde
9 Drysdale Road, Myross Bush, RD 2, Invercargill
Tel (03) 230 4788 Fax (03) 2304 788
Mob 025 667 0904 the.manor@xtra.co.nz
www.bnb.co.nz/themanor.html
Double $90-$110 Single $65-$75 (Full Breakfast)
Child negotiable Dinner $30 by arrangement
1 Queen 1 Double 2 Single (3 bdrm)
1 Guests share

Relax and enjoy our warm and comfortable home in a sheltered garden setting. Our 10 acre farmlet (sheep, lambs, horses & hens) is situated on the outskirts of Invercargill. We are retired farmers, our interests include: keen golfers, gardening, horses, travel and meeting people. We have underfloor heating, electric blankets, pleasant outdoor areas and meals of fresh home grown produce, private guest area with television, fridge, tea and coffee making facilities. We are five minutes drive from Invercargill along State Highway One. Sign at Kennington corner.

Invercargill *B&B Self-contained*

Montecillo Lodge
Bevron Sinclair
240 Spey Street, Invercargill,

Tel (03) 218 2503   0800 666 832   Fax (03) 218 2506
montecillo@hyper.net.nz
www.bnb.co.nz/montecillolodge.html

Double $100 Single $80 (Full Breakfast) Child $15
Dinner $25 four motel units $70
4 Queen 2 Double 8 Single (14 bdrm)
6 Ensuite

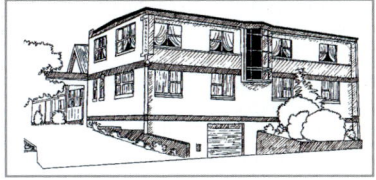

Your friendly hosts Bevron & Ray extend you a warm welcome to our comfortable lodge. We are situated in a quiet street just 5-10 minutes walk from the city centre, museum, park, golf course and swimming centre. Each of our centrally heated rooms has it's own ensuite, telephone, TV, tea and coffee-making facilities. Cooked breakfast is available in our dining room. Dinner by arrangement. We can arrange trips to Stewart Island and your next night accommodation. We go that extra step to make your stay more enjoyable.

Invercargill *B&B 1km N of Invercargill*

Bella Retreat B&B
Mary and Mark Hosie
70 Retreat Road, Invercargill

Tel (03) 215 7688   Fax (03) 215 7687
Mob 025 602 3419   info@bellaretreat.co.nz
www.bellaretreat.co.nz

Double $160 (Full Breakfast)
1 King/Twin 1 King 1 Queen 1 Single (3 bdrm)
1 Ensuite 1 Private

Take a break in this secluded modern retreat nestled in five acres of garden and woodlands. Bella Retreat provides a warm and welcoming environment where you can relax and feel at home. Your hosts Mark and Mary enjoy the many rich experiences of Southland and will happily share their knowledge while arranging transfers and booking attractions. Enjoy breakfast in the dining room or on the deck while watching native birds feed and sing in the grounds. Bella Retreat, on the outskirts of Invercargill offers a tennis court, and three rooms with the choice of a private bathroom with spa bath or ensuite.

Bluff *Self-contained continental breakfast optional 25km S of Invercargill*

The Lazy Fish
Robyn & Roy Horwell
35 Burrows Street, Bluff,

Tel (03) 212 7245   Fax (03) 212 8868
Mob 021 211 7424   thelazyfish@es.co.nz
www.bnb.co.nz/thelazyfish.html

Double $95 continental breakfast $8.50pp
1 Double (1 bdrm)
1 Private

Very homely fully self contained unit attached to our home, in a peacefull garden setting. Sleeps four, double bed in bedroom and sofa bed in lounge. Sunny shelterd courtyard. Animals in residence. Gateway to Stewart Island and Southern Scenic Route. Take a break and absorb our deep sea and fishing port. Coastal and native bush walks, maritime museum, restaurants and supermarket all within walking distance.Five minutes walk to Stewart island ferry. Continental breakfast by arrangement.

Riverton   *B&B Self-contained 35km S of Invercargill*

River Lodge Bed & Breakfast
Jocelyn and Russell Dore
93 Towack Street, Riverton

Tel (03) 234 8732   Fax (03) 234 8732
rbjmdore@actrix.co.nz
www.bnb.co.nz/dore.html

Double $85-$140 Single $50 (Continental Breakfast)
Credit cards accepted
3 Queen 1 King Single (4 bdrm)
2 Ensuite 1 Guests share 1 Host share

Relax and enjoy our comfortable home by the sea, situated on the waterfront with our 3 double bedrooms opening onto a sunny veranda with peaceful water and garden views. We also have a private, spacious upstairs studio unit with spa bath and views from the mountains to the sea. Come and enjoy a relaxed homestyle stay. We are only 20 minutes from Invercargill on the Southern Scenic Route. Enjoy a meal at Riverton's great cafes. Laundry facilities available. We look forward to meeting you.

Riverton - Waimatuku   *Farmstay 15km E of Riverton*

Kildonan Farm
Jacqui & Bruce Fallow
83 Fraser Rd, Waimatuku,

Tel (03) 224 6269   Fax (03) 224 6284
Mob 025 284 6882   fallow@southnet.co.nz
www.bnb.co.nz/user202.html

Double $90 Single $50 (Full Breakfast) Dinner $30
1 Double 1 Twin 1 Single (3 bdrm)

Looking forward to meeting you and sharing this unique part of New Zealand. Our 200ha deer and cropping farm is situated 4km N of the Southern Scenic Route, 25mins NW of Invercargill and 15mins from Riverton (a historic fishing village). Our home has modern facilities, is warm and comfortable, and set in a peaceful established garden. Conveniently located for excursions to Stewart Island, Hump Ridge track, Fiordland and Queenstown. Our interests include people, cooking, travel, gardening, fashion. Pets stay outside. Directions - please phone. Dinner by arrangement.

Riverton   *B&B 20min W of Invercargill*

Reo Moana
Jean & Alan Broomfield
192 Rocks Highway, Riverton,

Tel (03) 234 9044   Fax (03) 234 9047
www.bnb.co.nz/reomoana1.html

Double $140 Single $120 (Full Breakfast) Child neg.
(2 bdrm)
2 Ensuite

Reo Moana, meaning 'language of the sea', overlooks a beautiful secluded swimming and surfing beeach with extended views to the open sea beyond, and northward to the mountains and hills of Southland. Reo Moana, recently completed, was built to take advantage of the sea views and sun. Tastefully decorated and warm, the spacious guest rooms both have their own ensuite bathroom and sea views. Your hosts Jean and Alan have many years experience in the tourism industry, welcome you to Riverton, on the Southern Scenic Route.

Stewart Island *B&B Homestay Self-contained 1km N of Oban*

Thorfinn Charters & Accommodation
Barbara McKay & Bruce Story
PO Box 43, Halfmoon Bay, Stewart Island

Tel (03) 219 1210   Fax (03) 219 1210   Mob 025 201
1336   thorfinn@southnet.co.nz
www.thorfinn.co.nz

Double $160 Single $110 (Full Breakfast) Dinner by
arrangement 3 s/c units From $115 Credit cards accepted
2 Queen 3 Single (2 bdrm)
1 Private 1 Host share

Welcome to the tranquillity of our sunny open-plan home
'On the Beach' with panoramic views of Horseshoe Bay
out to the offshore islands from all rooms. Guest
bedrooms on the second floor are spacious with queen
and single bed in each. You may join us downstairs, or
use the upstairs sitting area for reading, writing or quiet
reflection in privacy.

With central heating, Sky TV, and transfers, you are
assured a comfortable stay. Evening meals are by
arrangement and feature local seafood.

For groups and families we offer 3 self-contained houses
just 10 minutes walk from the village. Two quality houses,
each 2-bedroom, sleep up to 7, while our 'Premium' house
has 3 bedrooms, 2 ensuite, dishwasher, etc. Sleeps up to
10. All feature Sky TV, central heating, superb sea views,
conservatory, bush surrounds and native birds.

Thorfinn, our luxury 12 metre launch provides 15 passengers with a comfortable ride,
and great visibility.

Our specialities are pelagic (seabirds) and terrestrial endemic birds and mammals with commentary
on island history, everywhere magnificent scenery, and always the option to catch a fish. The
highest number of available birds in any one place in NZ makes 30-40 species per day a possibility.
For 10 years we have operated nature trips with a guided nature walk on Ulva Island to explore
unspoilt forest, rare and endangered birds. We also do private charters including exclusive charters
for up to six pax with deluxe seafood meal and fine wine luncheon.

BJ, from the US East Coast and Hawaii, a medical doctor, brings botanical skill, while Bruce is a
former hill-country farmer with 40+ years' experience of the flora and fauna of Fiordland, the
Catlins and Stewart Island. Both are DoC Concessionaires, can access 'off the beaten track' areas,
and are foundation members of the NZ Birding Network. It will be our privilege to help you
discover Stewart Island.

Stewart Island   *B&B 500m Oban township*

Talisker Charters & Sails Ashore Accommodation
Iris and Peter Tait
11 View Street, Stewart Island,
Tel (03) 219 1151   Fax (03) 219 1151
tait@taliskercharter.co.nz
www.taliskercharter.co.nz/sailsashore.htm
Double $350 Single $350 (Full Breakfast)
Dinner By Arrangement
1 Queen 1 Twin (2 bdrm)
2 Ensuite

Enjoy with us our centrally located home with two new private apartments designed to maximise sun and scenery overlooking Halfmoon Bay. Stewart Island is New Zealands's newest National Park. Peaceful beaches, undisturbed forest and wonderful wildlife make the Island a haven. We have 33 years' of Island life as Ranger, District Nurse in charge, Commercial Fishers and now hosts of a charter yacht/ homestay. We and our Border Terriers will delight in sharing our Island and home with you.

Stewart Island   *B&B One km Oban*

Glendaruel Bed & Breakfast
Raylene & Ronnie Waddell
38 Golden Bay Road, Oban,
Tel (03) 219 1092   Fax (03) 219 1092
r.r.waddell@xtra.co.nz   www.glendaruel.co.nz
Double $150 Single $90 (Full Breakfast)
Dinner $25 B/A
1 King/Twin 1 Queen 1 Single (3 bdrm)
3 Ensuite

Peaceful bush setting, 10 minutes' walk from village, three minutes from Golden Bay on beautiful Paterson Inlet. Handy for water taxis, kayaks, sandy beaches and bush walks. Large guest lounge and three balconies with bush and sea views. Colourful garden - bird lover's paradise. Central heating. Courtesy transfers. Advice and assistance with local activities. We have travelled widely and love welcoming guests from around the world. Our friendly Cairn Terriers, Catriona and Morag, help us provide traditional Scottish and Kiwi hospitality. ìA Hundred Thousand Welcomes!î<\#13>

Stewart Island   *B&B Self-contained 5 min Oban*

Kowhai Lane Bed & Breakfast
Gary Huggins
6 Kowhai Lane, PO Box 66, Stewart Island
Tel (03) 219 1272   Fax (03) 219 1272
kowhai@taliskercharter.co.nz
www.taliskercharter.co.nz/lane.htm
Double $130 (Full Breakfast) Self contained flat $110
Children welcome
3 King/Twin (4 bdrm)

Welcome to Number 6 Kowhai Lane. A modern, comfortable, centrally located home overlooking Oban. Spacious guest rooms upstairs, and a private newly renovated self-contained flat downstairs. All centrally heated. Kowhai Lane management are happy to help with courtesy transfers and travel planning to make your stay memorable. The Department of Conservation Concessioned charter yacht complements Kowhai Lane & Sails Ashore. Explore Paterson Inlet and Ulva Island with us. Come over, enjoy Stewart Island, New Zealand's third Island and newest National Park.

Index

The New Zealand
Bed &Breakfast
Book

PLEASE HELP US
KEEP OUR STANDARDS HIGH

To help maintain the high reputation of *The New Zealand Bed & Breakfast Book* we ask for your comments about your stay. You can simply stick a stamp on this form or save all your comment forms and return them in an envelope.

Alternatively, leave your comment at our website
www.bnb.co.nz

Name of Host or B&B __ __ __ __ __ __ __ __ __ __ __ __ __

Address __ __ __ __ __ __ __ __ __ __ __ __ __ __ __

__ __ __ __ __ __ __ __ __ __ __ __ __ __ __ __

Considering things such things as breakfast, meals, beds, cleanliness, hospitality, value for money, what is your overall *satisfaction rating*, with 1 being the lowest and 10 being the highest rating?

1	2	3	4	5	6	7	8	9	10
☹				☺					☺

Do you have any comments?

We may display your comments on our website. The rating will be confidential and will be kept for administrative purposes.

Fill in your details to go into our regular prize draws!
Your details will not be passed on to anyone else. If you do not have email we suggest you use a friend's email address.

Your name __ __ __ __ __ __ __ __ __ __ __ __ __ __ __

Your town/city
and country __ __ __ __ __ __ __ __ __ __ __ __ __

Email __ __ __ __ __ __ __ __ __ __ __ __ __ __ __

Please post this form to:
The New Zealand B&B Book,
PO Box 6843, Wellington, New Zealand

Place stamp
here or send
forms in one
envelope.

Moonshine Press
PO Box 6843
Wellington
New Zealand

The New Zealand
Bed & Breakfast
Book

PLEASE HELP US
KEEP OUR STANDARDS HIGH

To help maintain the high reputation of *The New Zealand Bed & Breakfast Book* we ask for your comments about your stay. You can simply stick a stamp on this form or save all your comment forms and return them in an envelope.

Alternatively, leave your comment at our website
www.bnb.co.nz

Name of Host or B&B__ __ __ __ __ __ __ __ __ __ __ __ __

Address __ __ __ __ __ __ __ __ __ __ __ __ __ __ __

__ __ __ __ __ __ __ __ __ __ __ __ __ __ __

Considering things such things as breakfast, meals, beds, cleanliness, hospitality, value for money, what is your overall *satisfaction rating*, with 1 being the lowest and 10 being the highest rating?

1	2	3	4	5	6	7	8	9	10
☹				☺					☺

Do you have any comments?

We may display your comments on our website. The rating will be confidential and will be kept for administrative purposes.

Fill in your details to go into our regular prize draws!
Your details will not be passed on to anyone else. If you do not have email we suggest you use a friend's email address.

Your name __ __ __ __ __ __ __ __ __ __ __ __ __

Your town/city
and country __ __ __ __ __ __ __ __ __ __ __ __

Email __ __ __ __ __ __ __ __ __ __ __ __ __

Please post this form to:
The New Zealand B&B Book,
PO Box 6843, Wellington, New Zealand

Place stamp
here or send
forms in one
envelope.

Moonshine Press
PO Box 6843
Wellington
New Zealand

The New Zealand
Bed & Breakfast
Book

PLEASE HELP US
KEEP OUR STANDARDS HIGH

To help maintain the high reputation of *The New Zealand Bed & Breakfast Book* we ask for your comments about your stay. You can simply stick a stamp on this form or save all your comment forms and return them in an envelope.

Alternatively, leave your comment at our website
www.bnb.co.nz

Name of Host or B&B__ __ __ __ __ __ __ __ __ __ __ __

Address __ __ __ __ __ __ __ __ __ __ __ __ __ __ __ __

__ __ __ __ __ __ __ __ __ __ __ __ __ __ __ __ __ __

Considering things such things as breakfast, meals, beds, cleanliness, hospitality, value for money, what is your overall *satisfaction rating*, with 1 being the lowest and 10 being the highest rating?

1	2	3	4	5	6	7	8	9	10
☹				☺					☺

Do you have any comments?

We may display your comments on our website. The rating will be confidential and will be kept for administrative purposes.

Fill in your details to go into our regular prize draws!
Your details will not be passed on to anyone else. If you do not have email we suggest you use a friend's email address.

Your name __ __ __ __ __ __ __ __ __ __ __ __ __ __ __

Your town/city
and country __ __ __ __ __ __ __ __ __ __ __ __ __ __

Email __ __ __ __ __ __ __ __ __ __ __ __ __ __ __ __

Please post this form to:
The New Zealand B&B Book,
PO Box 6843, Wellington, New Zealand

Place stamp
here or send
forms in one
envelope.

Moonshine Press
PO Box 6843
Wellington
New Zealand

The New Zealand
Bed & Breakfast
Book

PLEASE HELP US
KEEP OUR STANDARDS HIGH

To help maintain the high reputation of *The New Zealand Bed & Breakfast Book* we ask for your comments about your stay. You can simply stick a stamp on this form or save all your comment forms and return them in an envelope.

Alternatively, leave your comment at our website
www.bnb.co.nz

Name of Host or B&B_ _ _ _ _ _ _ _ _ _ _ _ _ _

Address _ _ _ _ _ _ _ _ _ _ _ _ _ _ _ _

_ _ _ _ _ _ _ _ _ _ _ _ _ _ _ _ _

Considering things such things as breakfast, meals, beds, cleanliness, hospitality, value for money, what is your overall *satisfaction rating*, with 1 being the lowest and 10 being the highest rating?

1	2	3	4	5	6	7	8	9	10

Do you have any comments?

We may display your comments on our website. The rating will be confidential and will be kept for administrative purposes.

Fill in your details to go into our regular prize draws!
Your details will not be passed on to anyone else. If you do not have email we suggest you use a friend's email address.

Your name _ _ _ _ _ _ _ _ _ _ _ _ _ _

Your town/city
and country _ _ _ _ _ _ _ _ _ _ _ _ _ _

Email _ _ _ _ _ _ _ _ _ _ _ _ _ _ _

Please post this form to:
The New Zealand B&B Book,
PO Box 6843, Wellington, New Zealand

Place stamp here or send forms in one envelope.

Moonshine Press
PO Box 6843
Wellington
New Zealand

The New Zealand
Bed *&* Breakfast
Book

PLEASE HELP US
KEEP OUR STANDARDS HIGH

To help maintain the high reputation of *The New Zealand Bed & Breakfast Book* we ask for your comments about your stay. You can simply stick a stamp on this form or save all your comment forms and return them in an envelope.

Alternatively, leave your comment at our website
www.bnb.co.nz

Name of Host or B&B__ __ __ __ __ __ __ __ __ __ __ __ __

Address __ __ __ __ __ __ __ __ __ __ __ __ __ __ __ __

__ __ __ __ __ __ __ __ __ __ __ __ __ __ __ __ __

Considering things such things as breakfast, meals, beds, cleanliness, hospitality, value for money, what is your overall *satisfaction rating*, with 1 being the lowest and 10 being the highest rating?

1	2	3	4	5	6	7	8	9	10
☹					☺				☺

Do you have any comments?

We may display your comments on our website. The rating will be confidential and will be kept for administrative purposes.

Fill in your details to go into our regular prize draws!
Your details will not be passed on to anyone else. If you do not have email we suggest you use a friend's email address.

Your name __ __ __ __ __ __ __ __ __ __ __ __ __

Your town/city
and country __ __ __ __ __ __ __ __ __ __ __

Email __ __ __ __ __ __ __ __ __ __ __ __ __

Please post this form to:
The New Zealand B&B Book,
PO Box 6843, Wellington, New Zealand

Place stamp
here or send
forms in one
envelope.

Moonshine Press
PO Box 6843
Wellington
New Zealand